Navigating Computer Science Education in the 21st Century

Chantelle Bosch
North-West University, South Africa

Leila Goosen
University of South Africa, South Africa

Jacqui Chetty
University of Birmingham, UK

A volume in the Advances in Educational Technologies and Instructional Design (AETID) Book Series

IGI Global
PUBLISHER of TIMELY KNOWLEDGE

Published in the United States of America by
IGI Global
Information Science Reference (an imprint of IGI Global)
701 E. Chocolate Avenue
Hershey PA, USA 17033
Tel: 717-533-8845
Fax: 717-533-8661
E-mail: cust@igi-global.com
Web site: http://www.igi-global.com

Library of Congress Cataloging-in-Publication Data

Names: Bosch, Chantelle, 1984- editor. | Goosen, L. (Leila), editor. | Chetty, Jacqueline, 1968- editor.
Title: Navigating computer science education in the 21st century / Chantelle Bosch, Leila Goosen, Jacqueline Chetty.
Description: Hershey, PA : Information Science Reference, [2024] | Includes bibliographical references. | Summary: "This book project aims to position CSE as a critical component of the education system by raising awareness of its importance, advocating for its integration into the curriculum, and providing resources and training programs to support its implementation"-- Provided by publisher.
Identifiers: LCCN 2023052934 (print) | LCCN 2023052935 (ebook) | ISBN 9798369310663 (hardcover) | ISBN 9798369310670 (ebook)
Subjects: LCSH: Computer science--Study and teaching.
Classification: LCC QA76.27 .N385 2024 (print) | LCC QA76.27 (ebook) | DDC 004.071--dc23/eng/20240512
LC record available at https://lccn.loc.gov/2023052934
LC ebook record available at https://lccn.loc.gov/2023052935

This book is published in the IGI Global book series Advances in Educational Technologies and Instructional Design (AE-TID) (ISSN: 2326-8905; eISSN: 2326-8913)

British Cataloguing in Publication Data
A Cataloguing in Publication record for this book is available from the British Library.

For electronic access to this publication, please contact: eresources@igi-global.com.

Advances in Educational Technologies and Instructional Design (AETID) Book Series

Lawrence A. Tomei
Robert Morris University, USA

ISSN:2326-8905
EISSN:2326-8913

Mission

Education has undergone, and continues to undergo, immense changes in the way it is enacted and distributed to both child and adult learners. In modern education, the traditional classroom learning experience has evolved to include technological resources and to provide online classroom opportunities to students of all ages regardless of their geographical locations. From distance education, Massive-Open-Online-Courses (MOOCs), and electronic tablets in the classroom, technology is now an integral part of learning and is also affecting the way educators communicate information to students.

The **Advances in Educational Technologies & Instructional Design (AETID) Book Series** explores new research and theories for facilitating learning and improving educational performance utilizing technological processes and resources. The series examines technologies that can be integrated into K-12 classrooms to improve skills and learning abilities in all subjects including STEM education and language learning. Additionally, it studies the emergence of fully online classrooms for young and adult learners alike, and the communication and accountability challenges that can arise. Trending topics that are covered include adaptive learning, game-based learning, virtual school environments, and social media effects. School administrators, educators, academicians, researchers, and students will find this series to be an excellent resource for the effective design and implementation of learning technologies in their classes.

Coverage

- Social Media Effects on Education
- Instructional Design
- Instructional Design Models
- Educational Telecommunications
- E-Learning
- Collaboration Tools
- Digital Divide in Education
- Adaptive Learning
- Virtual School Environments
- K-12 Educational Technologies

The Advances in Educational Technologies and Instructional Design (AETID) Book Series (ISSN 2326-8905) is published by IGI Global, 701 E. Chocolate Avenue, Hershey, PA 17033-1240, USA, www.igi-global.com. This series is composed of titles available for purchase individually; each title is edited to be contextually exclusive from any other title within the series. For pricing and ordering information please visit http://www.igi-global.com/book-series/advances-educational-technologies-instructional-design/73678. Postmaster: Send all address changes to above address.

Titles in this Series

For a list of additional titles in this series, please visit:
http://www.igi-global.com/book-series/advances-educational-technologies-instructional-design/73678

Cutting-Edge Innovations in Teaching, Leadership, Technology, and Assessment
Asma Khaleel Abdallah (United Arab Emirates University, UAE) Ahmed Mohammed Alkaabi (United Arab Emirates University, UAE) and Rashid Al-Riyami (United Arab Emirates University, UAE)
Information Science Reference • © 2024 • 392pp • H/C (ISBN: 9798369308806) • US $165.00

Innovative Instructional Design Methods and Tools for Improved Teaching
Mohamed Khaldi (Abdelmalek Essaadi University, Morocco)
Information Science Reference • © 2024 • 441pp • H/C (ISBN: 9798369331286) • US $300.00

Technological Tools for Innovative Teaching
Mohamed Khaldi (Abdelmalek Essaadi University, Morocco)
Information Science Reference • © 2024 • 433pp • H/C (ISBN: 9798369331323) • US $300.00

The Role of Generative AI in the Communication Classroom
Sanae Elmoudden (St. John's University, USA) and Jason S. Wrench (SUNY New Paltz, USA)
Information Science Reference • © 2024 • 391pp • H/C (ISBN: 9798369308318) • US $230.00

AI in Language Teaching, Learning, and Assessment
Fang Pan (London School of Economics and Political Science, UK)
Information Science Reference • © 2024 • 384pp • H/C (ISBN: 9798369308721) • US $230.00

Restructuring General Education and Core Curricula Requirements
Julie Christina Tatlock (Mount Mary University, USA)
Information Science Reference • © 2024 • 243pp • H/C (ISBN: 9798369303856) • US $230.00

Inclusive Education in Bilingual and Plurilingual Programs
Lidia Mañoso-Pacheco (Autonomous University of Madrid, Spain) José Luis Estrada Chichón (University of Cádiz, Spain) and Roberto Sánchez-Cabrero (Autonomous University of Madrid, Spain)
Information Science Reference • © 2024 • 331pp • H/C (ISBN: 9798369305638) • US $230.00

Transforming Education With Generative AI Prompt Engineering and Synthetic Content Creation
Ramesh C. Sharma (Ambedkar University, Delhi, India) and Aras Bozkurt (Anadolu University, Turkey)
Engineering Science Reference • © 2024 • 550pp • H/C (ISBN: 9798369313510) • US $240.00

IGI Global
PUBLISHER of TIMELY KNOWLEDGE

701 East Chocolate Avenue, Hershey, PA 17033, USA
Tel: 717-533-8845 x100 • Fax: 717-533-8661
E-Mail: cust@igi-global.com • www.igi-global.com

Table of Contents

Detailed Table of Contents

In recent years, higher education has witnessed a shift towards open education and the proliferation of educational resources. Open educational resources (OERs) have gained prominence for their potential to revolutionize education by allowing students to create freely available, adaptable, and customizable content. Simultaneously, traditional assessment methods have come under scrutiny for their limited ability to measure critical thinking and practical skills. Computer science education, with its emphasis on innovation, is well-suited to embrace these changes. This chapter introduces creating OER as renewable assessment activities as an innovative approach, contributing to the discourse on open education, assessment, and pedagogy in computer science, emphasizing student empowerment, mastery, and intrinsic motivation.

To prepare students for the challenges of the Fifth Industrial Revolution, it is essential to cultivate deeper self-directed learning (DSDL) in computer science education. The process of DSDL empowers students to take ownership of their learning, enabling them to transfer their knowledge and skills to unfamiliar contexts. The proposed DSDL framework is anchored in cognitive load theory and social constructivism and draws upon three core concepts: the organization of course content; teaching and learning methods rooted in cooperative learning; and the characteristics of tasks. The importance of structuring course content to offer an initial holistic overview of key concepts, followed by deeper cycles of revisiting and reinforcing these concepts is underscored. Teaching and learning methods, such as cooperative pair programming and cooperative pair problem solving, are recommended. Moreover, the framework advocates for the adoption of a whole-task approach, involving authentic, complex tasks that encourage students to grapple with challenges and to learn from their failures.

This chapter focuses on the evolving landscape of computer science education in higher institutions, emphasizing the need to prepare students for a rapidly changing technology industry. It explores the integration of self-directed learning techniques in computer science courses to enhance outcomes, engagement, and critical skills like problem-solving. The chapter compares traditional instruction with self-directed learning, highlighting the benefits of the latter in terms of motivation, autonomy, and understanding complex computer science concepts. It reviews existing research in this area and introduces a conceptual framework aligning self-directed learning principles with core computer science concepts.

Despite social, historical, and cultural diversity, as well as poor educational attainment amongst high school learners, South African higher education is undergoing a digital revolution that fosters the cultivation of self-directed learning. This chapter contends that self-directed learning should not solely prioritize the accomplishment of tasks and the instructor's oversight of task completion. Instead, it should be centered around empowering learners to critically examine established conventions. Studies have demonstrated that learners from underserved regions are at a disadvantage when they enroll in higher education because they lack digital technology skills, which limits their level of critical thinking in problem-solving. The chapter further seeks to assist teachers and education policy makers in South Africa to keep up with the new pedagogical approaches that are suitable for 21st century learners and should enhance self-directed learning.

The fourth UNESCO goal for sustainable development addresses issues related to quality education for all. A worldwide effort strives to introduce computing from early studies. In this chapter, the authors will share and analyze approaches for embedding computational thinking (CT) in STEAM teaching, approaches drawn upon their experience as computing subject experts spanning their teaching careers. They will share experiences and best practices on the impact of CT on 1) Creativity supporting all the educational activities; 2) Challenges for educators and their students, with a particular emphasis on how to deliver an inclusive and accessible education addressing the expectation of all the students in the same class from the gifted one to those requiring a special education; 3) Convenience and how computing and CT promote special abilities within STEAM; 4) Custom and ethical principles supporting the teaching and learning process of all; and 5) Citizenship with an emphasis on digital citizenship and wisdom on how CT and computing can be taught, learned, and applied for the social good.

As the need for skilled computer programmers increases each year globally, so does the need for learning environments that serve the novice programmer. This literature review aims to contribute to the field of computer science education by highlighting successful practices reported in the literature and describing those practices through the lens of instructional design. As the demand for programmers increases, the success of novice programmers remains stagnant. By reviewing research-based instructional practices through the lens of instructional design, instructional designers, researchers, and CS, instructors can make purposeful design decisions in the future that help to meet the needs of the growing number of novice programmers. This chapter highlights the importance of instructional design theories and learning methods in meeting the diverse needs of computer science learners.

The purpose of this chapter is to report a study that examined the development of teacher education students' computational thinking (CT) knowledge and coding skills in a graduate educational technology class. In this class, the students learned about CT and coding over four consecutive weeks. Twenty-one students participated in the study. The results indicated that the participants developed a foundational understanding of CT and coding. They recognized the value of integrating CT and coding into education, but they would hesitate to engage their students in coding activities in classrooms. Teachers' knowledge and skills, students' knowledge and skills, technology accessibility and in-class time management were four major concerns that the participants expressed in the study. Practical implications of the results were discussed to provide a reference for including CT and coding in educational technology classes.

The introduction of computer science education (CSE) in schools is required to prepare the learners for future work and develop the required 21st century skills. However, for competent and confident learners, the educators need to be upskilled and trained to develop CSE teaching capacity and skills. The use of robotics education (RE) provides a more concrete (less abstract) environment for the introduction of CSE. Although CSE is introduced at schools, concern relates to the required access to quality training, required equipment and support from gatekeepers that delay or hinder the advancement of CSE. The good practices for the informal option of CE at higher education institutions (HEI), through engagement with and within a community of practice (COP), to provide access to quality CSE training and skills development to educators, visionary community leaders and learners is presented in terms of the balanced scorecard (BSC) perspectives of strategy, process, people, resources and growth and sustainability.

This study explored teachers' and learners' acceptance of the use of robotics based on their attitudes and experiences in two primary schools, which integrate robotics as a learning tool. Robotics is the current digital technology in the educational sector and offers new possibilities for modeling teaching and learning. The study used the technological acceptance model (TAM) as the theoretical framework and a qualitative approach. The researcher purposively sampled six learners and six teachers from the two identified schools in Pretoria, Gauteng. The study discovered that the integration of robotics in education is demanding, costly, and requires adequate resources. It necessitates additional time to design educational programs, requires more time for workshops and solving technical glitches, and puts more pressure on teachers. Teachers need support with the resolving of hardware and software issues as well as technical maintenance. Learners perceive robotics as a positive and exciting technological learning approach, which promotes teamwork and hands-on learning.

This study utilizes a scoping review of literature to explore the implementation of coding and robotics and its potential to foster and enhance teachers' self- directed learning skills through the implementation of coding and robotics within the South African educational context. This chapter presents a comprehensive synthesis of scholarly articles, reports, and studies published from 2013 to 2023. The study further aims to provide an extensive examination of the current status quo of coding and robotics implementation, as well as the possibilities that arise for professional development as well as the development of self-directed learning skills, also identifying gaps that will guide further studies in this field and later produce a systematic literature review. This scoping review utilizes a methodical and rigorous methodology to identify the current body of literature, discern significant themes, and provide a concise summary of the results.

The aim of this chapter is to examine the impact that AI coding assistants have on the manner in which novice programmers learn to read, write, and revise code. These discussions revolve around the concept of cognitive apprenticeship, a pedagogical framework informed by extensive research on tutoring dialogues and collaborative problem-solving practices. It involves guided instruction through modeling, coaching, and scaffolding. Within the realm of programming, these principles hold the key to nurturing skills in reading, writing, and revising code, thus making the learning process more effective and engaging. The chapter concludes by reflecting on the challenges and considerations of implementing cognitive apprenticeship within AI coding assistants. These insights are intended to benefit educators, developers, and researchers alike, offering a roadmap to enhance the learning experiences of novice programmers through AI support.

Preface

Welcome to *Navigating Computer Science Education in the 21st Century,* a comprehensive reference book curated by Chantelle Bosch, Leila Goosen, and Jacqui Chetty. As editors, we are delighted to present this collection that endeavors to address the dynamic landscape of Computer Science Education (CSE) in the contemporary world.

In an era characterized by rapid technological advancements and intricate concepts, CSE stands as a pivotal field, influencing our daily lives and shaping the future. Despite its paramount significance, CSE often receives less attention than other subjects within the education system. This book aspires to elevate the status of CSE, advocating for its integration into educational curricula and offering valuable resources and training programs to facilitate its implementation.

The editors recognize the urgency of introducing CSE in early childhood development, emphasizing its role in preparing children for the digital age. Early exposure to technology not only fosters problem-solving skills but also nurtures creativity, encourages collaboration, and contributes to reducing the digital divide. While acknowledging concerns about screen time for young children, the need for evidence-based practices to guide educators becomes apparent.

Success in computer science education hinges on effective teaching-learning activities. Learner-centered teaching strategies, encompassing individualized instruction, active learning, collaborative assessment, and communication, are paramount. This book delves into the complexity of the subject, exploring diverse teaching methodologies such as traditional lecture-based teaching, active learning, collaborative learning, and game-based teaching approaches.

The chapters presented in this book aim to provide insights into the impact of different teaching strategies on student engagement, motivation, and learning outcomes. By examining and comparing these methodologies, educators can make informed decisions to enhance their teaching practices, ultimately contributing to better-prepared students entering the technology workforce.

Furthermore, the book identifies gaps and areas for improvement, encouraging educators to refine their strategies to keep pace with the ever-evolving technology industry. Through collaboration with educators, industry professionals, and other stakeholders, we strive to contribute to the creation of a more skilled workforce and a more equitable society.

Positioning Computer Science in Education

Introducing coding and robotics in Grades R/K to 9, Computer Science/Information Technology/Computer Applications Technology in secondary schools, Computer Science/Information Technology etc. at tertiary institutions, Inclusive education, Underprivileged environments.

Teaching and Learning in Computer Science

Self-directed learning, Cooperative learning/Pair programming, Game-based learning, Problem-based learning, Blended learning, Online teaching and learning, Open Educational Resources (OERs).

Assessment in Computer Science Education

Renewable assessments, Meaningful assessments, Continuous assessment (CASS) vs examinations, Online assessment.

Innovation and New Technologies

AI/Chat GPT, Integrity in using AI, Utilizing AI in assessment practices.

We hope this book serves as a valuable resource for educators, institutions, and industry professionals, fostering innovation, collaboration, and excellence in Computer Science Education.

ORGANIZATION OF THE BOOK

Chapter 1: Exploring Educators' Pedagogical Capabilities to Develop University Students' 21st Century Skills: Navigating Within a Digital Learning Environment

Authored by Erkkie Haipinge and Leila Goosen, this chapter delves into the pedagogical capabilities of educators at a Namibian university in developing 21st-century skills among undergraduate tertiary students within a digital learning environment. Against the backdrop of navigating computer science education in the 21st century, the chapter explores topics such as self-directed learning, game- and problem-based learning, blended, and online teaching. The study aims to formulate a framework around the fully online learning community model and various learning types.

Chapter 2: Fostering the Teaching and Learning of Computer Programming with Open Educational Resources: Challenges and Solutions

Authored by William Deus, Fernando Balbino, Leonardo Barcelos, and Ellen Barbosa, this chapter addresses the synergy between Open Educational Resources (OER) and computer programming education. It explores the challenges students and teachers face in accessing these resources due to their dispersion in large digital collections. The chapter provides insights into strategies to overcome these challenges and enhance the integration of OER in computer programming education, ultimately contributing to the widespread use of OER in programming education.

Chapter 3: Creating Open Educational Resources as Renewable Assessment Activities for Computer Science Education: Enhancing Intrinsic Motivation through Co-Creation

Authored by Chantelle Bosch, this chapter explores the intersection of open education, assessment, and pedagogy in computer science education. It introduces the concept of "Creating OER as Renewable Assessment Activities" as an innovative approach, emphasizing student empowerment, mastery, and intrinsic motivation. The chapter contributes to the discourse on open education in computer science and advocates for assessing students through co-created, adaptable content.

Chapter 4: A Framework for Developing Deeper Self-Directed Learning in Computer Science Education

Sukie van Zyl presents a comprehensive framework in this chapter for fostering deeper self-directed learning (DSDL) in computer science education. Anchored in cognitive load theory and social constructivism, the framework emphasizes organizing course content, cooperative learning methods, and task characteristics. The chapter provides recommendations for structuring course content, incorporating cooperative learning methods, and adopting a whole-task approach to empower students to navigate the challenges of the Fifth Industrial Revolution.

Chapter 5: Teaching and Learning of Computer Science in Higher Education: A Self-directed Learning Perspective

Mncedisi Maphalala and Oluwatoyin Ajani's chapter focuses on the evolving landscape of computer science education in higher institutions. Emphasizing the need to prepare students for a rapidly changing technology industry, the chapter explores the integration of self-directed learning techniques in computer science courses. It compares traditional instruction with self-directed learning, highlighting the benefits of the latter in terms of motivation, autonomy, and understanding complex computer science concepts.

Chapter 6: Teaching Approaches of High School Teachers in the 21st Century: Fostering the Cultivation of Self-Directed Learning for Computer Science Education

Nomasonto Mthembu and Wanjiru Gachie's chapter addresses the digital revolution in South African higher education. It contends that self-directed learning should empower learners to critically examine established conventions, particularly important for learners from underserved regions lacking digital technology skills. The chapter aims to assist teachers and education policymakers in South Africa to adopt pedagogical approaches suitable for 21st-century learners, enhancing self-directed learning.

Chapter 7: Education with Passion: Computing as a Means for Addressing the Challenges of All

Authored by Francesco Maiorana, Andrew Csizmadia, Giusy Cristaldi, and Charles Riedesel, this chapter aligns with the fourth UNESCO goal for sustainable development, focusing on quality education for all. It shares experiences and best practices on embedding Computational Thinking (CT) in STEAM teaching, addressing creativity, challenges for educators and students, convenience, custom and ethical principles, and citizenship. The chapter emphasizes how CT and computing can be applied for the social good.

Chapter 8: Supporting Novice Programmers via the Lens of Instructional Design

Ghadah Almutairy and Alicia Johnson's literature review explores successful practices for novice programmers in computer science education through the lens of instructional design. Acknowledging the stagnant success of novice programmers despite the growing demand, the chapter highlights the importance of instructional design theories and learning methods. By synthesizing research-based practices, the chapter aims to guide instructional designers, researchers, and CS instructors in meeting the diverse needs of computer science learners.

Chapter 9: Introducing Computational Thinking and Coding to Teacher Education Students

Authored by Hua Bai, this chapter reports on a study examining the development of teacher education students' computational thinking (CT) knowledge and coding skills. The study, conducted in a graduate educational technology class, highlights the participants' foundational understanding of CT and coding. The chapter addresses teachers' concerns and practical implications for integrating CT and coding into educational technology classes.

Chapter 10: Introducing Computer Science Education through Robotics Education in Community Engaged Contexts: Reflecting on Good Practice

Patricia Gouws and Hugo Lotriet's chapter explores the introduction of Computer Science Education (CSE) in schools through Robotics Education (RE). Recognizing the need for upskilling educators, the chapter emphasizes community engagement within a community of practice (COP) at Higher Education Institutions (HEI). It presents good practices to provide access to quality CSE training and skills development, addressing strategy, process, people, resources, growth, and sustainability.

Chapter 11: Teachers' and Learners' Acceptance of the Use of Robotics in the Intermediate Phase

Doctor Mapheto and Maryke Mihai's study explores teachers' and learners' acceptance of robotics as a learning tool in primary schools. Utilizing the Technological Acceptance Model (TAM), the chapter reveals the demands, costs, and challenges associated with integrating robotics in education. Teachers' need for support and learners' positive perceptions of robotics as an exciting learning approach are key findings.

Chapter 12: Implementation of Coding and Robotics in South African Public Schools, Fostering Teachers' Self-Directed Learning: A Scoping Review

Averil Gorrah and Francios Papers conduct a scoping review in this chapter, exploring the implementation of coding and robotics in South African public schools. The chapter investigates the potential for fostering and enhancing teachers' self-directed learning skills through this implementation. It provides a synthesis of literature, identifies current trends, and highlights possibilities for professional development, self-directed learning, and future research directions.

Chapter 13: Cognitive Apprenticeship and Artificial Intelligence Coding Assistants

Authored by Eric Poitras, Brent Crane, David Dempsey, Tavis Bragg, Angela Siegel, and Michael Pin-Chuan Lin, this chapter examines the impact of AI coding assistants on the learning experiences of novice programmers. The chapter explores the concept of cognitive apprenticeship and its role in nurturing skills in reading, writing, and revising code. It reflects on the challenges and considerations of implementing cognitive apprenticeship within AI coding assistants, providing insights for educators, developers, and researchers.

Chapter 14: AI and Computer Science Education: The Need for Improved Regulation for the Use of AI in Computer Science Education

In the final chapter, Michael Laubscher addresses the significant role of AI in computer science education. Emphasizing the benefits and potential dangers, the chapter calls for improved regulation for the use of AI in this educational domain. It advocates for an ethic of care, ethical guidelines, and an approach that enhances human rights to ensure the responsible and effective use of AI in computer science education.

IN CONCLUSION

As editors of *Navigating Computer Science Education in the 21st Century,* we find ourselves at the culmination of a collaborative effort to illuminate the multifaceted landscape of computer science education. The diverse array of chapters within this reference book encapsulates the depth and breadth of contemporary discussions, research, and innovations that shape the trajectory of computer science education.

Throughout this journey, our esteemed authors have provided invaluable insights, addressing critical aspects ranging from pedagogical capabilities in a digital learning environment to the integration of open educational resources, fostering self-directed learning, and the strategic implementation of coding, robotics, and artificial intelligence in education. Each chapter serves as a building block contributing to the foundation of knowledge essential for educators, researchers, and policymakers navigating the evolving terrain of computer science education.

The emphasis on self-directed learning, open education, innovative teaching methodologies, and the ethical considerations in integrating emerging technologies underscores the transformative potential inherent in computer science education. We believe that the presented chapters not only provide a snapshot of the current state of the field but also serve as catalysts for ongoing conversations, explorations, and advancements.

As technology continues to evolve, our collective responsibility is to ensure that computer science education remains not only relevant but also inclusive, ethical, and empowering. The chapters presented here offer a rich tapestry of perspectives, methodologies, and best practices that will undoubtedly guide educators, institutions, and stakeholders in fostering a more skilled workforce and a more equitable society.

In conclusion, we extend our deepest gratitude to the contributing authors for their dedication, expertise, and commitment to advancing computer science education. We hope that this reference book serves as a source of inspiration, a springboard for further inquiry, and a roadmap for educators navigating the dynamic landscape of computer science education in the 21st century.

Chantelle Bosch
North-West University, South Africa

Leila Goosen
University of South Africa, South Africa

Jacqui Chetty
Birmingham University, United Kingdom

Acknowledgment

The editors would like to acknowledge the help of all the people involved in this project and, more specifically, to the authors and reviewers that took part in the review process. Without their support, this book would not have become a reality.

First, the editors would like to thank each one of the authors for their contributions. Our sincere gratitude goes to the chapters' authors, who contributed their time and expertise to this book.

Second, the editors wish to acknowledge the valuable contributions of the reviewers regarding the improvement of quality, coherence, and content presentation of chapters. Most of the authors also served as referees; we highly appreciate their double task.

Chantelle Bosch
North-West University, South Africa

Leila Goosen
University of South Africa, South Africa

Jacqui Chetty
Birmingham University, United Kingdom

Chapter 1
Exploring Educators' Pedagogical Capabilities to Develop University Students' 21st Century Skills:
Navigating Within a Digital Learning Environment

Erkkie Haipinge
University of South Africa, South Africa

Leila Goosen
https://orcid.org/0000-0003-4948-2699
University of South Africa, South Africa

ABSTRACT

The purpose of the study reported on in this chapter is exploring the pedagogical capabilities of educators at a university in Namibia to develop the 21st century skills of undergraduate tertiary students within a digital learning environment. Against the background of navigating computer science education in the 21st century, the chapter will discuss e.g., self-directed learning, game- and problem-based learning, as well as blended and online teaching and learning. One of the objectives of the study centers on developing a framework around the fully online learning community model and different types of learning.

INTRODUCTION

This section will describe the general perspective of the chapter and end by specifically stating the **aim and objectives**.

Navigating Computer Science Education in the 21st Century

Computer Science Education (CSE) is a rapidly growing field with ever-changing technologies and complex concepts that can be challenging for students to understand (Qurat-ul-Ain, et al., 2019, p. 1). With accent

DOI: 10.4018/979-8-3693-1066-3.ch001

similarities to the Eurasia journal article on Mathematics, Science and Technology education by the latter authors, the purpose of this chapter is to provide "a comprehensive review of several of the most popular teaching methodologies", including ones related to game- and problem-based learning, as well as "an analysis of different technological tools" and online learning tools, such as Massive Open Online Courses (MOOCs).

CSE has become increasingly important in society today as technologies continue to play a significant role in daily life (Burbules, Fan, & Repp, 2020, p. 93). The journal article by the latter authors against the background of Geography and sustainability pointed out that quality "education is one of the pillars in the United Nations 2030 Agenda for Sustainable Development" Goals (SDGs), which aim "to ensure inclusive and equitable quality education and promote lifelong learning opportunities for all.

Despite its importance, CSE is often not afforded the same level of attention as other subjects within the education system. The integration of CSE into the education system is critical to prepare students for the challenges of tomorrow (Qurat-ul-Ain, et al., 2019).

Exploring Educators' Capabilities to Develop University Students' 21st Century Skills Within a Digital Learning Environment

Namibia has aspirations to become a knowledge-based society by 2030 as per its Vision 2030 developmental policy that articulates the role of education towards this goal. Education is expected to develop students "with flexible enquiring minds and critical thinking skills, capable of adapting to new situations and demands and continuously learning from own initiative" (Government of the Republic of Namibia (GRN), 2004, p. 30). At a global level, the United Nations Educational, Scientific and Cultural Organization (UNESCO, 1999, p. 24) aims to "educate students to become well informed and deeply motivated citizens, who can think critically", analyze the "**problems** of society, look for **solutions** to the **problems** of society", as the role of higher education was outlined at its 1998 World Higher Education Conference (Teixeira & Shin, 2020).

To fulfil these developmental goals and global policy expectations, the revised National Curriculum for Basic Education in Namibia (Ministry of Education, Arts and Culture (MEAC), 2016, p. 8) identified core skills that learners need in order to operate in a knowledge-based society, that include learning to learn, personal skills, social skills, cognitive skills, communication skills and ICT skills, skills generally referred to as 21st century skills. In response to the basic education curriculum revision, the University of Namibia (UNAM) transformed its curriculum to be more competence based. This new curriculum implemented in 2023 seeks to embrace digital learning to promote learning approaches such as active and collaborative learning informed by social constructivism. The new curriculum also seeks to enhance students' 21st century skills of "creativity and innovation, critical thinking and **problem** solving, communication and collaboration and initiative and self-direction", amongst others (UNAM, 2020, p. 3).

Target Audience

Like that of the book that it proposes to form part of, the **target audience** of this chapter includes people, who, like the editors, believe that by working together with educators, industry, and other stakeholders, a more skilled workforce and more equitable society can be created.

Recommended Topics

From the **recommended topics** and sections suggested for the book, this chapter will specifically pay attention to:

1. Positioning Computer Science in Education
    - Computer Science/Information Technology/Computer Applications Technology in secondary schools
2. Teaching and Learning in Computer Science
    - **Game-based learning**
    - Problem-based learning
    - **Blended learning**
    - Online teaching and learning
3. Assessment in Computer Science Education
4. Innovation and New Technologies
    - Artificial Intelligence (AI)/Chat GPT

Aim and Objectives

As part of this book project, the chapter aims to position CSE as a critical component of the education system by raising awareness of its importance, advocating for its integration into the curriculum, and providing resources and training programs to support its implementation. As part of this book, the authors of the chapter would like to address **issues**, such as introducing CSE in early childhood development, as it is essential for preparing children for the digital age, developing **problem**-solving skills, fostering creativity, encouraging collaboration, and reducing the digital divide. By providing children with early exposure to technology and the skills necessary to use it effectively, we can help create a more skilled workforce and a more equitable society (Long & Magerko, 2020). CSE helps develop **problem**-solving skills in children and exposure to computer programming helps children learn how to break down complex **problems** into smaller parts and develop logical **solutions** (Sullivan & Bers, 2019; Chou, 2020). However, we acknowledge that introducing young children to computers, e.g., when screen time is not monitored, might raise major concerns. This is another reason why researched based evidence is needed to assist educators to succeed.

Game-Based Learning

The success in computer science education lies with the use of effective teaching-learning activities (Qurat-ul-Ain, et al., 2019). The importance of learner-centered teaching strategies in the computer science classroom cannot be overstated (Shah, Hussain, & Jabbar, 2022). By adopting a teaching approach that emphasizes individualized instruction, active learning, learner-centered **assessment**, collaboration, and communication, educators can create learning environments that meet the diverse needs of students and prepare them for success in the field of computer science. The complexity of the subject, coupled with the ever-changing nature of technology, poses a challenge for educators to find effective teaching strategies to expose students to knowledge. It is crucial to investigate and evaluate the effectiveness of various strategies in computer science education and to compare the effectiveness of traditional lecture-based teaching with active learning, collaborative learning, and **game-based** teaching and **learning** approaches (Karpava, 2022). The authors of this chapter want to present a study that examine the impact of these teaching strategies on student engagement, motivation, and learning outcomes. The findings of these studies will provide insights into the effectiveness of different teaching strategies in computer science education in various contexts. The results will help educators to make informed decisions on selecting appropriate teaching methodologies to enhance student engagement, motivation, and learning outcomes. These studies will also yield best practices for computer science education, which may lead to better-prepared students entering the workforce in the technology sector. As technology continues to evolve and play an increasingly important role in our lives, it is essential that we provide students with the skills and knowledge they need to succeed in this rapidly changing world. By identifying gaps and areas for improvement, educators can refine their teaching strategies and ensure that students are receiving the best possible education. The technology industry is constantly evolving, and it is essential that CSE programs keep pace with these changes. In line with the goal of the book, that of the chapter is not only to present research-based success stories of the teaching, learning and **assessment** that can assist computer science educators in implementing innovative strategies in their teaching but also to assist institutions in thinking about the way forward.

The study reported on in this chapter therefore **aims** to explore the pedagogical capabilities of lecturers at UNAM to effectively develop undergraduate students' 21st century skills within a digital learning environment (DLE). The **objectives** of the study therefore include to:

1. Evaluate the affordances of the Modular Object-Oriented Dynamic Learning Environment (MOODLE) learning management system (LMS) for supporting different types of learning for students' development of 21st century skills
2. Explore students' competence in terms of the self-directed learning necessary to develop 21st century skills
3. Develop a framework for supporting students' development of 21st century skills in a digital learning environment.

Now that an **introduction** to the chapter and study, as well as the research objectives, had been provided, the researcher describes the basic content of each chapter section as an outline of the study. The following section of the chapter will offer a look at the **background**, including presenting a literature review that will provide the conceptual and theoretical frameworks guiding the study, as well as scholarly research with empirical relevance to the current study. Next, the **problem** statement and significance of the study, as well as the research questions, which will be answered, will be stipulated. This section will also unpack the research methodology, addressing the research paradigm, approaches and design used in the study, as well as how data will be collected and analyzed, and how ethical **issues** would be addressed. After detailing solutions and **recommendations**, as well as opportunities related to **future research directions**, the final section of the chapter will deliver the conclusion.

BACKGROUND

This section of the chapter will seek to situate the study by exploring, broadly defining and discussing some of the key concepts within the context of this research topic on **exploring educators' pedagogical capabilities to develop university students' 21st century skills** while **navigating within a digital learning environment**. It will also incorporate the views of others (in the form of a review of the literature) into the discussion to support, refute, or demonstrate the authors' position on the topic, together with scholarly research that is related to and informs this study.

The Concept of 21st Century Skills

The concept of 21st century skills is highly debated. Debates on this topic include what these skills are, which appropriate term to use to describe these (whether these are skills or competencies), and in whose interest these are being promoted. Ananiadou and Claro (2009) defined 21st century skills as those that people need, both as citizens and as workers, to effectively operate in 21st century's knowledge society. The definition raises questions on the economic and market orientation and interests in the development of these skills. Some argue that 21st century skills are framed with the conception of people as human capitals seeking to make them efficient for economic production. From this perspective, "21st century skills in the context of" knowledge societies consolidate the notion of people as knowledge workers whose economic efficiency is enhanced by continually learning and developing new skills and competences (Watted, 2023, p. 797).

Frameworks for 21st Century Skills and Competencies

Assessment in Computer Science Education

Various frameworks exist that seek to define and categorize 21st century skills. In this literature review, the focus is limited on two frameworks, namely the Partnership for 21st Century Skills (P21), widely adopted and referenced, and the **Assessment** and Teaching of 21st Century Skills (ATC21S). The P21 frames 21st century skills into three main groups, namely learning skills, that include creativity, innovation, critical thinking; literacy skills that refers to information, media, and ICT literacy; and life skills, such as "flexibility and adaptability; initiative and self-direction" (Van Laar, Van Deursen, Van Dijk, & de Haan, 2020, p. 2).

The ATC21S framework consists of four categories, namely "ways of thinking (creativity and innovation; critical thinking," etc.) "ways of working (communication; collaboration), tools for working (information literacy; ICT literacy), and living in the world (citizenship; life and career skills", etc.) (Ibid). The necessity for these skills has been heightened by the proliferation of information communication technologies, increased access to an overwhelming amount of information that requires the ability to critically evaluate it and make decisions, and the demand on people to continually learn and develop new skills to meet and keep up with the demands of change.

There are, however, those that argue that the notion of 21st century skills has been accepted by educators and policy makers uncritically and there is a need to question them. Mehta, Creely and Henriksen

(2020) traced the discourse of 21st century to the United States in the early eighties with the roll out of neoliberal capitalist policies that took an instrumental view of people as human capitals to fuel economic growth, with 21st century skills see as instruments to make people efficient to the economy. Mehta, et al. (2020) further argued that 21st century skills are disputable and largely idealized and futuristic because there is no consensus on what these skills mean to most educators and how much they are decontextualized from areas of work or academic disciplines.

Computer Science/Information Technology etc. at Tertiary Institutions

In line with the theme of this book, Brian (2016) offered a critical approach to 21st century *tertiary* education towards **navigating** the tides of globalisation and neoliberalism.

Knowledge-Based Societies

Knowledge-based societies or knowledge societies are those with or seeking to develop "capabilities to identify, produce, process, transform, disseminate, and use information to build and apply knowledge for human development" (Bindé, 2005, p. 27). Knowledge societies are closely related with expanded access to information and the intense "use of information communication technologies" (Ntalindwa, Soron, Nduwingoma, Karangwa, & White, 2019, p. 1), two of the conditions that have been argued to support the need for developing 21st century skills as discussed above. In fact, capabilities to identify, produce, process, transform, disseminate, and use information pre-require some of the 21st century skills described earlier such as digital, communication, critical thinking, and analytical skills. From this perspective, for students, workers, or citizens to operate meaningfully in the knowledge-based societies, they need to develop 21st century skills (Sweet, 2014).

Given the discussion about knowledge and learning societies provided in this chapter, any alignment to be made to 21st century skills need to consider whether a set of such skills do indeed enable one to process knowledge resulting in enhanced capabilities to learn, innovate and adapt to change. This could be an added criteria for determining whether a given set of skills are to fall in the category of 21st century skills.

Rationale for Teaching 21st Century Skills

The debate on what to call the 21st century skills include the choice of terminology to use, with some preferring competencies for their wider application that is inclusive of skills, knowledge, and attitudes (Ananiadou & Claro, 2009), is likely to continue yet. At the same time, it is hard to deny the existence of ongoing societal changes, and the implications that these changes have on the expectations of the competencies or skills that education institutions are expected to develop in students. These societal changes are part of the rationale for the need to teach new competencies that may not have been in higher demand in the past. In comparing the functional emphasis of education in the two centuries, the 20th century is said to have promoted the attainment of skills such as reading, writing and arithmetic, but the 'three Rs' for the 21st century had shifted to rigor, relevance, and real-world skills (Teo, 2019). This shift necessitates the need for a consideration for what these "real-world skills" are, and how they can be developed.

Pedagogy for 21st Century Skills and Competencies

Pedagogical approaches that are supportive of the cultivation of 21st century skills require students' "active participation in the learning process" (Nedzinskaitė-Mačiūnienė & Šimienė, 2021, p. 201). From a learning theory perspective, such pedagogical choices should be informed by learning theories rooted in social constructivism. However, despite the adoption of educational technologies, research continues to find that educators continue to prefer transmissive teaching approaches that promote rote learning (Kim, Raza, & Seidman, 2019). This suggests that there is a need for reflective practice by educators towards introspection and determining where they are in terms of their pedagogical choices, regarding on the one hand, the expected learning outcomes of their students and on the other, including the cultivation of their 21st century skills and competences.

Digital Learning Environments

Digital learning environments can be defined as a dynamic digital learning platform that supports learning-centered pedagogies promoting interactions between students and educators as a learning community assisted by diverse technology tools (Brown, Dehoney, & Millichap, 2015). A digital learning environment is therefore not the same as a learning management system, such as MOODLE (Graf, Lachance, & Mishra, 2016). A digital learning environment is supposed to be a pedagogically informed perspective of the **LMS** that provides a diverse range of tools supportive of practices that help educators and students achieve active learning.

Universities globally, southern African and Namibia included, have adopted digitalization strategies that promote the use of digital technologies in learning and teaching. The digitalization process as a policy direction has been a thrust by the Covid-19 pandemic that compelled institutions to move teaching online. Dlamini and Ndzinisa (2020) acknowledged the affordances of learning management systems in complementing traditional face-to-face teaching and helping to cater for students that are geographically distributed (Luo, et al., 2022). However, Dlamini and Ndzinisa (2020) contend that the homogenous one size-fits-all implementation of digital learning needs to be critically reconsidered to ensure that students from vulnerable backgrounds such as those without ready access to internet or electricity, are not disadvantaged, and that suitable pedagogical innovations are used to cater for these diverse needs (Maguire, Gibbons, Glackin, Pepper, & Skilling, 2018).

Proposed Theoretical Framework

The study considers the Fully Online Learning Community (FOLC) model for a theoretical framework (Blayone, van Oostveen, Barber, DiGiuseppe, & Childs, 2016, p. 17). The FOLC is a digital learning framework where transactional distance is reduced through building a democratized learning community guided by constructivism and acknowledging "the digital context (and related competencies) as endogenous variables vital to the successful functioning of a fully online community". FOLC is composed of Social Presence (SP) and Cognitive Presence (CP) interacting in a digital space to foster collaborative learning using its asynchronous and synchronous affordances, and where critical inquiry is fostered by the community supported by their digital competencies (Blayone, van Oostveen, Barber, DiGiuseppe, & Childs, 2017). FOLC is found suitable as a theoretical framework for its orientation to both digital learning environments and to the social constructivist perspective of learning suitable for developing online learning communities harnessing 21st century skills development.

Additional to the FOLC model, the types of learning suggested by Laurillard (2013), namely Acquisition, Inquiry, Practice, Production, Discussion and Collaboration, are added to the framework to guide the evaluation of the affordances of the MOODLE LMS to support student development of 21st century competences, as well as to explore the extent to which lecturers utilize each type of learning in their teaching. The study discussed in this chapter makes an assumption that inquiry, collaboration, discussion and practice are critical learning types that provide an opportunity for the development and application of 21st century skills. The framework is summarized in Figure 1.

Figure 1. Framework combining the FOLC and the six learning types
Framework adapted from Blayone et al. 2017; learning types adapted from Luarillard, 2013)

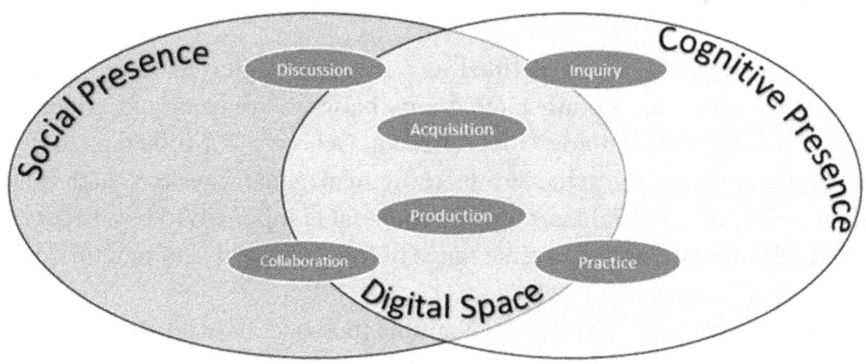

MAIN FOCUS OF THE CHAPTER

Issues, Problems

This section of the chapter will present the authors' perspective on the **issues**, **problems**, etc., as these relate to the main theme of **Navigating Computer Science Education in the 21st Century** and arguments supporting the authors' position on **exploring educators' pedagogical capabilities to develop university students' 21st century skills** while **navigating within a digital learning environment**. It will also compare and contrast with what has been, or is currently being, done as it relates to the specific topic of the chapter.

One of the other **issues** emanating from the conception of 21st century skills as described in the previous section of this chapter is whether these skills are only relevant in knowledge-based societies where people need a new set of skills to adapt and meet consumer demands and the needs of corporations they work for (Van Weert, 2005); Erdem, 2019). Therefore, this could lead one to **conclude** that, for societies that are not knowledge-based, 21st century skills do not matter.

Proponents of 21st century skills argue that these skills permeate all aspects of life due to the proliferation of information communication technologies that bring with it historically unmatched access to large volumes of information that people need to critically evaluate, to make decisions and find **solutions** to new **problems** (Erdem, 2019). Though there is a critique that labelling these skills as '21st century skills' may also suggest that they are new and have not been relevant prior to this century, Erdem (2019) maintained that, although these skills may not be new, the level of demand for their application to learning, work and everyday life is higher and more intense in comparison to periods past.

Educators are therefore challenged to move beyond helping students to master content through subject knowledge acquisition, as important as it remains to be, towards helping students to synthesize, evaluate, apply, transform, and create new knowledge (Teo, 2019). These "higher order thinking skills were" complemented by 21st century skills, such as critical thinking and **problem** solving and require a different pedagogical approach from the traditional transmissive one (Yue, 2022, p. 109). Educators are also expected to adopt more interdisciplinary approaches in their teaching and **assessment** of competences that students are expected to develop, not in one subject area but skills applicable across the curriculum (Caena & Redecker, 2019).

Issues of differential **access** aside, there is also a need to unpack how the learning management systems used to create digital learning environments are used in practice. Guillén-Gámez, Mayorga-Fernández, Bravo-Agapito and Escribano-Ortiz (2021) stated that, despite the opportunities presented by modern learning management systems like Moodle, educators continue to use them mainly as repository of learning content. Digital competence of educators does not always lead to pedagogical use of digital learning environments, indicating the need for continuous professional development for educators focusing on enhancing their pedagogical digital competence.

Problem-Based Learning

In an electronic journal article on e-learning, Barber and King (2016) considered student teachers' perspectives on the so-called 'invisible' pedagogy applicable in online **problem-based learning** environments.

Rationale of the Study

Blended Learning

UNAM recently transformed its curriculum to ensure its alignment to the country's national development goals – at whose center is to turn the country into knowledge-based society. Within the framework of this curriculum, the university has adopted digital learning strategies to prepare students for Industry 4.0 and enhance their 21st century skills, and these strategies include the implementation of **blended** learning across all its programs. The adoption of **blended** learning as a delivery approach would accelerate digital learning.

The study discussed in this chapter seeks to provide insight into the status quo at the university regarding lecturers, students, and the digitalization of "learning through the use of" MOODLE as a digital learning environment in the process of implementing the transformed curriculum (Li, 2022, p. 36). Without this insight, the university may not effectively evaluate its readiness to achieve its curricula and teaching goals, nor would it be able to make informed interventions to support students and lecturers who may lack the required competencies. The transformed curriculum refers to a lot of new concepts such as 21st century skills and Industry 4.0 that are not necessarily well understood by key stakeholders in is implementation.

This study therefore attempts to provide insights on how a digital learning environment at an institution of higher learning in Namibia can be empirically informed to facilitate the implementation of curriculum innovations. The study also seeks to develop a framework to inform and guide effective implementation of curricula seeking "to develop students' 21st century skills" within a digital learning environment (Reynolds, 2021). The framework would guide the institution, relevant stakeholders such as lecturers, academic developers, librarians, and students on how the transformed curriculum may be successfully implemented.

Statement of the Problem

Online Teaching and Learning

The transformed curriculum at the UNAM promotes the use of digital learning whereby courses in the transformed curriculum would be delivered through **blended** and **online learning**. Generally, traditional **teaching** approaches in conventional classrooms tend to be lecturer-centered focusing on individualization of students, lecturer-determined learning **problems** to be solved, and lecturer-controlled student engagement (Barber & King, 2016). Furthermore, there is a tendency for lecturers to replicate the traditional ways of teaching in the digital learning settings (Laurillard, et al., 2013), whilst the transformed curriculum at UNAM expects lecturers to utilize digital learning to develop students' higher order thinking and a range of 21st century skills.

These skills are best achieved through student-centered pedagogical approaches informed by social-constructivism that sees learning as a "the active process of meaning-construction in real-authentic **problems** and situations, and where learners are able to socially construct knowledge with others" and where the student takes responsibility and ownership of own learning (Tan & Hung, 2002, p. 50). The UNAM DLE is powered by the MOODLE (2018) learning management system. Although the design of MOODLE is informed by the social constructionist pedagogy (Zsolt & István, 2008), it can still be turned into an information deposit platform if lecturers maintain their transmissive teaching approaches. Transmissive teaching has dominated pedagogy in distance learning "and Massive Open Online Courses (MOOCs)" (Hass, Hass, & Joseph, 2023, p. 24) where teaching had focused on "the delivery of expert information to the masses" (Blayone, et al., 2017, p. 2). There is therefore a concern that lecturers at UNAM may retain transmissive teaching approaches, which will be incompatible with the student-centred learning expected to effectively develop students' 21st century skills.

Research Questions

This study is guided by the following research questions:

1. What are the affordances of the MOODLE LMS for supporting pedagogical strategies seeking to develop students' 21st century skills?
2. How are students' self-directed learning competence for enabling them to develop 21st century skills within a digital learning environment supported?
3. What does a framework for supporting a digital learning environment that fosters students' 21st century development look like?

Research Methodology and Design

This subsection of the chapter proposes the research methodology and design to be used in the study. "It describes the research approach, the" population and sampling technique to be used, the research instruments and data collection techniques, as well as how data would be analysed and interpreted (Fester, 2022, p. 9).

Philosophical Paradigm and Assumptions

This study is framed within the Social Constructivist/ Interpretivist philosophical paradigm whereby the subjective meanings of the research participants will be varied and multiple (Nelan, Wachtendorf, & Penta, 2018), thereby the objective of the researcher would be to "look for the complexity of views rather than narrow the meanings to a few categories or ideas" (Creswell & Poth, 2007, p. 20). However, to accommodate quantitative data, the researcher will adopt a pragmatic paradigm where the focus would be on adopting methods that best fulfil the objectives of the study.

In terms of philosophical assumptions, the study adopts the following ontological, epistemological, and axiological stances. Ontologically, the researcher assumes that there are multiple realities and perspectives towards the phenomenon under study. As such, the study would explore the phenomenon through the perspectives of the research participants and the artifacts they create.

Epistemologically, the researcher seeks to understand the research participants and the context within which they experience the phenomenon being studied, therefore the epistemological assumption requires me to have firsthand exposure to participants' reality. Axiologically, the researcher acknowledges that he brings along his own values, biases, and professional orientations to the study, and would attempt to position himself in the study.

Research Approach

The research approach adopted by the study is the qualitative approach complemented by quantitative methods, because the research sets out to explore phenomenon that is not well defined and whose variables are not yet well known to the researcher (Creswell, 2008). Therefore, a mixed method approach will be adopted. In terms of design, the qualitative portion will use the basic interpretive design with the focus on collecting rich descriptive accounts that would paint a picture of the phenomenon (Creswell, 2008, Ary, Jacobs, Irvine & Walker, 2018). The quantitative part of the study will use survey design for its ability to collect data efficiently and cheaply from a large sample (Ary, Jacobs, Irvine, & Walker, 2013).

Population and Sampling

The research *population* refers to "a group of individuals who have the same characteristic" (Creswell, 2008, p. 151). The target population for this study consists of all lecturers and all undergraduate senior students at a selected Namibian university. While the accessible population, the population accessible to the researcher for sampling purpose (Ary, Jacobs, Sorensen, & Razavieh, 2010), would be lecturers at a selected campus, as well as all undergraduate full-time degree students at a selected campus.

Non-probability sampling method would be used to identify a sample of lecturers to participate in the study. The sampling technique will be purposeful sampling informed by the knowledge of the participants where those to be selected are expected to provide information relevant to the study (Ary, et al., 2013). In this case, it would be lecturers who use MOODLE LMS for their teaching, and students who have courses delivered through MOODLE LMS. The purposive sampling to be used to select lecturers for the study would be maximum variation sampling to maximize the diversity of characteristics of participants, such as number of years using MOODLE LMS for teaching, participation in the teaching of core courses related to 21st century skills development, departments, or schools, etc. As for students, the stratified purposeful sampling strategy will be employed to ensure representation of students from different year groups and between students doing the new transformed curriculum and those not.

Instrumentation and Data Collection Techniques

Qualitative data will mainly be collected using semi-structured interviews for lecturers and focus-group interviews for students. Document analysis will be used to evaluate the MOODLE documentation and course activities related to the use of teaching and learning tools (Osode, 2021) to establish the affordances of MOODLE LMS used for supporting the six types of learning described by Laurillard (2013) and subsequently the potential of these for fostering students' 21st century skills development.

Data Analysis and Interpretation

Qualitative data analysis involves reducing, organizing, and synthesizing data to identify patterns and make sense of the data (Ary, et al., 2013). Recorded interview data will be transcribed. Together with all other qualitative data, such as field notes, journal entries and document analysis summaries, following the procedure as described by Ary et al. (2013), data analysis will start with organization and familiarizing, thereafter it will be coded, followed by interpretation and display of findings. The quantitative data generated by the **self-directed** learning readiness scale will be statistically analyzed using descriptive tables for factors and items (Kumar et al, 2021).

Reliability, Validity, Credibility, and Trustworthiness

This study, by virtue of using both qualitative and quantitative data, is answerable to both **reliability** and **validity** on the one hand (for quantitative data) and **credibility** and **trustworthiness** (for qualitative data). **Reliability**, the stability and consistency of the research instrument, and **validity** – the interpretation of data matches the intended purpose of the tool (Creswell, 2014) will be addressed by using the "Self-Directed Learning Readiness Scale (SDLRS)" that has been well tested by other researchers and the **reliability** and **validity** of which is well-established (Kumar, et al., 2021, p. 1).

For qualitative data, the focus is on **credibility** and **trustworthiness**, which is addressed through **credibility** (in preference to internal **validity**), transferability (in preference to external **validity**/generalizability), *dependability* (in preference to **reliability**), and confirmability (in preference to objectivity) (Shenton, 2004). In this study, these will be limited to **credibility** and *dependability*. As Shenton (2004) advised, the researcher will enhance the **credibility** of the study by establishing good rapport with research participants to build trust, by opening the research design to peers (such as fellow PhD students) for critical feedback, using triangulation through varying data collection methods, committing to frequent debriefing sessions with the research supervisor, and by using reflective commentary on the research process.

As far as *dependability* is concerned, the study will employ both individual and focus group interviews, as well as use document analysis, the resulting triangulation of which will enhance *dependability* of findings. Furthermore, the study will include a detailed description of the planning and implementation of the study, and details on the data gathering process, as proposed by Shenton (2004).

Research Ethics

Qualitative researchers tend to experience more ethical dilemmas than those using quantitative methods, due to their intensive interaction with participants in the field (Ary et al., 2013). This study will be guided by the national and institutional code of research ethics by which it shall seek to follow. The study will ensure the protection of research participants from physical or mental harm, will inform research participants about the nature and purpose of the study, and will respect their right to withhold consent to partake in the study. Access to the research site will only be done after permission by gate keepers have been granted. To ensure participant anonymity, the researcher shall provide an option for virtual interviews using a video conferencing software that will be set not to allow video sharing, and where participants shall use code names. Anonymity will be further addressed by not keeping records with personally identifiable information of research participants. Confidentiality will be maintained through using the data collected only for the purposes of the research and destroying such data within the stipulated period as per relevant institutional policies and procedures.

Limitations and Delimitations of the Study

This study is limited to educators (lecturers) and undergraduate degree students at a selected university in the capital of Namibia, Windhoek. Furthermore, only lecturers, who use the MOODLE LMS software for teaching and learning will be considered for partaking in the study, and only students registered in degree programs with courses offered on the MOODLE LMS at the selected campus will take part in the study.

The study use of qualitative research approach and limitations to one campus in the capital of the country will reduce the generalizability of the findings to other campuses and other universities in the country. Reliance on voluntary participation in the study is another inherent weakness in the study that may result in few participants. The researcher, being an actively involved in the administration of eL-earning services at the institution may impact the research process where bias towards use of technology may be present, and participants may have a positive or negative bias or prejudice towards the researcher, thereby potentially affecting the quality of data. These limitations will be addressed through considerate choice of research design methods and using reflective journal to document **issues** as these **emerge**, thereby enabling opportunities to address them timely.

SOLUTIONS AND RECOMMENDATIONS

This section of the chapter will discuss **solutions and recommendations** in dealing with the **issues** or **problems** presented in the preceding section.

Solutions

Artificial Intelligence/Chat GPT

With regards to societal changes, one such change is the much talked about fourth industrial revolution (IR 4.0) that accelerates the automation processes where a lot of routine and manual jobs risk automation. Teo, Unwin, Scherer and Gardiner (2021) made a case for education in IR 4.0 that should prepare graduates for human-centric tasks that cannot be automated, thus requiring the need to strengthen students' soft skills and 21st century competencies that machines cannot do as well as humans can. The proliferation of *artificial intelligence* **solutions**, such as the topical *ChatGPT* call for the need to develop new digital skills, going beyond basic computer skills towards data and AI literacy, to enable students as **future** active citizens and workers to use AI to complement their work, and not be replaced by it.

Leveraging ethical standards in *artificial intelligence* technologies towards a guideline for responsible teaching and learning applications was contained in the **solutions** suggested by Uunona and Goosen (2023) in their chapter as part of the *Handbook of Research on Instructional Technologies in Health Education and Allied Disciplines*.

Recommendations

In terms of **recommendations** for practitioners, Sullivan and Bers (2019, p. 114) indicated that successful

"early childhood computer science education programs must teach powerful ideas from the discipline of computer science in a developmentally appropriate way, provide means for self-expression, prompt debugging and problem solving, and offer a low-floor/high-ceiling interface for both novices and experts."

FUTURE RESEARCH DIRECTIONS

This section of the chapter will discuss **future** and **emerging trends** and provide insight about the **future** of the theme of **Navigating Computer Science Education in the 21st Century**, from the perspective of the chapter focus on **exploring educators' pedagogical capabilities to develop university students' 21st century skills** while **navigating within a digital learning environment**. The viability of a paradigm, model, implementation **issues** of proposed programs, etc., may also be included in this section. **Future research directions** within the domain of the topic will finally be suggested.

Burbules, et al. (2020, p. 93) pointed out five **emerging trends** related to education and technologies in a sustainable **future.**

21st century skills are argued to be of high relevance to both education and the workplace within the current and **emerging** economy (Van Laar, et al., 2020). These skills are considered distinctly unique to the 21st century because the capabilities that are needed for success at work, civil participation and functioning in daily lives, and for self-actualization are different from those that were required in the 20th century (Dede, 2010). Unless citizens acquire these soft and functional skills, some researchers argue that countries lacking such skills are likely to play subservient to those with such skills, as the former will tend to maintain economies that produce goods designed and created by the latter, while remaining consumer economies with their workers doing lowly paid routine jobs (Erdem, 2019).

In literature one would find that the concepts *'knowledge economy', 'knowledge society'* and *'learning society'* are used interchangeably (Oxley, Walker, Thorns, & Wang, 2008), or used closely in relation. Välimaa and Hoffman (2008) explained that these terms emanate from different research fields, with economists, sociologists and educators preferring the each of the three terms respectively, such that 'Knowledge Society' **emerged** from sociological theory while 'Knowledge Economy' from economic theory, with 'Learning Society' the subject of interest in education. Although the terms 'knowledge-based economy' and 'knowledge-based society' tend to be common, there is a logical expectation that the term Learning Society should be preferred in this study since it concerns itself with the field of education. In support of this notion, Hargreaves (2003) found the term knowledge society to be inappropriate, preferring learning societies that are characterized by the processing of information, knowledge to expand learning feed invention while capacitating people to both initiate and adapt to change.

Future research directions "should continue collecting Google Analytics from the ScratchJr app and track changes in usage." **Future research directions** "should also collect analytics from a wide range of programming applications for young children to see" whether the **emerging trends** identified in the study reported on by Sullivan and Bers (2019, p. 114) were consistent across different applications.

Mehta, et al. (2020) also maintained that the belief that 21st century skills give students an advantage in their **future** workplaces has been claimed to lack empirical evidence in support of it, especially considering the diverse nature of work practices and life realities that students tend to face upon graduation, compounded the difficulties of making accurate predictions about the **future** needs of students. The authors argue that educators must be critical of ideas promoted by corporate industries and the big tech companies and should seek to reconcile the agenda of the 21st century rhetoric with the foundational values of education. There is a need they argue, to bring to the fore the essence of education as a public good whose goal is to develop students as lifelong learners with well-developed ethical standards to benefit their communities.

CONCLUSION

This section of the chapter will provide a discussion of the overall coverage and concluding remarks.

This chapter situated the study by providing background on and the rationale for the study. The research objectives and questions that guide the study were presented and aligned to the research methodology. The literature review focused on clarifying the key concepts that guide the study and forming the units of analysis, while providing a tentative theoretical framework through which lens findings of the study would be interpreted and made sense of. An attempt has been made to explain some of the typical ethical **issues** considered and how these will be addressed.

REFERENCES

Aleem, M., Qurat-ul-Ain, Q.-A., Shahid, F., Islam, M. A., Iqbal, M. A., & Yousaf, M. M. (2019). A review of technological tools in teaching and learning computer science. *Eurasia Journal of Mathematics, Science and Technology Education, 15*(11). doi:10.29333/ejmste/109611

Ananiadou, K., & Claro, M. (2009). 21st Century Skills and Competences for New Millennium Learners in OECD Countries. In *Organisation for Economic Co-operation and Development (OECD) Education Working Papers, No. 41*. Paris: OECD Publishing. doi:10.1787/19939019

Ary, D., Jacobs, L. C., Irvine, C. K., & Walker, D. (2013). *Introduction to research in education* (9th ed.). Cengage Learning.

Ary, D., Jacobs, L. C., Irvine, C. K., & Walker, D. (2018). *Introduction to research in education*. Cengage Learning.

Ary, D., Jacobs, L. C., Sorensen, C., & Razavieh, A. (2010). *Introduction to research in education* (8th ed.). Wadsworth Cengage Learning.

Barber, W., & King, S. (2016). Teacher Student Perspectives of Invisible Pedagogy: New Directions in Online Problem Based Learning Environments. *Electronic Journal of e-Learning*, *14*(4), 235–243. https://academic-publishing.org/index.php/ejel/article/view/1759

Bindé, J. (2005). *Towards knowledge societies: The United Nations Educational, Scientific and Cultural Organization (UNESCO) world report*. UNESCO. Retrieved from UNESCO reference works series. https://unesdoc.unesco.org/images/0014/001418/141843e.pdf

Blayone, T., van Oostveen, R., Barber, W., DiGiuseppe, M., & Childs, E. (2016). *Developing learning communities in fully online spaces: Positioning the fully online learning community model*. Higher Education in Transformation Symposium, Oshawa, Ontario, Canada. https://arrow.tudublin.ie/cgi/viewcontent.cgi

Blayone, T. J., van Oostveen, R., Barber, W., DiGiuseppe, M., & Childs, E. (2017). Democratizing digital learning: Theorizing the fully online learning community model. *International Journal of Educational Technology in Higher Education*, *14*(1), 1–16. doi:10.1186/s41239-017-0051-4

Brian, T. (2016). Navigating the Tides of Globalisation and Neoliberalism: A Critical Approach to 21st century Tertiary Education. *New Zealand Journal of Teachers'. Work (Reading, Mass.)*, *13*(2), 134–146.

Brown, M., Dehoney, J., & Millichap, N. (2015, April). The next generation digital learning environment. A Report on Research. *Educause*, *5*(1), 1–13.

Burbules, N. C., Fan, G., & Repp, P. (2020). Five trends of education and technology in a sustainable future. *Geography and Sustainability*, *1*(2), 93–97. doi:10.1016/j.geosus.2020.05.001

Caena, F., & Redecker, C. (2019). Aligning teacher competence frameworks to 21st century challenges: The case for the European Digital Competence Framework for Educators (Digcompedu). *European Journal of Education*, *54*(3), 356–369. doi:10.1111/ejed.12345

Chou, P.-N. (2020). Using ScratchJr to foster young children's computational thinking competence: A case study in a third-grade computer class. *Journal of Educational Computing Research*, *58*(3), 570–595. doi:10.1177/0735633119872908

Creswell, J. W. (2008). *Educational research: planning, conducting and evaluating quantitative and qualitative research* (3rd ed.). Pearson/Merrill Prentice Hall.

Creswell, J. W. (2014). *Educational research: Planning, conducting, and evaluating quantitative and qualitative research* (4th ed.). Pearson.

Creswell, J. W., & Poth, C. N. (2007). *Qualitative inquiry and research design: choosing among five approaches*. SAGE.

Dede, C. (2010). Comparing frameworks for 21st century skills. *21st century skills: Rethinking how students learn, 20*, 51-76.

Dlamini, R., & Ndzinisa, N. (2020). Universities trailing behind: Unquestioned epistemological foundations constraining the transition to online instructional delivery and learning. *South African Journal of Higher Education, 34*(6), 52–64. doi:10.20853/34-6-4073

Erdem, C. (2019). Introduction to 21st Century Skills and Education. In 21st century skills and education (pp. 1-20). Cambridge Scholars Publishing.

Fester, M. O. (2022). *The Experiences of In-Service Teachers in Short Online Courses Aimed at Developing Online Teaching Skills*. University of Johannesburg.

Government of the Republic of Namibia (GRN). (2004). *Namibia Vision 2030: Policy framework for long-term national development.* Windhoek: Office of the President. https://www.npc.gov.na/wp-content/uploads/2021/11/Vision_2030_Summary.pdf

Graf, S., Lachance, P., & Mishra, B. (2016). Integrating Motivational Techniques into Learning Management Systems. In *State-of-the-Art and Future Directions of Smart Learning* (pp. 173–184). Springer Singapore. doi:10.1007/978-981-287-868-7_20

Guillén-Gámez, F. D., Mayorga-Fernández, M. J., Bravo-Agapito, J., & Escribano-Ortiz, D. (2021). Analysis of teachers' pedagogical digital competence: Identification of factors predicting their acquisition. *Technology. Knowledge and Learning, 26*(3), 481–498. doi:10.1007/s10758-019-09432-7

Hargreaves, A. (2003). *Teaching in the knowledge society: Education in the age of insecurity*. Teachers College Press.

Hass, D., Hass, A., & Joseph, M. (2023). Emergency online learning & the digital divide: An exploratory study of the effects of covid-19 on minority students. *Marketing Education Review, 33*(1), 22–37. doi:10.1080/10528008.2022.2136498

Karpava, S. (Ed.). (2022). *Handbook of Research on Teacher and Student Perspectives on the Digital Turn in Education*. IGI Global. https://www.igi-global.com/book/handbook-research-teacher-student-perspectives/290031 doi:10.4018/978-1-6684-4446-7

Kim, S., Raza, M., & Seidman, E. (2019). Improving 21st-century teaching skills: The key to effective 21st-century learners. *Research in Comparative and International Education, 14*(1), 99–117. doi:10.1177/1745499919829214

Kumar, A. P., Omprakash, A., Mani, P. K., Swaminathan, N., Maheshkumar, K., Maruthy, K. N., Sathiyasekaran, B. W. C., Vijayaraghavan, P. V., & Padmavathi, R. (2021). Validation of internal structure of self-directed learning readiness scale among Indian medical students using factor analysis and the structural equation modelling approach. *BMC Medical Education*, *21*(1), 1–13. doi:10.1186/s12909-021-03035-6 PMID:34895214

Laurillard, D. (2013). *Teaching as a design science: Building pedagogical patterns for learning and technology*. Routledge. doi:10.4324/9780203125083

Laurillard, D., Charlton, P., Craft, B., Dimakopoulos, D., Ljubojevic, D., Magoulas, G., Masterman, E., Pujadas, R., Whitley, E. A., & Whittlestone, K. (2013). A constructionist learning environment for teachers to model learning designs. *Journal of Computer Assisted Learning*, *29*(1), 15–30. https://doi-org.ezproxy.unam.edu.na/10.1111/j.1365-2729.2011.00458.x. doi:10.1111/j.1365-2729.2011.00458.x

Li, N. (2022). *How Technology Promotes Educational Change: Studies of Virtual Learning Environment in Higher Education*. The University of Liverpool.

Long, D., & Magerko, B. (2020, April). What is AI literacy? Competencies and design considerations. *Proceedings of the CHI conference on human factors in computing systems* (pp. 1-16). ACM. 10.1145/3313831.3376727

LuoF.JiangJ.YangL.LiangY.CaoY.ZhouX.WanQ. (2022). Dental interns' perception toward online learning of complete denture rehabilitation: a questionnaire survey. Retrieved from Research Square: https://www.researchsquare.com/article/rs-2169572/latest doi:10.21203/rs.3.rs-2169572/v1

Maguire, M., Gibbons, S., Glackin, M., Pepper, D., & Skilling, K. (2018). *EBOOK: Becoming a teacher: Issues in secondary education*. McGraw-Hill Education.

Mehta, R., Creely, E., & Henriksen, D. (2020). A profitable education: Countering neoliberalism in 21st century skills discourses. In *Handbook of research on literacy and digital technology integration in teacher education* (pp. 359–381). IGI Global. doi:10.4018/978-1-7998-1461-0.ch020

Ministry of Education, Arts, and Culture (MEAC). (2016). *The National Curriculum for Basic Education*. Okahandja: National Institute for Educational Development (NIED). http://www.nied.edu.na/assets/documents/05Policies/NationalCurriculumGuide/National_Curriculum_Basic_Education_2016.pdf

Nedzinskaitė-Mačiūnienė, R., & Šimienė, G. (2021). A Strategic and Goal-Directed Student: Expectations vs. Reality. In *Improving Inclusive Education through Universal Design for Learning* (pp. 187–215). Springer International Publishing. doi:10.1007/978-3-030-80658-3_8

Nelan, M. M., Wachtendorf, T., & Penta, S. (2018). Agility in disaster relief: A social construction approach. *Risk, Hazards & Crisis in Public Policy*, *9*(2), 132–150. doi:10.1002/rhc3.12135

Ntalindwa, T., Soron, T. R., Nduwingoma, M., Karangwa, E., & White, R. (2019). The use of information communication technologies among children with autism spectrum disorders: Descriptive qualitative study. *JMIR Pediatrics and Parenting*, *2*(2), e12176. doi:10.2196/12176 PMID:31573940

Osode, J. I. (2021). *Learning management systems in higher education: the attitudes, expectations and experiences of academic staff at selected Nigerian higher Eeducation institutions*. University of Johannesburg.

Oxley, L., Walker, P., Thorns, D., & Wang, H. (2008). The knowledge economy/society: The latest example of" Measurement without theory"? *Journal of Philosophical Economics*, *II*(1), 20–54. doi:10.46298/jpe.10568

Reynolds, D. W. (2021). *Using Entrepreneurship Education to Empower Students with 21st Century Skills.* [Doctoral dissertation, St. Thomas University].

Shah, M. A., Hussain, M., & Jabbar, A. (2022). Applications of Information Communication Technology in Education. *Journal of Computing & Biomedical Informatics*, *4*(1), 87–91.

Shenton, A. K. (2004). Strategies for ensuring trustworthiness in qualitative research projects. *Education for Information*, *22*(2), 63–75. doi:10.3233/EFI-2004-22201

Sullivan, A., & Bers, M. U. (2019). Computer science education in early childhood: The case of ScratchJr. *Journal of Information Technology Education. In Practice*, *18*, 113–138.

Sweet, D. (2014). *Strategies California superintendents use to implement 21st century skills programs*. University of Southern California.

Tan, S. C., & Hung, D. (2002). Beyond information pumping: Creating a constructivist e-learning environment. *Educational Technology*, *42*(5), 48–54.

Teixeira, P. N., & Shin, J. C. (Eds.). (2020). *The international encyclopedia of higher education systems and institutions*. Springer. doi:10.1007/978-94-017-8905-9

Teo, P. (2019). Teaching for the 21st century: A case for dialogic pedagogy. *Learning, Culture and Social Interaction*, *21*, 170–178. doi:10.1016/j.lcsi.2019.03.009

Teo, T., Unwin, S., Scherer, R., & Gardiner, V. (2021). Initial teacher training for twenty-first century skills in the Fourth Industrial Revolution (IR 4.0): A scoping review. *Computers & Education*, *170*, 104223. Advance online publication. doi:10.1016/j.compedu.2021.104223

United Nations Educational, Scientific and Cultural Organization (UNESCO). (1999). Higher education in the twenty-first century: vision and action, v. 1: final report. *World Conference on Higher Education in the Twenty-first Century: Vision and Action, Paris, 1998.* UNESCO. https://unesdoc.unesco.org/ark:/48223/pf0000116345

University of Namibia (UNAM). (2020). *Curriculum Transformation Framework: Towards increased access with success*. UNAM.

Uunona, G. N., & Goosen, L. (2023). Leveraging Ethical Standards in Artificial Intelligence Technologies: A Guideline for Responsible Teaching and Learning Applications. In M. Garcia, M. Lopez Cabrera, & R. de Almeida (Eds.), *Handbook of Research on Instructional Technologies in Health Education and Allied Disciplines* (pp. 310–330). IGI Global. doi:10.4018/978-1-6684-7164-7.ch014

Välimaa, J., & Hoffman, D. (2008). Knowledge society discourse and higher education. *Higher Education, 56*(3), 265–285. doi:10.1007/s10734-008-9123-7

Van Laar, E., Van Deursen, A. J., Van Dijk, J. A., & de Haan, J. (2020). Determinants of 21st-century skills and 21st-century digital skills for workers: A systematic literature review. *SAGE Open, 10*(1). https://journals.sagepub.com/doi/full/10.1177/2158244019900176. doi:10.1177/2158244019900176

Van Weert, T. (2005). Lifelong learning in the knowledge society: Implications for education. In *Education and the knowledge society: Information technology supporting human development* (pp. 15–25). Springer. doi:10.1007/0-387-23120-X_2

Watted, A. (2023). Examining motivation to learn and 21st century skills in a massive open online course. *International Journal of Instruction, 16*(3), 797–822. doi:10.29333/iji.2023.16343a

Yue, W. (2022). *A Comparative Case Study Analysis of the Effects of a Flipped Classroom Model on a College Foreign Language Course*. Delaware State University.

Zsolt, T., & István, B. (2008). *Moodle and social constructivism.* Research Gate. https://www.researchgate.net/profile/Zsolt-Toth-4/publication/345986283_Moodle_and_social_constructivism/links/5fb44fba299bf10c3689ac91/Moodle-and-social-constructivism.pdf

Chapter 2
Fostering the Teaching and Learning of Computer Programming With Open Educational Resources:
Challenges and Solutions

William Simão de Deus
University of São Paulo, Brazil

Fernando Cesar Balbino
https://orcid.org/0009-0009-1836-5669
University of São Paulo, Brazil

Leonardo Vieira Barcelos
Minas Gerais State University, Brazil

Ellen Francine Barbosa
Institute of Mathematics and Computer Sciences, University of São Paulo, Brazil

ABSTRACT

Open educational resources (OER) are materials designed for teaching, learning, or research. They are free and open, facilitating their use and reuse within a community of users. Due to these characteristics, OER can play a crucial role in supporting the teaching and learning of computer programming. They can provide, for instance, resources such as video classes, open books, and free online courses for students, along with various teaching materials for educators. However, these resources are hidden in large digital collections, generating a discovery problem for users. Considering this scenario, the purpose of this chapter is to discuss how to articulate OER and computer programming, emphasizing two main lines of necessary action: first, addressing the challenges that students and teachers still face when seeking such materials; second, outlining solutions that researchers or individuals interested in the topic can adopt to facilitate the reuse of these materials. Together, these two lines of action pave the way for the widespread use of OER in programming education.

DOI: 10.4018/979-8-3693-1066-3.ch002

INTRODUCTION

Open Educational Resources (OER) are both open and free materials for teaching, learning, and research (United Nations Educational, Scientific and Cultural Organization (UNESCO), 2019). In short, OER encompasses any kind of material that addresses educational content, such as videos, syllabi, open textbooks, among others. Additionally, the content must be open-licensed to enable their use, reuse, and sharing (Muñoz-Rujas, Baptiste, Pavani & Montero, 2020).

Despite the potential of OER to promote the democratization of education, OER are still far from being fully adopted by students and teachers (Cortinovis, Mikroyannidis, Domingue, Mulholland & Farrow, 2019). In fact, there is still a lack of OER in educational contexts as well as difficulties related to the use and identification of relevant resources (Ivanova, 2019; Wiley, Bliss & McEwen, 2013). In this sense, it is essential to establish strategies and solutions for disseminating OER within educational contexts, thereby facilitating their use and adoption by teachers, students, researchers, and other stakeholders (UNESCO, 2019).

According to Wiley et al. (2013), the discovery problem is one of the main factors limiting the potential of OER to be widely adopted. In summary, the discovery problem refers to the difficulty that users face when searching for OER in digital sources. In many cases, searches are ineffective and non-relevant results are produced.

The discovery problem is amplified due to many factors. For example, a teacher of Computing can search for 'Java' within an OER initiative. However, the results presented can be aligned with Geography, showing resources about the island of Indonesia. This occurs because there are many collisions among very distinct subjects within digital collections.

Some users may argue that a more specific search could solve the aforementioned scenario. For instance, searching for 'Java programming exercises' instead of just 'Java'. However, the problem still remains. On the one hand, the amount of educational resources available on the Web is vast and continuously increasing (Popescu & Buse, 2014). In this sense, adding more terms will probably show more resources, making the task of finding relevant and reliable resources a very complex issue. On the other hand, OER are highly heterogeneous (Molins-Ruano, Jurado & Rodriguez, 2019). This implies that each resource has its own logical structure and terminology. Some resources may adopt 'computer programming' instead of 'Java programming'. Other resources may use 'syllabi' or 'coding for students' instead of 'exercises'. In practice, several refinements should be made until to identify a relevant result.

In fact, computer programming is a cross-cutting skill taught in different undergraduate courses, being an evidence that industry expects programming skills and abilities from graduates of all computing related programs (Association for Computing Machinery (ACM) & Institute of Electrical and Electronics Engineers - Computer Society (IEEE-CS), 2020). As a consequence, it has a great impact on the use of OER for programming students. For example, an OER useful for Computer Engineering students may not be useful for Computer Science students because some topics, such as the use of pointers, are more detailed.

Another point related to the discovery problem of OER for programming education is the educational levels adopted. Computer programming can be addressed in different educational levels, as occurs with 'CS1' or 'CS2'. But, there is little agreement on the topics and subjects that should be mastered by beginners (CS1) or advanced (CS2) students in programming (Hertz, 2010). As a result, educational materials for programming education also reflect this trend. In many OER repositories, there is an unclear distinction between these resources. Most of the time, OER for CS1 and CS2 are mixed in the same category, covering similar topics and subjects.

Besides, current OER search engines are inefficient to identify relevant resources among digital collections. As synthesized by Okada, Connolly and Scott (2012), the problem is to filter the complexity of resources and provide relevant opportunities (results) for users to engage. In this context, filtering strategies are very ineffective because many filter manipulations must be carried out until a satisfactory result is reached, such as selection of licenses, types of resources, educational level, language, among others. After that, often users are unable to obtain a clear view of the presented results (Gunarathne, Chootong, Sommool, Ochirbat, Chen, Reisman & Shih, 2018). Therefore, the discovery problem remains present even in the latest OER search engines.

Although the discovery problem has introduced many issues for teachers and students of computer programming, it remains poorly understood. Given this context, this chapter presents an empirical approach, which combines focus group and grounded theory. By blending both methods, were identified and categorized ten challenges associated with the discovery problem. The chapter discusses each challenge and provides potential solutions for them.

Thus, the main objective of this chapter is to discuss how to articulate OER and computer programming, emphasizing two main lines of necessary action: First, addressing the challenges that students and teachers still face when seeking such materials. Second, outlining solutions that researchers or individuals interested in the topic can adopt to facilitate the reuse of these materials.

BACKGROUND

Open Educational Resources

According to UNESCO (2019), OER are learning, teaching and research materials in any format and medium that reside in the public domain or are under copyright that have been released under an open license, that permit no-cost access, re-use, re-purpose, adaptation and redistribution by others. In this sense, two aspects are very important for defining OER.

Firstly, the use of public domain or open licenses represents strategies for sharing content without barriers. Consequently, OER are released with the aim of providing educational content openly and freely, granting users five degrees of freedom, as synthesized by Wiley, Bliss & McEwen (2013):

- Retain: the right to make, own, and control copies of the content.
- Reuse: the right to reuse the content in its unaltered/verbatim form (e.g., make a backup copy of the content).
- Revise: the right to adapt, adjust, modify, or alter the content itself (e.g., translate the content into another language).
- Remix: the right to combine the original or revised content with other content to create something new (e.g., incorporate the content into a mashup).
- Redistribute: the right to share copies of the original content, the revisions, or the remixes with others (e.g., give a copy of the content to a friend).

Secondly, any format or medium for an OER is acceptable, as long as it serves the purpose of teaching, learning, or researching a specific subject. Consequently, a wide range of educational materials is available for use. This not only reduces the workload for creating new materials, as teachers, students, or general users can reuse existing materials, but also caters to students with diverse profiles by offering educational materials tailored to their interests and skills.

Collectively, these two characteristics help address various challenges in teaching programming, including the substantial workload that teachers face when instructing these subjects and the inherent difficulties experienced by individual students.

Computer Programming

Computer programming is associated with teaching and learning to program a computer. In this context, various topics such as 'variables', ''loops', 'arrays', among others, are introduced to students. Currently, the teaching and learning of these concepts are aligned with the use of a competency model. According to ACM and IEEE-CS (2020), a competency is composed of three dimensions: Knowledge, Skill and Dispositions:

- **Knowledge**: is the subject to be taught by teachers (also known as the 'know-what' dimension) (ACM and IEEE-CS, 2020). Generally, 'knowledge' is adapted to structure courses and their content.
- **Skill**: is the capability of applying knowledge to actively accomplish a task (ACM and IEEE-CS, 2020). In short, skill is the 'know-how' dimension. In order to specify the skills, the Bloom's taxonomy can be adopted. For instance, when a student names three types of loops (e.g., 'for', 'while' and 'do...while'), he or she is remembering loops.
- **Dispositions**: are habitual inclinations (e.g., socioemotional tendencies, predilections, and attitudes) (ACM and IEEE-CS, 2020). Commonly, 'dispositions' are related to the context explored and they are classified as 'know-why' dimension.

The competency is articulated when the three dimensions (Knowledge + Skills + Dispositions) are performed in a specific task. Often, teaching strategies (such as expository classes, educational projects, list of exercises, among others) are adopted to articulate each competency.

OER for computer programming can enhance this process. Since these resources come in various formats, instructors can provide students with diverse content, such as videos, exercise lists, or open books, to be used during classes. Moreover, these materials typically address topics that align with the curriculum of introductory programming. Therefore, the content of these resources is consistent with the expected knowledge level of students learning to program and can, at times, serve as support for testing or enhancing their skills.

State of the Art

However, to date, there is no consistent evidence of programming teachers and students using OER in the classroom. In practice, teachers often rely on proprietary materials like slides and exercises, rather than remixing or revising available OER from digital repositories. Reasons for this vary, from a lack of knowledge about using OER to concerns that students may perceive the teacher as not creating their own materials (Deus, Fioravanti, Oliveira & Barbosa, 2020). Nevertheless, various initiatives have emerged to address the utilization of OER in educational settings. These initiatives are detailed below.

Some authors have addressed the discovery problem in current literature. For example, Molins-Ruano et al. (2019) identified and classified challenges faced by users when they search for OER. As a result, they proposed a five-step model to support this operation. However, their model is focused on the development of digital recommenders. This work differs from Molins-Ruano et al. (2019) since it is interested in identifying challenges associated with the discovery problem in a broader context, encompassing users and their interaction with OER initiatives and collections.

Additionally, some authors have presented digital tools to reduce the discovery problem. For instance, Mouriño-García, Pérez-Rodríguez, Anido-Rifón, Fernández-Iglesias & Darriba-Bilbao (2018) proposed a repository aggregator to facilitate the discovery of OER. Similarly, Gunarathne et al. (2018) also introduced a digital tool to support the identification of OER through graphical visualization. Another line of action is the use of digital recommendation. In this perspective, the use of an external agent (automatic or manual) aims at identifying similar OER. Gasparetti, De Medio, Limongelli, Sciarrone & Temperini (2018), for example, adopted machine learning algorithms to annotate educational resources using digital sources and Rathod & Cassel (2013) proposed the use of social bookmarking and recommendations.

In this sense, the main distinction between this work and the aforementioned works lies in the perspective. On the one hand, Mouriño-García et al. (2018), Gunarathne et al. (2018), Gasparetti et al. (2018), and Rathod & Cassel (2013) have focused on the development of innovative tools to support the use and reuse of OER, thereby reducing the discovery problem. On the other hand, the intention of this chapter is to investigate the challenges associated with the discovery problem. In other words, the contribution to the literature is to strengthen this field by presenting a more comprehensive theory that can also guide the development of new tools.

Another related work was performed by Ivanova (2019). In short, the author analyzed possibilities of supporting the finding and use of relevant resources on the web. This work makes a significant contribution considering the technological aspects of the discovery problem, such as the use of metadata and the description of materials. This work contributes to this discussion by adding new perspectives on how human aspects also contribute to the discovery problem, such as the impact of user experience and problems with outdated interfaces.

RESEARCH METHODOLOGY

In order to investigate the discovery problem for OER in Computer Programming, an approach that combines a focus group and grounded theory was adopted. Herein, a summary of the main steps carried out during the research is described.

Research Question

Firstly, a Research Question (RQ) was formulated to guide the investigation:

- What challenges are associated with the discovery problem?

Data Collection

Secondly, to address the RQ, a focus group was conducted. For this purpose, a collaboration network at the Institute of Mathematics and Computer Sciences of University of São Paulo was established. Were invited participants who were experienced teachers. In total, five participants took part in the focus group, and their experiences are presented in Table 1.

One participant (P2) declared to be a Ph.D. student and serves as a teaching assistant (TA), helping undergraduate students with their doubts and providing support about programming. The other participants are teachers from universities who have taught introductory programming courses to undergraduate students. For this reason, this topic was selected in the focus group.

Next, were selected two OER initiatives for the focus group: the Merlot repository and the Mason OER Metafinder. These initiatives were selected because they have a large collection of OER for introductory programming and represent two current tendencies in OER collection: Central and Portal. In the first case, a unique OER database is adopted, as seen in the Merlot repository. In the second case, several OER databases are consulted, as observed in the Mason OER Metafinder.

Table 1. Participants and background

Participant	B.Sc.	M.Sc.	Ph.D.
P1	Computer Science	Augmented Reality	Virtual Production
P2	Analysis/System Development	Software Engineering	Software Engineering
P3	Information Systems	Image/Signal Processing	Artificial Intelligence
P4	Computer Science	Artificial Intelligence	Production Engineering
P5	Information Systems	Artificial Intelligence	-

The focus group was conducted in five distinct steps:

1. **Preparation:** Introduction to the research context, the concept of OER, and the collection of data about the experience of each participant.
2. **First Training:** Next, the Mason OER Metafinder was introduced (its interface, search options, and filters). Then, the participants accessed and browsed the Mason OER Metafinder.
3. **First Execution:** After the training, the following task was introduced: participants were asked to search for an OER suitable for an introductory programming class. The OER should have content focused on teaching loops (i.e., 'while', 'for', or 'do...while') in Java. This task was performed using the Mason OER Metafinder.
4. **Second Training:** This phase was similar to step 2. However, the participants received training and performed tests in the Merlot repository.
5. **Second Execution:** Similar to step 3, the participants were given the same task to perform in the Merlot repository.

The aforementioned steps were carried out under the supervision of two researchers (PhD students). In summary, each participant performed the steps while being individually accompanied by the researchers. Data were collected using two strategies: (1) personal notes taken by the researchers during the sessions, capturing participants' expressions and observations, and (2) feedback from participants themselves. After completing steps 3 and 5, each participant also filled out an electronic questionnaire about their experience, providing personal perceptions, difficulties, or barriers encountered during their OER searches. Figure 1 summarizes this process.

Figure 1. Survery process
Collecting data. Source: Authors

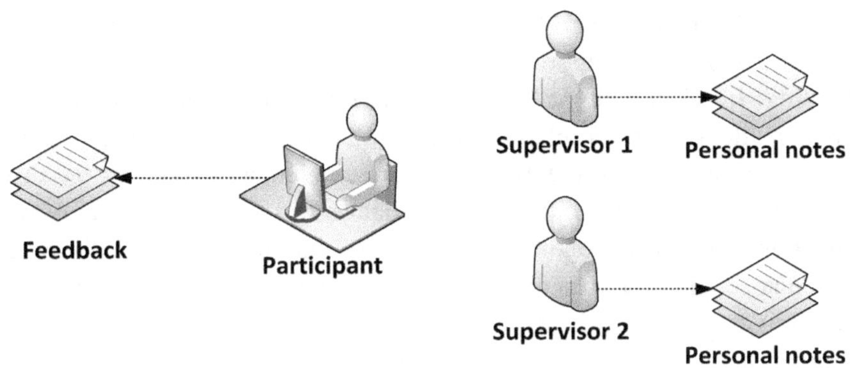

Data Analysis

In order to analyze the collected data, assumptions of grounded theory according to Pandit (1996) were followed. For this, the data were organized following the chronological order. Next, they were unified into a single document, adding an Identifier, Participant ID (P_1, P_2, P_3, P_4, or P_5), OER Source (Merlot or Metafinder), Origin (Researcher or Participant), and Description. In Figure 2, a synthesis of this process is presented.

To analyze the collected data, the grounded theory according to Pandit (1996) was adopted. The data were organized and unified into a single document, with each entry including an identifier, origin (researchers or participants), participant identification (p1, p2, p3, p4, or p5), OER source (portal or central), and description. Table 2 presents a synthesis of this process.

Table 2. Merging the collected data (example of entries)

ID	Origin	Who	OER Source	Description
1	Participants	P1	Portal	I have found problems with the interface and filters
2	Participants	P2	Central	The interface is outdated
...	...	...	...	...

Next, data analysis was started by adopting three strategies:

- **Open Coding:** In this activity, the collected data were carefully examined, following the recommendations of Khandkar (2009). Each description was marked with codes for further analysis.

During this process, pieces of data with similar codes were grouped together, leading to the generation of initial concepts.

- **Axial Coding:** In this activity, the open-coded data was revised to establish connections between categories and their sub-categories, following the approach proposed by Pandit (1996). The coded data were reorganized by grouping similar concepts into categories. During this process, the categories were refined, aligned, and organized according to their properties and dimensions, as suggested by Scott & Medaugh (2017). More specifically, this activity resulted in the development of an organized list of challenges reported by the participants.
- **Selective Coding:** In this activity, a descriptive narrative about the phenomenon by conceptualizing the main challenge and its relations was established, following the approach proposed by Pandit (1996). As a result, were identified the core challenge that causes the discovery problem and its consequences. Thus, each identified challenge was linked to the core through four possible classifications: (1) causal conditions (challenges that originated the discovery problem), (2) context (particular set of conditions to generate the discovery problem), (3) action/interaction (responses that occur as a result of the discovery problem), or (4) outcomes (intended or unintended consequences for the discovery problem) (Pandit, 1996).

An illustration of the data analysis is presented in Figure 2. Two researchers conducted the open, axial, and select activities independently. The data were coded by each researcher separately. After completing these procedures, the researchers merged the data. In short, they manually reviewed each code label to identify similar occurrences. This iterative procedure concluded when both researchers agreed that the final result was consistent.

Literature Comparison

Finally, evidence was gathered from the literature and OER community in order to validate the emerging theory, as suggested by Pandit (1996). Thus, after identifying each category, different OER initiatives and academic works were consulted. The literature comparison was conducted by examining various studies, as presented in the Solutions and Recommendations section.

PROBLEMS

After applying the grounded theory approach to collected data, 10 challenges were identified. These challenges are related to the discovery problem. These challenges vary, ranging from usability issues to difficulties in creating effective search strings. This section provides a summary of each identified challenge.

1) **User Experience:** The first challenge is the user experience. Many teachers and users are accustomed to searching for educational resources on popular platforms like Google or Youtube. When using an OER initiative, they expect a similar experience, where they can start their search and refine it based on the presented results. However, most OER initiatives fall short in this aspect. First, users often encounter multiple fields to fill out on the search page (e.g., title, subject, and license), unlike Google or Youtube, where a single search field suffices. Second, refining the search

Figure 2. Illustrating data analysis
Source: Authors

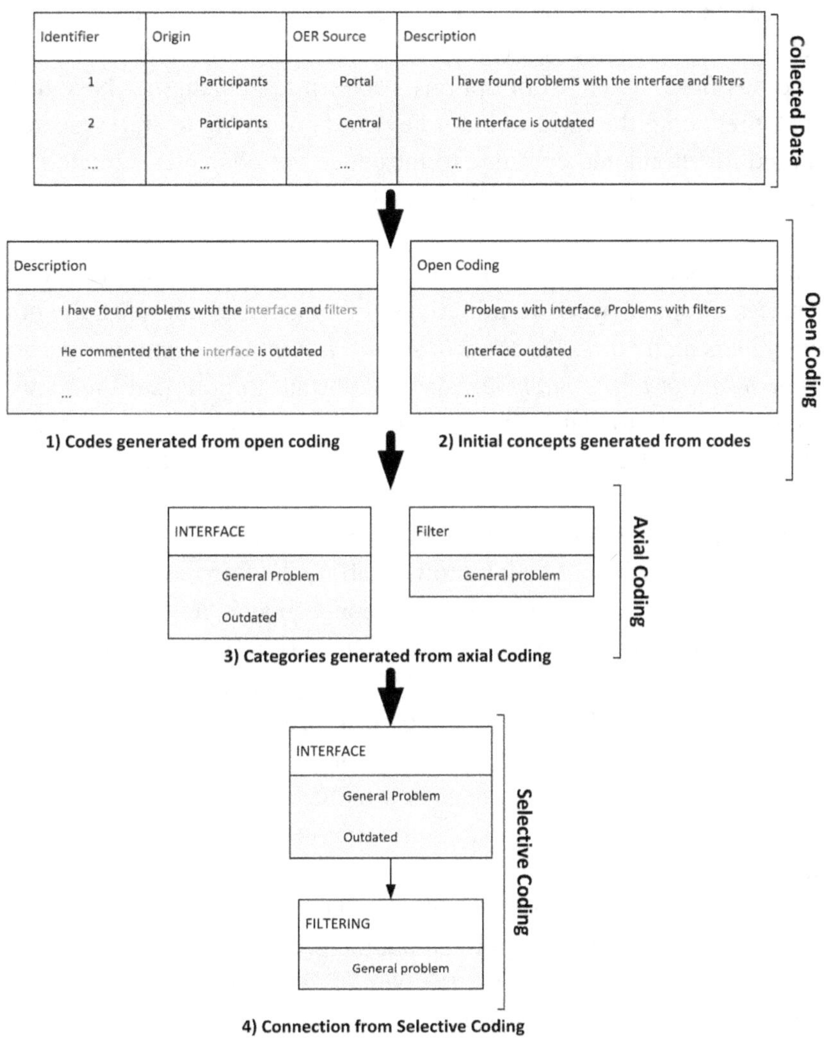

on OER platforms requires users to return to the homepage and re-enter filters and options, while Google or Youtube allow for quick and easy refinements on the same page. Furthermore, the lack of clear information about the meanings of fields, filters, and options in OER initiatives adds to the confusion.

One participant, for instance, stated: *'Initially, I had difficulties doing a new search. I tried to return to the home page to search with other parameters not initially established, but I was unable to do so'.* This problem is supported by a note from a researcher, who writes: *'Participants make faces and expressions of confusion when they see the results listed. Many results are not adhering to their search criteria, and the filtering options are confusing. For example, the repository may present an option to filter material in '.pdf' and/or 'open book'. They are different types, but in practice, they can represent the same thing. This generates mental confusion, typical of a user who is not understanding what the site is showing'.*

The aforementioned challenge becomes evident after comparing how the search process is started in YouTube and Google. YouTube and Google have provided a simple interface. In contrast, OER initiatives have presented numerous fields and a list of options. Modern search engines have minimized the effort required from users by reducing the need to input keywords or filters to start a search. However, OER initiatives have ignored this trend and continue to introduce various entries related to Open Education (e.g., Level, Resource Type, and Licenses), which can be confusing for users.

2) **Interface:** Another challenge is related to *interface*. Many users reported difficulties with the complex interfaces adopted by OER initiatives. For instance, one participant stated: *'The tool [OER repository] has many filters in the initial search interface.'* Another participant mentioned: *'I had little time to adapt to the interface'*. It is important to note that the focus group had a test period and the opportunity to clarify doubts about each repository and its interface. Despite this, the respective participant did not have any doubts during the execution of this research.

Additionally, one researcher also observed instances of 'miss clicks'. This indicates that participants clicked on something in the interface (e.g., a button or tab) and, after seeing the result, clicked again to undo the action or went back to the previous page. As a consequence, it was noticed that OER interfaces are very complex. Users often spend time clicking on buttons or tabs that do not effectively support the search process.

There are many issues with OER interfaces. For instance, some initiatives have two buttons for searching: a symbol and a label. Sometimes, a third option is provided (a link to 'start a new search'). Although they serve the same purpose, it is not clear whether there is a difference among them.

3) **Filtering:** The third challenge is related to the *lack of specific filters for users*. Participants highlighted that the current filters are not effective. Sometimes, they are unclear or too complex to understand. For instance, the following comments pointed out the problem: *'Filters presented aren't efficient'*; *'The search has no way for you to choose the type of OER you want to search for'*. Additionally, evidence of the issues with filter use was also presented in the previous challenges.

Filtering is a more robust challenge than it sounds. For instance, some participants used the term 'loop' in their searches, while many available OER were written using the synonym 'iteration'. Unfortunately, no filter was provided to help users identify similar resources. This problem is complex because efficient filter options may vary based on the area of each resource, requiring considerable expertise to develop.

This complexity is particularly evident in programming education, where a common vocabulary or standardization of terms is lacking. For instance, terms like 'function', ' method' and 'procedure' are used interchangeably in various OER, even though they often refer to similar concepts.

4) **Search String:** In essence, *search strings* are the set of words used to conduct searches. OER collections often lack standardized identification fields, such as titles, descriptions, and keywords, as they are organized by a community of users. Consequently, users may struggle to construct effective search strings, resorting to imprecise terms. As one researcher noted, *'When analyzing the participants' comments, I noticed a great difficulty in the process of constructing a search string.*

Participants were often lost as no function or resource was presented to help them. It was trial and error, brute force'. Similarly, a participant stated: *'Keywords can be used, but they can be found anywhere in the OER, causing the search to retrieve the keyword in the middle of sentences that do not reflect the real objective of the OER'.*

In fact, several challenges arises when it comes to supporting the creation of effective search strings. When comparing modern search engines, such as Google or Bing, distinct features were identified, such as suggestions, highlighting, and related searches. Unfortunately, OER initiatives often fall short in providing these extensive user supports. In fact, modern search engines have access to extensive user data, whereas OER initiatives have more limited access, primarily relying on teachers, students, and other educational stakeholders. Despite this disparity, the intention is not to stimulate the strategies used by commercial search engines in OER initiatives. Instead, OER initiative can introduce similar and simple strategies, such as highlighting the top result or providing a list of related searches, that can guide users in constructing more accurate search strings.

5) **Logical Operators:** A common strategy adopted by the participants was to adopt logical operators (AND/OR) to perform more effective searches. So, instead of searching for 'loop', the user could search for 'loop OR for OR while'. However, it was observed that the results remain unchanged after using these logical operators during the searches. This raises uncertainties about the efficiency of the OER initiatives in delivering relevant results. Feedback from participants illustrates this problem. For example, one participant expressed: *'When using more than one term with a logical operator to refine my search, I did not find the expected results. Using a single term returned several options, but when I added the second term with the AND operator, no results meeting the requested criteria appeared'*. Another participant added: *'While logical operators can be helpful, not using them seems to yield the same results'*.

Logical operators 'AND' and 'OR' are essential for listing results. They allow, among other functions, the creation of complex search strings using different synonyms and comparisons. However, despite the repositories' documentation presenting this possibility, the participants did not notice any evidence of its application.

6) **Open Educational Resources and Purpose:** OER are designed and developed to be used and adapted by users with distinct motivations. Therefore, it is essential to identify the purpose of each OER, specifically its main theme, topics, and target audience. One participant stated the following: *'Keywords can be used, but they can be found anywhere in the OER. This causes the search to find the keyword in the middle of sentences that do not reflect the real objective of the OER'*. According to the researchers, this participant succinctly highlights this problem. The challenge is to obtain relevant information from an OER and make it clear to identify its purpose. For instance, the search for an OER cannot solely focus on the occurrence of terms; instead, it should consider more robust characteristics, such as identifying the topics covered by that OER through its titles, subtitles, and content.

In some situations, OER initiatives presented results with different purposes, including resources for other subjects (e.g., Physics, Engineering, Mathematics, among others). This issue arises from the frequent overlap of terms across different fields and subjects. For instance, the term 'variable' carries distinct meanings in Programming, Physics or Mathematics. The problem is compounded by several factors. Firstly, users often misclassify resources. For example, a resource on 'how to declare a variable in Java' might pertain to computer programming in general, but its accurate classification should place it within introductory programming, a more specific category. Secondly, many OER materials are interdisciplinary. In the case of 'how to declare a variable in Java' it could belong to the broader field of programming and specifically to Java programming. Unfortunately, existing repositories struggle to effectively address this ambiguity.

7) **OER and Properties:** In addition to the purpose, each OER has a list of properties (e.g., link to access, remix, etc.). According to the analysis, such properties also impact the discovery problem because many of them are being ignored by OER initiatives. For example, many OER initiatives have presented resources with invalid access links. In this sense, one participant stated the following: *'[Merlot] returned null results multiple times'*. Another participant also said: *'None [OER] met the requirement completely, unavailable, or had problems like that'*. It was identified that the discovery problem is impacted because the user spends time clicking on links that do not load or that go to invalid addresses

This issue arises from the absence of data persistence in open repositories. Frequently, links to the original resource are provided. Consequently, if the resource's hosting location changes, the OER becomes inaccessible.

Another prevalent problem involves the integration of OER with additional materials like images, videos, and audio. In some cases, the OER is accessed and used, but the embedded resources (e.g., images) are hosted on a different server. This arrangement can lead to display issues if changes are made to the hosting server.

In both cases, the OER is often discarded by the user considering these problems.

8) **Size Collection:** Another problem reported by participants was related to the size of the digital collections. Both large and small collections presented challenges for users. Large collections often produced bad results, as one participant mentioned: *'Perhaps the large volume of links may have influenced the location of the material sought'*. This indicates that users had to make many refinements to establish an efficient search string. On the other hand, collections with few OER also reduced the possibility of identifying relevant resources. One participant stated: '*Due to the smaller number of links available, it became more difficult to locate material*'. In this case, the participant made several refinements, and sometimes no result was returned.

The problem is structural. Large digital collections tend to have localization problems due to a lack of standardization of terms and classification of resources. On the other hand, small collections tend to show few results and/or little variation in results after several search changes.

9) **Search Engine with Metadata:** Another challenge identified is related to the *dependency on metadata by many search engines*. While OER initiatives have adopted metadata to perform OER identification in their search engines, in many cases, the list of metadata provided is not relevant, as it may contain only descriptive information, discarding the real content of each resource.

Additionally, wrong information can be added, creating problems for identification. For instance, one participant mentioned: *'[...] when checking the type of material that the site indexes, I think that there are good OER, but they are among several others that do not meet what I expected'.*

This is a historical problem rooted in the perception that OER are similar to Learning Objects (LO). Consequently, the same identification structure is often applied to both types of resources. However, OER have a significant distinction: they can be edited through revisions and remixing, leading to a wide array of variations. In contrast, LO are typically developed to be used in their original format. As a result, an OER can have diverse forms and functionalities that cannot be adequately captured by metadata and search engines alone. For instance, can an open book be effectively identified solely by its title? Similarly, can a video lesson be accurately classified based solely on its description?

10) **Bad Perceptions:** Finally, the last challenge observed in the research is dedicated to the *bad perceptions of users in relation to the OER initiatives.* All participants were enthusiastic about the potential of using OER. However, they reported a sense of frustration after using OER initiatives. One participant stated that: *'I felt motivated at first, seeing that there was the possibility of getting materials to plan classes for free, but when checking the type of material that the site indexes, I think that there are good OER, but they are among several others that do not meet what I expected.'*. In addition, many participants have stated that there was not enough time to 'understand' how the repositories work. Even though they had taken the time to test the interface and ask the researchers questions.

This problem is an internal feeling expressed by participants after finishing the focal group. Many participants, who are experienced teachers, showed frustration in noticing that OER initiatives are far from reaching their goal of providing OER for users.

SOLUTIONS AND RECOMMENDATIONS

After presenting the challenges for the use of OER in programming education, this chapter discusses effective solutions for each.

1) **User Experience:** A good example of how to solve the problem associated with the user experience is available on the MIT OpenCourseWare, which has a clean and functional structure for starting a search (Massachusetts Institute of Technology (MIT), 2023). For others OER initiatives, it is essential to propose the following actions in order to solve the problems associated with user experience:
    - Reduce mental confusion during the search process by simplifying the number of filters or inputs on the search page. This will prevent users from spending too much time trying to understand the filters/inputs instead of conducting their search.
    - Minimize unnecessary clicks. For instance, instead of presenting a list of open licenses for the user to manually select each one, it is recommended that all licenses be pre-filled by default.

- Provide relevant information for each OER to support decision-making. This could include displaying the total number of remixes or visualizations for each resource. Currently, many OER initiatives present irrelevant information for users, such as authors' names and affiliations, which do not directly contribute to the user's search.

2) **Interface:** Some OER initiatives have adopted excellent designs for their interfaces. For instance, OpenStax has a clean and functional interface. Another example is Wikibooks, although it may appear outdated to some users, is highly functional. To address interface issues for future OER initiatives, two actions are proposed:
   - Design simple websites for users. This involves removing ambiguous fields, using labels easily understood by users, avoiding strong and striking colors, reducing information overload, and avoiding the use of complex structures (e.g., many tabs or buttons); and,
   - Remove any asymmetry. This means adopting a consistent standard for labeling search fields, buttons, and filters. For example, if the homepage has the filter labeled 'Licenses', this pattern should be consistently followed on other pages and in the presentation of results.

3) **Filtering:** To reduce challenges associated with filters, it is essential to create new solutions. Filters cannot solely rely on data classified by users, as many OER may be misclassified or inaccurately classified by users using wrong classifications or irrelevant keywords. Therefore, it is necessary to adopt mechanisms to verify the content of each OER, comparing it with the original classifications. An example is the idea from Gasparetti et al. (2018), in which the authors used an external database to enrich educational resources. Also, two actions can reduce the problems related to filters:
   - Go beyond their traditional use, extending to filters such as 'resource type' or 'license'. An important contribution is the construction of sophisticated mechanisms, including searching for the exact occurrence of a word, searching for synonyms of the terms used, or searching by intention use (remix, share, review, etc...);
   - Labels should be simple and easily understood by all users. In this sense, a suggestion is to use common standards, for example, 'Educational Levels' [''Primary Education, Secondary Education, and Tertiary Education'] instead of terms like ['School, High School, College, Lower Division or Upper Division'], which may be more region-specific, primarily used in the United States;

4) **Search String:** The elaboration of search strings may be optimized by adopting innovative strategies. An example is the idea from Gunarathne et al. (2018), in which the authors used a hierarchical knowledge graph, supporting the identification of new keywords. In order to solve problems related to search string, a recommendation is:
   - The development of strategies to create and refine search strings, such as providing examples of synonyms or similar searches, and highlighting top results.

5) **Logical Operators:** The use of logical operators is a simple challenge to be solved; it involves optimizing the keywords during the search. For this purpose, adopting the strategies of a Systematic Literature Review can serve as the best inspiration:

- The use of logical operators for searching OER, as occurs in Systematic Reviews. For this, it is necessary to create and develop more accurate mechanisms to identify results by using logical operators 'AND/OR' and parentheses '()'.
- At the same time, OER initiatives can provide new interfaces to elaborate complex search strings, suggesting synonyms, similar searchers and previous results.

6) **OER and Purpose:** Identifying the real purpose of an OER is not an easy task. However, the literature demonstrates that some solutions can be adopted. The best example is the work by Kastrati, Imran & Kuriti (2019). In their study, the authors integrate word embeddings and document topics with deep learning to help classify videos. A similar strategy can be adopted in OER to accurately extract the real purpose of the resource. In addition, the following is suggested:
    - Use HTML tags to extract more data about the OER content. Thus, developers can extract relevant data, such as terms in bold (which demonstrates that that term is relevant), subtitles (which presents the hierarchical classification of the contents), external links (which exposes related resources), among others.

7) **OER and Properties:** For reducing problems associated with the properties of each OER, several initiatives may be adopted. One of the most relevant is the development of a specific metadata schema, as proposed by Swain, Wagy, McClelland & Jacobs (2006). Thus, standard metadata schemas (such as Dublin Core or IEEE LOM) can be expanded or updated with specific entries following the nature of each resource. In addition, two actions can be developed:
    - OER initiatives must use links with persistent identifiers. This way, OER will be accessible, citable, and easily verifiable, reducing the occurrence of invalid resources due to changes in the original links;
    - In addition, another possible action is to revise collections using web crawlers. In summary, a web crawler can identify invalid resources (e.g., offline, broken references, etc.) that should be removed to prevent errors for users.

8) **Size Collection:** To solve problems related to the size of the OER collection, specific niches can be a solution. A programming teacher looking for OER about 'variables' is unlikely to be interested in resources that talk about variables in Mathematics or Physics. An interesting idea to solve this problem was presented by Chicaiza, Piedra, Lopez-Varga & Tovar-Caro (2014). These authors proposed the use of linked data to identify similar resources. Thus, collections can be created following a specific subject, linking data instead of adding new resources. Additionally, the following suggestion is provided:
    - Large OER collections are inefficient, especially those collections that have OER from several knowledge areas. In these collections, there is a great risk of collisions. As commented, one example is the term *'variable'* that has several definitions according to each area.

9) **Search Engines:** To solve the problems associated with search engines, the development of initiatives merging emergent technologies with OER is a relevant idea. For instance, the adoption of data visualization, as proposed by Gunarathne et al. (2018) or social bookmarking and recommendations, as presented by Popescu & Buse (2014). In addition, the following is suggested:

- Avoid using only metadata. While metadata is suitable for homogeneous digital resources, such as a digital library with similar metadata for each book (e.g., title, author, ISBN, pages, etc.), OER initiatives often encompass heterogeneous resources, such as videos, open books, courses, websites, among others.

10) **Bad Perception:** Users' feelings of frustration have been the object of little study in the literature. Despite searching, no no significant results or contributions exploring this challenge were found. Therefore, the following set of actions are proposed:
    - OER initiatives must be designed considering the aforementioned challenges. Merely creating new initiatives will not suffice as a viable solution for sharing OER.
    - The use, reuse, and sharing of OER for all users. Thus, it is recommended that new solutions follow the needs of specific users for adopting OER.
    - Mechanisms that integrate existing repositories can be designed. As demonstrated above, most of the challenges are common among several initiatives. Creating a plugin that filters OER according to their intended use, for example, is a viable alternative that can support several initiatives using the same technology, as is the case with DSpace, which is widely adopted to create OER repositories.

FUTURE RESEARCH DIRECTIONS

In a broader sense, the recommendations mentioned above represent future research directions that can have a direct impact on the routines of programming teachers and students intending to use OER. Moreover, developing work that contributes to and engages with the aspects mentioned above will enable the democratization of access to education for diverse audiences. This should be the most important and relevant motivation for developing new projects.

In addition, it is crucial to categorize the possibilities for future work into two distinct agendas. The first of these is applied research, which aims to generate products such as software, repositories, or applications to facilitate access and dissemination of OER for teaching introductory programming. For this line of research, it is recommended that the solutions developed consider users' interests, are user-friendly, and allow for adaptability.

The second line involves basic research, concentrating on the formulation of new theories or models aimed at abstracting the dynamics surrounding OER and the teaching of programming. In this context, contributions that can offer some form of theoretical framework for students, teachers, or even researchers in the field are highly valued.

Future Work

In the near future, the authors are interested in developing mechanisms to support the use and reuse of OER, reducing the challenges pointed out in this study. In this sense, the authors are working on two perspectives: the first one is related to the development of a web portal for teachers and students. This portal aggregates the practices adopted by such users (e.g., clean interface and design) and modern identification strategies. The second one is the investigation of open practices. In this sense, the authors intend to investigate several stakeholders, such as teachers, students, programmers, and specialists, in order to develop technical guidelines for OER.

CONCLUSION

The term 'OER' was first defined in 2002 and after two decades it is far from being widely adopted by users. In this study, it was investigate challenges related to the difficulty of finding relevant OER, also known as the discovery problem (Wiley et al., 2013). The discovery problem prevents OER from being identified. In a larger sense, it reduces the OER adoption among users due to difficulty of identifying relevant resources. As a consequence, the discovery problem becomes even more critical when observe the current technological scenario. Few companies are controlling web searching by using sophisticated search algorithms. Often, these algorithms do not follow ethical concepts or value free and open education (DiSalvo, Reid & Roshan, 2014). Instead, they almost always present sponsored results or pages that have an advanced Search Engine Optimization (SEO) strategy. Thus, there is a tendency for OER to be stored into specific repositories or digital collections. However, it does not consolidate OER as a viable alternative. It is necessary to go beyond the creation of websites that store OER, in the current paradigm of the society, it is essential to elaborate technical solutions that solve the discovery problem effectively.

For a long time, the problem of discovery has been cited as a significant barrier to the use of OER. However, in this chapter, this discussion was detailed by presenting a list of causes and potential solutions. OER are essentials to democratize access to education for everyone, reducing economical barriers and dependence on closed/proprietary materials (UNESCO, 2019). However, it is necessary to move forward with results that demonstrate practical advancement in the adoption of these materials by numerous users. Otherwise, OER may face serious issues due to their lack of adherence by students and teachers. This concern is already noted in the most recent OER recommendation provided by UNESCO (2019), but there is much work to be done.

Within this line of reasoning, it is essential to think of OER as a mechanism capable of reducing social inequalities, beyond providing accessible and free solutions to users. It is at this intersection that teaching and learning programming play a fundamental role.

According to the ACM & Association for Information Systems (AIS) (2020), most computing courses dedicate a significant portion of their workload to teaching aspects related to programming. This dynamic is repeated in STEM courses as well (Medeiros, Ramalho & Falcão, 2018), demonstrating that this is not just a trend, but a current and future necessity for various professions. Given this, OER can offer a new paradigm for programming education. In theory, professors from rural Brazil can utilize the same resources created by professors at MIT in the United States due to their potential for reuse and adaptation.

However, this encouraging scenario is still far from becoming a common reality around the world. Programming OER, along with other subjects, need to be efficiently disseminated and distributed globally. This requires a comprehensive overhaul of their current distribution methods. In this investigation, it was demonstrated, for example, that essential aspects of usability create significant barriers for materials to be effectively used. Currently, the use of OER produces dissatisfaction with users. In most cases, users are presented to open initiatives by giving opportunities to use, reuse, elaborate and adopt educational resources freely and openly. However, users face problems of interface, lack of support and difficulties to identify a relevant resource among digital collections. Such challenges prevent users from using OER, leading them to use closed/proprietary materials into web search engines.

Limitations

Considering the context, the main threat of this research is the coding process, which may have discarded relevant data. In order to reduce this threat, two independent researchers - both with OER background and teaching experience - performed the entire coding process. In addition, the categories and their relationships were decided based on the views of both researchers, who discussed each category as well as their relations.

Some researchers may find the total number of participants (5) a threat to validity. However, the epistemological paradigm for qualitative research was followed, which focuses on the complexity and details of the data collected (Pandit, 1996). For this reason, participants were highly relevant considering the phenomena observed. In addition, data were collected from a variety of sources, such as observations, feedback, and notes. Moreover, different researchers contributed to collect and analyze the data. In view of this, risks from sample size were considerably reduced.

ACKNOWLEDGMENT

This work was supported by grant #2019/26871-4, São Paulo Research Foundation (FAPESP).

REFERENCES

ACM & Association for Information Systems (AIS). (2020). *A Competency Model for Undergraduate Programs in Information Systems.* Association for Computing Machinery. https://dl.acm.org/doi/pdf/10.1145/3460863

Association for Computing Machinery & Institute of Electrical and Electronics Engineers - Computer Society (IEEE-CS). (2020). *Computing Curricula 2020: Paradigms for Global Computing Education.* Association for Computing Machinery. doi:10.1145/3467967

Chicaiza, J., Piedra, N., Lopez-Vargas, J., & Tovar-Caro, E. (2014). Domain categorization of open educational resources based on linked data. In *5th International Conference on Knowledge Engineering and the Semantic Web* (pp. 15-28). Springer International Publishing. 10.1007/978-3-319-11716-4_2

Cortinovis, R., Mikroyannidis, A., Domingue, J., Mulholland, P., & Farrow, R. (2019). Supporting the discoverability of open educational resources. *Education and Information Technologies, 24*(5), 3129–3161. Springer Science and Business Media. . doi:10.1007/s10639-019-09921-3

Deus, W., Fioravanti, M., Oliveira, C., & Barbosa, E. (2020). Emergency Remote Computer Science Education in Brazil during the COVID-19 pandemic: Impacts and Strategies. *Revista Brasileira de Informática na Educação, 28,* 1032–1059. doi:10.5753/rbie.2020.28.0.1032

DiSalvo, B., Reid, C., & Roshan, P. K. (2014). They can't find us: the search for informal CS education. *Proceedings of the 45th ACM Technical Symposium on Computer Science Education,* (pp. 487–492). ACM. 10.1145/2538862.2538933

Gasparetti, F., De Medio, C., Limongelli, C., Sciarrone, F., & Temperini, M. (2018). Prerequisites between learning objects: Automatic extraction based on a machine learning approach. *Telematics and Informatics*, *35*(3), 595–610. doi:10.1016/j.tele.2017.05.007

Gunarathne, W. K. T. M., Chootong, C., Sommool, W., Ochirbat, A., Chen, Y.-C., Reisman, S., & Shih, T. K. (2018). Web-Based learning object search engine solution together with data visualization: The case of MERLOT II. *IEEE 42nd Annual Computer Software and Applications Conference*. IEEE. 10.1109/COMPSAC.2018.00179

Hertz, M. (2010). What do 'CS1' and 'CS2' mean? Investigating differences in the early courses. *Proceedings of the 41st ACM technical symposium on Computer science education*, (pp. 199-203). ACM. /10.1145/1734263.1734335

Ivanova, T. (2019). Resources and Semantic-based knowledge models for personalized and self-regulated learning in the Web. *Proceedings of the 20th International Conference on Computer Systems and Technologies.* ACM. 10.1145/3345252.3345288

Kastrati, Z., Imran, A. S., & Kurti, A. (2019). Integrating word embeddings and document topics with deep learning in a video classification framework. *Pattern Recognition Letters*, *128*, 85–92. doi:10.1016/j.patrec.2019.08.019

Khandkar, S. H. (2009). Open Coding. *University of Calgary*. https://pages.cpsc.ucalgary.ca/~saul/wiki/uploads/CPSC681/open-coding.pdf

Massachusetts Institute of Technology (MIT). (2023). *Explore OpenCourseWare*. MIT. https://ocw.mit.edu/search/

Medeiros, R. P., Ramalho, G. L., & Falcão, T. P. (2018). A systematic literature review on teaching and learning introductory programming in higher education. *IEEE Transactions on Education*, *62*(2), 77–90. doi:10.1109/TE.2018.2864133

Molins-Ruano, P., Jurado, F., & Rodriguez, P. (2019). On the identification of several key issues on OER discovery for smart learning environments. *13th International Conference on Ubiquitous Computing and Ambient Intelligence*. MDPI. 10.3390/proceedings2019031086

Mouriño-García, M., Pérez-Rodríguez, R., Anido-Rifón, L., Fernández-Iglesias, M. J., & Darriba-Bilbao, V. M. (2018). Cross-repository aggregation of educational resources. *Computers & Education*, *117*, 31–49. doi:10.1016/j.compedu.2017.09.014

Muñoz-Rujas, N., Baptiste, J., Pavani, A., & Montero, E. (2020). Enhancing interactive teaching of engineering topics using digital materials of the MERLOT database. In *Advances in Intelligent Systems and Computing* (pp. 295–306). Springer International Publishing. doi:10.1007/978-3-030-57799-5_31

Okada, A., Connolly, T., & Scott, P. J. (Eds.). (2012). *Collaborative Learning 2.0: Open Educational Resources*. IGI Global. doi:10.4018/978-1-4666-0300-4

Pandit, N. (1996). The Creation of Theory: A recent application of the grounded theory method. *The Qualitative Report*. Nova Southeastern University. . doi:10.46743/2160-3715/1996.2054

Popescu, E., & Buse, F. E. (2014). Supporting students to find relevant learning resources through social bookmarking and recommendations. *18th International Conference on System Theory, Control and Computing*. IEEE. 10.1109/ICSTCC.2014.6982459

Rathod, N., & Cassel, L. (2013). Building a search engine for computer science course syllabi. *Proceedings of the 13th ACM/IEEE-CS Joint Conference on Digital Libraries*. http://dx.doi.org/10.1145/2467696.2467723

Scott, C., & Medaugh, M. (2017). Axial coding. The International Encyclopedia of Communication Research Methods, 1–2. Springer. doi:10.1002/9781118901731.iecrm0012

Swain, D. E., Wagy, J., McClelland, M., & Jacobs, P. (2006). Developing a metadata schema for CSERD: a computational science digital library. In *Proceedings of the 6th ACM/IEEE-CS joint conference on Digital libraries,* (pp. 350-350). IEEE. 10.1145/1141753.1141845

United Nations Educational, Scientific and Cultural Organization (UNESCO). (2019). *Recommendation on open educational resources (OER)*. UNESCO - Open Educational Resources. http://portal.unesco.org/en/ev.php-URL_ID=49556&URL_DO=DO_TOPIC&URL_SECTION=201.html

Wiley, D., Bliss, T. J., & McEwen, M. (2013). Open educational resources: A review of the literature. In *Handbook of Research on Educational Communications and Technology* (pp. 781–789). Springer New York. doi:10.1007/978-1-4614-3185-5_63

Chapter 3
Creating Open Educational Resources as Renewable Assessment Activities for Computer Science Education:
Enhancing Intrinsic Motivation Through Co-Creation

Chantelle Bosch
https://orcid.org/0000-0001-5743-1985
North-West University, South Africa

ABSTRACT

In recent years, higher education has witnessed a shift towards open education and the proliferation of educational resources. Open educational resources (OERs) have gained prominence for their potential to revolutionize education by allowing students to create freely available, adaptable, and customizable content. Simultaneously, traditional assessment methods have come under scrutiny for their limited ability to measure critical thinking and practical skills. Computer science education, with its emphasis on innovation, is well-suited to embrace these changes. This chapter introduces creating OER as renewable assessment activities as an innovative approach, contributing to the discourse on open education, assessment, and pedagogy in computer science, emphasizing student empowerment, mastery, and intrinsic motivation.

INTRODUCTION

This section is intended to provide an overview of the chapter's general perspective, culminating in a clear articulation of the stated aim and objectives.

Navigating Computer Science Education in the 21st Century

The changing landscape of modern education calls for innovation to stay relevant and recent in the 21st century. In Computer science education, which is known for its dynamic nature and continuously

DOI: 10.4018/979-8-3693-1066-3.ch003

expanding body of knowledge, using traditional pedagogies often strain educators to keep up with the ceaseless advances of the digital era. Educators and institutions are increasingly recognizing the need to empower students as active participants in their educational journeys, fostering knowledge and developing essential critical skills.

Target Audience

The study is particularly pertinent for educators who are interested in aligning their teaching practices with the principles of accessibility, affordability, and inclusivity. Individuals engaged in the design and implementation of assessment strategies, especially those dissatisfied with traditional forms such as standardized testing and final exams, may find the research beneficial. Moreover, educators in the field of computer science, given its emphasis on innovation, adaptation, and the cultivation of diverse skills beyond technical proficiency, are a primary target audience. Furthermore, this study may appeal to researchers and scholars in the broader domains of open education, assessment, and pedagogy. Professionals involved in shaping educational policies and practices, as well as those contributing to the discourse on student-centered learning, may also find insights in this research.

Aims and Objectives

This chapter aims to explores how engaging students in the collaborative creation of OER's, with an emphasis on renewal and ongoing improvement, can empower them as self-directed learners, enhance their mastery of computer science concepts, and foster a deeper sense of intrinsic motivation. From an extensive literature review on aspects including Self-directed learning, Intrinsic motivation, Renewable assessments and OER's, guidelines to Incorporating co-creation and renewable assessment activities will be proposed.

BACKGROUND

In recent years, there has been a significant shift in higher education toward open education and the widespread availability of educational resources (Maina et al.,2019). Open education initiatives, driven by principles of accessibility, affordability, and inclusivity, have prompted educators and institutions to explore new pedagogical strategies that align with these ideals (Kolesnykova, 2019). Among these strategies, the concept of open educational resources (OERs) has gained prominence. Creating OER's as renewable assessment activities have garnered attention for their potential to revolutionize the way educational content is created, shared, and accessed (Baran, & AlZoubi, 2020). Unlike traditional assessment activities, the OER's that are created by the students can be made freely available to others to use, are adaptable to diverse learning contexts, and amenable to continuous improvement and customization. They epitomize the principles of openness and collaboration, inviting educators and students to co-create and share knowledge (Katz & Van Allen, 2020). In tandem with the open education movement, evolving assessment practices have also begun to reshape the educational landscape. Traditional forms of assessment, such as standardised testing and final exams, have faced scrutiny for their limited capacity to measure students' critical thinking, problem-solving abilities, and practical application of knowledge (Sokhanvar et al., 2021). As a result, educators are seeking innovative assessment strategies that align with the principles of authentic learning, active engagement, and lifelong skill development. Computer science education, as a discipline that thrives on innovation and adaptation, is ideally positioned to embrace these transformative shifts in education. It is a field that demands not only the acquisition of technical skills but also the cultivation of creativity, collaboration, and problem-solving abilities. To address these multifaceted learning outcomes, computer science educators should explore assessment approaches that empower students to take ownership of their learning and engage in meaningful, real-world tasks. This chapter bridges these converging trends by proposing Creating OER as Renewable Assessment Activities as an innovative approach to assessment in computer science education. By examining the principles, practices, and outcomes of this co-creation process, this chapter contributes to the evolving discourse on open education, assessment, and pedagogy in the realm of computer science. It underscores the potential of this approach to empower learners, enhance mastery, and invigorate intrinsic motivation, paving the way for a more open, inclusive, and student-centered educational landscape in computer science education.

MAIN FOCUS OF THE CHAPTER

In the next section a discussion on the pertinent concepts in this chapter will be given

Self-Directed Learning

Self-directed learning is an educational approach in which individuals take primary responsibility for planning, initiating, and managing their own learning process. According to Knowles (1975:18) SDL is a process in which "individuals take the initiative, with or without the help of others, in diagnosing their learning needs, formulating learning goals, identifying human and material resources for learning, choosing and implementing learning strategies, and evaluating learning outcomes". SDL fosters autonomy, motivation, and a lifelong commitment to learning (Okwuduba et al., 2021). SDL holds immense value in diverse educational contexts, spanning formal education, workplace training, and personal development. It empowers individuals to cultivate self-reliance, intrinsic motivation, and a lifelong learning ethos, equipping them to adeptly respond to the constantly evolving demands of the contemporary world (Pan, 2020; Onah et al., 2021). In traditional classroom settings, where educators typically employ instructional approaches for knowledge dissemination, students often assume passive roles, receiving information in a predetermined manner regardless of their individual needs or challenges (Lopez, 2023). Yasmin et al. (2019) believes that, under such circumstances, students may lack the motivation to engage fully in the learning process. In contrast, when students take ownership of problem-solving for their own benefit, they proactively seek the acquisition of pertinent knowledge and skills (Calderón et al., 2020)). As a result, active learning comes to fruition when students embark on self-directed educational journeys motivated by their eagerness to tackle authentic or personally significant challenges (Yasmin et al., 2019). According to Guglielmino (1977), a highly self-directed student exemplifies qualities such as initiative, independence, and unwavering persistence in their pursuit of knowledge. They willingly assume responsibility for their learning, perceiving problems as opportunities rather than roadblocks (Guglielmino, 1977; Strickland, 2021). These individuals exhibit self-discipline, possess a robust sense of curiosity, and maintain a high level of self-confidence (Guglielmino, 1977; Loeng, 2020) They can adeptly employ fundamental study techniques, manage their time effectively, set a suitable pace for learning, and construct comprehensive learning plans (Guglielmino, 1977; Morris, 2019). Such students derive genuine enjoyment from the learning process and tend to be goal-oriented in their endeavors (Guglielmino, 1977; Schweder et al., 2022).

Notably, self-directedness is a trait that can both wane and be revitalized and further developed. The incorporation of self-directed learning techniques in an educational setting can be seen as an effort to emulate the innate way individuals naturally acquire knowledge (Dewi et al., 2019). It is imperative for students to acknowledge that their knowledge, attitudes, and self-directed learning skills are pivotal elements in their participation in the learning process. They must recognize the transformation of the educator's role into that of a facilitator or guide, signifying that students can no longer rely solely on the educator as the exclusive source of information (Robinson & Persky, 2020). It remains crucial for all students to understand that they possess the inherent potential for success in self-directed learning projects and programs. However, there persists a need for heightened student awareness regarding the purposes and processes that underlie or are essential for self-directed learning accomplishments (Loeng, 2020). To operate effectively, students must discern the multitude of components inherent in any given learning situation (Strickland, 2021).

Educators should guide the students to attain a higher level of self-direction in their learning (Leahy & Smith, 2021). One of the responsibilities of an educator involves assisting students in effectively planning, executing, and assessing their own learning. According to Yuliansyah and Ayu (2021), educators are advised to grant students greater autonomy in their learning experiences, primarily offering support in resource identification and the mastery of alternative learning methods for individuals or student groups. Granting students some level of control over their learning environment may be crucial in honing their self-directed learning skills (Okwuduba et al., 2021).

Student control constitutes a method for structuring education or educational materials within a formal academic environment. Integrating SDL into the classroom demands careful planning and a gradual implementation process. It is paramount for educators to offer students options regarding resource utilization, learning approaches, and even learning goals (Loeng, 2020). The educator's role extends to challenging students beyond their comfort zones, introducing them to novel learning scenarios, and fostering problem-solving opportunities. It is imperative for educators to offer constructive feedback and assist students in assessing their learning experiences, thereby promoting critical thinking (Song et al., 2022; van Woezik et al., 2021). Furthermore, educators should instil in students the belief in their own capabilities, motivating them to elevate their SDL skills to a higher level (Garcia, 2021). Creating an atmosphere characterized by openness and trust is crucial for educators, as it encourages students to confidently ask questions and actively participate in group activities and discussions (van Woezik et al., 2021). Ultimately, educators play a pivotal role in motivating students to cultivate a positive attitude, a sense of independence, and a genuine desire for continuous learning and the enhancement of their SDL skills (du Toit-Brits, 2019).

Through SDL people can develop the abilities and mindset necessary for lifelong learning. Independent learning is essential for both personal and professional development in today's environment of fast change (Morris, 2019). SDL gives students the ability to customize their educational experiences to meet their own needs, interests, and objectives. It encourages a specialized and individualized method of teaching (Wong et al., 2021). It is important that educators should guide students in setting meaningful goals and developing action plans to achieve those goals. By helping students identify their strengths and areas for growth, educators can support them in creating personalized learning paths tailored to their individual needs and aspirations (Lalitha & Sreeja, 2020). This fosters a sense of autonomy, self-regulation, and independence in decision-making, all of which are valuable life skills (Yaşar & Atay, 2023). Since SDL is inherently student-centered, incorporating co-creation into the SDL process can further enrich the learning experience.

Fostering SDL also holds immense importance in the 21st century. Learning does not stop with formal education in today's quickly changing society. SDL provides individuals with the skills and mindset required for life-long learning. This adaptability is critical in a world where new knowledge and technology arise on a regular basis. Rapid technical breakthroughs characterize the twenty-first century. In an era where technology plays a vital role, educators should utilize technology as a tool for self-directed learning. Online platforms offer a wealth of resources such as OER, Massive Open Online Courses (MOOCs), virtual communities of practice, and online forums that facilitate independent exploration and collaboration with others who share similar interests or expertise (Doo et al., 2023). SDL paves the way for a more informed, skilled, and adaptable society ready to face the challenges of the future. SDL promotes digital literacy, critical thinking, and problem-solving abilities—all of which are necessary for efficiently navigating the digital age. SDL empowers individuals to customize their learning to their unique needs, interests, and goals. This personalization ensures that learning is relevant and meaningful, whether for personal development or career advancement. Self-directed learners are distinguished by their capacity to detect problems, seek solutions, and make informed judgments. This problem-solving ability is invaluable when dealing with complex global issues. SDL is a catalyst for societal advancement, career achievement, and personal improvement in the twenty-first century, a time of continual change, rich knowledge, and numerous options. It gives people the skills they need to navigate successfully and resolutely a constantly changing world. Self-directed students ascertain their learning needs and objectives, make choices regarding their favoured learning methodologies, curate pertinent learning resources to attain these objectives, and evaluate their own learning achievements (Wiley et al., 2017). Furthermore, the literature emphasizes that intrinsic motivation (IM) stands out as a pivotal factor influencing Self-Directed Learning (SDL) (Ryan et al., 2022). Students who possess intrinsic motivation take ownership of their learning journey and demonstrate a heightened level of self-directedness (Schunk, 2023; Bosch et al., 2019; Dwilestari et al., 2021).

Self-directed learning (SDL) holds great relevance in the field of computer science education. Computer science is a dynamic field characterised by continuous advancements. SDL equips students with the skills and mindset to adapt to rapidly changing technologies (Mulaudzi, 2021). As students take charge of their learning, exploring new programming languages, tools, and technologies, they become intrinsically motivated to stay updated and relevant in the field (Onah et al., 2021). The field of computer science benefits from a wealth of online resources, including coding tutorials, open-source software, forums, and communities. SDL enables students to navigate and utilize these resources effectively, enhancing their intrinsic motivation to explore and learn independently(Calderón et al., 2020). In the technology industry, lifelong learning is a necessity due to the ever-evolving nature of the field. SDL fosters a culture of continuous learning, where students are motivated to seek new knowledge and skills throughout their careers (Singaravelu & Nair, 2021). In the computer science industry, professionals often work on complex, real-world challenges. SDL equips students with the skills and intrinsically motivation to tackle these challenges independently (Walters, 2023). Intrinsic motivation is one of the key characteristics of SDL and will be discussed in the next section.

Intrinsic Motivation

Intrinsic motivation (IM) is the inner drive that compels individuals to engage in an activity or pursue a goal solely for the inherent satisfaction and enjoyment it provides, without being influenced by external incentives or pressures (Malik et al., 2019). According to Bailey et al. (2021), IM arises when individuals are genuinely interested in a particular topic or activity and find fulfilment in pursuing it. In the realm of learning, IM reflects a student's desire for mastery, natural curiosity, and an innate inclination toward exploration (Kibga et al., 2021). This kind of motivation thrives when individuals engage in enjoyable, self-directed, and competence-boosting behaviours (Ryan et al., 2022). An intrinsically motivated person acts out of a genuine enthusiasm for the enjoyment or challenge the activity offers, rather than responding to external prods, pressures, or rewards (Asarkaya & Akaarir, 2021). Intrinsically motivated students seek personal satisfaction not only in the learning content but also in the learning process itself, making them more likely to demonstrate self-directed learning tendencies (Dwilestari et al., 2021).

Intrinsic motivation (IM) is not confined solely to individuals; it also manifests within the dynamic interplay between individuals and their activities (Shafi et al., 2020; Borah, 2021). People may exhibit intrinsic motivation for certain activities while lacking it for others, and the extent of intrinsic motivation can vary among individuals for a given task (Liu et al., 2020). When students are afforded the opportunity to select components that align with their interests within a group setting, their self-motivation receives a substantial boost (Riyanti, 2019). In these collaborative groups, students share their strengths and expertise, thereby intensifying their intrinsic motivation and enhancing group dynamics through the exchange of knowledge (Ehsan et al., 2019). Such group activities can foster intrinsic motivation and maintain students' productive engagement, motivating them to acquire emerging academic skills (Bosch et al., 2019). Intrinsically motivated students engage in learning driven by curiosity about the content and the challenge presented by the learning activities (Fulya Eyupoglu & Nietfeld, 2019).

Working on a task for intrinsic reasons is not only more enjoyable but it also relates positively to learning, achievement and perceptions of competence (Schunk, 2023). According to Schunk et al. (2012), these benefits presumably occur because intrinsically motivated students engage in activities that enhance learning, attend to instruction, rehearse new information, organise knowledge and apply it in different contexts. Educators can significantly improve intrinsic motivation (IM) by addressing specific aspects within their learning environments. These key factors, identified in the literature, include challenge, curiosity, control, and fantasy (Schunk, 2023; Waterschoot et al., 2019; Bougie & Ichise, 2020; Liu et al, 2020). When designing learning and assessment activities, educators should bear these factors in mind. To provide a structured approach, these factors will be organized and discussed individually.

Challenge

Activities that challenge students' skills have a propensity to evoke intrinsic motivation (Waterschoot et al., 2019). As per Asmus (2021), these activities should initially present an intermediate level of difficulty, gradually increasing as students develop their skills. It is crucial to afford students early opportunities for success, gradually elevating the complexity of assignments and exams over the course of the semester (Brophy, 2013).

This incremental progression progression serves as a means to bolster self-efficacy, nurturing in students a feeling of competence and accomplishment right from the start. As their competence develops, so does their confidence, enabling them to establish and pursue increasingly ambitious objectives (Schunk,

2023). Establishing goals signifies an intention to achieve and triggers ongoing learning. It directs students' efforts toward the desired outcome and provides opportunities for experiencing success. The key lies in finding a balance where each student feels that, with reasonable effort, they can succeed while still being encouraged to push their boundaries (Sengodan & Iksan, 2012). Facilitators can further enhance students' self-efficacy by offering precise feedback tailored to the task at hand (Goudini et al., 2019). It's essential to note that the timelier and more comprehensive the feedback provided by facilitators on homework and exams, the greater the likelihood of helping students reflect not only on their grasp of the material but also on their learning strategies (Afrouzeh et al., 2020).

Curiosity

Fostering curiosity in students can be achieved by presenting them with activities that introduce novel information or ideas beyond their current knowledge or beliefs (Bougie & Ichise, 2020). Such challenges motivate students to seek further understanding and bridge these knowledge gaps (Schunk, 2023). When designing coursework, it's crucial to consider students' interests, existing knowledge, and abilities. This consideration is essential to ensure that students perceive the knowledge gap as manageable and worth exploring (Liu et al., 2020). Moreover, by establishing connections between the course material and real-world experiences or the students' educational objectives, either through practical examples or in-class activities, educators can deepen their students' comprehension of the subject matter. This approach allows students to recognize the practical value of what they are learning (Zeng et al., 2020).

Control

Empowering students and granting them a sense of autonomy and control not only amplifies their intrinsic motivation but also fosters the development of self-directed learning (SDL) skills (Schunk, 2023; Alamri et al., 2020). Whether it involves allowing students to choose their own research topics or soliciting their input when crafting an evaluative rubric, students' motivation soars when they perceive themselves as having a degree of control over their educational outcomes (Brophy, 2013). Sharing classroom control with students entails involving them in decision-making processes, content organization, and even the selection of team members (Sun & Gao, 2020). Nonetheless, it is paramount for facilitators who share classroom control with students to provide timely assistance and guidance, as an excessive number of choices can lead to heightened anxiety and may not necessarily yield a positive impact on their intrinsic motivation (Schunk, 2023; Alamri et al., 2020).

Fantasy

IM can be fostered by engaging students in imaginative and make-believe activities, such as simulations and games involving scenarios that don't exist in reality (Schunk, 2023; Svendsen et al., 2020). Infusing an element of fantasy or fun into these activities captures students' interest, and when their curiosity is piqued, intrinsic motivation (IM) is heightened (Fulya Eyupoglu & Nietfeld, 2019). Game based learning are inherently engaging and enjoyable. They often feature elements like challenges, rewards, competition, and interactivity, which naturally captivate learners' attention and interest (Xiang, 2022; Zeng et al., 2020). When students find learning enjoyable, they are more intrinsically motivated to participate and persevere in the learning process (Svendsen et al., 2020). While it can be challenging for facilitators to nurture student motivation in a learning environment, given the diverse learning styles and individual differences among students, there remains an expectation among students for facilitators to provide constructive guidance and encouragement (Leahy & Smith, 2021).

IM plays a pivotal role in computer science education due to its profound impact on students' learning experiences, achievements, and long-term success in the field. The satisfaction of solving a complex problem, creating a functional software application, or optimizing code can be deeply rewarding. IM allows students to experience these intrinsic rewards, reinforcing their motivation to excel in the field. IM fosters a genuine interest and curiosity in students, motivating them to explore and delve deeper into various aspects of the discipline (Bougie & Ichise, 2020; Kibga et al., 2021). This sustained interest helps students stay engaged and committed to their learning. Computer science often involves tackling challenging problems and debugging complex code. IM encourages students to persevere through difficulties and setbacks, as they are intrinsically motivated to solve problems and achieve mastery.

Fostering IM through both teaching and learning activities as well as assessment activities is crucial for creating a holistic and sustainable approach to education (Makransky, 2019; Svendsen et al., 2020). Although Teaching and learning activities can spark initial interest and curiosity, assessment activities provide opportunities for students to continuously engage with the subject matter. This ongoing engagement helps maintain and deepen their intrinsic motivation.

Renewable Assessment

The transition from traditional assessments to meaningful and authentic assessments holds pivotal significance in modern education for several compelling reasons. This shift is driven by the acknowledgment that education should not solely focus on preparing students to excel in tests but should also equip them with the skills to thrive in the complexities of the real world (Sokhanvar et al., 2021). It underscores the value of integrating authentic assessment activities that emphasise practical skills, critical thinking, creativity, and the application of knowledge in diverse and meaningful ways, ultimately equipping learners with the essential tools for success in the 21st century (Stancil & Bartlett, 2022; Seraphin et al., 2019).

Authentic assessments are designed to mirror real-world scenarios, tasks, and challenges, demanding students to apply their knowledge and skills in contexts aligned with their potential future careers or daily lives (Farrell, 2020). This inherent relevance makes learning more practical and meaningful. As Ajjawi et al. (2020) point out, authentic assignments necessitate students to apply classroom knowledge to real-world situations, judiciously select pertinent information and procedures, making them a "high-impact practice" (McDaniel & Van Jura, 2022). Authentic assignments are often more valid than conventional assignments or unit tests because they require students to engage in higher-order thinking within a real-world context (Ornellas et al., 2019). This, in turn, amplifies students' motivation (Sokhanvar et al., 2021). Within the evolving landscape of educational assessment, one particular practice within the realm of authentic assessment has been gaining prominence is renewable assessment. While authentic assessments have long been recognized as a powerful means of gauging students' abilities in real-world contexts, the concept of renewable assessment takes this idea a step further. This approach, deeply rooted in the principles of authenticity, holds the promise of not only evaluating students' skills and knowledge but also enhancing their intrinsic motivation and engagement in the educational process (Arnett, 2022).

Renewable assessments are educational activities that not only evaluate a student's understanding but also contribute to their learning journey and the larger educational community (Katz & Van Allen, 2020). Such activities can serve as a bridge between traditional assessment methods and the cultivation of intrinsic motivation in learners. In the context of renewable assessment, embracing authentic assessments becomes particularly relevant and adding value to the world of knowledge (Wiley et al., 2017). By incorporating renewable assessments that faithfully replicate real-world challenges, compelling students to apply their knowledge in purposeful ways, educators can cultivate a profound sense of motivation and engagement among learners (Al Abri & Dabbagh, 2019). These renewable assessments, thoughtfully aligned with authentic learning objectives, empower students to recognize both the immediate and enduring value of their educational experiences, thereby further amplifying their intrinsic motivation to excel in their studies.

The defining characteristic of a renewable assignment is that "students compile and openly publish their work so that the assignment outcome is inherently valuable to the community" (Katz & Van Allen, 2020). The distinction between traditional "disposable" assignments and renewable assignments becomes evident when we trace their paths, as explained by Arnett (2022). In the case of disposable assignments, students complete the work, educators grade it, and then the work is discarded. In contrast, with renewable assignments, students complete the work, faculty assess it, and the work possesses inherent value for a broader community. It is openly published, making it accessible and usable by others beyond the confines of the classroom (Wiley et al., 2017). Renewable assessments are therefore intrinsically linked to OER as they both share the fundamental principle of openly sharing valuable educational content with a broader community, enriching the learning experience for all.

Open Educational Resources (OER)

Open Educational Resources (OER) have emerged as a transformative force in education, reshaping how knowledge is created, shared, and accessed (Bahrawy, 2019). OER are released with open licenses that grant users the permission to engage in a range of activities, including accessing, adapting, and sharing content freely (Huang et al., 2019). These resources are typically available in digital formats, which facilitate easy dissemination and modification. Open licenses are a fundamental component of OER that distinguish them from traditional copyrighted materials. These licenses enable creators and users of OER to exercise specific rights and freedoms regarding the use, modification, sharing, and distribution of educational resources (Downes, 2019). The most used open licenses for OER are Creative Commons licenses that offers a set of standardized open licenses that are widely adopted in the OER community (Huang et al., 2019). These licenses allow creators to choose the level of openness and flexibility they want to provide for their works.

Accessibility and equity represent foundational principles within the realm of OER, and their intricate interplay underscores the transformative potential of OER in the educational landscape (Kinskey & Miller,2019; Menzel, 2023). Traditional educational materials, typified by costly textbooks and resources, frequently pose insurmountable financial barriers to a significant portion of learners. OER, in stark contrast, champion unrestricted accessibility, dismantling the financial impediments associated with acquiring textbooks and educational materials (Serrano et al., 2019). This affordability extends the reach of education, making it an attainable pursuit for individuals of varying economic means (Huang et al., 2019). By adhering to best practices for designing accessible content, OER creators ensure that learners with diverse needs can actively and inclusively engage with the educational materials. This commitment promotes a learning landscape that accommodates a broader spectrum of learners (Ferri et al., 2020). OER also serves as a powerful equalizer by bridging educational disparities. Regardless of students' socioeconomic backgrounds, OER grants access to the same high-calibre educational resources.

This levelling of the playing field reduces discrepancies in educational opportunities and outcomes, thus advancing educational equity. OER also empowers educators to tailor materials to suit the distinctive needs of their students (Ujakpa et al, 2020). Educators can adapt OER to provide supplementary support for struggling learners or to challenge advanced students. This adaptability facilitates equitable access to personalized learning experiences, ensuring that every student receives education tailored to their requirements.

OER promotes open pedagogical practices that prioritize collaboration and student-cantered learning (Huang et al., 2019). These innovative approaches foster active engagement among learners from diverse backgrounds, engendering a sense of equity in the educational experience (Vlachopoulos & Makri, 2019). By embracing open pedagogies, educators create inclusive learning environments that honor the diversity of their students. Open pedagogies have evolved in response to the changing landscape of education, driven by advancements in technology and a growing demand for more participatory and learner-centric approaches (Bali et al., 2020). Early forms of open pedagogy emerged with the advent of open educational resources (OER) and have since expanded to encompass broader principles of openness in education (Nascimbeni & Burgos, 2019). The open access to educational materials laid the foundation for open pedagogical practices that extend beyond content to encompass collaborative, transparent, and inclusive teaching and learning approaches. Open pedagogies also prioritize transparency in teaching and learning processes (Seraphin et al., 2019). Educators openly share course materials, objectives, and assessment criteria, fostering a culture of trust and collaboration among learners. Learner agency is central to open pedagogies. These approaches empower students to co-create content, set learning goals, and shape their educational experiences, promoting a sense of ownership over their learning journey (Nascimbeni & Burgos, 2019). Learners therefore engage in collaborative projects, peer reviews, and the co-creation of open educational resources, enriching the learning experience.

Co-Creation in Education

In educational settings, the term "co-creation" refers to a collaborative method in which students actively contribute to the planning, preparation, and delivery of their learning experiences, materials, or curriculum (Medero et al., 2022). Together, students, teachers, and occasionally external stakeholders help to design the learning environment. Co-creation promotes shared responsibility, respect for one another, and a dedication to improving educational outcomes through cooperation (Abd Rahman et al., 2022), According to Longoria (2021) and Melis et al. (2023) co-creation is the process of developing new ideas alongside people rather than for them. It also refers to the distribution of value among interested parties and participants in these processes in a cooperative and evolutionary way. The pupils are actively involved in their own learning, which helps to promote learning (Bovill, 2020).

Transferring this idea to the world of higher education inevitably involves processes of knowledge creation with students rather than for students, where teachers and students interact, have a dialogue, and share opinions to jointly develop concepts and agreements that improve the teaching and learning model. When Co-creating educational content students are evaluated not just on their ability to regurgitate material, but also on their ability to actively engage, comprehend, and apply knowledge (Longoria, 2021). Students are given the tools to take an active role in their own learning when they co-create educational content. It changes the conventional paradigm of education from one in which students are passive recipients of knowledge to one in which they actively contribute to its creation and acquisition (Medero et al., 2022). By doing this, not only does students foster autonomy, drive, and a deeper understanding of the subject matter but they are in fact taking responsibility for their own learning and becoming more self-directed in their learning.

When introducing co-creation in the classroom, it is important to make use of structured collaborative learning strategies. Cooperative learning is one such a strategy that can lay the foundation for effective co-creation by cultivating collaboration, promoting active engagement, and developing the skills and mindset necessary for students to take an active role in shaping their educational experiences.

Cooperative Learning as a Strategy for Co-Creation

Cooperative learning, as an instructional approach, centres on peer-to-peer learning where students engage in explaining subject content to each other (Riley & Anderson, 2006). Rooted in theories like social cognitive theory, which underscores the significance of social behaviour acquisition, cooperative learning emphasizes learning through observation and within a social context (Heath, 2010). This method not only encourages academic development but also fosters social outcomes such as collaborative work, group interactions, and self-esteem building (Wessner & Pfister, 2000).

Within the collaborative learning setting, students articulate and exchange their ideas, providing immediate feedback to peers and engaging in discussions that enhance mutual teaching and learning (Heath, 2010). Cooperative learning ensures continuous interaction and engagement among all group members, facilitating "deeper learning" through the reshaping of concepts and the discovery of new connections via critical thinking (Mundy, 2012).

Effectively implementing cooperative learning requires careful preparation and planning by facilitators (Yi & Luxi, 2012). Facilitators typically play several crucial roles, including defining learning outcomes, grouping students, explaining tasks, monitoring group work, and evaluating achievements and cooperation (Ding et al, 2007:38). Johnson and Johnson (2009) further outline the facilitator's responsibilities, encompassing decisions regarding learning outcomes, group size, student roles, classroom arrangements, and resource utilization before instruction commences. The facilitator's role extends beyond task explanation; it involves clarifying the concept of positive interdependence, defining expected social skills, and articulating the assignment's criteria for success. Additionally, facilitators must oversee group interactions, assist in enhancing students' interpersonal and group skills, and support the evaluation of group interactions and individual learning.

Johnson, Johnson, Smith, and Smith (2013) emphasize that effective cooperative learning enables students to work collaboratively, contribute meaningfully, take responsibility for their tasks, and aid in the meaningful learning of their peers. While facilitators need to plan and structure the learning environment, their role primarily entails providing assistance and intervention rather than being authoritarian sources of information (Felder & Prince, 2006). Facilitators primarily focus on stimulating individual accountability, promoting interdependence and interpersonal interactions, and ensuring the smooth functioning of the group (Yi & Luxi, 2012). Cooperative learning aims to deepen students' understanding of subject content and expand their existing knowledge base (Ding et al., 2007).

Johnson et al., (2014) delineate the five fundamental components of cooperative learning (CL): positive interdependence, individual accountability, face-to-face promotive interaction, social skills, and group processing. Substantial research has demonstrated that the effective integration of these five elements into tasks can significantly enhance various aspects of learning, including academic achievement, self-esteem, attitudes toward peers, and the development of social skills (Heath, 2010). Johnson et al. (2013) underscores the vital importance of facilitators comprehending how to integrate these five foundational elements of CL into the learning environment while also tailoring cooperative learning to suit the unique circumstances and requirements of the students.

Positive Interdependence

Positive interdependence encompasses the phenomenon in which students establish a sense of connection with their fellow group members. It signifies that students perceive their success as contingent upon their ability to synchronize their efforts within the group to effectively accomplish a task (Kishore, 2012). Johnson and Johnson (2012) aptly describe this concept as "sink or swim" together, highlighting that students must collaborate to attain the desired outcome. To fulfill this collaborative effort, students are entrusted with two key responsibilities: firstly, achieving the designated goal, and secondly, ensuring that all group members reach their assigned objectives (Johnson & Johnson, 2012). Understanding these dual responsibilities instills in students the awareness that the contribution of each group member is vital for the group's overall success. It underscores the significance of each individual's role within the group, emphasizing that their unique resources, roles, or task responsibilities are integral to the group's performance (Johnson & Johnson, 2012).

Individual Accountability

Individual accountability signifies a student's personal responsibility in achieving the group's objectives (Johnson & Johnson, 2012). This concept encompasses two vital dimensions: first, the individual's obligation to manage their own learning, and second, their duty to support fellow group members in their learning endeavours (Abrami et al., 2011). It entails not only being answerable for their designated section of the work (Tsay & Brady, 2010) but also ensuring the completion of the entire task (Yi & Luxi, 2012).

Individual accountability plays a pivotal role in ensuring the overall success of the group while maintaining an equitable workload distribution among all members (Onwuegbuzie et al., 2009). The development of individual accountability occurs along a continuum, ranging from a facilitator-centred structure to a point where students assume responsibility for their own learning (Abrami et al., 2011). To establish individual accountability, facilitators must structure and facilitate tasks in a manner that fosters and sustains student responsibility for appropriate behaviour, engagement, and outcomes (Wang, 2012). It serves as a crucial mechanism for determining whether students actively participate in the learning process or engage in "free riding" by relying on the work of other group members (Heath, 2010).

Promotive Interaction

Promotive interaction in cooperative learning is characterized by collaborative efforts among group members, where they engage in activities such as challenging, teaching, encouraging, and providing feedback to one another (Tsay & Brady, 2010). This form of interaction fosters a supportive environment in which students actively contribute to each other's success in achieving common goals (Johnson & Johnson, 2012). As promotive interaction intensifies, it enhances peer accountability, making students more cognizant of their responsibility for their fellow group members' success (Johnson & Johnson, 2012). Research by Johnson and Johnson (2009) has shown that as promotive interaction increases, group members tend to develop higher levels of trust in one another, experience reduced individual stress, and make more high-quality decisions.

Effective Use of Social Skills

Effective use of social skills is vital for the success of cooperative learning (CL) as it hinges on students' ability to interact, communicate, trust, make decisions, and handle conflicts within interpersonal and small group settings (Johnson et al., 2013). Cooperation in CL involves not only task completion but also the quality of interaction and teamwork among group members (Johnson & Johnson, 2009). Therefore, students need to be taught and motivated to employ essential social skills for productive collaboration (Johnson & Johnson, 20012).

Social skills development should be integrated into the tasks assigned to students, promoting qualities like active listening, taking individual and collective responsibility, participating in decision-making, giving and receiving constructive feedback, and providing encouragement and motivation to peers (Wang, 2012). Particularly when collaborating with classmates of diverse attitudes, personalities, cultural backgrounds, and learning styles, the cultivation of social skills becomes paramount (Baghheghi et al., 2011). Working in heterogeneous groups encourages students to engage with peers who may hold different perspectives and emotions. This interaction facilitates mutual understanding, confidence-building, effective communication, peer support, acceptance of differences, and constructive conflict resolution (Yi & Luxi, 2012).

Group Processing

Group processing in cooperative learning (CL) involves a thoughtful review of the individual contributions and actions of group members, assessing what aspects should be continued and which need adjustments, and recognizing the members who made commendable contributions (Johnson & Johnson, 2009). Through this reflective process, peers provide feedback that can be employed to refine activities and progress toward the intended objectives (Yi & Luxi, 2012). Group processing has the potential to enhance and refine the effectiveness of group members in accomplishing their shared objectives (Nam & Zeller, 2011).

Cooperative learning serves as a compelling strategy for co-creation in education due to its inherent focus on collaboration, active engagement, and the development of shared knowledge. In a cooperative learning environment, students are encouraged to work together, pooling their diverse skills, perspectives, and experiences to tackle complex problems and tasks (Wang, 2012).. This collaborative process aligns with the principles of co-creation, where students actively contribute to the design and development of their educational experiences. By participating in cooperative learning activities, students not only engage in peer teaching and learning but also take on roles as co-designers of their learning environments (Yi & Luxi, 2012).

This approach empowers learners to have a say in shaping the content, format, and assessment methods, fostering a sense of ownership and intrinsic motivation (Baghheghi et al., 2011). Moreover, cooperative learning enhances social interaction, communication skills, and the ability to appreciate diverse viewpoints, which are essential aspects of effective co-creation. Ultimately, cooperative learning provides a supportive and dynamic framework for students to co-create meaningful educational experiences, promoting a deeper sense of motivation and engagement in the learning process (Johnson & Johnson, 2012).

Statement of the Problem

The contemporary landscape of higher education is undergoing a transformative shift towards open education, marked by the widespread availability of educational resources and the adoption of principles centered on accessibility, affordability, and inclusivity (Maina et al., 2019; Kolesnykova, 2019). This transition has led educators and institutions to explore innovative pedagogical strategies, with a particular emphasis on open educational resources (OERs) as potential agents of change (Baran & AlZoubi, 2020). Notably, the creation of OERs as renewable assessment activities has gained attention for its capacity to revolutionize the creation, sharing, and access of educational content.

However, despite the growing interest in OERs and renewable assessments, there exists a critical gap in understanding how engaging students in the collaborative creation of OERs, with an emphasis on renewal and ongoing improvement, can impact their development as self-directed learners, enhance their mastery of computer science concepts, and foster intrinsic motivation. The current assessment landscape in higher education, particularly in the field of computer science, faces challenges with traditional forms such as standardized testing and final exams, which are criticized for their limited ability to measure critical thinking, problem-solving abilities, and practical application of knowledge (Sokhanvar et al., 2021).

To address this gap, this research seeks to explore and propose guidelines for incorporating co-creation and renewable assessment activities in the context of computer science education. The study aims to investigate the potential of Creating OERs as Renewable Assessment Activities to empower students, promote mastery of computer science concepts, and cultivate intrinsic motivation. Through an extensive literature review encompassing self-directed learning, intrinsic motivation, renewable assessments, and OERs, this research aims to contribute insights that bridge the converging trends of open education, innovative assessment practices, and the evolving pedagogical landscape within the realm of computer science. Ultimately, the study seeks to provide educators and institutions with a comprehensive understanding of the benefits and challenges associated with this innovative approach, thereby paving the way for a more open, inclusive, and student-centered educational environment in computer science education.

Research Questions

This study is guided by the following research questions:

1. How does the collaborative creation of Open Educational Resources (OERs) in computer science education contribute to students' development as self-directed learners?
2. In what ways does engaging students in the renewal and ongoing improvement of OERs impact their mastery of computer science concepts?
3. What guidelines can be proposed for incorporating co-creation and renewable assessment activities in computer science education that aligns with principles of self-directed learning, intrinsic motivation, and open education?

Research Methodology and Design

This section of the chapter suggests the methodology and design that will be employed in the study.

Research Approach

This literature-based study adopts a comprehensive and systematic research approach to explore the intersection of open education, innovative assessment practices, and the evolving pedagogical landscape within computer science education. The methodology involves an in-depth review and synthesis of existing scholarly literature to provide insights, perspectives, and guidelines on the proposed topic. The following key elements characterize the research approach:

Extensive Literature Review: The study begins with an extensive and thorough review of relevant literature on open education, self-directed learning, intrinsic motivation, renewable assessments, and the creation of Open Educational Resources (OERs). Academic databases, peer-reviewed journals, conference proceedings, and reputable educational repositories are systematically searched to identify relevant studies, theoretical frameworks, and empirical findings.

Synthesis of Literature: The identified literature is synthesized to extract key themes, concepts, and insights related to the collaborative creation of OERs as renewable assessment activities in computer science education. The synthesis involves categorizing and organizing information, identifying patterns, and noting variations in the existing literature.

Data Analysis and Interpretation

Drawing on the insights obtained from the literature review, the study data analysis and Interpretation includes the following:

Guidelines Proposal: The study proposes guidelines for incorporating co-creation and renewable assessment activities in computer science education. These guidelines aim to provide practical recommendations for educators and institutions interested in implementing the innovative approach.

Contribution to the Discourse: The study contributes to the evolving discourse on open education, assessment, and pedagogy within the realm of computer science. It emphasizes the potential impacts of the proposed approach on student empowerment, mastery of computer science concepts, and intrinsic motivation.

Limitations and Delimitations of the Study

This study acknowledges certain limitations inherent in the available literature, including the scope of the reviewed materials, potential publication bias, temporal constraints up to early 2022, and a focus on English-language publications, which may introduce language bias. The delimitations of the study include a geographical focus on English-speaking academic communities, a specific concentration on the field of computer science education, a literature-based approach without empirical data collection, and the contextual applicability of the developed conceptual framework to the reviewed literature. While efforts have been made to offer a comprehensive review within these constraints, readers should interpret the findings considering these limitations and recognize that the study's scope is specifically delimited to the delineated parameters, potentially limiting its generalizability to other contexts and disciplines.

SOLUTIONS AND RECOMMENDATIONS

Enhancing intrinsic motivation in computer science education through co-creation and the creation of OERs as renewable assessment activities represents a powerful and transformative approach. This pedagogical strategy aligns perfectly with the dynamic and innovative nature of the field of computer science. By actively involving students in the design, development, and sharing of educational content, educators can tap into students' intrinsic motivation, fostering a deep and enduring passion for learning.

Co-creation in computer science education empowers students to become active participants rather than passive recipients of knowledge. They take on the roles of content creators, collaborating with their peers and instructors to produce OERs that have real-world relevance. Cooperative learning is a structured collaborative strategy, that can contribute to the process of co-creation. Both cooperative learning and co-creation recognize the power of collaborative efforts in enhancing the educational journey and fostering a deeper sense of intrinsic motivation among learners. This sense of ownership and autonomy over their learning journey naturally ignites intrinsic motivation. Students are no longer merely seeking to fulfil course requirements but are driven by a desire to make a meaningful contribution to their field.

The renewable assessment aspect of this approach amplifies intrinsic motivation further. Traditional assessments often result in disposable outcomes—assignments that have no purpose beyond the grade. In contrast, renewable assessments that require students to create OERs can benefit future learners, both within and beyond their educational institution. Knowing that their work has the potential to make a positive impact on others motivates students intrinsically. They see the tangible value in what they are doing, which fuels their dedication and enthusiasm.

Furthermore, co-creation and renewable assessment in computer science education align with the principles of self-directed learning. Students actively seek out resources, engage in critical thinking, and take responsibility for their learning. This self-directed approach not only enhances their skills and knowledge but also reinforces their intrinsic motivation. They become more self-regulated learners, driven by a genuine thirst for knowledge and a sense of personal agency.

Incorporating co-creation and renewable assessment activities into computer science education also nurtures 21st-century skills such as collaboration, creativity, and problem-solving—skills that are highly valued in the technology industry. Students gain experience in working collaboratively, adapting to new challenges, and thinking innovatively, further deepening their intrinsic motivation to excel in the field. By co-creating OERs that have a lasting impact, students are not only preparing for successful careers but also becoming advocates for open and collaborative learning practices, fostering a culture of continuous improvement and innovation in computer science education.

From the literature discussed above the following set of guidelines to implement this practice in CSE classrooms is proposed (Table 1).

By following these guidelines, educators can create a learning environment in computer science education where co-creation and the development of OERs as renewable assessment activities not only enhance intrinsic motivation but also equip students with essential skills for success in the 21st century.

FUTURE RESEARCH DIRECTIONS

The current findings highlight the potent impact of integrating co-creation and the creation of Open Educational Resources (OERs) as renewable assessment activities in enhancing intrinsic motivation in

Table 1. Guidelines to Incorporating co-creation and renewable assessment activities

Number	Guideline	Sources
1	Clear Learning Objectives: Define clear learning objectives for the course or project, ensuring they align with both course content and the development of 21st-century skills.	Nam & Zeller, 2011. Yi & Luxi, 2012. Zeng et al., 2020; Wong et al, 2021.
2	Choice and Autonomy: Emphasize the real-world relevance of the projects. Help students see how their work can impact others, the industry, or society.	Walters, 2023. Al Abri & Dabbagh, 2019; Sokhanvar et al., 2021; Arnette 2022.
3	Co-creation Encourage co-creation and collaboration among students by making use of cooperative learning tasks. Collaborative projects promote a sense of community and shared learning experiences.	Abd Rahman et al., 2022, Medero et al., 2022. Yi & Luxi, 2012:165.
4	Open Pedagogies: Embrace open pedagogies that encourage active participation, critical thinking, and student-led discussions. These pedagogies align with co-creation and intrinsic motivation.	Seraphin et al., 2019; Huang et al., 2019; Vlachopoulos & Makri, 2019.
5	Regular Feedback: Provide regular feedback and support. Timely and constructive feedback keeps students engaged and motivated to improve.	Yi & Luxi, 2012; Wang, 2012; Goudini et al., 2019; Song et al., 2022; van Woezik et al., 2021).
6	Continual Improvement: Promote a culture of continual improvement. Encourage students to revisit and enhance their OERs even after the course ends.	Mundy, 2012:26; Singaravelu & Nair, 2021; Van Allen & Katz, 2020.
7	Flexibility and Adaptation: Be flexible and adaptable in response to students' interests and needs. Adjust the course based on feedback and evolving project goals.	Huang et al., 2019; Mulaudzi, 2021.
8	Open Licensing: Educate students about open licensing and the benefits of sharing knowledge openly. Help them understand the broader implications of their work.	Huang et al., 2019; Downes, 2019; Kinskey & Miller,2019; Menzel, 2023.
9	Assessment as Learning: Position assessment as a learning process rather than a final judgment. Encourage students to view feedback and assessment as opportunities for growth	Sokhanvar et al., 2021; Stancil & Bartlett, 2022; Seraphin et al., 2019.

computer science education. This pedagogical strategy, well-aligned with the dynamic nature of the field, serves as a transformative approach, actively involving students in designing, developing, and sharing educational content. As further research avenues, the following recommendations are proposed:

Longitudinal studies: Embarking on comprehensive longitudinal studies is recommended to delve into the enduring effects of integrating co-creation and renewable assessment activities in computer science education. By tracking students beyond the immediate educational context, researchers can uncover valuable insights into the sustained intrinsic motivation cultivated by these pedagogical approaches, shedding light on their lasting influence on students' professional journeys.

Comparative Analyses: Undertaking insightful comparative analyses across diverse institutions, cultures, and educational contexts is suggested. Such examinations would provide a nuanced understanding of the effectiveness of co-creation and renewable assessment activities in computer science education. Exploring variations in implementation and their impact on intrinsic motivation can offer tailored insights, fostering practices that resonate with the diversity of learning environments.

Integration with Emerging Technologies: A compelling avenue for research involves exploring the integration of emerging technologies, such as artificial intelligence, virtual reality, or augmented reality, within the realm of co-creation and renewable assessment activities. This exploration is poised to uncover how these cutting-edge technologies can elevate engagement, foster collaboration, and further enhance intrinsic motivation among students in computer science education.

Interdisciplinary Applications: To broaden the scope of inquiry, researchers are encouraged to explore the potential interdisciplinary applications of co-creation and renewable assessment in computer science education. Investigating how these strategies might be adapted and effectively implemented in diverse STEM disciplines or non-STEM fields will contribute valuable insights into the transferability of intrinsic motivation enhancement across academic domains.

Faculty Perspectives and Professional Development: Examining the perspectives of educators and faculty members on the integration of co-creation and renewable assessment activities is vital. This recommendation emphasizes the importance of understanding the challenges and benefits perceived by instructors. Additionally, exploring the impact of professional development programs designed to equip educators with the necessary skills and knowledge for effective implementation is crucial for ensuring successful adoption.

Impact on Diverse Student Populations: Researchers are urged to investigate the impact of co-creation and renewable assessment activities on diverse student populations. This inclusive exploration should encompass students with varying levels of prior knowledge, diverse cultural backgrounds, and distinct learning styles. Insights gained from this research will contribute to the creation of educational environments that cater to the diverse needs of learners, fostering inclusivity.

These research suggestions collectively aim to deepen our understanding of the intricacies surrounding co-creation and renewable assessment activities in computer science education, paving the way for innovative and inclusive teaching practices.

CONCLUSION

The journey towards enhancing intrinsic motivation through co-creation and renewable assessment activities in computer science education is not merely a pedagogical strategy; it represents a transformative approach to teaching and learning in the digital age. This chapter has explored the importance of SDL, the synergy between co-creation, the development of Open Educational Resources (OERs), and the cultivation of intrinsic motivation among students in the field of computer science.

Throughout our exploration, it has become evident that fostering a sense of ownership, autonomy, and purpose in learners can ignite their passion for learning. By actively involving students in the creation of OERs—educational materials that have real-world impact—educators tap into the inherent drive within individuals to seek mastery and make meaningful contributions to their field. Co-creation empowers students to become knowledge creators and collaborators, breaking down the traditional barriers between educators and learners. Renewable assessment activities, where students share their OERs openly with the global community, amplify the motivational factors at play. Knowing that their work can benefit not only their peers but also learners worldwide ads a layer of purpose and responsibility that is intrinsically motivating. It transforms assessment from a mere evaluation into an opportunity for personal growth, community engagement, and the creation of lasting educational resources. In the context of computer science education, where adaptability, creativity, and problem-solving are paramount, co-creation and renewable assessment align seamlessly with the skills demanded by the field. Moreover, they prepare students to navigate a rapidly changing technological landscape by fostering a mindset of lifelong learning, innovation, and collaboration.

As I conclude this chapter, it is clear that the integration of co-creation and renewable assessment activities into computer science education has the potential not only enhances intrinsic motivation but also empowers students to become active contributors to the global knowledge ecosystem. It equips them not only with technical skills but also with the passion, resilience, and creativity necessary for success in their academic journeys and future careers. In embracing this transformative approach, educators are not only nurturing the next generation of computer scientists but also fostering a culture of openness, collaboration, and continuous improvement in education. As we look ahead, the journey towards enhancing intrinsic motivation through co-creation and renewable assessment activities promises to remain at the forefront of progressive education, bridging the gap between the classroom and the real world, and empowering learners to shape the future of computer science and beyond.

REFERENCES

Abd Rahman, E., Yunus, M., Hashim, H., & Khadirah, N. (2022). *Learner autonomy between students and teachers at a defense university*. Research Gate.

Abrami, P. C., Bernard, R. M., Bures, E. M., Borokhovski, E., & Tamim, R. M. (2011). Interaction in distance education and online learning: Using evidence and theory toimprove practice. *Journal of Computing in Higher Education*, *23*(2-3), 82–103. doi:10.1007/s12528-011-9043-x

Afrouzeh, M., Konukman, F., Lotfinejad, M., & Afroozeh, M. S. (2020). Effects of knowledge of results feedback on more accurate versus less accurate trials on intrinsic motivation, self-confidence and anxiety in volleyball serve. *Physical Culture and Sport Studies and Research*, *87*(1), 24–33. doi:10.2478/pcssr-2020-0016

Ajjawi, R., Tai, J., Huu Nghia, T. L., Boud, D., Johnson, L., & Patrick, C. J. (2020). Aligning assessment with the needs of work-integrated learning: The challenges of authentic assessment in a complex context. *Assessment & Evaluation in Higher Education*, *45*(2), 304–316. doi:10.1080/02602938.2019.1639613

Al Abri, M. H., & Dabbagh, N. (2019). Testing the intervention of OER renewable assignments in a college course. *Open Praxis*, *11*(2), 195–209. doi:10.5944/openpraxis.11.2.916

Alamri, H., Lowell, V., Watson, W., & Watson, S. L. (2020). Using personalized learning as an instructional approach to motivate learners in online higher education: Learner self-determination and intrinsic motivation. *Journal of Research on Technology in Education*, *52*(3), 322–352. doi:10.1080/15391523.2020.1728449

Arnett, E. J. (2022, July). Failure Is Always an Option: Lessons from Creating Authentic, Renewable Assignments. In *2022 IEEE International Professional Communication Conference (ProComm)* (pp. 221-227). IEEE. 10.1109/ProComm53155.2022.00046

Asarkaya, Ç., & Akaarir, S. (2021). The effect of ethical leadership on intrinsic motivation and employees job satisfaction. *Working Paper Series Dergisi, 2*(1), 14-30.

Asmus, E. P. (2021). Motivation in music teaching and learning. *Visions of Research in Music Education*, *16*(5), 31.

Bailey, D., Almusharraf, N., & Hatcher, R. (2021). Finding satisfaction: Intrinsic motivation for synchronous and asynchronous communication in the online language learning context. *Education and Information Technologies, 26*(3), 2563–2583. doi:10.1007/s10639-020-10369-z PMID:33169066

Bali, M., Cronin, C., & Jhangiani, R. S. (2020). Framing Open Educational Practices from a Social Justice Perspective. *Journal of Interactive Media in Education, 2020*(1), 10. doi:10.5334/jime.565

Baran, E., & AlZoubi, D. (2020). Affordances, challenges, and impact of open pedagogy: Examining students' voices. *Distance Education, 41*(2), 230–244. doi:10.1080/01587919.2020.1757409

Borah, M. (2021). Motivation in learning. *Journal of Critical Reviews, 8*(2), 550–552.

Bosch, C., Mentz, E., & Reitsma, G. M. (2019). Integrating cooperative learning into the combined blended learning design model: Implications for students' intrinsic motivation. [IJMBL]. *International Journal of Mobile and Blended Learning, 11*(1), 58–73. doi:10.4018/IJMBL.2019010105

Bougie, N., & Ichise, R. (2020). Skill-based curiosity for intrinsically motivated reinforcement learning. *Machine Learning, 109*(3), 493–512. doi:10.1007/s10994-019-05845-8

Bovill, C. (2020). Co-creation in learning and teaching: The case for a whole-class approach in higher education. *Higher Education, 79*(6), 1023–1037. doi:10.1007/s10734-019-00453-w

Brophy, J. E. (2013). *Motivating students to learn*. Routledge.

Calderón, A., Meroño, L., & MacPhail, A. (2020). A student-centred digital technology approach: The relationship between intrinsic motivation, learning climate and academic achievement of physical education preservice teachers. *European Physical Education Review, 26*(1), 241–262. doi:10.1177/1356336X19850852

Dewi, P. Y., & Primayana, K. H. (2019). Effect of learning module with setting contextual teaching and learning to increase the understanding of concepts. *International Journal on E-Learning, 1*(1), 19–26. doi:10.31763/ijele.v1i1.26

Ding, M., Li, X., Piccolo, D., & Kulm, G. (2010). Teacher interventions in cooperative-learning. *The Journal of Educational Research, 100*(3), 37–41.

Doo, M. Y., Zhu, M., & Bonk, C. J. (2023). Influence of self-directed learning on learning outcomes in MOOCs: A meta-analysis. *Distance Education, 44*(1), 86–105. doi:10.1080/01587919.2022.2155618

Downes, S. (2019). A look at the future of open educational resources. *The International Journal of Open Educational Resources, 1*(2). doi:10.18278/ijoer.1.2.4

du Toit-Brits, C. (2019). A focus on self-directed learning: The role that educators' expectations play in the enhancement of students' self-directedness. *South African Journal of Education, 39*(2), 1–11. doi:10.15700/saje.v39n2a1645

Dwilestari, S., Zamzam, A., Susanti, N. W. M., & Syahrial, E. (2021). The students'self-directed learning in english foreign language classes during the covid-19 pandemic. *Jurnal Lisdaya, 17*(2), 38–46. doi:10.29303/lisdaya.v17i2.42

Ehsan, N., Vida, S., & Mehdi, N. (2019). The impact of cooperative learning on developing speaking ability and motivation toward learning English. *Journal of language and education, 5*(3 (19)), 83-101.

Farrell, C. (2020). Do international marketing simulations provide an authentic assessment of learning? A student perspective. *International Journal of Management Education*, *18*(1), 100362. doi:10.1016/j.ijme.2020.100362

Felder, R. M., & Prince, M. J. (2006). Inductive teaching and learning methods: Definitions,comparisons, and research bases. *Journal of Engineering Education*, *95*(2), 123–138. doi:10.1002/j.2168-9830.2006.tb00884.x

Ferri, F., Grifoni, P., & Guzzo, T. (2020). Online learning and emergency remote teaching: Opportunities and challenges in emergency situations. *Societies (Basel, Switzerland)*, *10*(4), 86. doi:10.3390/soc10040086

Fulya Eyupoglu, T., & Nietfeld, J. L. (2019). Intrinsic motivation in game-based learning environments. *Game-based assessment revisited*, 85-102.

Garcia, R. S. (2021). Influence of self-directed learning skills on the academic adjustment in an online learning platform among level I and II student nurse. *International Journal of Recent Advances in Multidisciplinary Research*, *8*(6), 6925–6929.

Goudini, R., Ashrafpoornavaee, S., & Farsi, A. (2019). The effects of self-controlled and instructor-controlled feedback on motor learning and intrinsic motivation among novice adolescent taekwondo players. *Acta Gymnica*, *49*(1), 33–39. doi:10.5507/ag.2019.002

Guglielmino, L. M. (1977). *Development of the self-directed learning readiness scale*. University of Georgia.

Heath, T. (2010). The impact of a cooperative learning training program on teacher perceptions aboutc ooperative learning [Doctoral thesis, NWU]. http://search.proquest.com.nwulib.nwu.ac.za/pqdtft/advanced

Huang, R., Liu, D., Tlili, A., Knyazeva, S., Chang, T. W., Zhang, X., & Holotescu, C. (2020). *Guidance on open educational practices during school closures: Utilizing OER under COVID-19 pandemic in line with UNESCO OER recommendation*. Smart Learning Institute of Beijing Normal University.

Johnson, D., & Johnson, R. (2009). An educational psychology success story: Social interdependence theory and cooperative learning. *Educational Researcher*, *38*(5), 365–379. doi:10.3102/0013189X09339057

Johnson, D. W., Johnson, R. T., & Smith, K. A. (2014). Cooperative learning: Improving university instruction by basing practice on validated theory. *Journal on Excellence in University Teaching*, *25*(4), 1–26.

Johnson, D. W., Johnson, R. T., Smith, K. A., & Smith, K. (2013). Cooperative learning:Improving university instruction by basing practice on validated theory. *Journal on Excellence in University Teaching*, *25*(3-4), 1–26.

Katz, S., & Van Allen, J. (2020). *Evolving into the open: a framework for collaborative design of renewable assignments*.

Kibga, E. S., Gakuba, E., & Sentongo, J. (2021). Developing students' curiosity through chemistry hands-on activities: A case of selected community secondary schools in Dar es Salaam, Tanzania. *Eurasia Journal of Mathematics, Science and Technology Education*, *17*(5), em1962. doi:10.29333/ejmste/10856

Kinskey, C., & Miller, C. L. (2019). Creating Faculty Development on OER. *The International Journal of Open Educational Resources*, *1*(2). doi:10.18278/ijoer.1.2.10

Kishore, K. (2012). *Cooperative Learning*. Alden Books.

Knowles, M. S. (1975). *Self-directed learning: A guide for learners and teachers.*

Kolesnykova, T. O. (2019, December). The Role of Libraries as Publishers in the Open Education Landscape: Reflecting Modern World Practice of Open Textbooks. In *University Library at a new stage of social communications development. Conference proceedings* (*№. 4,* pp. 88-99). IEEE.

Lalitha, T. B., & Sreeja, P. S. (2020). Personalised self-directed learning recommendation system. *Procedia Computer Science*, *171*, 583–592. doi:10.1016/j.procs.2020.04.063

Leahy, K. S., & Smith, T. D. (2021). The self-directed learning of adult music students: A comparison of teacher approaches and student needs. *International Journal of Music Education*, *39*(3), 289–300. doi:10.1177/0255761421991596

Liu, Y., Hau, K. T., Liu, H., Wu, J., Wang, X., & Zheng, X. (2020). Multiplicative effect of intrinsic and extrinsic motivation on academic performance: A longitudinal study of Chinese students. *Journal of Personality*, *88*(3), 584–595. doi:10.1111/jopy.12512 PMID:31498427

Loeng, S. (2020). Self-directed learning: A core concept in adult education. *Education Research International*, *2020*, 1–12. doi:10.1155/2020/3816132

Longoria, L. C., López-Forniés, I., Sáenz, D. C., & Sierra-Pérez, J. (2021). Promoting sustainable consumption in Higher Education Institutions through integrative co-creative processes involving relevant stakeholders. *Sustainable Production and Consumption*, *28*, 445–458. doi:10.1016/j.spc.2021.06.009

Lopez, I. (2023). The Science Disseminators Academy: a teacher training program to use astronomy for implementing phenomenon-based learning.

Maina, M. F., Santos-Hermosa, G., Mancini, F., & Guàrdia Ortiz, L. (2020). Open educational practices (OEP) in the design of digital competence assessment. *Distance Education*, *41*(2), 261–278. doi:10.1080/01587919.2020.1757407

Makransky, G., Borre-Gude, S., & Mayer, R. E. (2019). Motivational and cognitive benefits of training in immersive virtual reality based on multiple assessments. *Journal of Computer Assisted Learning*, *35*(6), 691–707. doi:10.1111/jcal.12375

McDaniel, A., & Van Jura, M. (2022). High-impact practices: Evaluating their effect on college completion. *Journal of College Student Retention*, *24*(3), 740–757. doi:10.1177/1521025120947357

Medero, G. S., Albaladejo, G. P., Medina, P. M., & Solana, M. J. G. (2022). Blogging as an Instrument for Co-Creation and Collaborative Learning in University Education. *Contemporary Educational Technology*, *14*(4), ep393. doi:10.30935/cedtech/12555

Melis, G., McCabe, S., Atzeni, M., & Del Chiappa, G. (2023). Collaboration and learning processes in value co-creation: A destination perspective. *Journal of Travel Research*, *62*(3), 699–716. doi:10.1177/00472875211070349

Menzel, M. (2023). Developing a metadata profile for higher education OER repositories. In *Distributed Learning Ecosystems: Concepts, Resources, and Repositories* (pp. 263–278). Springer Fachmedien Wiesbaden. doi:10.1007/978-3-658-38703-7_14

Morris, T. H. (2019). Self-directed learning: A fundamental competence in a rapidly changing world. *International Review of Education*, *65*(4), 633–653. doi:10.1007/s11159-019-09793-2

Mulaudzi, M. A. (2021). *The implementation of hybrid problem-based learning to foster Senior Phase Technology student teachers' self-directed learning abilities* [Doctoral dissertation, North-West University (South Africa)].

Mundy, M. (2012). Faculty perceptions of cooperative learning and traditional discussion strategies. *Turkish Online Journal of Distance Education*, *13*(2), 84–95.

Nam, C. W., & Zellner, R. D. (2011). The relative effects of positive interdependence and groupprocessing on student achievement and attitude in online cooperative learning. *Computers & Education*, *56*(3), 680–688. doi:10.1016/j.compedu.2010.10.010

Nascimbeni, F., & Burgos, D. (2019). Unveiling the relationship between the use of open educational resources and the adoption of open teaching practices in higher education. *Sustainability (Basel)*, *11*(20), 5637. doi:10.3390/su11205637

Okwuduba, E. N., Nwosu, K. C., Okigbo, E. C., Samuel, N. N., & Achugbu, C. (2021). Impact of intrapersonal and interpersonal emotional intelligence and self-directed learning on academic performance among pre-university science students. *Heliyon*, *7*(3), e06611. doi:10.1016/j.heliyon.2021.e06611 PMID:33869848

Onah, D. F., Pang, E. L., Sinclair, J. E., & Uhomoibhi, J. (2021). An innovative MOOC platform: The implications of self-directed learning abilities to improve motivation in learning and to support self-regulation. *The International Journal of Information and Learning Technology*, *38*(3), 283–298. doi:10.1108/IJILT-03-2020-0040

Onwuegbuzie, A. J., Collins, K. M. T., & Jiao, Q. G. (2009). Performance of cooperative learning groups in a postgraduate education research methodology course: The role of social interdependence. *Active Learning in Higher Education*, *10*(3), 265–277. doi:10.1177/1469787409343190

Ornellas, A., Falkner, K., & Edman Stålbrandt, E. (2019). Enhancing graduates' employability skills through authentic learning approaches. *Higher education, skills and work-based learning*, *9*(1), 107-120.

Pan, X. (2020). Technology acceptance, technological self-efficacy, and attitude toward technology-based self-directed learning: Learning motivation as a mediator. *Frontiers in Psychology*, *11*, 564294. doi:10.3389/fpsyg.2020.564294 PMID:33192838

Riley, W., & Anderson, P. (2006). Randomized study on the impact of cooperative learning: Distance education in public health. *Quarterly Review of Distance Education*, *7*(2), 129.

Riyanti, D. (2019). The role of motivation in learning English as a foreign language. [JELTIM]. *Journal of English Language Teaching Innovations and Materials*, *1*(1), 29–35. doi:10.26418/jeltim.v1i1.27788

Robinson, J. D., & Persky, A. M. (2020). Developing self-directed learners. *American Journal of Pharmaceutical Education, 84*(3), 847512. doi:10.5688/ajpe847512 PMID:32313284

Ryan, R. M., Duineveld, J. J., Di Domenico, S. I., Ryan, W. S., Steward, B. A., & Bradshaw, E. L. (2022). We know this much is (meta-analytically) true: A meta-review of meta-analytic findings evaluating self-determination theory. *Psychological Bulletin, 148*(11-12), 813–842. doi:10.1037/bul0000385

Schunk, D. H. (2023). Self-regulation of self-efficacy and attributions in academic settings. In *Self-regulation of learning and performance* (pp. 75–99). Routledge.

Schweder, S., & Raufelder, D. (2022). Adolescents' enjoyment and effort in class: Influenced by self-directed learning intervals. *Journal of School Psychology, 95*, 72–89. doi:10.1016/j.jsp.2022.09.002 PMID:36371126

Sengodan, V., & Iksan, Z. H. (2012). Students' learning styles and intrinsic motivation in learning mathematics. *Asian Social Science, 8*(16), 17. doi:10.5539/ass.v8n16p17

Seraphin, S. B., Grizzell, J. A., Kerr-German, A., Perkins, M. A., Grzanka, P. R., & Hardin, E. E. (2019). A conceptual framework for non-disposable assignments: Inspiring implementation, innovation, and research. *Psychology Learning & Teaching, 18*(1), 84–97. doi:10.1177/1475725718811711

Serrano, D. R., Dea-Ayuela, M. A., Gonzalez-Burgos, E., Serrano-Gil, A., & Lalatsa, A. (2019). Technology-enhanced learning in higher education: How to enhance student engagement through blended learning. *European Journal of Education, 54*(2), 273–286. doi:10.1111/ejed.12330

Shafi, M., Lei, Z., Song, X., & Sarker, M. N. I. (2020). The effects of transformational leadership on employee creativity: Moderating role of intrinsic motivation. *Asia Pacific Management Review, 25*(3), 166–176. doi:10.1016/j.apmrv.2019.12.002

Singaravelu, S. L., & Nair, A. S. (2021). Technology deployment in self-directed learning: A guide for new path in medical education. *SBV J Basic Clin Appl Health Sci, 4*(2), 51–53. doi:10.5005/jp-journals-10082-03112

Sokhanvar, Z., Salehi, K., & Sokhanvar, F. (2021). Advantages of authentic assessment for improving the learning experience and employability skills of higher education students: A systematic literature review. *Studies in Educational Evaluation, 70*, 101030. doi:10.1016/j.stueduc.2021.101030

Song, Y., Lee, Y., & Lee, J. (2022). Mediating effects of self-directed learning on the relationship between critical thinking and problem-solving in student nurses attending online classes: A cross-sectional descriptive study. *Nurse Education Today, 109*, 105227. doi:10.1016/j.nedt.2021.105227 PMID:34972030

Stancil, S. K., & Bartlett, M. E. (2022). An Integrative Literature Review of Non-Disposable and Reusable Assignments. *Journal on Excellence in College Teaching, 33*(1), 155–175.

Strickland, T. N. (2021). *The self-directed goal theory experiment: a mixed methods study of personal development goal-setting programs and self-efficacy* [Doctoral dissertation, Lindenwood University].

Svendsen, B., Burner, T., & Røkenes, F. M. (2020). *Intrinsically Motivating Instruction—Thomas Malone. Science Education in Theory and Practice: An Introductory Guide to Learning Theory*, (pp. 45-50). Research Gate.

Tsay, M., & Brady, M. (2010). A case study of cooperative learning and communication pedagogy: Does working in teams make a difference? *The Journal of Scholarship of Teaching and Learning*, *10*(2), 78–89.

Ujakpa, M. M., Osakwe, J. O., Iyawa, G. E., Hashiyana, V., & Mutalya, A. N. (2020, May). Industry 4.0: university students' perception, awareness and preparedness-A case of Namibia. In 2020 IST-Africa Conference (IST-Africa) (pp. 1-10). IEEE.

van Woezik, T. E., Koksma, J. J. J., Reuzel, R. P., Jaarsma, D. C., & van der Wilt, G. J. (2021). There is more than 'I' in self-directed learning: an exploration of self-directed learning in teams of undergraduate students. Medical Teacher, 43(5), 590-598.Vlachopoulos, D., & Makri, A. (2019). Online communication and interaction in distance higher education: A framework study of good practice. *International Review of Education*, *65*(4), 605–632.

Walters, J. (2023). *Becoming: Using Self-directed Learning to Develop Learners' Research and Leadership Capabilities and Confidence*. Active Learning for Real-World Inquiry.

Waterschoot, J., Vansteenkiste, M., & Soenens, B. (2019). The effects of experimentally induced choice on elementary school children's intrinsic motivation: The moderating role of indecisiveness and teacher–student relatedness. *Journal of Experimental Child Psychology*, *188*, 104692. doi:10.1016/j.jecp.2019.104692 PMID:31539835

Wessner, M., & Pfister, H. (2000). Points of cooperation: Integrating cooperative learning into web-based courses. Paper presented at the International Workshop on New Technologies for Collaborative Learning, Awaji-Yumebutai, Japan.

Wiley, D., Webb, A., Weston, S., & Tonks, D. (2017). A preliminary exploration of the relationships between student-created OER, sustainability, and students success. International Review of Research in Open and Distributed Learning, 18(4), 60–69. https://doi.org/. V18i4.3022 doi:10.19173/irrodl

Wong, F. M. F., Tang, A. C. Y., & Cheng, W. L. S. (2021). Factors associated with self-directed learning among undergraduate nursing students: A systematic review. *Nurse Education Today*, *104*, 104998. doi:10.1016/j.nedt.2021.104998 PMID:34139583

Xiang, Y. (2022). Research on the Design of Education Games for Vocabulary Learning from the Perspective of Intrinsic Motivation Theory. In 2022 4th International Conference on Computer Science and Technologies in Education (CSTE) (pp. 164-167). IEEE. 10.1109/CSTE55932.2022.00036

Yaşar, M. Ö., & Atay, D. (2023). Evaluating Learner Autonomy during the Covid-19: An Examination of Student Teachers' Self-Directed Learning Readiness for MOOCs. Anatolian Journal of Education, 8(1).

Yasmin, M., Naseem, F., & Masso, I. C. (2019). Teacher-directed learning to self-directed learning transition barriers in Pakistan. Studies in Educational Evaluation, 61, 34-40.Yi, Z., & Luxi, Z. (2012). Implementing a cooperative learning model in universities. *Educational Studies*, *38*(2), 165–173.

Yuliansyah, A., & Ayu, M. (2021). The implementation of project-based assignment in online learning during covid-19. *Journal of English Language Teaching and Learning*, *2*(1), 32–38. doi:10.33365/jeltl.v2i1.851

Zeng, J., Parks, S., & Shang, J. (2020). To learn scientifically, effectively, and enjoyably: A review of educational games. *Human Behavior and Emerging Technologies*, *2*(2), 186–195. doi:10.1002/hbe2.188

Chapter 4
A Framework for Developing Deeper Self-Directed Learning in Computer Science Education

Sukie van Zyl
https://orcid.org/0000-0001-7070-2719
Research Unit Self-Directed Learning, Faculty of Education, North-West University, Potchefstroom, South Africa

ABSTRACT

To prepare students for the challenges of the Fifth Industrial Revolution, it is essential to cultivate deeper self-directed learning (DSDL) in computer science education. The process of DSDL empowers students to take ownership of their learning, enabling them to transfer their knowledge and skills to unfamiliar contexts. The proposed DSDL framework is anchored in cognitive load theory and social constructivism and draws upon three core concepts: the organization of course content; teaching and learning methods rooted in cooperative learning; and the characteristics of tasks. The importance of structuring course content to offer an initial holistic overview of key concepts, followed by deeper cycles of revisiting and reinforcing these concepts is underscored. Teaching and learning methods, such as cooperative pair programming and cooperative pair problem solving, are recommended. Moreover, the framework advocates for the adoption of a whole-task approach, involving authentic, complex tasks that encourage students to grapple with challenges and to learn from their failures.

INTRODUCTION

Computer Science is characterized by change and new technological developments. Disruptive changes that affect various sectors often originate within computer science (Majumdar, Banerji & Chakrabarti, 2018). Students in Computer Science should therefore be lifelong learners and should have a sound knowledge base of information and communications technologies (ICTs). They further need to acquire a multitude of skills, such as problem-solving, computational thinking, and critical thinking. Computer Science educators therefore have the daunting task of facilitating challenging subject content, fostering a multitude of skills, and preparing students for an unknown future.

DOI: 10.4018/979-8-3693-1066-3.ch004

Self-directed learning (SDL) is the process during which students take ownership of their learning by identifying their learning needs and applying strategies to address these needs (Knowles, 1975). Research underscores the importance of SDL to address the challenges of a changing world. It is however argued that SDL is not sufficient to address the challenges of the Fourth Industrial Revolution (4IR) (Van Zyl & Mentz, 2022). Even as society and education are trying to address the complexities of the 4IR, Nosta (2023, para. 3) argues, "we are on the cusp of yet another transformative era", namely the Fifth Industrial Revolution (5IR), which is envisioned to be cognitive in nature and characterized by profound change. Consequently, students are now, more than ever, expected to embody the characteristics of lifelong learners, equipped with the competence to transfer knowledge and skills for addressing future challenges in unfamiliar contexts. This necessitates the cultivation of deeper self-directed learning (DSDL) competencies demanding that students identify their learning needs, resourcefully locate, and employ materials and strategies to attain their learning objectives, transfer knowledge and skills to solve novel problems, and evaluate whether successful knowledge transfer occurred (Van Zyl, 2020).

The recognition of the significance of knowledge transfer within educational institutions has grown substantially (Cheng, 2021). Moreover, strategies intended to enhance knowledge transfer must adopt modified perspectives (Van Merriënboer & Kirschner, 2018). Prior activities and misconceptions could influence transfer attempts (Beker, Kim, Van Boekel, van den Broek, & Kendeou, 2019), particularly in Computer Science education (CSE), where even minor misconceptions can yield significant consequences. Students in CSE must grapple with complex tasks where prior knowledge of various interrelated concepts is required.

In this chapter, it is therefore argued that the objective of CSE should revolve around cultivating DSDL. This chapter does not aim to provide specific recommendations on teaching computer programming or delve into the challenges associated with such instruction. Rather, the intention is to underscore the comprehensive nature of CSE, extending beyond mere computer programming, and consequently, accentuating the complexity of CSE. The aim is to propose a conceptual framework for an educational environment within CSE, with the primary objective of fostering DSDL.

The following research question subsequently guides this chapter: Which framework can be proposed to develop DSDL in Computer Science education?

To answer this research question, the following objectives are discussed in this chapter:

- the importance of DSDL in CSE;
- a theoretical framework for developing DSDL based on cognitive load theory (CLT) and social constructivist theory; and
- a framework to promote DSDL in CSE, and which focuses on structuring course content, the role of cooperative learning, and the characteristics of tasks or assignments.

BACKGROUND, CONCEPTUAL AND THEORETICAL FRAMEWORK

This section illuminates the extensive array of knowledge and skills essential to CSE to shed light on the multifaceted nature of the discipline. The significance of developing DSDL in CSE will subsequently be emphasized. To underpin discussions and provide a theoretical foundation for the forthcoming proposal of a DSDL framework, CLT and social constructivist theory will be examined.

Computer Science Education

Computer Science is considered a "fundamental skill" and "the study of principles and practices that underpin an understanding of computation" (Lloyd, Weatherby, Curry & Buckley, 2021, p. 1). Traditionally, CSE centered on computer programming, and the subject was often perceived as inaccessible (Tissenbaum, Weintrop, Holbert & Clegg, 2021). However, it is imperative for CSE to evolve and adapt, equipping students for a world in which it is projected that millions of new jobs will emerge by 2025 in fields such as data science, artificial intelligence (AI), and the Internet of Things (IoT) (Salcito, 2021).

New pedagogical approaches are said to overcome previous arguments on learner capabilities, which excluded students from CSE (Webb, Davis, Bell, Katz, Reynolds & Sysło, 2017). Calls are increasingly being made to include Computer Science as a core subject (Tissenbaum et al., 2021). Furthermore, a plethora of topics and courses in CSE are implemented globally in all educational contexts, ranging from basic software application skills up to "the most extreme complexity imaginable" in AI (Lloyd et al., 2021, p. 1).

Apart from challenges in terms of the content and digital skills that should be included (Webb et al., 2017), there is a lack of consensus on when and how to introduce concepts, and on how to structure the curriculum. Research by Vogel, Santo & Ching (2017) identified seven main areas on which CSE has an influence. Apart from "economic and workforce development", "competencies and literacies", they also identified areas not commonly associated with CSE, such as "equity and social justice", "school improvement and reform", and "fun, fulfillment and personal agency" (Vogel et al., 2017, p. 609). It is further contended that curricula should move beyond the conventional perspectives of CSE to nurture creative computing concepts and cultivate individuals who are "data literate athletes" (Tissenbaum et al., 2021, p. 1170). Although it is beyond the scope of this chapter to give a detailed overview of CSE curriculums across different countries, curricula focus on digital skills, software applications and programming skills, developing computational thinking, problem-solving, and topics that have a strong theoretical underpinning, such as system technologies and computer networks (Webb et al., 2017).

Compiling a computer science curriculum that endures the test of time and incorporates all essential topics is a formidable undertaking (Salcito, 2021). The dynamic nature of computer science, marked by constant evolution and the emergence of new technologies, presents an ongoing challenge for education to keep pace with these changes (Koby, Hazan & Hazzan, 2020). Despite the evident need for updates and reforms in CSE curricula, initiatives globally face resistance grounded in practical implications and governmental policies (Moller & Crick, 2018). The importance of pedagogical knowledge for quality learning and teacher capability has been identified as "a key limiting factor for curriculum change" (Webb et al., 2017, p. 465). Innovative pedagogical approaches can subsequently be seen as pivotal for CSE. The focus should therefore not only be on 'why', 'what', and 'when' in the CSE curriculum, but also on sound pedagogical practices to develop DSDL.

To provide a theoretical grounding for this book chapter, CLT and social constructivist theory are first elaborated on, before discussing DSDL.

Cognitive Load Theory

CLT is especially relevant in the teaching and learning of challenging subject matter, such as computer programming (Berssanette & De Francisco, 2022). To enhance the process of learning, it is essential to consider the cognitive architecture of the human mind, which in simplified terms involves the interplay between working memory (WM) and long-term memory (LTM) (Sweller, Van Merriënboer & Paas, 2019). New information is processed by the WM as the "processing engine" (Sweller, 2020, p. 5) before being stored in the LTM for future retrieval. Low WM resources, however, hampers learning and transfer, implicates academic performance, and increases learning anxiety (Moran, 2016; Sweller et al., 2019).

The main goal of CLT is thus to provide guidelines for instructional design to optimize the learning of complex tasks (Paas & Van Merriënboer, 2020). Optimal learning is shaped by two contrasting features: the constraints of the WM, which is limited in both duration and capacity, in contrast to the boundless capacity of the LTM (Sweller et al., 2019). However, when new information becomes integrated with existing knowledge stored in LTM, and the WM is tasked with processing familiar information, the constraints on WM no longer apply (Sweller, 2020).

CLT must be considered when designing instructional environments when new and complex concepts are introduced to novice students (Sweller, 2020). Computer programming fits the profile, as computer programming is described as "a highly cognitive skill" that is "difficult to learn" because it "requires mastery of multiple domains" (Berssanette & De Francisco, 2022, p. 441). Difficulties encountered by students however mostly stem from the complexity of content in the unfamiliar environment coupled with a student's prior knowledge. The level of complexity subsequently relies not only on the nature of the information but also on a student's prior knowledge and places renewed emphasis on the importance of cultivating a large knowledge base in the LTM (Sweller et al., 2019).

LTM has furthermore been described "as the central factor in problem-solving skill" (Sweller et al., 2019, p. 263). Research has shown that what sets master chess players apart from novices is their extensive knowledge of chessboard configurations stored in their LTM, which they can draw upon when solving problems (Sweller, 2020). Although chess is a game that focuses on problem-solving, the information store principle is foundational to chess. CLT thus underscores the acquisition of domain-specific knowledge rather than relying solely on the development of general cognitive strategies. This perspective aligns with arguments against unguided environments, such as discovery learning, and minimally structured problem-based learning, which rely exclusively on cognitive strategies (Kapur, 2015). It is thus imperative to guide novice students to build sufficient prior knowledge to construct new knowledge later (Sweller, 2020).

To promote transfer of learning, it is crucial to manage the cognitive load and to allow enough processing capacity for the WM (Sweller et al., 2019). The available resources in the WM will be allocated to three categories of cognitive load, namely intrinsic cognitive load, extraneous cognitive load, and germane cognitive load. Intrinsic cognitive load is determined by the difficulty of the content, the consequent complexity of tasks, and the expertise of the learner. Extraneous cognitive load is imposed by the instructional design and by what students are required to do. Effective instructional design can therefore decrease the extraneous cognitive load and provide optimal resources to the WM. Conversely, ineffective instruction could lead to an increase in element interactivity, and subsequently increase the extraneous cognitive load. Ineffective instruction could thus lead to the perception that content is challenging. Current research indicates that the germane cognitive load facilitates learning by reallocating WM resources from the extraneous cognitive load to address the intrinsic cognitive load (Sweller et al., 2019).

Besides limited WM and unlimited storage in LTM, another crucial aspect is an individual's capability to learn from other people (Sweller, 2020). CLT subsequently acknowledges the significance of learning in collaborative environments (Kirschner, Sweller, Kirschner & Zambrano, 2018). Environment-related factors, such as anxiety uncertainty, could restrict WM capacity and increase the cognitive load (Moran,

2016). These factors could however be mitigated through collaboration and the support of peers (Paas & Van Merriënboer, 2020). Collaborative learning environments, where groups are functioning effectively, would reduce intrinsic cognitive load, and subsequently, the application of social constructivist learning strategies is recommended (Kirschner et al., 2018).

Social Constructivism

Learning is viewed as an individual activity that occurs during collaboration. Knowledge is socially constructed when peers and teachers discuss, explain, debate, and reflect (Churcher, Downs & Tewksbury, 2014). While CLT primarily centers on retention of knowledge in the LTM, social constructivism encompasses both intrapersonal and interpersonal domains by highlighting reflective thinking and collaboration with peers as central components of the learning process (Vygotsky, 1978). According to social constructivist theory, learning leads to the development of "an internal dialogue" or "an *intrapsychological* tool" that could be applied to solve future problems in various contexts (Churcher et al., 2014, p. 35). It could thus be argued that social constructivism addresses the transfer of knowledge across cognitive, intrapersonal and interpersonal domains.

Social constructivism furthermore posits that students' potential capabilities can be reached faster by collaborating with peers who are more knowledgeable than they are, described as the "zone of proximal development" (Vygotsky, 1978, p. 86). Learning is subsequently fast-tracked when peers collaborate and share knowledge. Information is shared, which overcomes the difficulty of obtaining information individually. It is even argued that knowledge is obtained more easily when collaborating with others than when attempting troubleshooting and problem-solving individually (Sweller, 2020). When groups discuss explanations about problem-solving scenarios, multiple perspectives are shared which leads to better understanding, and thus to transfer (Johnson & Johnson, 2019). Accordingly, when teaching concepts and skills to their peers, students practice retrieval of knowledge. The more knowledge is retrieved, the more retrievable it becomes, and transfer of knowledge is fostered (Agarwal, 2019).

According to CLT, collective working memories of group members provide increased processing capacity (Kirschner et al., 2018). Collaborative learning can subsequently become a scaffold for learning difficult content and solving problems with a high intrinsic cognitive load. Collaborative learning environments should however be designed carefully, as unstructured environments could increase the extraneous cognitive load to such an extent that the benefits of collective working memories are eliminated (Sweller et al., 2019). Students should subsequently be aware of what their group roles are, and they should have collaboration skills (Kirschner et al., 2018).

Deeper Self-Directed Learning

DSDL incorporates the concepts of deeper learning and self-directed learning (SDL) (Van Zyl & Mentz, 2022). In literature, the concepts 'deep learning' and 'deeper learning' in the educational context are often used interchangeably. 'Deep learning' or 'deep learning approaches' refers to learning environments that aim for deep understanding and high-quality outcomes (Guo & Wu, 2017). Deep approaches to learning subsequently result in integration with prior knowledge, applying knowledge to real-world situations, and transfer of ideas (Varunki, Katajavuori & Postareff, 2017).

The American National Research Council (NRC) indicated transferable knowledge as an important twenty-first-century skill (NRC, 2012). Deeper learning has accordingly advanced the concept of deep learning approaches, by drawing on a rich legacy of research and emphasizing the acquisition of transferable knowledge and skills in the cognitive, intrapersonal, and interpersonal domains as a key learning outcome. Examples include critical thinking, creativity, a growth mindset, a desire to learn, perseverance, metacognition (intrapersonal), collaboration, social skills, and empathy toward others (interpersonal) (NRC, 2012). Pedagogical approaches should accordingly be balanced to address cognitive, interpersonal, and intrapersonal competencies, and be specifically designed to promote transfer of such competencies (Morris, 2021).

SDL is a continuous process where individuals apply strategies to fulfill their identified learning needs (Van der Westhuizen & Mentz, 2020). During the SDL process, learners formulate their learning goals, identify academic resources, collaborate with peers, identify and implement appropriate learning strategies, and evaluate whether learning goals have been met (Knowles, 1975). Self-directed learners are adaptive and find ways to respond to the needs of a rapidly changing world (Morris, 2021). They are furthermore characterized by a multitude of skills in the cognitive, intrapersonal and interpersonal domains (Van Zyl, 2020). One characteristic not commonly mentioned in the literature on SDL, that is emphasized by deeper learning, is the ability to transfer knowledge to new contexts (NRC, 2012). Consequently, the concept of DSDL encompasses the need to bridge the gap in transferable knowledge and skills. DSDL is subsequently defined as a process where students intentionally take charge and ownership of the learning process, resulting in transferable twenty-first-century competencies in the cognitive, intrapersonal, and interpersonal domains (Van Zyl & Mentz, 2022).

CSE is positioned centrally in a rapidly changing technological environment, and transferable knowledge and skills in CSE are therefore imperative (Berssanette & De Francisco, 2022). Continuous change is the one constant in all topics related to CSE, presenting an ongoing challenge to stay abreast of developments in the field. Even though a particular programming language may be the focal point of a course, the reality is that students are likely to utilize a different programming language in their professional roles. This necessitates a continuous transfer of knowledge of programming concepts and transfer of programming skills to new environments. Accordingly, network technologies will evolve, hardware will become more sophisticated, and software will increasingly integrate with AI.

Considering the above, pedagogical approaches solely focused on knowledge construction are recognized as insufficient. The incorporation of CLT acknowledges the intricacies of computer science and emphasizes the management of the cognitive load to facilitate schema construction in LTM. This, in turn, enhances higher cognitive processes and promotes knowledge transfer. In a structured, social constructivist environment, the utilization of multiple working memories, collective knowledge, and emotional support from group members emerges as a vital scaffold. Social constructivist learning environments subsequently leverage individual learning, facilitate knowledge transfer, and ultimately cultivate DSDL. It is within such a pedagogical framework that CSE, often perceived as a challenging subject limited to an exclusive student audience (Shin, Jung & Lee, 2023), becomes accessible and inclusive for students across diverse professions. This transformation offers a long-overdue opportunity for a broader spectrum of learners to engage with and excel in the field of computer science (Berssanette & De Francisco, 2022).

THE DEEPER SELF-DIRECTED LEARNING FRAMEWORK

Although "innovative changes in pedagogy" were predicted (Majumdar et al., 2018, p. 199), it seems that technology was merely integrated into education. In contrast to the disruptive influences of computer science in the world around us, CSE has remained focused on traditional methods and teacher-centered pedagogies where transmission of knowledge is still the norm (Lloyd et al., 2021). Especially when learning computer programming, knowledge-driven and teacher-centered approaches often lead to fragile knowledge and unsatisfactory programming competencies (Peng, Wang & Sampson, 2017).

Strong arguments can be made against teaching and learning methods that employ direct instruction and focus on knowledge transmission (Al-Sakkaf, Omar, & Ahmad, 2019). Accordingly, instructional methods that focus on improving knowledge retention, such as practicing one version of a task repeatedly, step-by-step guidance, and frequent and complete feedback, will not have a positive effect on problem-solving and knowledge transfer. This is described as the "transfer paradox" (Van Merriënboer & Kirschner, 2018, p. 18). CSE should therefore apply student-centered teaching and learning methods (Al-Sakkaf et al., 2019), should encourage learners to be thoughtful and adaptive (Morris, 2021), should foster SDL (Breed & Bailey, 2018), and should develop transferable knowledge and skills that can be applied to solve novel real-life problems (Morris, 2021).

The framework for the development of DSDL draws upon prior research that proposed guidelines aimed at fostering DSDL within the context of database design in CSE (Van Zyl, 2020). In this chapter, these guidelines are enriched by incorporating insights gleaned from additional literature, thereby encompassing a wide array of themes in CSE. These enriched guidelines are presented as a framework for the cultivation of DSDL within CSE. The DSDL framework is underpinned by a theoretical foundation rooted in the principles of CLT and social constructivism, and focuses on three key aspects:

- The structuring of course content: this facet emphasizes the way course content is structured and sequenced to facilitate DSDL.
- Cooperative learning as teaching and learning strategy: this element highlights the adoption of cooperative learning strategies when aiming to promote DSDL.
- Task characteristics: the framework emphasizes understanding of the characteristics of the tasks involved and recognizes their role in shaping the learning experience.

In sum, this chapter presents a framework for the development of DSDL in CSE, combining established guidelines with contemporary research insights and anchored in a solid theoretical foundation.

Structuring Course Content

Academic courses typically follow a sequential structure, starting with the introduction of simple and fundamental concepts before gradually incorporating more advanced material. The more advanced concepts tend to be deferred until the later stages of the course. However, this traditional "atomistic approach" (Van Merriënboer, 2019, p.15) introduces concepts in a fragmented manner and often leads to an excessive amount of time being spent on the initial concepts (Kapur, 2015). Given that it takes approximately 21 days to establish a new concept in the LTM and around 42 days to develop thinking habits (Leaf, 2018), there is limited time available for students to absorb new knowledge and enhance their competencies. This is especially relevant for novice students who are learning to program and need to construct several mental models without sufficient prior knowledge of programming and programming concepts. Subsequently, students find all the programming concepts overwhelming and find it challenging to construct procedural and declarative knowledge (Qian & Lehman, 2017). Challenging concepts should therefore be incorporated earlier and scaffolded throughout the course (Van Merriënboer & Kirschner, 2018).

The following practical example in this regard could apply. Since the 1970s, computer programming textbooks have traditionally introduced students to programming by tasking them with writing code to display the phrase 'hello world' (Fry, 2018). Programming courses are usually structured by first explaining what a variable is, then focusing on input and output statements, then explaining how to program arithmetic expressions, and then moving to decision structures and the different types of loops.

The suggestion is, therefore, to follow a holistic, whole-task sequencing approach where various aspects are integrated and studied holistically from the outset (Van Merriënboer, 2019). Instead of over-explaining stand-alone concepts (such as variables), examples of programming code that contain several concepts simultaneously – for example, variables, input, processing, output, and decision-making or repetition structures – could be studied. Learners are initially provided with an overview of concepts, and examples increase in complexity by adding more variables, more complex decision-making, and more complex repetition structures. In the context of database courses, it is beneficial to commence with the introduction of fundamental objects simultaneously, such as tables, forms, queries, and reports, to provide learners with an immediate overview of these various objects and how they are interrelated (Van Zyl, 2020). Thereafter, a more in-depth exploration of these objects can be conducted while concurrently integrating other components.

Van Merriënboer (2019, p. 12) refers to the approach described above as "backward chaining with snowballing". This pedagogical method recommends starting at the lowest level of complexity, where learners initially engage in tracing simple algorithms. This approach differs from conventional teaching methods that often begin with explaining abstract concepts, such as variables, or instructing students to write a basic 'hello world' program. As learners progress, more complex algorithms are introduced, and they gradually advance to the debugging of provided algorithms. It is only at the highest level of complexity that learners are encouraged to design, code, and debug complete computer programs.

The order in which course content is presented should also account for the correction of misconceptions (Van Merriënboer & Kirschner, 2018). Considering that prior knowledge is considered a major source of misconceptions, the critical importance of instilling accurate programming concepts right from the outset is therefore emphasized to avoid the need for students to unlearn misconceptions later in their learning journey (Qian & Lehman, 2017). For instance, many database design courses typically commence with the introduction of tables, with forms introduced at a later stage. This sequencing could inadvertently foster the misconception that the primary function of database tables is data input, while forms are solely for data display (Van Zyl, 2020).

In summary, a holistic approach to structuring course content is recommended. This approach entails the strategic sequencing of topics to facilitate schema construction in the LTM, the integration of core concepts across the curriculum, and a focus on elucidating the underlying theoretical and practical purposes of these concepts.

Cooperative Learning as Foundational Teaching and Learning Strategy

The learning environment plays a pivotal role in shaping the processes through which learners engage in and complete tasks. This, in turn, significantly influences the outcomes of the learning process, which in turn will determine the outcomes of the learning process. Cooperative learning is a structured and effective form of group learning in which students work in small groups to enhance their learning and that of their peers. Cooperative learning builds upon the concept of positive goal interdependence, according to which students perceive that they can only achieve their goals if other group members also attain theirs. Cooperation with a focus on social interdependence, thus promotes high levels of achievement, higher-level reasoning, retention and transfer, positive relationships, attitudes, and values (Johnson & Johnson, 2018).

It is argued that learners do not engage optimally in unguided collaboration processes (Kirschner et al., 2018). As stated by Kapur (2015, p. 52), "structure helps learners to accomplish what they might not otherwise be able to in the absence of structure". Unstructured group work may furthermore increase the extraneous load imposed by transactive group activities (Kirschner et al., 2018). The mere placing of learners or students in groups and requiring them to work together therefore does not necessarily promote cooperation and have the desired learning outcomes (Xing, Zhu, Arslan, Shim & Popov, 2023). The phenomenon of social free-riding comes into play when only some students within a group actively engage in the work, leaving others to contribute less or not at all (Le, Janssen & Wubbels, 2018). Additionally, it is common to encounter partial knowledge within such groups, where members have only completed specific portions of an assignment and may therefore have limited, or no understanding of the contributions made by their fellow group members.

Cooperative learning not only prepares students better for their future professional endeavors, but also facilitates the development and transfer of competencies in the intrapersonal, interpersonal, and cognitive domains (Van Zyl, 2020). Consequently, for optimal learning and effective functioning of groups, collaborative teaching and learning environments should be structured to incorporate five specific elements (Johnson & Johnson, 2018).

The Five Elements of Cooperative Learning

Cooperative learning successfully addresses the common hurdles associated with conventional group work through the integration of five specific elements: positive interdependence, individual accountability, face-to-face promotive interaction, social skills, and group processing (Johnson & Johnson, 2018).

Element One: Positive Interdependence

Positive interdependence promotes mutual help and assistance between group members, leading to desired outcomes (Johnson & Johnson, 2019). Group members should feel responsible for each other's success and should have the view that the work they are doing mutually benefits each other. The state of positive interdependence between group members will thus create the momentum for members to work together, while they encourage each other to complete their part of the task. Positive interdependence can be facilitated by incorporating task interdependence, role interdependence, goal interdependence, joint rewards, and cooperative constructive controversy (Bertucci, Johnson, Johnson, & Conte, 2016; Johnson & Johnson, 2017).

Role interdependence is achieved when group members are allocated individual roles to fulfill. Examples are the roles of checker, recorder, and observer in their groups. Roles can either be assigned formally by the facilitator or they can be assigned spontaneously, where individuals drift into roles based on their interests and skills. Roles should however be complementary, meaning that one role cannot be performed without the other (Johnson & Johnson, 2014).

Task interdependence exists when a task is divided into subtasks and allocated to group members. The group can only achieve its goal if all members complete their individual subtasks (Bertucci et al., 2016). One example is the jigsaw method, where students switch between different groups while acting as expert teachers and novice students (Jainal & Shahrill, 2021). Each group member is accountable for a unique part of the learning material. He or she must study the allocated part of the content and then meet in another expert group, where all members of that group have to study the same content. Group members then return to their original groups, where they have to present their part of the content to the group, acting as expert teachers or listening to other students presenting their content, in this case acting as novice students.

Task interdependence can also be fostered by increasing the cognitive level of tasks, as will be explained further in the section below on task characteristics. When working on simple tasks, learners will not necessarily benefit more from working in groups as opposed to individual learning. However, regarding complex learning tasks, which have a high intrinsic cognitive load, collaborative learning is superior to individual learning (Johnson & Johnson, 2017; Kirschner et al., 2018). Complex tasks are thus said to increase the interdependence between group members, because group members rely on each other to solve the task at hand.

Goal interdependence unites group members into a "dynamic whole" (Johnson & Johnson, 2018, p. 62) and exists when group members believe that they can only reach their goals if their fellow group members also reach their goals. The goal of the group could, for example, be that all members have to learn the assigned material. Yet another goal might be the earning of bonus points by all members of a team with an average assignment grade above a certain percentage. Linking the bonus points to the team average, gives all members an incentive to get the best grade they can, and to teach each other, without putting too much pressure on weaker members, who may not be able to obtain a certain percentage (Felder & Brent, 2007).

Constructive controversy has the cooperative group goal of reaching consensus on issues that individuals disagree on, by synthesizing the arguments from different sides. Heterogeneous small groups are randomly assigned by the facilitator, and each group receives a controversial issue to discuss and on which they have to report. The groups are then subdivided, with each sub-group taking a different stand on the issue. Each small group then must defend their stand and collect supporting arguments. Outcomes of constructive controversy are improved decision-making, enhanced creativity, higher cognitive reasoning, positive relationships, and social support (Johnson & Johnson, 2018).

Element Two: Individual Accountability

The purpose of cooperative learning is to improve group cooperation so that individuals can perform higher and be strengthened (Johnson & Johnson, 2019). Individual accountability subsequently refers to each individual's responsibility to be accountable and to perform individually. Each group member should accept the responsibility to complete his or her part of the task, master the material that has to be learned, and assist other group members to do the same (Johnson & Johnson, 2019).

Several suggestions can be found for fostering individual accountability. The performance of each group member should, for example, be assessed, and feedback on results should be given to individuals and the group for group members to account for their share of the work (Johnson & Johnson, 2019). Another suggestion is to use a combination of group assignments and individual assignments. Facilitators could also randomly nominate any group member, instead of assigning a group leader. This will ensure that each member of the group should be able to report on what the group did, thereby fostering individual accountability (Felder & Brent, 2007).

Element Three: Face-to-Face Promotive Interaction

Face-to-face communication remains a key aspect for groups to be effective, as it requires engagement, energy, focus, and attention (Johnson & Johnson, 2014). Promotive interaction requires that members share resources, praise each other's efforts, and teach and encourage each other by supporting and evaluating each other's learning efforts critically. This should be done by listening to each other, providing constructive feedback, exchanging ideas, challenging reasoning and conclusions, and connecting present learning with past learning (Johnson & Johnson, 2018).

Element Four: Social Skills

The fourth element, appropriate use of social skills, requires that students learn and express interpersonal group or teamwork skills. It should not be assumed that students will have the necessary social skills required to work in cooperative groups, but a trust-building climate should first be created, and a rationale be provided to foster a willingness to cooperate, to ask for help, and to handle conflict (Johnson & Johnson, 2018). Social skills are further considered a critical element of cooperative learning concerning problem-solving success, gaining achievement, establishing effective working relationships between group members, and fostering metacognition. Students should be actively listening, considering each other's ideas and perspectives, stating ideas clearly without making degrading comments, accepting responsibility for behavior, constructively evaluating ideas, sharing resources, and taking turns (Gillies, 2014).

Element Five: Group Processing

Embedding the fifth element, group processing, means that groups reflect on and discuss how well they have achieved their goals, which behaviors need to change to improve the performance of the group and celebrate hard work and success. Group members can, for example, be asked to discuss which actions of group members have contributed to the achievement of all group members, what they have been doing well, what needs improvement, and what they will do differently next time (Johnson & Johnson, 2018).

Group members are expected to show appreciation and respect for each other's contributions, which tends to increase members' self-esteem and the joint efficacy of the group (Johnson & Johnson, 2019). When engaging in group processing and receiving feedback, group members become increasingly aware of their thinking about the topic being discussed, and they obtain insight into how to improve their social skills (Gillies, 2014). When giving feedback skillfully, the focus is directed towards constructive action, and group members are empowered to be more effective in future (Johnson & Johnson, 2019).

Because group processing is seen as the final phase of a cooperative learning lesson, it can easily be neglected due to time constraints or insufficient planning. Group processing is, however, of high importance, and the full benefits of cooperative learning will not be reaped if this element is left out. Without consolidation, learning is compromised (Kapur, 2015). Accordingly, group processing in cooperative learning leads to higher achievement, better relationships between group members, and less social loafing. Even when the group has not performed satisfactorily, learning can still take place when consolidating and reflecting on the performance of the group (Johnson & Johnson, 2018).

Although resistance from students can be expected at first when implementing cooperative learning, this can be overcome when cooperative learning is implemented appropriately, and it will be minimized once students experience the benefits of cooperative learning. The perspective is that cooperative learning is considered appropriately implemented only when all five elements are incorporated (Johnson & Johnson, 2018).

Apart from structuring cooperative learning as discussed above, the composition of the group could also influence the effectiveness of the group.

Group Composition

When deciding on group composition, three key factors are: group size, diversity within the group, and duration for which the group will be active. The size of the group must be considered in relation to the group task, and four or fewer members are preferred (Johnson & Johnson, 2014). Groups of four may initially need time to develop strategies for working together, and therefore initially working in pairs is suggested. For activities where a diversity of ideas is required, groups of three or four members should rather be formed. Group members should preferably be allocated by the facilitator, as students usually select their friends or popular classmates, and leave other students out (van Zyl, 2020).

The diversity of the group can be described as determining how group members will be assigned, that is, homogeneously or heterogeneously. Sources of diversity can be demographic, for example, age, gender and ethnic differences; differences in abilities or skills, which can be social or technical; and differences in personality traits. No group can however be considered truly homogeneous, as there will always be differences between individuals (Johnson & Johnson, 2018).

Although arguments can be made against heterogeneous groups (Kirschner et al., 2018), it seems that research favors such groups (van Zyl, 2020). Heterogeneous groups are more likely to perform better in problem-solving, creativity, and decision-making than homogenous groups, because of the range of skills, knowledge, and perspectives that are available. Although challenges exist within heterogeneous groups, the promise of diversity outweighs the problems, when group members value diversity and understand how to avoid pitfalls and capitalize on benefits. Diverse personalities can be united by incorporating a high level of positive interdependence, creating mutual goals, developing common ground, and creating a group identity. An effective way to assign students to a group is by using a random method, such as drawing a number from a box. Creative group allocation using a gamified approach could serve as an icebreaker and provide common ground for the selection of heterogeneous groups.

Cooperative Pair Programming and Cooperative Pair Problem Solving

Collaborative teaching and learning strategies have been shown to enhance learning when incorporating the elements of cooperative learning (Van der Westhuizen & Mentz, 2020). In this section, cooperative pair programming (suggested for teaching and learning of programming) and cooperative pair problem solving (suggested for teaching and learning of non-programming concepts) are highlighted.

Pair programming, where two programmers work together on one computer and collaborate to solve a problem, is commonly accepted as an effective strategy for teaching and learning programming (Denner, Green & Campe, 2021). The roles of the pair are assigned as 'driver' and 'navigator'. The navigator assumes the role of a strategic, forward-thinking individual who engages the driver through a series of insightful questions, prompting them to articulate their actions. In addition to seeking explanations, the navigator offers valuable guidance, assesses available resources, and scans for potential errors. The driver takes charge of the computer, executing tasks such as inputting commands and crafting designs through typing. The driver and the navigator could also engage in brainstorming activities at any time and swap roles from time to time (Denner et al., 2021).

Pair programming will however be more effective when the five elements of cooperative learning are embedded in pair programming. In these conditions, cooperative pair programming has also been shown to influence students' critical thinking skills positively (Bailey & Mentz, 2017). Accordingly, cooperative pair problem-solving incorporates the principles of pair programming and cooperative learning when working collaboratively on non-programming tasks (Breed & Bailey, 2018).

Task Characteristics

In addition to how the course content is structured and the teaching and learning strategy that is applied, the nature of the task is another key aspect that should be examined.

Students are usually reluctant to work collaboratively on simple tasks that they could have completed on their own. Regardless of the form of the task, complexity is thus viewed as the key aspect of fostering group collaboration (Kirschner et al., 2018). Furthermore, when students collaborate on challenging, authentic tasks, they are doing tasks that prepare them for real professions, and deeper learning is promoted (Peng et al., 2017). Authentic tasks are ill-defined, complex tasks that are relevant to the real world. Providing an authentic context for activities simulates how the knowledge will be applied in the real world and allows students to model real-world practice (Van Merriënboer & Kirschner, 2018). Additionally, it is highly advisable to expose learners to a diverse range of learning conditions, that focus on a variety of problems and solutions, which they should practice in a random order (Van Merriënboer, 2019). This approach enhances their ability to transfer knowledge and skills effectively across different contexts, promoting a deeper and more flexible understanding of the subject matter. While this may result in more challenging and time-consuming initial learning, the transfer gain can be substantial.

Such complex, ill-structured tasks can assist students in reconciling attitudes towards failure, and to develop persistence and resilience by failing forward (Beghetto, 2018). Failure needs to be incorporated deliberately to provide instructional and emotional support for future problem-solving situations where failure will be experienced. Under specific circumstances, tasks that are purposively designed for productive failure could contribute to deeper learning (Kapur, 2015) and developing creativity. Research found that transfer of problem-solving skills occurred when students had to solve a well-structured problem individually after solving a complex, ill-structured problem collaboratively (Kapur, 2015). Especially when preparing novice students to acquire new knowledge, experiencing failure could profoundly influence their conceptual understanding (Steenhof, Woods & Mylopoulos, 2020).

While educational problems need to be intellectually challenging, it is equally crucial that they do not lead to student frustration (Kapur, 2015). To mitigate this challenge, cooperative pair programming is recommended as an effective scaffolding technique. Moreover, gamification, which focuses on enhancing student motivation and fostering a "desire and willingness" to engage in tasks, as emphasized by Dichev and Dicheva (2017, p. 26), offers another avenue to address frustration in complex tasks and sustain intrinsic motivation.

In addition to the primary task, it is essential to incorporate metacognitive self-questioning techniques to reflect on failure (Beghetto, 2018), and "to prompt students to move beyond mere cognition" (Breed & Bailey, 2018, p. 4). These metacognitive questions encompass inquiries, such as "Do we understand exactly what outcomes we have to reach with the solution of this problem?" and "Do we know strategies/procedures that are appropriate to solve this problem?" Furthermore, reflective questions are also asked, such as, "What happened when you failed?" and "What did you learn from that situation?" (Beghetto, 2018, p. 22).

Finally, task characteristics to manage cognitive load are addressed. The formulation of a task could impose an unnecessary high cognitive load. When designing conventional problems using the "goal-free effect", as advocated by Sweller et al. (2019, p. 265), the focus shifts toward generating solutions that facilitate knowledge construction. For instance, instead of framing the final part of a problem with a specific goal (e.g., How many times will the loop execute?), the question should be rephrased as a goal-free statement (e.g., Determine all possible outputs).

A whole-part approach to learning tasks is recommended. Right from the outset, learners should engage with complete and meaningful tasks to develop a comprehensive understanding of the entire task (Van Merriënboer, 2019). Subsequent tasks should gradually increase in complexity, demanding further knowledge than the preceding simpler task. This means that 'scaffolding' will take place by giving simple problems that include more concepts, followed by more advanced problems that also include those concepts. This approach contrasts with scaffolding tasks by gradually introducing new concepts.

From the outset, whole and meaningful tasks should thus be given, for learners to develop a holistic view of the whole task.

Another effective scaffolding technique, according to CLT, is providing students with worked-out examples. Worked-out examples offer comprehensive solutions with detailed steps that novice learners have to study before attempting their solutions (Sweller et al., 2019). Learning is scaffolded by gradually reducing the guidance provided in subsequent partial solutions until learners can solve a task independently (Van Merriënboer, 2019). Research conducted by Shin et al. (2023) reported that the integration of metacognitive self-questioning and reflection, coupled with worked-out examples, resulted in several positive outcomes. Participants demonstrated a deeper understanding of the subject matter, exhibited more effective control over their learning beliefs, and showcased improvements in knowledge transfer.

In summary, tasks should be authentic, complex, designed to incorporate failure, and have to focus on different contexts to include a variety of practice. However, making the complex process of authentic tasks accessible to avoid discouraging students, is a key issue (Peng et al., 2017). Subsequently, authentic and complex tasks, worked-out examples, a whole-part approach, and metacognitive self-questions are suggested. Incorporating gaming and playful elements could enhance intrinsic motivation and reduce cognitive load. Furthermore, these tasks should be done in cooperative learning environments to provide scaffolding and accessibility in a supportive group environment to promote DSDL.

SOLUTIONS AND RECOMMENDATIONS

Computer Science education needs to prepare students to strive within a field that is positioned at the forefront of disruptive technological developments. Renewed and innovative pedagogical approaches are required to support students to acquire competencies to rise above AI. While machines are exponentially acquiring knowledge and skills through deep learning algorithms, educational environments should be purposefully designed to develop students' DSDL.

DSDL is a recursive, infinite process that aims at developing self-directed learners who can transfer cognitive, intrapersonal, and interpersonal competencies to solve problems in new contexts. The proposed framework to develop DSDL is portrayed in Figure 1. The cornerstones of the DSDL framework are the structuring of the course content, cooperative learning as teaching and learning strategy, and

Figure 1. Deeper self-directed learning framework
(Own contribution)

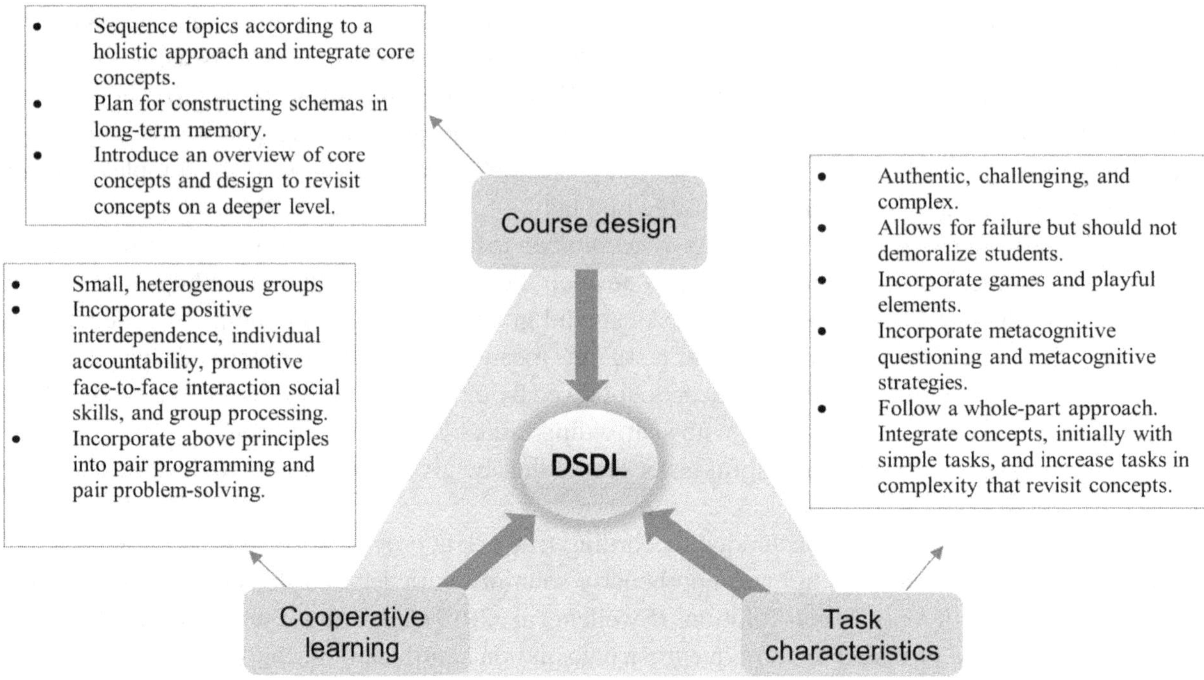

characteristics of tasks or assignments. DSDL should be developed in social constructivist environments, that incorporate CLT, and create opportunities to fail forward while solving complex, authentic tasks.

Instructional environments need to be intentionally designed to develop DSDL and all of the three suggested key aspects should be incorporated. The focus is on designing learner-centered, active teaching and learning environments that emphasize a significant shift away from teacher explanations or direct instruction. To accomplish this, it is necessary to redesign the sequence and structure of the course content while considering the specific characteristics of the suggested tasks. Depending on the nature of the content being taught, various teaching and learning methods rooted in cooperative learning can be employed. Theoretical content can, for instance, be effectively facilitated by applying the Jigsaw method. Cooperative pair programming is suggested for facilitating programming concepts and cooperative pair problem solving for facilitating topics such as spreadsheets, database design, and other problem-solving activities.

Problem-solving activities, tasks, or assignments should be thoughtfully compiled ensuring they meet specific characteristics. Task characteristics should however be applied according to the topic in CSE that is being studied. In general, tasks should be authentic, complex, and purposefully designed to embrace the potential for setbacks, without disheartening students. The incorporation of gamified elements has the potential to not only bolster intrinsic motivation but also foster persistence in the problem-solving process.

An overarching strategy is to employ a holistic, whole-part approach. This approach allows for the inclusion of several concepts right from the outset. As learners tackle such tasks, scaffolding is systematically introduced by elevating the complexity of the challenges they encounter. Consequently, this approach not only saves valuable time by introducing several concepts simultaneously, but it also promotes effective retrieval practice as students revisit these concepts at a deeper level of understanding.

It is further advisable to provide worked-out examples that offer a comprehensive overview of potential solutions. Worked-out examples should be gradually scaffolded, by also incorporating metacognitive scaffolding, necessitating students to complete specific sections of the task before being able to tackle the entire assignment independently. This gradual progression empowers students to build their knowledge and skills incrementally and with confidence.

RECOMMENDATIONS BEYOND THE CLASS LEVEL

The influence of computer science permeates across all professions and societal spheres, with its reach and applications experiencing exponential growth. Consequently, at the institutional and curriculum policy levels, computer science should transcend its status as an exclusive field of study. Instead, it ought to be made accessible to all students and seamlessly integrated into diverse courses, fostering digital literacy, skills, and a robust understanding of pertinent information and ICT.

Assumptions regarding students' inherent computer literacy and knowledge to incorporate computer science and artificial intelligence into their studies and future careers must be dispelled. Faculty members should not shy away from embracing artificial intelligence but rather proactively equip students to adeptly navigate ICT, integrating it to enhance higher-order thinking skills, foster digital skills, and promote DSDL.

Consequently, the educational focus should shift away from mere rote learning and memorization, placing a greater emphasis on promoting DSDL. This necessitates a substantial mindset shift in designing educational programs, curricula, and assessments. Recognizing that much of the foundational knowledge is readily available online and within expansive language models, higher education programs must adapt, discarding outdated courses in favor of innovative, relevant ones.

The very concept of knowledge requires a redefinition, evolving towards a higher-level understanding of how to acquire and critically evaluate information, as well as the ability to transfer competencies for solving authentic problems. The urgency lies in empowering educators with the requisite knowledge and skills to overhaul traditional teaching practices (Morris, 2021; Shin et al., 2023), centering instruction around active, student-centric strategies that promote DSDL.

Through the implementation of the DSDL framework, students can acquire the knowledge and competencies necessary to become lifelong learners, ready to confront the challenges of a swiftly evolving digital society.

FUTURE RESEARCH DIRECTIONS

Further research can explore the integration of the proposed DSDL framework into practical educational resources, including textbooks, study guides, websites, curriculum design, and online learning environments. This framework could be incorporated within various subject disciplines and educational contexts and could benefit students and learners across the educational spectrum. Moreover, research must be done on the relevance of courses and curricula, and aspects of computer science that should be incorporated, especially in higher education, to better prepare students for unknown career paths.

Further research could delve into the integration of the proposed DSDL framework into tangible educational resources such as textbooks, study guides, websites, curriculum design, and online learning environments. The adaptability of this framework makes it suitable for incorporation across diverse subject disciplines and educational contexts, presenting potential benefits for students and learners spanning the entire educational spectrum.

Moreover, it is imperative to conduct research on the pertinence of existing courses and curricula, with a focus on identifying aspects of computer science that should be integrated, particularly within higher education. This exploration aims to better equip students for the uncertainties of future career paths. By understanding the evolving demands of the professional landscape, educators can ensure that the content of courses remains relevant and aligned with the dynamic nature of technology and its applications.

Further research into the incorporation of the DSDL framework into educational resources and the ongoing relevance of computer science courses in higher education can contribute significantly to the enhancement of educational practices. This research provides a foundation for creating adaptable and forward-looking educational materials, fostering an environment where students are not just prepared for current challenges but are also equipped to navigate the uncharted territories of future career opportunities.

CONCLUSION

In this chapter, a framework for developing DSDL in CSE was proposed. CLT and social constructivist theory were discussed as foundational to the framework. The framework is based on three primary aspects, namely structuring the course content according to a holistic approach by incorporating key concepts from the very beginning, applying cooperative learning as a foundational teaching and learning strategy, and compiling tasks to meet specific characteristics. One inherent limitation is that the DSDL framework has only been empirically tested in database design (Van Zyl, 2020). However, this chapter serves as a launching pad for potential future research endeavors, offering the opportunity to rigorously test and validate the framework's effectiveness in promoting DSDL in other topics in the field of CSE and other subject areas.

REFERENCES

Agarwal, P. K. (2019). Retrieval practice & Bloom's taxonomy: Do students need fact knowledge before higher order learning? *Journal of Educational Psychology, 111*(2), 189–209. https://psycnet.apa.org/doi/10.1037/edu0000282. doi:10.1037/edu0000282

Al-Sakkaf, A., Omar, M., & Ahmad, M. (2019). A systematic literature review of student engagement in software visualization: A theoretical perspective. *Computer Science Education, 29*(2-3), 283–309. doi:10.1080/08993408.2018.1564611

Bailey, R., & Mentz, E. (2017). The value of pair programming in the IT classroom. *The Independent Journal of Teaching and Learning, 12*(1), 90–103.

Beghetto, R. A. (2018). Taking beautiful risks in education. *Educational Leadership*, 18–24.

Beker, K., Kim, J., Van Boekel, M., van den Broek, P., & Kendeou, P. (2019). Refutation texts enhance spontaneous transfer of knowledge. *Contemporary Educational Psychology*, *56*, 67–78. doi:10.1016/j.cedpsych.2018.11.004

Berssanette, J. H., & De Francisco, A. C. (2022). Cognitive load theory in the context of teaching and learning computer programming: A systematic literature review. *IEEE Transactions on Education*, *65*(3), 440–449. doi:10.1109/TE.2021.3127215

Bertucci, A., Johnson, D. W., Johnson, R. T., & Conte, S. (2016). Effect of task and goal interdependence on achievement, cooperation, and support among elementary school students. *International Journal of Educational Research*, *79*, 97–105. doi:10.1016/j.ijer.2016.06.011

Breed, B., & Bailey, R. (2018). The influence of a metacognitive approach to cooperative pair problem-solving on self-direction in learning. *TD: The Journal for Transdisciplinary Research in Southern Africa*, *14*(1), 1–11. doi:10.4102/td.v14i1.516

Cheng, E. C. (2021). Knowledge transfer strategies and practices for higher education institutions. *VINE Journal of Information and Knowledge Management Systems*, *51*(2), 288–301. doi:10.1108/VJIKMS-11-2019-0184

Churcher, K. M., Downs, E., & Tewksbury, D. (2014). "Friending" Vygotsky: A social constructivist pedagogy of knowledge building through classroom social media use. *The Journal of Effective Teaching*, *14*(1), 33–50.

Denner, J., Green, E., & Campe, S. (2021). Learning to program in middle school: How pair programming helps and hinders intrepid exploration. *Journal of the Learning Sciences*, *30*(4-5), 611–645. doi:10.1080/10508406.2021.1939028

Dichev, C., & Dicheva, D. (2017). Gamifying education: What is known, what is believed and what remains uncertain: A critical review. *International Journal of Educational Technology in Higher Education*, *14*(9), 1–36. doi:10.1186/s41239-017-0042-5

Felder, R. M., & Brent, R. (2007). Cooperative learning. In P. A. Mabrouk (Ed.), *Active learning: Models from the analytical sciences, 970* (pp. 34–53). American Chemical Association. doi:10.1021/bk-2007-0970.ch004

Fry, H. (2018). *Hello world: How to be human in the age of the machine*. Random House.

Gillies, R. M. (2014). Cooperative learning: Developments in research. *International Journal of Educational Psychology*, *3*(2), 125–140. doi:10.4471/ijep.2014.08

Guo, Y., & Wu, S. (2017). Creating the learning situation to promote student deep learning: Data analysis and application case. In AIP Conference Proceedings. American Institute of Physics. doi:10.1063/1.4982529

Jainal, N. H., & Shahrill, M. (2021). Incorporating Jigsaw strategy to support students" learning through action research. [IJonSES]. *International Journal on Social and Education Sciences*, *3*(2), 252–266. doi:10.46328/ijonses.75

Johnson, D. W., & Johnson, R. T. (2014). Cooperative learning in 21st century. [Aprendizaje cooperativo en el siglo XXI]. *Anales de Psicología/Annals of Psychology, 30*(3), 841–851. doi:10.6018/analesps.30.3.201241

Johnson, D. W., & Johnson, R. T. (2017). The use of cooperative procedures in teacher education and professional development. *Journal of Education for Teaching*, *43*(3), 284–295. doi:10.1080/02607476.2017.1328023

Johnson, D. W., & Johnson, R. T. (2018). Cooperative learning: The foundation of active learning. In S. M. Brito (Ed.), *Active learning: Beyond the future* (pp. 59–71). IntechOpen. doi:10.5772/intechopen.81086

Johnson, D. W., & Johnson, R. T. (2019). The impact of cooperative learning on self-directed learning. In E. Mentz, J. de Beer, & R. Bailey (Eds.), *Self-directed learning for the 21st century: Implications for higher education* (pp. 37–66). AOSIS. doi:10.4102/aosis.2019.BK134.02

Kapur, M. (2015). Learning from productive failure. *Learning: Research and Practice*, *1*(1), 51–65. doi:10.1080/23735082.2015.1002195

Kirschner, P. A., Sweller, J., Kirschner, F., & Zambrano, R. J. (2018). From cognitive load theory to collaborative cognitive load theory. *International Journal of Computer-Supported Collaborative Learning*, *13*(213), 213–233. doi:10.1007/s11412-018-9277-y PMID:30996713

Knowles, M. S. (1975). *Self-directed learning: A guide for learners and teachers.* Association Press.

Koby, M., Hazan, T., & Hazzan, O. (2020). Equalizing data science curriculum for Computer Science pupils. In *Proceedings of the 20th Koli Calling International Conference on Computing Educational Research.* ACM. 10.1145/3428029.3428045

Le, H., Janssen, J., & Wubbels, T. (2018). Collaborative learning practices: Teacher and student perceived obstacles to effective student collaboration. *Cambridge Journal of Education*, *48*(1), 103–122. doi:10.1080/0305764X.2016.1259389

Leaf, C. (2018). *Think, learn succeed: Understanding and use your mind to thrive at school, the workplace, and life.* Baker.

Lloyd, M., Weatherby, K., Curry, J., & Buckley, D. (2021). *Reimagining Computer Science in the curriculum.* Microsoft Computer Science Curriculum Toolkit. https://info.microsoft.com/rs/157-GQE-382/images/EN-CNTNT-Other-SRGCM4491.pdf

Majumdar, D., Banerji, P. K., & Chakrabarti, S. (2018). Disruptive technology and disruptive innovation: Ignore at your peril! *Technology Analysis and Strategic Management*, *30*(11), 1247–1255. doi:10.1080/09537325.2018.1523384

Moller, F., & Crick, T. (2018). A university-based model for supporting computer science curriculum reform. *Journal of Computers in Education*, *5*(4), 415–434. doi:10.1007/s40692-018-0117-x

Moran, T. P. (2016). Anxiety and working memory capacity: A meta-analysis and narrative review. *Psychological Bulletin*, *142*(8), 831–864. doi:10.1037/bul0000051 PMID:26963369

Morris, T. H. (2021). Meeting educational challenges of pre- and post-COVID-19 conditions through self-directed learning: Considering the contextual quality of educational experience necessary. *On the Horizon*, *29*(20), 52–61. doi:10.1108/OTH-01-2021-0031

National Research Council. (2012). *Education for life and work: Developing transferable knowledge and skills in the 21st century*. National Academies Press.

Nosta, J. (2023, October 6). The 5th industrial revolution: The dawn of the cognitive age. *Psychology Today.* https://www.psychologytoday.com/intl/blog/the-digital-self/202310/the-5th-industrial-revolution-the-dawn-of-the-cognitive-age?eml

Paas, F., & Van Merriënboer, J. J. G. (2020). Cognitive-load theory: Methods to manage working memory load in the learning of complex tasks. *Current Directions in Psychological Science*, *29*(4), 394–398. doi:10.1177/0963721420922183

Peng, J., Wang, M., & Sampson, D. (2017). Visualizing the complex process for deep learning with an authentic programming project. *Journal of Educational Technology & Society*, *20*(4), 275–287. https://www.jstor.org/stable/26229223

Qian, Y., & Lehman, J. (2017). Students' misconceptions and other difficulties in introductory programming: A literature review. [TOCE]. *ACM Transactions on Computing Education*, *18*(1), 1–24. doi:10.1145/3077618

Salcito, A. (2021, February 16). *Reimagining computer science in the curriculum*. Microsoft Education Blog. https://educationblog.microsoft.com/en-us/2021/02/reimagining-computer-science-in-the-curriculum

Shin, Y., Jung, J., & Lee, H. J. (2023). Exploring the impact of concept-oriented faded WOE and metacognitive scaffolding on learners' transfer performance and motivation in programming education. *Metacognition and Learning*, 1–22. doi:10.1007/s11409-023-09362-x

Steenhof, N., Woods, N. N., & Mylopoulos, M. (2020). Exploring why we learn from productive failure: Insights from the cognitive and learning sciences. *Advances in Health Sciences Education : Theory and Practice*, *25*(5), 1099–1106. doi:10.1007/s10459-020-10013-y PMID:33180211

Sweller, J. (2020). Cognitive load theory and educational technology. *Educational Technology Research and Development*, *68*(1), 1–16. doi:10.1007/s11423-019-09701-3

Sweller, J., Van Merriënboer, J. J., & Paas, F. (2019). Cognitive architecture and instructional design: 20 years later. *Educational Psychology Review*, *31*(2), 261–292. doi:10.1007/s10648-019-09465-5

Tissenbaum, M., Weintrop, D., Holbert, N., & Clegg, T. (2021). The case for alternative endpoints in computing education. *British Journal of Educational Technology*, *52*(3), 1164–1177. doi:10.1111/bjet.13072

Van der Westhuizen, C., & Mentz, E. (2020). Implementing cooperative learning elements in Google Docs to optimise online social presence in a self-directed learning environment. In J. Olivier (Ed.), *Self-directed multimodal learning in higher education* (pp. 201–234). AOSIS. doi:10.4102/aosis.2020.BK210

Van Merriënboer, J. J. (2019). *The four-component instructional design model: An overview of its main design principles*. School of Health Professions Education. https://www.4cid.org/wp-content/uploads/2021/04/vanmerrienboer-4cid-overview-of-main-design-principles-2021.pdf

Van Merriënboer, J. J., & Kirschner, P. A. (2018). *Ten steps to complex learning: A systematic approach to four-component instructional design*. Routledge.

Van Zyl, S., & Mentz, E. (2022). Deeper self-directed learning for the 21st century and beyond. In P. Hughes & J. Yarbrough (Eds.), *Self-directed learning and the academic evolution from pedagogy to andragogy* (pp. 50–77). IGI Global. doi:10.4018/978-1-7998-7661-8.ch004

Van Zyl, S. C. (2020). *Developing deeper self-directed learning in Computer Applications Technology education* [Doctoral dissertation, North-West University].

Varunki, M., Katajavuori, N., & Postareff, L. (2017). First-year students' approaches to learning, and factors related to change or stability in their deep approach during a pharmacy course. *Studies in Higher Education, 42*(2), 331–353. doi:10.1080/03075079.2015.1049140

Vogel, S., Santo, R., & Ching, D. (2017). Unpacking arguments for and projected impacts of CS4All initiatives. In *Proceedings of the 2017 ACM SIGCSE Technical Symposium on Computer Science Education* (SIGCSE'17). ACM. 10.1145/3017680.3017755

Vygotsky, L. S. (1978). *Mind in society: Development of higher psychological processes*. Harvard University Press.

Webb, M., Davis, N., Bell, T., Katz, Y. J., Reynolds, N. C. D., & Sysło, M. M. (2017). Computer Science in K-12 school curricula of the 21st century: Why, what and when? *Education and Information Technologies, 22*(2), 445–468. doi:10.1007/s10639-016-9493-x

Xing, W., Zhu, G., Arslan, O., Shim, J., & Popov, V. (2023). Using learning analytics to explore the multifaceted engagement in collaborative learning. *Journal of Computing in Higher Education, 35*(3), 633–662. doi:10.1007/s12528-022-09343-0

ADDITIONAL READING

Berger, R., & Hänze, M. (2015). Impact of expert teaching quality on novice academic performance in the jigsaw cooperative learning method. *International Journal of Science Education, 37*(2), 294–320. doi:10.1080/09500693.2014.985757

Fernandez-Rio, J., Sanz, N., Fernandez-Cando, J., & Santos, L. (2017). Impact of a sustained Cooperative Learning intervention on student motivation. *Physical Education and Sport Pedagogy, 22*(1), 89–105. doi:10.1080/17408989.2015.1123238

Güney, Z. (2019). Four-Component Instructional Design (4C/ID) Model Approach for Teaching Programming Skills. *International Journal of Progressive Education, 15*(4), 142–156. doi:10.29329/ijpe.2019.203.11

Herrington, A. J., & Herrington, J. A. (2006). What is an authentic learning environment? In A. J. Herrington & J. A. Herrington (Eds.), *Authentic learning environments in higher education* (pp. 1–13). Information Science., doi:10.4018/978-1-59140-594-8.ch001

Mason, R., Seton, C., & Cooper, G. (2016). Applying cognitive load theory to the redesign of a conventional database systems course. *Computer Science Education*, *26*(1), 68–87. doi:10.1080/08993408.2016.1160597

Mentz, E., Van der Walt, J. L., & Goosen, L. (2008). The effect of incorporating cooperative learning principles in pair programming for student teachers. *Computer Science Education*, *18*(4), 247–260. doi:10.1080/08993400802461396

Pai, H. H., Sears, D. A., & Maeda, Y. (2015). Effects of small-group learning on transfer: A meta-analysis. *Educational Psychology Review*, *27*(1), 79–102. doi:10.1007/s10648-014-9260-8

Plonka, L., Sharp, H., Van der Linden, J., & Dittrich, Y. (2015). Knowledge transfer in pair programming: An in-depth analysis. *International Journal of Human-Computer Studies*, *73*, 66–78. doi:10.1016/j.ijhcs.2014.09.001

Qian, Y., Hambrusch, S., Yadav, A., Gretter, S., & Li, Y. (2020). Teachers' perceptions of student misconceptions in introductory programming. *Journal of Educational Computing Research*, *58*(2), 364–397. doi:10.1177/0735633119845413

KEY TERMS AND DEFINITIONS

Authentic Tasks: Ill-defined, complex tasks that are relevant to the real world and allow students to model real-world practice.

Cognitive load theory: The learning theory is particularly relevant in scenarios involving challenging content and complex tasks. This theory offers valuable insights and guidance on effectively managing the cognitive load experienced by students during the learning process, specifically addressing the interplay between working memory and long-term memory.

Cooperative Learning: A structured and effective form of group learning in which students work in small groups to enhance their learning and that of their peers. Cooperative learning builds upon the concept of positive goal interdependence, according to which students perceive that they can only achieve their goals if other group members also attain theirs. Cooperative learning addresses the common hurdles associated with conventional group work through the integration of five specific elements: positive interdependence, individual accountability, face-to-face promotive interaction, social skills, and group processing.

Deeper Self-Directed Learning: The process where students take ownership of their learning by identifying their learning needs, resourcefully locate and employ materials and strategies to attain their learning objectives, transfer knowledge and skills to solve novel problems, and evaluate whether successful knowledge transfer occurred.

Knowledge Transfer: To apply knowledge and skills learned in one context to solve problems in different contexts.

Pair Programming: Where two programmers work together on one computer and collaborate to solve a problem. The roles of the pair are assigned as driver and navigator.

Positive Interdependence: When group members feel responsible for each other's success and have the view that the work they are doing mutually benefits each other.

Self-Directed Learning: The process as defined by Knowles (1975) during which students take ownership of their learning by taking the initiative to identify their learning needs, formulate learning goals, identify resources for learning, choose and apply strategies to address these needs, and evaluate whether their learning needs were met.

Social Constructivism: A learning theory that encompasses both intrapersonal and interpersonal domains by highlighting reflective thinking and collaboration with peers as central components of the learning process.

Chapter 5
Teaching and Learning of Computer Science in Higher Education:
A Self-Directed Learning Perspective

Mncedisi Christian Maphalala
https://orcid.org/0000-0002-1078-1985
University of South Africa, South Africa

Oluwatoyin Ayodele Ajani
Durban University of Technology, South Africa

ABSTRACT

This chapter focuses on the evolving landscape of computer science education in higher institutions, emphasizing the need to prepare students for a rapidly changing technology industry. It explores the integration of self-directed learning techniques in computer science courses to enhance outcomes, engagement, and critical skills like problem-solving. The chapter compares traditional instruction with self-directed learning, highlighting the benefits of the latter in terms of motivation, autonomy, and understanding complex computer science concepts. It reviews existing research in this area and introduces a conceptual framework aligning self-directed learning principles with core computer science concepts.

INTRODUCTION

Computer science teaching and learning in higher education have evolved significantly over the years, particularly in the context of self-directed learning (Barnes, 2021). In the ever-evolving landscape of higher education, the field of computer science stands as a dynamic crucible where innovation, adaptation, and lifelong learning are not just encouraged but imperative (Hebda, 2023). With technology advancing at an unprecedented pace and the job market continually shifting its demands, it has become increasingly clear that equipping computer science students with skills to thrive in this ever-changing

DOI: 10.4018/979-8-3693-1066-3.ch005

environment is paramount. Moreover, instilling a passion for learning and fostering the ability to adapt to new challenges are skills that will not only serve students during their academic journey but throughout their entire careers (Markova et al., 2019). To address these evolving needs, integrating self-directed learning techniques into computer science courses has emerged as a promising pedagogical approach.

The field of computer science education in higher institutions is constantly evolving to meet the changing demands of technology and the job market (Noone & Mooney, 2018). To address this, integrating self-directed learning approaches has emerged as a valuable strategy to empower students and enhance their readiness for the dynamic field of computer science (Onah, Pang & Sinclair, 2020).

Traditional computer science education often relies on teacher-led instruction, which may not fully engage students or adequately prepare them for the rapidly evolving industry (Oda, Noborimoto, & Horita., 2021). In contrast, self-directed learning places emphasis on student autonomy, motivation, and active participation in their education, allowing them to take control of their learning process (Bergamin et al., 2019). This approach can enhance student motivation, critical thinking skills, and adaptability to new technologies and concepts, vital attributes in computer science.

Research in various educational contexts has demonstrated the benefits of self-directed learning. It has been associated with improved student achievement, increased self-directed learning readiness, and more positive attitudes towards learning (Cigdem & Öztürk, 2016; Oda et al., 2021; Kayacan & Ektem, 2019). In the specific context of computer science education, self-directed learning offers several advantages (De Beer, 2016). It allows students to explore their interests, set personal learning goals, and select resources and strategies that align with their individual needs. This approach can lead to a deeper understanding of complex computer science concepts and the development of effective problem-solving skills (Bosch, 2017). Moreover, self-directed learning cultivates lifelong learning habits, which are crucial in a constantly evolving field.

Self-directed learning (SDL) is an educational approach that places the responsibility for learning on the student, allowing them to take control of their learning journey (Ona et al., 2020). This approach has gained prominence in computer science education due to its potential to foster independent and lifelong learning skills, which are crucial in a rapidly evolving field like computer science. This chapter embarks on a comprehensive exploration of the teaching and learning of computer science in higher education, with a keen focus on the invaluable perspective of self-directed learning. Self-directed learning is a multifaceted approach that emphasises students' active participation in their own learning process, allowing them to take ownership of their education (Oosthuizen, 2016; Ntombana, Gwala & Sibanda, 2023). As we delve into this perspective, we will uncover the multifarious benefits of self-directed learning, its challenges, and the considerations required for its successful implementation.

Implementing self-directed learning in computer science curricula comes with its own set of challenges. Assessment difficulties, scaffolding, accommodating diverse learning styles, and the ongoing professional development of academics are some of the obstacles that need to be addressed (Santhanam, Sasidharan & Webster, 2008; Thomson & Tippins, 2013; Markova et al., 2019; Threekunprapam & Yasri, 2020; Estisari, Wengrum & Nurhantanto, 2023). Despite these challenges, the potential benefits of self-directed learning in computer science education make it worthwhile. The key aim of this chapter is to provide a comprehensive view of self-directed learning in the teaching and learning of computer science in higher education. It reviews existing research on self-directed learning in computer science education, explores the potential synergies between self-directed learning principles and core computer science concepts, and discusses the challenges and considerations of implementing self-directed learning in computer science curricula.

By examining the integration of self-directed learning techniques into computer science education, this chapter seeks to contribute to the ongoing efforts to enhance the teaching and learning of computer science in higher education institutions. It provides insights for academics, curriculum designers, and policymakers to design effective and student-centred computer science curricula that prepare students for the demands of the field and foster their autonomy, motivation, and critical thinking skills. The following vital **objectives** guided this chapter to:

- explore self-directed learning and its techniques in computer science.
- examine self-directed learning outcomes, engagement, and skills development.
- discuss comparative traditional instruction with self-directed instruction.
- highlight challenges and considerations for self-directed learning in higher education.
- proffer recommendations for effective implementation.

BACKGROUND

The Ever-Evolving Landscape of Computer Science Education

Computer science is a rapidly evolving field, and students must develop the skills and knowledge to learn independently and keep up with the latest trends and technologies (Lee, Lau & Yip, 2016; Hebda, 2023). Self-directed learning is a process in which students take responsibility for their learning and seek resources and opportunities to learn new things (Kayacan & Ektem, 2019). It is a valuable skill for all students but significant for computer science students. The landscape of computer science education is ever-evolving, driven by the rapid pace of innovation in the field of computer science (Threekunprapam & Yasri, 2020). New technologies and programming languages are constantly emerging, and the skills and knowledge that computer scientists need are constantly changing (Safitri Lestari, 2021). This poses a challenge for computer science teachers, who must keep their curricula up-to-date and ensure their students learn the skills they need to succeed in the workforce. However, it also presents an opportunity to create innovative and engaging learning experiences that prepare students for the future (Zainuddin, Hermawan, Nuraini & Prayitno, 2019). One of the key trends in computer science education is the shift towards more hands-on and project-based learning (Thomson & Tippins, 2013). This is in response to the growing demand for computer scientists who can think critically and solve problems creatively. Teachers also emphasise teaching computational thinking, a set of problem-solving skills that can be applied to a wide range of domains (Oda et al., 2021).

Another trend is the increasing popularity of online and blended learning (Barnes, 2021). This is making computer science education more accessible to students from all backgrounds. Additionally, there is a growing movement to make computer science education more inclusive and equitable (Brisimis et al., 2020). This includes initiatives to attract more girls and underrepresented minorities to the field (De Beer, 2016). There are so many specific ways in which the landscape of computer science education is evolving. Computer science focuses on computational thinking for students in higher education (Noone & Mooney, 2018). Computational thinking is a problem-solving approach that involves breaking down problems into smaller steps, identifying patterns, and developing algorithms. It is a valuable skill for all students to learn and significant for computer science students (Condie & Livingstone, 2007). In essence, computational thinking emerges as a universal problem-solving approach with far-reaching applications rather than a specialized skill for computer science students. Its development in educational settings enables students to approach problems analytically, fostering an adaptable and applicable mindset across multiple fields. As the educational landscape evolves, the incorporation of computational thinking demonstrates its enduring relevance in preparing students for the complexities of today's world.

Furthermore, computer science education provides a shift to more hands-on and project-based learning. Teachers are moving away from traditional lectures and towards more hands-on and project-based learning (Santhanam et al., 2008). This allows students to learn by doing and to develop the skills they need to succeed in the workforce. In addition, computer science education increases the popularity of online and blended learning in higher education (Larson et al., 2017).

Online and blended learning make computer science education more accessible to students from all backgrounds (Holmes & Fray, 2018). This is especially important for students in rural areas or with other commitments. Thus, providing a focus on inclusion and equity in higher education. Teachers are working to make computer science education more inclusive and equitable (Hmelo-Silver, 2004). This includes initiatives to attract more girls and underrepresented minorities to the field. However, the ever-evolving landscape of computer science education presents challenges and opportunities (Lee et al., 2016). By embracing new technologies and teaching methods, teachers can prepare students for the future of work (Condie & Livingstone, 2007).

The field of computer science education exists within an ever-evolving landscape characterised by rapid technological advancements, shifting industry demands, and an insatiable hunger for innovation (Santhanam et al., 2008). This dynamic terrain challenges teachers, students, and institutions to continually adapt, re-imagine, and enhance how computer science is taught and learned in higher education (Oda et al., 2021). At the heart of this evolving landscape lies the profound impact of technology on society. As digitalisation sweeps across industries, computer science education becomes not just a choice but a necessity for students aspiring to navigate the modern job market (Markova et al., 2019). The demand for skilled computer scientists is upward, with emerging fields such as artificial intelligence, data science, cybersecurity, and cloud computing reshaping the employment landscape. Simultaneously, computer science's tools, languages, and methodologies are in constant flux (Hebda, 2023). Programming languages gain and lose popularity, new paradigms emerge, and the tools used for software development evolve at a breakneck pace. Keeping curricula up-to-date with these changes is a formidable challenge for teachers.

Moreover, the very nature of learning itself is transforming (Maphalala & Ajani, 2023). Students, especially those in the digital-native generation, approach education with different expectations and learning styles (Lee et al., 2016). They seek to acquire knowledge and actively engage in the learning process, demanding a more participatory and adaptable educational experience.

In response to these challenges, computer science education is undergoing a paradigm shift that embraces self-directed learning as a cornerstone (Hebda, 2023). Self-directed learning empowers students to take ownership of their educational journey, encouraging them to explore, experiment, and innovate independently (Holmes & Fray, 2018). This approach nurtures technical skills, critical thinking, problem-solving abilities, and the adaptability needed to thrive in an ever-evolving technological landscape. In this higher education environment, teachers, curriculum designers, and policymakers are tasked with re-imagining computer science education, integrating self-directed learning principles, and equipping students with the adaptable skills they need to excel (Kayacan & Ektem, 2019). This ongoing transformation underscores computer science education's dynamic and exciting nature, where pursuing knowledge and innovation is a journey without a final destination.

The Necessity of Equipping Students With Adaptable Skills

The emergence of the Fourth Industrial Revolution in the education system has transformed education, focusing on making students globally competent for the labour market (Koole et al., 2018). Hence, equipping students with adaptable skills in computer science education within higher education has become imperative due to the rapidly evolving technological landscape and the shifting demands of the job market (Maphalala et al., 2021). The necessity of fostering these adaptable skills arises from several key factors. In Africa, there is a growing emphasis on harnessing technological advancements to promote sustainable student development in higher education (Ajani, 2023). Given the rapid innovations in computer science, it has become imperative for higher education institutions to equip students with adaptable skills to thrive in the ever-evolving technological landscape (Ajani & Khoalenyane, 2023). These skills are essential to meet the changing demands of the digital age, encompassing technical and soft skills, interdisciplinary collaboration, and various knowledge domains within computer science (Gurcan & Cagiltay, 2019). To achieve competency-based software engineering education, there is a need for demand-driven interdisciplinary collaboration.

Traditional educational approaches alone are insufficient to prepare students for the technology-driven era. Integrating interdisciplinary studies and project-based learning is becoming increasingly crucial in computer science education (Üşengül & Bahçeci, 2020). Competitive events like hackathons provide an engaging way to develop both technical and soft skills among computer science students (Seidametova et al., 2022). Furthermore, the incorporation of game-based learning has effectively enhanced student motivation and engagement in computer science education (Hosseini et al., 2019). Traditional game design methods can improve student engagement and perception of learning computer science concepts (Hosseini et al., 2019). Additionally, digital peer assessment serves as a valuable formative assessment tool in engineering and computer science education (Van Helden et al., 2023).

The concept of computational thinking (CT) education has gained recognition in various fields, including computer science, science, mathematics, and technology (Park & Kwon, 2022). CT education reforms have been implemented in K–12 schools in countries like Korea, Taiwan, Hong Kong, and China (So et al., 2019). Bridging the gap between higher education institutions and industry expectations is essential to effectively equip students with adaptable skills in computer science education (Sahin & Celikkan, 2020). Often, the skills taught in higher education do not align with industry requirements for IT professionals. Identifying and addressing these gaps is crucial to ensure that graduates are well-prepared for the job market. While computer science education at the primary level is relatively new and curriculum models are still evolving, many countries recognize the importance of offering computer science education from primary to tertiary institutions (Ohadugha et al., 2020). Such education equips students with fundamental computer literacy and problem-solving skills, which are vital in an interconnected digital world. Adaptable skills in computer science education are paramount in today's rapidly evolving technological landscape, and achieving this goal involves interdisciplinary collaboration, project-based learning, competitive approaches like hackathons, game-based learning, integrating computational thinking, and aligning with industry expectations. Furthermore, extending computer science education to all levels, from primary to tertiary institutions, is crucial for preparing students for the challenges of the modern world (Deliwe, 2020).

The Role of Self-Directed Learning in Enhancing Computer Science Education

Self-directed learning is critical to higher education, particularly in computer science. It refers to the ability of students to take control of their learning process, set goals, identify resources, and evaluate their progress (Conradie, 2014; Bosch, 2017; Cigdem & Ozturk, 2016). In computer science education, SDL plays a crucial role in enhancing students' knowledge and skills and their motivation and engagement in the learning process. Self-directed learning enhances computer science education in higher education, providing motivation and self-efficacy to students (Bembenutty, 2023). Motivation and self-efficacy are important factors that influence students' engagement and success in computer science education (Armoed, 2021). Several studies have shown that students' motivation for online learning and their computer/Internet self-efficacy positively relate to their achievements in online courses (Condie & Livingston, 2007; Cigdem & Öztürk, 2016; Chiu, 2021). Similarly, students' self-efficacy in technology and their STEM attitudes are associated with their active and vicarious learning experiences (Harry & Chinyamurindi, 2021). These findings suggest that students' beliefs in their own abilities and their motivation to learn are crucial for their success in computer science education.

Self-directed learning readiness (SDLR) is a critical determinant of students' capacity to engage in self-directed learning. SDLR encompasses the skills and dispositions necessary for individuals to participate effectively in self-directed learning (Ghazal et al., 2018). Research has demonstrated that SDLR correlates positively with students' self-directed learning behaviors and their attitudes toward scientific experiments (Kayacan & Ektem, 2019). Additionally, SDLR has been identified as a moderator of the impacts of various implementations of computer-assisted inquiry learning activities on students' educational outcomes (Safitri & Lestari, 2021; Richter et al., 2022). These findings underscore the significance of students' readiness for self-directed learning in the context of computer science education.

Self-directed learning provides students with metacognitive strategies and self-regulation capabilities (Chiu, 2021). These metacognitive strategies and self-regulation skills play pivotal roles in facilitating self-directed learning and enhancing students' outcomes in computer science education. Students who possess metacognitive strategies are better equipped to plan, monitor, and assess their learning processes (Condie & Livingston, 2007; Thomson & Tippins, 2013; Markova et al., 2019). Studies have established a positive relationship between students' utilization of metacognitive strategies and their academic achievements and self-directed learning behaviors (Mayet, 2021; Olawunmi & Mavuso, 2022; Ntombana et al., 2023). Moreover, self-regulated learning environments have demonstrated a positive impact on students' academic success within the field of computer science education (Bembenutty, 2023). These findings underscore the importance of nurturing metacognitive strategies and self-regulation skills to enhance students' self-directed learning within computer science education.

Self-directed learning has significant implications for the teaching methods and learning environments within higher education (Maulana et al., 2016). The selection of teaching methods and the design of learning environments can profoundly influence students' capacity to engage in self-directed learning in the context of computer science education. Instructional methods such as problem-based learning, learning tasks, discovery learning, computer simulations, project work, and direct instruction have been identified as particularly suitable for computer science education (Oosthuizen, 2016). These approaches empower students to actively participate in the learning process, make decisions, and take ownership of their educational journey. Additionally, the utilization of technology-enhanced learning environments, including online platforms and computer-based simulations, can provide students with the flexibility and resources essential for self-directed learning (Prentice et al., 2018). These findings emphasize the necessity of aligning teaching methods and learning environment designs with the principles of self-directed learning to enhance students' engagement and success in computer science education.

Self-directed learning plays a pivotal role in enriching computer science education within higher education. Students' motivation, self-efficacy, SDLR, metacognitive strategies, and self-regulation skills are crucial factors influencing their ability to engage in self-directed learning (Ryan & Deci, 2000; Maulana et al., 2016). Moreover, the selection of appropriate teaching methods and the design of conducive learning environments are instrumental in fostering self-directed learning within the realm of computer science education. By promoting self-directed learning, educators empower students to take charge of their learning processes, develop lifelong learning competencies, and excel in the field of computer science (Olawunmi & Mavuso, 2022). Further research is warranted to explore effective strategies and interventions aimed at enhancing self-directed learning in computer science education.

Theoretical Framework

To understand the phenomenon better, the authors employed self-directed learning and constructivist learning theories as the underpinning theoretical frameworks for this discursive chapter. This subsection delves into the theoretical foundations of self-directed learning, emphasising its relevance and applicability to computer science education. The chapter adopted self-directed learning theory to shed light on the psychological and pedagogical principles that support self-directed learning.

Self-directed learning theory is a critical framework for teaching and learning computer science in higher education (Murniati et al., 2023). This theory strongly emphasises students' autonomy, motivation, and ability to control their learning processes. In computer science education, self-directed learning theory has significant implications and advantages (Masina et al., 2023). Self-directed learning theory recognises that students are more motivated and engaged when they have a sense of autonomy and ownership over their learning (Zhu et al., 2023). In computer science, students can choose projects, explore topics of interest, and set their own learning goals (Markova et al., 2019). This theory aligns with the idea that intrinsically motivated students tend to perform better and better understand the subject matter. In computer science, students can develop a genuine interest in programming languages, algorithms, and problem-solving when exploring these areas on their own terms (Hebda, 2023).

Computer science is fundamentally about problem-solving. Pellet & Parriaux, (2023) concurs that the competence to solve problems is of fundamental importance in software engineering and the broader field of computer science.Self-directed learning encourages students to seek out challenges, identify problems, and find solutions independently (Oda & Mavuso, 2022). This approach helps students develop critical problem-solving skills, a cornerstone of success in the field. The field of computer science is dynamic and constantly evolving. Self-directed students are better equipped to adapt to new technologies, languages, and paradigms because they have experience learning and seeking the latest information and tools (Onah et al., 2020). Self-directed learning theory promotes lifelong learning (Lin, 2023). In computer science, where technological advancements occur rapidly, the ability to continue learning independently is crucial for staying relevant. Different students have varying interests and learning paces (Ajani, 2023). Self-directed learning allows for customising educational experiences to meet individual needs (Holmes & Fray, 2018). In computer science, this means accommodating various skill levels and interests.

Self-directed learning theory prepares students for real-world challenges they will face in their careers (Kiesler et al., 2023). In computer science, where professionals often encounter complex, unstructured problems, this approach helps students become more self-reliant and adaptable problem solvers. Self-directed learning theory is highly relevant and advantageous in the teaching and learning of computer science in higher education (Van Der Berg et al., 2023). It empowers students to take charge of their learning, fosters intrinsic motivation, and equips them with the skills needed to thrive in the dynamic and rapidly evolving field of computer science. By embracing this perspective, teachers can create more engaging, effective, and adaptable learning experiences for their students (Mncube & Maphalala, 2023). Self-directed learning theory in computer science education plays a crucial role in higher education. It empowers students to take control of their learning process, allowing them to explore and acquire knowledge independently (Liu et al., 2023).

This theory holds particular significance in the field of computer science, given its rapid technological advancements (Verster et al., 2023). Through self-directed learning, students can keep abreast of the latest developments, fostering critical thinking, adaptability and problem-solving – vital traits in the ever-evolving computer science realm. In computer science education, the self-directed learning theory underscores the importance of student accountability and active engagement. It empowers students to set learning goals, select pertinent resources and strategies, and evaluate their progress (Murniati et al., 2023). Furthermore, this theory aligns seamlessly with the constructivist didactics approach, which stimulates active student cognition and creates optimal learning environments (Zhu et al., 2023). Self-directed learning enables students to actively immerse themselves in the subject matter, explore their interests, and attain a deeper grasp of computer science concepts (Mahlaba, 2020; Masina et al., 2023). Additionally, it harmonizes with the concept of digital literacy.

Research Methodology

This conceptual research study employed a literature-based review approach to explore and synthesise existing concepts, theories, and ideas about integrating self-directed learning principles in computer science education within higher education institutions. The methodology analysed scholarly literature, theories, and models to construct a comprehensive conceptual framework that illuminates the self-directed learning perspective in computer science education (Gicevic et al., 2016). This research conducted a thorough systematic literature review, a robust method for identifying and analysing relevant findings on a specific research topic. Systematic literature reviews enhance the scientific value of gathered data by providing comprehensive insights into the research subject (Gluckman et al., 2021). The review adhered to the Preferred Reporting Items for Systematic Reviews and Meta-Analyses (PRISMA) framework, consisting of a 27-item checklist and a four-phase flowchart. PRISMA is designed to improve the reporting of systematic reviews and meta-analyses, enhancing clarity and transparency (Martucci et al., 2023). The search for relevant literature sources encompassed various reputable databases, including Scopus, Elsevier, ACM, IEEE Xplore, Web of Science, the ERIC database, and the Wiley library, from 2003 to 2023 (as used in Helbach et al., 2023). Additionally, Xie et al. (2023) argued that other data sources, such as Google Scholar and ResearchGate.net, were considered. Lee et al. (2023) posit that this extensive search strategy encompassed various research materials, including journal articles, conference papers, and open publications like doctoral theses and dissertations.

The review followed a structured methodology of identifying the research questions drawn from the initial phase of formulating research questions that guided the systematic review (Page et al., 2023). Selected articles underwent data extraction using a standardised form, capturing publication details, research objectives, methodologies, key findings, and implications. Data were organised into categories aligned with the review's sub-topics. Belle and Zhao (2023) opine that qualitative analysis identified the literature's themes, patterns, and trends. The quality assessment evaluated methodological rigour, considering research design and sample size (as followed in Lee et al., 2023). Since this review analysed publicly available scholarly publications, ethical considerations concerning human subjects and privacy did not apply. The systematic literature review included 80 articles that met the inclusion criteria. The PRISMA process was employed to identify research questions and discussion points derived from these articles (Page et al., 2023). The PRISMA process was adopted to ensure a comprehensive and rigorous literature review (Xie et al., 2023). This systematic review provided valuable insights into self-directed learning and computer science education in higher education, aiding teachers, policymakers, and researchers in advancing this critical domain.

FINDINGS

Self-Directed Learning in Computer Science Education: A Review of Literature

This section presents a comprehensive review of the existing literature on self-directed learning in the context of computer science education within higher institutions. It establishes a foundational understanding of the topic, examining the theoretical underpinnings and practical applications of self-directed learning within this domain. Computer science education is an ever-evolving field due to the rapid advancements in technology and the changing landscape of the job market (Cigdem & Ozturk, 2016). To keep pace with these developments, it is imperative to equip students with the skills, motivation, and autonomy necessary for continuous learning. Self-directed learning has emerged as a pedagogical approach that aligns well with the dynamic nature of computer science (Masina et al., 2023). This literature review explores the existing body of knowledge on self-directed learning in computer science education (Musitha & Mafukata, 2018). By comparing traditional instructional methods with self-directed learning, this review sheds light on how SDL can enhance student engagement, motivation, and understanding of complex computer science concepts (Mayet, 2021).

According to Knowles (1975), self-directed learning is a process in which people take the initiative to diagnose their learning needs, set learning goals, find learning resources, choose and use learning strategies, and assess learning outcomes (Masina et al., 2023; van Der Berg et al., 2023; Zhu et al., 2023). This student-centric approach emphasises autonomy, intrinsic motivation, and the development of problem-solving and critical-thinking skills. In the context of computer science education, SDL places students in the driver's seat of their learning journey, allowing them to explore and adapt to the ever-changing landscape of technology. Many scholars believe self-directed learning benefits computer science education (Lin, 2023; Verster et al., 2023). One of the critical principles of SDL is the fulfilment of basic psychological needs, including autonomy. In computer science education, students often thrive when they can choose projects, set goals, and direct their learning path. This empowerment can lead to increased motivation and a sense of ownership over one's education (Ryan & Deci, 2000; Ntombana et al., 2023). Improved problem-solving skills are derived from self-directed learning (Mayet, 2021). Computer science is fundamentally about problem-solving. SDL encourages students to seek solutions independently, fostering the development of problem-solving skills, which are crucial in this field (Lin, 2023).

While some studies identify adaptability to technological changes as a critical benefit of SDL to students (Cigdem & Ozturk, 2016; Chiu, 2021), technology evolves rapidly, and computer science students must be prepared to adapt to new tools and programming languages (Deliwe, 2020). SDL cultivates the ability to self-learn, enabling students to stay current with emerging technologies (Musitha & Mafukata, 2018). Lifelong learning orientation is provided to students through SDL. Computer science professionals must engage in lifelong learning to remain relevant. SDL instils a continuous learning mindset, equipping students with the skills and motivation to embrace lifelong learning (Verster et al., 2023).

Traditional instructional methods in computer science education often follow a structured curriculum with lectures, assignments, and assessments. While these methods provide a foundational understanding of core concepts, they may not fully prepare students for the demands of a constantly evolving field (Sun et al., 2023). In contrast, self-directed learning encourages students to explore topics beyond the curriculum, work on self-selected projects, and seek resources independently (Bosch, 2017). This approach allows students to develop a deeper understanding of computer science concepts and nurtures their ability to adapt to new challenges. Self-directed learning offers a promising pedagogical approach to computer science education in higher institutions. It empowers students to become autonomous, lifelong students equipped to thrive in a rapidly evolving field (Santhanam et al., 2008; Threekunprapam & Yasri, 2020). While challenges exist, the benefits of SDL in enhancing motivation, problem-solving skills, adaptability, and a lifelong learning orientation make it a valuable framework for computer science education (Van Wyk, 2017).

This literature review provides insights into the potential of self-directed learning in computer science education and highlights the need for further research and exploration. It encourages academics, curriculum designers, and policymakers to consider integrating SDL principles to prepare students for success in the dynamic world of computer science.

Benefits and Outcomes of Self-Directed Learning

The reviews of various extant literature have established the benefits associated with integrating self-directed learning techniques into computer science education (Condie & Livingston, 2007; Conradie, 2014; Markova et al., 2019). It examines how self-directed learning fosters critical thinking, problem-solving skills, student engagement, and motivation. Additionally, it explores the potential for self-directed learning to enhance students' autonomy and understanding of complex computer science concepts. An analysis of various literature sources provides an in-depth comparative analysis of traditional instructional methods and self-directed learning approaches in computer science education. It highlights empirical evidence and case studies that showcase the advantages of self-directed learning models in enhancing student outcomes, motivation, and autonomy. Thus, the debate between traditional instruction and self-directed instruction in the field of computer science education has sparked significant interest among researchers and teachers (Noone & Mooney, 2018; Oda et al., 2021). Both approaches have merits and drawbacks, and their effectiveness often depends on various factors, including the learning context and the student's individual needs. This comparative discussion delves into the key differences, advantages, and challenges of traditional and self-directed instruction in computer science education.

Traditional instruction in computer science typically follows a structured curriculum with predefined topics and a linear progression. In contrast, self-directed instruction allows students to explore topics of personal interest at their own pace (Markova et al., 2019). While structured content ensures comprehensive coverage, self-directed learning allows a more profound exploration of specific areas. The choice between these approaches hinges on the learning objectives and the extent to which students require guidance versus autonomy (Mncube & Maphalala, 2023). Traditional instruction often involves passive learning, where students absorb information from teachers through lectures or textbooks. Self-directed instruction promotes active learning as students take responsibility for their learning journey, actively seeking information and resources. Ajani and Khumalo (2023) opine that research suggests that active learning leads to better retention and comprehension, making self-directed instruction an attractive option for fostering a more profound understanding of computer science concepts.

Traditional instruction tends to be teacher-centred, with teachers leading the learning process. In contrast, self-directed instruction places students at the centre of the educational experience. While traditional instruction offers expert guidance, self-directed learning empowers students to become more self-reliant and resourceful (Sun et al., 2023). The choice here depends on the desired balance between guidance and independence in the learning process. Traditional instruction often employs standardised assessments, such as exams and quizzes, to evaluate students' understanding. Self-directed instruction may employ more personalised evaluation methods like project-based assessments, reflective journals, or peer reviews (Masina et al., 2023). The latter approach can provide a more holistic view of students' skills and competencies, aligning with the multifaceted nature of computer science. Traditional instruction may need help to engage students, primarily when content is delivered passively. Self-directed learning fosters intrinsic motivation, as students have a say in what they study and how they approach it (Liu et al., 2023). Research indicates that motivated students are more likely to excel in computer science education, making self-directed instruction a promising avenue for enhancing student engagement (Masina et al., 2023).

Traditional instruction offers a structured support system, with teachers readily available for guidance. In self-directed learning, students may encounter challenges related to self-discipline and resource management (Zhu et al., 2023). However, these challenges can be mitigated with suitable support mechanisms, such as mentorship, peer collaboration, and well-curated learning resources. In computer science, real-world application is paramount (Murniati et al., 2023). Self-directed instruction allows students to apply their knowledge to practical projects and real-world scenarios (Verster et al., 2023). Traditional instruction can benefit from integrating more hands-on, project-based elements to bridge the gap between theory and practice (Bergamin et al., 2020). Self-directed instruction can be more easily individualised to accommodate diverse learning styles and paces. Traditional instruction may need help to cater to the unique needs of each student. In computer science education, accommodating diverse learning styles and fostering inclusivity are crucial (Dombestein et al., 2019). The choice between traditional and self-directed instruction in computer science education should be informed by the specific educational goals, the characteristics of the students, and the available resources (Thomson & Tippins, 2013). While both approaches have their strengths and limitations, there is a growing recognition of the value of self-directed learning in empowering computer science students to become lifelong students and adaptable professionals in a rapidly evolving field (Williams et al., 2006; Sheldon & Prentice, 2019; Zainuddin et al., 2019; Chiu, 2021).

Challenges and Considerations in Implementing Self-Directed Learning

Implementing self-directed learning in computer science education is challenging and requires careful consideration. While self-directed learning offers numerous benefits, teachers and institutions must address several critical challenges to ensure effectiveness. One of the primary challenges in self-directed learning is motivating students to take responsibility for their education (Brisimis et al., 2020). Some students may need help with self-discipline, finding it difficult to set goals, manage their time effectively, and stay motivated without external guidance (Bembenutty, 2023). Teachers must create strategies and environments that foster intrinsic motivation and help students develop self-discipline. De Beer (2016) asserts that self-directed students rely heavily on access to various learning resources, including textbooks, online materials, tutorials, and tools. Ensuring that students have equitable access to these resources is crucial, as disparities in access can lead to unequal learning outcomes (Ajani, 2023). Institutions should invest in digital infrastructure and provide support to bridge the resource gap.

While self-directed learning emphasises autonomy, students may still require guidance, particularly in complex subjects like computer science (Van Wyk, 2017). Establishing mentorship programmes or providing access to knowledgeable teachers who can offer support, answer questions, and provide direction when needed is essential. Traditional assessment methods, such as exams, may need to align better with self-directed learning (Williams et al., 2006; Zainuddin et al., 2019). Designing meaningful and fair assessment strategies that evaluate students' ability to set goals, research, problem-solve, and apply knowledge is challenging. Incorporating peer assessments, project-based evaluations, and regular feedback mechanisms becomes crucial.

The physical and digital learning environments play a significant role in self-directed learning (Lin, 2023). Institutions must create spaces that foster independent study and collaboration among students. Additionally, they should invest in learning management systems (LMS) and online platforms that support self-directed learning, making resources easily accessible (Deliwe, 2020). Xie et al. (2023) posit that effective self-directed learning requires solid time-management skills. Students must allocate sufficient time to set goals, plan their learning path, acquire resources, and assess their progress. Institutions should offer time-management workshops or integrate time-management skills into the curriculum. Students have diverse learning styles and preferences (Ajani & Khumalo, 2023). Some may thrive in self-directed settings, while others may struggle. Institutions should recognise these differences and offer a variety of learning pathways to accommodate various learning styles, including collaborative projects, experiential learning, and traditional instruction (Ghazal et al., 2018). Measuring the effectiveness of self-directed learning can be challenging. Institutions must develop clear assessment criteria and methods to accurately evaluate students' progress and outcomes (Van De Berg, 2023). This may involve a combination of self-assessment, peer assessment, and teacher evaluation. Self-directed students may experience feelings of isolation, especially in online or asynchronous learning environments (Estisari et al., 2023). Building a sense of community through forums, discussion boards, or collaborative projects can mitigate this challenge and foster a supportive learning ecosystem.

Fabriz et al. (2021) avow that teachers must be prepared to facilitate self-directed learning effectively. This requires ongoing professional development to enhance their skills in guiding, mentoring, and assessing self-directed students. Institutions should invest in training programmes for faculty members. Self-directed learning in computer science education offers numerous advantages, but it requires a thoughtful and supportive infrastructure to address the associated challenges (Oda et al., 2021). By considering these challenges and implementing strategies to overcome them, institutions can harness the potential of self-directed learning to empower students in their computer science education journey.

Conceptual Framework for Integrating Self-Directed Learning in Computer Science

This chapter introduces a conceptual framework that aligns the principles of self-directed learning with core computer science concepts. It explores the potential synergies and integration points between these two approaches, offering insights into designing effective self-directed learning experiences in computer science education. Integrating self-directed learning into computer science education requires a robust conceptual framework that aligns educational principles with the core concepts of computer science (Murniati et al., 2023). This section delves into the literature review concerning developing a conceptual framework for effectively integrating self-directed learning in computer science education.

Alignment of Self-Directed Learning and Computer Science: The first step in constructing a conceptual framework is establishing the alignment between self-directed learning and computer science. Lin (2023) highlights the importance of fulfilling basic psychological needs for autonomy, competence, and relatedness to maintain intrinsic motivation. These needs can be translated into computer science education by allowing students autonomy in choosing learning paths, designing projects that challenge their competence, and fostering a sense of community within the computer science learning community.

Incorporating Self-Directed Learning Principles: The literature review suggests that self-directed learning principles can be effectively integrated into computer science education. According to Musitha and Mafukata (2018), Oda et al. (2021), and Mncube and Maphalala (2023), need-supportive teaching practices can fulfil multiple fundamental psychological needs. In computer science courses, teachers can employ strategies like open-ended projects, problem-solving challenges, and collaborative coding activities to simultaneously address autonomy, competence, and relatedness.

Designing Adaptive Learning Environments: It is essential to design adaptive learning environments to create a conceptual framework for integrating self-directed learning in computer science. A study by Ajani and Khoalenyane (2023) underscores the need for open pedagogical approaches in online learning. This chapter suggests that online computer science courses should provide diverse learning resources, interactive platforms, and opportunities for peer collaboration to accommodate various learning styles and preferences.

Assessment and Feedback Mechanisms: Assessment methods are crucial in integrating self-directed learning in computer science. The literature review indicates that traditional assessment approaches may need to align with self-directed learning goals. Ajani and Khumalo (2023) suggest that teachers should consider alternative methods, such as project-based assessments and self-assessment, to evaluate students' ability to set goals, research, and apply knowledge effectively. Moreover, regular feedback mechanisms should be incorporated to guide students' self-directed learning journeys.

Faculty Professional Development: A vital aspect of the conceptual framework involves faculty development (Zhu et al., 2023). Masina et al. (2023) emphasise the role of teachers in supporting self-directed learning. Faculty members should receive training and professional development opportunities to enhance their skills in guiding, mentoring, and assessing self-directed students effectively. This requires a shift in pedagogical approaches and cultivating a supportive learning ecosystem.

Continuous Improvement and Evaluation: Integrating self-directed learning in computer science education is an ongoing process that demands continuous improvement and evaluation. Liu et al.'s (2023) research findings highlight the importance of evaluating the effects of self-directed learning on student engagement and achievement. A conceptual framework should include mechanisms for gathering feedback from students and faculty to refine and adapt self-directed learning strategies over time.

This chapter reveals that a well-structured conceptual framework for integrating self-directed learning in computer science education should focus on aligning self-directed learning principles with core computer science concepts, designing adaptive learning environments, re-imagining assessment and feedback mechanisms, providing faculty professional development, and emphasising continuous improvement and evaluation. Such a framework can empower students to take ownership of their learning, fostering intrinsic motivation and better preparing them for the dynamic field of computer science (Sun et al., 2023).

PROPOSED SOLUTIONS AND RECOMMENDATIONS

Based on the in-depth literature review, the chapter provides recommendations for teachers, curriculum designers, and policymakers interested in adopting self-directed learning perspectives in computer science education. It summarises best practices gleaned from the literature and emphasises the advantages of embracing self-directed learning to prepare students for success in the dynamic field of computer science. Based on the comprehensive literature review of self-directed learning in computer science education, several key recommendations and best practices emerge to guide teachers, curriculum designers, and policymakers in enhancing computer science education with a self-directed learning perspective.

One of the primary recommendations is the seamless integration of self-directed learning principles into computer science curricula. Teachers should design courses that allow students to make choices about their learning paths, explore topics of personal interest, and set their learning objectives. This approach fosters autonomy and intrinsic motivation among students. Computer science programmes should provide a wide range of learning resources to support self-directed learning. These may include interactive online platforms, coding tutorials, open-access textbooks, and access to real-world projects. Offering diverse resources accommodates various learning styles and preferences. The literature suggests that computer science courses should offer flexibility in terms of pacing and content. Students should be free to delve deeper into topics of interest and progress at their own speed. Incorporating elements like asynchronous learning and self-paced modules can enhance flexibility. Teachers should rethink assessment methods to align with self-directed learning goals. Rather than relying solely on traditional exams, consider implementing project-based assessments, peer evaluations, and self-assessment tools. Regular feedback mechanisms should be in place to guide students' self-directed learning journeys.

Professional development programmes for computer science faculty are critical. These programmes equip teachers with the skills and knowledge to facilitate self-directed learning effectively. Faculty members should learn how to mentor, guide, and provide constructive feedback to self-directed students. While self-directed learning empowers students, they still benefit from guidance and mentorship. Assigning mentors or advisors who can assist students in setting goals, monitoring progress, and navigating challenges can enhance the effectiveness of self-directed learning initiatives. Furthermore, incorporating learning analytics and data-driven insights to monitor students' progress in self-directed learning environments can assist in learning computer science education in higher education. These tools can provide valuable information on how students engage with course materials, where they might struggle, and where improvements can be made. Encourage collaborative learning experiences within computer science courses. Group projects, peer learning communities, and coding clubs can create a sense of relatedness and peer support, enhancing the social aspect of learning.

Computer science programmes should establish mechanisms to evaluate and improve self-directed learning initiatives continuously. Regularly collect feedback from students and faculty to identify areas that need refinement and adjustment. Given the dynamic nature of technology and education, staying informed about the latest research and trends in self-directed learning and computer science is crucial. Be prepared to adapt and evolve self-directed learning strategies as new insights emerge. Thus, integrating self-directed learning into computer science education offers numerous benefits, including enhanced student motivation, autonomy, and critical thinking skills. Implementing these recommendations and best practices can help institutions create a supportive and effective learning environment that prepares students to excel in the ever-evolving field of computer science.

Discussion

Self-directed learning in computer science education represents a significant shift from traditional instructional methods (Santhanam et al., 2008). This discussion delves into the various aspects, implications, and outcomes of integrating self-directed learning principles into computer science curricula. One of the primary advantages of self-directed learning is its positive impact on student motivation and autonomy (Zhu et al., 2023). When students have the freedom to choose their learning paths, set goals, and take ownership of their education, they are more likely to be intrinsically motivated. This motivation leads to deeper engagement with course materials and greater autonomy in the learning process (Armoed, 2021). As a result, students become active participants in their education, which is especially crucial in a field as dynamic as computer science.

Li (2023) asserts that self-directed learning plays a crucial role in nurturing students' critical thinking abilities and problem-solving skills. It involves exploring subjects of personal interest and addressing real-world challenges, allowing students to apply theoretical knowledge to practical contexts effectively. This practice equips them with the capacity to identify issues, seek pertinent information, and devise innovative solutions. These competencies are particularly valuable in the field of computer science, where adaptability and creativity are highly esteemed (Bergamin et al., 2019).

Deliwe (2020) argues that computer science is characterized by rapid evolution, and self-directed learning serves as a means to imbue students with the flexibility and adaptability necessary to keep pace with industry advancements. Through self-directed projects and exploration, students can remain updated on the latest technologies, programming languages, and trends (De Beer, 2016). This adaptability stands as a significant advantage in the job market, where employers seek professionals who can rapidly acquire and apply new skills. However, the adoption of self-directed learning is not without challenges. Its implementation necessitates careful consideration of factors such as assessment methodologies, scaffolding, and accommodating diverse learning styles (Chiu, 2021). Assessing self-directed projects can be intricate since conventional exams may not fully capture the depth of knowledge acquired through self-directed exploration (Lin, 2023). Moreover, certain students may struggle to exercise the autonomy and independence essential for self-directed learning. Hence, providing guidance and mentorship becomes imperative (Liu et al., 2023).

An integral aspect of self-directed learning in computer science involves promoting collaboration and social learning. Students are encouraged to collaborate on group projects, share insights, and participate in coding communities (Ajani & Maphalala, 2023). Additionally, Dombestein et al. (2019) advocate for collaborative experiences that foster a sense of connection among students, offering opportunities for peer support and knowledge exchange. Despite its self-directed nature, the learning process retains its inherently social character, mirroring the teamwork prevalent in the technology industry (Van Der Berg et al., 2023). Zhu et al. (2023) suggest incorporating learning analytics into self-directed learning environments can offer valuable insights into student progress and engagement. These tools provide data on how students interact with course materials, allowing teachers to identify areas where additional support or resources may be needed. Continuous evaluation and improvement are crucial to refining self-directed learning initiatives and ensuring they meet the evolving needs of computer science education (Noone &

Mooney, 2018). Faculty members play a pivotal role in facilitating self-directed learning. They must be equipped with the necessary skills and knowledge to mentor and guide self-directed students effectively. Professional development programmes should focus on helping teachers create a supportive learning environment that balances autonomy with guidance.

Self-directed learning in computer science education holds great promise for preparing students to excel in this dynamic and ever-evolving field (Chiu, 2021). It fosters motivation, critical thinking, and adaptability while promoting collaboration and social learning. However, it requires careful planning, ongoing support, and a commitment to continuous improvement to realise its full potential in preparing the next generation of computer scientists.

FUTURE RESEARCH DIRECTIONS

The landscape of computer science education is currently undergoing a profound transformation, catalyzed by emerging trends poised to reshape how students interact with the learning process. This discussion delves into these pivotal trends and their far-reaching implications for the future of self-directed learning in computer science education. The requirement for advanced learning analytics tools is critical to this transformative shift. The need stems from a desire to gain deeper insights into student progress, preferences, and areas for improvement. These sophisticated analytics tools have the potential to usher in a new era of personalized self-directed learning. Allowing educators to identify individual needs, they can tailor support and resources with previously unattainable precision. Another focus is the incorporation of Artificial Intelligence. Incorporating Artificial Intelligence (AI) into self-directed learning platforms is another focus. This integration paves the way for adaptive learning experiences in which AI algorithms are key in recommending personalized learning paths and resources. The potential of AI-powered platforms is found in their ability to improve the efficiency of self-directed learning. These platforms, which provide real-time feedback and dynamically adjust content based on individual learning styles and pace, represent a significant advancement in personalized education. Another noteworthy trend is the incorporation of gamification elements and interactive simulations. This strategy can potentially increase engagement and make self-directed learning more enjoyable. Gamification emerges as a key driver in sustaining motivation and interest among students in computer science, where problem-solving and creativity are essential.

Global collaborative learning networks are more critical than ever before. The expansion of these networks, which connect students, educators, and industry professionals all over the world, presents unprecedented opportunities. Students participating in cross-cultural collaboration within these networks gain insights into diverse perspectives and global industry trends, resulting in a more enriching learning experience. The viability of the self-directed learning paradigm in computer science education is emphasized by its alignment with the industry's need for adaptable, creative, and autonomous professionals. This paradigm allows students to take ownership of their learning journey, a valuable skill in the fast-paced world of computer science. Looking ahead, there are exciting opportunities for research in the field.

Investigating the impact of AI-powered self-directed learning platforms on student outcomes, such as skill acquisition, retention, and real-world application, represents a new avenue for learning. Longitudinal studies on the recognition and value of self-directed learning micro-credentials can provide insights into their impact on career progression and industry acceptance. In conclusion, the future of self-directed learning in computer science education holds enormous promise, thanks to advances in analytics, AI integration, and global collaboration. Ongoing research efforts and a concerted focus on addressing implementation challenges will be critical in realizing the transformative benefits of this paradigm, ultimately preparing students for success in an ever-changing technological landscape.

CONCLUSION

Integrating self-directed learning principles into computer science education in higher institutions is a transformative approach with the potential to prepare students effectively for the rapidly evolving technology landscape. This systematic literature review has provided a comprehensive overview of the benefits, challenges, and considerations associated with self-directed learning in computer science. Self-directed learning empowers students with motivation, autonomy, critical thinking skills, and adaptability. It enables them to take ownership of their education, engage deeply with course materials, and develop problem-solving abilities crucial for success in the computer science field. The flexibility of self-directed learning equips students to stay current with industry advancements and fosters a culture of continuous learning—a hallmark of successful computer scientists.

However, implementing self-directed learning also poses challenges related to assessment, scaffolding, and accommodating diverse learning styles. It demands faculty training and support to guide and mentor self-directed students effectively. To harness the full potential of self-directed learning in computer science education, institutions must invest in pedagogical strategies, learning analytics, and a supportive learning environment that balances autonomy with guidance. By doing so, they can equip the next generation of computer scientists with the skills and mindset needed to thrive in this dynamic and innovative field. In summary, self-directed learning has the potential to revolutionise computer science education by fostering student-centred, adaptive, and collaborative learning experiences. Its adoption requires careful planning and ongoing evaluation. However, it promises to prepare students for academic success, lifelong learning, and success in the ever-changing world of technology.

REFERENCES

Ajani, O. A., & Khoalenyane, N. B. (2023). Using WhatsApp as a tool of learning: A systemic literature review of prospects and challenges. *International Journal of Innovative Technologies in Social Science*, *3*(39). doi:10.31435/rsglobal_ijitss/30092023/8025

Ajani, O. A., & Khumalo, N. P. (2023). Aftermaths of the Post-Covid-19 Pandemic Experiences: Assessing and Repositioning South African Higher Education. *International Journal of Social Science Research and Review*, *6*(6), 674–683.

Ajani, O. A. (2023). Challenges mitigating against effective adoption and usage of e-learning in curriculum delivery in South African universities. *International Journal of Innovative Technologies in Social Science*, *2*(38), 1–15. doi:10.31435/rsglobal_ijitss/30062023/8005

Armoed, Z. (2021). The COVID-19 pandemic: Online teaching and learning at higher education institutes. *IOP Conference Series. Earth and Environmental Science*, *654*(1), 012026. doi:10.1088/1755-1315/654/1/012026

Barnes, L. (2021). Challenges South African youth face in education and their quest to eradicate issues of the past. *Alternate Horizons*, (1). Advance online publication. doi:10.35293/ah.vi.3540

Belle, A. B., & Zhao, Y. (2023). Evidence-based decision-making: On the use of systematicity cases to check the compliance of reviews with reporting guidelines such as PRISMA 2020. *Expert Systems with Applications*, *217*, 119569. doi:10.1016/j.eswa.2023.119569

Bembenutty, H. (2023). Self-regulated learning with computer-based learning environments. *New Directions for Teaching and Learning*, *2023*(174), 11–15. doi:10.1002/tl.20543

Bergamin, P. B., Bosch, C., Du Toit, A., Goede, R., Golightly, A., Johnson, D. W., & van Zyl, S. (2019). *Self-directed learning for the 21st century: Implications for higher education*. AOSIS.

Bosch, C. (2017). *Promoting self-directed learning through the implementation of cooperative learning in a higher education blended learning environment* [Doctoral dissertation, North-West University (South Africa), Potchefstroom Campus].

Brisimis, E., Krommidas, C., Galanis, E., Karamitrou, A., Syrmpas, I., & Zourbanos, N. (2020). Exploring the relationships of autonomy-supportive climate, psychological need satisfaction and thwarting with students' self-talk in physical education. *Journal of Education Society and Behavioural Science*, *2*(3), 112–122. doi:10.9734/jesbs/2020/v33i1130276

Chiu, T. (2021). Applying the self-determination theory (SDT) to explain student engagement in online learning during the COVID-19 pandemic. *Journal of Research on Technology in Education*, 54 (sup1), S14-S30. . doi:10.1080/15391523.2021.1891998

Cigdem, H., & Öztürk, M. (2016). Critical components of online learning readiness and their relationships with learner achievement. *Turkish Online Journal of Distance Education*, *20*(10). doi:10.17718/tojde.09105

Condie, R., & Livingston, K. (2007). Blending online learning with traditional approaches: Changing practices. *British Journal of Educational Technology*, *38*(2), 337–348. doi:10.1111/j.1467-8535.2006.00630.x

Conradie, P. W. (2014). Supporting self-directed learning by connectivism and personal learning environments. *International Journal of Information and Education Technology (IJIET)*, *4*(3), 254–259. doi:10.7763/IJIET.2014.V4.408

De Beer, J. (2016). Re-imagining science education in South Africa: The affordances of indigenous knowledge for self-directed learning in the school curriculum. *Journal for New Generation Sciences*, *14*(3), 34–53.

Deliwe, A. (2020). The use of a learner management system (moodle) in promoting teaching and learning. *Universal Journal of Educational Research*, *8*(12B), 8383–8392. doi:10.13189/ujer.2020.082644

Dombestein, H., Norheim, A., & Husebø, A. (2019). Understanding informal caregivers' motivation from the perspective of self-determination theory: An integrative review. *Scandinavian Journal of Caring Sciences*, *34*(2), 267–279. doi:10.1111/scs.12735 PMID:31313852

Estisari, K., Wengrum, T., & Nurhantanto, A. (2023). Economic Students' perceptions towards learning management system (LMS). *JAE*, *3*(1). doi:10.33365/jae.v3i1.198

Fabriz, S., Mendzheritskaya, J., & Stehle, S. (2021). Impact of synchronous and asynchronous settings of online teaching and learning in higher education on students' learning experience during COVID-19. *Frontiers in Psychology*, *12*, 733554. doi:10.3389/fpsyg.2021.733554 PMID:34707542

Ghazal, S., Aldowah, H., & Umar, I. (2018). Satisfaction of learning management system usage in a blended learning environment among undergraduate students. *The Turkish Online Journal of Design Art and Communication*, *8*(Sept), 1147–1156. doi:10.7456/1080SSE/156

Gicevic, S., Aftosmes-Tobio, A., Manganello, J., Ganter, C., Simon, C., Newlan, S., & Davison, K. (2016). Parenting and childhood obesity research: A quantitative content analysis of published research 2009–2015. *Obesity Reviews*, *17*(8), 724–734. doi:10.1111/obr.12416 PMID:27125603

Gluckman, H., Pontes, C., & Scheyer, E. (2021). An overview of COVID-19 infection in dental practices - a questionnaire survey. *SADJ; Journal of the South African Dental Association*, *76*(07), 404–408. doi:10.17159/2519-0105/2021/v76no7a2

Gurcan, F., & Cagiltay, N. E. (2019). Big data software engineering: Analysis of knowledge domains and skill sets using LDA-based topic modeling. *IEEE Access : Practical Innovations, Open Solutions*, *7*, 82541–82552. doi:10.1109/ACCESS.2019.2924075

Harry, T., & Chinyamurindi, W. (2021). "still haven't found what I am looking for": Rural black students' perceived work readiness and assessment of labour market access. *Education + Training*, *64*(2), 276–289. doi:10.1108/ET-10-2021-0387

Hebda, M. (2023). Technology talent development: Beyond an hour of code. *Gifted Child Today*, *46*(2), 108–118. doi:10.1177/10762175221149256

Helbach, J., Hoffmann, F., Pieper, D., & Allers, K. (2023). Reporting according to the preferred reporting items for systematic reviews and meta-analyses for abstracts (PRISMA-A) depends on the abstract length. *Journal of Clinical Epidemiology*, *154*, 167–177. doi:10.1016/j.jclinepi.2022.12.019 PMID:36584734

Hmelo-Silver, C. E. (2004). Problem-based learning: What and how do students learn? *Educational Psychology Review*, *16*(3), 235–266. doi:10.1023/B:EDPR.0000034022.16470.f3

Holmes, K., & Fray, L. (2018). Student and staff perceptions of a learning management system for blended learning in teacher education. *The Australian Journal of Teacher Education*, *43*(3), 21–34. doi:10.14221/ajte.2018v43n3.2

Hosseini, H., Hartt, M., & Mostafapour, M. (2019). Learning is child's play: Game-based learning in computer science education. [TOCE]. *ACM Transactions on Computing Education*, *19*(3), 1–18. doi:10.1145/3282844

Kayacan, K., & Ektem, I. (2019). The effects of biology laboratory practices supported with self-regulated learning strategies on students' self-directed learning readiness and their attitudes towards science experiments. *European Journal of Educational Research*, *8*(1), 313–323. doi:10.12973/eu-jer.8.1.313

Kiesler, N., Mackellar, B. K., Kumar, A. N., McCauley, R., Raj, R. K., Sabin, M., & Impagliazzo, J. (2023, June). Computing Students' Understanding of Dispositions: A Qualitative Study. *In Proceedings of the 2023 Conference on Innovation and Technology in Computer Science Education,* V1, (pp. 103–109). Academic Press.

Knowles, M. S. (1975). *Self-directed learning: A guide for learners and teachers.*

Koole, S., Schlinkert, C., Maldei, T., & Baumann, N. (2018). Becoming who you are: An integrative review of self-determination theory and personality systems interactions theory. *Journal of Personality, 87*(1), 15–36. doi:10.1111/jopy.12380 PMID:29524339

Larson, L., Seipel, M., Shelley, M., Gahn, S., Ko, S., Schenkenfelder, M., Rover, D. T., Schmittmann, B., & Heitmann, M. (2017). The academic environment and faculty well-being: The role of psychological needs. *Journal of Career Assessment, 27*(1), 167–182. doi:10.1177/1069072717748667

Lee, J. H., Ostwald, M. J., & Zhou, L. (2023). Socio-Spatial Experience in Space Syntax Research: A PRISMA-Compliant Review. *Buildings, 13*(3), 644. doi:10.3390/buildings13030644

Lee, Y., Lau, K., & Yip, V. (2016). Blended learning for building student-teachers' capacity to learn and teach science-related interdisciplinary subjects. *Asian Association of Open Universities Journal, 11*(2), 166–181. doi:10.1108/AAOUJ-09-2016-0029

Lin, X. (2023). Exploring the Role of ChatGPT as a Facilitator for Motivating Self-Directed Learning Among Adult Learners. *Adult Learning*, 10451595231184928. doi:10.1177/10451595231184928

Liu, B., Gui, W., Gao, T., Wu, Y., & Zuo, M. (2023). Understanding self-directed learning behaviours in a computer-aided 3D design context. *Computers & Education, 205*, 104882. doi:10.1016/j.compedu.2023.104882

Liu, G., Teng, X., & Zhu, D. (2019). Effect of self-esteem and parents' psychological control on the relationship between teacher support and Chinese migrant children's academic achievement: A moderated mediation. *Frontiers in Psychology, 10*, 2342. doi:10.3389/fpsyg.2019.02342 PMID:31736816

Luo, Y., Lin, J., & Yang, Y. (2021). Students' motivation and continued intention with online self-regulated learning: A self-determination theory perspective. *Zeitschrift für Erziehungswissenschaft, 24*(6), 1379–1399. doi:10.1007/s11618-021-01042-3 PMID:34483723

Mahlaba, S. C. (2020). Reasons why self-directed learning is important in South Africa during the COVID-19 pandemic. *South African Journal of Higher Education, 34*(6), 120–136. doi:10.20853/34-6-4192

Maphalala, M. C., & Ajani, O. A. (2023). The COVID-19 pandemic: Shifting from conventional classroom learning to online learning in South Africa's higher education. *International Journal of Innovative Technologies in Social Science*, 2(38), 1–15. doi:10.31435/rsglobal_ijitss/30062023/8002

Maphalala, M. C., Mkhasibe, R. G., & Mncube, D. W. (2021). Online Learning as a Catalyst for Self-directed Learning in Universities during the COVID-19 Pandemic. *Research in Social Sciences and Technology, 6*(2), 233–248. doi:10.46303/ressat.2021.25

Markova, O., Semerikov, S., Маркова, О., Semerikov, S., Семеріков, С., Семериков, С., & Тронь, В. (2019). Implementation of cloud service models in training of future information technology specialists. *Cte Workshop Proceedings*, (*vol. 6*, 499-515). IEEE. 10.31812/123456789/3270

Martucci, A., Gursesli, M. C., Duradoni, M., & Guazzini, A. (2023). Overviewing Gaming Motivation and Its Associated Psychological and Sociodemographic Variables: A PRISMA Systematic Review. *Human Behavior and Emerging Technologies*, *2023*, 1–156. doi:10.1155/2023/5640258

Masina, R., Mukaro, J. P., & Mawonedzo, A. (2023). Self-directed assessment framework for practical tasks for Clothing and Textile Technology undergraduate teacher trainees under COVID-19 conditions. *Teacher Education through Flexible Learning in Africa* (*TETFLE*), *4*(1), 102-120.

Maulana, R., Helms-Lorenz, M., Irnidayanti, Y., & Grift, W. (2016). Autonomous motivation in the Indonesian classroom: Relationship with teacher support through the lens of self-determination theory. *The Asia-Pacific Education Researcher*, *25*(3), 441–451. doi:10.1007/s40299-016-0282-5

Mayet, R. (2021). Supporting at-risk learners at a comprehensive university in South Africa. *Journal of Student Affairs in Africa*, *4*(2). doi:10.18820/jsaa.v4i2.2

Mncube, D. W., & Maphalala, M. C. (Eds.). (2023). *Advancing Self-Directed Learning in Higher Education*. IGI Global. doi:10.4018/978-1-6684-6772-5

Murniati, C. T., Hartono, H., & Nugroho, A. C. (2023). The challenges, supports, and strategies of self-directed learning among college students. [EduLearn]. *Journal of Education and Learning*, *17*(3), 365–373.

Musitha, M., & Mafukata, M. (2018). Crisis of decolonising education: Curriculum implementation in Limpopo Province, South Africa. Africa's Public Service Delivery. *Performance Research*, *6*(1). doi:10.4102/apsdpr.v6i1.179

Noone, M., & Mooney, A. (2018). Visual and textual programming languages: A systematic review of the literature. *Journal of Computers in Education*, *5*(2), 149–174. doi:10.1007/s40692-018-0101-5

Ntombana, L., Gwala, A., & Sibanda, F. (2023). Positioning the #feesmustfall movement within the transformative agenda: Reflections on student protests in South Africa. *Education as Change*, *27*. Advance online publication. doi:10.25159/1947-9417/10870

Oda, M., Noborimoto, Y., & Horita, T. (2021). International trends in k–12 computer science curricula through comparative analysis: Implications for the primary curricula. *International Journal of Computer Science Education in Schools*, *4*(4). doi:10.21585/ijcses.v4i4.102

Olawumi, K., & Mavuso, M. (2022). Education in the new normal: a need for alternative strategies in supporting teaching and learning in South African schools in the post-COVID-19 era. *E-Journal of Humanities Arts and Social Sciences*, (pp. 116–125). IEEE. . doi:10.38159/ehass.2022SP31110

Onah, D., Pang, E., & Sinclair, J. (2020). Cognitive optimism of distinctive initiatives to foster self-directed and self-regulated learning skills: A comparative analysis of conventional and blended-learning in undergraduate studies. *Education and Information Technologies*, *25*(5), 4365–4380. doi:10.1007/s10639-020-10172-w

Oosthuizen, I. (2016). *Self-directed learning research: An imperative for transforming the educational landscape*. AOSIS.

Page, M. J., McKenzie, J. E., Bossuyt, P. M., Boutron, I., Hoffmann, T. C., Mulrow, C. D., & Moher, D. (2023). A declaração PRISMA 2020: Diretriz atualizada para relatar revisões sistemáticas. *Revista Panamericana de Salud Pública*, *46*, e112. PMID:36601438

Pellet, J. P., & Parriaux, G. (2023). Informatics in Schools. *Beyond Bits and Bytes: Nurturing Informatics Intelligence in Education: 16th International Conference on Informatics in Schools: Situation, Evolution, and Perspectives, ISSEP 2023*, Lausanne, Switzerland.

Prentice, M., Jayawickreme, E., & Fleeson, W. (2018). Integrating whole trait theory and self-determination theory. *Journal of Personality*, *87*(1), 56–69. doi:10.1111/jopy.12417 PMID:29999534

Ryan, R., & Deci, E. (2000). Self-determination theory and the facilitation of intrinsic motivation, social development, and well-being. *The American Psychologist*, *55*(1), 68–78. doi:10.1037/0003-066X.55.1.68 PMID:11392867

Safitri, I., & Lestari, P. (2021). Optimising learning management system to teach English grammar. *Edulink Education and Linguistics Knowledge Journal*, *3*(1), 51. doi:10.32503/edulink.v3i1.1490

Santhanam, R., Sasidharan, S., & Webster, J. (2008). Using self-regulatory learning to enhance e-learning-based information technology training. *Information Systems Research*, *19*(1), 26–47. doi:10.1287/isre.1070.0141

Sheldon, K., & Prentice, M. (2019). Self-determination theory as a foundation for personality researchers. *Journal of Personality*, *87*(1), 5–14. doi:10.1111/jopy.12360 PMID:29144550

Sun, W., Hong, J. C., Dong, Y., Huang, Y., & Fu, Q. (2023). Self-directed learning predicts online learning engagement in higher education mediated by the perceived value of knowing learning goals. *The Asia-Pacific Education Researcher*, *32*(3), 307–316. doi:10.1007/s40299-022-00653-6

Thomson, N., & Tippins, D. (2013). Envisioning science teacher preparation for twenty-first-century classrooms for diversity: Some tensions. *Science Education for Diversity*, *2*(3), 231–249. doi:10.1007/978-94-007-4563-6_11

Threekunprapam, A., & Yasri, P. (2020). Patterns of Computational Thinking Development While Solving Unplugged Coding Activities Coupled with the 3S Approach for Self-Directed Learning. *European Journal of Educational Research*, *9*(3), 1025–1045. doi:10.12973/eu-jer.9.3.1025

Van Helden, G., Zandbergen, B., Shvarts, A., Specht, M., & Gill, E. (2023). *An Embodied Cognition Approach To Collaborative Engineering Design Activities*.

Van Wyk, M. M. (2017). An e-portfolio as empowering tool to enhance students' self-directed learning in a teacher education course: A case of a South African university. *South African Journal of Higher Education*, *31*(3), 274–291. doi:10.20853/31-3-834

Verster, M. C., Laubscher, D. J., & Bosch, C. (2023). Facilitating Blended Learning in Underprivileged Contexts: A Self-Directed Curriculum as Praxis View. In Competence-Based Curriculum and E-Learning in Higher Education (pp. 20-50). IGI Global. doi:10.4018/978-1-6684-6586-8.ch002

Williams, G., McGregor, H., Sharp, D., Levesque, C., Kouides, R., Ryan, R., & Deci, E. (2006). Testing a self-determination theory intervention for motivating tobacco cessation: Supporting autonomy and competence in a clinical trial. *Health Psychology*, *25*(1), 91–101. doi:10.1037/0278-6133.25.1.91 PMID:16448302

Xie, Z., Man, W., Liu, C., & Fu, X. (2023). A PRISMA-based systematic review of measurements for school bullying. *Adolescent Research Review*, *8*(2), 219–259. doi:10.1007/s40894-022-00194-5

Zainuddin, Z., Hermawan, H., Nuraini, F., & Prayitno, S. (2019). Students learning experiences with LMS tes teach in flipped-class instruction. *Elinvo Electronics Education*, *4*(1), 1–11. doi:10.21831/elinvo.v4i1.24405

Zhu, M., Berri, S., Koda, R., & Wu, Y. J. (2023). Exploring students' self-directed learning strategies and satisfaction in online learning. *Education and Information Technologies*, *5*, 1–17. doi:10.1007/s10639-023-11914-2

Chapter 6
Teaching Approaches of High School Teachers in the 21st Century:
Fostering the Cultivation of Self-Directed Learning for Computer Science Education

Nomasonto Mthembu
University of KwaZulu-Natal, South Africa

Wanjiru Gachie
University of KwaZulu-Natal, South Africa

ABSTRACT

Despite social, historical, and cultural diversity, as well as poor educational attainment amongst high school learners, South African higher education is undergoing a digital revolution that fosters the cultivation of self-directed learning. This chapter contends that self-directed learning should not solely prioritize the accomplishment of tasks and the instructor's oversight of task completion. Instead, it should be centered around empowering learners to critically examine established conventions. Studies have demonstrated that learners from underserved regions are at a disadvantage when they enroll in higher education because they lack digital technology skills, which limits their level of critical thinking in problem-solving. The chapter further seeks to assist teachers and education policy makers in South Africa to keep up with the new pedagogical approaches that are suitable for 21st century learners and should enhance self-directed learning.

INTRODUCTION

Literature has witnessed that digital technologies have permeated society to the point where their use in everyday life and education is nearly unavoidable (Meintjes, 2023; Oki, Uleanya, & Mbanga, 2023). This suggests that a re-evaluation of teaching and learning approaches in high schools is necessary,

DOI: 10.4018/979-8-3693-1066-3.ch006

with an emphasis on implementing teaching methods that foster self-directed learning. Furthermore, the field of computer science is characterized by continuous growth, making it imperative to conduct an analysis of the potential benefits that these innovations may bring to the educational landscape (van Heerden & Mulumba, 2023). Literature further revealed that numerous research has been undertaken on the educational benefits of online learning technologies for enhancing student learning beyond the classroom (Nuryatin, Rokhmansyah, Hawa, Rahmayanti, & Nugroho, 2023). ICTs and social media for educational purposes is a concept that is not only riddled with difficulties but also possesses enormous unrealised potential globally and, more especially, in South Africa.

As time goes on, classrooms in the 21st century will become more like laboratories. Thus, teachers in South Africa are strongly urged to enrol in additional ICT short courses to meet the growing need for digital technologies among learners. This is essential for both widespread computer science education and international efficiency, and autonomous learning. Moreover, Olivier, Oojorah and Udhin (2022) argued that teachers need to experiment with new teaching and learning approaches which in this case includes: self-directed learning, which will encourage critical thinking amongst learners.

In addition, the study conducted by Widodo, Gustari, and Chandrawaty (2022) posited that teachers' professional competence, perceived advantages of information and communication technology (ICT) utilisation, and teacher collaboration significantly impact teachers' attitudes towards implementing self-directed teaching approaches through the integration of technology. Teachers in South Africa still need more digital technology training from the Department of Education if they are to appropriately educate learners for the digital age (Dlamini & Mbatha, 2018) and if they are to be motivated to adopt more positive perceptions towards self-directed learning. This will assist South African learners who are currently in the process of applying to colleges and universities which are highly characterised by self-directed learning. Hence, will serve to close the gap between urban and rural educational facilities. As a result, most universities in South Africa now refer to their students as digital natives, putting significant pressure on high schools in the country to provide learners with the skills they will need to thrive in the digital age.

The Motivation of the Chapter

There is a need for more authentic critical literature in which the authors produce writing that is beneficial to the context in which the writer is working. This suggests that high school teachers, education stakeholders, learners, and students will not be disadvantaged by their background, ethnicity, or culture, but rather will gain from the project and that it is important to inspire and motivate them as they venture into self-directed learning through the use of digital technology (Pischetola, 2018). On the contrary, a lack of proper teacher training in South Africa for digital technology may also contribute to a decline in self-directed learner motivation. This chapter discusses the teaching approaches of teachers through digital technology that foster the cultivation of self-directed in South African high schools.

Henceforth, it will be necessary to bridge the gap in knowledge for digital technology for high school learners. This will partly be achieved by looking at the holistic development of the learner through the lens of the constructivist theory. Thus, by looking at the personal, social and the professional rationale of teaching. This chapter will discuss the literature in the field of digital technology and how digital technology fosters the cultivation of self-directed learning. Furthermore, explores teaching and learning approaches of matric teachers that foster the cultivation of self-directed learning.

Objectives

1. To discuss teaching and learning approaches that fosters the cultivation of self-directed learning for computer science education.
2. To explore the holistic development of a learner through the lens of the constructivist theory

BACKGROUND

Self-Directed Learning

In contemporary society, individuals are increasingly burdened with higher expectations compared to preceding generations, necessitating the active cultivation of their own lives, the exercise of personal agency in decision-making, and the assumption of accountability for the outcomes of those decisions. The contemporary cohort of students is confronted with the imperative of engaging in lifelong learning, necessitating a perpetual acquisition of novel knowledge and abilities throughout their whole career path (Chukwunemerem, 2023). This places significant demands on South African learners' capacity to self-manage. In light of this context, the acquisition of self-direction abilities is frequently referred to as an essential competency for high school learners to acquire within the classroom setting. Simultaneously, self-directed learning is perceived as a strategy to enhance learner motivation within the school setting. By affording learners greater autonomy and accountability, they are more likely to adopt a proactive and engaged stance toward their education (Voskamp, Kuiper, & Volman, 2022). The reasons behind the self-directed learning approach are undoubtedly varied, with one significant factor being children's desire to exert authority over the selection and manner of acquiring knowledge. Furthermore, it aligns with the natural desire and necessity experienced by the majority of people to persist in their pursuit of knowledge. The concept of self-directed learning embraces essential learners' basic learning qualities. Thus, this chapter aims to link self-directed learning with the constructivist theory in conjunction with the three (personal, social and professional) rationales of teaching and learning. Teachers have to take into consideration that learners exist within their individual selves (personal rationale), therefore, they can never be viewed as empty boxes that need to be filled. Furthermore, learners come from a social context (social rationale), which drives the ways they learn and perceive the world. In addition, an explicit unpacking of knowledge through subject discipline (professional rationale) and activities should assist learners to be able to make their own informed decisions, innovate, and be critical.

In essence, this article aims to connect self-directed learning with learners' responsibility and accountability for their own learning. In this particular scenario, learning activities would function solely as a means to facilitate learner autonomy and foster critical thinking skills. According to Razak et al. (2022) critical thinking is a manifestation of the cognitive component within the process of acquiring knowledge. Furthermore, critical thinking involves the intricate cognitive process that goes into building individualised meaning and valuable knowledge that is derived from a shared consensus.

In order to fully foster the cultivation of self-directed learning with the use of digital technology, which then interprets Self-directed learning beyond task control but includes the process of responsibility and innovation. In order to fully comprehend self-directed learning, this chapter draws in the constructivism theory of teaching and learning.

Cultivating Self-Directed Learning Through Constructivist Approaches in Teaching and Learning

Constructivism is based on the idea that learners actively construct or make their own knowledge, and that reality is determined by their experiences (Erdal, Mehmet, & Bulent, 2021). This suggests that for learning to occur, new learning experiences must take into consideration human factors and assist the learners in assimilating new knowledge to their existing knowledge constructs. Hence, fostering the cultivation of self-directed learning by making abstract concepts and facts more grounded in personal experiences and the values of learners and by allowing the learning experience to be differentiated for individual learners.

Social constructivism as described by Vygotsky (1978) realises the learning processes that are influenced by social interaction using three concepts, namely, Zone of Proximal Development (ZPD), inter-subjectivity, and enculturation which refers to the distance between the actual developmental level, as determined by independent problem solving, and the level of potential development, as determined through problem solving under adult guidance or in collaboration with more capable peers (Vygotsky, 1978; Abtahi, 2018; Svanhild, 2020). This suggests that the teacher cannot teach knowledge, but learners must acquire it for themselves. This further gets learners to think critically; creatively; experiment; solve; question; discover; evaluate; analyse; and present what they've learned in a variety of ways, using the principles of constructivism. Hence, the primary objective of this chapter is to assist teachers teaching Computer Application Technology (CAT) and Information Technology (IT) with pedagogical approaches that aim to enhance self-directed learning amongst learners in high school. This could be achieved by empowering teachers to encourage learners to create personal constructions of reality; simulated authentic learning environments; multiple representations of data; active learning and collaboration as discussed by Wang et al. (2021).

Furthermore, social constructivism theory suggests that knowledge is the result of processes within communities rather than those of individuals functioning in isolation. Thus, this chapter recognises the learning environment in high schools through social interactions and in the manner by which those interactions with teachers, learners, and peers are interpreted. Social constructivism (Vygotsky, 1978, p. 86) recognises the learning processes that are influenced by social interaction using three concepts, namely the zone of proximal development, inter-subjectivity, and enculturation. The zone of proximal development refers to "the distance between the actual developmental level, as determined by independent problem solving, and the level of potential development, as determined through problem solving under adult guidance or in collaboration with more capable peers". The zone of proximal development represents the extent of learning that is possible for an individual with proper instructional.

Moreover, the coordination of the two terms (inter-subjectivity and enculturation) does not progress independently of the social environment and culture of the individual. The social environment influences cognition through the resources used in the classroom for effective teaching which, at this point, could be integrating ICT tools and digital language. This replaces the traditional everyday language of the school, as well as churches to change perceptions about the emerging digital age as alluded by van der Westhuizen and Hannaway (2021). This suggests that knowledge and understanding are socially constructed and arise within particular cultural beliefs to reflect the communal knowledge of that culture. In order to cultivate self-directed learning through constructivism, this chapter arranges constructs that assist in the development of self-directed learning. These constructs consist of properties aimed at building a new framework for self-directed learning.

LEARNING IS CONSTRUCTED

Learners' Unique Learning (Personal Rationale)

Research in the field of psychology indicates that individuals exhibit several distinct characteristics in their decision-making, problem-solving, and learning abilities (Wood, 2022). In the pursuit of creating optimal learning experiences, educators and instructional designers must take into consideration the unique variances among learners. When learners are instructed according to their unique abilities, interests, and preferences, it is possible to attain greater and more impactful self-directed learning. Giulia (2021) asserted that the learning styles of learners are a significant factor that directly impacts their self-directed learning experiences. The concept of learning style refers to the preferred and prioritized approach that an individual learner employs during the process of acquiring knowledge. Furthermore, the learning style is a complex component inside the learning environment that has an impact on the learner's motivation and capacity to learn efficiently. The aforementioned statement explains the cognitive, emotive, and physiological manifestations displayed by learners when watching and engaging with the learning environment (Zhang & Van Reet, 2021). Learners exhibit diverse learning styles, particularly in terms of their incorporation and processing of various sorts of knowledge in unique ways.

The correlation between the instructional methodology and the preferred learning style of the student serves as a determinant in fostering basic motivation, which enhances the learner's inquisitiveness, cultivates a thirst for knowledge through self-directed learning. Conversely, when there is a discrepancy between the instructional approach and the learner's chosen learning style, this inconsistency can result in a poor learning environment for the student. It has been determined that conflicts in teaching styles between educators and students lead to a sense of dissatisfaction among students with regards to the educational experience (Giulia, 2021).

Learners' Ideological Learning (Social Rationale)

When there is a reason to believe that a cultural paradigm gives one group of learners' preferential treatment at the expense of other groups of learners, to cultivate a successful self-directed learning, teachers have an ethical obligation to change the cultural paradigm into a basic framework. Hence, it is deemed unethical to refrain from critically analysing learners' beliefs, particularly pertaining to language and culture. Additionally, Fangfang (2022) commented that ideologies and computer science ideologies are systemic and change over time because views are implicit and grow through historical and cultural interactions. The examination of these entities is necessary as they overtly prioritize a specific group or language, therefore warranting scholarly investigation. Hegemonic social dynamics will happen if the dominant group or language is not questioned. This means that the interests of one group will be put ahead of those of the other group. This leads to a culture imbalance among students who are interested in computer science.

Moreover, rules and social media are examples of cultural models that help people interact on a larger societal level. These models show up in the smaller-scale semiotic practices of daily life. This effect is especially clear in schools where students are present. The texts, dialects, and conversation patterns that are used, as well as how learners are placed in connection to their nonstandard linguistic and cultural backgrounds, can all show how children feel about computer science subjects in a larger sense, which can lead to arguments and disagreements about these views (Weismueller, Harrigan, Coussement, & Tessitore, 2022).

Learners' Competent Learning (Professional Rationale)

Students' relevant prior knowledge is described as what learners already know from their lives and prior schooling. Thus, creating deep and meaningful academic experiences for learners is important (Castillo-Montoya & Ives, 2021). However, few schools are formally prepared in knowing how to use learners' prior knowledge to support their learning. Teachers can surface and incorporate students' prior knowledge to increase students' active engagement in the classroom with implications for content learning as alluded by Heitzman, Richters, Radkowitsch, Schmidmaier, Weidenburch and Fischer (2021) or to specifically enhance the quality of learners' content learning. The latter suggests that constructivism's central idea is that human learning is constructed, that learners build new knowledge upon the foundation of previous learning. This prior knowledge influences what new or adopted knowledge an individual will construct from new learning experiences. Although Castillo-Montoya and Ives (2021) argue that drawing on students' prior knowledge can enhance learning, we know little about how instructors learn to teach with this knowledge in mind.

Heitzmann, et al. (2021) conceptualised learner diagnosis through teacher using eight diagnostic activities as listed in Table 1:

Table 1. Diagnostic activities to draw learners' prior knowledge

	Diagnosis	Diagnostic Activity
1.	Problem identification	A learner portrays a specific behaviour.
2.	Questioning	A teacher considers why or what is the cause of the learner's behaviour.
3.	Hypothesis generation	A teacher suspects a particular learning ability or disability.
4.	Construct and design artefacts	A teacher assigns differentiated assessment to learners
5.	Evidence generation	A teacher uses other teaching and learning approaches and resources to further examine different learning abilities,
6.	Evidence evaluation	A teacher evaluates her teaching methods and resources to test if they were valid for the type of learning differences existing in her classroom,
7.	Drawing conclusion	The teacher decides on the appropriate teaching and learning approaches and resources to use in class to enhance creativity and cater for all learning abilities.
8.	Communication and scrutiny	The teachers then reflect on his/her practice, encourage learner evaluation, and peer evaluation.

Source: Heitzmann, et al. (2021)

Table 1 outlines certain diagnostic principles, however it is not necessary to do all eight of them. These eight diagnostic activities serve the purpose of proper integration of technology. Depending on prior knowledge, diagnostic activities may be missed or repeated in a circular way. It also seems possible that over the course of a learning session, the order or frequency of diagnostic activities that a learner shows may alter. For a successful diagnostic process to take place in the classroom, a teacher should find ways to actively engage learners through activities that translate into deeper levels of learning, motivation and achievement (Castillo-Montoya & Ives, 2021).

LEARNING IS ACTIVE

Self-Assurance

Akbari and Sahibzada (2020) affirmed that competence, knowledge, and performance are interconnected concepts that play a pivotal role in a learner's success. As a result of the absence of certain resources or opportunities, learners may encounter numerous difficulties in their lives. This suggests that learners who possess deficiencies in self-confidence may encounter a range of difficulties in attaining the desired personal goals they have set for themselves. Consequently, the absence of self-confidence within learners can have negative implications not just for learners themselves, but also for high schools and the successful cultivation of self-directed learning. The prevailing problem in the educational system mostly stems from diminished self-confidence, resulting in insufficient student engagement and mediocre academic advancement despite prolonged classroom attendance. Apart from this, confidence is a significant determinant in the process of learning, as it can exert a profound influence on the level of students' engagement and academic advancement.

According to Senent, Kelley and Abo-Zena (2021), self-confidence plays a crucial role in a learner's readiness to undertake risks and actively participate in learning activities that are self-motivated. This suggests that learners who possess self-confidence exhibit a sense of assurance in their skills, enabling them to establish objectives and exert diligent effort towards their attainment, without being too concerned about the potential outcomes. One the one hand, children are inherently endowed with a certain level of self-confidence, which is subject to fluctuations throughout the course of their lifespan. In a similar manner, Learners may experience reduced self-confidence due to anxiety, fear, feelings of social isolation in the classroom, and self-insecurity. Self-confidence has the power to significantly alter an individual's behaviour and is a very influential aspect in human motivation. Students that possess self-confidence are those who demonstrate assurance in their capacity to participate in a variety of academic and extracurricular activities in an efficient manner, all in the service of learning.

Collaboration

The prioritization of learner participation as a measure of learning efficacy aligns with the current and growing focus on pedagogies that promote collaborative learning. In addition, collaborative learning refers to the diverse range of instructional practices implemented by teachers to foster learners' collective efforts in enhancing self-directed learning in particular subject area (Osman, Duffy, Chang, & Lee, 2011). The emphasis on comprehension necessitates the use of many collaborative and cooperative learning methodologies, while excluding strategies that primarily emphasize repetitive exercises or superficial grasp of the material. The many collaborative learning methodologies facilitate learner engagement through interactive exchanges, promoting the expression of individual viewpoints and the resolution of discrepancies in comprehension. From a social constructivist perspective, the requirement to articulate one's thoughts to others and to consider and include the perspectives of others aids students in developing a more comprehensive and intricate comprehension of a subject matter.

Facilitating

This second notion is that learning is an active rather than a passive process. The passive view of teaching views the learner as an empty vessel to be filled with knowledge, whereas constructivism states that learners construct meaning only through active engagement with the world. Hence, active learning, as a pedagogical approach, gives learners the opportunity to utilise their cognitive and higher-order skills and strategies by creating meaning from their experiences and the environment and from thereon, construct their own knowledge and knowledge (Stanberry, 2018). Furthermore, stated that active learning encompasses a broad range of pedagogical practices and instructional methods that connect with an individual learner's active learning strategies. Figure 1 illustrates pedagogical approaches of active learning through scaffolding, together with matching teaching designs as described in Shroff et al. (2021).

Figure 1. Concepts of scaffolding for pedagogical approaches of active learning scaffolding
(Adopted from Shroff, et al., 2021)

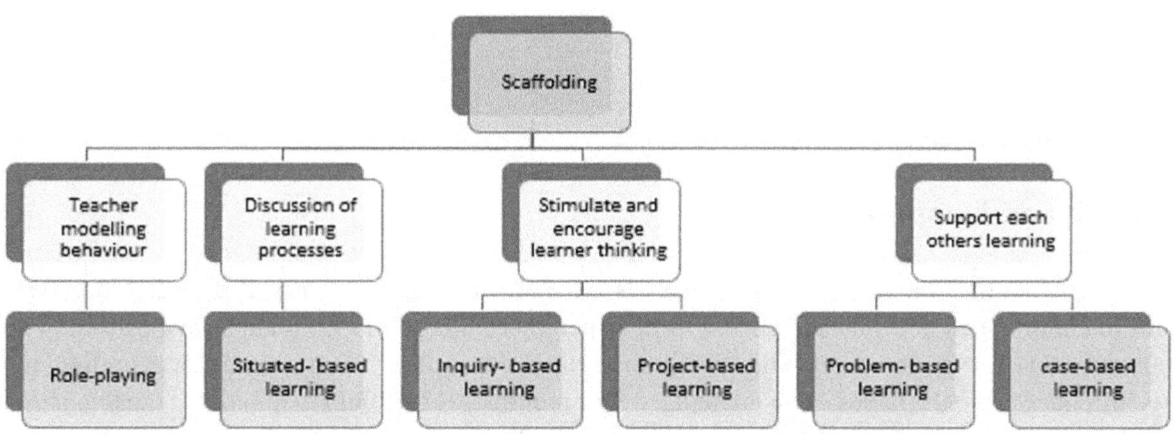

Figure 1 further discusses the pedagogical approaches and scaffolding with the properties associated with them. These approaches hold appropriate teaching and learning methods that were relevant for this research. As a teacher assists in the process that can guide learners in integrating digital literacy in their learning, by applying the six learning designs: role-playing; where a learners assume characters within a context, in situated learning; where learners are exposed to the experts in their learning discipline, in inquiry- based learning; learners formulate research questions from open-ended ideas, in project-based learning; learners engage in activities to create artefacts, in problem-based learning; learners work in groups facilitated by a teacher to solve real life problems, and in cased-based learning; students work collaboratively to solve a problem.

The concept of scaffolding was relevant in this research context because scaffolding is together with teaching designs and is often the practical application of teaching and learning related theories. Moreover, the focus of this research was on matric teachers integrating digital literacy in their teaching to prepare matric learners for HEIs. The objective of this research was to assess pedagogical approaches that teachers use when teaching digital literacy. It was therefore appropriate for this research to increase theoretical knowledge of learning effectiveness through the application of constructivist learning theory during digital literacy integration through scaffolding. Olsen, Rummel and Eleven (2021) define scaffolding as the concept of helping learners to develop their knowledge bases through interactions. With regards to learning, Vygotsky (1978) posits learning course development across two levels, actual and potential develeopment, with proximal development explaining the gap between the two levels. Proximal development relies on a learner's problem solving abilities, often guided by adult supervision.

Thus, Heilmann (2018) states that active learning coupled with guided learning are foundational to the concept of scaffolding. That being said, the significance of scaffolding in this research is that matric teachers act as facilitatiors of active learning, that will enable learners to explore freely through the world of digital literacy. The success of scaffolding can be completed by the following: a teacher modelling behaviour through discussion with students identifying the processes used approaching problem-solving or processs orientated ask. Many studies have addressed modeling learner behaviour through open online courses for example the likes of Zhao et al. (2017), Conati, et al. (2018) and Collins et al. (2019). This suggests that digital literacy can be used as learners' modeling tool in a matric classroom. This will enable active and authentic learners, a learning that will create meaning to matric learners. Thus, the teacher is able to engage matric learners in discussion of learning processes through collaboration, and the provision of timely feedback and coaching.

LEARNING IS INNOVATIVE THINKING

Curiosity and Inspiration

Children do not undergo learning events in a passive manner. On the contrary, it is the autonomous actions of children that generate and choose these experiences. Piaget (1952) delineated a pattern of baby behaviour that serves as a compelling illustration of this assertion. A toy that made a rattling sound was introduced into the hands of an infant aged four months. As the child manipulated the toy, it would simultaneously enter the field of vision and emit an auditory stimulus, eliciting a state of arousal and agitation in the infant. Consequently, the infant would engage in additional bodily movements, resulting in the toy oscillating between being visible and invisible, and generating further auditory stimuli.

More importantly, the infant lacked prior familiarity with the toy, but via active engagement, they were able to discern the purpose and objective of shaking the to produce sound. When the child inadvertently manipulated the toy, perceiving and experiencing the resulting effects, the infant exhibited a heightened interest in the activity and its outcomes. Consequently, it may be argued that the infant acquired deliberate mastery over the act of shaking the toy with the specific objective of producing sound. This particular instance, characterized by a bodily motion that results in a captivating conclusion, has the potential to serve as a fundamental element in both the developmental process and the evolutionary mechanisms that operate within it.

However, the level of interest in computer science subjects, is contingent upon other factors. Once all the potential patterns of toy shaking have been accurately anticipated and all the corresponding results have been foreseen, the act of playing with a toy becomes considerably less captivating, as demonstrated by the lack of enthusiasm displayed by older infants towards toys. The concept of what is deemed intriguing is contingent upon the learner's existing knowledge and areas of unfamiliarity. In the field of computer science, there is a keen interest in phenomena that exist outside the current boundaries of knowledge. This curiosity arises from the delicate balance between familiarity and excessive complexity. Therefore, teachers should be conscious of the differentiated development of their learners when assigning assessments and learning activities. In many situations, teachers are pushed to use narrow, skill-based lesson plans along with strict standards and monitoring measures. On the other hand, some teachers help kids learn and grow in all areas by letting them play and ask questions.

Impacting

The evolution of technology is playing an increasingly significant role in driving changes to modern curricula. The rapid increase in the use of personal digital devices and the extensive accessibility of communication infrastructure have resulted in significant changes in global society. The aforementioned alterations have underscored the imperative for schools to guarantee that every learner is adequately equipped for the present-day digital landscape. Moreover, the imperative to impart digital skills to every student necessitates a departure from the conventional approach of teaching computer science as a distinct subject, and instead calls for its integration throughout all disciplines within the curriculum. The acknowledgment of the significance of digital skills for high school learners of all backgrounds has resulted in the formulation of novel curricular domains in numerous nations, with a specific emphasis on cultivating these skills. Nevertheless, a significant disparity persists among teachers regarding the alignment of technical skills emphasized in curricula and the pragmatic approaches required to effectively incorporate these abilities into their overall classroom practices.

Procedure

Knowledge is not a copy or a true reflection of some independent reality. According to this perspective, truth as an objective correspondence to a distinct reality does not exist. Teachers usually observe and recognise the world from a particular sociocultural and historically placed vantage point (Antonini, 2019). Therefore, human knowledge should always be seen as something that comes from the human mind. But one can agree with this conceptual relativism argument without being forced into a subjective or relativistic view of how one knows what he or she knows. For instance, Maps of the world are made by people and use different assumptions and simplifications to show the globe.

However, teachers do not have to think that there is not a globe or a planet Earth because these are not the best pictures people can make of them. In the same way, their conceptual points of view are limited, but since they are views, they are views of the world or some part of it. Even though teachers cannot know things in themselves or reality as it is, this doesn't mean teachers have to give up their deep assumption that things in themselves exist or that there is a world outside of their minds and the minds of the learners. Moreover, the background assumption of external realism is very important for how teachers live, how learners learn, and the conversations that happen between them. Teachers are not required to perceive in external realism; rather, everything they do, say, and investigate is predicated on the assumption that it is true. Educators may never be able to convey to students the precise nature of this reality, regardless of what they believe about it. As a starting point, however, it is nearly impossible to avoid external realism.

LEARNING IS PERSONAL

Learner Experience

Each individual learner has a distinctive point of view, based on existing knowledge and values. For educators, individualistic learning is crucial since August (2020) suggests that students can gain different knowledge and experience by participating in the same lesson or activity. Furthermore, each student, although receiving the same formal instruction or reading the same book, arrives at their own, subjective interpretation. However, social constructivists, who tend to be Vygotskian in their outlook, stress the importance of context and culture in the educational process. Thus, it is argued by Alam et al. (2022) that a person's capacity for knowledge is seen as something that is built up by their participation in social interactions and the language they use to communicate with others; the person is thus seen as a social product (Alam, et al., 2022). Moreover, according to many, teaching and learning is recognised to be a process of sharing and negotiating knowledge that is socially produced because all meanings are social. Since the 'shared building of knowledge is now the dominant metaphor for education, this also has significant consequences for educators. Keeping both latter discussed and the current viewpoint in mind at the same time will help teachers spot the improbable extreme that each one tends toward. The notion of learning is personal seems to deny the idea of knowledge being shared and communicated from one person to another by emphasizing the uniqueness of each learner's experiences. This leads directly to the conclusion that one's own subjective experience is the sum of all possible experience and, by extension, the entire universe. This means that same lesson, teaching or activity may result in different learning by each pupil, as their subjective interpretations differ.

Learning Area Preference

The efficacy of Self-directed learning in computer science education, as imparted by teachers to students, is significantly dependent upon the teaching methods employed by teachers within the classroom setting. Therefore, to adequately equip 21st century learners for future success, it is essential for teachers specializing in computer science subjects to prioritize the effectiveness of their teaching methods. Furthermore, it is important for teachers to possess a comprehensive understanding of how learners think in relation to computer science subjects, as well as effective pedagogical strategies for its instruction. The ongoing professional concern among high school teachers pertains to the change of teaching techniques and curriculum content in the field of computer science. It is important to initiate proactive measures aimed at shifting the method of instruction of computer science subjects' lessons from conventional approaches to a learner-centered pedagogical approach. The understanding of learners' attitudes holds significance in facilitating their academic accomplishments and fostering their engagement in a specific field of study. The attitudes of teachers have undergone a great deal of research on digital technology, with early emphasis mostly placed on its integration into general teaching practices (Bui, 2022). However, comparatively less effort has been devoted to exploring its application within specific disciplines such as computer Application Technology (CAT) and information technology (IT). The phenomenon can serve as a partial means of masking students' dispositions towards those specific subject areas.

ALL KNOWLEDGE IS SOCIALLY CONSTRUCTED

Family

One significant issue of concern pertains to the potential future scarcity of adequately skilled computer science professionals within the context of South Africa. The decline in student enrolment in computer science subjects is a cause for concern, as it can be ascribed to the negative opinions held by high school learners towards computer science subjects. The majority of individuals lack awareness regarding the various employment prospects associated with computer science, often mistakenly equating it just with computer literacy.

Certain parents assume the responsibility of determining the academic courses or disciplines that their children will undertake during their high school. It should be noted that the issue of learners' limited interest in computer science subjects should be entrusted to school management teams and computer science teachers. They should employ study findings to raise awareness and cultivate more learners interest in pursuing computer science subjects at high school level. Consequently, the field of computer science education in tertiary colleges experiences lower enrolment rates compared to other areas of study. This can be attributed to the prevailing apathetic perceptions towards computer science subjects, as it is often regarded as a less prestigious career choice. This perception is particularly prevalent among families residing in both rural and urban areas, leading to a discouragement of their children from pursuing computer science as a viable career option. One of the contributing factors to this discouragement is the belief that computer science is a non-profitable field, as many IT specialists often struggle to find employment opportunities. Moreover, parents are not well informed of the significance of computer science subjects since it is part of new developments. Hence, Educators should assume a vital role in providing career guidance to their children and students.

Social Culture

As for the previously discussed principle of constructivism, that knowledge is personal, the assumption that social variables or influences alone govern all learning and all conscious thought moves towards an impossible extreme: the view that all knowledge is a socially constructed, insists on the essentially social nature of all knowledge and, by extension, all learning. This would completely remove the learner from the learning process. However, this seems excessive given the importance of memories to learning and the fact that they, along with perceptual systems, are contained within each person's unique biological brain. Researchers, in support of Marx, have often had a key role to play in changing people's ideas, changing knowledge, and so changing civilisations (Brown, 2021). The latter is true even for those who follow Marx in saying that man's consciousness is a product of the social reality. Despite claims that linguistic experience shapes human minds, the reasons for privileging linguistic over other types of experience remain unclear. If taken at face value, this position suggests that animals are incapable of knowing the world around them and dismisses the intellect of pre-verbal infants (Piaget's entire sensory motor intelligence). It also fails to account for the vast body of unspoken knowledge that each of us possesses about the world. By emphasising education as the collaborative construction of knowledge, the education system run the risk of downplaying the significance of learners' own time spent on guided practice and problem-solving.

LEARNING EXISTS IN THE MIND

The constructivist theory posits that knowledge can only exist within the human mind, and that it does not have to match any real-world reality. Thus, learners will be constantly trying to develop their own individual mental model of the real world from their perceptions of that world. As they perceive each new experience, learners will continually update their own mental models to reflect the new information, and will, therefore, construct their own interpretation of reality.

Making sense is a concept that has its roots in language, in activities like reading, and in noticing patterns in general. As learners puzzle over a text, an image, or a set of numbers, they make sense of it by adding the new information to what they already know. In this case, constructivism focuses on the part of learning that is about knowledge. Hence, it is moving past the idea that learning is just about memorising facts or drinking in new information without any problems. The latter was definitely a big step toward a more realistic view of how people learn. However, if you take it too literally or only look at one side, it can make you think that knowledge is all there is to learning and that teachers do not have to worry about getting learners to learn. This could suggest teachers are at the mercy of what they already know. Moreover, the easiest and most effective ways to recognise what constructivism is trying to say is to think about one of the many visual illusions or unclear images that are studied in the psychology of visual perception. Figure 2 shows an example of this. In Kanizsa's design, people see or make up a set of white star points that aren't really there. The effect is strong because people's eyes show them not only the shape of a white star, but also the edges of white against a white background and a brighter white figure (the star) against a darker white background.

Figure 2. Kanizsa's design experiments
(Li, Qian and Liang, 2018)

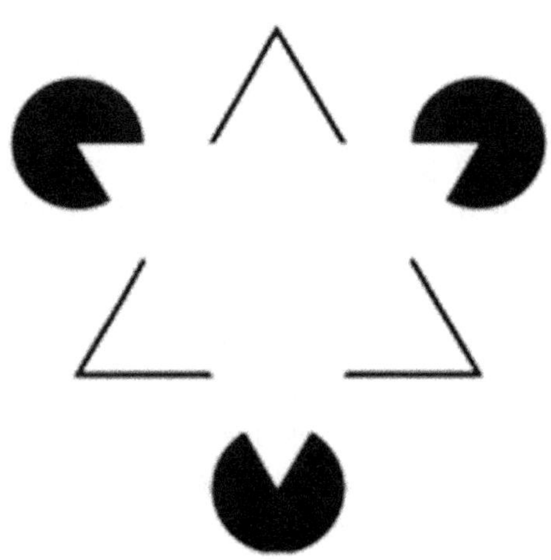

Figure 2 is impressive evidence of the way in which learners construct their view of the world using stored knowledge, but teachers should also keep in mind that virtually all humans report seeing this phenomenon and that peoples' visual system delivers this visual experience up to us without conscious effort (Antonini, 2019).

As learners practise their application of concepts, skills, and methods, making performance effortless is a key aspect of learning. Thus, practice is essential for two reasons: first, it is the primary means by which learners eradicate errors from habitual routines, and second, it assists learners to transfer their limited conscious focus away from routine competencies. Consequently, the practicing musician does not precisely duplicate each scale or musical piece, but rather seeks to alter the performance with each attempt to make it more fluid, error-free, and simple to execute. In fact, nothing has been learned when a trial is an exact replica of a prior trial.

CONCLUSION

The discussions have come up to a conclusion that fostering the cultivation of Self-directed learning (SDL) for a successful teaching and learning of computer science in high school, requires a holistic approach to child development and learning. Thus, recognising the connectedness of individual learner's unique learning style, the society and cultural background of the learners and ensuring proper implementation of the computer science curriculum. In addition, the professional competency of teachers, the perceived benefits of utilizing information and communication technology (ICT), and teacher collaboration have a substantial influence on teachers' attitudes towards the implementation of self-directed teaching approaches through the integration of technology. In order to effectively educate learners for the digital age and foster good attitudes towards self-directed learning, it is imperative that teachers in South Africa receive additional digital technology training from the Department of Education. This will provide support to South African students who are presently engaged in the application process for schools and universities that emphasize self-directed learning. Therefore, it will effectively bridge the disparity between educational resources in urban and rural areas. Consequently, a majority of universities in South Africa have adopted the term "digital natives" to describe their student body, so imposing considerable demands on high schools throughout the nation to equip students with the necessary competencies essential for success in the era of digitalization.

REFERENCES

Abtahi, Y. (2018). Pupils, tools and the Zone of Proximal Development. *Research in Mathematics Education, 20*(1), 1–13. doi:10.1080/14794802.2017.1390691

Akbari, O., & Sahibzada, J. (2020). Students' Self-Condidence and Its Impacts on Their Learning Process. *American International Journal of Social Science Research*, 1-15 .

Alam, R., Ansarey, D., Halim, H. A., Rana, M., Milon, K. R., & Mitu, R. K. (2022). Exploring Bangladeshi university studnt's Willingness to communicate (WTC) In English Classes through a qualitative study. *Asian-Pacific Journal of Second and Foreign Language Education*, 1-17 . doi:10.1186/s40862-022-00129-6

Antonini, S. (2019). Intuitive acceptance of proof by contradiction. *ZDM Mathematics Education, 51*(5), 798–821. doi:10.1007/s11858-019-01066-4

Brown, M. H. (2021). *Marxist Forged Through Personal Struggle: Counterstorytelling through Learning Experiences of Becoming Class Conscious.* Research Gate. file:///D:/for%20chapter%203/1-s2.0-S0959475222000536-main.pdf.

Bui, T. H. (2022). English teachers' intergration of digital technologies in the classroom. *International Journal of Educational Research Open*, *3*, 1–15. doi:10.1016/j.ijedro.2022.100204

Castillo-Montoya, M., & Ives, J. (2021). Instructor's conceptions of Minoritized College Students' Prior Knowledge and their related Teaching Practice. *The Journal of Higher Education*, *92*(5), 735–759. doi :10.1080/00221546.2020.1870850

Chukwunemerem, O. P. (2023). Lessons from Self-Directed Learning Activities and Students Think Critically. *Journal of Education*, 80–87. doi:10.5539/jel.v12n2p79

Dlamini, R., & Mbatha, K. (2018). The discource on ICT teacher professional development need: The case of a South African teacher's Union. *International Journal of Education and Development Using Information and Communication Technology*, 17–37. https://files.eric.ed.gov/fulltext/EJ1190045.pdf

Erdal, B., Mehmet, B., & Bulent, D. (2021). The reason for gaining and losing the popularity of paradigm in constructivism: Why? and How? *Psycho-* [doi:https://www.journals.lapub.co.uk/index.php/PERR]. *Educational Research Review*, 8–24.

Fangfang, L. (2022). Ideas and Cases of Ideological and Political Construction in Computer Science Courses. *Adult and Higher Education*, *61-64*. doi:10.23977/aduhe.2022.041211

Giulia, C. (2021). Hope and reponsibility: Embracing different types of knowledge whilst generating my own living-educational-theory. *Educational Action Research*, 1–16. doi:10.1080/09650792.2021.1880458

Heilmann, S. (2018). A Scaffolding Approach Using Interviews and Narrative Inquiry. *Online Journal for teacher research*, 2470-6353 https://newprairiepress.org/networks/vol20/iss2/3/

Heitzmann, N., Richters, C., Radkowitsch, A., Schmidmaier, R., Weidenbusch, M., & Fischer, M. (2021). Learners' adjustment strategies following impassesses in simulations-effects of prior knowledge. *Learning and istructions*, 1-11 . doi:10.1016/j.learninstruc.2022.101632

Meintjes, H. H. (2023). Learner Views of a facebook page as a supportive Digital pedagogy at a Public South African School in a Grade 12 Business Studies Class. *Business Studies Journal*, 1-16. doi:10.4018/978-1-6684-7123-4.ch073

Nuryatin, A., Rokhmansyah, A., Hawa, A. M., Rahmayanti, I., & Nugroho, B. A. (2023). Google Classroom as an online Learning Media for Indonesian Language Learning During Covid-19 Pandemic. *Journal of Language Teaching and research*, 73-80. . doi:10.17507/jltr.1401.27

Oki, A. O., Uleanya, C., & Mbanga, C. (2023). Echoing the effect of information and communications technology on rural education development. *Information and Communication technology*, 1-18. doi:10.15587/2706-5448.2023.269698

Olivier, S. J., Oojorah, A., & Udhin, W. (2022). Multimodal Learning Environments in Southern Africa Embracing digital Pedagogies. *Digital educaiton and learning*, 1-16 . doi:10.1007/978-3-030-97656-9

Olsen, J. K., Rummel, N., & Eleven, V. (2021). Designing for the co-orchestration of social transitions between individual, small-group and whoe-class learning in the classroom. *International Journal of Artificial Intelligence in Education, 24-56*, 24-56 . doi:10.1007/s40593-020-00228-w

Osman, G., Duffy, T. M., Chang, Y., & Lee, J. (2011). Learning through collaboration: studnet perspectives. *Asian Pacific Education Review*, 547-558 . doi:10.1007/s12564-011-9156-y

Pischetola, M., & Heinsfeld, B. (2018). Technology and teacher's motivational style: A research study in Brazilian Public Schools. *Journal of Education*, (17), 163–178. doi:10.7358/ecps-2018-017-pisc

Razak, A. A., Ramdan, R. M., Mahjom, N., Zabit, N. M., Muhammad, F., Hussin, M. Y., & Abdullar, N. L. (2022). Improving Critical Thinking skills in Teaching through problem-Based Learnng for Students: A Scoping Review. *International Journal of Learning, Teachng and Educational Research*, 342-362.

Senent, G. I., Kelley, K., & Abo-Zena, M. (2021). Sustaining curiosity: Reggio-Emilia inspired learning. *Earlhy child development and care*, 1247-1258 . doi:10.1080/030044430.2021.1900835

Svanhild, B. (2020). Student-teacher dialectic in the co-creation of a Zone of proximal development an example from from kindergaten mathematics. *Education Research Journal*, 413-356.

van der Westhuizen, L. M., & Hannaway, D. M. (2021). Digital play for language development in early grades . *South African journal of Childhood Education*, 2-45 https://doi.org/ lil.925. doi:10. 4102/sajce.v1

Van Heerden, J., & Mulumba, M. (2023). Science, Technology and Innovation (STI): Its Role in South Africa's Development Outcomes and STI Diplomacy. *Research for Development*, 144–154. doi:10.1007/978-981-19-6802-0_9

Voskamp, A., Kuiper, E., & Volman, M. (2022). Teaching Practices for Self-Direcred and Selft-Regulated Learnng: Case Studies in Dutch Innovative Secondary Schools. *Educational Studies*, *48*(6), 772–789. doi:10.1080/03055698.2020.1814699

Vygotsky, L. S. (1978). *Mind in Society: The development of higher psychological processes*. Harvard Univesity Press., http://outleft.org/wp-contents/uploads/Vygotsky

Weismueller, J., Harrigan, P., Coussement, K., & Tessitore, T. (2022). What makes people share political content on social media? The role of emotion, authority and ideology. *Computers in Human Bahaviour*, 1-11 . doi:10.1016/j.chb.2021.107150

Widodo, W., Gustari, I., & Handrawty, C. (2022). Adversity Quotient Promotes Teachers' Professional Competence More Strongly Than Emotional Intelligence: Evidence form Indinesia. *Journal of Intelligents*, 1-17 . doi:10.3390/jintelligence10030044

Wood, R. (2022). Practitioners respond to Sarah Mercer's Psychology for language learning: Spare a thought for the teacher. *Language Teaching*, *422-425*(3), 422–425. Advance online publication. doi:10.1017/S0261444821000203

Zhang, L., & Van Reet, J. (2021). How is Knowledge constructed During Science activities? Detecting Instructional Effects of Play and Telling to Optimize integration of Scientific investigations. *Research in Science Education*, 1–15. doi:10.1007/s11165-021-09990-w

Zhao, Y., Davis, D., Chen, G., Lofi, C., Hauff, C., & Houben, G. J. (2017). Certificate Achievement Unlocked: How does MOOC Learner's Behaviours Change? *Late-Breaking Results, Demonstration and Theory, Opinion and Reflection Paper*, 83-88. Research Gate.

Chapter 7
Education With Passion:
Computing as a Means for Addressing the Challenges of All

Francesco Maiorana
https://orcid.org/0000-0001-7327-2611
University of Urbino, Italy

Andrew Csizmadia
Newman University, Birmingham, UK

Giusy Cristaldii
Pegaso International, Malta

Charles Riedesel
University of Nebraska, USA

ABSTRACT

The fourth UNESCO goal for sustainable development addresses issues related to quality education for all. A worldwide effort strives to introduce computing from early studies. In this chapter, the authors will share and analyze approaches for embedding computational thinking (CT) in STEAM teaching, approaches drawn upon their experience as computing subject experts spanning their teaching careers. They will share experiences and best practices on the impact of CT on 1) Creativity supporting all the educational activities; 2) Challenges for educators and their students, with a particular emphasis on how to deliver an inclusive and accessible education addressing the expectation of all the students in the same class from the gifted one to those requiring a special education; 3) Convenience and how computing and CT promote special abilities within STEAM; 4) Custom and ethical principles supporting the teaching and learning process of all; and 5) Citizenship with an emphasis on digital citizenship and wisdom on how CT and computing can be taught, learned, and applied for the social good.

DOI: 10.4018/979-8-3693-1066-3.ch007

INTRODUCTION AND BACKGROUND

The primary issue for this chapter is in what resources exist and how they can contribute to academic enrichment practices for fostering development of Computational Thinking (CT) in students so that they can excel in (hopefully) all Science, Technology, Engineering, Arts and Mathematics (STEAM) education and, in general, in education. More fundamentally, can educators be empowered with best practices and materials so as to impart CT to their students, regardless of the subject area? For example, students who only learn how to follow instructions (as in a program), may become proficient in following instructions, but probably not gain proficiency in solving the underlying problems independently. In such a restricted environment, they gain only the capabilities of a (non-thinking) computer, not of the computer programmer, or more generally of the creators of all STEAM solutions. Is this what students are looking for or do they prefer to look for other ways to express their creativity? Can this be considered quality education?

One of UNESCO's sustainability goals is quality education for all (UNESCO, 2017), (Owens, 2017). The paramount importance of education is clearly stated by researchers (Howells, 2018a). Quality education allows for "an integrated approach" with mutual sustainment involving different activities pursuing different goals. This international effort for quality education is comprehensive, incorporating the dissemination of computing knowledge to all citizens, involving all educators, using all levels of education, extending into all types of educational systems, and considering all stages of life, have all been indicated to be pursued from early development (Cutts et al., 2018) and has been the focus of the Computer Science education community during its entire existence.

Some notable examples around the world in this direction are the following:

1. Computing At School (CAS), (Crick, 2011), (Anonymized, 2015) which was, is and will be the driving force of the National Curriculum in England and Scotland.
2. Computer Science Teachers Association (CSTA) which released a framework (CSTA, 2016) and a Standard, both for students (CSTA, 2016) and teachers (CSTA, 2020), covering Computer Science (CS) education from kindergarten through 12th grade, which drives the effort in the USA.
3. Code.org (Franke & Osborne, 2015) with an incisive action to have everyone learn CS, working with educational departments across the USA and around the world with initiatives covering Europe (Sirocchi et al., 2022) and Italy (Corradini & Nardelli, 2021), and the United Kingdom.
4. CSforAll (Santo et al., 2018), a movement dedicated to bringing high quality Computer Science to all school students in order to prepare them for college.
5. Informatics for All (M. E. Caspersen et al., 2018) coalitions supported by the ACM Europe Council, Informatics Europe, and the Council of European Professional Informatics Societies (CEPIS) aims at introducing Informatics as a fundamental discipline for all learners.
6. The Consortium for Computing Sciences in Colleges (CCSC) promotes CS in two and four years Colleges and Universities in the USA and represents the glue between K-12 school and higher education.
7. Additional leading educational organizations like OECD (Howells, 2018), (OECD learning, 2030) and ACM, and more specifically SIGCSE.

A focus on competencies is driving the effort in new curricula development and comparison on 21st-century competencies, and skills (Binkley et al., 2014), such as Computational Thinking (CT), play a key role (Wing, 2020) despite a debate (Denning, 2017) lasting more than 80 years (Tedre & Denning,

2016). It is their (and our) position that CT should be included with an interdisciplinary approach in all disciplines and should involve all stakeholders. According to the various operational definitions of CT it is possible to argue that:

- CT can be interpreted as a transversal and transversal set of skills that can be used as a means to acquire and to develop broad competencies like the one proposed in (Bocconi, 2016).
- "more tools in the mental toolbox seems like a worthy goal" (Tedre & Denning, 2016).

Despite the remarkable effort cited above and despite the excellent results obtained thus far (according to objective data analysis (Guzdial, 2020)) "we have not yet created popular computing education. We reach very few students". Sustained by these efforts, the authors under the umbrella of CT and in the light of their experiences covering three nations and two continents and spanning decades up to an entire life will present:

1. **Creativity** and how computing and CT promote creativity within STEAM.
2. **Challenges** faced by learners and educators, and ways to overcome those challenges.
3. **Convenience** and how computing and CT promote convenience and accessibility for students with Special Educational NeeDs (SEND) but considered with special abilities
4. **Customs** and ethical principles laying the foundation of the educational process with a particular emphasis on the computing domain.
5. **Citizenship** with an emphasis on digital citizenship and wisdom on how CT and computing can be taught, learned, and applied for the social good.

presenting best practices to promote creativity, accessibility, ethical and active citizenship. While leveraging on the author experiences and on a selection of research papers found in literature, the work offers a reference point for current literature on these topics and synthetize lesson learned in decades of experiences to overcome the challenges faced in teaching computing and CT.

Creativity represents a driving force for all human activities, including computing and allows to overcome challenges. All, if adequately and conveniently supported, are creative, and this creativity, if guided by custom and ethical principles, leads to active and good citizens.

The above topics will be organized in sections. Each section will have a brief overview and state of the art regarding the topic, a sub-section for each country, namely England, Italy and the USA, with a particular emphasis on Nebraska and Kansas when appropriate, and a final section with lessons learned and best practices. Concluding remarks and further work will be presented in the last section.

All the above will be presented to provide an epistemological and comprehensive narrative review as emerging from the comparison of educational experiences of researchers around the world, i.e., Italy (Anonymized, 2019), (Anonymized, 2021) & Europe, Nebraska & USA, England & United Kingdom. The approach spurred from a systematic review conducted according to the Preferred Reporting Items for Systematic Reviews and Meta-Analyses (PRISMA) guidelines developed in a narrative and epistemological review distilled from more than 30 tears of experiences of the authors both as on the field educator and as researcher, arising from international discussions and comparisons. The effort culminated in an annotated bibliography to a large literature on computational thinking providing a solid research foundation framing successive research (Anonymized, 2023).

CREATIVITY

There exist various definitions of creativity:

1. According to the Cambridge dictionary: "the ability to produce or use original and unusual ideas"
2. According to the Merriam-Webster dictionary: "the ability to create"
3. According to the Treccani definitions, the intellectual process divergent from the normal abstract logical process.
4. According to J.P. Guilford (Guilford, 1967), it is characterized by: particular sensitivity to problems, ability to produce ideas, flexibility of principles, originality in ideation, ability to synthesize, ability to analyze, ability to define and structure one's experiences and knowledge in a new way, breadth of the field of ideation, ability to evaluate.
5. According to (Romero et al., 2017) is "a context-related process in which a solution is individually or collaboratively developed and considered as original, valuable, and useful by a reference group".

The OECD PISA has recently released the third edition of the Creative Thinking Framework (OECD, PISA, 2021). From the above definitions it is clear that creativity is a high order cognitive competency that is required in STEAM, and it permutates all disciplines and all aspects of our life. Among the projects linking CT and creativity, it is possible to recall (Miller et al., 2013). Where the authors demonstrate that the addition of creative exercises to computing courses for Computing, STEM and Humanities majors students, not only improves CT knowledge and skills, but by combining hands-on problem solving, guided analysis and reflection, real-world CS applications allows students to leverage their creative thinking skills to "unlock" their understanding of CT. The same path of linking of CT and creativity and other soft skills is advocated in (Lemay & Basnet, 2017) even if the authors did not find a link between CT skill development and academic performance. In (Pecanin et al., 2019) the authors report that by applying business process methodologies coupled with a constructive and multidisciplinary approach they found an increase in innovation and the student ability to develop innovative ideas.

How Does Computing and CT Promote Creativity Within STEAM?

On the basis of the teaching and educational experience of the authors, the following educational practices are suggested:

1. Foster and require students to look for, find and share at least two solutions of each given problem. Besides developing creativity, the approach fosters critical thinking and decision making, requiring the students to compare strengths and weaknesses of each solution and choose the best one based on objective and subjective parameters (Giordano & Maiorana, 2013b). The same process is suggested for the teaching practice by presenting as many examples as possible (Savage & Csizmadia, 2018).
2. Foster moments for presentations and classroom reflection. Use web-based tools to promote discussion beyond the classroom time (Giordano & Maiorana, 2013a). Besides developing critical thinking, these activities facilitate metacognitive strategies, sharing with students not only the results of this approach but also the "basic functioning" of a meta-level analysis (Hoppe & Werneburg, 2019).

3. Build a collection of the best solutions and share these solutions with students. Reading solutions performed by others fosters creative and critical thinking. Allowing reuse and repurposing of resources greatly helps in producing better solutions while offering a richer set of services (Maiorana, 2018).
4. Emphasizes process over product (Giordano & Maiorana, 2013b), (Savage & Csizmadia, 2018).

CHALLENGES

According to recent works (Yadav, 2016) where 24 teachers were interviewed according to a semi structured protocol in order to collect insights on challenges faced in daily educational activities. The challenges were coded into 3 categories namely:

1) challenges of teaching in a computer science classroom,
2) compounding factors that influence teaching in a computer science classroom
3) professional needs of computer science

On the same track the Cambridge handbook of computing education research (Fincher, 2019) 5 systemic issues have been selected and discussed in separate chapter, namely:

1) Novice programmers and introductory programming (Robins, 2019)
2) Programming paradigms and beyond (Krishnamurthi, 2019)
3) Assessment and plagiarism (Lancaster, 2019)
4) Pedagogic approaches (Falkner, 2019)
5) Equity and diversity (Lewis, 2019)

According to the experience of the authors and as emerged from the literature review there are many challenges in computing education. Admittedly far from being comprehensive, we will provide a summary as distilled from research literature, findings from surveys completed by teachers, and from the authors' experiences of some of these challenges deemed most important in relation to the topics presented in this work:

1) Equity and inclusion are to be intended in the broadest sense possible. This has been identified as a challenge by most authors in many domains from K-12 to higher education. This challenge has emerged from researchers (Gal-Ezer & Stephenson, 2014) and referenced in careful analysis of teachers' perception in Europe (Sentance & Csizmadia, 2015), (Sentance & Csizmadia, 2017a), the USA (Yadav et al., 2016) and South American countries (Sentance et al., 2020). Equity and inclusion are meant to include in the educational process more students, including women and underrepresented minorities, learners facing socio-economic difficulties, and students with special abilities. Equity and inclusion mean an even stronger substantial effort for developing customizable and accessible learning resources, offering tools accessible to all students, economically sustaining learners. Despite the fact that a lot has been done (Guzdial, 2020) and a lot we have learned from the computing education community, there is still a great deal to be done by educators and researchers to include all learners regardless of their ability (Upadhyaya et al., 2020)

2) Supporting teachers and educators, is the cornerstone of the educational process. This support should not necessarily be enforced by rules; another venue of resource should leverage on the profound desire of educators to positively impact the lives of their students. With adequate support from peers, colleagues and the whole educational community, teachers are and will be able to overcome all the difficulties addressed in literature: from lack of subject knowledge (Sentance & Csizmadia, 2017a), when present (Sentance et al., 2020) due to different studies and life experience, to lack of resources offered by schools and institutions and sense of isolation, a feeling that could affect educators from elementary school to higher education (Almstrum et al., 2005). In higher education the major reported challenges span curriculum engagement and retention, and course administration (Deitrick & Stowell, 2019). All these challenges have been addressed and will be addressed involving the educational community and society starting from the local context. Solutions could range from technological support from other institutions. For example, by donation of replaced technologies of data-center, resources that could represent a great solution in smaller situations. Institutions themselves support students with resources, such as by renting hardware, books and material.
3) Understanding the algorithm design, problem solving and programming process (Mcgettrick et al., 2005), transfer this in carefully designed individualized learning resources and assessment activities aimed at developing the competencies needed in a quickly evolving scientific and technological world. This requires a balancing of design and development, latest innovations often tightened to new and quickly evolving technologies with core lasting concepts and rigorous methodological approaches, tests, written and oral examinations, flexibility in exam date with at least a second chance for each semester, and resources and activities aiming at improving students life. Students have to be adequately supported in all educational settings from face to face, to blended, and online context, from developed to developing countries, from urban neighborhoods to rural areas (LeBlanc et al., 2020) scaffolding them in overcoming the many educational challenges they face in computing education (Piwek & Savage, 2020).
4) Engaging and retaining students with success measured both in the ability to attract new students and in strategies to avoid a high attrition rate. All available channels have to be used to meet this goal: from using multiple strategies to prepare and delivering content, to choosing a mix of pedagogical approaches to meet the needs of more learners, to preferring, especially in the first computing course, the simplest and most effective educational technology and tool rather than the most professional one (Bruce, 2018), and in general by providing "simpler models of computing as a discipline without neglecting the need for mathematical formalism (Mcgettrick et al., 2005) and rigorous scientific approach.
5) Continue and sustain the effort of the computing community in recognizing Computational Science "on par with other scientific disciplines" (Gal-Ezer & Stephenson, 2014) granting to all student at all educational levels, from elementary school through higher education, at least one computing course, possibly on an interdisciplinary setting (Amoussou et al., 2010). This still requires harmonizing both pre-university and university instruction where some countries are still lagging in this process.

CONVENIENCE

It is important that a quality education for all guarantees that all students have access to resources and instructions that enable all to fulfil their potential (Ibe et al., 2018), (Wobbrock et al., 2011). Missing this goal means denting access to invaluable resources for members of educational communities. To enable Special Educational Need or Disability (SEND) students to participate, it is necessary to:

1. Adhere to both the universal design in learning principles (S. E. Burgstahler & Cory, 2010)], (Rogers-Shaw et al., 2018) and Universal Design Instruction principles (S. Burgstahler, 2009)
2. Participate and put effort into one of the 25 ways that the Disabilities, Opportunities, Internetworking, and Technology (DO-IT, 2017) is changing the world (Dlab et al., 2020) through its programs.
3. Develop accessible resources. Having accessible resources and putting significant effort in developing such resources have a positive effect on the whole educational community. Many tools and resources are available. The Daisy consortium provides a comprehensive list of tools and resources for creation, conversion and validation of accessible publications (Park et al., 2019a). In this direction we could list some initiatives and tools:
    a. Poet Image description tool (Diagram center, 2015) and their guidelines for describing images, such as the flow chart guidelines (Diagram center, 2015).
    b. Captioning software like the Caption and Description Editing Tool (Cadet), developed by the National Center for Accessible Media (NCAM) at WGBH educational foundation (Foster & Connolly, 2017), (Linebarger, 2000) helps in completing an automated captioned video.
    c. Interactive video transcripts. Interactivity allows for searching the video using text phrases, running transcripts with synchronously highlighted text, and the possibility to click on the text and jump to the selected part on the video (Wildemuth et al., 2003).
    d. Tactile reading and digital talking book or spoken book (Argyropoulos et al., 2019) with a crowd-sourced volunteer effort in Europe and around the world. Crowd-sourcing the effort will allow a rich set of books to be available to a wide community beyond dyslexic and people facing visual difficulties. They can serve as great teaching and learning tools in-line courses with the multimedia requirements of 21st century learners.
    e. Use 3D Printing for creating tactile experiences.
4. Develop accessible hardware and software tools that will assist both in daily practice activities and in educational activities. Listing all the initiatives here would not be feasible. In the Computing domain we could cite some remarkable examples such as Integrated Development Environment (IDE) specifically designed for SEND learners (Milne & Ladner, 2019a).

Experience Report: The Master Lab for In-Service and Pre-Service and student Teachers for Special Ability Certification

In Italy, a significant nationwide effort has recently been implemented to train in-service, pre-service and teacher students for teaching SEND learners (Shinohara et al., 2018a) at all school levels from primary through high school. The effort culminated in multiyear educational initiatives spread nationwide with master courses for teachers. The courses, usually run in one or two years, provide in many cases a nationally recognized certification for teachers of SEND learners.

A laboratory in this master course was designed with these goals:

1) Provide the learners with information seeking tools and techniques applied to the domain of interest, eliciting the main reference points and information sources in the domain of interest. Provide an overview on who and what is taught around the world (Kawas et al., 2019a), (Shinohara et al., 2018a).

2) Provide the learners with Computational Thinking abilities using tools and techniques applied in an interdisciplinary setting to construct software and hardware tools as well as learning resources useful for people with special abilities. Test and get feedback from the students involved in their daily class activities, asking feedback with others in the same community.
3) Promote communication, collaborations and networking among teachers. Reflection and experience reports peer-lead meetings had a positive impact on the whole educational process.
4) Organize the activities around a curriculum delineated by special abilities focusing on technologies, pedagogies and content.
5) Favor project based pedagogies in group settings.
6) Leverage on tools such as concept maps (Cañas et al., 2004), (Liu et al., 2011), (Novak & Cañas, 2006) as a design tool useful for teachers and students.

The main difficulties faced during the programme were due to a severe lack of time for the participants. An overbooked schedule and a tight and tough master program contributed to a heavy cognitive overload in all participants, resulting in lost momentum in the educational activities despite the commitment of teachers and the dedication to their students. Self and group reflection using on-line communication means should be pursued for after-experience reflections. Blended and on-line instruction initiatives should be sought to avoid depleting time, energy and resources to teachers simply for reaching the campus location.

How Does Computing and CT Promote Convenience and Access for all Learners Within STEAM?

From the above discussions and from the authors' own experiences, the authors would raise the following points:

1) Computing tools, software, hardware and unplugged are all essential parts of the teaching practices.
2) CT can and should be used by teachers to co-develop with their colleagues simple and effective Apps and tools for solving real-life problems with their students, thereby improving their educational experiences. The developed products need to be tested with the students.
3) Involve in the design and development processes all the class members, infusing a culture of inclusiveness.

CUSTOMS

Educational systems and practices are culturally dependent. Even what we recognize as knowledge and skills (i.e. education) are colored by our life experiences. In some systems the emphasis is on rote learning with recitations used for assessment, while in others it is in guiding the students in constructing their own models of how the world works. In some cultures, learning is very individual while in others it is collaborative. Similarly, there is a range of practices from being competitive to being cooperative. These differences may lead to misunderstandings of standards of academic integrity. How cultural and ethical differences impact the teaching and learning of CT, and vice versa, is the subject of this section.

CT is grounded in constructivist educational theory in which the learner does not simply accumulate facts, but takes an active role in building models of subject knowledge. The ability to discern patterns, make inferences, generalize, sequentialize steps, etc. is integral with CT. There are cultures in which the goals of education tend toward making the grade or ultimately getting the job. In these cases, there may be increased impatience, temptation to seek shortcuts, to cut corners, to seek easier more convenient paths to their goals. Attempting to memorize everything is another resort which might work to some extent in some subjects, but is not possible in others including mathematics and Computer Science. The same can be said about learning by trial and error. However, CT is more immediate, being about the process rather than a more distant goal.

The perceived role and status of the teacher vis a vis the student, expectations for the students, classroom environment, assessment strategies, social stratification of the students, family involvement, pressure for personal excellence or cooperation, perception of education as being for technical/job skills vs. liberal arts or research, even the concept of work or job as the means to afford entertainment and sustenance rather than itself being the fulfillment of life's ambitions, all these culturally dependent characteristics have an impact on the receptiveness of students and teachers alike to CT (R. Morelli et al., 2009).

Cheating and other forms of academic integrity violations are defined by the school and understood in the context of the culture and ethics of the institution, the faculty, and the students (Gotterbarn et al., 2018), (ACM Code 2018 task force, 2018), (ACM Committee on Professional Ethics, 2018), (University South Australia, 2020), (Head, 2018), (S. J. Simon & M, 2016), (Riedesel, 2009). Our purpose is not to judge the ethical rightness or wrongness of academic practices (or mispractice), but instead to consider the impact on learning and inculcation of CT in the students (Bruce, 2018). In so much as such practices and tolerance of them results in students attempting to bypass the higher functioning of their minds, they are not appropriate for teaching CT. At the same time, it is essential for instructors to carefully consider the constraints on student behaviors, as to whether they are justified for ethical and academic purposes, or if they are imposed primarily because of traditional practice.

Teamwork can take many different forms. In its simplest implementation, all team members are expected to learn and be responsible for all aspects of the team project. This results in comparable learning by all students in the team and can be accomplished by the team members educating each other from their own individual discoveries and accomplishments. This may or may not be the objective of the learning experience, either case being justifiable depending on the circumstances. In some cultures, and educational environments, it is the practice for teams to have a more distributed learning experience in which multidisciplinary students contribute according to their own expertise, and none are expected to be responsible for the totality of the learning. Again, this may be justifiable depending on the circumstances.

Sometimes advantage can be made of customs of the region. For example, if there is a strong interest in competition (Burguillo, 2010) through the school sports program, that competitive spirit can be leveraged for programming competitions. Or if the students come from a culture of cooperation (D. W. Johnson et al., 2000), (Qin et al., 1995) and sharing, the projects can be created that both build on that culture and simultaneously incorporate features that ensure breadth of learning, and/or cater to the inclination to build for the common social good. Some institutions are located where there is emphasis and/or resources for special needs/abilities learners. These can be seen as opportunities for developing products that serve those populations.

The authors' experience suggests that attention be paid to all the above cultural and ethical considerations both for areas of concern and opportunities for learning (Guillén et al., 2007), (Bruce, 2018).

CITIZENSHIP

Today's digital technologies offer opportunities in all aspects of our daily life, and it is important to teach students how to be responsible digital citizens starting in primary school (Ribble & Bailey, 2007), educating them to be part of a sustainable technology development (Giordano & Maiorana, 2013c).

Humanitarian Free and Open Source Software (HFOSS) (H. J. Ellis et al., 2015a), (R. Morelli et al., 2009) collects projects designed and developed with a social benefit in mind. Projects are developed in the fields of health care, disaster management, accessibility assistance, economic development, education, and other areas of social need. The approach can be used in the daily teaching practice of students, including non-computing majors, in all types of activities, from commenting and documenting their projects, reading the code, reverse engineering it or contributing to existing projects or developing new ones. Activities and real life humanitarian projects that can be used from the first day of classes and activities in this regard can be found in (Goldweber et al., 2019). HFOSS projects represent a way to tackle the real challenges, i.e. addressing the real life challenges, such as granting jobs to the students, allowing them to spend their time learning while working instead of looking for jobs that are disconnected from their learning path. Too many times the lack of resources for students results in a real depletion of diversity to the computing and educational community.

According to (Maiorana, 2024) we elaborate on an experience report related to the development of educational resources related to digital citizenship with a leading international publishing house .

A Publishing Experience With an International Editor

Quality education for all should be supported by learning resources that are able to attract and retain all students offering them a rich set of low floor and high ceiling activities (Anonymized, 2019) spanning different domains, covering different topics and approaching education with a truly interdisciplinary and systemic approach that supports students in honing their talents and transforming their weaknesses into strengths. The experience emerged from the aspiration of the authors to craft and share learning resources with a wider public than the one their students met in class.

Context and Motivating Factors

The experience regards a project carried out with the collaboration of a leading international publishing house which involved a group of teachers and researchers in the development of a book related to digital education for teachers and their students in secondary education, with particular emphasis on grades 8 to 13. The publishing house has freely distributed the book to all the teachers of STEM disciplines in the Italian territory. Reflection on the experiences can be found in (Anonymized et al., 2022). A wealth of resources related to critically conscious computing in the realm of secondary education can be found in (KO et al., 2021).

The developed learning aims to (Gousetti, 2021) "capture the bigger and more complex picture of critical digital literacy as well as the complexity of the educational practice" in all areas of teaching.

Methods: Content, Pedagogies, and Technologies

During the experience, the above mentioned protocol was used in:

1) The call for experience which was launched in August 2021 by the chief editor of the publishing house who managed to invite a set of experts from all over Italy, including two authors of this work, The grade band of the audience was indicated.
2) The Asynchronous online negotiations on topics among the authors and decision on topics and index which were carried out in collaboration with the authors and managed by the chief editors and their team.
3) Discussion on a reporting template which was carried out during the negotiation phase in a three-month period with biweekly meetings with the authors.
4) The learning resources which were crafted by the authors and submitted for reviews by the editorial team and by a blind external review managed by the publishing house according to necessity. The drafting and reviewing process lasted another three months.
5) Alongside content, pedagogies and technologies were discussed with the editorial team through written reports during the drafting of the learning resources, the camera ready preparation and during the whole distribution phase, allowing the implementation of the sixth step of the protocol during the following four months
6) Finally, the sixth step for discussion and refinement was conducted during the next year, exploring improvement and collaboration possibilities.

Content

The experience regarded the design and development of three learning resources related to:

1) Source validation and verification and the online inquiry process.
2) Open and big data and their importance in developing competencies in searching, selecting, interpreting, analyzing and visualizing data sources for active digital citizenship.
3) Ecological footprint of Information and Communication Technologies and their ecological use.
4) Behaviors: how we use our time on the web.
5) Why it is important to share kindness.

Pedagogies

The learning resources (LR) were designed according to the following principles:

- Leverage on reviews and state of the art in research. i.e. supporting educational practice with research
- Use-case approach: adapt the same topic and learning path to different audiences: a) From lower to higher secondary school; b) Formal, non-formal and informal education
- Pre-test and post-test
- A flipped content approach (Maiorana, 2020): when possible, the topics are introduced using animations and short tests to guide student reflection. At the end of these preliminary steps, students are able to describe the content of the animation, including referencing technical details, and are ready to engage in meaningful class discussion, reflection and a deepening of their knowledge and understanding.

- ➢ Rich set of student-centered assessment activities, both formative and summative
- ➢ Solutions with a focus on the process rather than on the solution
- ➢ Rich set of references and web links

The LR and the associated activities have been designed with a flipped content approach in mind (Anonymized, 2020), facilitating student-centered approaches such as problem and project based learning. The plan is to involve teachers in the evaluation of the impact of the LR on the student learning path towards digital literacies in order to distill best practices to maximise the impact on students and develop their talents.

Other LRs related to the Digital selfhood and Digital overexposure sub-domains of Digital wellbeing and safety described in (Gouseti et al., 2021) are under development.

Technologies

The set of technologies suggested either directly, or implied, is ample, e.g.

1) Source validation: from the use of search engines to auto generative networks in artificial intelligence
2) Data: data visualization and analysis tools from spreadsheets to coding and databases with textual and visual block languages highly recommended for mastering advanced concepts such as parallel analysis of large volumes of data through maps and reduce primitive
3) Ecological footprint: exposure to all the technologies mentioned in the text and applications of tools spanning data retrieval, analysis and reporting to chemistry[1]
4) Time on the web: from data analysis to communication, collaboration, presentation and concepts organization tools
5) Kindness: from blog and online communication tools to artificial intelligence software

Findings and Reflections

In this chapter a research guided learning journey lasting decades have been summarized and several milestones can be identified, some of which have been highlighted in the chapters of this paper. By summarizing the work presented here, the main reflections and conclusion will be shared:

1) From the international comparison of the intended curricula guidelines and frameworks, the importance of formal reporting must be highlighted. The work presented in this chapter can be understood as a proof of concept and advocacy for self-reflection and reporting through research.
2) From the international comparison of the enacted curricula and on the field experience, the importance of teacher flexibility has emerged. To cope with this need, coupled with the even greater flexibility, required to address students' needs, when designing learning resources, it is imperative to have great variety at all levels: content, learning paths, type of media used in delivering the learning resources, type of assessment, level of deepening, formative and summative assessment, technologies, and so on.
3) The underlying and under the wood research based international comparison of intended and enacted curricula for each grade band can inspire, support, and sustain learning resource design, development, and assessment across adjacent grade bands, i.e., for this work, the first two years of

high school, final years of high school, undergraduate studies in this work. This chapter is intended as a proof of concepts in this direction.

4) The comparison of successive editions of computing curricula, e.g. the ACM computing curricula (Anonymized, 2020) and the process used for this comparison can be applied in other contexts, e.g., in relation to the previous point.
5) The competencies building process (Anonymized, 2020) performed through the curriculum design process must guide learning resource design, development and assessment enacting the identified competencies building process.
6) The importance of a research based collaborative effort demonstrates that teachers and educators are a key resource in the development of enacted curricula and the authors strongly support and sustain a view of their role as curriculum designers and as guides and coaches for curriculum consumption. Resources and reduced workload should be granted to teachers and educators, allowing for a sharper impact as learning resource designers offering their contributions in fulfilling the needs identified as most important for quality learning resources (Falkner, 2019b).
7) Data and data analysis should complement and support educators and whole learning communities in their daily activities.

FUTURE RESEARCH DIRECTIONS

As further steps we plan to map the curricula and learning material to international reference frameworks, such as the Informatics reference framework for Schools (Caspersen, 2022) while reflecting on Coding, Computational, Algorithmic, Design, Creative, and Critical Thinking in K-16 education acting as guest editor for the IEEE Transaction on Education special issue (Maiorana, 2023)[2].

In the long run, the ultimate goal of each and every educational action is to reduce the number of people neither in employment nor education and training. Besides providing inclusive access to quality education for all, actions must be taken to support students in their learning path after compulsory education. Leveraging previous international experiences in introducing computing in the USA (Morelli, 2014), where teachers received a stipend to attend a summer professional development course on computing and then taught the subject in the following school year, we advocate for financing, at the national level, school-led projects, assuring resources and grants for graduating students to attend the first three years of undergraduate education. The same students during the three years grant period will serve as near mentors for students attending school. In this way, the undergraduate students will develop their leadership role (Maiorana, 2022) and, instead of performing unrelated work, they can work on domains related to their learning path and contribute, under the supervision of the school teachers, to a quality learning path for the students aiming for high school graduation. We invite further discussion of this, and further ideas related to the theme, in Italian and International conferences, starting with the Scientix one, calling for a round table among educational research institutes, e.g., INDIRE, national evaluation institutes, e.g., INVALSI, ministry, and political representatives. Assessing the impact of some of the curricula design principles applied in designing the enacted curricula e.g., the flipped content (Maiorana, 2020), the interactive, inverted and spiral curriculum (Caspersen, 2022), along with pedagogical approaches (Caspersen, 2022), and technologies in setting up and implementing learning activities through adjacent grade levels could be an underlying research idea to be implemented and tested in one of the above envisaged school-led projects.

CONCLUSION

In this work the authors, with the support of research literature and their educational experience, have presented, compared, and contrasted the similarities and differences in educational perspectives in two continents, Europe, and America, in regard to CT and the interplay with respect to Content, Pedagogies and Technologies and how CoP can sustain the whole computing community composed of learners and educators. After reviewing the main tools that can be used, we shared the main lessons learned regarding the capability of CT to foster and sustain the development of 21st computing competencies, creativity, collaboration and communication, and digital citizenship and how CT can be fostered through competition, and assessed. The main conclusions are the following:

1. The need for educators to develop accessible and inclusive resources, content, pedagogical practice and technologies, and differentiated learning trajectories suitable to all learners and differentiable to their educational needs. To reach this ambitious goal the richest set of tools and activities, including formative assessments, educational games, and competitions, must be used.
2. Despite the effort already in place, there is still space to expand the exposition to computing in an interdisciplinary setting to all learners from kindergarten through higher education. A rationalization of the curriculum for non-majors in many countries and in international settings should couple the effort to introduce computing in schools at all levels, especially where some countries are still lagging.
3. All students should be exposed to ethics during all learning paths.

As a further work we plan to do the following:

1) Develop accessible and inclusive learning resources and assessment activities, suitable for use in face to face, blended and online activities.
2) Test the effectiveness of the developed content using a qualitative and quantitative approach.
3) Leverage on data mining and learning analytics to better personalize student learning experience and scaffold on the learning process to improve it.

REFERENCES

ACM Committee on Professional Ethics. (2018) *Using the Code.* ACM. http://ethics.acm.org/code-of-ethics/using-the-code/

Almstrum, V. L., Guzdial, M., Hazzan, O., & Petre, M. (2005). Challenges to computer science education research. In *Proceedings of the Thirty-Sixth SIGCSE Technical Symposium on Computer Science Education* (SIGCSE) (pp. 191-192). ACM. 10.1145/1047344.1047415

Amoussou, G. A., Boylan, M., & Peckham, J. (2010). Interdisciplinary computing education for the challenges of the future. In *Proceedings of the 41st ACM Technical Symposium on Computer Science Education* (pp. 556-557). ACM. 10.1145/1734263.1734449

Argyropoulos, V., Paveli, A., & Nikolaraizi, M. (2019). The role of DAISY digital talking books in the education of individuals with blindness: A pilot study. *Education and Information Technologies*, *24*(1), 693–709. doi:10.1007/s10639-018-9795-2

Binkley, M., Erstad, O., & Herman, J. (2014). Defining twenty-first century skills. In *Assessment and Teaching of 21st Century Skills* (pp. 17–66). Springer Netherlands. doi:10.1007/978-94-007-2324-5_2

Bocconi, S., Chioccariello, A., Dettori, G., Ferrari, A., & Engelhardt, K. (2016). Developing Computational Thinking in Compulsory Education. No. JRC104188). [Seville site]. *Joint Research Centre*, *2016*, 1–68. doi:10.2791/792158

Bruce, K. B. (2018). Five big open questions in computing education. *ACM Inroads*, *9*(4), 77–80. doi:10.1145/3230697

Burgstahler S. (2009). *Universal Design of Instruction (UDI): Definition, Principles, Guidelines, and Examples*. DO-IT. 2009.

Burgstahler, S. E., & Cory, R. C. (2010). Universal Design in Higher Education: From Principles to Practice. Harvard Education Press; 2010.

Burguillo, J. C. (2010). Using game theory and competition-based learning to stimulate student motivation and performance. *Computers & Education*, *55*(2), 566–575. doi:10.1016/j.compedu.2010.02.018

Cañas AJ, Hill G, & Carff R. (2004). *CmapTools: A knowledge modeling and sharing environment.*

Caspersen, M. E., Gal-Ezer, J., McGettrick, A., & Nardelli, E. (2018)... *Informatics for All The Strategy.*, *2018*. doi:10.1145/3185594

Corradini, I., & Nardelli, E. (2021). Promoting digital awareness at school: A three-year investigation in primary and secondary school teachers. *Proceedings of EDULEARN21 Conference, 5, 6th*. Iated. 10.21125/edulearn.2021.2162

Crick, T., & Sentance, S. (2011, November). Computing at school: stimulating computing education in the UK. In *Proceedings of the 11th Koli Calling International Conference on Computing Education Research* (pp. 122-123). ACM. 10.1145/2094131.2094158

Csizmadia, A., Curzon, P., Dorling, M., Humphreys, S., Ng, T., Selby, C., & Woollard, J. (2015). *Computational thinking-A guide for teachers.*

CSTA. (2016). *K-12 Computer Science Framework*. Computer Science Teachers Association. https://K12cs.org/downloads/

CSTA. (2020). *Computer Science Teachers Association. Standards for Computer Science Teachers*. CSTA. https://csteachers.org/teacherstandards

Cutts, Q., Patitsas, E., & Cole, E. (2017). Early developmental activities and computing proficiency. In: *ITiCSE-WGR 2017 - Proceedings of the 2017 ITiCSE Conference on Working Group Reports. Vol 2018-January*. Association for Computing Machinery. 10.1145/3174781.3174789

Deitrick, E., & Stowell, J. (2019). *Survey of Computer Science teaching: challenges and resources in U.S. colleges and Universities. 2019.* Codio INC. www.codio.com/research/2019-computer-science-teaching-survey

Denning, P. J. (2017). Remaining trouble spots with computational thinking. *Communications of the ACM, 60*(6), 33–39. doi:10.1145/2998438

Dlab, M., Boticki, I., Hoic-Bozic, N., & CL-C&, E. (2020). *Exploring group interactions in synchronous mobile computer-supported learning activities.* Elsevier. https://www.sciencedirect.com/science/article/pii/S036013151930288X

Do-IT. (2017). *DO-IT Retrospective Our First 25 Years.* University of Washington.

Ellis, H. J. C., Hislop, G. W., Jackson, S., & Postner, L. (2015). Team project experiences in humanitarian free and open source software (HFOSS). *ACM Trans Comput Educ., 15*(4), 1–23. doi:10.1145/2684812

Falkner, K., Sentance, S., Vivian, R., Barksdale, S., Busuttil, L., Cole, E., Liebe, C., Maiorana, F., McGill, M. M., & Quille, K. (2019b). An International Study Piloting the MEasuring TeacheR Enacted Computing Curriculum (METRECC) Instrument. *Proceedings of the Working Group Reports on Innovation and Technology in Computer Science Education, 2019,* 111–142. doi:10.1145/3344429.3372505

Falkner, K., & Sheard, J. (2019). Pedagogic Approaches. The Cambridge handbook of computing education research, 445. Cambridge. doi:10.1017/9781108654555.016

Fincher, S. A., & Robins, A. V. (Eds.). (2019). *The Cambridge handbook of computing education research.* Cambridge University Press. doi:10.1017/9781108654555

Foster, J., & Connolly, R. (2017). Digital Media for STEM Learning: Developing scientific practice skills in the K-12 STEM classroom with resources from WGBH and PBS LearningMedia. In: *AGU Fall Meeting Abstracts.*

Franke, B., & Osborne, B. (2015). Decoding CS principles: A curriculum from Code. org. In *Proceedings of the 46th ACM Technical Symposium on Computer Science Education (ACM);* (pp. 713-713). ACM. 10.1145/2676723.2678309

Gal-Ezer, J., & Stephenson, C. (2014). A tale of two countries: Successes and challenges in K-12 computer science education in Israel and the United States. *ACM Trans Comput Educ., 14*(2), 1–18. doi:10.1145/2602483

Giordano, D., & Maiorana, F. (2013a). Teaching database: a pedagogical and curriculum perspective. In *Proceedings of the International Conference on Information and Communication Technology for Education, (ICTE),* (pp. 237-248). IEEE.

Giordano, D., & Maiorana, F. (2013b). Business Process Modeling and Implementation A 3-Year Teaching Experience. In *Proceedings of the 5th International Conference on Computer Supported Education (CSEDU-2013),* (pp. 429-436). IEEE.

Giordano, D., & Maiorana, F. (2013c). An interdisciplinary project in sustainable development based on modern visual programming environments and web 2.0 technologies. In: *2013 3rd Interdisciplinary Engineering Design Education Conference.* IEEE.

Goldweber, M., Kaczmarczyk, L., & Blumenthal, R. (2019). Computing for the social good in education. *ACM Inroads, 10*(4), 24–29. doi:10.1145/3368206

Gotterbarn, D. W., Brinkman, B., Flick, C., Kirkpatrick, M. S., Miller, K., Vazansky, K., & Wolf, M. J. (2018). ACM code of ethics and professional conduct.(2018). ACM. Https://Www. Acm. Org/Code-of-Ethics

GousetiA.BruniI.IlomäkiL.LakkalaM.MundyD.RaffaghelliJ.RanieriM.RoffiA.RomeroM.RomeuT. (2021). Critical Digital Literacies framework for educators - DETECT project Report 1. Developing Teachers' Critical Digital Literacies (DETECT) project, Erasmus+, KA2, European Union. Zenodo. doi:10.5281/zenodo.5070329

Guilford, J. P. (1967). Creativity: Yesterday, Today and Tomorrow. *The Journal of Creative Behavior, 1*(1), 3–14. doi:10.1002/j.2162-6057.1967.tb00002.x

Guillén M, Fontrodona J, Rodríguez-Sedano A. (2007). *The Great Forgotten Issue: Vindicating Ethics in the European Qualifications Framework (EQF).* Springer. doi:10.1007/s10551-007-9515-0

Guzdial, M. (2020). Sizing the U.S. student cohort for computer science. *Communications of the ACM, 63*(2), 10–11. doi:10.1145/3374764

Head, G. (2018). Ethics in educational research: Review boards, ethical issues and researcher development. *European Educational Research Journal.* doi:10.1177/1474904118796315

Hoppe, H. U., & Werneburg, S. (2019). Computational thinking—More than a variant of scientific inquiry. Computational Thinking Education, 13–30.

Howells, K. (2018). *The Future of Education and Skills: Education 2030: The Future We Want.* Create Canterbury. http://create.canterbury.ac.uk/17331/1/E2030 Position Paper (05.04.2018).pdf

Ibe, N. A., Howsmon, R., Penney, L., Granor, N., De Lyser, L. A., & Wang, K. (2018). Reflections of a diversity, equity, and inclusion working group based on data from a national CS education program. In: *SIGCSE 2018 - Proceedings of the 49th ACM Technical Symposium on Computer Science Education. Vol 2018-Janua.* Association for Computing Machinery, Inc. 10.1145/3159450.3159594

Johnson D W, Johnson, R T, Stanne, M B (2000). *Cooperative learning methods: A meta-analysis.*

Kawas, S., Vonessen, L., & Ko, A. J. (2019). Teaching accessibility: A design exploration of faculty professional development at scale. In: *Proceedings of the 50th ACM Technical Symposium on Computer Science Education.* ACM. 10.1145/3287324.3287399

Krishnamurthi, S., & Fisler, K. (2019). Programming Paradigms and Beyond. The Cambridge handbook of computing education research, 377. Cambridge Press. doi:10.1017/9781108654555.014

Lancaster, T., Robins, A. V., & Fincher, S. A. (2019). Assessment and Plagiarism. The Cambridge handbook of computing education research. Cambridge Press. doi:10.1017/9781108654555.015

LeBlanc, C. A., Newcomb, J., & Rheingans, P. (2020). First Generation-Rural Computer Science Students. Association for Computing Machinery (ACM). doi:10.1145/3328778.3372662

Lemay, D., & Basnet, R. (2017). Algorithmic thinking, cooperativity, creativity, critical thinking, and problem solving: Exploring the relationship between computational thinking skills and academic performance. *Journal of Computers in Education*, *4*(4), 355–369. doi:10.1007/s40692-017-0090-9

Lewis, C. M., Shah, N., & Falkner, K. (2019). Equity and Diversity. The Cambridge handbook of computing education research, 481. Cambridge Press. doi:10.1017/9781108654555.017

Linebarger, D. L. (2000). Summative evaluation of Between the Lions: A final report to WGBH Educational Foundation. *Univ Kansas Kansas City, Kansas*, *3*, 2010.

Liu, C.-C., Chen, H. S. L., Shih, J.-L., Huang, G.-T., & Liu, B.-J. (2011). An enhanced concept map approach to improving children's storytelling ability. *Computers & Education*, *56*(3), 873–884. doi:10.1016/j.compedu.2010.10.029

Maiorana, F. (2018). *Computational Thinking and Humanities*. Didamatica.

Maiorana, F. (2019). Interdisciplinary Computing for STE (A) M: a low Floor high ceiling curriculum. *Innovations, Technologies and Research in Education, 37*.

Maiorana, F. (2020). A flipped design of learning resources for a course on algorithms and data structures. International Conference on Interactive Collaborative and Blended Learning, (pp. 268–279). Springer. 10.1007/978-3-030-67209-6_29

Maiorana, F. (2021). From High School to Higher Education: Learning Trajectory for an Inclusive and Accessible Curriculum for Teachers and Their Students. [IJSEUS]. *International Journal of Smart Education and Urban Society*, *12*(4), 36–51. doi:10.4018/IJSEUS.2021100104

Mcgettrick, A., Boyle, R., Ibbett, R., Lloyd, J., Lovegrove, G., & Mander, K. (2005). Grand Challenges Grand Challenges in Computing: Education-A Summary. *The Computer Journal*, *48*(1), 42–48. doi:10.1093/comjnl/bxh064

Miller, L. D., Soh, L.-K., Chiriacescu, V., Ingraham, E., Shell, D. F., Ramsay, S., & Hazley, M. P. (2013). Improving learning of computational thinking using creative thinking exercises in CS-1 computer science courses. *2013 Ieee Frontiers in Education Conference (Fie),* (pp. 1426–1432). IEEE.

Milne, L. R., & Ladner, R. E. (2019). Position: Accessible Block-Based Programming: Why and How. In: 2019 IEEE Blocks and Beyond Workshop (B&B). IEEE.

Morelli, R., Tucker, A., Danner, N., De Lanerolle, T. R., Ellis, H. J. C., Izmirli, O., Krizanc, D., & Parker, G. (2009). Revitalizing computing education through free and open source software for humanity. *Communications of the ACM*, *52*(8), 67–75. doi:10.1145/1536616.1536635

Novak, J. D., & Cañas, A. J. (2006). The theory underlying concept maps and how to construct them. *Florida Inst Hum Mach Cogn.*, *1*(1), 1–31.

OECD. (2021). *PISA 2021 Creative Thinking Framework* (*Vol. 53*, pp. 1689–1699). OECD.

OECD. (2020). OECD learning compass 2030. *COMPASS 2030 Conceptual Learning Framework*. OECD. www.oecd.org/education/2030-project.

Owens, T. L. (2017). Higher education in the sustainable development goals framework. *European Journal of Education*, *52*(4), 414–420. doi:10.1111/ejed.12237

Park, J. H., Kim, H.-Y., & Lim, S.-B. (2019). Development of an electronic book accessibility standard for physically challenged individuals and deduction of a production guideline. *Computer Standards & Interfaces*, *64*, 78–84. doi:10.1016/j.csi.2018.12.004

Pecanin, E., Spalevic, P., Mekic, E., Jovic, S., & Milovanovic, I. (2019). E-learning engineers based on constructive and multidisciplinary approach. *Computer Applications in Engineering Education*, *27*(6), 1544–1554. doi:10.1002/cae.22168

Piwek, P., & Savage, S. (2020). Challenges with Learning to Program and Problem Solve. *An Analysis of Student Online Discussions Conference or Workshop Item Challenges with Learning to Program and Problem Solve: An Analysis of Student Online Discussions.*, *2020*, 494–499. doi:10.1145/3328778.3366838

Qin, Z., Johnson, D. W., & Johnson, R. T. (1995). Cooperative versus competitive efforts and problem solving. *Review of Educational Research*, *65*(2), 129–143. doi:10.3102/00346543065002129

Ribble, M., & Bailey, G. (2007). *Digital Citizenship in Schools, Mike Ribble and Gerald Bailey*. Info-World. www.infoworld.com/article/05/11/22/hnonlineshoppers_1.html.

Riedesel, C. P., Manley, E. D., Poser, S., & Deogun, J. S. (2009). A model academic ethics and integrity policy for computer science departments. *SIGCSE Bulletin*, *41*(1), 357–361. doi:10.1145/1539024.1508994

Robins, A. V. (2019). Novice programmers and introductory programming. The Cambridge handbook of computing education research, 327. Cambridge Press. doi:10.1017/9781108654555.013

Rogers-Shaw, C., Carr-Chellman, D. J., & Choi, J. (2018). Universal design for learning: Guidelines for accessible online instruction. *Adult Learning*, *29*(1), 20–31. doi:10.1177/1045159517735530

Romero, M., Lepage, A., & Lille, B. (2017). Computational thinking development through creative programming in higher education. *International Journal of Educational Technology in Higher Education*, *14*(1), 42. Advance online publication. doi:10.1186/s41239-017-0080-z

Santo, R., Vogel, S., DeLyser, L. A., & Ahn, J. (2018). Asking “CS4What?” as a basis for CS4All: Workshop tools to support sustainable K-12 CS implementations. In *Proceedings of the 49th ACM Technical Symposium on Computer Science Education* (pp. 678-686). ACM.

Savage, M., & Csizmadia, A. (2018). Computational thinking and creativity in the secondary curriculum. In *Debates in Computing and ICT Education* (pp. 137–152). Routledge. doi:10.4324/9781315709505-10

Sentance, S., & Csizmadia, A. (2015). Teachers’ perspectives on successful strategies for teaching Computing in school. (2015, June). In IFIP TCS.

Sentance, S., & Csizmadia, A. (2017). Computing in the curriculum: Challenges and strategies from a teacher’s perspective. *Education and Information Technologies*, *22*(2), 469–495. doi:10.1007/s10639-016-9482-0

Sentance, S., Singh, L., & De Freitas, P. (2020). *Challenges Facing Computing Teachers in Guyana*. ACM. doi:10.1145/3328778.3372613

Shinohara, K., Kawas, S., Ko, A. J., & Ladner, R. E. (2018). Who teaches accessibility? A survey of US computing faculty. In: *Proceedings of the 49th ACM Technical Symposium on Computer Science Education*. ACM. 10.1145/3159450.3159484

Simon, S. J. & Morgan, M. (2016). Negotiating the maze of academic integrity in computing education. In: *Proceedings of the 2016 ITiCSE Working Group Reports, ITiCSE 2016*. Association for Computing Machinery. 10.1145/3024906.3024910

Sirocchi, C., Pofantis, A. O., & Bogliolo, A. (2022). Investigating Participation Mechanisms in EU Code Week. arXiv preprint arXiv:2205.14740.

Tedre, M., & Denning, P. J. (2016). The long quest for computational thinking. In: *ACM International Conference Proceeding Series*. Association for Computing Machinery. 10.1145/2999541.2999542

Ulrich Hoppe, H., & Werneburg, S. (2019). Computational Thinking—More Than a Variant of Scientific Inquiry! In *Computational Thinking Education* (pp. 13–30). Springer Singapore. doi:10.1007/978-981-13-6528-7_2

University of South Australia. Resource on Academic Integrity. Retrieved on April 2, 2020 at https://lo.unisa.edu.au/course/view.php?id=6751&section=6

Upadhyaya, B., McGill, M. M., & Decker, A. (2020). A longitudinal analysis of k-12 computing education research in the united states: Implications and recommendations for change. In: *Annual Conference on Innovation and Technology in Computer Science Education, ITiCSE*. Association for Computing Machinery. 10.1145/3328778.3366809

Wing, J. M. (2016). *Computational thinking, 10 years later*. Microsoft Research. https://www.microsoft.com/en-us/research/blog/computational-thinking-10-years-later/.

Wobbrock, J. O., Kane, S. K., Gajos, K. Z., Harada, S., & Froehlich, J. (2011). Ability-based design: Concept, principles and examples. *ACM Transactions on Accessible Computing*, *3*(3), 1–27. doi:10.1145/1952383.1952384

Yadav, A., Gretter, S., Hambrusch, S., & Sands, P. (2016). Expanding computer science education in schools: Understanding teacher experiences and challenges. *Computer Science Education*, *26*(4), 235–254. doi:10.1080/08993408.2016.1257418

ENDNOTES

1 https://www.chimicaconimattoncini.it/

2 https://ieee-edusociety.org/special-issue-coding-computational-algorithmic-design-creative-and-critical-thinking-k-16-education

Chapter 8
Supporting Novice Programmers via the Lens of Instructional Design

Ghadah Fayez Almutairy
https://orcid.org/0000-0003-3692-8567
Imam Abdulrahman Bin Faisal University, Saudi Arabia

Alicia L. Johnson
Virginia Tech, USA

ABSTRACT

As the need for skilled computer programmers increases each year globally, so does the need for learning environments that serve the novice programmer. This literature review aims to contribute to the field of computer science education by highlighting successful practices reported in the literature and describing those practices through the lens of instructional design. As the demand for programmers increases, the success of novice programmers remains stagnant. By reviewing research-based instructional practices through the lens of instructional design, instructional designers, researchers, and CS, instructors can make purposeful design decisions in the future that help to meet the needs of the growing number of novice programmers. This chapter highlights the importance of instructional design theories and learning methods in meeting the diverse needs of computer science learners.

INTRODUCTION

The need for skilled computer programmers has shown continued growth over the last several years. The necessity to fill the many jobs created through the growth of the computer industry with skilled programmers has led to colleges and universities around the world developing computer science degree programs as well as non-degree programs that highlight the skills attributed to computer programming such as problem-solving, computational thinking, and creativity (Verma et al., 2019).

The need for success in the education of future programmers has invited decades of research that seeks to determine what instructional approaches are most successful in producing the skilled global

DOI: 10.4018/979-8-3693-1066-3.ch008

workforce being sought after by employers (Peslak et al., 2018). The meta-analyses of research by Scherer et al. (2020, p.15) focused on computer programming interventions (such as blended learning, collaboration, feedback, game-based learning, metacognition, problem solving, and others) in a variety of settings from 1965-2017, they concluded that they found no evidence "for the superiority of specific interventions, such as collaborative activities, feedback-based instruction, or game-based learning in programming". As these findings resemble other "no significant difference" studies in education, such as the comparison between distance education and face-to-face education (Lockee et al., 1999), it may be helpful to consider Computer Science (CS) research and education from a different perspective.

Scherer et al. (2020) suggest the following as 'important' in the instruction of computer science: student prior knowledge, student self-efficacy, the learning context, aligning instructional approaches with specific learners, process feedback for gaining metacognitive skills, as well as multiple approaches to enhance student programming skills.Those elements are all standard practices suggested by the field of instructional design (Larson & Lockee, 2014). As more non-majors are taking CS courses and students are arriving at college less prepared than previous generations of CS learners (Ashcraft et al., 2016; Lahtinen et al., 2005), it may be an excellent time to determine who is succeeding at learning in CS, who is not and why? And what lessons can educators take into future course designs and instructional practices? Approaching these new audiences from the perspective of Instructional Design may be relevant for future instructional designs and research in this area.

The objective of this chapter is to look at the literature of computer science learning, CS learner characteristics, and specific challenges present in CS instruction with novice learners. It also includes strategies supported by the learning sciences that have been shown to be successful in CS instruction and learning. This chpater is not designed to solve design problems per se, but more to explore the literature for the purpose of possible future interventions.

BACKGROUND

Increased Demand for Computer Science Education

Before 2008 computer programming was already considered a critical skill for the labor market (Liao & Bright, 1991; Robins et al., 2003). The U.S. The Bureau of Labor Statistics (BLS, 2023) indicates that computer and information technology (IT) jobs are expected to increase by 11 percent between 2019 to 2029; far faster than the rate for all occupations (BLS, 2020). The past decade has seen an increase in the need for not only skilled programmers in the workforce (National Academies of Sciences, Engineering, and Medicine (NASEM), 2018), but also for fields that value the same skills attributed to computer programming activities such as "reasoning skills, logical thinking and planning skills, and general problem-solving skills" (Liao & Bright, 1991, p. 262; Scherer et al., 2020). The Computing Research Association's 2015 survey reports graduate programs in the U.S. and Canada show non-degree graduate students enrolled in CS mid-level courses from 2005-2015 grew by 265% and upper-level CS courses by 146% (Computing Research Association, 2017). This trend is likely to continue as the National Academies of Sciences, Engineering, and Medicine's 2018 report on the growth of undergraduate CS numbers shows only 37% of their survey participants identified as workers in the CS field, indicating the demand for computer science courses is not confined to those in the profession (NASEM, 2018). The National Center for Women and Information Technology indicates about 58% of the new positions in

STEM are related to computing jobs as well as many non-STEM jobs in industries requiring computer skills (Ashcraft et al., 2016). The participation in CS courses has risen at a comparable pace among non-majors and those majoring in the field, indicating the increasing value of programming skills in the overall workforce and workers' daily lives.

Computer Science Education

Computer science programs are attracting students with relevant background knowledge as well as those new to the field. With this in mind, it is becoming increasingly more important to be able to teach those non-majors and novices entering CS courses in a successful way.

Among the various computer science courses students can take is computer programming, which is considered to be a complex and demanding activity that includes many sub-tasks related to different levels of knowledge and cognitive processes (Ambrósio et al., 2011; Pea & Kurland, 1983). Logical reasoning, analytical and imaginative thought, problem analysis, solution generation, critical thinking, mathematical skills, and procedural skills are the most essential skills in learning programming (Ambrósio et al., 2011; Akar & Altun, 2017). As the study of programming languages requires complex cognitive skills, the individual differences between learners at various stages of programming and problem-solving skill development must be considered when designing CS curricula (Akar & Altun, 2017) as thinking like a programmer "may be an entirely different experience than thinking like a non-programmer" (Onorato & Schvaneveldt, 1987, p. 357).

From this point it is important to understand the nature of the programming and coding field. Coding is more about following steps in order to apply a specific command or solve a specific logical or mathematical problem. In other words, the user is "telling a computer what to do" (Nyisztor, 2019, p.5). While programming consists of a hierarchy of sub-skills, and the mastery of programming comes in a sequence rather than holding a particular block of knowledge (Jenkins, 2001). There are also intermediate skill levels that track the progression from novice to expert which include: novice level, advanced beginner, competence level, proficiency level, and expert level (Dreyfus & Dreyfus, 1986). The time it takes to acquire new skills varies throughout the progression from novice to expert, for example, experienced programmers can respond and "acquire new skills" by exploiting their previous experiences in contrast with novices (Kato, & Watanabe, 2006, p.827). Learners with more expertise can follow the steps taught to them more easily when applying a command or writing a program. These same steps may serve as a learning obstacle to novices or less experienced learners (Akar & Altun, 2017). Studies dealing with various levels of programmers advocate for instructors to develop and implement specific instructions to support the less-skilled programmers and reduce cognitive load in the novice learners (Mason et al., 2016).

Novice Programmers

The term novice learner is used to describe a beginner who has no previous knowledge or experience about the current content (Laakso et al.,2007). Learning theorists explain through schema theory that each learner comes to the learning experience with prior knowledge and experiences. These experiences are organized in the learner's memory as schemata. These schemata "guide and govern performance as one undertakes some task or attempts to solve some problem" (Driscoll, 2014, p. 130). Therefore, one of the main differences between the novice and the expert programmer is "novices have only low-level representations of programming knowledge, whereas experts have representations at both abstract and concrete levels" (Rist, 1989, p. 392). In programming instruction that focuses on problem-solving, novices sometimes provide simplistic solutions based on inadequate comprehension and interpretation of the problem that needs to be solved (Kokotovich, 2008). In other words, novice learners are "typically limited to surface knowledge of programs" (Lahtinen et al., 2005, p. 15). Prior knowledge and expertise are often content specific which means an expert can be a specialist in the computer science field, however, the same learner could be a "novice at upper division material such as network design or parallel programming" (Winslow, 1996, p.18). As instructors with CS expertise recognize these differences in students' skills and knowledge, they may find it challenging to put themselves in the novices' shoes as Guzdial (2015 p.33) stated that it is"hard to see with the novices' eyes. It's hard for expert computer scientists to see the students' misconceptions, but it's critical".

Learner Characteristics

Novice learners have many characteristics. One fundamental feature that characterizes novice programmers from the experts is the ability to develop solutions. Expert programmers have deeper and more developmental skills in writing programs and finding solutions as well as the expert physics scientist with their advanced ability in reasoning (Rist, 1989). To illustrate, Anderson (1983, p.295) indicated that experts "tend to develop problem solutions breadth first, whereas novices develop their solutions depth first". That means novice learners use the simplest tricks to solve coding issues compared to experts who tend to be more familiar with codes and would operate broader and deeper functions than the simplest approaches. The second critical difference is the decision-making process, where learners face problems that require high-level cognitive skills to solve. The logical analysis of the expert learner differs from that of the novice learner. Where the expert learner resorts to thinking in a deeper analytical manner and maybe 'outside the box' compared to the novice learner who may have difficulty in making decisions (Perez & Emery, 1995).A third important difference involves the mental model structure between the novices and the experts. The novice learners' mental models may be incomplete and unstable (Norman, 1983) compared to the expert learners who have the more advanced organized mental models (Kessler & Anderson, 1986; Visser & Hoc, 1990). A fourth difference is that expert learners have more in-depth experience and knowledge related to the subject matter. In contrast, novice learners may have limited information to draw from to develop appropriate responses to solving problems (Winslow, 1996). A fifth difference concerns strategies for dealing with problems. Since the nature of programming languages is basically about problems and solutions, both the novice and the expert have their individual approaches to solving problems. Experts often use a classification method with problems to gain deeper insight, while novices often deal with problems from the surface level. Experts tend to find answers to not only how do they solve that? But also, why do they know that? (Chi et al., 1981; Sweller, 1988).

Lastly, the procedure of dealing with the provided instruction. Experts like to chunk and divide instruction. It helps them to have a clever perspective and allows more timely and creative solutions. Novices often look at the problem as a whole chunk, thus affecting their problem-solving approach and attempted solutions (Eylon & Reif, 1984).

Novice Learner Challenges

Many beginner programmers experience substantial difficulties in the learning process (Nandigam & Bathula, 2013). This is not restricted to a particular form of programming language or a particular programming society. It is a challenge addressed by many undergraduates (Sarpong et al., 2013). Some novice CS learner challenges are not necessarily different than the many challenges all first and second year students face when learning the foundational skills of a new major (Fields, 2018; Stephenson et al., 2018).

Challenges related to the nature of acquired skills gained by the novices includes the lack of problem-solving skills, lack of analytical skills, lack of logic and reasoning skills, and lack of algorithmic skills (Ismail et al., 2010; Butler & Morgan, 2007; Sarpong et al., 2013). Arriving to courses with a lack of these skills, negatively affects the students' continued learning of these skills. Deek and colleagues (1998) point out that it's not just important to gain these skills, specifically problem-solving skills, to do well in a *current* semester, but "there is also the concern that students retain the knowledge and skills that they acquire so that they can be applied in later courses and in the real world" (Deek, Kimmel, & McHugh, 1998, p. 313). Consequently, the weakness of a novice's prior knowledge may affect their ability to gain further skills in a timely manner. This may result in a low-level learning progression causing a negative rippling effect in future course success compared with the achievements of learners who have more prior knowledge who may be able to progress more successfully (Lister et al., 2004). The aim of teaching programming languages and codes is to provide opportunities for students to build skills and develop abilities in producing computer programs (Sarpong et al., 2013). It is essential to recognize the multiple achievement level differences among individuals in computer programming courses (Bishop-Clark, 1995). When numerous advanced learners are experiencing better performance, conversely, other learners may *not* be.

In Lahtinen, Ala-Mutka and Jarvinen's (2005) international study of the difficulties of novice programmers, they found the biggest problem of novice programmers from 6 different universities from 6 different countries did "not seem to be the understanding of basic concepts, but rather learning to apply them" (p. 17). Their study also showed, more than half (58.6%) of the 559 student participants reported having previous programming experience before attending the university. This means close to half of the students *did not.* The study also reported (40.6%) of the student participants reporting prior experience, believed that their programming skills were at least moderate. Researchers concluded that "students in a programming class often may have very different experience levels, which makes it difficult to design the teaching so that it would be challenging and interesting for everyone." Of course, if faculty is focused on making the course "challenging and interesting for everyone" in a course where half are experienced and half are not, they may not fully meet the needs of the novice learner whose challenges may exceed their ability in the early stages of learning (Lahtinen et al., 2005).

The struggle novice students have in developing necessary problem-solving skills for programming may be a result of lack of experience in problem-solving in general that results in a slower acquisition of higher level problem-solving skills (Chi, Bassok, Lewis, Reimann, & Glaser, 1989; Pirolli & Recker, 1994; Gerdes, Jeuring, & Heeren, 2010). Learners hoping to gain the knowledge base necessary for programming and coding courses require significant time to experience building codes and programs in practice settings. The learner's ability to acquire necessary problem-solving skills, may not be the results of lack of prior knowledge alone, but rather its relationship to the significant role of practice (Nandigam & Bathula, 2013). The novice learners may require more time to learn than the more experienced students. As the struggles of novice CS learners have remained steady throughout the literature, the variety of strategies has changed over time. The strategies that seem to represent promise and success in the literature seem to be theoretically based and purposefully included in the course design to serve the novice learners.

Instructional Strategies

There are several decades of research supporting the use of theory-based instructional practices and the instructional design process. Research has already shown that building a program is one of the most challenging tasks that novice learners can deal with (Caspersen & Bennedsen, 2007; Robins et al., 2003). The rationale behind this complexity remains motivated by many reasons like the precious essence of the language, the learner, the instructor, the tutor, the environment, as well as other factors that influence the challenge of learning such languages. For more than 40 years, and even with rapid technological advancements, teaching programming is still known as a challenging task and subject for both teacher and learner (Mcgettrick et al., 2005; Butler & Morgan, 2007; Tan et al., 2009; Qian & Lehman, 2017). Despite researchers' efforts and attempts to find solutions to this issue using many strategies and tools, this problem still exists (Deek et al., 1998; Lawrence et al., 1994; Stephenson et al., 2018). The question remains, what do teachers need to make learning programming languages more accessible, especially for beginners? What does the learner need to develop his or her programming skills and move from a beginner to an expert learner? Reviewing the literature from the perspective of theoretically based practices for CS instruction follows.

Theoretically-Based Computer Science Instructional Practices

Computer science instructors play a significant role in affecting learners' progression in developing codes and programs. Many years of studies in programming language instruction have shown the way the instructor facilitates learning is important (Chang, Chiao, Chen, & Hsiao, 2000; Ismail et al., 2010; Robins et al., 2003). This role may include providing specific strategies to students learning programming languages or building an appropriate learning environment to enable learners in reaching the instructional goals. (Chang et al.,2000). However, teaching programming languages to novice learners can be a challenging task for teachers (Bennedsen & Caspersen, 2008; Kranch, 2011; Robins et al., 2003).

The teaching strategies of programming languages have taken many forms over the years, for example, advanced intelligent tutoring technology, collaborative style, and technology enhanced learning strategies, all have proven to show an efficient impact on the educational process. Many of the successful strategies described in the literature can be associated with theoretically based practices. This section will offer how some of the solutions from the literature on teaching programming align with ID practices.

The theories ID relies on in practice offer a focal point for various studies attempting to use ID to solve CS learning and performance problems, for example, Caspersen and Bennedsen's (2007) study on using a theoretic approach to designing a programming course. They focused on three theories from the learning sciences: cognitive load theory, cognitive apprenticeship, and worked examples. These theories (discussed in more detail later in the paper) were utilized by Caspersen and Bennedsen (2007) to guide their approach to designing a programming course (p. 111). They noted that they found no studies in the literature at the time of their study which applied cognitive load theory to the instructional design of introductory computer programming courses. As mentioned previously, many novice students arrive to courses with little or no prior knowledge which means when they are sitting in class, they are most likely experiencing cognitive load. The learner with little or no prior knowledge (schemata) "must hold in mind all elements of the task individually and simultaneously" (Driscoll, 2014, p. 136). Designing courses that allows the novice learner time to build their schema might serve to create a strong foundation for them to progress through a CS program. Caspersent and Bennedsen (2007) state their course design has been successfully used at their university for 4 years with over 400 students experiencing cognitive theories of learning strategies designed into their courses.

Cognitive Theories of Learning in Computing Education

It is important for computer science instructors to be conscious of the challenges and problems that novice and inexperienced programmers may have as "it is difficult to teach computer programming to students with either little prior knowledge of programming or weak problem-solving skills" (Sands, 2019, p.44). Several studies in the area of computer science have explored the challenges of novices to understand their learning limitations to reach desired instructional objectives (Skiena & Revilla, 2003; Albusays & Ludi, 2016). One common explanation behind problems novices face is cognitive load which is frequently discussed in the literature as a lack of prior knowledge (Lahtinen et al., 2005; Rist, 1989; Scherer et al., 2020).

The concept of cognitive load is derived from cognitive psychology and was originally developed by John Sweller. Cognitive load is associated with the working memory where all the mental cognitive processes occur (Chandler & Sweller, 1996). It is also based on the idea of the limited capacity of short-term memory, which can only perceive and process limited elements of information (Miller, 1956). Such working memory limitations cause a significant restriction on mental functioning. In addition, cognitive load theory differentiates three types of cognitive load: Intrinsic Load (IL), Extraneous Load (EL), and Germane Load (GL) (Leppink, Paas, Van der Vleuten, Van Gog, & Van Merriënboer, 2013). Intrinsic Load (IL) involves the "task complexity and the learner's prior knowledge," while Extraneous Load (EL) involves the "instructional features that are not beneficial for learning," and Germane Load (GL) involves the "instructional features that are beneficial for learning" (Leppink et al., 2013, p.1058). In the case of programming, Intrinsic Load (IL) will be affected by a student's prior knowledge (Kalyuga, 2009). Extraneous Load (EL) may be affected by excessive or confusing instruction as well as the learning environment that may negatively affect the learning process and contribute to distractions (Kalyuga, & Hanham, 2011). Germane Load (GL) should be affected (increased) as the learner engages with the learning more successfully and "constructs and automates the appropriate schema or mental model that pertains to the particular class of problems to be solved" (Driscoll, 2014, p. 137; Van Merrienboer & Sweller, 2005). Researchers assert that reducing cognitive load during the programming learning process is challenging (Cakiroğlu, Suiçmez, Kurtoğlu, Sari, Yildiz, & Öztürk, 2018; Mead et al.,, 2006; Renkl & Atkinson, 2003; Stachel et al., 2013). Additionally, in developing computer programming instructions, Garner (2002) emphasized the significance of considering the cognitive load principles and its effects on various learners' levels of performance. Moreover, Chandler and Sweller (1996) noted that instructional design often plays a crucial function when there is a high level of involvement between learning components, resulting in certain factors being consistently retained in working memory because "All problem-based searching makes heavy demands on working memory" (Kirschner, Sweller,

& Clark's, 2006, p. 77). Consequently, for novice programmers in particular, an educator may look for the recommended solutions that can solve or at least minimize the cognitive loads. In addition to cognitive load theory, strategies such as worked examples, pair programming, and cognitive apprenticeships can reduce cognitive load, build schema, and enhance learning for novice programmers (Caspersen & Bennedsen, 2007).

Worked Examples

The worked examples approach has been discussed in the programming education literature. "The worked examples literature is particularly relevant to programs of instruction that seek to promote skill acquisition, e.g., music, chess, and programming (Atkinson et al., 2000, p.181)." Worked examples are defined as "instructional devices that provide an expert's problem solution for a learner to study" (Atkinson et al., 2000, p.181). Worked examples act as a scaffolding system for learning as students interact with programming problems and acquire new coding commands (Sands, 2019). Worked examples facilitate problem-solving by helping learners experience a decreased cognitive load, which may enhance learning abilities in the solution manufacturing process (Sweller & Cooper, 1985). In agreement with Atkinson, Derry, Renkl and Wortham (2000) suggest the worked examples must be optimized to ensure guidance despite the additional information. Worked examples assist and empower learners' capabilities to perform fundamental tasks in coding, and achieve subgoals successfully (Catrambone, 1998) as the inexperienced and novice learners appear to require more assistance and advice when learning compared to the more experienced learners (Kirschner, Sweller, & Clark, 2006).

There is considerable discussions among researchers in the CS and Education fields as to how to best implement worked examples into programming instruction. Segal and Ahmad (1993) noted that in learning programming languages, worked examples may be considered as the primary source of the learning material, mainly when the provided exercises resemble the required assignments. The first step in developing worked examples is to associate the chunks of the information or the problem with the desired sub goals of the lesson (Catrambone, 1998; Caspersen & Bennedsen, 2007). The second step is to apply the worked examples within the developing instructions effectively. It is important for instructors and instructional designers to recognize the instructional strategy and match it with the suitable examples as a scaffolding system and support technique specifically when the instructions are designed for novice problem-solving with a surface approach instead of with depth like the experts (VanLehn, 1998). Worked examples is one instructional strategy that addresses cognitive load. Often successful instruction is achieved through a combination of strategies. In addition to designing instruction that reduces the student's cognitive load, designing instruction that includes modeling and explicit guidance to students as they maneuver through the type of ill-structured problems necessary to computer science learning. Such practices can be developed through cognitive apprenticeships

Cognitive Apprenticeship

"Cognitive apprenticeship is a model of instruction that works to make thinking visible" (Collins et al.,1991, p. 1). In the cognitive apprenticeship, instructors model their ways to solve problems or complete a task, observe, facilitate, and encourage learners to articulate and reflect their tasks (Kirschner & Hendrick, 2020).

According to Lee (2011), in the application of cognitive apprenticeship "resolving complex, real-world tasks requires implicit knowledge that is not easily recognizable to novice learners" (p.529). Basically, the cognitive apprenticeship is based on " the ancient model of apprenticeship education where a profession is learned while working under the guidance of a senior master." (Vihavainen et al., 2011, p.94). In particular, the central principle in this approach is to provide beginner and inexperienced learners with all the resources they need to conduct various complicated tasks (Collins et al., 1991).

The use of cognitive apprenticeships is shown to have a positive impact in the programming discipline (Astrachan & Reed, 1995; Black, 2006; Caspersen & Bennedsen, 2007; Kölling & Barnes, 2004). There are 6 elements present when applying cognitive apprenticeships successfully: Modeling (Explanation), Coaching, Scaffolding, Articulation, Reflection, and Exploration (Collins, 2006). The social characteristics of the learning environment has also been shown to be beneficial to the cognitive apprenticeship practice (Collins et al., 1991). The social characteristics of cognitive apprenticeship capitalizes on students being able to help each other reach their learning goals (Brown et al.,1989; Kirschner & Hendrick 2020; Knobelsdorf et al., 2014).

Social Cognitive Approach

One instructional approach used to enhance novice learning is a paired or collaborative approach. This approach is an example of a social cognitive learning strategy. Social Cognitive Theory (SCT) is a learning theory that describes learning as a constant interaction between the learner's environment, behavior and cognitions (Bandura, 1997). Collaborative programming is a planned interaction between two programmers who are engaging together within the learning process, designing, developing codes, and building programs (Lui & Chan, 2006). Beck and Chizhik (2013) emphasized that learners' engagement in solving problems is a type of collaborative learning where both learners benefit from each other in order to modify their learning. Collaborative work supports learners and encourages a collaborative effort to succeed in difficulties and challenges (Kirschner et al., 2018). The two programmers identified as the "driver" (who is responsible for writing the code) and the "observer" or the "navigator" (who is responsible for reviewing the code line by line as it is being typed) (Williams, 2001, p.27, Hulkko & Abrahamsson, 2005). Sands (2019) suggests using the strategy of having the two programmers switch between their roles frequently in order to enhance their learning skills and interactivity through programming tasks. The shared process and responsibilities between two programmers allow both of them to participate and share their thoughts, which eventually draw the path for the correct solutions.

Individual levels are different in each educational setting, but within the pair programming technique it is better to indicate the partners from the same level. Pair programming is a collaborative approach where two programmers work together on a single computer project ().Although Noesk (1998) pointed out that the procedure of the pair programming within the beginner programmers is more efficient compared with the performance of the other individuals' skill levels, a practice of pair variation can include all skills levels. Pair variations include three levels: expert to expert, expert to novice, and novice to novice (Lui & Chan, 2006; Williams & Kessler, 2003; Cockburn & Williams, 2000). According to Williams and Kessler (2003), the expert to novice level provides many opportunities for both novice and expert; it can likewise propose new concepts, as the novice is more likely to ask questions while the expert is assumed to explain the tasks. While the novice-to-novice level is shown to be more beneficial than individualized novice coding, a proper role model is needed to encourage novices to develop their skills together (Cockburn & Williams, 2000). Pair programming technique has been shown to have a positive impact on learning programming compared to the individualized coding method (Canfora, Cimitile, Garcia, Piattini, & Visaggio, 2007; Cockburn & Williams, 2001; Williams & Kessler, 2003). Working in pairs is efficient particularly to learners with low levels of prior experience (Lui & Chan, 2006; Williams, 2000). In the time of COVID-19 this practice can be achieved remotely as well (Flor, 2006). Lastly, pair programming is a social pedagogical practice that requires instructors to train learners to make sufficient interactions to ensure engagement in order to enhance learners' abilities to code efficiently (Hanks et al., 2004; Tsai, Yang, & Chang, 2015).

Behaviorism and Computing Education

Perhaps one of the well-known statements within behaviorism theory is that our behavior "is more likely to reoccur if it has been rewarded or reinforced" (Driscoll, 2014, p.35). The advent of behaviorism as a theory of learning has influenced learning and instruction, and the field of instructional design, for decades. Examples of applications of behavioral principles include programmed instruction, task analysis, behavioral objectives, practices and feedback (Richey,et al, 2010, p. 54-56).

Programmed instruction is a method of presenting new subject matter to students through a sequence of steps with corresponding activities. Students work through the programmed material at their own pace and test their knowledge through formative assessments after each step (Miller & Malott, 2006). Programmed instruction was originally created by B. F. Skinner to make the teaching and learning process more effective through timely feedback and allowing for more individual responses. Although Skinner's machine didn't stay in the mainstream, later versions of the idea have been created which include improvements such as "incorporating more human interaction, social reinforcers and other forms of feedback, larger and more flexible chunks of instruction, and more attention to learner appeal" (Molenda, 2008, p. 52). An attribute of programmed instruction is the provision of micro-instructions within those specific features of "content being presented in small, soundly, designed segments, learner interactions with the content, feedback provided to the learner through their interactions, and learner control over the pace of the content" (Kapp & Defelice, 2019, p.23). Providing learners with the ability to use self-paced practice is a vital strategy for novice learners. In the CS field, these types of approaches have proven successful (Emurian, 2007).

One example of programmed instruction in a CS learning environment is a web-based PI system (programmed instructions) designed to teach one of the fundamental programming languages: JAVA (Emurian, 2007). The PI system was built based on behaviorist principles and has been researched under a variety of contexts (Emurian, Holden, & Abarbanel, 2008; Emurian, Wang & Durham, 2003; Hu, Wang & Durham, 2000). Researchers of the PI system suggest that it should be designed to "the extent to which the knowledge or skill gained is generalizable to solve problems not explicitly taught or encountered with the tutor itself" (Emurian, 2007, p.70). The research indicated that the developed programmed instructions are represented based on the learner's interactions, and self-paced engagement. As the target users are various professional learners, the most significant feature of this research is the entry-skill evaluation of behavior, which is seen as a critical pre-step before beginning the instruction, primarily to provide appropriate instruction for an inexperienced programmer.

Emurian (2007) stated that the e-tutor included a rule-base questionnaire as an entry behavior examination which allows identification of the "baseline" knowledge of the learners (p.71). This step plays a significant role in identifying the learner's level from beginner to expert and helps to ensure that the provided instructions are appropriate to the learner's level of knowledge. The principles of behaviorist theory can be applied to the way instruction is provided via web-based or digital devices, especially when learners are coding. Such methods "focused on stimulus, response pairs," and trial and error learning (Conole & Oliver, p.85). Emurian's study does not just highlight the implementation of theoretical principles within the instructional design content, but also the ID practice of identifying the learners' prior knowledge and skill-levels, which is essential to avoid any learning obstacles.

E-tutoring systems have been a part of CS instruction and research for some time, for example, the Intelligent Tutoring Systems (ITS). ITS is a computer-based system that provides timely feedback and support to the interactive users (Psotka et al., 1988). The common features between the ITS examples is their supportive role for novice programmers. However, this support is missing practice with figuring out the programming mistakes that occurred while learning. Being able to analyze the causes behind common programming errors, may contribute to a more thorough interpretation of learners' performances (Bush et al., 2000).

Besides the Intelligent Tutoring Systems (ITSs), there are other approaches that instructors incorporate in their courses to enhance novice learning. Emerging technologies have proven to be a sufficient technique to enhance the learning process. Computer science instructors take advantage of the technology enhanced learning strategy by utilizing many tech tools in delivering instructions, for instance, mobile devices. A successful experience of investigating the impact of mobile devices in delivering computer science-based instruction appears in Fabic, Mitrovic, and Neshatian's (2018) study. In their research, Fabric and his colleagues aimed to develop an interactive tutor application via mobile smartphones in order to teach Python programming language. The Python tutoring purposed in developing learners' programming skills outside the classroom settings, where they can interact with the content anytime and anywhere. The result of this research indicates a significant impact of the Python tutoring application on acquiring coding skills specifically for the novice learners, and a positive correlation between pretest and posttest of the knowledge base of the provided instruction. The practice time students invest impacts their future progress. (Fabic, et al., 2018; Yildiz Durak, 2018). As new technology is examined through the lens of Instructional Design and Computer Science there will likely be more human-computer interactions in the design, development, instruction, and learning of computer science content.

Reconsidering the Instructional Design Role

As has been previously described, novice learner's lack many of the necessary skills that hinder their progress and have a negative effect on their ability to construct a program compared to the expert (or more experienced) learners (Jonassen, 2000). Researchers and educators from the CS field have worked towards solving this problem (Byrd, Ballantyne, Rosenblatt, & Might, 2017). Very little can be found in the literature that specifically focuses on Instructional Design theories to help solve novice CS student learning and performance problems. Instructional Design is "the process of solving instructional problems by systematic analysis of the conditions of learning" (Seels & Glasgow, 1998, p. 2). The systematic approach to solving learning and performance problems often uses an iterative process of analysis, design, development, implementation, and evaluation (Reiser, 2001, p. 57). Disciplines contributing to the field include educational psychology, general systems theory, and communication to name a few (Seels & Glasgow, p. 2). Various learning theories have been developed by researchers in cognitive psychology, psychology, and education which focus on how to create learning environments that enhance learning (Greeno et al., 1996).

Instructional design is "an applied, decision-oriented field," where learning theories are paradigms that provide information about human learning and knowledge acquisition (Smith & Regan, 2005, p.18). As a systemic progression, the instructional design domain analyzes learning requirements and performance challenges and offers concrete instructional approaches for instructional problems. Learning theories function as the fundamental theoretical basis for educators and also is a "significant element in ID practice, especially as it guides designers in the selection of instructional solutions" (Richey, et al, 2010, p. 63). All of the decisions made in the ID process are based on a thorough understanding of the learner and the learning process. The human learning process is explained through theories of learning and the ID process is guided by those theories. The successful design and instruction of CS courses can be studied through the lens of Instructional Design theories and practices, to inch CS instruction closer to achieving the desired goals.

SOLUTIONS AND RECOMMENDATIONS

The findings of this chapter emphasize the essential significance of instructional design in facilitating computer science education and programming. This is achieved by utilizing well-established theories as the fundamental principles for successful teaching methods. The incorporation of educational theories and models, such as constructivism, cognitive load theory, and worked examples has shown a substantial influence on the understanding and practicing of programming among students (Garcia et al., 2018). To enhance instructional design in computer science education, it is crucial to customize techniques according to the varied learning styles and cognitive abilities of the learners (Thomas et al., 2002). This entails integrating experiential exercises, cooperative ventures, and practical implementations to heighten involvement and foster deep comprehension.

For educators and instructional designers, it is recommended to consistently incorporate new technologies and interactive platforms to create an engaging learning environment. Adopting adaptive learning tools, virtual laboratories, and customized coding assignments can effectively cater to the unique prerequisites of learners with varying demands.

Additionally, continuous professional development for educators is crucial to guarantee competence in using modern instructional design approaches. Workshops and collaborative networks can enhance the sharing of exemplary methods and advanced approaches for integrating theories into programming instruction. At some point, the fusion of instructional design with fundamental theories in computer science education is crucial for fostering a vibrant and efficient learning encounter. By applying these suggestions, educators can establish an all-encompassing and engaging atmosphere that cultivates learners' programming capabilities and encourages a long-lasting enthusiasm for computer science.

CONCLUSION

This chapter has examined the crucial significance of instructional design in promoting the progress of computer science education and programming, based on fundamental theories. By following instructional design knowledge, educators and designers can develop pedagogical frameworks that accommodate various learning styles, learning techniques, and strategies to promote more effective knowledge. The significance of matching instructional practices with theoretical underpinnings has been highlighted, emphasizing the symbiotic relationship between theory and practice. The importance of instructional design approaches' adaptability grows as technology advances. By acquiring a thorough comprehension of theories, educators and designers can customize methods that not only improve technical skills but also foster critical thinking and problem-solving capabilities for all learners. This integration of theory and practical application is essential for the ongoing enhancement and advancement of computer science education, guaranteeing its efficacy in equipping learners for the ever-changing environment of the digital age.

REFERENCES

Akar, S. G. M., & Altun, A. (2017). Individual Differences in Learning Computer Programming: A Social Cognitive Approach. *Contemporary Educational Technology*, *8*(3), 195–213.

Albusays, K., & Ludi, S. (2016). Eliciting programming challenges faced by developers with visual impairments: exploratory study. In *Proceedings of the 9th International Workshop on Cooperative and Human Aspects of Software Engineering* (pp. 82-85). ACM. 10.1145/2897586.2897616

Ambrósio, A. P., Costa, F. M., Almeida, L., Franco, A., & Macedo, J. (2011, October 11-15). *Identifying cognitive abilities to improve CS1 outcome*. [Conference session].41st Annual Frontiers in Education Conference: Celebrating 41 Years of Monumental Innovations from Around the World, FIE 201, Rapid City, SD, United States. https://doi.org/10.1109/FIE.2011.6142824

Anderson, J. R. (1983). *The architecture of cognition*. Harvard University press.

Ashcraft, C., McLain, B., & Eger, E. (2016). *Women in tech: The facts*. National Center for Women & Technology (NCWIT).

Astrachan, O., & Reed, D. (1995, March). AAA and CS 1: the applied apprenticeship approach to CS 1. *In Proceedings of the twenty-sixth SIGCSE technical symposium on Computer science education* (pp. 1-5). ACM. 10.1145/199688.199694

Atkinson, R. K., Derry, S. J., Renkl, A., & Wortham, D. (2000). Learning from examples: Instructional principles from the worked examples research. *Review of Educational Research*, *70*(2), 181–214. doi:10.3102/00346543070002181

Bandura, A. (1997). A sociocognitive analysis of substance abuse: An agentic perspective. *Psychological Science*, *10*(3), 214–217. doi:10.1111/1467-9280.00138

Beck, L., & Chizhik, A. (2013). Cooperative learning instructional methods for CS1: Design, implementation, and evaluation. [TOCE]. *ACM Transactions on Computing Education*, *13*(3), 1–21. doi:10.1145/2492686

Bennedsen, J., & Caspersen, M. E. (2008). Optimists have more fun, but do they learn better? On the influence of emotional and social factors on learning introductory computer science. *Computer Science Education*, *18*(1), 1–16. doi:10.1080/08993400701791133

Bishop-Clark, C. (1995). Cognitive style, personality, and computer programming. *Computers in Human Behavior*, *11*(2), 241–260. doi:10.1016/0747-5632(94)00034-F

Black, T. R. (2006). Helping novice programming students succeed. *Journal of Computing Sciences in Colleges*, *22*(2), 109–114.

Brown, J. S., Collins, A., & Duguid, P. (1989). Situated cognition and the culture of learning. *Educational Researcher*, *18*(1), 32–42. doi:10.2307/1176008

Bureau of Labor Statistics, U.S. Department of Labor. (2023). *Occupational outlook handbook*. BLS. https://www.bls.gov/ooh/about/ooh-faqs.htm

Bush, W. R., Pincus, J. D., & Sielaff, D. J. (2000). A static analyzer for finding dynamic programming errors. *Software, Practice & Experience*, *30*(7), 775–802. doi:10.1002/(SICI)1097-024X(200006)30:7<775::AID-SPE309>3.0.CO;2-H

Butler, M., & Morgan, M. (2007). Learning challenges faced by novice programming students studying high level and low feedback concepts. *Proceedings ascilite Singapore*, (99-107).

Byrd, W. E., Ballantyne, M., Rosenblatt, G., & Might, M. (2017). A unified approach to solving seven programming problems (functional pearl). *Proceedings of the ACM on Programming Languages, 1*(ICFP), (pp. 1-26). ACM. 10.1145/3110252

Cakiroğlu, Ü., Suiçmez, S. S., Kurtoğlu, Y. B., Sari, A., Yildiz, S., & Öztürk, M. (2018). Exploring perceived cognitive load in learning programming via Scratch. *Research in Learning Technology*, 26.

Camp, T., Frieze, C., Lewis, C., Cannon Mindell, E., Limbird, L., Richardson, D., Sahami, M., Villa, E., Walker, H., & Zweben, S. (2018). *Retention in computer science undergraduate programs in the U.S.: Data challenges and promising interventions*. ACM.

Canfora, G., Cimitile, A., Garcia, F., Piattini, M., & Visaggio, C. A. (2007). Evaluating performances of pair designing in industry. *Journal of Systems and Software*, *80*(8), 1317–1327. doi:10.1016/j.jss.2006.11.004

Caspersen, M. E., & Bennedsen, J. (2007, September). Instructional design of a programming course: a learning theoretic approach. *In Proceedings of the third international workshop on Computing education research* (pp. 111-122). ACM. 10.1145/1288580.1288595

Catrambone, R. (1998). The subgoal learning model: Creating better examples so that students can solve novel problems. *Journal of Experimental Psychology. General*, *127*(4), 355–376. doi:10.1037/0096-3445.127.4.355

Chandler, P., & Sweller, J. (1996). Cognitive load while learning to use a computer program. *Applied Cognitive Psychology*, *10*(2), 151–170. doi:10.1002/(SICI)1099-0720(199604)10:2<151::AID-ACP380>3.0.CO;2-U

Chang, K. E., Chiao, B. C., Chen, S. W., & Hsiao, R. S. (2000). A programming learning system for beginners-a completion strategy approach. *IEEE Transactions on Education*, *43*(2), 211–220. doi:10.1109/13.848075

Chi, M. T., Bassok, M., Lewis, M. W., Reimann, P., & Glaser, R. (1989). Self-explanations: How students study and use examples in learning to solve problems. *Cognitive Science*, *13*(2), 145–182.

Chi, M. T., Feltovich, P. J., & Glaser, R. (1981). Categorization and representation of physics problems by experts and novices. *Cognitive Science*, *5*(2), 121–152. doi:10.1207/s15516709cog0502_2

Cockburn, A., & Williams, L. (2001). The costs and benefits of pair programming. In G. Succi & M. Marchesi (Eds.), *Extreme programming examined* (pp. 223–243). Pearson Education.

Collins, A. (2006). Cognitive apprenticeship. In K. R. Sawyer (Ed.), *The Cambridge handbook of the learning sciences* (pp. 47–60). Cambridge University Press.

Collins, A., Brown, J. S., & Holum, A. (1991). Cognitive apprenticeship: Making thinking visible. *American Educator*, *15*(3), 6–11.

Computing Research Association. (2017). *Generation CS: Computer Science Undergraduate Enrollments Surge Since 2006*. CRA. https://cra.org/data/Generation-CS/

Conole, G., & Oliver, M. (2006). *Contemporary perspectives in e-learning research: themes, methods and impact on practice*. Routledge. doi:10.4324/9780203966266

Da Silva Estácio, B. J., & Prikladnicki, R. (2015). Distributed pair programming: A systematic literature review. *Information and Software Technology*, *63*, 1–10. doi:10.1016/j.infsof.2015.02.011

Deek, F., Kimmel, H., & McHugh, J. A. (1998). Pedagogical changes in the delivery of the first-course in computer science: Problem solving, then programming. *Journal of Engineering Education*, *87*(3), 313–320. doi:10.1002/j.2168-9830.1998.tb00359.x

Dreyfus, H. L., & Dreyfus, S. E. (1986). *Mind over machine: the power of human intuition and expertise in the era of the computer*. Free Press.

Driscoll, M. P. (2014). *Psychology of Learning for Instruction*. Pearson.

Emurian, H. H. (2007). Programmed instruction for teaching Java: Consideration of learn unit frequency and rule-test performance. *The Behavior Analyst Today*, *8*(1), 70–88. doi:10.1037/h0100103

Emurian, H. H., Holden, H. K., & Abarbanel, R. A. (2008). Managing programmed instruction and collaborative peer tutoring in the classroom: Applications in teaching Java™. *Computers in Human Behavior*, *24*(2), 576–614. doi:10.1016/j.chb.2007.02.007

Emurian, H. H., Hu, X., Wang, J., & Durham, A. G. (2000). Learning JAVA: A programmed instruction approach using applets. *Computers in Human Behavior*, *16*(4), 395–422. doi:10.1016/S0747-5632(00)00019-4

Emurian, H. H., Wang, J., & Durham, A. G. (2003). Analysis of learner performance on a tutoring system for Java. In *Current issues in IT education* (pp. 46–76). IGI Global. doi:10.4018/978-1-93177-753-7.ch005

Eylon, B., & Reif, F. (1984). Effects of knowledge organization on task performance. *Cognition and Instruction*, *1*(1), 5–44. doi:10.1207/s1532690xci0101_2

Fabic, G. V. F., Mitrovic, A., & Neshatian, K. (2018). Investigating the effects of learning activities in a mobile Python tutor for targeting multiple coding skills. *Research and Practice in Technology Enhanced Learning*, *13*(1), 23. doi:10.1186/s41039-018-0092-x PMID:30613261

Field, K. (2018). A Third of Your Freshmen Disappear. How Can You Keep Them? *The Chronicle of Higher Education*, *64*(35), A8–A13.

Flor, N. V. (2006). Globally distributed software development and pair programming. *Communications of the ACM*, *49*(10), 57–58. doi:10.1145/1164394.1164421

Garcia, R., Falkner, K., & Vivian, R. (2018). Systematic literature review: Self-Regulated Learning strategies using e-learning tools for Computer Science. *Computers & Education*, *123*, 150–163. doi:10.1016/j.compedu.2018.05.006

Garner, S. (2002). Reducing the cognitive load on novice programmers (pp. 578-583). Association for the Advancement of Computing in Education (AACE).

Gerdes, A., Jeuring, J. T., & Heeren, B. J. (2010). Using strategies for assessment of programming exercises. *In Proceedings of the 41st ACM technical symposium on Computer science education* (pp. 441-445). ACM. 10.1145/1734263.1734412

Greeno, J. G., Collins, A. M., & Resnick, L. B. (1996). Cognition and learning. Handbook of educational psychology, 77, 15-46.

Guzdial, M. (2015). Learner-centered design of computing education: Research on computing for everyone. *Synthesis Lectures on Human-Centered Informatics*, *8*(6), 1–165. doi:10.1007/978-3-031-02216-6

Hanks, B., McDowell, C., Draper, D., & Krnjajic, M. (2004, June). Program quality with pair programming in CS1. *In Proceedings of the 9th annual SIGCSE conference on Innovation and technology in computer science education* (pp. 176-180). ACM. 10.1145/1007996.1008043

Hulkko, H., & Abrahamsson, P. (2005, May). A multiple case study on the impact of pair programming on product quality. *In Proceedings of the 27th international conference on Software engineering* (pp. 495-504). ACM.

Ismail, M. N., Ngah, N. A., & Umar, I. N. (2010). Instructional strategy in the teaching of computer programming: A need assessment analyses. *The Turkish Online Journal of Educational Technology*, *9*(2).

Jenkins, T. (2001). The motivation of students of programming. *In Proceedings of the 6th annual conference on Innovation and technology in computer science education* (pp. 53-56). ACM. 10.1145/377435.377472

Jonassen, D. H. (2000). Toward a design theory of problem solving. *Educational Technology Research and Development*, *48*(4), 63–85. doi:10.1007/BF02300500

Kalyuga, S. (2009). Knowledge elaboration: A cognitive load perspective. *Learning and Instruction*, *19*(5), 402–410. doi:10.1016/j.learninstruc.2009.02.003

Kalyuga, S., & Hanham, J. (2011). Instructing in generalized knowledge structures to develop flexible problem solving skills. *Computers in Human Behavior*, *27*(1), 63–68. doi:10.1016/j.chb.2010.05.024

Kansanen, P. (1999). Teaching as teaching-studying-learning interaction. *Scandinavian journal OF educational Research, 43*(1), 81-89.

Kapp, K. M., & Defelice, R. A. (2019). *Microlearning: Short and Sweet.* American Society for Training and Development.

Kato, K., & Watanabe, T. (2006, October). Structure-based categorization of programs to enable awareness about programming skills. In *International Conference on Knowledge-Based and Intelligent Information and Engineering Systems* (pp. 827-834). Springer, Berlin, Heidelberg. 10.1007/11893011_105

Kessler, C. M., & Anderson, J. R. (1986). Learning flow of control: Recursive and iterative procedures. *Human-Computer Interaction*, *2*(2), 135–166. doi:10.1207/s15327051hci0202_2

Kirschner, P. A., & Hendrick, C. (2020). Cognitive Apprenticeship" Revisited. *American Educator*, *44*(3), 37.

Kirschner, P. A., Sweller, J., & Clark, R. E. (2006). Why minimal guidance during instruction does not work: An analysis of the failure of constructivist, discovery, problem-based, experiential, and inquiry-based teaching. *Educational Psychologist*, *41*(2), 75–86. doi:10.1207/s15326985ep4102_1

Kirschner, P. A., Sweller, J., Kirschner, F., & Zambrano, J. (2018). From cognitive load theory to collaborative cognitive load theory. *International Journal of Computer-Supported Collaborative Learning*, *13*(2), 213–233. doi:10.1007/s11412-018-9277-y PMID:30996713

Knobelsdorf, M., Kreitz, C., & Böhne, S. (2014, March). Teaching theoretical computer science using a cognitive apprenticeship approach. In *Proceedings of the 45th ACM technical symposium on Computer science education* (pp. 67-72). ACM. 10.1145/2538862.2538944

Kokotovich, V. (2008). Problem analysis and thinking tools: An empirical study of non-hierarchical mind mapping. *Design Studies*, *29*(1), 49–69. doi:10.1016/j.destud.2007.09.001

Kölling, M., & Barnes, D. J. (2004). Enhancing apprentice-based learning of Java. *In Proceedings of the 35th SIGCSE technical symposium on Computer science education* (pp. 286-290). ACM. 10.1145/971300.971403

Laakso, M. J., Rajala, T., Kaila, E., & Salakoski, T. (2012) Novice Learning. In: Seel N.M. (Ed.), Encyclopedia of the Sciences of Learning. (2012). Springer. doi:10.1007/978-1-4419-1428-6_1520

Lahtinen, E., Ala-Mutka, K., & Järvinen, H. M. (2005). A study of the difficulties of novice programmers. *Acm sigcse bulletin, 37*(3), 14-18.

Larson, M. B., & Lockee, B. B. (2014). *Streamlined id: A practical guide to instructional design*. Routledge.

Lawrence, A. W., Badre, A. M., & Stasko, J. T. (1994, October). Empirically evaluating the use of animations to teach algorithms. *In Proceedings of 1994 IEEE Symposium on Visual Languages* (pp. 48-54). IEEE. 10.1109/VL.1994.363641

Lee, Y. J. (2011). Empowering teachers to create educational software: A constructivist approach utilizing Etoys, pair programming and cognitive apprenticeship. *Computers & Education*, *56*(2), 527–538. doi:10.1016/j.compedu.2010.09.018

Leppink, J., Paas, F., Van der Vleuten, C. P., Van Gog, T., & Van Merriënboer, J. J. (2013). Development of an instrument for measuring different types of cognitive load. *Behavior Research Methods*, *45*(4), 1058–1072. doi:10.3758/s13428-013-0334-1 PMID:23572251

Liao, Y. K. C., & Bright, G. W. (1991). Effects of computer programming on cognitive outcomes: A meta-analysis. *Journal of Educational Computing Research*, *7*(3), 251–268. doi:10.2190/E53G-HH8K-AJRR-K69M

Lister, R., Adams, E. S., Fitzgerald, S., Fone, W., Hamer, J., Lindholm, M., & Simon, B. (2004). A multinational study of reading and tracing skills in novice programmers. *SIGCSE Bulletin*, *36*(4), 119–150. doi:10.1145/1041624.1041673

Lockee, B. B., Burton, J. K., & Cross, L. H. (1999). No comparison: Distance education finds a new use for 'no significant difference'. *Educational Technology Research and Development*, *47*(3), 33–42. doi:10.1007/BF02299632

Lui, K. M., & Chan, K. C. (2006). Pair programming productivity: Novice–novice vs. expert–expert. *International Journal of Human-Computer Studies*, *64*(9), 915–925. doi:10.1016/j.ijhcs.2006.04.010

Mason, R., Seton, C., & Cooper, G. (2016). Applying cognitive load theory to the redesign of a conventional database systems course. *Computer Science Education*, *26*(1), 68–87. doi:10.1080/08993408.2016.1160597

Mcgettrick, A., Boyle, R., Ibbett, R., Lloyd, J., Lovegrove, G., & Mander, K. (2005). Grand challenges in computing: Education a summary. *The Computer Journal*, *48*(1), 42–48. doi:10.1093/comjnl/bxh064

Mead, J., Gray, S., Hamer, J., James, R., Sorva, J., Clair, C. S., & Thomas, L. (2006). A cognitive approach to identifying measurable milestones for programming skill acquisition. *SIGCSE Bulletin*, *38*(4), 182–194. doi:10.1145/1189136.1189185

Miller, G. A. (1956). The magical number seven plus or minus two: Some limits on our capacity for processing information. *Psychological Review*, *63*(2), 81–97. doi:10.1037/h0043158 PMID:13310704

Miller, M. L., & Malott, R. W. (2006). Programmed instruction: Construction responding, discrimination responding, and highlighted keywords. *Journal of Behavioral Education*, *15*(2), 109–117. doi:10.1007/s10864-006-9010-1

Milne, I., & Rowe, G. (2002). Difficulties in learning and teaching programming—Views of students and tutors. *Education and Information Technologies*, *7*(1), 55–66. doi:10.1023/A:1015362608943

Molenda, M. (2008). When effectiveness mattered. *TechTrends*, *52*(2), 53.

Murata, A., Bofferding, L., Pothen, B. E., Taylor, M. W., & Wischnia, S. (2012). Making connections among student learning, content, and teaching: Teacher talk paths in elementary mathematics lesson study. *Journal for Research in Mathematics Education*, *43*(5), 616–650. doi:10.5951/jresematheduc.43.5.0616

Nandigam, D., & Bathula, H. (2013). Competing dichotomies in teaching computer programming to beginner-students. *American Journal of Educational Research*, *1*(8), 307–312. doi:10.12691/education-1-8-7

National Academies of Sciences, Engineering, and Medicine. (2018). *Assessing and Responding to the Growth of Computer Science Undergraduate Enrollments*. The National Academies Press. . doi:10.17226/24926

Naveed, M. S., Sarim, M., & Ahsan, K. (2016). Learners Programming Language a Helping System for Introductory Programming Courses. *Mehran University Research Journal of Engineering and Technology, 35*(3), 347–358. doi:10.22581/muet1982.1603.05

Norman, D. A. (1983). Some observations on mental models. *Mental models, 7*(112), 7-14.

Nosek, J. T. (1998). The case for collaborative programming. *Communications of the ACM, 41*(3), 105–108. doi:10.1145/272287.272333

Nyisztor, K. (2019). *The non-programmer's programming book.*

Onorato, L. A., & Schvaneveldt, R. W. (1987). Programmer-nonprogrammer differences in specifying procedures to people and computers. *Journal of Systems and Software, 7*(4), 357–369. doi:10.1016/0164-1212(87)90034-3

Pea, R. D., & Kurland, D. M. (1983). On the cognitive prerequisites of learning computer programming. *New Ideas in Psychology, 2*(2), 137–168. doi:10.1016/0732-118X(84)90018-7

Perez, R. S., & Emery, C. D. (1995). Designer thinking: How novices and experts think about instructional design. *Performance Improvement Quarterly, 8*(3), 80–95. doi:10.1111/j.1937-8327.1995.tb00688.x

Peslak, A., Kovalchick, L., Kovacs, P., Conforti, M., Wang, W., & Bhatnagar, N. (2018). Linking Programmer Analyst Skills to Industry Needs: A Current Review. *In Proceedings of the EDSIG Conference ISSN* (Vol. 2473, p. 3857).

Pirolli, P., & Recker, M. (1994). Learning strategies and transfer in the domain of programming. *Cognition and Instruction, 12*(3), 235–275. doi:10.1207/s1532690xci1203_2

Psotka, J., Massey, L. D., & Mutter, S. A. (Eds.). (1988). *Intelligent tutoring systems: Lessons learned.* Psychology Press.

Qian, Y., & Lehman, J. (2017). Students' misconceptions and other difficulties in introductory programming: A literature review. [TOCE]. *ACM Transactions on Computing Education, 18*(1), 1–24. doi:10.1145/3077618

Renkl, A., & Atkinson, R. K. (2003). Structuring the transition from example study to problem solving in cognitive skill acquisition: A cognitive load perspective. *Educational Psychologist, 38*(1), 15–22. doi:10.1207/S15326985EP3801_3

Richey, R. C., Klein, J. D., & Tracey, M. W. (2010). *The instructional design knowledge base: Theory, research, and practice.* Routledge. doi:10.4324/9780203840986

Rist, R. S. (1989). Schema creation in programming. *Cognitive Science, 13*(3), 389–414. doi:10.1207/s15516709cog1303_3

Robins, A., Rountree, J., & Rountree, N. (2003). Learning and teaching programming: A review and discussion. *Computer Science Education, 13*(2), 137–172. doi:10.1076/csed.13.2.137.14200

Sands, P. (2019). Addressing cognitive load in the computer science classroom. *ACM Inroads, 10*(1), 44–51. doi:10.1145/3210577

Sarpong, K. A. M., Arthur, J. K., & Amoako, P. Y. O. (2013). Causes of failure of students in computer programming courses: The teacher-learner Perspective. *International Journal of Computer Applications*, *77*(12).

Scherer, R., Siddiq, F., & Viveros, B. (2020). A meta-analysis of teaching and learning computer programming: Effective instructional approaches and conditions. *Computers in Human Behavior*, *109*, 1–18. doi:10.1016/j.chb.2020.106349

Segal, J., & Ahmad, K. (1993). The Role of Examples in the teaching of Programming Languages. *Journal of Educational Computing Research*, *9*(1), 115–129. doi:10.2190/X63F-X1QX-V4KL-BJEX

Skiena, S. S., & Revilla, M. A. (2003). Programming challenges: The programming contest training manual. *ACM SIGACT News*, *34*(3), 68–74. doi:10.1145/945526.945539

Smith, P. L., & Ragan, T. J. (2005). *Instructional design*. John Wiley & Sons.

Stachel, J., Marghitu, D., Brahim, T. B., Sims, R., Reynolds, L., & Czelusniak, V. (2013). Managing cognitive load in introductory programming courses: A cognitive aware scaffolding tool. *Journal of Integrated Design & Process Science*, *17*(1), 37–54. doi:10.3233/jid-2013-0004

Stephenson, C., Derbenwick Miller, A., Alvarado, C., Barker, L., Barr, V., Seels, B., & Glasgow, Z. (2018). *Making instructional design decisions* (2nd ed.). Prentice Hall, Inc.

Sweller, J. (1988). Cognitive load during problem solving: Effects on learning. *Cognitive Science*, *12*(2), 257–285. doi:10.1207/s15516709cog1202_4

Sweller, J., & Cooper, G. A. (1985). The use of worked examples as a substitute for problem solving in learning algebra. *Cognition and Instruction*, *2*(1), 59–89. doi:10.1207/s1532690xci0201_3

The National Academic of Science, Engineering, and Medicine. (2017, October 26). *New Report: Colleges and Universities Should Take Action to Address Surge of Enrollments in Computer Science*. National Academics. https://www.nationalacademies.org/news/2017/10/colleges-and-universities-should-take-action-to-address-surge-of-enrollments-in-computer-science

Thomas, L., Ratcliffe, M., Woodbury, J., & Jarman, E. (2002). Learning styles and performance in the introductory programming sequence. *SIGCSE Bulletin*, *34*(1), 33–37. doi:10.1145/563517.563352

Tsai, C. Y., Yang, Y. F., & Chang, C. K. (2015, October). Cognitive load comparison of traditional and distributed pair programming on visual programming language. *In 2015 International Conference of Educational Innovation through Technology (EITT)* (pp. 143-146). IEEE. 10.1109/EITT.2015.37

Van Merrienboer, J. J., & Sweller, J. (2005). Cognitive load theory and complex learning: Recent developments and future directions. *Educational Psychology Review*, *17*(2), 147–177. doi:10.1007/s10648-005-3951-0

VanLehn, K. (1989). Problem solving and cognitive skill acquisition. In M. Posner (Ed.), *Foundations of cognitive science* (pp. 527–580). MIT Press. doi:10.7551/mitpress/3072.003.0016

Verma, A., Yurov, K. M., Lane, P. L., & Yurova, Y. V. (2019). An investigation of skill requirements for business and data analytics positions: A content analysis of job advertisements. *Journal of Education for Business*, *94*(4), 243–250. doi:10.1080/08832323.2018.1520685

Vihavainen, A., Paksula, M., & Luukkainen, M. (2011, March). Extreme apprenticeship method in teaching programming for beginners. *In Proceedings of the 42nd ACM technical symposium on Computer science education* (pp. 93-98). ACM. 10.1145/1953163.1953196

Visser, W., & Hoc, J. M. (1990). Expert software design strategies. In *Psychology of programming* (pp. 235–249). Academic Press. doi:10.1016/B978-0-12-350772-3.50020-3

Williams, L. (2001, February). Integrating pair programming into a software development process. *In Proceedings 14th Conference on Software Engineering Education and Training.'In search of a software engineering profession'(Cat. No. PR01059)* (pp. 27-36). IEEE.

Williams, L., & Kessler, R. R. (2003). *Pair programming illuminated.* Addison-Wesley Professional.

Winslow, L. E. (1996). Programming pedagogy—A psychological overview. *SIGCSE Bulletin*, *28*(3), 17–22. doi:10.1145/234867.234872

Yildiz Durak, H. (2018). Digital story design activities used for teaching programming effect on learning of programming concepts, programming self-efficacy, and participation and analysis of student experiences. *Journal of Computer Assisted Learning*, *34*(6), 740–752. doi:10.1111/jcal.12281

Chapter 9
Introducing Computational Thinking and Coding to Teacher Education Students

Hua Bai
https://orcid.org/0000-0003-1779-1892
Northeastern Illinois University, USA

ABSTRACT

The purpose of this chapter is to report a study that examined the development of teacher education students' computational thinking (CT) knowledge and coding skills in a graduate educational technology class. In this class, the students learned about CT and coding over four consecutive weeks. Twenty-one students participated in the study. The results indicated that the participants developed a foundational understanding of CT and coding. They recognized the value of integrating CT and coding into education, but they would hesitate to engage their students in coding activities in classrooms. Teachers' knowledge and skills, students' knowledge and skills, technology accessibility and in-class time management were four major concerns that the participants expressed in the study. Practical implications of the results were discussed to provide a reference for including CT and coding in educational technology classes.

INTRODUCTION

The interest in computer science (CS) education in K-12 contexts has greatly increased in the last decade (Kwon, Ottenbreit-Leftwich, Brush & Jeon, 2021; Upadhyaya, McGill & Decker, 2020; Weintrop, Hansen, Harlow & Franklin, 2018). Teachers, administrators, parents, policymakers and other stakeholders have recognized the importance of having students learn CS before they graduate from high school. According to the 2022 State of Computer Science Education report (Code.org, CSTA, & ECEP Alliance, 2022), 53% of high schools in the United States offer a foundational CS class, 3.9% of middle school students across 17 states, and 7.3% of elementary school students across 8 states took a foundational CS class. It was expected that in the next decade, almost every K-12 student would take CS classes (Tissenbaum & Ottenbreit-Leftwich, 2020).

DOI: 10.4018/979-8-3693-1066-3.ch009

CS "is the broad discipline that encompasses computing, CT, coding, and other branches dealing with computing connectivity and hardware" (Mason & Rich, 2019, p. 792). The K-12 Computer Science Framework (2016) consists of seven core practices to guide computer science education. Computational thinking (CT) is essential in the practices of the framework. Therefore, CT has become the focus of K-12 CS education.

To support K-12 CS education, it is important and necessary to prepare teacher education students. The purpose of this chapter is to report a study that examined the development of teacher education students' CT knowledge and coding skills in an educational technology class.

BACKGROUND

Computational Thinking

In current literature, researchers defined CT literally in different ways. According to Wing (2014), computational thinking was defined as "the thought processes involved in formulating a problem and expressing its solution(s) in such a way that a computer -human or machine - can effectively carry out" (section 1.1). This was echoed by Lodi (2020, p. 128), who analyzed different definitions of CT and concluded that "the most famous definitions share many characteristics. All agree CT is a form of thinking for solving problems by expressing the solution in a way that can be automatically carried out by an (external) processing agent". Although there is no consensus on a definition of CT and the fundamental components of CT, the common components that have been used by some researchers include abstraction, generalization, algorithms and decomposition (Cansu & Cansu, 2019).

Wing (2006) argued that CT is a fundamental skill for everyone in modern society and it should be in a child's analytical ability. Since then, there has been growing interest in developing students' CT knowledge and skills in K-12 education. It "is a skill today's students need to be taught, in order to adequately prepare for the workplace but also to be able to participate effectively in the modern digital world" (Papadakis, Kalogiannakis & Zaranis, 2016, p.190). Greater attention has been placed on integrating CT into elementary education (Tsortanidou, Daradoumis & Barberá, 2021). It was advocated that CT concepts should be introduced to students as early as elementary school (Flórez et al., 2017). Although CT derives from computer science, it can be developed in other subject areas including STEM disciplines (Kjällander, Mannila, Åkerfeldt & Heintz, 2021; Li et al., 2020; Sung, Ahn &. Black, 2017; Sung & Black, 2021), social studies and language arts (Moreno-León, Robles & Román-González, 2016), as well as art and social science (Sáez-López, Román-González & Vázquez-Cano, 2016) in elementary education. Butler and Leahy (2020, p. 63) concluded that "concepts of computational thinking are not developed in a decontextualized manner but are embedded within the prescribed curriculum across a range of subject content in a relevant and meaningful manner."

In general, there are two pedagogies to develop CT. One is the unplugged approach to teaching CT knowledge and skills through activities without using computers. The other is a commonly used approach to develop CT through learning to code or program on computers (Huang & Looi, 2021; Kjällander et al., 2021; Tsortaanidou et al., 2021).

Coding/Programming and Computational Thinking

Flórez et al. (2017, p. 836) argued that computer programming is the best approach to developing CT. The latter authors defined computer programming as "the process through which a person is able to provide a set of instructions that will communicate, as specifically and accurately as possible, a procedure, method, practice, or task to a machine". Technically, coding is "a type of computer programming" and is often used interchangeably to refer to the activities of providing "instructions for the computer to perform a specific task following a task" (Balanskat & Engelhardt, 2014, p. 9). In this chapter, the terms 'coding' and 'programming' refer to the same concepts.

Coding can be taught to students as early as preschool education (Papadakis et al., 2016; Papadakis, 2021). Although some researchers argued that coding or programming is not necessary to develop CT (Huang & Looi, 2021; Relkin, Ruiter & Bers, 2020; Tsortanidou, et al., 2021), "offering computational thinking strategies with coding as part of the curriculum in elementary schools, K-5 students will have the exposure to 21st century skills that enable them to be successful in their future careers" (Alexiou-Ray, Raulston, Fenton & Johnson, 2020; p.70). They are not only the problem-solving process but also enable students to express themselves and support their cognitive and social-emotional development (Herro, Quigley, Plank & Abimbade, 2021; Papadakis, 2021; Papavlasopoulou, Giannakos & Jaccheeri, 2019). Therefore, it is worth developing students' CT through programming or coding activities.

Scratch

Since teaching and learning programming syntax can be challenging in schools, block-based coding language is appropriate for K-12 education and has been widely used to teach programming concepts and computing (Mladenović, Boljat & Žanko, 2018; Papavlasopoulou et al., 2019; Rich et al., 2019; Sáez-López et al., 2016; Sung & Black, 2021). Block-based coding interface was found to be more effective in helping students learn computer science content than text-based interface (Weintrop, 2019). Scratch is a free block-based coding language that provides an interactive programming environment online. According to Weintrop (2019), Scratch is "the most successful (to date) block-based programming environment" (p. 23). The designers of Scratch intended to make it easy for everyone to program (Resnick et al., 2009). Users with limited or no programming background can explore and learn to code through trial and error (Mladenović et al., 2018).

Scratch was created to support CT (Resnick et al., 2009). The characteristics of Scratch have made it the most commonly used tool to support the development of CT through programming or coding (Sáez-López et al., 2016, Tikva & Tambouris, 2021). Prior research reported positive results in improving students' CT skills (Pérez-Marín, Hijón-Neira, Bacelo & Pizarro, 2020; Li, Xie, Vongkulluksn, Stein & Zhang, 2021) and CT self-efficacy (Özmutlu, Atay & Erdoğan, 2021) by using Scratch to code activities. Introducing coding through Scratch was found not only to develop CT but also to improve academic performance (Moreno-León et al., 2016; Rodríguez-Martínez, González-Calero & Sáez-López 2020).

Teacher Preparation

Teachers play a pivotal role in developing students' CT and coding skills (Ray, Rogers & Hocutt, 2020; Yadav, Gretter, Good & McLean, 2017). Ray et al. (2020) suggested that "before teachers can integrate coding into their instructional practice, they first must feel knowledgeable about and skilled, to some degree, in the concepts themselves" (p. 21). Some researchers reported professional development that supported in-service teachers in developing an understanding of CT (Hestness, Ketelhut, McGinnis & Plane, 2018; Ketelhut et al., 2020; Marcelino, Pessoa, Vieira, Salvador & Mendes, 2018; Yadav, Krist, Good & Caeli, 2018;) and how to integrate it into practice through coding (Jocius et al., 2021; Kong, Lai & Sun, 2020).

Lloyd and Chandra (2020) pointed out that, "The urgency of the requirement to teach coding and computational thinking means that this is an immediate issue for teacher education" (p. 189). If this knowledge and skills are preferred to be developed in elementary school (Flórez et al., 2017), elementary education students should be exposed to CT and coding in teacher preparation programs. It has been suggested that CT knowledge could be introduced to teacher education students in introductory educational psychology courses, educational technology courses, or content-specific methods courses (Yadav et al., 2017). Practical efforts have been taken to develop teacher education students' CT in methods classes (Kaya, Newley, Yesilyurt & Deniz, 2020; McGinnis et al., 2020). For example, Kaya et al. (2020) examined preservice teachers' CT teaching beliefs after they were introduced to CT, engaged in building robotics, coding in code.org and playing a video game in the last three weeks in an elementary science teaching methods class. They found that the preservice teachers improved their CT knowledge and increased CT teaching efficacy. However, there was no improvement in CT teaching outcome expectance.

Although CT concepts are naturally fit for STEM disciplines, CT knowledge and coding skills need to be integrated into teacher education for teachers of all subject areas (Ray et al., 2020). Since the students in educational technology courses learn various technologies available for use in practice to support student learning in different subject areas, such courses could better meet the expectations of preparing teacher education students to teach CT and coding. In an undergraduate educational education class, Zha, Jin, Moore and Gaston (2020) examined a flipped classroom CT module of one week and 75 minutes in which the preservice teachers used Hopscotch to learn about coding. Significant growth in CS/CT knowledge was found after the delivery of the module. However, they did not find significant changes in preservice teachers' attitudes toward CT or self-efficacy. Chang and Peterson (2018) exposed the teacher education students to CT using two different designs in an undergraduate educational technology class. After examining the students' reflections, they suggested that when building future teachers' expertise in CT, the educators could provide practical examples of CT integration, engage them in purposeful activities and allow the future teachers to explore CT concepts as their students. Ray et al. (2020) reported that coding experience across eight weeks in an online master's level technology integration course increased non-STEM teacher education students' perceptions of the value of coding and improved their motivation to integrate coding into teaching practice. Nevertheless, some of them were uncertain about their ability to introduce coding to their students. Guided by the framework of TPACK, Mouza, Yang, Pan, Ozden and Pollock (2017) redesigned an undergraduate-level educational technology course for K-8 preservice teachers to make it a CT-infused technology integration course. In this course, the preservice teachers learned CT concepts, computing tools and applications of CT in specific disciplines and pedagogy. This course developed preservice teachers' understanding of CT and its value in teaching, although they demonstrate different abilities to integrate CT with content and pedagogy. Interestingly, when the preservice teachers designed lessons, they did not choose to use any programming tools that were introduced to them. It was suggested that educational technology courses could offer training explicitly targeting programming in the learning of CT, which in turn would enable future teachers to help their students become creators of technology through the use of programming tools such as Scratch. These studies provided references for fostering teacher education students' knowledge and skills of CT and coding in educational technology classes.

Research Purpose

A stand-alone educational technology course is offered in most teacher education programs in the US. Such courses not only serve as the primary means to prepare teacher education students for technology integration but also influence the students' attitudes toward and beliefs about technology (Jin & Harp, 2020). If it is imperative that teacher education students need to be prepared to incorporate CT and coding in the classroom, the educational technology course should play an important role. This study intended to expand the understanding of developing teacher education students' CT knowledge and coding skills and preparing them to transfer the skills to future teaching practice in the educational technology class. Specifically, there are two questions:

1. How did the educational technology class help the participants develop knowledge and skills in CT and coding?
2. What were the participants' perceptions of CT and coding in education, as well as the integration of coding into teaching?

METHODS

Participants and Setting

The study was conducted in a graduate-level educational technology class at a four-year university. The class familiarized students with media technology for instructional use in K-8 classroom settings. When the study was conducted, there were twenty-six students in this class. The class met once each week remotely and each class session lasted 2 hours and 40 minutes. In this class, the students learned about CT and coding in a 4-week learning module by being engaged in various learning activities such as reading, lectures, online posts, projects, and self-assessments. The concept of CT was introduced to the students at the start of the learning module. Then they were exposed to coding with the use of Scratch. In the first two weeks, the students followed the tutorials in Scratch to learn to code and create simple coding activities, such as making a chase game or animating a character. Then, the students created a digital story. This enabled them to become familiar with the interface of Scratch and learn to code using different categories of blocks including motion, looks, sound, events, and control. In the third and fourth weeks, the students created a coding-integrated lesson plan and shared the work with their classmates.

A convenient sampling method was used. Of the twenty-six students, twenty-one students signed the research consent form and participated in this study. They took this educational technology class in the first semester of their graduate study. Five of them self-reported having prior experience in coding/programming on a computer or a mobile device including LOGO, SQL, and Maple. However, only one of them used a block-based coding program, Alice. In this class, it was their first time using Scratch.

Data Collection and Analysis

A mixed methodology was adopted. Data collected came from the participants' online posts, a quiz, a survey and course projects. In online posts, the participants shared their understanding of CT and coding, as well as their perceptions of the integration of coding into education. In addition to the online posts, the participants worked on two projects. In the first project, they used Scratch to create activities including a story. In the second project, the participants created a lesson plan in which coding activity is integrated to support student learning in a core content area. To assess learning, a quiz was administered to measure the participants' basic knowledge of CT and Scratch. At the end of the learning module, the participants took a survey that examined their perceptions of CT and coding activities in education. There were three parts in the survey. Part one consisted of six items from Yadav, Mayfield, Chou, Hambrusch and Korb's (2014) instruments and measured the participants' understanding of the definition of CT and their attitude toward using CT in classrooms. Part two and part three consisted of ten items that were modified from the instruments used by Ari, Arsian-Ari and Vasconcelos (2022) to examine participants' perceptions of coding in education and their perceptions of integrating coding into teaching practice. All the survey items were five-point Likert scale items ranging from 1 (Strongly disagree) to 5 (Strongly agree).

In data analysis, the participants' performance on the quiz was analyzed by identifying the questions that most participants got correct and the questions that most participants got wrong to find out the strengths and the gaps in learning. The mean value of the participants' responses to each survey item was calculated. To examine their perceptions in greater detail, the participants' online posts were analyzed to find emerging patterns to correlate responses to the survey. In addition, the projects provided extra information regarding their coding skills and the intended incorporation of coding into teaching and learning.

RESULTS

Knowledge of Computational Thinking

The analysis of the participants' performance on the quiz and their online posts revealed that overall, the participants understood the concept of CT and its techniques. They agreed that CT involved thinking logically to solve problems. All but one participant thought that CT was using a set of techniques and approaches to help solve problems. The only participant who considered CT as thinking like a computer also described CT as a problem-solving process. In the online posts, the participants were able to explain abstraction, generalization, decomposition and algorithmic thinking. Many of them also gave examples of CT in real life. Most of the participants did not see CT as understanding how computers work or using computers to solve problems. One participant posted, "While computational thinking is necessary to program, one does not need to be a programmer to use this method, nor is it necessary to become one."

Knowledge of Coding

Most of the participants perceived coding as a way to communicate with computers and give instructions or commands to the computers to get the desired outcome. Only one participant stated in the post that teachers can begin to teach the core concepts of coding without a computer. The participants learned to code using Scratch on computers, which naturally made them connect coding activities with the use of computers. The quiz results showed that the participants' knowledge about positioning the sprites using coordinates needs to be enhanced.

In the first two weeks, all except two participants were able to create a complete activity and a digital story, although many of them demonstrated basic skills. It was found that when creating the stories, some participants focused on cording to let the sprites say scripts but did not have the sprites move or change position. This may explain the low performance on the quiz questions that involved using coding blocks of motion to determine the sprite's movement and position. In addition, the short display time of the scripts was also identified in some participants' stories. Unexpectedly, a few participants used blocks of variables and operations, although there were errors in their codes. Overall, the participants were able to code as beginners and create activities that did not require the complex use of coding blocks.

When sharing their experience with Scratch in the online post, most of the participants commented that the program was fun and they enjoyed learning to use it, although a few participants felt it was challenging to learn at the start. They thought it was a great tool for students to learn to code, as one stated, "I think that Scratch is a good, fun, introduction to both coding and the practical application of computational thinking to solve problems." The participants also made comments on the video tutorials in the program. One participant thought the tutorials were somewhat helpful but they were not enough. Another participant pointed out that "there aren't many tutorials on the more complicated stuff'.

Perceptions of Connection Between Computational Thinking and Coding

When discussing the connections between CT and coding, most of the participants thought that CT is essential in coding. Typical comments are "Coding is one of the most natural expressions of computational thinking", "you need computational thinking in order to code", and "I see computational thinking as both the fundamental precursor to coding and a tool that assists during coding." Five participants also elaborated on the CT components in coding when describing the connections. One participant gave an example of having students create a book report through coding:

Students would have to decompose the book report project into smaller, more manageable parts. They would also have to use abstraction to identify which parts of the plot are worth including and which parts should be left out. Algorithmic thinking comes into play when they plan out how they want each animation to function before writing the code. Generalization could be applied to utilize similar blocks of code in multiple scenes if the same outcome is desired. Lastly, evaluation is a necessary step to make sure the animations function as desired or to determine where the code needs to be edited.

It needs to be noted that four participants did not explicitly describe the connections between CT and coding. Instead, they described the similarities between the two concepts. The comments included, "They both involve creating algorithms in order to achieve the task and breaking things down into smaller parts" and "They are both used to solve problems, whether it be in a computer program or in actual life." This indicated that they did not seem to have considered CT and coding in an integrated way.

Incorporation of Computational Thinking and Coding in Education

The participants' responses to the survey questions revealed that they agreed CT can be incorporated in the classroom by allowing students to problem solve (M=4.6) and by using computers in the lesson plan (M=4.0). They also agreed that coding should be integrated into education (M=4.0) and it would help students to become good problem solvers (M=4.0). They agreed on the ideas of infusing coding and CT into teaching (M=4.2) and having background knowledge and understanding of doing that (M=4.5). They tended to agree that teaching students coding is essential in today's world (M=3.8) and they should take courses on how to code and how to teach coding (M=3.7). However, they had neutral perceptions that coding would help students choose good careers in the future (M=3.2), which suggested that they were not certain about the influence of being able to code on students' selection of future career paths. The findings from the analysis of the participants' online posts echoed their responses to the survey questions. They all thought that coding could be integrated into education to support CT, help the students improve their problem-solving skills and bring out the creativity in the students. They also thought that coding could support student learning in subject content, as the skills involved are what students need to develop in each content area. Two participants commented that integrating coding into education can ignite a passion for a future career path in a student, as one participant stated, "It is my hope that by doing so, my students will carry that passion on to high school, secondary education, or their future careers." That only two participants connected the students' coding experience to their future careers may help to explain why overall the participants had neutral perceptions that coding would help students choose good careers. When describing how they would integrate coding into classrooms, most of the participants indicated that they would engage students in coding activities to demonstrate or express their learning creatively and assess students' understanding of content knowledge. This may result from their experience in creating a lesson plan in which coding activity was integrated to support student learning in a core content area, letting students construct and express their knowledge and ideas.

In the lesson plan, they included the use of Scratch in the learning activities, however, none of them specified how to guide the students' CT through coding. It seems that they intended to use Scratch as a web-based program to support the students' creation of content, instead of a coding program to develop the students' CT skills. Although some participants planned to have the students use Scratch to create an activity to assess their learning of the content, the achievement of the learning objectives in the lesson could not be measured in the activity. For example, two participants designed lessons to help the students learn about coordinate planes. They planned to have the students create a chasing game to demonstrate their knowledge about the coordinate plane. As part of the lesson plan project, they created a game as an example. However, the game by itself did not examine whether the students understood the plotting in four quadrants. This may be because the participants took this class in their first semester of graduate study. Not all of them were Education majors in undergraduate study or had a background in education before they entered graduate school. Some of them may need more training in writing learning objectives and aligning the assessment with the objectives.

Challenges and Concerns

According to the participants' responses to the survey questions, they were inclined to agree that they could do well in infusing coding and computing into teaching (M=3.7). However, they had neutral responses to the statements "I expect to use coding and computing skills in my daily life as a teacher" (M=3.5), and "I hope that my future career as a teacher will require the use of coding and computing concepts" (M=3.5). A deep dive into their online posts helped to explain these results.

There were four major challenges and concerns that the participants would foresee if they were to integrate coding into the classroom. They were concerned about the students' knowledge and skills, such as different levels of understanding about coding and analytical mindset, variation in the students' literacy skills and mathematical knowledge when using the coding blocks that feature vocabulary words and logical operators. The students' technology skill was also an element. One participant believed that the most prevalent challenge would be the student not able to adapt to the technical features of Scratch, "I still see individuals struggle with advanced technology and Scratch isn't exactly easy for someone who isn't comfortable using technology."

Teachers' lack of knowledge and skills in coding was considered another challenge. They thought that teachers must feel confident and be proficient in using Scratch if they wanted to integrate coding into a lesson, as one participant posted, "It is one thing to have an idea of a worthwhile activity, but actually coding/designing and then implementing the activity may be difficult." Some participants made it clear that they would need to learn more about how to use Scratch if they were to engage students in the coding activities. Due to these concerns, some participants clearly expressed the need for professional development. One participant stated, "I would want to attend personal development workshops geared toward using Scratch in the classroom in order to learn how other individuals have successfully done this in their classroom." Another participant considered that it would be helpful if lesson modules could be obtained with coding activities already built into the lesson plan objectives.

As with the use of any other technologies, accessibility issue is also a concern about using coding programs. Having access to computers and a good connection to the Internet in classrooms was considered a possible challenge by some participants. The participants were also concerned about the accessibility at home, as one participant explained, "While at school it may be possible for every student to use a computer, but not every family will have internet access, or even a computer for students." Such concern made them feel it would be hard to make students work on coding projects at home.

In addition, the participants were concerned about time management when integrating coding into lessons, as they thought coding took a lot of class time. Part of this concern was associated with the concern of students' skills, as one participant posted:

"As an educator, you must give your students time to become familiar with the program, especially if they are just beginning to study it. You must provide the other students in the class time and space to assist them, even if I am aware that certain students will pick up information more quickly than others."

One participant expressed concerns about adjusting the existing curriculum, "Many times we are given strict curricula to follow and implement in a very particular time frame because of testing and district demands. I foresee having to explain and justify my reasoning for taking an extra 2 weeks because I am adding coding."

DISCUSSIONS AND IMPLICATIONS

Effects of Educational Technology Class

In this study, almost all the participants were able to explain the concept of CT and its main components. This suggested that introducing CT in the educational technology class helped the teacher education students to develop CT knowledge. This supported the results reported by Zha et al. (2020) that a significant growth in students' CT knowledge was found after a learning module on CT and coding in an educational technology class. The participants also gained an understanding of what coding means and developed some basic coding skills using Scratch. In this study, it was their first time using Scratch. The participants were not engaged in complex coding. Nevertheless, the participants' performance in this study implied insufficient skills in using motion blocks to control the position and movement of the sprites. Those who used variables and operations also needed more practice. When learning to code, more time should be provided to the participants to work on coding activities (Marcelino et al., 2018). In this study, the participants were immersed in coding experience for four weeks. Given the time limit, future practice may need to be better structured to help teacher education students develop target skills within a dedicated time frame.

When discussing the connection between CT and coding, there was a general consensus among most of the participants that CT was fundamental to coding. This was aligned with the observation of the preservice teachers in the previous research (Lloyd & Chandra, 2020) that CT could be used outside of coding but the coding was impossible without CT. However, four participants did not point out that CT components were folded in coding. They seemed to perceive CT and coding as distinct concepts that have common characteristics. The discussion of the connection between CT and coding took place at the end of the second week of the four-week learning module. The time length may not be enough for them to attend to the application of CT in coding (Zha et al., 2020).

Although the participants were uncertain that learning to code would help students choose their future career paths, overall, they were positive or tended to be positive about integrating CT and coding into education. Although most of them realized that CT is fundamental in coding, when creating the lesson plan, they did not intentionally and explicitly integrate CT into the coding activity. The lack of CT requirements in the coding-integrated lesson plan project may contribute to this result. In the future, the participants may need to be required to specify how they would guide students' CT in coding when they describe the learning activities in the lesson plan so that they would consciously weave CT into the coding activity. Meanwhile, more scaffolding should be provided to the participants, especially to those who do not have a background in education before the graduate study, to support the development of the lesson plan.

The participants acknowledged the importance of integrating CT and coding into education and created a lesson plan. However, they were uncertain about using coding skills as a teacher in their future career, which backed up the findings from prior research (Ray et al., 2020). This indicated that the participants would hesitate to engage students in coding activities in classrooms. In current literature, teacher knowledge, student knowledge, time and resources were identified as frequent challenges to teaching coding (Rich et al., 2019; Rich, Mason & O'Leary, 2021). Similar results were found in this study. The participants were concerned about students' knowledge and skills that are important to be used in coding, including literacy and mathematical knowledge, analytical skills and technology skills. The participants were also concerned about teachers' knowledge and skills. While developing some basic skills in the learning module, they realized that they would need to learn more about coding. This concern coupled with the challenge of time management in classrooms naturally made them feel the need for professional development and coding-integrated lesson plans available in the curriculum. Additionally, the participants had concerns about technology accessibility. This may be because most of the participants lived in urban communities and had experiences in urban schools. This concern was associated with the resources in urban education.

Recommendations and Future Research Directions

The results of this study supported that teacher education students could develop their knowledge of CT and some basic coding skills in a stand-alone educational technology class (Mouza et al., 2017; Ray et al., 2020; Zha et al., 2020). The findings carried some implications for future practice in the education technology class. In this study, the participants learned about CT and coding over a period of four weeks. Since such a class usually exposes students to multiple topics and various technologies, it is unlikely that CT and coding are the only topics in the class. Given the time limit, the teacher educator needs to consider how to support teacher education student learning of CT and coding to the greatest extent.

Guided and Structured Coding Activities

It has been suggested that guided hands-on coding experience would help to increase teachers' confidence to teach coding (Rich et al., 2021). In Scratch, the video tutorials are short and provide segmented training. For first-time users, there are no tutorials that offer an overview of different categories of blocks and step-by-step demonstrations of advanced features such as variables and operations. In this study, some participants' comments on the use of Scratch also reflected that they felt the Scratch tutorials did not provide enough training. The participants first watched a video online that introduced the interface of Scratch. Then they followed the Scratch tutorials to create two simple activities and a story. The simple activities helped them to get started in Scratch, such as animated names or flying objects. When creating the story, however, the participants did not demonstrate the same level of learning, as observed by some researchers in elementary school teachers who learned to use Scratch online (Marcelino et al., 2018). To help the students create a complete coding product that can be used in education, such as a story, in a limited time frame, the teacher educator can provide students with structured directions to let them know the minimum requirements including the minimum number of sprites, look, motion and sound of sprites. The structured directions define the scope of the coding activity and guide the students to design and develop the story. Following step-by-step instructions helps to reduce students' anxiety and motivates them to practice coding (Zha et al., 2020). To support student learning, it will be helpful if the educator can present an example to the students and create a demonstration video to walk students through the process of creating the story. Watching the video allows the students to practice coding at their own pace, which helps to address the needs of students who have different comfort levels with using technology.

Modeling

The participants in this study created a coding-integrated lesson plan. Since not all the participants had a background in education before they entered graduate school, a template of the lesson plan was provided. The template outlined the components of the lesson plan, such as learning objectives and learning activities. It is noteworthy that although most of the participants recognized the connection between CT and coding, none of them explicitly related the coding activity to the development of the students' CT skills. In the future, when engaging teacher education students in creating a coding-integrated lesson plan, it may be necessary to have them specify how their students' CT skills will be developed through coding activity.

Additionally, and most importantly, teacher educators need to take a modeling approach in their teaching practice. It has been suggested that practical examples of activities and modeling of teaching CT and coding should be included in training (Mason & Rich, 2019; Ketelhut et al., 2020). The participants in this study were trained to become general education teachers in K-8 settings. Computer science was not included in their graduate study curriculum. In such a case, it would be helpful if the teacher educator of the educational technology class could model the integration of CT into coding when having teacher education students work on the coding activities. Also, the teacher education students can be exposed to external resources that provide examples of classroom teachers' teaching of CT and coding in practice, such as videos or ready-made lesson plans. The participants in this study watched videos on teachers' perceptions of the effects of coding on student learning and videos on students' thoughts and reflections. This helped to cultivate the participants' awareness of including CT and coding in education. To create meaningful CT-infused coding activities, they need concrete examples and vignettes to engage students in CT and coding in the classroom. This will not only help to strengthen their understanding of the connection between CT and coding but also support the development of their confidence in implementing such activities in future teaching.

Set Realistic Goals

Depending on the length of time dedicated to the topics of CT and coding in an educational technology class, the teacher educator may need to set realistic goals. Novice coding teachers had difficulties with the concepts of functions, conditionals and variables in Scratch (Rich et al., 2021; Tsortanidou et al., 2021). Teacher educators can start by introducing basic concepts and having students create coding activities in which they can apply those concepts. The linear nature of storytelling would make coding stories a good starting point (Burke, O'Byrn & Kafai, 2016). Teacher educators can have students create stories that require them to apply CT techniques and basic coding concepts by using coding blocks of motion, look, sound and events. The experience with unsophisticated coding activity will motivate the teacher education students and help to build their confidence. Since "coding stories represent a particularly effective way of introducing adolescents to programming" (Burke et al., 2016, p. 372), the coding experience may also help the teacher education students to transfer the skills to future teaching practice. The teacher education students can be expected to develop a foundational understanding in educational technology classes. They will develop a greater understanding and more confidence in integrating CT and coding into lessons in their future teaching practice (Mason & Rich, 2019; Lloyd & Chandra, 2020; Rich et al., 2021).

Teacher Educator Knowledge and Skills

Yadav et al. (2017) suggested that it "is time for teacher educators to transform educational technology toward computing education and to structure courses to engage preservice teachers in computational thinking tools and ideas" (p.218). This may require revision of the curriculum in the teacher education program, especially if the educational technology class is the only technology class in the program. It has to be pointed out that not all educational technology educators may have been trained to teach CT and coding. Teacher educators can collaborate with computer science educators (Mouza et al., 2017; Yadav et al., 2017). To better prepare teacher education students, teacher educators need support to develop their expertise. In current literature, there is a dearth of research on teacher educators' professional development in CT and coding. Future research may be conducted to address the gap in the literature.

CONCLUSION

It has been proposed that teacher education students can be exposed to CT early in the teacher preparation program so that they would be able to see the relevance of CT in their own disciplines (Yadav et al., 2014). Coding is an important tool to help develop CT knowledge and skills. In this study, the participants learned about CT and coding in their first semester of the graduate teacher education program. Although they recognized the value of integrating CT and coding into education, they had some concerns and were not certain about integrating coding into teaching practice. The results of this study implied that introducing CT and coding to the teacher education students in an educational technology class could help to develop a foundational understanding of CT and coding. The participants' concerns and the challenges that they foresaw had practical meanings. Future research may engage teacher education students in more structured hands-on experience with a modeling approach to achieve realistic goals within a given time frame. Additionally, future research may be needed to examine teacher educators' professional development in preparing education students to integrate CT and coding into the classroom, as they work closely with the students in teacher preparation programs.

Since the research was conducted in a class required for teacher education students in the graduate program, a convenient sampling method was used. The number of participants was small. In addition, due the the scope of the content in this class, only a 4-week learning module was dedicated to CT and coding. The time may not be enough for beginners to develop a deep understanding of infusing CT and coding into content learning of a subject area. All of these may pose a limitation on the generalization of the results from this study. Hopefully, the findings and the implications provide a reference for future practice and contribute to the current literature by expanding the knowledge about this topic.

ACKNOWLEDGMENT

I sincerely thank Dr. Eleni Makris, Professor of the Educational Foundations program and Community and Teacher Leaders program, Northeastern Illinois University, Chicago, IL, for the help with data collection.

REFERENCES

Alexiou-Ray, J., Raulston, C., Fenton, D., & Johnson, S. (2020). Coding: Coding in the K-12 classroom. In A. Ottenbreit-Leftwich & R. Kimmons (Eds.), *The K-12 educational technology handbook* (pp. 68–77). EdTech Books.

and learning outcomes of programming concepts, practices and pedagogy. *Computers & Education, 151*. doi:10.1016/j.compedu.2020.103872

Ari, F., Arsian-Ari, I., & Vasconcelos, L. (2022). Early childhood preservice teachers' perceptions of computer science, gender stereotypes, and coding in early childhood education. *TechTrends*, *66*(3), 539–546. doi:10.1007/s11528-022-00725-w PMID:35499061

Balanskat, A., & Engelhardt, K. (2014). *Computing our future: Computer programming and coding – priorities, school curricula and initiatives across Europe*. European Schoolnet. http://www.eun.org/

Burke, Q., O'Byrne, W. I., & Kafai, Y. (2016). Computational participation: Understanding coding as an extension of literacy instruction. *Journal of Adolescent & Adult Literacy*, *59*(4), 371–375. doi:10.1002/jaal.496

Cansu, S. K., & Cansu, F. K. (2019). An overview of computational thinking. *International Journal of Computer eScience Education in School, 3*(1), 17-30. doi:10.21585/ijcses.v3i1.53

Chang, Y.-H., & Peterson, L. (2018). Pre-service teachers' perceptions of computational thinking. *Journal of Technology and Teacher Education*, *26*(3), 353–374.

Code.org. CSTA, & ECEP Alliance. (2022). *2022 State of computer science education: Understanding our national imperative*. https://advocacy.code.org/stateofcs

computational thinking and scratch at distance. *Computers in Human Behaviors, 80*, 470-477. doi:10.1016/j.chb.2017.09.025

design-based learning approach to enhance elementary students' self-perceived computational thinking. *Journal of Research on Technology in Education, 55*(2), 344-368. doi:10.1080/15391523.2021.1962453

Duschl, R. A. (2020). On computational thinking and STEM education. *Journal for STEM Education Research*, *3*(2), 147–166. doi:10.1007/s41979-020-00044-w

Flórez, F. B., Casallas, R., Hernández, M., Reyes, A., Restrepo, S., & Danies, G. (2017). Changing a generation's way of thinking: Teaching computational thinking through programming. *Review of Educational Research*, *87*(4), 834–860. doi:10.3102/0034654317710096

Herro, D., Quigley, C., Plank, H., & Abimbade, O. (2021). Understanding students' social interactions during making activities designed to promote computational thinking. *The Journal of Educational Research, 114*(2), 183–195. doi:10.1080/00220671.2021.1884824

Hestness, E., Ketelhut, D. J., McGinnis, J. R., & Plane, J. (2018). Professional knowledge building within an elementary teacher professional development experience on computational thinking in science education. *Journal of Technology and Teacher Education*, *26*(3), 411–435.

Huang, W., & Looi, C.-K. (2021). A critical review of literature eon "unplugged" pedagogies in K-12 computer science and computational thinking education. *Computer Science Education*, *31*(1), 83–111. doi:10.1080/08993408.2020.1789411

Jin, Y., & Harp, C. (2020). Examining preservice teachers' TPACK, attitudes, self-efficacy, and perceptions of teamwork in a stand-alone educational technology course using flipped classroom or flipped team-based learning pedagogies. *Journal of Digital Learning in Teacher Education*, *36*(3), 166–184. doi:10.1080/21532974.2020.1752335

Jocius, R., O'Byrne, W. I., Albert, J., Joshi, D., Robinson, R., & Andrews, A. (2021). Infusing Computational Thinking into STEM Teaching: From Professional Development to Classroom Practice. *Journal of Educational Technology & Society*, *24*(4), 166–179.

Kaya, E., Newley, A., Yesilyurt, E., & Deniz, H. (2020, July). teaching efficacy beliefs of preservice elementary teachers. *Journal of College Science Teaching*, *49*(6), 55–64. doi:10.1080/0047231X.2020.12290665

Ketelhut, D. J., Mills, K., Hestness, E., Cabrera, L., Plane, J., & McGinnis, J. R. (2020, February). Teacher change following a professional development experience in integrating computational thinking into elementary science. *Journal of Science Education and Technology*, *29*(1), 173–187. doi:10.1007/s10956-019-09798-4

Kjällander, S., Mannila, L., Åkerfeldt, A., & Heintz, F. (2021, February 19). approach to computational thinking and programming. *Education Sciences*, *11*(2), 80. doi:10.3390/educsci11020080

Kong, S-C., Lai, M., & Sun, D. (2020). *Teacher development in computational thinking: Design*. Research Gate.

Kwon, K., Ottenbreit-Leftwich, A. T., Brush, T. A., Jeon, M., & Yan, G. (2021, October). based learning in elementary computer science education: Effects on computational thinking and attitudes. *Educational Technology Research and Development*, *69*(5), 2761–2787. doi:10.1007/s11423-021-10034-3

Lloyd, M., & Chandra, V. (2020). Teaching coding and computational thinking in primary classrooms: Perceptions of Australian preservice teachers. *Curriculum Perspectives*, *40*(2), 189–201. doi:10.1007/s41297-020-00117-1

Lodi, M. (2020). Informatical thinking. *Olympiads in Informatics*, *14*, 113–132. doi:10.15388/ioi.2020.09

Mason, S. L., & Rich, P. (2019). Preparing elementary school teachers to teach computing, coding, and computational thinking. *Contemporary Issues in Technology & Teacher Education*, *19*(4), 790–824. https://citejournal.org/publication/volume-19/issue-4-19/

McGinnisJ. R.HestnessE.MillsK.KetelhutD. J.CabreraL.JeongH. (2020).

Mladenović, M., Boljat, I., & Žanko, Ž. (2018). Comparing loops misconceptions in block-based and text-based programming languages at the K-12 level. *Education and Information Technologies*, *23*(4), 1483–1500. doi:10.1007/s10639-017-9673-3

Moreno-León, J., Robles, G., & Román-González, M. (2016). Code to learn: Where does it belong in the K-12 curriculum? *Journal of Information Technology Education*, *15*, 283–303. doi:10.28945/3521

Mouza, C., Yang, H., Pan, Y.-C., Ozden, S. Y., & Pollock, L. (2017). Resetting educational technology coursework for pre-service teachers: A computational thinking approach to the development of technological pedagogical content knowledge (TPACK). *Australasian Journal of Educational Technology*, *33*(3), 61–76. doi:10.14742/ajet.3521

Özmutlu, M., Atay, D., & Erdoğan, B. (2021). Collaboration and engagement based coding training to enhance children's computational thinking self-efficacy. *Thinking Skills and Creativity*, *40*, 100833. doi:10.1016/j.tsc.2021.100833

Papadakis, S. (2021). The impact of coding apps to support young children in computational thinking and computational fluency. A literature review. *Frontiers in Education*, *6*, 657895. doi:10.3389/feduc.2021.657895

Papadakis, S., Kalogiannakis, M., & Zaranis, N. (2016). Developing fundamental programming concepts and computational thinking with ScratchJr in preschool education: A case study. *International Journal of Mobile Learning and Organization*, *10*(3), 187–202. doi:10.1504/IJMLO.2016.077867

Papavlasopoulou, S., Giannakos, M. N., & Jaccheeri, L. (2019). Exploring children's learning experience in constructionism-based coding activities through design-based research. *Computers in Human Behavior*, *99*, 415–427. doi:10.1016/j.chb.2019.01.008

Pérez-Marín, D., Hijón-Neira, R., Bacelo, A., & Pizarro, C. (2020). Can computational thinking be improved by using a methodology based on metaphors and scratch to teach computer programming to children? *Computers in Human Behavior*, *105*(C), 105849. doi:10.1016/j.chb.2018.12.027

Ray, B. B., Rogers, R. R. H., & Hocutt, M. M. (2020). Perceptions of non-STEM discipline teachers on coding as a teaching and learning tool: What are the possibilities? *Journal of Digital Learning in Teacher Education*, *36*(1), 19–31. doi:10.1080/21532974.2019.1646170

Relkin, E., Ruiter, L., & Bers, M. U. (2020). TechCheck: Development and validation of an unplugged assessment of computational thinking in early childhood education. *Journal of Science Education and Technology*, *29*(4), 482–498. doi:10.1007/s10956-020-09831-x

Resnick, M., Maloney, J., Monroy-Hernández, A., Rusk, N., Eastmond, E., Brennan, K., Millner, A., Rosenbaum, E., Silver, J., Sillverman, B., & Kafai, Y. (2009). Scratch: Programming for all. *Communications of the ACM*, *52*(11), 60–67. doi:10.1145/1592761.1592779

Rich, P. J., Browning, S. F., Perkins, M., Shoop, T., Yoshikawa, E., & Belikov, O. M. (2019). Coding in K-8: International trends in teaching elementary/primary computing. *TechTrends*, *63*(3), 311–329. doi:10.1007/s11528-018-0295-4

Rich, P. J., Mason, S. L., & O'Leary, J. (2021). Measuring the effect of continuous professional development on elementary teachers' self-efficacy to teach coding and computational thinking. *Computers & Education*, *168*, 104196. doi:10.1016/j.compedu.2021.104196

Rodríguez-Martínez, J. A., González-Calero, J. A., & Sáez-López, J. M. (2020). Computational thinking and mathematics using Scratch, an experiment with sixth-grade students. *Interactive Learning Environments*, *28*(3), 316–327. doi:10.1080/10494820.2019.1612448

Sáez-López, J.-M., Román-González, M., & Vázquez-Cano, E. (2016). Visual programming languages integrated across the curriculum in elementary school: A two year case study using "Scratch" in five schools. *Computers & Education*, *97*, 129–141. doi:10.1016/j.compedu.2016.03.003

Sung, W., Ahn, J., & Black, J. B. (2017). Introducing computational thinking to young learners: Practicing computational perspectives through embodiment in mathematics education. *Technology. Knowledge and Learning*, *22*(3), 443–463. doi:10.1007/s10758-017-9328-x

Sung, W., & Black, J. B. (2021). Factors to consider when designing effective learning: Infusing computational thinking in mathematics to support thinking-doing. *Journal of Research on Technology in Education*, *53*(4), 404–426. doi:10.1080/15391523.2020.1784066

Tikva, C., & Tambouris, E. (2021). Mapping computational thinking through programming in K 12 education: A conceptual model based on systematic literature review. *Computers & Education*, *162*, 104083. Advance online publication. doi:10.1016/j.compedu.2020.104083

Tissenbaum, M., & Ottenbreit-Leftwich, A. (2020). A vision of k-12 computer science education for 2030. *Communications of the ACM*, *63*(5), 42–44. doi:10.1145/3386910

Tsortanidou, X., Daradoumis, T., & Barberá, E. (2021). A K-6 computational thinking curricular framework: pedagogical implications for teaching practice. *Interactive Learning Environments*. Taylor & Francis. https://www.tandfonline.com/doi/full/10.1080/10494820.2021.1986725

Upadhyaya, B., McGill, M. M., & Decker, A. (2020). A longitudinal analysis of k-12 computing education research in the United State: Implications and recommendations for change. *SIGCSE '20: Proceedings of the 51st ACM Technical Symposium on Computer Science Education*, (pp. 605-611). ACM. 10.1145/3328778.3366809

Weintrop, D. (2019). Block-based programming in computer science education. *Communications of the ACM*, *62*(8), 22–25. doi:10.1145/3341221

Weintrop, D., Hansen, A. K., Harlow, D. B., & Franklin, D. (2018). Starting from Scratch: Outcomes of early computer science learning experiences and implications for what comes next. *ICER '18: Proceedings of the 2018 ACM Conference on International Computing Education Research*, (pp. 142-150). ACM. 10.1145/3230977.3230988

Wing, J. M. (2006). Computational thinking. *Communications of the ACM*, *49*(3), 33–35. doi:10.1145/1118178.1118215

Wing, J. M. (2014, January 10). Computational thinking benefits society. *Social Issues in Computing*. http://socialissues.cs.toronto.edu/index.html

Yadav, A., Gretter, S., Good, J., & McLean, T. (2017). Computational thinking in teacher education. In P. J. Rich & C. B. Hodges (Eds.), *Emerging research, practice and policy on computational thinking* (pp. 205–220). Springer. doi:10.1007/978-3-319-52691-1_13

Yadav, A., Krist, C., Good, J., & Caeli, E. N. (2018). Computational thinking in elementary classrooms: Measuring teacher understanding of computational ideas for teaching science. *Computer Science Education*, *28*(4), 371–400. doi:10.1080/08993408.2018.1560550

Yadav, A., Mayfield, C., Chou, N., Hambrusch, S., & Korb, J. T. (2014). Computational thinking in elementary and secondary teacher education. *ACM Transactions on Computing Education*, *14*(1), 1–16. doi:10.1145/2576872

Zha, S., Jin, Y., Moore, P., & Gaston, J. (2020). Hopscotch into coding: Introducing pre-service teachers computational thinking. *TechTrends*, *64*(1), 17–28. doi:10.1007/s11528-019-00423-0

Chapter 10
Introducing Computer Science Education Through Robotics Education in Community-Engaged Contexts:
Reflecting on Good Practice

Patricia M. Gouws
https://orcid.org/0000-0003-4948-2699
University of South Africa, South Africa

Hugo H. Lotriet
University of South Africa, South Africa

ABSTRACT

The introduction of computer science education (CSE) in schools is required to prepare the learners for future work and develop the required 21st century skills. However, for competent and confident learners, the educators need to be upskilled and trained to develop CSE teaching capacity and skills. The use of robotics education (RE) provides a more concrete (less abstract) environment for the introduction of CSE. Although CSE is introduced at schools, concern relates to the required access to quality training, required equipment and support from gatekeepers that delay or hinder the advancement of CSE. The good practices for the informal option of CE at higher education institutions (HEI), through engagement with and within a community of practice (COP), to provide access to quality CSE training and skills development to educators, visionary community leaders and learners is presented in terms of the balanced scorecard (BSC) perspectives of strategy, process, people, resources and growth and sustainability.

DOI: 10.4018/979-8-3693-1066-3.ch010

INTRODUCTION

Computer science (CS), especially through computational thinking (CT), is significant in the context of 21st century skills. The elements of CT related to the thinking methods of a computer scientist, such as analysis, and algorithmic approaches to problem solving, are considered as core 21st century skills (Bocconi et al., 2016). Teaching of CS and the development of related skills, including the teaching of programming, is considered challenging (Robins, 2015). The equipping and empowering of educators (despite limited resources, limited exposure to technology, and limited CS backgrounds) to teach the CS curriculum is a hinderance in the teaching and learning of CS.

The intuitive link between CSE and RE has been described as reciprocal (El-Hamamsy *et al.*, 2021). Efforts have been made in the context of formal education to include RE as a method to teach CS. In science, technology, engineering, and mathematics (STEM), RE is considered a practical vehicle to engage and develop 21st century skills for learners.

Within South African tertiary institutions, emphasis is placed on more informal engagement with communities. Community engagement (CE), and communities of practice (COP) entails engagement with communities around skills development and knowledge transfer. An academic responsibility is the pursuit of CE within tertiary institutions, to address knowledge mobilization and the addressing of social injustices.

Within South African schools, the Department of Basic Education (DBE) introduced a coding and robotics curriculum. The Department of Science and Innovation (DSI) promotes Science Olympiads and Competitions. Significant resources are made available for science engagement to advance science (Department of Science and Technology, 2015). Recently, DSI introduced a focussed approach, ensuring that robotics and coding have a focussed segment of implementation.

This chapter proposes that equipping, supporting, and development of educators, mentors, and coaches through CE provides a less formal engagement context. The combination of good practices related to the elements of CE, RE and CSE (which is the focus of this paper) allows for equipping educators, mentors, and coaches to teach and mentor CSE fundamentals through practical content and the domain of RE. To ensure competent and confident RE and CSE learners, community leaders can be equipped and supported to be competent and confident. Although not the focus of this paper, the structure within which this support and equipping would occur would typically be a Community of Practice (COP). The establishment of COPs in this context is an extensive topic which would warrant a paper on its own.

The chapter proposes a comprehensive literature-founded framework for good practices of RE with a specific focus for the development and support of CSE through and in the context of CE. The contribution makes CSE through RE a more explicit endeavour, specifically in less formal engagement with communities. This approach will complement and strengthen the existing literature on using RE to support CSE in more formal CE contexts.

Community Engagement (CE) Context

The elements that enhance CE include the definition of role players and partners, the use of infrastructure, the understanding the complexities of engaging with communities, conducting research to support best practices, understanding the history and social context of the community, respectful engagement and power sharing, and the inclusion of the community in all aspects of the engagement, and networking (Michener *et al.*, 2012). The aim is for engagement practices to be sustainable and in the best interests of all role players. In tertiary institutions in South Africa, CE that addresses the social injustices related to, e.g., race, gender, disability, economic factors, and location that result in inequality in education is a strategic focus. Thus, the context of CE can be used to engage with SA communities to advance 21st century skills.

The South African government engages in the development and support of digital and future skills. This is undertaken based on the National Digital and Future Skills (Ministry of Communication and Digital Technologies, 2020). The strategy discussed eight elements including the development of basic and advanced digital skills related to the Fourth Industrial Revolution (4IR), and the support needed to create a digitally skilled society (including awareness, research and monitoring, co-ordination, and funding). Potential benefits of being digitally skilled, not only for individuals, but for all communities, are highlighted. The benefits relate to empowerment in terms of politics, social development, economic opportunities, and enhanced opportunities for education and improved knowledge. Investment in the learning of digital skills accessible to communities, both in terms of informal and formal learning and programmes is emphasized.

Current trends around digitalisation (and specifically 4IR) are developing rapidly. Without the necessary access to quality training and capacity building, disempowered communities will lag further and further behind in the development of required digital skills. Thus, the digital divides widen, and negatively impact on these communities (Molala and Makhubele, 2021). An intention has been expressed that digital skills training should be promoted in underserved communities, specifically to ensure that the benefits would transcend race, gender, disability, economic factors, income, and geography, i.e., the social injustices that impact on education.

Robotics Education (RE)

Robotics spans the knowledge domains of engineering and programming, and the development of 21st century skills (Angel-Fernandez and Vincze, 2018). Problem-solving skills (also referred to as CT) can be developed through robotics (Kopcha, Wilson and Yang, 2022). Although the interest in robotics in tertiary institutions is growing, robotics is still taught mostly from an engineering perspective (Esposito, 2017). Within the school education curriculum, RE is considered a tool to support creativity and 21st century learning skills (Khan and Bari, 2023). RE may be implemented with physical robots or simulations thereof (Choi *et al.*, 2021) and RE may be introduced early into the school curriculum (Alam, 2022). Through the introduction of RE, learners grapple with and discover the fundamentals of engineering and the principles of programming, through concrete (less abstract) learning, developing the required 21st century skills (including problem solving, creativity, CT, imagination, innovation, collaboration, teamwork). These 21st century skills are required to ensure that the learners thrive beyond the 21st century as a skilled future workforce. Using RE to effectively develop learner CT skills (Chiazzese *et al.*, 2019) has been reviewed and measured for learners of all grade levels. Robotics and coding education has been introduced into a limited number of schools. CS learners can also be introduced to robotics as part of the CS curriculum (Correll, Wing and Coleman, 2013). However, the development of competent and confident RE learners requires competent and confident robotics coaches and educators.

Access to quality RE resources is required for the teaching and learning of robotics. Online RE resources have been classified into three categories, namely, random access (e.g. TedX talks), sequential access (e.g. Massive Open Online Courses (MOOCs), and practical learning (including robotics competitions, robotics simulations) (Pozzi, Prattichizzo and Malvezzi, 2021). The classification of online robotics resources can be used to guide the user to the most suitable online robotics resources. The issue of language (and thus cultural relevance) of the resources is noted.

Computer Science Education (CSE)

CSE requires the development of CT skills, including abstraction, decomposition, generalization, pattern recognition, algorithms, flow control, and data representation, which are associated with programming (Piedade *et al.*, 2020). CT is aligned with 21st century skills (problem solving, critical thinking, creativity, communication, innovation, and digital skills) (Piedade *et al.*, 2020).

Guidelines for the teaching and learning of an ever-evolving discipline of CS for under-graduates in tertiary institutions have been previously defined in literature and can be used to guide CSE for K-12 learners (Raj and Kumar, 2022). The curriculum for the introduction of CSE for K-12 learners that has been defined in the literature includes algorithms and programming, information and data, machines, systems and networks (El-Hamamsy *et al.*, 2021). The inclusion of CSE and the development of CT within compulsory education is considered a vital component for the digital transformation of the future work force (Bocconi *et al.*, 2022).

Globally, the shortage of CSE educators hinders the implementation. In-service educators require continuous professional development (CPD) to develop the required skills and competencies, while pre-service educators require CSE training. Support for all educators is required to ensure ongoing improvement of the teaching of CSE. Through CPD, the teaching of other school subjects such as mathematics can be supported (Kopcha, Wilson and Yang, 2022). The lack of access to quality CSE learning for educators through CPD is highlighted (Kopcha, Wilson and Yang, 2022).

To support the learning of CT, options including robotics and game design were proposed in a culturally responsive teaching of CSE in a rural setting (Leonard *et al.*, 2018). The research highlights the need for education self-efficacy for CSE educators, as relevant knowledge, skills, and competencies do not guarantee the implementation of best practice. The educator self-efficacy is measured in terms of personal judgement of the ability to teach CSE, and outcome expectancy that an expected outcome will be achieved. Informal (rather than formal) learning of CSE is considered (Newton *et al.*, 2020).

The perceptions and attitudes of various role players at schools towards CSE are important and need to be considered when implementing CSE. These may include gatekeepers (both at schools and in the wider community surrounding the school, principals, and councillors (McGarr *et al.*, 2023). From this research, several CSE perceptions were identified, including the perception that CSE is limited for access to specific learner groups (rather than all learners) (McGarr *et al.*, 2023). However, the determination to ensure the successful implementation of CSE education must be supported by relevant funding, resources, and stakeholder engagement.

The issue of underrepresentation of females and underserved learners also needs to be addressed (Fletcher and Warner, 2021). The underrepresentation may be due to the perceptions and attitudes of the CSE gatekeepers (McGarr *et al.*, 2023). Another aspect that needs to be considered in the introduction of CSE for all learners is the lack of social justice in society, and the need for a justice-centred approach to CSE that will consider the relevant communities, and citizenship within a world society (Yadav, Heath and Hu, 2022). It is noted that CSE has striven to address the problems of social injustices by increasing the access and support to quality CSE through awareness and exposure to content curricula, skills development, and required technology(Yadav, Heath and Hu, 2022).

RE in the CE Context in South Africa

RE has been used in CE initiatives to promote science and STEM awareness and participation. The argument is made that given the success of RE in the CE context, explicit and formal CSE can then also be presented through informal CE. Thus, through CE, educators can be equipped with the skills and knowledge to teach CSE in schools. In South Africa, the government has explicitly indicated the importance of robotics in classrooms as part of the digital transformation of (McNulty, 2021). Reference is made to the importance of educator development to teach "various branches of CS" and the use of "digital tools and applications" to teach various subjects in schools. There is mention of the need for artificial intelligence (AI), a branch of CS, and coding. As part of CE at tertiary institutions, robotics and activities are used in an informal CE context to overcome some of the barriers associated with the digital divide.

An example of CE using RE is the Inspired toward Science, Engineering and Technology (I-SET) CE flagship project that has been engaging with communities of learners and educators since 2009 to create awareness and develop capacity to compete in robotics competitions. To equip coaches (educators, facilitators, and community leaders), the I-SET robotics project hosts weekly I-SET Robotics Live Online Learning sessions. All sessions are recorded, and links are available on the I-SET Unisa YouTube channel. The session content is available on the Unisa Massive Open Online Course (MOOC) portal. On successful submission of a portfolio, a certificate of completion is issued (Gouws *et al.*, 2021).

Using RE for CSE

Although the impact of RE on CS has long been predicted (Hopcroft, 1986), the teaching of CS **with** robotics (Fagin, Merkle and Eggers, 2001) present early research using the physical robot to teach CS concepts to undergraduate students. However, the robot has evolved, and robotics is now more accessible to all learners as part of the selected school curriculum. The introduction of CSE concepts is explored, including flow control and procedure. The issues pertaining to effective learning of CS are considered as part of the recommendations for future research.

At a tertiary level, robotics is usually presented from an engineering perspective, however, robotics can also be presented from a CSE perspective to include topics such as mathematics of robotics (including kinematics), sensors, and artificial intelligence (AI) (including neural networks) (Kay, 2003). The CSE approach to robotics assumes knowledge of calculus, linear algebra, programming, data structures, and algorithms.

However, CSE can also be taught using RE, where robots provide a concrete (less-abstract) environment for exploring CSE concepts. The domain of robotics is used to enhance the teaching of CS and Engineering at a tertiary level (Berenguel *et al.*, 2016). When students enter CS classes, it is assumed that the students have the skills and knowledge to progress. However, it was found that students coming to tertiary institutions lack the required CT skills to ensure success in studies in CS (Csapó, 2019). Robotics were used to introduce CS at a tertiary level, suggesting that robots as learning catalysts can be used to equip diverse learners and educators (Arlegui *et al.*, 2008). Block based programming is used to program robots, however, in the process CSE topics are introduced to learners still in school (Weintrop, 2019). This leads to the need for the teaching and learning of CSE at the earliest possible opportunity.

At a school level, RE can also be deployed to trigger the early learning of CS concepts. In this regard, the introduction of RE in the schooling systems of other countries can provide insights and examples

(Crick, 2022). The development of educators (and thus learners) in CT using RE is proposed (Esteve-Mon *et al.*, 2019).

The culturally responsive teaching and learning of CSE in a rural setting may use robotics, game design, or a combination thereof, and engagement in engineering and CS tasks (Leonard *et al.*, 2018). The use of physical robots and participation in robotics competitions provides learning experiences to gain 21st century skills, as well as explore engineering and programming knowledge (Graffin, Sheffield and Koul, 2022).

El-Hamsamy *et al.* (2021) provide a Swiss example where CSE and RE are integrated into the school curriculum, and the associated compulsory CSE CPD programme focussed on the identification of barriers to CSE implementation and mitigation strategies for successful implementation of CSE (El-Hamamsy *et al.*, 2021) . The pathway of using robotics competitions for learners to develop 21st century skills, in schools or as extra-mural activity or community initiative can be used to extend the school implementation (Usart *et al.*, 2019).

For the implementation of both CSE and RE requires the equipping of the educators. While formal qualifications are ideal, a CE opportunity using a less formal approach may be valuable in facilitating the equipping process in less formal community engagement contexts. Using RE to further the learner grasp of CSE concepts, robotics may be presented to learners in terms of the content of RE and as a tool to introduce other subjects (such as CSE).

Using RE for CSE in a CE Context: Towards Good Practices

Simply increasing access to computing without adequate **support** *for* **educators** *and centring students' identities and cultures in the curriculum is just a veneer of broadening participation.*

(Yadav, Heath and Hu, 2022, 43)

Given that CE is already used to address the needs of RE, and that RE can be used for CSE, then by inference, CE can also be used to advance CSE. However, it should be clear that this undertaking is not trivial and will have to be undertaken in ways that would result in the growing and sustainable development of CS skills in communities. Understanding what constitutes good practice requires a complex multilevel, multi-layered understanding of good practices that relate to, inter alia the use of ER, good education practices, and especially the development of educators in all communities, and good CSE practices. Furthermore, there is a requirement to understand the CE elements that would contribute to an enabling environment that would support sustainable practices.

The extent to which RE can adjust or redesign the schooling education should be evaluated beyond merely a mathematics and physics perspective (Karim, Lemaignan and Mondada, 2016a). RE can effectively be used for the advancement of CSE (Fagin and Merkle, 2003). (Karim, Lemaignan and Mondada, 2016b) suggest that RE can ensure that the introduction of technology can support a new approach to education. The introduction of robotics needs to be evaluated both in terms of platforms and environments, and the need for equipping and training of educators for effective implementation of teaching and learning

As previously indicated, our intention in this chapter is to highlight good practices at the intersection of CSE, RE and CE that can inform the introduction of CSE through RE in CE context for (especially) South African schools.

We broadly base our approach to good practices in this chapter on the work of Kaplan and Norton on BSC method (Kaplan, 2009). The BSC method has its roots in organisational research on the measurement of organisational performance for enabling continuous improvement of the management of intangible organisational assets. The BSC method entails employing different perspectives on the organisation that informs the creation of sustainable stakeholder value (Kaplan, 2009, *op. cit.*)

The BSC method has been applied over diverse domains, including in education (Karathanos and Karathanos, 2005). Our view considers an intersection between CSE, RE, and CE as shown in Figure 1.

Figure 1. CSE, RE and CE: Intersection of domains

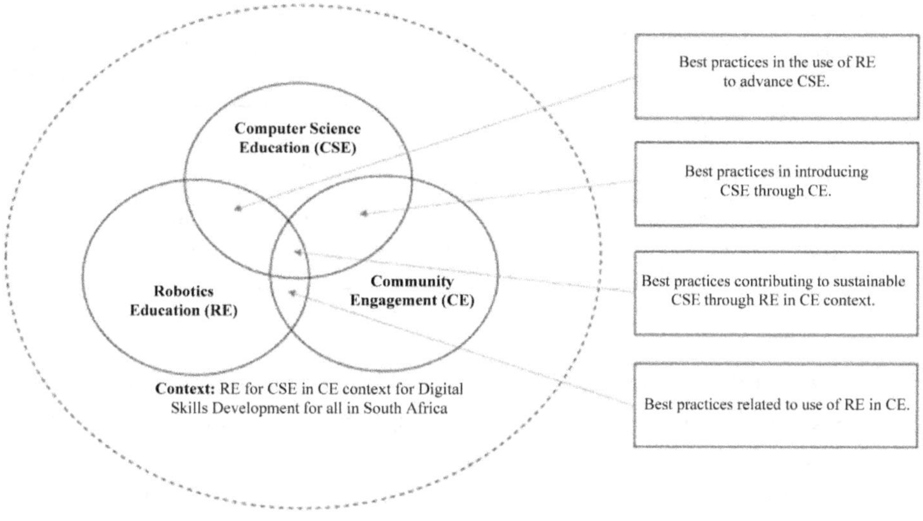

As presented in Figure 1, this chapter presents the achievement of a good practice strategy to advance CSE using RE in a CE context using the BSC from the four defined BSC perspectives (Kaplan, 2009), namely process (all related processes, not only internal processes as viewed in the organization), people (more broadly defined than the "customers" of Kaplan and Norton to account for all role players and stakeholders), resources (not only organizational financials), and growth and sustainability (broadly corresponding to "learning and growth"). The BSC perspectives are detailed from the literature for the three research focus concepts of CSE, RE, and CE, three 2-way intersections, and the one 3-way intersection as set out in Table 1. The perspectives are detailed in Table 2 to Table 6.

From Table 1 it is noted that each research focus (CSE, RE, and CE), the three 2-way intersection, and one 3-way intersection are considered strategically in terms of the four defined BSC perspectives that contribute to the strategy, namely process, people, resources and outcome for sustainability and growth. The BSC perspectives are detailed in Table 2 to Table 6.

Strategy

Table 2 presents an overview of the focus on the strategic best practices requirements (introduced in Table 1). The overall best practices requirements for each of the research concepts (RE, CSE, and CE)

Table 1. CSE, RE and CE: Strategy and 4 BSC perspectives

	Strategy (Table 2)	Process (Table 3)	People (Table 4)	Resources (Table 5)	Sustainability and Growth (Table 6)
CSE	Good practices to advance CSE	Processes in CSE	Role-players in CSE	Resources for CSE	Sustainability and growth of CSE
RE	Good practices to advance RE	Processes in RE	Role-players in RE	Resources for RE	Sustainability and growth of RE
CE	Good practices for impactful CE	Processes for CE	Role-players in CE	Resources for CE	Sustainability and growth of CE
RE and CE	Good practices to introduce RE in CE context	Processes for RE in CE context	Role-players for RE in CE context	Resources for RE in CE context	Sustainability and growth of RE in CE context
CSE and RE	Good practices to integrate RE and CSE	Processes to integrate RE and CSE	Role-players for RE for CSE	Resources for RE for CSE	Sustainability and growth of CSE using RE
CSE and CE	Good practices to introduce CSE in CE context	Processes for CSE in CE context	Role-players for CSE in CE context	Resources for CSE in CE context	Sustainability and growth of CSE in CE context
CSE, RE and CE	Good practices to advance CSE using RE in CE context	Processes for CSE using RE in CE context	Role-players for CSE using RE in CE context	Resources for CSE using RE in CE context	Sustainability and growth of CSE using RE in CE context

guide the best practices for the two-way intersections, and lead to recommendations for best practice for the three-way intersection (the advancement of CSE using RE in CE context). Some examples from the literature are included in the Requirements column of the table.

From Table 2, it is noted that the strategic best practices for each research focus (CSE, RE, and CE) and the three 2-way intersections are considered. From the literature, there are examples of best practice strategies for each of the research focuses (CSE, RE and CE), and the three 2-way intersections. The one 3-way interaction is recommended as the synthesis of the literature presented. It should be noted that the introduction of CSE via RE in a CE context represents the intersection of several diverse strategies, which represents a significantly complex multidisciplinary undertaking.

Process

Table 3 presents a focus on the process perspective, with reference to the current literature. The processes are supported by procedures that are identified as best practices. The defined processes for each of the research concepts (RE, CSE, and CE) then guide the processes required for each of the two-way intersections, and lead to the definition of the processes required for the three-way intersection.

From Table 3, it is noted that the best practices in terms of processes for each research focus (CSE, RE, and CE) and the three 2-way intersections are considered. From the literature, there are best practice processes for each of the research focuses (CSE, RE and CE), and the three 2-way intersections. The one 3-way interaction is recommended as the synthesis of the literature presented. From the literature examples, the processes need to be human-centred (i.e., active, collaborative, and involving all relevant role-players). Furthermore, the consideration of stages (and phases) and measurement and evaluation of processes is significant.

Table 2. Strategy

Strategy	Requirements
Good practices to advance CSE	Understand the cognitive models and processes involved in CSE (Robins, A., Rountree, J. and Rountree, 2003) Understand of the interaction between personality types and CS (Robins, A., Rountree, J. and Rountree, 2003). Distinguish between the comprehension and application of CS (Robins, A., Rountree, J. and Rountree, 2003) Consider procedural and object-oriented programming approaches (Robins, A., Rountree, J. and Rountree, 2003) Designing appropriate curriculum and tuition methods (Robins, A., Rountree, J. and Rountree, 2003) Allow educators access to quality CS activities, knowledge, and skills (Kopcha, Wilson and Yang, 2022). Ensure buy-in from all gate-keepers to overcome the identified barriers of CSE (McGarr *et al.*, 2023). Identify CSE role models to address under-representation (McGarr *et al.*, 2023) Develop CSE materials to encourage participation (McGarr *et al.*, 2023)
Good practices to advance RE	Understand the affordances of RE, including 21st century skills (Yang *et al.*, 2020) Apply appropriate learning strategies (constructivism and constructionism) (Goldman, Eguchi and Sklar, 2012) and (Luciano *et al.*, 2019) Understand barriers to the introduction, adoption, and use of RE in context (Alsoliman, 2018) Follow good practices: ensure practical application, allow exploration, engage with learners in context, and use opportunities (Thomas, 2021)
Good practices for impactful CE	Use strategies for best practices in impactful CE, including early engagement, understanding the community and the context, ensuring a flow of information around programmes, understanding community perspectives, allowing for community participation and shared ownership, acquiring permission, and ongoing review of engagement (Lavery *et al.*, 2010) Measure and evaluate the impact of CE (Hanover Research, 2011)
Good practices to introduce RE in CE context	Use RE to engage with learners with low RE opportunities in school (Goldman, Eguchi and Sklar, 2012) Use RE to engage with minority groups (Goldman, Eguchi and Sklar, 2012) Promote of RE through local (and localized) competitions and coach training (Maximova and Kim, 2021) Create multiple pathways for the participation of communities (Rusk *et al.*, 2008)
Good practices to integrate RE and CSE	Use scaffolding as a strategy (Angeli *et al.*, 2016; Angeli and Giannakos, 2020; Angeli and Valanides, 2020) Design learning scenarios (Piedade *et al.*, 2020) Combine constructionism with core patterns of CT (Piedade *et al.*, 2020) Use CSE RE integration model for educator CPD (El-Hamamsy *et al.*, 2021) Use RE activities to support CPD development of CS knowledge and skills (Kopcha, Wilson and Yang, 2022).
Good practices to introduce CSE in CE context	Ensure local support and enhanced capacity building (Maximova & Kim, 2020) Create learning through service opportunities (Oakes, Zoltowski and Drummond, 2014) Identify a plan for the advancement of CSE using RE in CE context (rather than a hit-and-and-run approach) (Oakes, Zoltowski and Drummond, 2014) Align with the requirements of the CSE curriculum (Clear *et al.*, 2019)
Good practices to advance CSE using RE in CE context	*Integrate the CSE with RE practical best practice activities, to strategically achieve the good practices of RE and CSE in the relevant CE context.*

People

Table 4 presents the focus on the people (role-players) perspective of Table 1. The overall people requirements for each of the research concepts (RE, CSE, and CE) guide the people requirements for each of the two-way intersections and leads to the synthesis of the people requirements for the three-way intersection.

From Table 4, it is noted that the best practices in terms of people (role-players) for each research focus (CSE, RE, and CE) and the three 2-way intersections are considered. From the literature, there are best practice role-players for each of the research focuses (CSE, RE and CE), and the three 2-way intersections. The one 3-way interaction is recommended as the synthesis of the literature presented. A

Table 3. Process

Process	Requirements
Processes in CSE	Develop ways of teaching that correspond to learning paths (Carbone and Kaasboll, 1998) Document good practices in accessible ways (Carbone and Kaasboll, 1998) Focus on CSE learning processes from a student perspective as complex and challenging (Piedade *et al.*, 2020) Develop processes to ensure support from all gatekeepers to address the barriers of CSE implementation (McGarr *et al.*, 2023) Integrate educators early in the CSE implementation process, and pilot the process before implementation to increase the probability of successful adoption (El-Hamamsy *et al.*, 2021) Use CPD of educators as centralised and systematic, and include MOOCs and distance learning (El-Hamamsy *et al.*, 2021) Ensure the process of CPD is active, collaborative, adapted, confidence building, and support for educators (El-Hamamsy *et al.*, 2021)
Processes in RE	Consider the project stages (Goldman, Eguchi and Sklar, 2012) Teach engineering fundamentals (Berry, Remy and Rogers, 2016) Introduce programming principles, starting with icon-based drag and drop coding (Silvis *et al.*, 2022)
Processes for CE	Ensure continuous learning (and adjustment of processes) as part of CE (Cavaye, 2004)
Processes for RE in CE context	Introduce RE in the community context as a technology diffusion process. Elements include enhancing the potential of adoption of RE, local actions, systemizing actions, and support actions (Maximova and Kim, 2021)
Processes to integrate RE and CSE	RE contributes towards a more active role of learners in the processes of mastering CS (Piedade *et al.*, 2020) Processes of construction of a robot entail significant aspects of CS (both CT and programming) and there is therefore an interaction between the processes associated with RE and the processes associated with CS (CT) (Piedade *et al.*, 2020) The educators require ongoing professional development using RE activities (Kopcha, Wilson and Yang, 2022)
Processes for CSE in CE context	Measure and evaluate the impact of CE (Hanover Research, 2011)
Processes for CSE using RE in CE context	*Integrate the CSE with RE practical processes to strategically achieve the good practices of RE and CSE in the relevant CE context. The processes should be well-defined, adaptive, interactive, relevant, and culturally appropriate (for age and language) curriculum including activities and assessments that have an annual roll-out plan with timelines, goals, objectives, and target measurements.*

diverse set of role players is involved, including experts (RE and CSE), community members, educators, coaches, and mentors. Ensuring a trusting environment where all these role players understand their relevance and are free to contribute to the success of the undertaking is essential. As indicated elsewhere in the chapter, a meaningful way of creating a cohesive structure would be the establishment of a Community of Practice (CoP). However, this (extensive) topic is not dealt with as part of this chapter.

Resources

Table 5 presents a focus on the required resources perspective of Table 1, with reference to the current literature. The resources required for each of the research concepts (RE, CSE, and CE) then guide the resources required for each of the two-way intersections, and lead to the synthesis of the resources required for the three-way intersection.

From Table 5, it is noted that the best practices in terms of resources for each research focus (CSE, RE, and CE) and the three 2-way intersections are considered. From the literature, there are best practices for resources for each of the research focuses (CSE, RE and CE), and the three 2-way intersections. The one 3-way interaction is recommended as the synthesis of the literature presented.

Table 4. People

People	Requirements
Role-players in CSE	Identify the educators and learners (Robins, A., Rountree, J. and Rountree, 2003) Identify the perceptions of CSE gatekeepers of school implementations, and wider stakeholder support and commitment (McGarr *et al.*, 2023) Identify the CSE role-models to motivate and encourage underrepresented groups (McGarr *et al.*, 2023) Ensure support for the reformation initiative (introduction of CSE in schools) of policy-makers and collaboration between all relevant stakeholders (unions, school leaders, educators, and CS experts) (El-Hamamsy *et al.*, 2021) Develop a COP for the exchange of activities and experiences (El-Hamamsy *et al.*, 2021)
Role-players in RE	Identify the learners, educators, experts, technical support, and researchers (Jing *et al.*, 2015; dos Santos and dos Santos, 2021; Koç and Büyük, 2021) Include pre-service educators (Kim *et al.*, 2015)
Role-players in CE	Identify networks of complex interaction (Cavaye, 2004) that may involve government (at various levels), individuals, private entities, community groups, and others. Include the tertiary institutions (Clifford and Petrescu, 2012)
Role-players for RE in CE context	Educators and educator trainers, volunteers and mentors, and visionary community leaders (Gouws *et al.*, 2021) Mentors (Goldman, Eguchi and Sklar, 2012) Trainers and coaches, and experts that can supply knowledge, skills and experience (Maximova and Kim, 2021)
Role-players for RE for CSE	STEM coaches (in this instance CSE) for educator support and technology experts (Kopcha, Wilson and Yang, 2022)
Role-players for CSE in CE context	Trainers and coaches, and experts that can supply knowledge, skills, and experience (Maximova and Kim, 2021) STEM coaches (in this instance CSE) for educator support and technology experts (Kopcha, Wilson and Yang, 2022)
Role-players for CSE using RE in CE context	*Integrate the role-players of CSE with the role-players of RE, to strategically achieve the good practices of RE and CSE in the relevant CE context. The role-players should be confident and competent learners, educators need to be competent and confident through relevant and effective CPD and access to a COP, with networking with stakeholders and policy makers.*

From the examples in literature, it may be noted that a diverse range of resources is required, including funding (for all aspects of the undertaking), infrastructure, information and computing technologies, and robotics technologies, and that the supply of resources should be explicitly planned for.

Growth and Sustainability

Table 6 presents an overview of the BSC perspective of growth and sustainability for the achievement of strategic best practices. The requirements for growth and sustainability for each of the research concepts (RE, CSE, and CE) then guide the requirements for growth and sustainability for each of the two-way intersections, and lead to the synthesis of the requirements for growth and sustainability of the three-way intersection.

From Table 6, it is noted that the best practices in terms of growth and sustainability for each research focus (CSE, RE, and CE) and the three 2-way intersections are considered. From the literature, there are best practices for growth and sustainability for each of the research focuses (CSE, RE and CE), and the three 2-way intersections. The one 3-way interaction is recommended as the synthesis of the literature presented.

From the examples provided in literature it may be observed that sustainability is largely dependent on human-related elements and relates to for instance, engagement between role-players, interaction and sharing of ideas and resources, and training and capacity building. Similar to the examples related

Table 5. Resources

Resources	Requirements
Resources for CSE	Create effective learning environment (Robins, A., Rountree, J. and Rountree, 2003) Provide support through funding required for the implementation of CSE in a school (McGarr *et al.*, 2023) Ensure any initiative of reform (introduction of CSE in schools) requires financial support and relevant infrastructure (El-Hamamsy *et al.*, 2021) Design a well-defined curriculum that includes corresponding resources,, and assessments (El-Hamamsy *et al.*, 2021)
Resources for RE	Secure robotics kits (Goldman, Eguchi and Sklar, 2012) Provide appropriate RE learning materials (Yang *et al.*, 2020) Ensure quality online robotics resources (Pozzi, Prattichizzo and Malvezzi, 2021) Follow a plan (Gouws and Mentz, 2021) Use ASTEMI (in South Africa) science Olympiads and competitions, as a resource for collaboration for the advancement of robotics competitions (Qidwai, Riley and El-Sayed, 2013; Graffin, Sheffield and Koul, 2022) and (Nugent *et al.*, 2016)
Resources for CE	Use of community centres (Goldman, Eguchi and Sklar, 2012)
Resources for RE in CE context	Use of supportive technologies (mobile) in rural areas, using mobile resources that can be transported to CE contexts (Rodríguez, 2013)
Resources for RE for CSE	Use and adapt the integration of the RE and CSE defined curricula to ensure the availability of well-defined curriculum materials (El-Hamamsy *et al.*, 2021)
Resources for CSE in CE context	A well-defined curriculum should include corresponding resources,, assessments to meet the needs of the community (El-Hamamsy *et al.*, 2021)
Resources for CSE using RE in CE context	*Integrate the existing resources of CSE with the existing resources of RE, to strategically achieve the good practices of RE and CSE resources in the relevant CE context. The resources include support (finance, infrastructure, HR, volunteers, mentors), time, and space. The required resources should be included in the process planning and should be measured and evaluated in terms of availability and effectiveness.*

to "process" previously presented, the importance of finding meaningful ways to measure sustainability is important.

CONCLUSION

This chapter focused on good practices related to the potential use of RE to introduce CSE in less formal contexts (in this instance CE).

In navigating CSE into and beyond the 21st century, RE can be used as a catalyst for the advancement of CSE, by equipping educators to be competent and confident. To ensure that RE advances CSE effectively and optimally, all perspectives of CSE, RE, and CE that support or hinder the implementation of CSE need to be identified and evaluated. CSE should be made widely available, given that it is considered core to 21st century skills. This chapter focused on the informal aspects. To ensure that the benefits of CSE are available to all learners, a concerted effort should be made to ensure that it is available to all communities. In this context, RE as a potential vehicle for CSE becomes important, because of the DBE explicit interest in including robotics and coding into the school curriculum from Grade R. RE is already being used to engage with communities of educators and learners to advance science engagement.

The contribution of this chapter has been to demonstrate the complexity of the interaction between CSE, RE, and CE that needs to be navigated for successful implementation of initiatives in less formal ways that are suitable for schools in communities. We also provide some examples of how good practices related to CSE, RE, and CE

Table 6. CSE, RE and CE: Growth and sustainability

Sustainability and Growth	Requirements
Sustainability and growth of CSE	Measure and evaluate the impact of teaching standards on outcomes (Robins, A., Rountree, J. and Rountree, 2003) Understand the characteristics of experts in CS (e.g. programmers) as an outcome of growth (Robins, A., Rountree, J. and Rountree, 2003) Build knowledge, capabilities, and CS-related behaviour in learners through innovative curricula (Robins et al., 2003) Identify and overcome barriers and perceptions of CSE gatekeepers that hinder CSE teaching (McGarr *et al.*, 2023) Present educator CPD to ensure ongoing support in CSE implementation (El-Hamamsy *et al.*, 2021) Investigate non-CSE adopters to ensure sustainability (El-Hamamsy *et al.*, 2021)
Sustainability and growth of RE	Growth in the mature use of RE requires ongoing training and development to ensure ongoing innovation during engagement (Goldman, Eguchi and Sklar, 2012) Reflect on progress (Danahy *et al.*, 2014)
Sustainability and growth of CE	Strengthen relationships between role players (Clifford and Petrescu, 2012) Trust and collaboration (Mbah, 2019) Ongoing incentives for engagement with and in communities. The need for a play-it-forward model (Hall, 2010; Tamarack, 2010)
Sustainability and growth of RE in CE context	Improve adoption and use of RE in CE, through appropriate processes for adoption and use of RE, and increase the number of initiatives for access and opportunity (Maximova and Kim, 2021)
Sustainability and growth of CSE using RE	Improve the adoption and use of RE for CSE, sharing of ideas and resources through a COP and MOOC repository (Gouws *et al.*, 2021)
Sustainability and growth of CSE in CE context	Ongoing incentives for engagement with and in communities. The need for a play-it-forward model (Hall, 2010; Tamarack, 2010)
Sustainability and growth of CSE using RE in CE context	*Integrate the growth and sustainability plans for CSE and RE, to strategically achieve the growth and sustainability required to advance CSE using RE within a defined CE context. For sustainability and growth, define realistic goals, and ensure regular evaluation and monitoring of the impact on learners and educators, with input from all relevant role players. Regular review and analysis of the progress towards goals. Hinderances must be identified and addressed, risks must be identified, and mitigation plans must be set in place.*

can be synthesized in terms of BSC perspectives towards a strategic, measurable, and unified BSC framework (Kaplan, 2009). The strategic good practices of CSE and RE within CE, can ensure that all communities have access to quality CSE. This engaged CE undertaking, however, requires the commitment of role-players and resources dedicated to the strategic best practices and processes to ensure the growth and sustainably of the initiative, learners and the educators that require vision, energy, and commitment from all role players.

REFERENCES

Alam, A. (2022). Educational Robotics and Computer Programming in Early Childhood Education: A Conceptual Framework for Assessing Elementary School Students' Computational Thinking for Designing Powerful Educational Scenarios. *1st IEEE International Conference on Smart Technologies and Systems for Next Generation Computing, ICSTSN 2022*, (pp. 1–7). IEEE. 10.1109/ICSTSN53084.2022.9761354

Alsoliman, B. (2018). The utilization of educational robotics in Saudi Schools: Potentials and Barriers from the perspective of the Saudi Teachers. *International Education Studies*, *11*(10), 105–111. doi:10.5539/ies.v11n10p105

Angel-Fernandez, J., & Vincze, M. (2018). Towards a Definition of Educational Robotics. P. Zech, & J. Piater (eds) *Proceedings of the Austrian Robotics Workshop*. Innsbruck Press. 10.15203/3187-22-1

Angeli, C. (2016*). International Forum of Educational Technology & Society A K-6 Computational Thinking Curriculum Framework : Implications for Teacher Knowledge.* International Forum of Educational Technology & Society.

Angeli, C., & Giannakos, M. (2020). Computational thinking education: Issues and challenges. *Computers in Human Behavior*, *105*, 106185. doi:10.1016/j.chb.2019.106185

Angeli, C., & Valanides, N. (2020). Developing young children's computational thinking with educational robotics: An interaction effect between gender and scaffolding strategy. *Computers in Human Behavior*, *105*, 105954. doi:10.1016/j.chb.2019.03.018

Arlegui, J. (2008). Robotics, Computer Science curricula and Interdisciplinary activities. Workshop Proceedings of SIMPAR, Venice, Italy. https://www.terecop.eu/downloads/simbar2008/arlegui_menegatti_moro_pina_final.pdf

Berenguel, M., Rodríguez, F., Moreno, J. C., Guzmán, J. L., & González, R. (2016). Tools and methodologies for teaching robotics in computer science & engineering studies. *Computer Applications in Engineering Education*, *24*(2), 202–214. doi:10.1002/cae.21698

Berry, C. A., Remy, S. L., & Rogers, T. E. (2016). Robotics for All Ages: A Standard Robotics Curriculum for K-16. *IEEE Robotics & Automation Magazine*, *23*(2), 40–46. doi:10.1109/MRA.2016.2534240

Bocconi, S. (2022) *Reviewing Computational Thinking in Compulsory Education.* EC. https://publications.jrc.ec.europa.eu/repository/handle/JRC128347

Carbone, A., & Kaasboll, J. (1998). A survey of methods used to evaluate computer science teaching. *6th Annual Conference on the teaching of computing and the 3rd Annual Conference on intergrating technology with computer science education: Changing the delivery of computer science education*, (pp. 41–45). ACM. 10.1145/282991.283014

Cavaye, J. (2004). Governance and Community Engagement: The Australia experience. Participatory governance: Planning, conflict mediation and public decision making in civil society, (pp. 85–102). IEEE.

Chiazzese, G., Arrigo, Chifari, Lonati, & Tosto. (2019). Educational robotics in primary school: Measuring the development of computational thinking skills with the bebras tasks. *Informatics (MDPI)*, *6*(4), 43. Advance online publication. doi:10.3390/informatics6040043

Choi, H. S., Crump, C., Duriez, C., Elmquist, A., Hager, G., Han, D., Hearl, F., Hodgins, J., Jain, A., Leve, F., Li, C., Meier, F., Negrut, D., Righetti, L., Rodriguez, A., Tan, J., & Trinkle, J. (2021). On the use of simulation in robotics: Opportunities, challenges, and suggestions formoving forward. *Proceedings of the National Academy of Sciences of the United States of America*, *118*(1), 1–9. doi:10.1073/pnas.1907856118 PMID:33323524

Clear, A. (2019) Computing Curricula 2020: Introduction and Community Engagement. *Proceedings of the 50th ACM Technical Symposium on Computer Science Education (SIGCSE '19). Association for Computing Machinery*, (pp. 653–654). ACM. 10.1145/3287324.3287517

Clifford, D., & Petrescu, C. (2012). The keys to university-community engagement sustainability. *Non-profit Management & Leadership, 23*(1), 77–91. doi:10.1002/nml.21051

Correll, N., Wing, R. & Coleman, D. (2013). A one-year introductory robotics curriculum for computer science upperclassmen. *IEEE Transactions on Education, 56*(1), 54–60. . doi:10.1109/TE.2012.2220774

Crick, T. (2022). Cwricwlwm i Gymru 2022: A New Era for Computer Science in Schools in Wales?' *ACM International Conference Proceeding Series*. ACM. 10.1145/3555009.3555024

Csapó, G. (2019). Placing event-action-based visual programming in the process of computer science education. *Acta Polytechnica Hungarica, 16*(2), 35–57. doi:10.12700/APH.16.2.2019.2.3

Danahy, E., Wang, E., Brockman, J., Carberry, A., Shapiro, B., & Rogers, C. B. (2014). LEGO-based Robotics in Higher Education: 15 Years of Student Creativity. *International Journal of Advanced Robotic Systems, 11*(2), 27. doi:10.5772/58249

Department of Science and Technology. (2015). Science Engagement Strategy. *Science and society engaging to enrich and improve our lives, 2015*(1), 1–46. https://www.saasta.ac.za/saasta_wp/wp-content/uploads/2017/11/Science_Engagement_Strategy-11.pdf

dos Santos, P., & dos Santos, T. (2021). Analysis of a didactic sequence using educational robotics to teach graphs in kinematics. *Physics Education, 56*(1), 015015. https://iopscience.iop.org/article/10.1088/1361-6552/abc8fb/meta. doi:10.1088/1361-6552/abc8fb

El-Hamamsy, L., Chessel-Lazzarotto, F., Bruno, B., Roy, D., Cahlikova, T., Chevalier, M., Parriaux, G., Pellet, J.-P., Lanarès, J., Zufferey, J. D., & Mondada, F. (2021). A computer science and robotics integration model for primary school: Evaluation of a large-scale in-service K-4 teacher-training program, Education and Information Technologies. *Education and Information Technologies, 26*(3), 2445–2475. doi:10.1007/s10639-020-10355-5 PMID:33162777

Esposito, J. (2017). The State of Robotics Education: Proposed Goals for Positively Transforming Robotics Education at Postsecondary Institutions. *IEEE Robotics & Automation Magazine, 24*(3), 157–164. https://ieeexplore.ieee.org/abstract/document/7970162. doi:10.1109/MRA.2016.2636375

Esteve-Mon, F. M. (2019). The development of computational thinking in student teachers through an intervention with educational robotics. *Journal of Information Technology Education: Innovations in Practice, 18*, 139–152. doi:10.28945/4442

Fagin, B., & Merkle, L. (2003). Measuring the effectiveness of robots in teaching computer science. SIGCSE Bulletin (Association for Computing Machinery, Special Interest Group on Computer Science Education), (pp. 307–311). ACM. doi:10.1145/611892.611994

Fagin, B. S., Merkle, L. D., & Eggers, T. W. (2001). Teaching computer science with robotics using Ada/Mindstorms 2.0. *ACM SIGAda Ada Letters, XXI*(4), 73–78. doi:10.1145/507546.507592

Fletcher, C. L., & Warner, J. R. (2021). CAPE: A Framework for Assessing Equity throughout the Computer Science Education Ecosystem. *Communications of the ACM, 64*(2), 23–25. doi:10.1145/3442373

Goldman, R., Eguchi, A., & Sklar, E. (2012). *Using Educational Robotics to engage inner-city students with technology*. Embracing Diversity in the Learning Sciences.

GouwsP. (2021). Towards Defining the Place and Role of Robotics MOOCs in OdeL. UnisaRxiv. https://www.scienceopen.com/hosted-document?doi=10.25159/UnisaRxiv/000017.v1 doi:10.25159/UnisaRxiv/000017.v1

Gouws, P., & Mentz, J. (2021). Towards a comprehensive conceptual framework for Robotics Education. Proceeedings of EdMedia and Innovate Learning. Association for the Advancement of Computing in Education (AACE).

Graffin, M., Sheffield, R., & Koul, R. (2022). '"More than Robots": Reviewing the Impact of the FIRST® LEGO® League Challenge Robotics Competition on School Students' STEM Attitudes, Learning, and Twenty-First Century Skill Development', *Journal for STEM Education Research. Journal for STEM Education Research*, *5*(3), 322–343. doi:10.1007/s41979-022-00078-2

Hall, M. (2010). Community Engagement in South African Higher Education. *Kagisano. CHE Pretoria*, (6).

Hanover Research. (2011) *Best Practices in Measuring University-Community Engagement*. Hanover Research. https://intranet.ecu.edu.au/__data/assets/pdf_file/0006/208689/Measuring-University-Community-Engagement-Edith-Cowan-University.pdf

Hopcroft, J. E. (1986). The impact of robotics on computer science. *Communications of the ACM*, *29*(6), 486–498. doi:10.1145/5948.5949

Jing, Q. (2015). A Case Study on LEGO Activity in Physics Class: Taking the "Rotational Kinetic Energy" for Example. *2015 IEEE 15th International Conference on Advanced Learning Technologies*, (pp. 293-295). IEEE. https://ieeexplore.ieee.org/abstract/document/7265329

Kaplan, R. S. (2009). Conceptual Foundations of the Balanced Scorecard. *Handbooks of Management Accounting Research*, *3*, 1253–1269. doi:10.1016/S1751-3243(07)03003-9

Karathanos, D., & Karathanos, P. (2005). Applying the Balanced Scorecard to Education. *Journal of Education for Business*, *80*(4), 222–240. https://www.tandfonline.com/doi/abs/10.3200/JOEB.80.4.222-230. doi:10.3200/JOEB.80.4.222-230

Karim, M. E., Lemaignan, S., & Mondada, F. (2016a). A review: Can robots reshape K-12 STEM education? *Proceedings of IEEE Workshop on Advanced Robotics and its Social Impacts, ARSO*. IEEE. 10.1109/ARSO.2015.7428217

Karim, M. E., Lemaignan, S., & Mondada, F. (2016b). A review: Can robots reshape K-12 STEM education? *Proceedings of IEEE Workshop on Advanced Robotics and its Social Impacts, ARSO*. IEEE. 10.1109/ARSO.2015.7428217

Kay, J. S. (2003). Teaching Robotics from a Computer Science Perspective. *J. Comput. Sci. Coll.* ACM. https://dl.acm.org/citation.cfm?id=948785.948831

Khan, P., & Bari, M. (2023). Impact of Emergence With Robotics At Educational Institution And Emerging Challenge. *International Journal of Multidisciplinary Engineering in Current Research*, *6*(12), 42–46.

Kim, C. (2015). Robotics to promote elementary education pre-service teachers. STEM engagement, learning, and teaching: Computers and Education. Elsevier Ltd. doi:10.1016/j.compedu.2015.08.005

Koç, A., & Büyük, U. (2021). Effect of Robotics Technology in Science Education on Scientific Creativity and Attitude Development. *Journal of Turkish Science Education*, *18*(1), 54–72. doi:10.36681/tused.2021.52

Kopcha, T. J., Wilson, C. Y., & Yang, D. (2022). Improving teacher use of educational robotics to teach computer science in K-5 mathematics. *Computational Thinking in Pre, K-5*, 47–54. doi:10.1145/3507951.3519287

Lavery, J., Tinadana, P. O., Scott, T. W., Harrington, L. C., Ramsey, J. M., Ytuarte-Nuñez, C., & James, A. A. (2010). Towards a framework for community engagement in global health research. *Trends in Parasitology*, *26*(6), 279–283. doi:10.1016/j.pt.2010.02.009 PMID:20299285

Leonard, J., Mitchell, M., Barnes-Johnson, J., Unertl, A., Outka-Hill, J., Robinson, R., & Hester-Croff, C. (2018). Preparing Teachers to Engage Rural Students in Computational Thinking through Robotics, Game Design, and Culturally Responsive Teaching. *Journal of Teacher Education*, *69*(4), 386–407. doi:10.1177/0022487117732317

Luciano, A. P. (2019). The educational robotics and Arduino platform: Constructionist learning strategies to the teaching of physics. *Journal of Physics: Conference Series*, *1286*(1), 012044. doi:10.1088/1742-6596/1286/1/012044

Maximova, M., & Kim, Y. H. (2021). The effective diffusion of educational robotics in rural areas: A case study in the Sakha Republic of Russia. *European Journal of Educational Research*, *10*(1), 145–159. doi:10.12973/eu-jer.10.1.145

Mbah, M. (2019). 'Can local knowledge make the difference? Rethinking universities' community engagement and prospect for sustainable community development'. *The Journal of Environmental Education*, *50*(1), 11–22. https://www.tandfonline.com/doi/full/10.1080/00958964.2018.1462136?scroll=top&needAccess=true. doi:10.1080/00958964.2018.1462136

McGarr, O., Exton, C., Power, J., & McInerney, C. (2023). 'What about the gatekeepers? School principals' and school guidance counsellors' attitudes towards computer science in secondary schools'. *Computer Science Education*, *33*(2), 168–185. doi:10.1080/08993408.2021.1953296

McNulty, N. (2021) *Introduction to the CAPS Coding and Robotics Curriculum*. Niall McNulty. https://www.niallmcnulty.com/2021/05/introduction-to-the-caps-coding-and-robotics-curriculum/

Michener, L., Cook, J., Ahmed, S. M., Yonas, M. A., Coyne-Beasley, T., & Aguilar-Gaxiola, S. (2012). Aligning the goals of community-engaged research: Why and how academic health centers can successfully engage with communities to improve health. *Academic Medicine*, *87*(3), 285–291. doi:10.1097/ACM.0b013e3182441680 PMID:22373619

Ministry of Communication and Digital Technologies. (2020). National Digital and Future Skills Strategy. *Government Gazette*, (43730), 3–38.

Molala, T. S., & Makhubele, J. C. (2021). The Connection Between Digital Divide and Social Exclusion: Implications for Social Work. *Humanities & Social Sciences Reviews*, *9*(4), 194–201. doi:10.18510/hssr.2021.9427

Newton, K. J. (2020). Informal STEM: learning with robotics and game design in an urban context. *Journal of Research on Technology in Education*. Routledge, *52*(2), 129–147. . doi:10.1080/15391523.2020.1713263

Nugent, G., Barker, B., Grandgenett, N., & Welch, G. (2016). 'Robotics camps, clubs, and competitions: Results from a US robotics project', *Robotics and Autonomous Systems. Robotics and Autonomous Systems*, *75*, 686–691. doi:10.1016/j.robot.2015.07.011

Oakes, W. C., Zoltowski, C. B., & Drummond, M. (2014). Dissemination of community engagement in engineering and computing. *2014 IEEE Frontiers in Education Conference (FIE) Proceedings*, (pp. 1–7). IEEE. https://ieeexplore.ieee.org/abstract/document/7044371

Piedade, J., Dorotea, N., Pedro, A., & Matos, J. F. (2020). On teaching programming fundamentals and computational thinking with educational robotics: A didactic experience with pre-service teachers. *Education Sciences*, *10*(9), 1–15. doi:10.3390/educsci10090214

Pozzi, M., Prattichizzo, D., & Malvezzi, M. (2021). Accessible Educational Resources for Teaching and Learning Robotics. *Robotics (Basel, Switzerland)*, *10*(38), 1–21. doi:10.3390/robotics10010038

Qidwai, U., Riley, R., & El-Sayed, S. (2013). Attracting Students to the Computing Disciplines: A Case Study of a Robotics Contest. Procedia - Social and Behavioral Sciences, 102, 520–531. doi:10.1016/j.sbspro.2013.10.768

Raj, R. K., & Kumar, A. N. (2022). Toward computer science curricular guidelines 2023 (CS2023). *ACM Inroads*, *13*(4), 22–25. doi:10.1145/3571092

Robins, A., Rountree, J., & Rountree, N. (2003). Learning and Teaching Programming : A Review and Discussion. *Computer Science Education*, *13*(2), 137–172. doi:10.1076/csed.13.2.137.14200

Rodríguez, A. (2013). Learning by teaching robotics with mobile devices in rural areas. *International Conference on Information Society (i-Society 2013)*. IEEE. https://ieeexplore.ieee.org/abstract/document/6636353

Rusk, N., Resnick, M., Berg, R., & Pezalla-Granlund, M. (2008). New pathways into robotics: Strategies for broadening participation. *Journal of Science Education and Technology*, *17*(1), 59–69. doi:10.1007/s10956-007-9082-2

Silvis, D., Lee, V. R., Clarke-Midura, J., & Shumway, J. F. (2022). The technical matters: Young children debugging (with) tangible coding toys. *Information and Learning Science*, *123*(9–10), 577–600. doi:10.1108/ILS-12-2021-0109

Tamarack. (2010). *Approaches to Measuring more Community Engagement, Tamarak Institute for Community Engagement*. Tamarack Community. http://tamarackcommunity.ca/downloads/index/Measuring_More_Community_Engagement.pdf.

Thomas, S. (2021). Best Practices in Robotics Education: Perspectives from an IEEE RAS Women in Engineering Panel. *IEEE Robotics and Auto*, *8*(1). http://0-ieeexplore-ieee-org.oasis.unisa.ac.za/stamp/stamp.jsp?tp=&arnumber=9382158&isnumber=9382150

Usart, M. (2019). Are 21st century skills evaluated in robotics competitions? The case of first lego league competition. *CSEDU 2019 - Proceedings of the 11th International Conference on Computer Supported Education, 1*(Csedu), 445–452. 10.5220/0007757404450452

Weintrop, D. (2019). Education block-based programming in computer science education. *Communications of the ACM, 62*(8), 22–25. doi:10.1145/3341221

Yadav, A., Heath, M., & Hu, A. D. (2022). Toward justice in computer science through community, criticality, and citizenship. *Communications of the ACM, 65*(5), 42–44. doi:10.1145/3527203

Yang, Y., Long, Y., Sun, D., Van Aalst, J., & Cheng, S. (2020). 'Fostering students' creativity via educational robotics: An investigation of teachers' pedagogical practices based on teacher interviews'. *British Journal of Educational Technology, 51*(5), 1826–1842. doi:10.1111/bjet.12985

Chapter 11
Teachers' and Learners' Acceptance of the Use of Robotics in the Intermediate Phase

Maryke Anneke Mihai
https://orcid.org/0000-0003-0254-6122
University of Pretoria, South Africa

Doctor Mapheto
University of Pretoria, South Africa

ABSTRACT

This study explored teachers' and learners' acceptance of the use of robotics based on their attitudes and experiences in two primary schools, which integrate robotics as a learning tool. Robotics is the current digital technology in the educational sector and offers new possibilities for modeling teaching and learning. The study used the technological acceptance model (TAM) as the theoretical framework and a qualitative approach. The researcher purposively sampled six learners and six teachers from the two identified schools in Pretoria, Gauteng. The study discovered that the integration of robotics in education is demanding, costly, and requires adequate resources. It necessitates additional time to design educational programs, requires more time for workshops and solving technical glitches, and puts more pressure on teachers. Teachers need support with the resolving of hardware and software issues as well as technical maintenance. Learners perceive robotics as a positive and exciting technological learning approach, which promotes teamwork and hands-on learning.

INTRODUCTION

The integration of robotics in education has been a topic of growing interest and discussion in recent years (Ali et al., 2023). With advancements in technology, robotics has become more accessible and affordable for educational institutions, particularly in the Intermediate Phase. This phase, which typically

DOI: 10.4018/979-8-3693-1066-3.ch011

encompasses children between the ages of 10 and 14, is a critical stage in their educational journey, as they transition from the foundational knowledge of the Primary Phase to more specialised subjects in the later stages of their schooling. While the potential benefits of incorporating robotics into the curriculum are widely acknowledged, questions remain regarding the extent to which teachers and learners are embracing this approach. Robots are defined as programmable machines or tools that can substitute humans in executing a variety of activities by integrating input commands (Barreto, & Benitti, 2012).

In addition, as part of transformation, learning institutions are supposed to prepare learners to participate in a digital world by considering technology integration in their curriculum (Ketelhut & Mills, 2020). As a result, robotics has been introduced in education to enhance the utilisation of technology and to prepare learners to participate in a digital world. Robotics incorporates Science, Technology, Engineering and Mathematics (STEM) spectrum and is a tactic to instil and strengthen STEM subjects (Cejka et al., 2012). According to Mauch (2015) robotics in education is a purely technological approach of instilling knowledge with 21st century skills, which involves problem solving, critical thinking, innovation and creativity. According to Agenda (2023), the World Economic Forum list analytical thinking, creative thinking, resilience, flexibility and agility, motivation and self-awareness, curiosity and lifelong learning and technological literacy as the top skills needed in 2023, while artificial intelligence and big data will be on top of the list by 2027. These skills need to be instilled in the learners of today.

The objectives of the chapter were to explore the perceptions of teachers and learners in accepting the use of robotics in the Intermediate Phase, to identify factors that affect the acceptance of the use of robotics in the Intermediate Phase, to assess the ease of which Intermediate Phase teachers and learners find in using robotics and to establish the use of incorporating robotics into teaching and learning in the Intermediate Phase.

BACKGROUND

Digital technologies have a crucial influence on the educational sector and significantly model educational principles at different phases (Samuels, 2016). Robotics is the outcome of development, inquisitiveness, capabilities and creativity of human thought on how to make tools and machineries be able to resolve challenges and perform precise activities freely (Hongshuai, 2021). The progression of transformation through technical and material conquests, has led to the construction of tools that are equipped with autonomy and skills. The evolution of robotics is entangled with the histories of technological developments, engineering and science. Technology used in computer science, manufacturing of cars, even advanced electronical gadgets, engineering and fluid mechanics could all be regarded as the key components of the initiative of robotics.

Robotics is the current digital technology in the educational sector and offers new possibilities for modelling teaching and learning. User acceptance is one of the key aspects, which should be taken into consideration when new technology is introduced, because this can influence the success of the implementation of robotics. The aspects of user acceptance are the attitudes and experiences related to using robotics. To facilitate a positive integration of robotics in education necessitates considering the attitudes of teachers and learners. Teachers' and learners' attitudes towards robotics will regulate the future acceptance of robotics for teaching and learning. Moreover, according to Jaipal-Jamani and Angeli (2017) a person's technological acceptance is the main aspect in establishing the success or failure of technology practice.

Few scholars have researched the acceptance of robotics in the educational setting (Ali et al., 2023; Rao & AbJalil, 2021; Mavrida et al., 2010, Lei et al., 2022). Most of these studies are based on skills that learners acquire when learning with robotics in the classroom whereby the acceptance of teachers represents robotics as a learning aid to assist the teacher to administer effective teaching. Very little research is gathered on teachers' acceptance and attitudes towards the utilization of robotics as an educational tool, even though robotics in educational sectors was implemented for teaching and learning. The Technology Acceptance Model (TAM) by Davis (1989) is an appropriate framework to identify and explore the acceptance of teachers and learners towards the use of robotics in education. The TAM model encompasses different sections that demonstrate the process of technology acceptance by people who are using it; involving external factors, perceived usefulness, perceived ease of use and attitude towards using (Lai, 2017).

This chapter is based on two primary schools in Gauteng, Pretoria East. The schools offer robotics as part of their curriculum to promote and furnish learners with 21st century skills. All the adequate and necessary resources are available to facilitate learning in robotics such as tablets, laptops, EV3 bricks, data projectors, white boards, Lego Mindstorms and Wi-Fi connection for internet access. In terms of human resources, educators are going through training and workshops so that they can administer lessons about robotics. Teachers' and learners' acceptance of the use of robotics were explored based on their experiences when teaching and learning with robotics.

The study identified the following gaps:

- The impact of robotics on 21st skills development in learners.
- Teachers' readiness and attitudes towards robotics integration.
- Practical challenges in the implementation of robotics in education.

LITERATURE REVIEW

The History of Robotics

According to Carey and Clarke (2019), the origin of robotics initiated back from the Greek theorist Aristotle's philosophies about computerised tools.

The Russian biochemistry professor Asimov predicted the moral and social insinuations that could result from the integration of automated tools in society in 1940 (Portelli, 1980). As a result, Asimov proposed to organise the basic principles of how people should interact with robots by introducing the three laws of robotics in 1942. The first law asserted: "A robot may not injure a human being or through inaction, allow a human being to be harmed" (Portelli, 1980, p.150).

The second law: "A robot should obey the instructions allocated to it by people except where such commands would clash with the First Law". The third law: "A robot should shield its own existence as long as such defence does not battle with the First or Second Laws" (Portelli, 1980, p. 150). These three laws of robotics by are still applicable in the current application of robotics and coding of different technological gadgets in education, science and engineering fields (Carey & Clarke, 2019). Figure 1 below shows the history, biggest developments and milestones of robotics up until the present day.

Figure 1. A brief history of robotics
(Carey and Clarke, 2019)

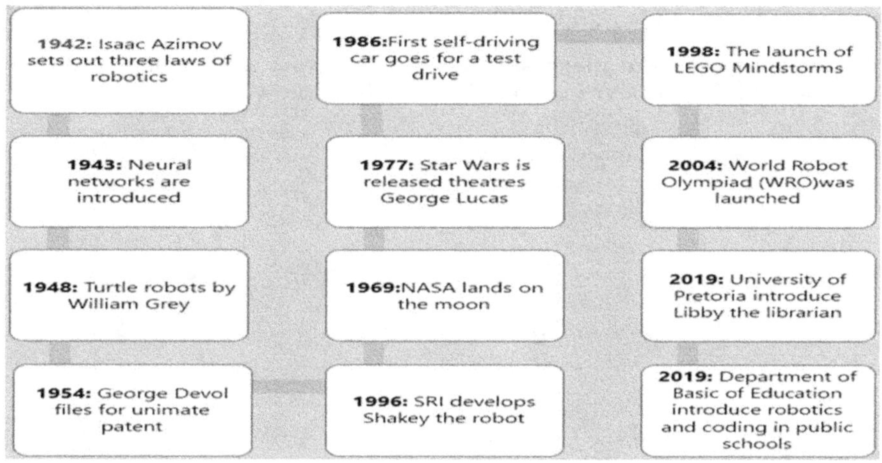

The State of Robotics Curriculum in the South African Education System

The White Paper on Science, Technology and Innovation (Department of Science and Technology, 2019) outlines the long-term strategies to give a way forward for the South African government to ensure that there is an increasing role of Science Technology and Innovation (STI) in a more effective and comprehensive culture. As a result, it emphasises utilising STI to assist South Africans to benefit from transformations such as fast technological developments and the important developments that are linked with the 4IR. In response to the 4IR South Africa has developed a coding and robotics curriculum to be integrated from grades R-9. According to the South African national Department of Basic Education (DBE, 2021a), the curriculum will provide learners with knowledge and skills of coding and robotics and will prepare them for the 4IR.

The piloting of schools for coding and robotics for Grade R-3 has taken place in two hundred schools across all the provinces in South Africa whereas, in Grade 7 one thousand schools have been piloted (Staff Writer, 2021). The piloted schools were provided with tablets and robotics equipment. According to DBE (2021a), there will be no additional instructors or coaches that will be employed to facilitate robotics in schools. As a result, some of the universities such as the University of Pretoria, University of South Africa, University of Witwatersrand and non-governmental organisations have partnered with the DBE to offer teachers training and technological services to administer coding and robotics (Veldman et al., 2021). Figures 2 and 3 below show the number of pilot schools per province from grades R-7.

Due to the Covid-19 pandemic the initial strategies and plans to pilot robotics in public schools have been affected negatively in terms of time. The DBE initially planned to start with the integration of robotics in 2020 by commencing with grades R-3 and followed by grades 4-6 in the 2021 academic year (DBE, 2021a). The piloting approach for grades 7-9 should have been done in 2022. Nevertheless, the drafted coding and robotics curriculum that was submitted to Umalusi for assessment and quality assurance was only approved and gazetted in 2021. These transitions led to a backlog and the DBE came up with new plans to pilot robotics in all schools across South Africa. In 2021 the piloting process started

Figure 2. The number of pilot schools per province Grade R-3
(DBE, 2021a)

PILOT GRADE R -3

The Grade R-3 Pilot will take place in 200 schools across all provinces. The number of pilot schools per province are as outlined in the table below.

	PROVINCE	NO OF GRADE R -3 SCHOOLS
1	EASTERN CAPE	25
2	FREE SATE	15
3	GAUTENG	33
4	KWAZULU-NATAL	33
5	LIMPOPO	22
6	MPUMALANGA	17
7	NORTHERN CAPE	10
8	NORTH WEST	15
9	WESTERN CAPE	30
TOTAL		**200**

NATIONAL DEVELOPMENT PLAN 2030 8 Read to Lead

Figure 3. The number of pilot schools per province Grade 7
(DBE, 2021a)

PILOT GRADE 7

The Grade 7 Pilot will take place in 1000 schools across all provinces. The number of pilot schools per province are as outlined in the table below.

	PROVINCE	NO OF GRADE R -3 SCHOOLS
1	EASTERN CAPE	111
2	FREE STATE	111
3	GAUTENG	111
4	KWAZULU-NATAL	112
5	LIMPOPO	111
6	MPUMALANGA	111
7	NORTHERN CAPE	111
8	NORTH WEST	111
9	WESTERN CAPE	111
TOTAL		**1 000**

NATIONAL DEVELOPMENT PLAN 2030 9 Read to Lead

with grades R – 7, followed by grade 8 in 2022 and lastly, grade 9 will be piloted in the 2023 academic year (Staff Writer, 2021).

The Coding and Robotics Curriculum Grade R-9 in South Africa

The coding and robotics subject plays an essential role in a digital and information driven world by integrating technological skills and transmits these skills to handle day-to-day situations in the development of learners (DBE, 2021b). As a result, it is concerned with the enhancement and instilling of STEM related subjects in education. The subject coding and robotics in grades R-9 has been divided into five content areas. Figure 4 below shows the focus content areas in grade R-9.

Figure 4. Coding and robotics focus areas Grade R-9
(DBE, 2021b)

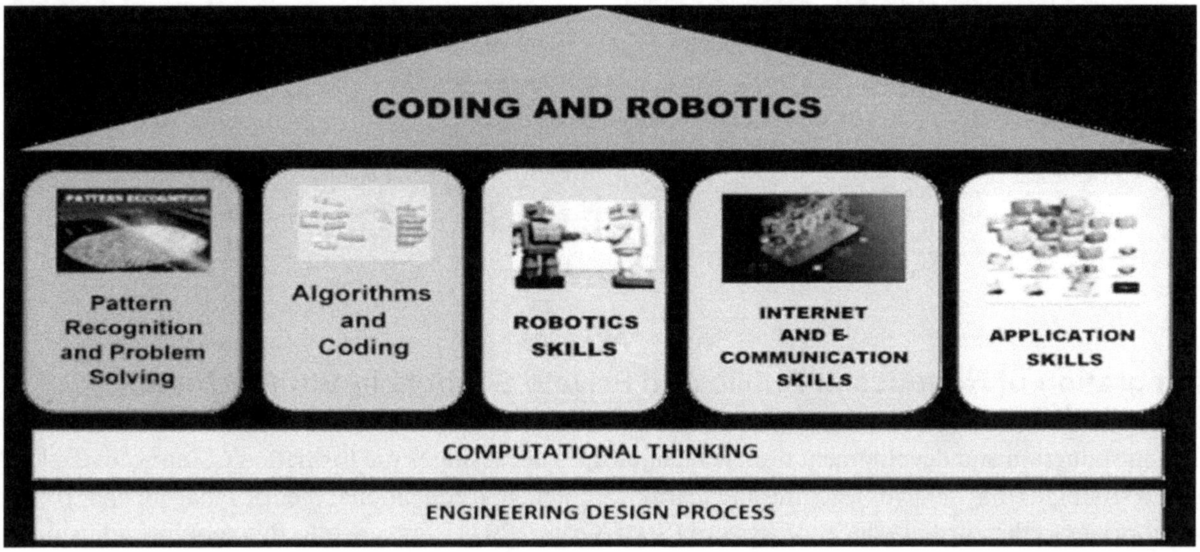

The method of teaching and learning of the subject is constructed on the foundation of computational thinking and engineering designing processes (DBE, 2021b). The components of each content area are imparted in its strand but is also strengthened in other components. For example, pattern recognition and problem-solving constitutes certain abilities which still need to be established, but also creates the groundwork for algorithms and coding. Algorithms and coding are integrated to align a logical sequence that robots utilize, and the application skills show learners how to cooperate and communicate with different technological gadgets. Therefore, Internet and e-communications focus on the implementation of technological gadgets that are imparted in application skills and integrate the same skills to direct and generate messages. However, the content areas from grade R-9 are the same but they differ in skills and content knowledge per grade.

The coding and robotics curriculum is based on hands-on learning and involves the Practical Assessment Task (PAT), which are recorded as formal tasks and should be administered during the formal teaching and learning time according to the Annual Teaching Plan (ATP). The administration of informal tasks persists during lessons when learners are not engaging in PAT. Therefore, time allocation becomes one of the key elements when administering the lessons in the coding and robotics curriculum.

The pedagogical approach of teaching and learning robotics is based on the foundation of computational thinking. The integration of computational thinking is a fundamental skill in robotics to solve problems, create effective systems and innovative ideas. According to Chalmers (2018) there are four pillars of computational thinking which are as follows: decomposition, pattern recognition, algorithm design and abstraction. Figure 5 below shows the four pillars of computational thinking.

Figure 5. The four pillars of computational thinking
(Chalmers, 2018)

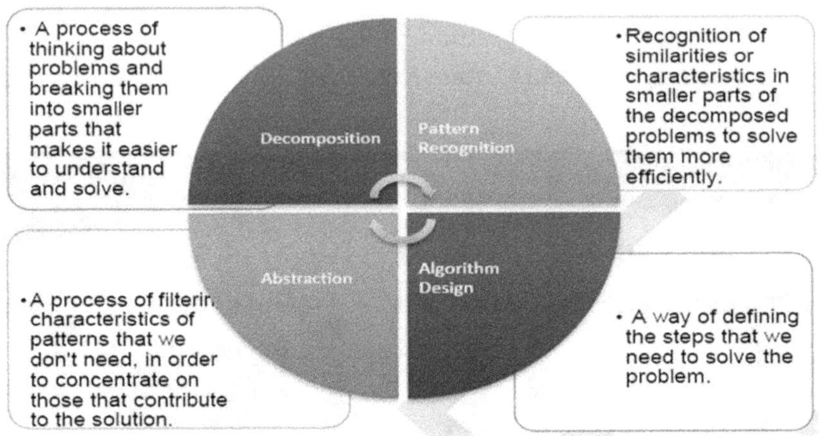

Integration of Robotics in Public and Private Schools in South Africa

The introduction and development of new technologies necessitates the formation of innovative educational strategies that involves teaching and learning content and educational theories that are creative and appropriate to the current education system (Staff Writer, 2021). As a result, this requires adjustments to influential philosophies to allow a successful 21st century period of teaching and learning. According to Zawacki-Richter and Latchem (2018) the utilization of computers and technological devices such as overhead projectors, PowerPoint presentations, tablets, clickers, and smartboards are the normal use of technology in the current education system, specifically in private schools. The incorporation of robotics in teaching and learning to enhance the 21st century skills, has become a preferred pedagogical device in the current education system (Jung & Won, 2018).

The integration of robotics in public and private schools in South Africa shows a huge digital divide (Staff Writer, 2021). Most private schools in South Africa introduced robotics into their curriculum from 2010, whereas the DBE piloted robotics in 2021 across all the nine provinces in South African public schools. Hence, this shows a huge difference in terms of the time frame of integration and not all schools that have been piloted are integrating robotics due to circumstantial issues such as limited resources, internet access, facilities and human resources. The piloting of schools involved schools, which are mainly situated in urban areas. During the piloting of robotics in schools the DBE provided the schools with robot equipment and tablets as part of the resources to be used to incorporate robotics. The DBE provided teachers with training workshops after school hours in partnership with higher institutions to gain knowledge and develop skills in robotics. However, according to Chisango and Marongwe (2018), afternoon training could contribute negatively on the time available for teachers to be fully engaged in learning, since they were facilitating their lessons during the day.

South Africa has many public schools, and some are rooted in deep rural areas whereby there are social and economic issues that should be taken into consideration and therefore the integration of robotics in those schools becomes a pipe dream to be achieved in the future. This was also confirmed during the Covid-19 pandemic lockdown whereby the method of teaching and learning was moved from physical teaching and learning to online learning (Mahaye, 2020). The public schools in rural areas suffered tremendously and this even created a digital divide between urban and rural schools. Teachers from the rural areas were unable to use digital technology for online classes and struggled to adapt to online teaching due to a lack of adequate digital knowledge and skills. Some challenges experienced by teachers were associated with the lack of facilities to conduct online classes such as digital gadgets, access to data and lack of network and internet use especially in some rural areas where there is no electricity (Du Plessis & Mestry, 2019). In some of the rural schools, the integration of technology is at a minimal stage and is used for basic operations such as entering of learners' marks though the South African School Administrative and Management System (SASAMS) and typing and printing out of question papers. However, according to Du Plessis and Mestry (2019) some schools lack teachers who are technologically competent and able to support their fellow colleagues in integrating technology efficiently into their lessons.

In private schools the integration of robotics was initiated by offering teachers who specialize in technology, science and mathematics, training and after training sessions teachers were assessed theoretically (Pather, 2020). The schools also have policies which give them guidance and direction on the implementation process and teachers have access to support sessions online which includes videos, tutorials and activities. In private schools they also employ human resources specifically for maintenance and technical glitches that may occur during the learning process with robotics (Pather, 2020). Hence, teachers only focus on facilitating their planned lessons according to ATP efficiently without worrying about the maintenance of gadgets or any technical glitches. Whereas in public schools, according to the DBE (2021a) there will be no additional teachers or coaches that will be employed to facilitate robotics within school premises. As a result, teachers will be responsible for facilitating the lessons and solving technical problems such as software updates, poor connections and hardware malfunctions. However, the study by Chambers and Carbonaro (2018) shows that for the smooth running and integration of technology the school should have a qualified technician within the school premises to solve technical glitches.

Many private and former Model C schools in South Africa are already competing in the WRO competition. The WRO competition was first established in 2004 in Singapore. There were some private schools, which represented South Africa on an international level with robotics in countries like Malaysia, India and Russia, and some took part in Costa Rica to enhance their participation in robotics (ORT South Africa, 2017). According to Ntekane (2018) the integration of robotics in private schools is also influenced by positive parental involvement in terms of support, funding and availability. The study by Ates (2021) shows that parents have a crucial influence in encouraging their children's interest in the usage of technology or taking part in extra-mural activities by influencing them through both their own actions and the amount of inspiration they provide to them.

Robotics as an Educational Learning Tool in the World

The integration of robotics in education has attracted many countries over the world with the aim of aligning their educational curriculum with the 4IR and preparing leaners for the digital world (You et al., 2021). However, the integration of robotics is not the same across all countries due to financial stability, affordability, politics and educational policies. For example, in Asia the implementation of technology and robotics as a learning tool is pervasive in high income populations whereby more innovative and digital forms of technological gadgets and broadband connectivity are available (Afari & Khine, 2017). As a result, learners and teachers in such populations become more advanced, knowledgeable and creative in how they integrate technology for teaching and learning. The presence of specialised human capital is one of the most important aspects for the growth and progression of science, technology and engineering in the world (You et al., 2021).

In developing countries such as Sri Lanka securing necessary capital is often considered to be the major obstacle for integrating advanced technological initiatives in education such as robotics (Lanka, 2021). However, the study by Gyamfi et al. (2022) shows a low literacy rate in Ghana within the people from rural areas, and the expenses of integrating technology/robotics in education such as hardware, software and strong network connections are perceived as an obstacle to integrate technology for teaching and learning. The study by Hbaci and Abdunabi (2020) asserts that in Libya teachers still perceive the utilization of technology in education as a difficult task, and most learning institutions do not have adequate resources such as computers, accessibility to internet, and reasonable allocation of funds to improve the educators' technological skills in teaching and learning. Hence, the integration of advanced technological initiatives in education such as robotics is still a gigantic task to be achieved.

Policymakers internationally have largely acknowledged that the utilization of technology in teaching and learning could have a positive impact on people coping in a universal economy by creating a trained labour force and enabling societal mobility (Qureshi et al., 2021). However, there has been an increase in interest from developing countries in knowing the way in which robotics, internet and subject matter are linked together to expand the knowledge and skills in science, technology and engineering (ORT South Africa, 2017). The old pedagogical approaches of integrating technology into education have been transformed and necessitates educational transformation globally (Qureshi et al., 2021). Robotics in developed countries such as Germany is perceived to be one of the most key learning tools to enhance the minds of the young ones since they are open-minded which allows them to develop new information, and to show their creativity and improves critical thinking (Chaldi & Mantzanidou, 2021). The integration of robotics in Germany is based on the establishment of training workshops, learners' competitions and annual conferences.

Teachers' Acceptance Towards the Use of Robotics

Different learning institutions have changed swiftly by meeting the current demands of the digital world and aiming to promote 21st century skills (Erwin et al., 2013; Petre & Price, 2014; Rogers & Portsmore, 2014). Some countries afford resources, tuition and budgets so that they can supplement the implementation of technologies and prepare for the digital world and uplift the standard of their education. Irrespective of all the determinations, several countries are experiencing the same predicament whereby teachers are not creating the best practice of the technology provided (Hamidi, 2016).

The integration of robotics creates a meaningful and hands-on learning approach, which benefits teachers and learners by simplifying concepts in Mathematics, Science and Technology (Erwin et al., 2013). According to Sullivan (2012) the focal point towards the use of robotics is based on teachers' beliefs, since the teachers are the human beings who incorporate the transformation in their teaching and learning practice (Petre & Price, 2014). Furthermore, previous research by Marcinkiewicz (2010) shows that the connection between teachers' attitudes and the utilisation of technology are vital.

In addition, according to Lambert and Guiffre (2013) the teachers' attitudes towards the integration of robotics are reliant on their experiences and teachers develop positive attitudes towards the use of robotics when they are integrating robotics more often in their teaching and learning. Lambert and Guiffre (2013) assert that skills and knowledge gained from training can influence perceived ease of use and perceived usefulness, which will result in influencing the attitudes of teachers towards the use of robotics in education.

Teachers' and Learners Experience With the Use of Robotics

The perceptions of teachers and learners of the integration of technology are gained from their current and previous experience of using technology. According to Sangkawetai et al. (2018) a field experience has a huge impact on the actual integration and implementation of technology in a learning environment. As a result, user experience is vital in determining the issues that might influence the acceptance of robotics in an educational setting by teachers and learners.

The study by Jaipal-Jamani and Angeli (2017) reveal that teachers lack self-efficacy and have misunderstandings towards the use of technology. As a result, this contributes to their inability to integrate technology in their respective classrooms and their actual experience. According to Lai (2017), some teachers believe that by just simply setting up technological tools for learners, effective teaching and learning will take place and there will be a huge educational transformation. Hence, lack of training and technological skills has an influence on the acceptance of technology and will result in negative experiences.

The professional development for teachers in robotics is significant and provides them with skills and knowledge on how to teach robotics and how to integrate it into subject matter. According to Chambers and Carbonaro (2018) robotics teacher training equips teachers with necessary skills and information about robotics programming and creates positive experiences. The research by Samuels (2016) shows that having knowledge and skills about robotics encourages teachers to create scientific inquiries and their self-efficacy in both learning and teaching robotics and programming have improved after attending training in robotics. Moreover, the training had a positive impact on teachers' pedagogic philosophies towards teaching robotics and improved their STEM integration and emotional engagement.

The key role of the learning environment is to provide learners with skills and knowledge and prepare them for the future world (Denis & Hubert, 2016). Thus, learners' views about robotics should not be disregarded. However, according to Sangkawetai et al. (2018) teachers are accountable for equipping learners with knowledge in their respective classrooms with the objectives and aims of learners becoming knowledgeable and responsible citizens of the community. Learners' perceptions about the role of technology at school and their life outside of school can have an impact on their participation and curiosity. Hence, exploring learner's interests about technology and the impact it has on their day-to-day activities is a significant aspect, which teachers should take into consideration.

The study by Hamidi (2016) shows that learners who took part in the WRO, and study STEM in meaningful learning are capable of learning how things can be joined together to build a moving device that could be programmed. According to Bers et al. (2015) when learners are engaged in robotics, they acquire skills and knowledge on how to work as a team with their fellow classmates and to understand that in a team everyone has a role that serves the same purpose. Robotics creates a positive learning experience for the learners and provides numerous and different methods of acquiring skills and knowledge, in such a way that could not be replicated by traditional textbook based approaches (Jaipal-Jamani & Angeli, 2017).

Importance of Robotics in Education

Robotics in the educational setting provides learners with a chance to take part in problem-solving by participating effectively with their peers (De Walle et al., 2011). The most significant and challenging topics in a subject could be learned through problem-solving (De Walle et al., 2011). Learning by solving problems permits learners to have optimistic perceptions towards the subject, uplifts their higher order thinking skills and supports them to intensely grasp the content knowledge by creating meaningful learning rather than rote learning (De Walle et al., 2011). According to Grubbs (2013) integrating robotics for problem-solving learning is an effective approach to instill the content knowledge and to allow learners to show their creativity and build their communication skills as they communicate with their peers.

During the learning process of robotics, learners work in groups, conduct investigations and collect data by brainstorming, create robots with their own designs using elementary electrical apparatuses such as wires, insulators, sensors and wheels, and integrate mathematics for counting rotations, numbers of turns and angles and plan a robot program which involves programming using computer software (Grubbs, 2013; De Walle et al., 2011). The study by Rogers and Portsmore (2014) shows that robotics smartly and genuinely assimilates STEM in hands-on learning and can uplift learners' commitment, creativeness, collaboration, accurate investigation, collecting and evaluating information, solving problems and in-depth indulgence in subjects related to Science, Mathematics, Engineering and Technology.

Cejka et al. (2012) assert that the goal of STEM in learning robotics is not only about furthering learners' understanding of Physics, Mathematics and Engineering subjects, but also to accommodate them by giving them opportunities to promote and sustain permanent knowledge in STEM disciplines. Furthermore, according to Lambert and Guiffre (2013) robotics is an interactive device that constructs a stimulating educational setting, advances learners' perspectives and interest towards STEM disciplines and inspires them to take part in STEM projects and follow professions linked to STEM disciplines. Grubbs (2013) states that robotics generates a thrilling and realistic setting, which accommodates learners with the opportunity to integrate facts and perspectives that they thought are ineffectual and impractical.

Robotics has received a lot of attention from educators and scholars as a respected educational tool to advance cognitive and communication skills for learners from kindergarten to higher grades, and to support education in Physics, Mathematics, Technology, Informatics and other school subjects (Petre & Price, 2014; Eguchi, 2014; Cejka et al., 2012). The core philosophies that support robotics in education are constructivism and constructionism (Barreto & Benitti, 2012). Robotics builds an educational setting whereby learners can cooperate with their environment and work with real-world situations which results in a constructionist learning practice (Barreto & Benitti, 2012).

Robots are valuable technological resources for teaching Mathematics and Science; they can be utilized in classrooms for clarifying problematic topics since they grasp the attention of many children (Bers et al., 2015). According to Chambers and Carbonaro (2018) robotics is a suitable learning field to integrate current technological developments for learners and offers them advantages by energetically participating in the STEM spectrum and develops them to explore and contemplate in a constructivist way (Petre & Price, 2014). The study by Rogers and Portsmore (2014) showed that learners as early as Grade 1 could easily study significant Science and Mathematics topics relevant to their curriculum by utilising LEGO resources. Denis and Hubert (2016) assert that robotics not only assists learners to study Science and Technology, but also meaningfully supports them to study sequencing that is significant for numerous fields, which involve reading, arithmetic, and basic life skills.

Factors That Influence the Use of Robotics in Education

The integration of robotics in education is demanding, costly, time consuming and requires adequate resources (Barreto & Benitti, 2012; Petre, & Price, 2014; Samuels, 2016). Hence, it necessitates additional time to design educational activities for workshops and solving technical glitches and puts pressure on teachers. The study by Chambers and Carbonaro (2018) shows that the main problematic issue that might obstruct educators from integrating robotics in education is teachers' enthusiasm and ability to learn. In contrast, the study by Lambert and Guiffre (2013) shows that the lack of sufficient educational robots and suitable software/hardware is the main stumbling block for integrating robotics in education for teaching and learning.

According to Eguchi (2014) the lack of technical support, teachers' lack of self-reliance in their technological abilities, and their lack of understanding in creating the link between robotics and the subject matter are also key hindrances to integrate robotics in education. Teachers need support with the resolving of hardware and software issues as well as technical maintenance (Eguchi, 2014). The technological support needs to be provided in the learning environment and it should be continuing practice, delivered during contact time and meet the needs of the educators. Lambert and Guiffre (2013) believe that the amount of work that teachers administer in their daily school schedule reduces their interest in engaging in new methodological approaches and new technologies.

Robotics as the current phenomena in the education field, which aims to equip learners with the 21st century skills and to promote STEM subjects, requires teachers to uplift their technological skills and competency (Samuels, 2016). Hence, in relation to preparing learners for the digital world, teachers play the most significant part by integrating robotics in their teaching and learning (Levin & Wadmany, 2011). Teachers' readiness and skills in integrating robotics are very crucial for the application of technology in education. Furthermore, teachers need suitable technological knowledge to incorporate technology and to be highly inspired to utilise it in their teaching and learning. The study by Chambers and Carbonaro (2018) supports this view by showing that teachers who went through robotics training which includes programming, assembling of robots and coding are extremely competent in integrating and linking robotics with their subject matter, as opposed to those that did not attend any form of training.

Certain Partnerships and Initiatives to Help With the Preparation and Rollout of Robotics

In 2013 Hadi and Ali Partovi launched Code.org in the USA with a virtual video "What Most Schools Don't Teach". They also launched the "Hour of Code" reaching 20 million students in the first week. In 2014, they reached 90 million hours served. They also launched Computer Science Fundamentals for Grades K-5. Many achievements followed, and in 2023 they helped one billion students to prepare for Artificial Intelligence (Code.org, 2023).

Every afternoon after class in Diepsloot in Gauteng, a group of girls gather in a shipping container crammed with computers, and they are learning to code. Code for Change is a non-profit organization based in Sandton. Jonathan Novoty, co-founder of Code for Change, said everything is about practical skills that teenagers can implement as soon as possible in the real world. Code of Change has been working with local organizations in South Africa to help introduce coding in schools, and not only urban schools, but rural schools as well. Mobile phones have been the key to this success. Much of Code of Change's platform is focused on mobile connectivity. Code of Change is very proud of the high rate of involvement of girls in Computer Science programs. Tanzania and Ghana are also in the game. Despite differences in history and development, South Africa, Tanzania and Ghana have comparable demographics, with youg people making up the majority of their populations. In regions where education disparities and exclusion are among the highest in the world, Code of Change, CodeJIKA, Jenga Hub and Ghana Code Club are focussing on levelling the playing field for all kids (Herman, 2022).

Code for Change proudly initiated the Computer Science Education Week (CSEd week) that took place from 4 to 10 December 2023. This initiative equipped 100 000 students with essential coding skills. Mr. Joel Mavuso, Deputy Chief Education Specialist- E- learning from the Ekurhuleni South District, describes CSED Week as an opportunity to join forces with educators, community leaders and business professionals to foster a nationwide movement focused on Computer Science education.

For many scholars, Open Education Resources (OER) are the only way in which they can progress. Just to name a few: On the website of Worchester Polytechnic Institute you can find open textbooks, open courseware, general Engineering OER, interactive lab materials and simulations, all about robotics (https://libguides.wpi.edu/c.php?g=355457&p=9805369). At Widener University you find print books, e-books and videos (https://widener.libguides.com/robotics/OER). You can also visit Co-Dream OER Collaborative Development of Robotics, mEchatronics and Advanced Manufacturing Open Educational Resources (https://libraries.clemson.edu/teaching/open-ed/oer-development-projects/co-dream-oer/). On the OER Commons you find 15 affiliated resources. Under UNISA Open there is an iniative "Learn to speak Robotics indigenously" (https://www.unisa.ac.za/sites/corporate/default/Unisa-Open).

THEORETICAL FRAMEWORK

In this study, to identify and explore the acceptance of teachers and learners towards the use of robotics in education, the Technology Acceptance Model (TAM) by Davis (1989) was integrated. The TAM model encompasses different sections that demonstrate the process of technology acceptance by people who are using it; involving "behavioral intension, perceived usefulness, perceived ease of use and attitude towards using" (Lai, 2017). While perceived usefulness conforms to the level where the person considers the benefits of utilizing a certain technology by improving the work presentation, perceived ease of use relates to the significance for technology to be accessible and friendly for people" (Dillion, 1996). TAM asserts that the integration of technology is controlled by the intention to utilize technology (Davis, 1989). Hence, the intention is determined by individuals' attitudes and perceived usefulness.

The model explores factors that lead people to accept or discard the use of various technological resources in a working environment. According to Davis (1989) perceived usefulness reflects people's use of technology constructed from their beliefs of the technological abilities to elevate their work performance. Therefore, when the integration of technology tends to be beneficial and improving the productivity, people are more likely to integrate these technologies more often (Purba & Hwang, 2017). However, if the introduced technologies are not user friendly and challenging to integrate, negative attitudes towards using them will be stimulated and will influence the perceived usefulness, behavioural intentions and acceptance of the technologies (Purba & Hwang, 2017). People enjoy and promote using technologies that are easier to use and effortless when integrating them.

The TAM is significant and most relevant to this study, since teachers' and learners' acceptance of the use of robotics is directly influenced by the four crucial principles of the model: perceived usefulness, external variables, perceived ease of use and users' attitudes (Purba & Hwang, 2017). Figure 6 below shows the Technology Acceptance Model.

Figure 6. Technology acceptance model
(Davis, 1989)

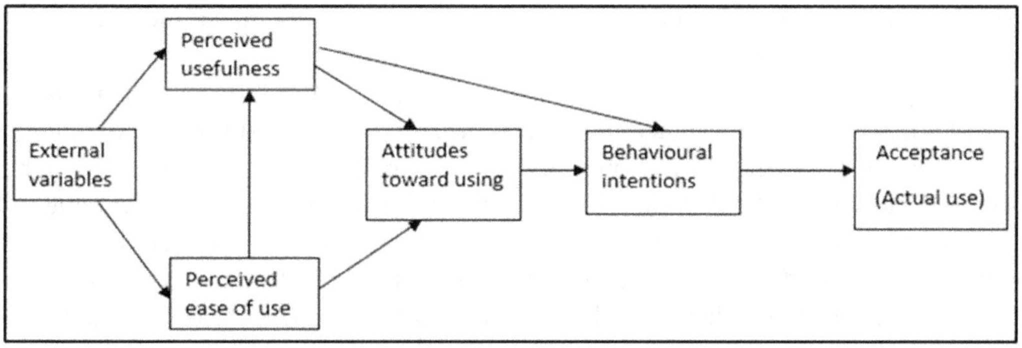

The objective of integrating robotics in education is fundamental for effective teaching and learning and maintains the core principles in the theory above like ease of use (Adams & Nelson, 2003). Moreover, the intentions of teachers to integrate robotics are robustly affected by their perception of the ease of use and usefulness of the resources and apparent accessibility and deciding on their actual use of technology (Chau, 2009). The theoretical framework directed this study in exploring and identifying teachers' and learners' attitudes towards the use of robotics, as well as the external and internal challenges that influence the perceived usefulness and ease of the use of robotics.

RESEARCH METHODOLOGY

Qualitative Research

Qualitative research refers to the type of research that is determined more with the intrinsic worth, the qualities and the characteristics of the phenomena, instead of measurements or scientific enquiry (Seale, 2000). This methodological approach intends to understand and represent the truths as formulated by the members who are involved in the participant's behaviour from the insider's point of view (Denzin & Lincoln, 2005). The researcher integrated this method because it explains why and how robotics occur in the classroom. For example, some teachers may find it difficult to utilise robotics in the classroom for teaching and learning because of their fear of technology. Moreover, the aim was to understand teachers and learners from their point of view and own voice. Information in a qualitative research design is gathered as it happens naturally, and situations cannot be manipulated.

Research Design

A case study is an experiential methodology of investigation that investigates contemporary phenomena from an original actual life situation whereby the limitations amongst phenomena and situations are not obviously clear where numerous resources of support are utilised to gather data (Hennink & Hutter, 2011). Therefore, a case study focuses on how individuals relate and cooperate with each other in a certain context and how they make sense of the phenomena being studied. This study explored teachers' and learners' attitudes towards the use of robotics. The data was gathered by exploring the case through the personal experiences of the teachers and learners when teaching and learning with robotics. The case consisted of two schools in Pretoria East, which offers robotics as part of their curriculum, which makes them unique from other schools.

An exploratory research design was applied to gather a better understanding of the current problematic issue, but will not provide decisive outcomes (Creswell, 2017). For this study, an exploratory research design was integrated to gather information as it seeks to understand how and why certain behaviours are happening. Teachers in schools have different experiences and views about integrating robotics in education. Therefore, the researcher wanted to know and understand the underlying phenomena by exploring the causes and effects. Moreover, the exploratory research design was able to accommodate questions such as what and how that were also part of the research questions of this study.

Population and Sampling

Population refers to an inclusive cluster of people, organisations or items with the same characteristics that are the interest of a researcher (Leedy & Ormrod, 2015). The entire cohort of teachers and learners in the intermediate phase from the two identified schools were part of the population group of this study as they have common characteristics, which were of interest to the researcher.

Sampling is a method of choosing individual members or a portion of the population to represent the whole population (Leedy & Ormrod, 2015). The researcher used purposive and convenience sampling. In purposive sampling the participants are selected with a specific purpose. Convenience sampling is administered when participants are easily accessible and located in one geographic area to avoid time and cost constraints (Maree & Pietersen, 2016). Convenience sampling is one of the non-probability sampling approaches whereby the participants are selected within a cluster of individuals easier to collaborate or to contact (Denzin & Lincoln, 2005). This sampling method has been chosen based on the following reasons. Firstly, the participants are close to the researcher in terms of distance, which means transport money does not have to be used to get to them. Secondly, it will be much easier for them to participate since workshops and teacher training are attended together. Lastly, it could save time and the data will be collected very quickly and with less cost.

The researcher purposively sampled six learners in the intermediate phase from the two identified schools. The schools were labelled as School A and School B. Three learners from School A represent Grade 5 and the other three learners represent Grade 6 from School B. Six teachers from the two identified schools were sampled. Three teachers represent Grade 5 and the other three represent Grade 6. The teachers were selected to represent different grades since the robotics activities differs from one grade to another and that result in different experiences for teachers. In purposive sampling, the researcher chooses individuals that take part in the research who have experience, wisdom or content about the research topic and study. On the foundation of the researcher's information of the people, he/she decides which participants must be chosen to supply the best and accurate data (Creswell, 2017).

Purposive sampling has been chosen for gathering data because the participants that have been selected are administering robotics in their respective schools. The learners also have background knowledge about robotics, and they take part in different robotics competitions. Hence, the selected participants were able to answer the research questions since they had experience. The integration of robotics is done in all phases; but differs in terms of curriculum and activities that are specified for a certain phase. Therefore, this study is specifically based on robotics in the Intermediate Phase. The teachers have the following characteristics: Firstly, they have knowledge about the application of technology in the classroom. Secondly, they have experience about integration of robotics in education for teaching and learning. Lastly, they are all qualified and professional educators as approved by the South African Council of Educators (SACE).

Data Collection Strategies

Data collection strategies are the approaches that the researchers utilise to collect data (Wellington, 2014). In this study, the researcher used semi-structured interviews, field notes, focus group interviews, documents and lesson observations as data-collection methods.

Semi-Structured Interviews

The semi-structured interview is a method of gathering data from participants whereby the researcher focuses on open-ended questions to allow the participant to give more details about their experiences and underlying phenomena (Denzin & Lincoln, 2005). Semi-structured interviews hardly ever take prolonged periods and typically entail the contributor to fill in all groups of prearranged questions and enable questioning and explanation of the results (Hennink & Hutter, 2011).

The researcher integrated the semi-structured interviews to gather data as it allows the participants to give in-depth knowledge based on their actual personal experiences, which is crucial in responding to the research questions. This is a very good method of gathering data as it ensures that questions are detailed and prepared in advance. Therefore, the participants and the researcher had a flow in terms of responding to the research questions. The researcher was able to make follow up questions as the conversation flowed. Moreover, the participants were interviewed individually, and all the information collected from the interviews was audio-recorded and later transcribed in the data analysis phase. The semi-structured interviews were integrated to gather information from the six teachers.

Field Notes

Field notes refer to qualitative based data on behavioural observations and activities of the participants documented by researchers in the context or situation that they are investigating (Phillippi & Lauderdale, 2017). The notes are planned to be interpreted as proof that provides meaning and support in the accepting or acknowledging of the observable behaviours. The researcher used field notes to capture data that cannot be recorded on the voice recorder. Hence, the researcher noted the participants' non-verbal reactions during the interviews as these also play an important role when collecting data and shows the actual truth or experiences of the participants.

Focus Group Interviews

A focus group interview is a data collection approach used to gather information by means of group interaction (Maree & Pietersen, 2016). The focus group interview approach is grounded in the notion that group interaction is fruitful in broadening the variety of responses, triggering overlooked facts of experience and freeing inhibitions that might reduce participants from revealing information (Maree & Pietersen, 2016).

The researcher used focus group interviews to gather information from learners in the intermediate phase, considering their age and confidence some of the learners might be shy to participate as individuals. Hence, focus group interviews allowed learners to develop their responses on each other's notions and comments to provide detailed viewpoints that cannot be attained through individual interviews.

Observations

Observations refer to the use of human sensory systems such as ears and eyes to examine and record the behaviour in a fieldwork (Cohen et al., 2018). The researcher observed the learners' behaviours based on their interactions, confidence and attitudes during the robotics lessons. To fully comprehend the underlying phenomena, teachers were observed in terms of their methodological approach, skills and knowledge to facilitate their lessons in robotics. The researcher managed to observe the lessons in the natural setting of the participants without interfering with the lessons. Moreover, the researcher used Notebook to record and took notes while observing the lesson. Data collected through observations were crucial to this study since the information is based on the actual scenes and actions. Hence, information that might not have been collected through the interviews was gathered through observations.

Document Analysis

Document analysis refers to formal written information based on the content of a particular field that could be retrieved in a public or digital platform to answer certain specific research questions (Cohen et al., 2018). The researcher consulted the official and approved DBE documents such as Curriculum Assessment Policy statement (CAPS), teachers' lesson plans, Annual Teaching Plans (ATP), circulars and timetable to regulate how teachers facilitate their lessons in robotics guided by the documents provided.

Data Analysis

Content Analysis

Content analysis is a methodical tactic to qualitative data analysis that classifies and summarises the content of the message (Creswell, 2017). After gathering data, it is important to analyse it and look at the difference and similarities so that we can reach conclusions. Content analysis was used to summarise the data collected and draw up conclusions based on the findings. The following data analysis steps by Creswell (2017) were followed to analyse the data:

1. The data were organised and large components were broken into smaller sections.
2. Categories were created and linked to patterns or themes in the data.
3. Data was combined.
4. A summary of the information was created.

Semi-Structured Interviews

Technological Training and Impact on Teaching. The researcher posed this question to the participants to get their background information in terms of their expertise and experience of teaching and learning with technology. Participants were able to reflect on their training and how technology influenced their teaching.

Most of the participants had received technological training as part of their teacher professional development. The training has influenced their teaching and learning positively, since they integrate technology to facilitate their lessons, administration and integrate robotics as part of learning with technology.

The technological training motivates teachers to administer meaningful and interesting lessons by integrating technology and assists them to execute their day-to-day activities within their learning institution. Since Covid-19, they can communicate online through WhatsApp, Zoom and Microsoft Teams with parents and learners.

Experiences in Using Robotics in the Intermediate Phase. The majority of the participants highlighted that they had nurtured skills and knowledge with robotics since they had been teaching it for a couple of years and participated in the World Robot Olympiad (WRO). However, teachers have different experiences of using robotics in the intermediate phase as some have their own way of outsourcing information to uplift their knowledge in robotics. One teacher indicated that she has four years' of experience in coaching Lego Robotics in the Intermediate Phase and participating in WRO competitions.

The integration of robotics in the Intermediate Phase plays an essential role in the curriculum delivery by enhancing the technological skills and knowledge for teachers and learners. One of the participants is of the opinion that robotics motivates Intermediate Phase learners to reach their maximum potential, they strive to lead, learn and master skills on their own, and this promotes independence among them.

The Usefulness of Robotics for Teaching and Learning. The importance and usefulness of robotics for teaching and learning will determine its future use and sustainability in the education system.

All the participants recommended and valued robotics as an important educational tool to enhance technological skills for teaching and learning. The participants believe that through robotics learners can develop their career path in STEM related careers at an early age. The participants believe that their learners should acquire 21st century skills such as the utilisation of ICT, independence, problem solving skills, collaboration, communication, creativity, and abstract and analytical thinking already from primary school.

Some of the participants also asserted that the integration of robotics in the Intermediate Phase has a huge influence on building learners' academic performance in Mathematics and Science. Learners also acquire engineering skills in building a robot and programming it at an early age. To some of the participants the integration of robotics in education has a huge impact on developing the country for a better future in terms of job creation and economy. Moreover, the participants perceive robotics as a weapon to strengthen and create relationships with other countries since learners can travel abroad to participate in competitions and solve real life challenges.

Robotics Ease of Use in the Intermediate Phase. Four of the participants felt that the use of robotics is not easy and requires constant training and practise. The participants received various training sessions from different service providers. However, they believe that robotics is not plug and play and one should always revisit the manual and online tutorials to administer lessons and prepare thoroughly.

Two of the participants felt that it is simpler for them to integrate robotics and they believe that robotics requires enough time since it is based on a trial-and-error approach. One of the participants also highlighted that the involvement of learners to do the robotics activities as a team make it easier for them to utilise robotics.

Teachers' Attitudes Towards the Use of Robotics. All the participants are positive about the integration of robotics for teaching and learning. The participants believe that robotics is very important for the education system; it should be officially integrated in all schools as a subject and it creates better opportunities for the learners. It urges learners to learn using technology, and then they will survive the current and future education system. The participants' attitudes are based on the possibilities they perceive robotics could add to the education system and the skills and knowledge learners attain in robotics. The participants highlighted that the integration of robotics in education provides multiple skills in our education system and gives teachers an opportunity to uplift their skills in technology.

Learners' and Teachers' Perceptions Towards the Teaching and Learning of Robotics. The participants were questioned about their colleagues' and learners' perspectives in relation to the integration of robotics for teaching and learning. There are different perspectives concerning the integration of robotics for teaching and learning. Some of their colleagues are sceptical about robotics and believe that it is just for fun and entertainment for learners to learn with technology. The perceptions of robotics are based on individuals' background or experience with technology. However, all the participants highlighted that learners are very positive about robotics, and they are always looking forward to learning more when they take part in robotics, they enjoy working as a team and every learner wants to be part of the competition.

Benefits/ Opportunities of Robotics in the Intermediate Phase. All the participants highlighted that the integration of robotics in the Intermediate Phase has great benefits and opportunities for the learners. Robotics as an educational tool improves teachers' and learners' competency and prepares learners to become future engineers and teaches them independence at an early age.

The participants believe that robotics encompasses all learning capabilities such as reading, writing, drawing, calculating, theoretical thinking, problem-solving skills and critical thinking as well as working independently and as a team. Robotics puts teachers and learners on a global scale, it makes them able to compete and be in line with the global trends.

Challenges When Integrating Robotics for Teaching and Learning. The challenges of integrating robotics for teaching and learning differs based on the school context. Learning institutions may have access to various technological resources. However, there are numerous internal and external challenges that could influence the smooth integration of technologies in classrooms. The internal challenges are based on individuals' beliefs, perceptions and personal preferences about the integration of technology, which are mainly determined by the ease of use and usefulness (Foss & Rasmus, 2019). Moreover, the internal challenges are barriers, which are based within the school environment, whereas the external challenges are concomitant with hindrances outside the school environment like any support originating from the educational authorities (Foss & Rasmus, 2019).

The following factors have been highlighted and categorised under internal challenges: lack of support and motivation from the SGB, SMT and co-workers and time allocation for robotics lessons. The following factors are regarded as external challenges: unscheduled power cuts during robotics lessons, cost and affordability of robotics equipment, lack of technological resources and lack of continuous training for teachers. The internal and external challenges both have a negative impact on the effective teaching and learning with technologies, and for the successful integration of technology they should all be examined. Moreover, internal challenges depend on external challenges. For instance, when teachers are fully trained and supported for integration of technology, they will have positive attitudes and perspectives towards the utilisation of technology.

The participants highlighted that there are some challenges, which could not be avoided when integrating robotics such as few allocated resources, lack of training and time allocation for robotics lessons. Most of the participants highlighted the issue of time as one of the major challenges since robotics requires learners to work as a team which necessitate more discussions and planning.

The issue of cost and affordability was also highlighted as one of the major obstacles when integrating robotics for teaching and learning. The robotics teaching and learning support materials are very expensive, for example just a single set of Lego Mindstorms cost about R6 000 and it could only accommodate about four learners and one robot costs about R4 000. In addition, learners sometimes have to share some of the robotics materials, which delays the process of teaching and learning.

The participants also highlighted that the lack of support from their colleagues. The School Management Team (SMT), parents and School Governing Body (SGB) influences the integration of robotics for teaching and learning negatively. The SGB is responsible for governance and LTSM procurement and they do not purchase enough materials for robotics, which inconveniences the smooth running of robotics. Moreover, the issue of continuous and consistent training for teachers also raises a big concern since most of the participants believe that robotics is not a fixed curriculum or content like textbooks. Hence, more continuous training should be provided for teachers.

The two identified schools are well resourced and in a very conducive environment for teaching and learning. However, they do not have power backup during load shedding which inconveniences robotics lessons since they require overhead projectors, use of the internet, laptops and EV3 robots.

Focus Group Interviews

The researcher conducted focus group interviews to collect data from the learners in the intermediate phase. Three leaners were sampled from School A representing the Grade 5s and the other three learners were sampled from School B representing the Grade 6s. The learners were called Participants 1 to 6.

Learners' Experience with Robotics. Learners showed a vast experience in robotics and highlighted that they had been participating in many competitions, like the WRO, which gave them a lot of confidence. The lessons offered by teachers contributed positively on learners' experience with robotics and encouraged them to fully participate. Learners enjoy working with their peers to compete in robotics since it gives them exposure to solve problems collectively and share ideas. Learners indicated that they had started robotics at the beginner level and initially it was something complicated until they had hands-on experience.

Ease of Use and Usefulness for Learners when Learning with Robotics. Some learners find robotics easy to use, since they make use of manuals and videos to guide them, and others believe that robotics could sometimes be tricky, especially when you have to put more sensors in one robot. Learners' experiences with technology contributes positively to their effective use of robotics for learning. Most learners have always been surrounded by technological gadgets and enjoy navigating applications.

Learners believe that their teachers and coaches also make things easier for them to use robotics since they guide them step by step until they master the skills. However, once learners have mastered the skills, they are able to work on their own and gain confidence. Learners' willingness to learn and their passion with the integration of technology builds their confidence in robotics. Learners find robotics an effective and creative educational tool that makes learning fun and easy. The activities and missions provided when learning with robotics provide learners with experiential and meaningful learning since it is based on hands-on learning and grants them opportunities to develop an interest in STEM related careers such as programmers and engineers. Moreover, robotics increases learners' interests and understanding of mathematics concepts practically, since some of the activities mainly revolve around mathematics.

Challenges While Learning with Robotics. Learners have highlighted some challenges that they experience when learning with robotics. The challenges experienced by learners are mainly related to external challenges. Some of these challenges are interrelated with the ones that were highlighted by their teachers when integrating robotics for teaching and learning. The challenges experienced by learners are as follows: fewer allocated technological resources, time allocated for robotics lessons, internet connections and malfunctioning of technological gadgets for robotics. Fewer allocation of technological resources was also highlighted as one of the challenges experienced by learners, which forces them to share with their peers and also consumes a lot of time. Learners' challenges while learning with robotics are beyond their control.

Attitudes Towards the Use of Robotics for Learning. Learners' attitudes towards the use of robotics are positive and they are excited about it and perceive robotics as an educational tool to enhance and promote 21st century skills and build their confidence in Mathematics, Science and Technology. Some participants perceive robotics as a great approach to learn since it is based on hands-on learning, and they get an opportunity to construct their own designs. This improves their creativity and innovation skills. Robotics competitions stimulates learners' confidence and attitudes towards the use of robotics for learning. The support and guidance learners are provided with by their teachers and parents allow them to be positive and they perceive robotics as one of the educational tools that can open opportunities for them.

Documents

The documents that were requested are the annual teaching plans (ATPs), lesson plans, subject policy, formal and informal assessments tasks. The researcher requested the documents to understand the outline of the subject and how it had been structured. The ATP has been designed according to the total number of weeks in a term and the content that should be administered in that week. The number of hours are also included per week. The content has been outlined into five content areas per term, which are as follows: internet and e-communication, algorithms and coding, applications skills, pattern recognition and problem solving, and robotics skills. Learners are initially given the scenario and therefore they should be able to identify the problem and come up with possible solutions. This links to their subject Technology since they apply five technological processes (investigate, design, make, evaluate and communicate).

The subject policy provided outlines of the key aspects that should be taken into consideration when entering the robotics lab, the role and responsibilities of the SMT in the learning process of robotics and how the subject should be managed. The robotics lab should have enough space for learners to work as a team and have strong internet connections for teachers and learners to download online resources. All the robotics resources should be included in the LTSM procurement, and it is the responsibility of the SMT along with the SGB. The resources should be checked and maintained at the end of each term.

The formal and informal assessment tasks are officially pre-meditated by teachers and they cover all the five content areas according to their cognitive levels and weightings. The assessments are pre-moderated by the Departmental Head (DH) as per policy before they are administered. The informal assessments are practical and theoretical and they serve as a form of practice for the formal assessment.

Field Notes

The researcher has managed to collect data through field notes, which encompass the facial expressions and gestures of the participants during the semi-structured and focus group interviews. Teachers expressed their optimistic ideas with confidence when asked about technological training and impact on their teaching. When teachers were asked about their experience in using robotics in the Intermediate Phase, some took time to respond to the question while putting a hand on their head. It showed that they needed time to think thoroughly as compared to when they were asked about their technological training and impact on their teaching. One participant was a bit nervous and confused when discussing her experience with robotics. Another was very confident and explained in detail about his experience with robotics in the Intermediate Phase.

The ease of use of robotics question raised frustrations and dropped the confidence and participation of most of the participants. When teachers were asked about the ease of use of robotics, they seemed like they really needed some help and expressed the issues that affect them when administering lessons with robotics. As a result, most of the teachers expressed that robotics is not easy and provided their reasons to back up their opinions. When teachers were asked about the importance of integrating robotics in the Intermediate Phase for teaching and learning, they were very confident and active in responding to the question and provided the advantages of robotics. Overall, teachers value the integration of robotics into teaching and learning regardless of the challenges they experience when administering robotics lessons.

Learners were asked six questions through the focus group interviews. The first question, learners were asked was about their favourite subjects and they were very active and excited when responding to the question. The learners' facial expressions were very positive throughout the interviews even though some were just giving one-word answers. However, some were a bit shy to contribute or answer the questions while the interview progressed. Some learners were using gestures such as head and hand movements when responding to the questions to show that they were thinking or agreeing with their peers on certain ideas. Overall, the participants were very kind, enthusiastic and patient during the interviews. The interviews went smoothly, there were no negative attitudes, gestures or language to show disrespect or anger.

Observations

The researcher managed to observe three lessons as part of the data collection strategy. In the first lesson, all learners had their technological devices, and access to the internet was very strong. The lesson was very interactive, and learners were participating on their own. The teacher only introduced a lesson by showing a video clip through an overhead projector and explained the activity for the day. The learners then went to their respective groups and started working on their own. The learners' facial expressions were very positive and the teacher was confident when conducting the lesson. The pictures below depict what transpired in this class.

In the second class, the learners were working individually and each one had a tablet and the robot. The lesson started with the teacher showing learners how to attach the colour sensor and to program the robot to follow specified colours on the mat. The teacher showed positivity and a high quality of content knowledge and even delivered a practical example after programming her own robot. The learners were able to follow the instructions and some managed to finish the activity as instructed. However, others were complaining about their robots not being able to upload the program they had programmed. As a result, the teacher replaced the robots, and all learners were assisted.

In the third class, the lesson was based on the preparation for the upcoming WRO competition. Therefore, learners had their own mat and worked in groups to compete with their classmates. The winning team was nominated as the one that would represent the school for the upcoming competition. However,

Figure 7. Robotics mat

Figure 8. Learner workstation

during their internal competition learners had the issue of internet connection and found it difficult to download the online videos as their tutorials. The issue was partially sorted out later whereby the teacher connected learners to the internet with his personal phone.

The researcher was fortunate to be invited by one of the schools as a guest to the WRO competition. The WRO competition consisted of many schools from the different provinces and learners were participating as groups. Each team consisted of four learners and their coach/teacher. Learners and coaches were very excited about this competition. When learners arrived at the competition, they were given workstations and their coaches stood on the other side. There are judges and timekeepers and coaches were not allowed to intervene.

FINDINGS

The study investigated the teachers' and learners' acceptance of the use of robotics in the Intermediate Phase. As a result, this section of the study tends to summarize the answers to the primary research

Figure 9. WRO competition

question: **What influences teachers' and learners' acceptance towards the use of robotics?** The main research question was divided into four research sub-questions, which were as follows:

1. What are internal and external factors that influence the use of robotics in primary school education?
2. What are the attitudes of teachers and learners towards the use of robotics?
3. How easy do intermediate phase teachers and learners find it to use robotics?
4. How useful do intermediate phase teachers and learners find robotics in their teaching and learning?

Internal and External Factors That Influence the Use of Robotics in Primary School Education

The findings of this study show that there are various internal and external factors, which influence the use of robotics in primary school education. The lack of technological resources, continuous training for educators, time allocation for lessons, cost and affordability of robotics resources are major challenges, which influence the implementation, teaching and learning with robotics in primary school education. Moreover, lack of support from colleagues, SMT and SGB and unscheduled power cuts during robotics lessons are also regarded as major challenges, which influence the implementation of robotics. The article by a Staff Writer (2021) shows that lack of adequate technological resources and accessibility to internet are the main challenges which schools experience when integrating technology for teaching and learning.

Technological skills and training for teachers is a major key element for the successful integration and implementation of robotics into teaching and learning (Chambers & Carbonaro, 2018). This statement is supported by Piatti (2020) who indicated that teaching and learning with robotics requires an ongoing and consistent practise in order to master the essential skills. Curto and Moreno (2016) particularise on this notion by highlighting that teachers should get adequate support for integrating recently introduced technologies.

The study also revealed that time allocation for robotics lessons is one of the hindrances for adequate teaching and learning with robotics. The lessons could not be completed during the time allocated due to technical glitches, internet connectivity and lack of adequate resources. The study by Chisango and Marongwe (2018) shows that time is one of the constraints for successful implementation of technology in education and poses a huge obstacle. According to the Staff Writer (2021), time is necessary for teacher professional development and co-curricular activities. However, the study by Foss and Rasmus

(2019) shows that exploration and learning with robotics requires ample time as compared to traditional teaching preparation because learners work in groups; technical setup and troubleshooting are required and ensuring that all learners are connected to the internet before the lesson commences. Moreover, robotics is based on a trial-and-error learning approach.

Lastly, the research revealed that the cost of robotics resources and lack of support from colleagues, SMT and SGB influences the integration of robotics in primary schools. The technological resources for robotics seems to be more expensive and schools do not have enough budget to include them on their LTSM procurement. As a result, most schools rely on sponsors and donations from different service providers for robotics resources. Akilbekovna (2021) supports the statement that technological developments are increasing rapidly within the education sector, and this may put more pressure on a school's budget and affordability to keep up with the latest technology.

The lack of support from SMTs also affects the integration of robotics in schools as teachers often feel helpless, rely on the internet for support and outsource information on their own. The study by Amutha (2020) shows that the SMT plays a vital role in ensuring that the technology is fully integrated for teaching and learning at schools by supporting, guiding and providing training for teachers. However, according to Foss and Rasmus (2019) without proper guidance and support from the SMT the integration of robotics in schools will not be productive and meaningful to learning. The lack of support from the SGB or SMT denies learners and teachers opportunities to enhance teaching and learning with robotics. The study by Akilbekovna (2021) shows that the SGB should promote and ensure effective teaching and learning by providing adequate resources for quality education.

Attitudes of Teachers and Learners Towards the Use of Robotics

The study by Ahmed and Kazmi (2020) found that teachers' attitudes towards the acceptance and use of technology could be regarded as one of the obstacles for future use and integration of technology in schools. Farjon et al. (2019) who supports this notion asserted that the integration of technology in the learning environment is strongly affected by the attitudes of teachers. Moreover, teachers' attitudes towards the use of technology are mainly grounded in their current and previous use of technology. Positive attitudes of teachers determine the future use of technology in the learning environment.

The study discovered that teachers' and learners' attitudes towards the use of robotics are positive and inspirational. Teachers' technological experience and skills have significant impact on the integration of robotics for teaching and learning which also influences their attitudes towards the utilization of technology. The study by Jaipal-Jamani and Angeli (2017) shows that early integration of robotics in primary schools will boost learners' confidence in the use of technology and allow teachers to keep up with 21st century skills and technological developments. According to Chambers and Carbonaro (2018) teachers' willingness and their depth in pedagogical content knowledge in robotics influences learners' attitudes towards the use of robotics. Learners enjoy experiential learning and feel comfortable when learning with technology. The integration of robotics into education adds value to learning by enriching learners' interest in the lesson (Lanka, 2021).

Robotics Ease of Use in the Intermediate Phase

Teachers have different experiences when integrating technologies for teaching and learning which are related to perceived ease of use, effectiveness and challenges they experience when integrating technology (Eguchi, 2016). This notion is supported by Akilbekovna (2021) who asserted that the utilization of technology in classrooms has its own challenges and achievements, which are based on the schools' context. In this study, the teachers have a variety of experiences in terms of the ease of use of robotics in the Intermediate Phase.

The lack of consistent and continuous robotics training for teachers has a huge impact on the perceived ease of use, skills and knowledge when integrating robotics into their lessons. As a result, some of the teachers find it difficult when conducting lessons with robotics. A study by Lanka (2021) highlighted that teachers' lack of technological training and skills development workshops is the obstacle for integration and facilitation of technology in the learning environment, which in turn affects the ease of use.

Two of the teacher participants find robotics easy to integrate into their lessons and enjoy working with technology. The participants are innovative, creative and outsource information from different sources such as watching online videos, colleagues and workshops to gain more content knowledge in robotics. Teachers who uplift their technological skills through professional development workshops have better understanding of technology and integrate it more often into their lessons (You et al., 2021). Moreover, according to Ahmed and Kazmi (2020) teacher professional developmental workshops on technology have a positive influence on teachers' perceived ease of use of technology.

The Usefulness of Robotics in the Intermediate Phase for Teachers and Learners

The study discovered that regardless of challenges that teachers and learners experience during teaching and learning with robotics, the participants perceive robotics as a fundamental technological learning tool. The integration of robotics builds learners' confidence and enhances essential 21st century skills (Nouri et al., 2020).

The study also revealed that robotics incorporates practical strands from different subjects such as mathematics, technology, science and engineering, which helps learners to develop content knowledge. Robotics creates opportunities for learners to develop a foundation of engineering and programming at an early age. This view is supported by Akilbekovna (2021) who asserted that the integration of robotics in teaching and learning will provide learners with stimulating and very engaging environments of science, technology and engineering and allow them to directly experience the practical applications of theoretical concepts in the STEM spectrum.

SOLUTIONS AND RECOMMENDATIONS

The following recommendations have been made based on the findings of this research.

Adequate and ongoing training should be provided for teachers who administer robotics. Training should have the objectives and assessments whereby teachers are assessed theoretically and practically after being trained. The training should also accommodate teachers according to their level of competency with robotics. Such programs should encompass not only technical training but also pedagogical guidance, facilitating the seamless integration of robotics with established teaching methods. There should be trained personnel amongst the staff members in schools who deal timeously with technical issues to assist with any technical glitches. The trained personnel could also train other staff members. Data indicate a disparity between teachers' enthusiasm for integrating robotics and their level of preparedness and comfort with these technologies (Michalec et al., 2021). Furthermore, continual professional development opportunities are essential to keep teachers updated with the latest advancements in educational technology (Hew et al., 2019).

A further recommendation entails the meticulous integration of robotics within existing curricula and the adaptation of pedagogical strategies to accommodate this emergent technology. This process involves aligning robotics with educational standards and learning outcomes, thereby ensuring its application is fundamental to the learning process rather than supplementary. Curricula should be structured such that robotics enhances understanding in disciplines like Mathematics and Science and fosters the development of critical thinking and problem-solving skills (Anwar et al., 2019). Additionally, instructional strategies ought to evolve to include more hands-on, project-based learning approaches, which have been proven effective in engaging students and enriching their learning experiences through robotics (Michalec et al., 2021).

Addressing the challenges of resource allocation and infrastructure is crucial for the successful implementation of robotics in educational environments. The study underscores the disparities in resources among schools, particularly those underfunded or in rural areas. To counteract these disparities, it is recommended that governments and educational authorities devise strategies for equitable resource distribution. This strategy should encompass the provision of financial resources for the acquisition of robotics kits and the enhancement of technological infrastructure within schools. Moreover, there should be a commitment to ensuring ongoing maintenance and support for these technologies, a critical factor for their sustained application in educational settings (Anwar et al., 2019). The SGB, SMT, ICT committee alongside the school principal should have a budget to purchase robotics resources and ensure that the ICT committee is functional and proactive. They should also come up with fundraising activities or ask for sponsors and donations if the school has limited funds. Learners should be supported with all the learning support materials they need during the robotics lessons to ensure that they all take part and are included in the lesson.

The fortification of collaborations between public entities and private sector organisations in the realm of robotics education is also advised. Such cooperative efforts between educational institutions, governmental bodies, and industry entities could form a solid foundation for the rollout of robotics programs (Jawaid et al., 2020). These alliances have the potential to facilitate the sharing of resources, expertise, and funding, thereby addressing financial and infrastructural challenges that may confront schools. Engagements with industry partners can additionally provide practical insights into the application of robotics, thereby enhancing the pragmatic aspect of robotics education.

Another recommendation advocates for the utilization of robotics as a tool to promote collaborative learning and augment student engagement. Primary data suggests that robotics fosters an environment conducive to collaboration, where students engage in teamwork, idea sharing, and problem-solving tasks. To optimise these benefits, educational initiatives involving robotics should be designed to encourage teamwork, communication, and peer-to-peer learning. The incorporation of elements such as robotics competitions and collaborative projects can further stimulate student motivation and engagement, providing a dynamic and competitive platform for the application of learning (Alam, 2022).

The development of robotics programs that are specifically tailored to suit the distinct educational and socio-cultural contexts of various regions is recommended. Such an approach aims to address the disparate levels of access and exposure to technology prevalent in schools across diverse regions, with particular reference to countries like South Africa (Gunal, 2019). Programs of robotics that are customized to align with the local conditions, resource availability, and educational requisites could significantly augment the relevance and efficacy of integrating technology within educational frameworks. The goal is to move away from a universal application of robotics education, instead adopting a model that is flexible and responsive to the unique needs and circumstances of each educational environment.

It is imperative to implement ongoing assessment and evaluation of robotics programs. This process should involve consistent monitoring and analytical review of the outcomes associated with robotics education, ensuring alignment with the objectives of augmenting student learning and skill acquisition (Tzagkaraki et al., 2021). It is essential to establish mechanisms for evaluation that assess the impacts of robotics on student learning, teacher effectiveness, and the overall quality of education, both in the short and long term. Utilizing feedback from these evaluations can inform necessary modifications and improvements to the robotics programs.

Planning in robotics lessons is absolutely crucial. Teachers should have weekly and daily plans for their robotics lessons and accommodate all learners. Teachers should prepare their robotics lessons and put all teaching and learning materials in place. All systems should be tested before the actual lesson begins to avoid technical glitches during the lesson, which will affect time constraints.

Finally, it is advocated to cultivate a culture within educational institutions that promotes innovation and experimentation, particularly in the context of robotics education. Such a cultural shift would encourage teachers and learners to experiment with novel ideas and methodologies in the teaching and learning processes involving robotics (Stewart et al., 2021). Educational settings should provide an environment where taking risks is supported, and perceived failures are considered valuable learning opportunities. This innovative ethos could inspire creative applications of robotics in education, potentially leading to more stimulating and impactful educational experiences for students.

CONCLUSION

Technology is increasing rapidly, and new inventions are explored daily. This puts pressure on the education system to adapt to newly introduced technologies and to meet the standards set. Robotics is the current influential technological learning tool across the world used by different institutions because of its possibilities and influence on education.

REFERENCES

Adams, D. A., Nelson, R. R., & Todd, P. A. (2003). Perceived Usefulness, Ease of Use, and Usage of Information Technology: A Replication. *Management Information Systems Quarterly*, *16*(2), 227–250. https://www.jstor.org/stable/249577. doi:10.2307/249577

Adegbenro, J. B., Tumbo, M. T., & Olakanmi, E. E. (2017). In-service secondary school teachers' technology integration needs in an ICT-enhanced classroom. *The Turkish Online Journal of Educational Technology*, *16*(3), 79–87. https://files.eric.ed.gov/fulltext/EJ1152645.pdf

Afari, E., & Khine, M. S. (2017). Robotics as an educational tool: Impact of Lego Mindstorms. *International Journal of Information and Education Technology (IJIET)*, *7*(6), 437–442. doi:10.18178/ijiet.2017.7.6.908

Agenda, D. (2023). *Future of jobs 2023: These are the most in-demand skills now- and beyond.* World Economic Forum. https://www.weforum.org/agenda/2023/05/future-of-jobs-2023-skills/

Ahmed, S., & Kazmi, H. (2020). Teacher Educators' Attitude towards the Pedagogical use of ICTs: A Study. *Journal of Education and Educational Development*, *7*(2), 369–386. doi:10.22555/joeed.v7i2.67

Akilbekovna, B. (2021). The Usage of ICT in The Classrooms of Primary School. *International Journal On Orange. Technologies*, *3*(3), 291–294. doi:10.31149/ijot.v3i3.1545

Alam, A. (2022). Social robots in education for long-term human-robot interaction: Socially supportive behaviour of robotic tutor for creating robo-tangible learning environment in a guided discovery learning interaction. *ECS Transactions*, *107*(1), 12389–12403. doi:10.1149/10701.12389ecst

Ali, N., Santos, I. M., AlHakmani, R., Abu Khurma, O., Swe Khine, M., & Kassem, U. (2023). Exploring technology acceptance: Teachers' perspectives on robotics in teaching and learning in the UAE. *Contemporary Educational Technology*, *15*(4), ep469. doi:10.30935/cedtech/13646

AmuthaD. (2020). The Role and Impact of ICT in Improving the Quality of Education. SSRN. doi:10.2139/ssrn.3585228

Anwar, S., Bascou, N. A., Menekse, M., & Kardgar, A. (2019). A systematic review of studies on educational robotics. *Journal of Pre-College Engineering Education Research (J-PEER), 9*(2), 2.

Ates, A. (2021). The Relationship between Parental Involvement in Education and Academic Achievement: A Meta-Analysis Study. *Journal of Education and Instruction*, *11*(3), 50–66.

Barreto, F., & Benitti, V. (2012). Exploring the educational potential of robotics in schools: A systematic review. *Computers & Education*, *5*(8), 78–88. https://www.researchgate.net/publication/220140191

Bers, U. M., Ponte, I., Juelich, C., Viera, A., & Schenker, J. (2015). Teachers as designers: Integrating robotics in early childhood education. *Information Technology in Childhood Education Annual*, *3*(4), 23–45. https://core.ac.uk/download/pdf/33556818.pdf

Carey, S., & Clarke, L. (2019) A brief history of robotics timeline of key achievements in the field of science. *Tech advisor*. https://www.techadvisor.com/feature/small-business/brief-history-of-robotics-timeline-of-key-achievements-in-field-since-1941-3788761/

Cejka, E., Rogers, C., & Portsmore, M. (2012). Kindergarten robotics: Using robotics to motivate math, science, and engineering literacy in elementary school. *International Journal of Engineering Education*, *22*(4), 711–722. https://www.researchgate.net/publication/233616845

Chaldi, D., & Mantzanidou, G. (2021). Educational robotics and STEAM in early childhood education. *Advances in Mobile Learning Educational Research*, *1*(2), 72–81. doi:10.25082/AMLER.2021.02.003

Chalmers, C. (2018). Robotics and computational thinking in primary school. *International Journal of Child-Computer Interaction*, *17*, 93–100. doi:10.1016/j.ijcci.2018.06.005

Chambers, J. M., & Carbonaro, M. (2018). Designing, developing, and implementing a course on LEGO robotics for technology teacher education. *Journal of Technology and Teacher Education*, *11*(2), 25–29. https://www.ijiet.org/vol7/908-T108.pdf

Chau, P. Y. (2009). Examining a Model of Information Technology Acceptance by educators. *Journal of Management Information Systems, 18*(4), 192–220. doi:10.1080/07421222.2002.11045699

Chisango, G., & Marongwe, N. (2018). The impact of inadequate information and communication technologies on teaching and learning of pre-service teachers at a rural university in South Africa. *Journal of Communication, 9*(2), 1–10. 11.258359/KRE-31

Creswell, J. W. (2017). *Qualitative inquiry & research design: choosing among the five approaches.* Sage Publications, Inc.

Curto, B., & Moreno, V. (2016). Robotics in education. *Journal of Intelligent & Robotic Systems, 81*(1), 3–4. doi:10.1007/s10846-015-0314-z

Davis, F. D. (1989). Acceptance of Information Technology. *Management Information Systems Quarterly, 13*(3), 319–340. doi:10.2307/249008

De Walle, J. A. V., Folk, S., Karp, K. S., & Bay-Williams, J. M. (2011). *Elementary and middle school mathematics: Teaching developmentally.* Pearson Canada Inc.

Denis, B., & Hubert, S. (2016). Collaborative learning in an educational robotics environment. *Computers in Human Behavior, 17*(5-6), 465–480. doi:10.1016/S0747-5632(01)00018-8

Denzin, N. K., & Lincoln, Y. S. (2005). *Handbook of qualitative research.* Sage.

Department of Basic Education. (2021a). *DBE and partners workshop Coding and Robotics Curriculum for the GET Band.* DBE. https://www.education.gov.za/CodingCurriculum010419.aspx

Department of Basic Education. (2021b). Draft Curriculum and assessment Policy Statement Grades 7-9 Coding and Robotics. DBE. https://www.education.gov.za/LinkClick.aspx?fileticket=dp2IJGuK0Lw%3D&tabid=2689&portalid=0&mid=9573

Department of Science and Technology. (2019). *White paper on Science, Technology and Innovation.* DST. https://www.dst.gov.za/images/2019/White_paper_web_copyv1.pdf

Dillion, A. (1996). User Acceptance of Information Technology Theories and models. *Annual Review of Information Science & Technology, 3*(12), 9–21. https://www.researchgate.net/publication/277983543

Du Plessis, P., & Mestry, R. (2019). Teachers for rural schools – a challenge for South Africa. *South African Journal of Education, 39*(S). doi:10.15700/saje.v39ns1a1774

Eguchi, A. (2014). Educational robotics for promoting 21 century skills. *Journal of Automation. Mobile Robotics & Intelligent Systems, 8*(1). doi:10.14313/JAMRIS_1-2014/1

Eguchi, A. (2016). RoboCupJunior for promoting STEM education, 21st century skills, and technological advancement through robotics competition. *Robotics and Autonomous Systems, 75*, 692–699. doi:10.1016/j.robot.2015.05.013

Erwin, B., Cyr, M., & Rogers, C. (2013). LEGO engineer and RoboLab: Teaching engineering with LabVIEW from kindergarten to graduate school. *International Journal of Engineering Education, 16*(3), 181–192.

Farjon, D., Smits, A., & Voogt, J. (2019). Technology integration of pre-service teachers explained by attitudes and beliefs, competency, access, and experience. *Computers & Education*, *130*, 81–93. doi:10.1016/j.compedu.2018.11.010

Foss, A., & Rasmus, J. (2019). The academic and behavioural implications of robotics in the classroom: An elementary case study. *Technology and Innovation*, *20*(3), 321–332. doi:10.21300/20.3.2019.321

Gleason, N. W. (2018). *Higher Education in the Era of the Fourth Industrial Revolution*. Palgrave Macmillan. doi:10.1007/978-981-13-0194-0

Grubbs, M. (2013). Robotics intrigue middle school students and build STEM skills. *Technology and Engineering Teacher, 72*(6), 12-16. https://eric.ed.gov/?id=EJ1006898

Gunal, M. M. (2019). Simulation and the fourth industrial revolution. In *Simulation for Industry 4.0: Past, Present, and Future* (pp. 1–17). Springer International Publishing. doi:10.1007/978-3-030-04137-3_1

Gyamfi, N. K., Dayie, R., & Asiedu, E. K. (2022). Application of Artificial Intelligence Techniques in Educational Delivery; Ghana Perspective. *Webology, 19*(1).

Hamidi, T. K. (2016). Information technology in education. *Procedia Computer Science*, *2*(3), 110–123. doi:10.1016/j.procs.2010.12.062

Hbaci, I., & Abdunabi, R. (2020). Evaluating higher education educators' computer technology competencies in Libya. *Journal of Computing in Higher Education*, 1–18. doi:10.1007/s12528-020-09261-z

Hennink, M., & Hutter, I. (2011). *Qualitative research methods*. Sage.

Herman, C. (2022). *From South Africa to Ghana and Tanzania, computer science unlocks the future for youth*. Code.org.

Hew, K., & Brush, T. (2007). Integrating technology into K-12 teaching and learning: Current knowledge gaps and recommendations for future research. *Educational Technology Research and Development*, *55*(3), 223–252. doi:10.1007/s11423-006-9022-5

Hew, K. F., Lan, M., Tang, Y., Jia, C., & Lo, C. K. (2019). Where is the "theory" within the field of educational technology research? *British Journal of Educational Technology*, *50*(3), 956–971. doi:10.1111/bjet.12770

Hongshuai, Y. (2021). Research on the Application of Industrial Robots in Automation Control. *Curriculum and Teaching Methodology, 4*(4), 132-138. https://openarchive.nure.ua/bitstream/document/19396/1/SotLyash1.pdf

Hubbard, A. (2018). Pedagogical content knowledge in computing education: A review of the research literature. *Computer Science Education*, *28*(2), 117–135. doi:10.1080/08993408.2018.1509580

Jaipal-Jamani, K., & Angeli, C. (2017). Effect of robotics on elementary pre-service teachers' self-efficacy, science learning, and computational thinking. *Journal of Science Education and Technology*, *26*(2), 175–192. doi:10.1007/s10956-016-9663-z

Jawaid, I., Javed, M. Y., Jaffery, M. H., Akram, A., Safder, U., & Hassan, S. (2020). Robotic system education for young children by collaborative-project-based learning. *Computer Applications in Engineering Education, 28*(1), 178–192. doi:10.1002/cae.22184

Jung, S. E., & Won, E. S. (2018). Systematic review of research trends in robotics education for young children. *Sustainability (Basel), 10*(4), 905. doi:10.3390/su10040905

Ketelhut, D., Mills, K., Hestness, E., Cabrera, L., Plane, J., & McGinnis, J. R. (2020). Teacher change following a professional development experience in integrating computational thinking into elementary science. *Journal of Science Education and Technology, 29*(1), 174–188. doi:10.1007/s10956-019-09798-4

Lai, P. C. (2017). The literature overview of technology adoption models and theories for the novelty technology. *Journal of Information Systems and Technology Management, 14*(1), 21–38. https://www.scielo.br/pdf/jistm/v14n1/1807-1775-jistm-14-01-00021.pdf. doi:10.4301/S1807-17752017000100002

Lambert, L., & Guiffre, H. (2013). Computer science outreach in an elementary school. *Journal of Computing Sciences in Colleges, 24*(3), 118–124.

Lanka, S. (2021). The impact of education technology in teaching and learning. *European Journal of Research and Reflection in Educational Sciences, 9*(1).

Leedy, P., & Ormrod, J. (2015). *Practical research: planning and design.* Pearson Education.

Lei, M., Clemente, I. M., Liu, H., & Bell, J. (2022). The Acceptance of Telepresence Robots in Higher Education. *International Journal of Social Robotics, 14*(4), 1025–1042. doi:10.1007/s12369-021-00837-y PMID:35103081

Levin, T., & Wadmany, R. (2011). Changes in educational beliefs and classroom practices of teachers and students in rich technology-based classroom. *Technology, Pedagogy and Education, 14*(3), 281–307. doi:10.1080/14759390500200208

Mahaye, N. E. (2020). The Impact of COVID-19 Pandemic on Education: Navigating Forward the Pedagogy of Blended Learning. *ResearchGate*, 1-24. https://www.researchgate.net/publication/340899662_

Marcinkiewicz, H. R. (2010). Technology and teachers: Factors influencing technology use in the classroom. *Journal of Research on Computing in Education, 26*(2), 220–237. doi:10.1080/08886504.1993.10782088

Maree, K., & Pietersen, J. (2016). Sampling. In K. Maree (Ed.), *First steps in research 2* (2nd ed.). Van Schaik.

Mauch, E. (2015). Using technological innovation to improve the problem-solving skills of middle school students. *The Clearing House: A Journal of Educational Strategies, Issues and Ideas, 75*(4), 211–213. doi:10.1080/00098650109599193

Mavridis, N., Petychakis, M., Tsamakos, A., Toulis, P., Emami, S., Kazmi, W., Datta, C., BenAbdelkader, C., & Tanoto, A. (2010). FaceBots: Steps towards enhanced long-term human-robot interaction by utilizing and publishing online social information. *Paladyn : Journal of Behavioral Robotics, 1*(3), 169–178. doi:10.2478/s13230-011-0003-y

Michalec, O., O'Donovan, C., & Sobhani, M. (2021). What is robotics made of? The interdisciplinary politics of robotics research. *Humanities & Social Sciences Communications*, *8*(1), 65. doi:10.1057/s41599-021-00737-6

Nouri, J., Zhang, L., Mannila, L., & Norén, E. (2020). Development of computational thinking, digital competence and 21st century skills when learning programming in K-9. *Education Inquiry*, *11*(1), 1–17. doi:10.1080/20004508.2019.1627844

Ntekane, A. (2018). Parental Involvement in Education, A dissertation/thesis of North-West University Vaal. *Vanderbijlpark, South Africa*. doi:10.25304/rlt.v29.2544

Pather, M. R. (2020). Education in South Africa. *Fourth Industrial Revolution*, 19.

Petre, M., & Price, B. (2014). Using robotics to motivate 'Back Door' learning. *Education and Information Technologies*, *9*(2), 147–158. doi:10.1023/B:EAIT.0000027927.78380.60

Phillippi, J., & Lauderdale, J. (2017). A Guide to Field Notes for Qualitative Research: Context and Conversation. *Qualitative Health Research*, *23*(8), 381–388. doi:10.1177/1049732317697102 PMID:29298584

Piatti, A. (2020). Fostering computational thinking through educational robotics: A model for creative computational problem solving. *International Journal of STEM Education*, *7*(1), 1–18.

Portelli, A. (1980). The Three Laws of Robotics: Laws of the Text, Laws of Production, Laws of Society. *Science Fiction Studies*, *7*, 150.

Purba, S. W. D., & Hwang, W. Y. (2017). Investigation of learning behaviors and achievement of vocational high school students using an ubiquitous physics tablet PC app. *Journal of Science Education and Technology*, *26*(3), 322–331. doi:10.1007/s10956-016-9681-x

Qureshi, M. I., Khan, N., Raza, H., Imran, A., & Ismail, F. (2021). Digital Technologies in Education 4.0. Does it Enhance the Effectiveness of Learning? A Systematic Literature Review. *International Journal of Interactive Mobile Technologies*, *15*(4), 31. doi:10.3991/ijim.v15i04.20291

Rao, L., & Ab Jalil, H. (2021). A survey on Acceptance and Readiness to Use Robot Teaching Technology Among Prinary School Science Teachers. *Asian Social Science*, *17*(2), 115. doi:10.5539/ass.v17n11p115

Rogers, C., & Portsmore, M. (2014). Bringing engineering to elementary school. *Journal of STEM Education: Innovations and Research*, *5*(2), 17–28.

Ruggiero, D., & Mong, C. J. (2015). The teacher technology integration experience: Practice and reflection in the classroom. *Journal of Information Technology Education*, 14. doi:10.28945/2227

Samuels, P., & Haapasalo, L. (2016). Real and virtual robotics in mathematics education at the school–university transition. *International Journal of Mathematical Education in Science and Technology*, *43*(3), 285–301. doi:10.1080/0020739X.2011.618548

Sangkawetai, C., Neanchaleay, J., Koul, R., & Murphy, E. (2018). Predictors of K-12 Teachers' Instructional Strategies with ICTs. *Technology, Knowledge and Learning*, 1-29.

Seale, C. (2000). Quality in qualitative research. *Qualitative Inquiry*, *5*(4), 465–478. https://citeseerx.ist.psu.edu/viewdoc/download?doi=10.1.1.460.3511&rep=rep1&type=pdf. doi:10.1177/107780049900500402

South Africa O. R. T. (2017). *ORT South Africa*. ORTSA. https://www.ortsa.org.za/ort-sa-owns-thetechnology-revolution

Staff Writer. (2021). South Africa moves ahead with coding and robotics at schools. *Business Tech*. https://businesstech.co.za/news/technology/469860/south-africa-moves-ahead-with-coding-and-robotics-at-schools/

Stewart, W. H., Baek, Y., Kwid, G., & Taylor, K. (2021). Exploring factors that influence computational thinking skills in elementary students' collaborative robotics. *Journal of Educational Computing Research, 59*(6), 1208–1239. doi:10.1177/0735633121992479

Sullivan, F. R. (2012). Robotics and science literacy: Thinking skills, science process skills and systems understanding. *Journal of Research in Science Teaching, 45*(3), 373–394. doi:10.1002/tea.20238

Tzagkaraki, E., Papadakis, S., & Kalogiannakis, M. (2021, February). Exploring the Use of Educational Robotics in primary school and its possible place in the curricula. In *Educational Robotics International Conference* (pp. 216-229). Cham: Springer International Publishing. 10.1007/978-3-030-77022-8_19

Veldman, S., Dicks, E., Suleman, H., Greyling, J., Freese, J., & Majake, T. (2021). *The Status of Coding and Robotics in South African Schools*. Academy of Science of South Africa. https://www.youtube.com/watch?v=hMHgnEY41U&ab_channel=AcademyofScienceofSouthAfrica

Vidal-Hall, C., Flewitt, R., & Wyse, D. (2020). Early childhood practitioner beliefs about digital media: Integrating technology into a child-centred classroom environment. *European Early Childhood Education Research Journal, 28*(2), 167–181. doi:10.1080/1350293X.2020.1735727

Wellington, J. (2014). Educational research: Contemporary issues and practical approaches. *Continuum*.

You, H. S., Chacko, S. M., & Kapila, V. (2021). Examining the Effectiveness of a Professional Development Program: Integration of Educational Robotics into Science and Mathematics Curricula. *Journal of Science Education and Technology, 30*(4), 567–581. doi:10.1007/s10956-021-09903-6

Zawacki-Richter, O., & Latchem, C. (2018). Exploring four decades of research in Computers & Education. *Computers & Education, 122*, 136–152. doi:10.1016/j.compedu.2018.04.001

KEY TERMS AND DEFINITIONS

21st Century Skills: Various skills that allow learners to be updated with the changes and transformations in response to global advancements and prepares them to be able to participate in the digital world, which involves creativity, communication and critical thinking (Sullivan, 2012).

Acceptance: Refers to the ability to welcome or adopt something with a positive or negative attitude and it is based on previous experience (Lai, 2017). In this study, acceptance refers to the ability of teachers and learners to adopt and integrate robotics in the Intermediate Phase.

Attitudes: Refers to how an individual feels or thinks about something (Hew & Brush, 2007). In this study, attitudes refer to how teachers and learners feel and think about the integration of robotics in the Intermediate Phase.

Computational Thinking: Computational thinking is a dynamic process, which consists of different techniques of problem-solving approaches, which include articulation of challenges and their resolutions in a manner that a computer might also accomplish (Chalmers, 2018).

Experience: To be acquainted with information about certain things through observations, hands-on activities and practicals (Ruggiero & Mong, 2015). In this study, teachers' and learners' experience is based on knowledge of the training, lessons and teacher developmental workshops with robotics.

Fourth Industrial Revolution: Refers to quick technological developments in science, technology, engineering and processes in the 21st century due to connectivity and advanced computerization (Gleason, 2018). The Fourth Industrial Revolution (4IR) in this study refers to rapid technological developments which impact on education and necessitates a paradigm shift.

Lego Mindstorm EV3: The Lego Mindstorm is a practical, cross-curricular STEM approach, which involves learners by introducing resources to plan, create and program their inventions while assisting them to cultivate important abilities such as creativeness, communication and critical thinking (Chambers & Carbonaro, 2018).

Robotics: An engineering, science and technology spectrum specializing in the construction and software design of robots, tools which can robotically follow instructions to perform activities.

Self-efficacy: Is based on a set of beliefs, which control how individuals feel, contemplate, boost their self-esteem and behave, which have an impact on their attitude towards something (Jaipal-Jamani & Angeli, 2017). In this study, self-efficacy refers to teachers' and learners' beliefs towards the use of robotics.

Technology Integration: Is the utilization and incorporation of technological resources to advance teaching and learning (Adegbenro et al., 2017). In this study, the integration of technology refers to teachers' and learners' utilization and incorporation of robotics for teaching and learning.

Chapter 12
Implementation of Coding and Robotics in South African Public Schools, Fostering Teachers' Self-Directed Learning: A Scoping Review

Averil Gorrah
North-West University, Potchefstroom Campus, South Africa

Francois Papers
https://orcid.org/0000-0002-2904-5523
North-West University, Potchefstroom Campus, South Africa

ABSTRACT

This study utilizes a scoping review of literature to explore the implementation of coding and robotics and its potential to foster and enhance teachers' self- directed learning skills through the implementation of coding and robotics within the South African educational context. This chapter presents a comprehensive synthesis of scholarly articles, reports, and studies published from 2013 to 2023. The study further aims to provide an extensive examination of the current status quo of coding and robotics implementation, as well as the possibilities that arise for professional development as well as the development of self-directed learning skills, also identifying gaps that will guide further studies in this field and later produce a systematic literature review. This scoping review utilizes a methodical and rigorous methodology to identify the current body of literature, discern significant themes, and provide a concise summary of the results.

INTRODUCTION

Information Technology (IT) and Computer Applications Technology (CAT) initially comprised the South African public-school Computer Science Education (CSE) curriculum. These two subjects were implemented in the South African public school system for Grade 10 in 2006 (Chiles, 2013) and the Grade

DOI: 10.4018/979-8-3693-1066-3.ch012

12`s sat for the inaugural paper in November 2008 (Havenga and Mentz, 2009). The CSE curriculum was expanded when two new CSE subjects, Digital Technology (DT) (Botha, 2020) and Coding and Robotics (C & R) (Department of Basic Education, 2021a), were introduced as part of the Curriculum and Assessment Policy Statement (CAPS). CAT and IT are presented as elective subjects in the Further Education and Training band (FET) for grades 10-12 while DT was introduced in the Senior Phase (SP) for grades 8 and 9. However, C & R has been introduced in the General Education and Training band (GET), which includes the Foundation Phase (FP) for grades R-3, the Intermediate Phase (IP) for grades 4-6, and the SP for grades 7-9 (Figure 1).

This curriculum change marks a dynamic paradigm shift in the teaching and learning of CSE subjects, where the elective CSE subjects, CAT and IT, taught mostly by a small percentage of subject specialists (Van Wyk, 2012) to a small percentage of grade 10-12 learners (Gustafsson, 2014), pivot to what will become a mandatory subject, C & R, taught to every learner entering the South African public school system in the FP (Department of Basic Education, 2023). This move of the Department of Basic Education (DBE) essentially establishes the base of the CSE pyramid (BoCSEP) and the foundation of the South African CSE (Figure 1), where the fundamentals of information and communication technology (ICT) and digital skills (DS) will be introduced and subsequently form the foundation for future teaching and learning of the DT, CAT, and IT subjects in the upper education levels (Figure 1). Furthermore, this curriculum change infers that the onus of teaching the foundations of CSE also shifts to the BoCSEP and becomes the responsibility of all FP teachers.

Figure 1. Base of the Computer Science Education Pyramid (BoCSEP)
(Author)

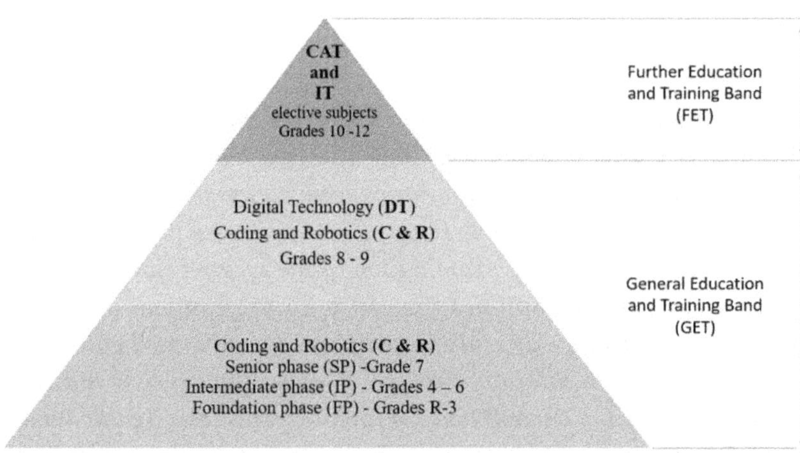

Computer Science Education in the South African Public School system

FP teachers encounter challenges when introducing new subjects and educational programs. Makeleni & Sethusha (2014) identified several challenges faced by teachers during curriculum implementation while Geldenhuys & Fatar (2021) identified factors crucial for an efficient introduction of the C & R curriculum in South African schools, obstacles encountered by educators, and aspects requiring attention to ensure successful implementation. These challenges encompass the requirement for ongoing training, assistance, and access to necessary materials.

Teachers, however, need the resources and a solid knowledge base of ICT and the relevant skills to facilitate theoretical and practical content to teach CSE subjects (Breed, 2015). According to Gorrah (2022), teachers, as custodians of the curriculum, have a crucial responsibility in implementing the South African C & R curriculum; therefore, it is critical that they possess adequate expertise and knowledge to facilitate C & R. Numerous educators currently tasked with teaching C & R lack the basic digital knowledge (DK) and DS that they would have acquired through the completion of a three to four-year specialized course. Jantjies (2019) therefore acknowledge that many teachers in the education system received few or no ICT-infused learning experiences while also studying. This impediment could be addressed through PD programs and activities, however teachers in schools are not efficiently trained for the pilot C & R implementation plan (Mokonyane-Motha & De Jager, 2023; Gorrah, 2022). Dlamini and Mbatha (2018) maintain that the requirements for teachers to enhance their ICT skills and competencies are not adequately met through a substantial and organized approach to their Professional development (PD) in ICT.

Therefore, teachers would need to engage in acquiring DS and DK regularly even after PD programs. Moreover, teachers should reinforce the essential knowledge and skills required to teach C & R attained through multifaceted PD programs by becoming self-directed learners who recognize their learning requirements, establish objectives, find resources, choose learning strategies, and evaluate their learning (Knowles 1975).

As C & R is an emerging component of CSE, literature pertaining to the introduction and implementation of C & R suggests that CSE teachers encountered challenges (Khanlari, 2016) with PD and training programs, DK and DS and face challenges with curriculum implementation (Stokes et al., 2022). It is therefore imperative to understand how the implementation of C & R at the BoCSEP, in South African public schools, will foster the SDL of teachers who will be responsible for facilitating C & R. Subsequently, this chapter presents a theoretical framework aimed primarily at serving as a comprehensive guide for researchers interested in exploring the initial introduction and future implementation of C & R in South African public schools.

The Background section of this study focuses on C & R, SDL, and other Literature Reviews pertaining to the introduction and future implementation of C & R directed at SDL. The Methodology section explains the methodology used in this article, specifically describing the protocol followed in conducting the scoping review. Furthermore, this research effort aims to provide a comprehensive scoping review that focusses on the introduction and future implementation of C & R in public schools within the South African context and how this will foster self-directed learning of teachers identified to teach C & R in the GET band. The review draws upon the limited array of existing national and a broad array of international literature sources to ensure a diverse and comprehensive literature mapping, as well as to identify gaps that will guide further studies in this field.

BACKGROUND

What Are Coding and Robotics?

C & R emerged as a critical subject introduced or implemented in the changing international educational landscape in recent years. Using robots in the classroom is often referred to as educational robotics (ER) as many studies (Tang et al., 2020; Theodoropoulos et al., 2017) explored ER and the connection between programming, C & R, and its application in the classroom. Hence, Sapounidis and Alimisis (2021) state that ER is a teaching tool that affords students to use an easy-to-understand coding language to build and program a robot. In the South African context, the subject has been introduced as C & R that aligns with the view of Sapounidis and Alimisis (2021) as the DBE (2023) envisions that including C & R in the curriculum will equip learners with the necessary skills and knowledge to succeed in the workplace. Subsequently, the DBE noted the value of introducing learners to C & R from grade R-9 that covers interrelated IT (coding) and engineering (robotics) topics. The subject examines logical and computational problem-solving focusing on algorithms and coding, robotic skills, application skills and internet and e-communication skills pattern recognition and problem solving being added in the FP (Department of Basic Education, 2023). Consequently, computer science lessons, such as programming and robotics skills, would progressively increase in difficulty as learners progress through each grade level. Learners in grades R-3 would engage in analog and unplugged activities that impart fundamental concepts of coding and algorithms. Learners in grades 4 through 6 would utilize block-based programming tools. During grades 7 to 9, students would utilize coding platforms (Fares et al., 2021).

Coding and Robotics Skills and Knowledge

As it will be the responsibility of teachers to implement and teach the C & R subject (Gorrah, 2022), teachers should acquire the essential DK and DS required to teach C & R. As teachers need specific knowledge and skill sets to prepare today's learners for the world of work, one should acknowledge that teachers should rely on these professional aptitudes, upskill, and stay current with present teaching and learning demands. The C & R proficiency, one of these skills, is becoming more imperative for individuals to secure employment opportunities in the current and future job market (Xia, Wan, Kochhar & Lo, 2019). Consequently, computational, and critical thinking, problem solving, and digital literacy are poised to be crucial in future job markets. Moreover, integrating C & R offers a favorable solution to address and promote these skills of the 21st century. Additionally, basic coding skills facilitate a more effective orientation between educational qualifications and labour market demands (Demertzi et al., 2018). However, such a dynamic shift in curriculum requires a new way of thinking about education in general. Therefore, one would argue that exposure to new skills and knowledge would encourage and require teachers to view themselves as self-directed lifelong learners.

Teachers must develop competence in and master C & R to teach effectively and facilitate the C & R subject. Internationally, it is now best practice for educators to further improve their C & R skills and knowledge through participation in workshops, online courses, and communities of practice (Pankratova et al., 2021; Scaradozzi et al., 2019). Morze and Strutynska (2023) focus on providing future teachers with the essential competencies to successfully teach educational robotics. These experiences do more than improve teachers' abilities; they also foster a mindset that values and allows for SDL.

Coding and Robotics Training and Professional Development

Wu et al. (2020), emphasized that many schools now teach coding and other 21st-century skills. However, there is a noticeable gap in official and sufficient training for teachers in effectively incorporating C & R activities into their teaching practices at the school level as studies in broader literature have identified challenges that must be addressed to achieve complete integration and implementation of the C & R curriculum (Greyling,2022; Stokes et al., 2022). Giannandrea, Gratani, and Renieri (2020) noted that teachers' knowledge and abilities improved by participating in teacher training in design, C & R. As a result, these changes created increased self-assurance regarding their professional aptitudes. Camilleri (2017) proposed a framework for teacher learning and training to facilitate the integration of robotics in primary school. Therefore, Hill, Kim, and Yuan (2019), recommended the integration of C & R into the primary school curriculum, with a particular emphasis on the importance of adequate teacher preparation, further underscoring the potential influence of incorporating C & R into primary education. The role of teachers in integrating C & R into the curriculum is crucial. Teachers are the ones to lead learners in educational programs and projects that provide opportunities to discover, experiment, and develop computational and 21st century skills (Ogegbo & Aina, 2022). Most teacher training courses focus on teaching basic skills and knowledge, and the training content is mostly planned and organised by outside providers, leaving teachers' roles as subjects (Giannandrea et al., 2020).

The DBE and their training partners initiated diverse C & R training initiatives (Department of Basic Education, 2021b), but despite participating in PD programs the problem is that teachers often revert to their old and familiar teaching methods (de Beer 2019). However, Fares et al. (2021) indicated that the South African government's efforts to incorporate Computer Science (CS) into the curriculum have not been complemented by effective PD programs to adequately train teachers for CSE. Mokonyane-Motha and De Jager (2023), demonstrated the importance of DK and DS acquisition and transferring these knowledge and skill sets to students and learners. The newly suggested C & R curriculum would significantly reinforce the demand for teachers with expertise in CSE and computational thinking (CT) (Fares et al., 2021). Enhancing teacher preparedness for the subject is thus the utmost priority for the government and nonprofit partners to provide quality CSE to more learners. However, Stokes et al. (2022) recognized a shortage of resources, inadequate curriculum integration, and limited opportunities for PD as obstacles that impede the broader implementation of robotics education. This is also evident in the South African context as Greyling (2022) highlights challenges to be overcome with implementing C & R including the lack of resources and lack of trained teachers.

Research emphasizes the importance of C & R teacher education and continuous learning of C&R teachers (Boz & Allexsaht-Snider, 2022). However, resources confined to and beyond PD courses, teacher collaboration, C & R platforms, and teaching approaches can either facilitate or impede teachers' learning of C & R. According to Avalos (2011), PD involves acquiring knowledge from teachers, developing their learning skills, and applying this knowledge to their instructional practices to facilitate the growth and development of their learners.

The process of teacher professional learning is multifaceted, as it necessitates the active engagement of teachers both individually and collectively, the ability and willingness to critically assess one's convictions and beliefs, and the exploration and implementation of suitable alternatives for enhancing or modifying current practices. The onus is therefore on teachers to navigate the challenges and craft a professional path for their own C & R education and SDL.

CODING AND ROBOTICS AND SELF-DIRECTED LEARNING

Conceptualizing self-directed learning

Self-directed learning (SDL) is one of the most researched topics due to its impact on education (Doo et al., 2023) observing that SDL is becoming an increasingly important concept in education (Van der Westhuizen and Bailey, 2022). SDL is best defined by Knowles (1975) and Boyer et al. (2014) as the student taking initiative, diagnosing learners' needs, formulating learners' goals, identifying resources for learning, appropriate learning, and evaluating learning outcomes.

SDL is an important goal to improve the quality of preparation of students for the future (Sumuer, 2018) and it is essential that the learner's SDL skills be developed to release students' full potential (Williamson 2007) as learners are growing up to be more independent to allow for SDL development (Kruger et al., 2022). Morris & Rohs (2023) maintain that SDL is a fundamental competence to live and work in the modern world, especially in the digital age. Candy (2004) pronounces that in the rapid times we are living, considering the constant new development of technology, learners should become aware of the benefits of SDL. Van Zyl & Mentz (2019) reports that promoting SDL in education will prepare students for a changing world. SDL competencies benefit someone who wants to pursue a rapidly changing career, such as information technology. SDL is important to improve the quality of student learning and prepare students for the future. SDL is vital for 21st-century education (Mentz & Bailey, 2019).

Self-Directed Learning Skills

Van der Westhuizen and Kemp (2022), du Toit Brits (2019); Van Zyl &Mentz (2019) justifies that SDL skills are an important skill to survive in the 21st century. Bailey & Breed (2022) challenges that the South African curriculum should introduces subjects such as coding, robotics, and digital technology in all schools. SDL skills are crucial for success in the rapidly changing social and economic areas concerning education we acquire lifelong and SDL learners (Kruger et al., 2022). The SDL developments are one strategy that could be implemented in teaching and learning to promote skills of the 21st century. There is a need to provide teaching and learning experiences that help learners learn to use SDL skills (Bosch et al. (2019). There is a concern that education lacks the development of skills of the 21st century (Van Zyl & Mentz, 2019).

Self-Directed Learning and Technology

With the demanding world, it is noticed that the advancement of technology requires the education sector to become more adopting in how we engage in teaching and learning for the future (Kruger et al., 2022). A study by Sumuer (2018) points out that SDL with technology warrants further investigation because SDL, as a process, is particularly enhanced with the convenience of ICTs. Geng (2019) asserts that a learning environment integrated with technology can provide students with ample opportunities and capabilities to develop self-directed learning skills. With the introduction of the C & R in schools, many teachers were required to independently acquire proficiency in various programs. Geng (2019) asserts that a high management level is crucial for SDL, and teachers should employ diverse strategies to acquire these skills. Geng (2019) found that research on self-directed learning with technology (SDLT) indicates that the perception of collaborative learning promotes SDL.

Van der Westhuizen and Bailey (2022) mentioned that the education landscape has not kept up with the rapid changes and the demands to equip our students for the fourth industrial revolution. More exposure to SDL and technology increases students' technological development and directly influences SDL. Doo et al. (2023) emphasized that self-directed learning needs to reflect whether they have learnt the skills and competencies. Schools should prepare learners with the skills needed for a successful life and employment in the 21st century (du Toit, 2019).

RESEARCH METHODOLOGY

The outline section illustrates the study design, data collection procedure, and data analysis procedures adopted for this study.

Study Design

The research process was based on suggestions from (Arksey and O'Malley, 2009; Levac et al., 2010; Pharm et al., 2014; Peters et al., 2020) in consultation with the Proposed Methodology of the Scoping Reviews based on the Joanna Briggs Institute (JBI) Framework of Evidence Synthesis. A scoping review methodology was used for this study. This paper aims to furnish a scoping literature review on how implementing C & R fosters educators' SDL skills.

Munn et al. (2018) maintain that scoping reviews are a novel approach and ever increasingly popular in synthesizing evidence. (Pharm et al., 2014; Tricco et al., 2018). Khalil et al. (2016) validate that scoping reviews will ensure further research and identify gaps that will contribute to the body of knowledge. Scoping reviews present a large, diverse body of literature on a specific research question (Pharm et al., 2014). Sannicandro et al. (2022) supports that scoping reviews can provide researchers with insights into the characteristics of a body of evidence, concepts of terms used, and topics reported on. Subsequently the aim of this scoping review is to look at existing knowledge, significant trends, and research gaps concerning the incorporation of C & R into the South African public-school curricula and how this move will be cultivating SDL in teachers' task to teach the new subject. Consequently, with these aims in mind, we embarked on this scoping review study to address the following research question:

1. How does the implementation of Coding and Robotics foster and enhance teachers' self-directed learning within the South African public educational context?
2. How can Coding and Robotics implementation influence self-directed learning skills of teachers?

Data Search Strategy

Researchers used a database covering education to ensure the relevant literature search to the research questions. Boolean operators (AND, OR) were used to refine the search. The search terms included: Coding AND Robotics, Coding AND Robotics AND South AND Africa, Computer AND Science, Robotics AND Education, Robotics AND Education AND South AND Africa, Self AND Directed AND Learning, Fostering AND Self AND directed AND Learning AND Skills and ("coding and robotics") AND "South Africa" AND "self-directed learning" AND "robotics education".

On 18th October 2023, the initial search yielded 2 430 articles related to Coding and Robotics, Coding and Robotics in South Africa, Robotics Education, Computer Science, Self-directed learning, and Fostering Self-directed learning skills.

Inclusion and Exclusion Criteria

During our literature search, researchers included teachers involved in teaching C & R at the school's national and international levels. C & R form under the different strands of CSE. The main concept for this study is the implementation of C & R and its effect on fostering SDL skills. Literature evidence clearly describes teaching C & R, which usually takes place in the classroom/computer laboratory. The only language selected for the literature search was English. Empirical research published between 2013–2023 must be peer–reviewed. The exclusion criteria thus include studies that fall outside the identified period, publications in languages other than English, and studies that do not directly focus on the implementation of C & R in the South African context.

Data Collection

Mensah-Williams and Derera (2023) suggest steps are needed for a scoping literature review. The study thus incorporated a series of steps, including the identification of research questions, identification of relevant studies, selection of studies, organization and analysis of data, and summarization and reporting of the results. (Figure 2).

Figure 2. Phases the researchers followed towards completing the article

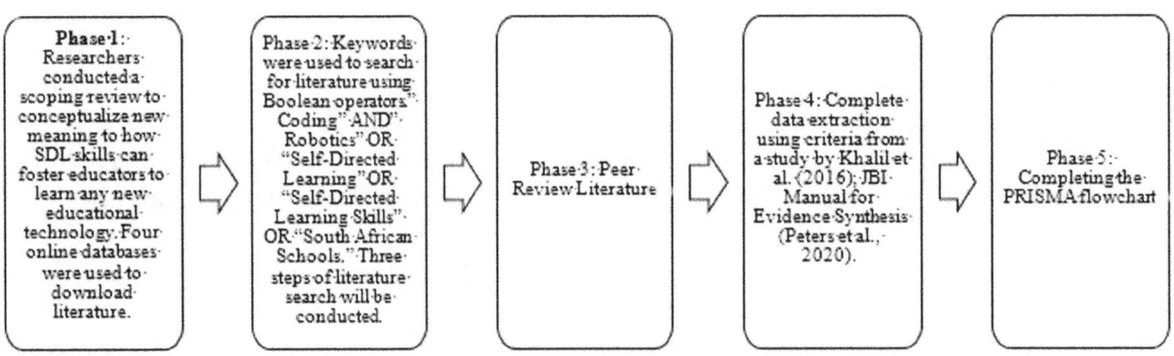

This study used online databases *Scopus, African Journal, EBSCOhost, and Google Scholar* (Table 1). Separate phases were performed for the Scoping review. The researchers identified the following keywords: Self-directed learning, Self-directed learning skills, Self-directed technology, Computer Science Education, Coding and Robotics, and Robotics Education. The search was conducted from October to December 2023. The extensive search ended in December 2023. Table 1 displays the analysis of results when researchers conducted a literature search.

Table 1. Data collected

Key Words	**African Journal**	**Scopus**	**EBSCOhost**	**Google Scholar**
Coding AND Robotics	4767	1178	73	19 100
Coding AND Robotics AND South AND Africa	35 503	35 503	0	19 400
Computer AND Science	77 297	119 943	6083	53 700
Robotics AND Education	9324	7882	2627	37 400
Robotics AND Education AND South AND Africa	8084	27	6	17 600
Self AND Directed AND Learning	27 946	11 162	1557	17 800
Fostering AND Self AND directed AND Learning AND Skills	7900	86	2	17 800
("coding and robotics") AND "South Africa" AND "self-directed learning"	0	1	60	42

Data Extraction

The PRISMA 2020 checklist, depicted in Figure 3, employed in this scoping review, presents a systematic and lucid approach for extracting and reporting data. By following the PRISMA guidelines, researchers aimed to achieve higher levels of reliability and reproducibility in their results, which aims to improve the understanding of the implementation of C & R in South African schools. The utilization of the PRISMA 2020 checklist aids in the systematic arrangement of collected data. The objective is to identify trends, patterns, and gaps in the current literature. This enables a thorough analysis of the incorporation of C & R in South African schools and the affordance of fostering SDL and SDL skills in the teachers' task with introducing, implementing and subsequently teaching the C & R curriculum at the BoCSE in the GET in South African public schools.

This review included an extensive search across prominent academic databases (Table 1), which resulted in an initial set of records. A comprehensive full-text review as illustrated in Figure 3 was performed which resulted in the inclusion of studies that satisfied our predetermined inclusion and exclusion criteria. This was accomplished after the elimination of duplicates and the completion of an initial screening. Records were disregarded prior to screening because they did not have any relevance to introduction, implementation, integration, and SDL. When these findings were synthesized, a nuanced understanding of the South African landscape of C & R introduction, implementation or integration was provided. This understanding revealed a concept of self-directed learning fostering based on the introduction and implementation of C & R. The purpose of this scoping review is to serve as a foundational resource for future research endeavors, and it does so by contributing valuable insights into current trends and focal points within the C & R field.

Data Analysis

The study comprised of 10 articles published from qualitative, quantitative, and mixed-method studies in different educational journals with reference to the introduction, implementation, integration, or SDL of C & R. The articles were reviewed and scanned by the researchers with the research librarian's

Figure 3. PRISMA flow diagram of article inclusion and exclusion
Note: Adapted from: Page MJ, McKenzie JE, Bossuyt PM, Boutron I, Hoffmann TC, Mulrow CD, et al. The PRISMA 2020 statement: an updated guideline for reporting systematic reviews. BMJ 2021;372:n71. doi: 10.1136/bmj.n71

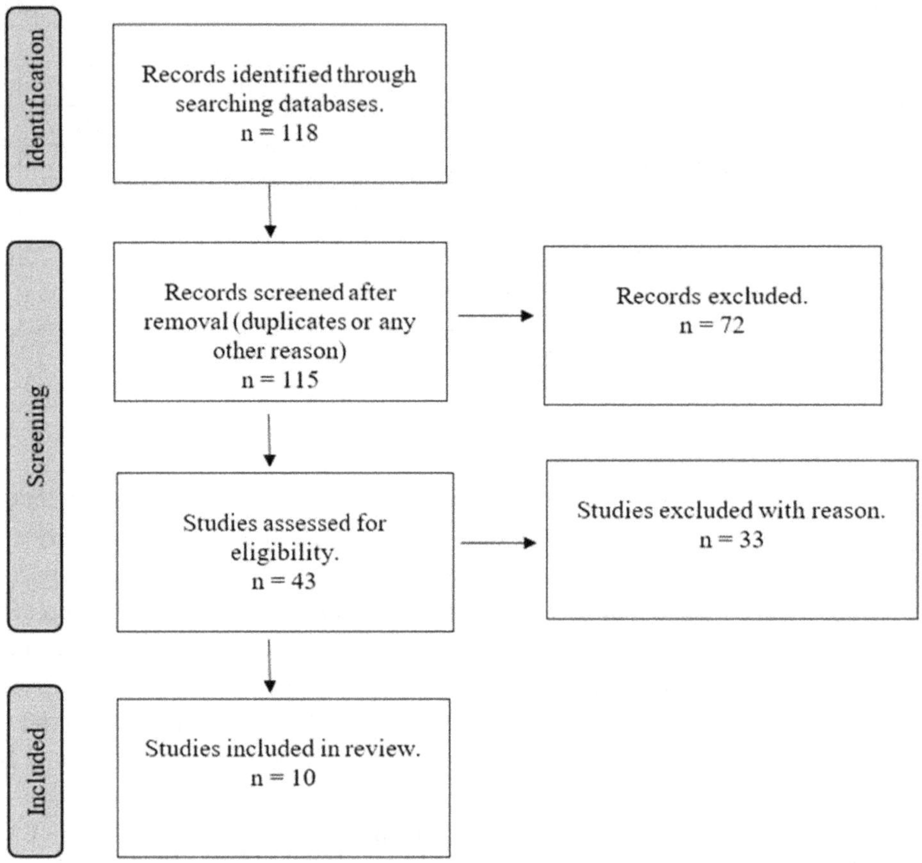

assistance; during this process, duplicate articles were removed. Table 2 shows the data extracted into a tabular form focusing on how the implementation of C & R foster and enhance teachers' SDL within the South African public educational context, whilst Table 3 presents data pertaining to how C & R implementation influence SDL skills in teachers.

SOLUTIONS AND RECOMMENDATIONS

The implementation of C & R in South African public schools faces numerous challenges (Fares, 2021; Greyling, 2022), including but not limited to teacher training and PD, as well as curriculum integration. The lack of skilled teachers with specialized DK and DS presents a significant challenge, requiring the implementation of thorough and continuous PD initiatives to empower teachers to enhance their understanding of the incorporation of C & R, as well as their proficiency in utilizing these tools to supplement their teaching (Willemse, 2023). Heyns (2023) expresses concern about the limited availability of teachers in the South African context who possess the required enthusiasm and digital skills. They argued that the

Table 2. Coding and robotics introduction, implementation or intergration (n=4)

First Author and Year	Title	Implementation of Coding and Robotics	Fostering Self-directed learning
Fares, K, (2021)	How South Africa implemented its computer science education program	The paper addresses CSE challenges and opportunities in South Africa in a comprehensive manner. It prioritizes teacher training, infrastructure, curriculum, and public-private partnerships.	Prioritizing teacher training is crucial when introducing CSE, according to the study. It stresses the importance of qualified teachers in computer science education. It also emphasizes the need for extensive professional development to equip educators with computer science skills.
Greyling, J. (2023)	Coding Unplugged—A Guide to Introducing Coding and Robotics to South African Schools	The study aims to aid in the introduction of C & R into South African Schools by offering a comprehensive guide for introducing the subject in an unplugged way. The authors argue that the unplugged approach can serve to bridge the digital divide and offer C & R `s to learners who lack access to technology. The study also emphasizes the significance of early implementation of C & R in schools to equip learners for the future labour market.	This study underscores the significance of teacher training in context of implementing C & R in South African schools and the necessity to equip educators with the requisite DS and DK to proficiently instruct coding principles through unplugged activities. This highlights the importance of investing in teachers' professional development to guarantee the effective implementation of C & R in schools.
Havenga, M. (2013)	Metacognitive and Problem-Solving Skills to Promote Self-Directed Learning in Computer Programming: Teachers' Experiences	The study proposes that instructing students in metacognitive and problem-solving skills could enhance their ability to manage their own learning. Additionally, teaching students' management processes and activities may contribute to their academic success and performance improvement. Moreover, combining instruction in both metacognitive and problem-solving skills could potentially enhance students' programming performance and their capacity to exert cognitive control.	Students who develop metacognitive and problem-solving skills become more responsible for their own learning, taking ownership of their progress and development.
Havenga, M. (2023)	Introducing Coding and Robotics: Prospective Mathematics Teachers' Metacognitive Thinking in Scratch	The study emphasized the significance of students' metacognitive abilities in facilitating their thinking during coding tasks. It underscored the importance of metacognitive knowledge and thinking in effectively tackling challenges and resolving complex problems, especially in C & R. The results also indicated that students possessed metacognitive awareness and utilized metacognitive strategies when engaging in coding tasks. This involved planning their actions, monitoring their progress, reflecting on their thought processes, and assessing the quality of their work.	The inclusion of higher cognitive skills such as problem solving, decision making, critical and creative thinking, innovation, and computational thinking, along with metacognitive skills, is crucial for C & R. Students demonstrated metacognitive thinking and their own metacognitive knowledge awareness or lack thereof.

overall level of teacher proficiency in SA is not reassuring when it comes to the capacity of in-service teachers to acquire the skills needed to teach a new subject. It is necessary to modify both pre-service and in-service training to ensure that future teachers are prepared to teach C & R. Additionally, current teachers should be empowered and trained to handle this new subject. Khanlari (2016) found that teachers perceived C & R to have positive effects on students' lifelong learning skills and indicated barriers to integrating robotics into their teaching activities.

Table 3. Fostering self-directed learning skills (n=6)

First Author and Year	Title	Conceptualization of Self-Directed Learning	Fostering Self-directed learning Skills
Stefanie L. Boyer, Diane R. Edmondson, Andrew B. Artis, and David Fleming,2013	Self-Directed Learning: A Tool for Lifelong Learning	Since its 1967 introduction by Tough within the adult learning literature, SDL has been shown to be a highly effective method to engage and train adult learners (Ellinger, 2004). In SDL is a process by which learners manage their own learning process from beginning to end (Knowles, 1975). Research has shown that SDL is positively related to many education-related constructs: academic performance, aspiration, creativity, curiosity, and life satisfaction (Edmondson, Boyer, & Artis, 2012); however, limited research exists on how SDL is related to workplace-learning constructs.	College students who are taught how to be proactive and self-directed learners will be better prepared as employees to anticipate their organization's needs, tailor their learning to meet their own unique learning styles, and acquire the necessary skills, knowledge, and abilities to create value for their customers, employers, and organizations (Artis & Harris, 2007; Cron, Marshall, Singh, Spiro, & Sujan, 2005).
Charlotte Silén & Lars Uhlin.2008.	Self-directed learning – a learning issue for students and faculty!	The importance of becoming a self-directed learner is a learning process, and the need for teachers to take part in the learning is crucial. students' development as self-directed learners have been neglected.	The students need challenges, support, and feedback in their struggle to become self-directed learners and thus require ongoing attention. If the intention is to enhance the students' ability to become self-directed learners, and prepare for lifelong learning in their professions, it is essential to recognise that students becoming responsible and independent is a learning process.
KAILASH CHAROKAR1, MS, FAIMER Fellow; PUJA DULLOO2, MD, MHPE (UK), FAIMER Fellow.2022	Self-directed Learning Theory to Practice: A Footstep towards the Path of being a Life-long Learner	Self-directed learning cuts across all domains of learning and have a significant potential in shaping transformational learning experiences. The concepts of SDL are based on adult learning principles and experiential learning fostering skills for lifelong learning.	SDL through an explicit approach and dedicated teaching hours in the disciplines which gives the opportunity to develop skills for developing lifelong learners. The The prime goal of the SDL is to make students lifelong learners and gain subject topic knowledge as an immediate outcome.
Thomas Howard Morris, Nicholas Bremner & Nozomi Sakata.2023	Self-directed learning and student-centered learning: a conceptual comparison	Both SDL and SCL are poorly understood among many stakeholders (e.g., Neumann 2013; Gandomkar and Sandars 2018)	Rogers (1969) advocated that SDL is the most important competence in formal education to prepare young people to cope effectively with rapidly changing societies, stating that 'no knowledge is secure' and 'only the process of seeking knowledge gives a basis for security' Scholars of SDL view formal education settings as a primary opportunity to practice and foster competence for SDL: to form a foundation for successful lifelong learning (Bagnall and Hodge 2022).
Faiyaz Ahammad.2023.	SELF-DIRECTED LEARNING: A CORE CONCEPT IN ADULT EDUCATION	The idea of self-directed learning is significant in the context of adult education. Self-directed learning, often referred to as learning by oneself, encompasses a broad spectrum of skills and attributes within individuals. It involves the proactive identification of one's learning needs, the establishment of personal learning objectives, the selection of appropriate learning resources, the utilization of effective learning strategies, and the assessment of learning outcomes, either independently or with external support (Knowles, 1975).	Importance of 21st century skills in today's knowledge-based societies is on the rise, and lifelong education encompasses a wide range of topics
Thomas Howard Morris & Matthias Rohs.2023	The potential for digital technology to support self-directed learning in formal education of children: a scoping review	SDL has been recognized as a fundamental competence for living and working in the modern world, which enables persons to adapt to changing conditions (e.g., Boyer et al., 2014; Kranzow & Hyland, 2016).	Self-directed learning is a critical competence for living and working in an increasingly complex and unpredictable world. Understanding how SDL can be fostered through formal schooling in childhood is particularly important because studies have historically and consistently identified that many people do not fully foster SDL competence during their childhood (e.g., Bonk et al., 2018; Canty et al., 2019; Gatewood, 2019). Bonk and Lee (2017) note that this is surprising given that the importance of SDL has been noted by scholars for decades.

Therefore, implementing targeted training programs and support systems for educators will not only improve their skills but also cultivate a favorable educational atmosphere, equipping learners to meet the challenges of the digital era (Department of Basic Education, 2023) within the limitations of the South African educational context. The current C & R implementation milieu can provide teachers with exceptional opportunities and capabilities to become self-directed as one can argue that the state of PD relating to C & R will not fully equip teachers with DS and DK. Many teachers therefore are required to independently acquire C & R proficiency.

SDL can therefore enhance performance, making it crucial for educators to explore effective ways of incorporating C & R into their classrooms. It is recommended as a frequent approach to cultivate lifelong learning skills. The SDL approach, viewed as a teaching method, aligns with certain competencies, and offers a dual component in the curriculum: one to achieve lifelong learning goals. Education plays a vital role in developing the skills necessary for SDL, further research is needed to deepen our understanding, emphasizing its importance in fostering SDL skills to comprehend recent technologies such as C & R. Due to constantly changing innovative technology, if an educator is equipped with SDL skills it would be easier for a teacher to understand and implement C & R at the BoCSE pyramid.

FUTURE RESEARCH DIRECTIONS

In this chapter, the challenges and obstacles that teachers face in introducing and implementing the C & R subjects are documented. C & R, as the newest addition to the CSE in the South African public-school context, has shifted the teaching of DS, DK, and ICT principles from a relative few (grades 10-12) as an elective component to a mandatory subject to be implemented from grade R-9 at a broader base in South African public schools, referred to in this chapter as the BoCSE.

As this novel subject was rolled out, introduced, and implemented, the current teacher in-service corps were trained to teach C & R. They were not afforded the benefit of a full three or four-year digital and ICT course; instead, training was presented in short intervals. The quality of the professional development (PD) and training initiatives was brought into question, and it is evident that these challenges are a matter of concern for many stakeholders regarding how this will affect the implementation of C & R.

Numerous existing international studies in the broader literature have examined the implementation of C & R and ER, as these were implemented well before it was the case in South Africa. The authors found that there is thus a limited number of studies available relating to the implementation of C & R in the South African public-school environment and even fewer pertaining to the fostering of SDL to supplement and enhance delivered PD and activities. Subsequently, fostering SDL skills are necessary for teachers to navigate their own 21st-century learning path in this ever-changing digital era.

The authors, therefore, suggest that research should explore the role of C & R in fostering SDL among South African teachers who are tasked to implement the C & R subject, as this area was identified as a knowledge gap. C & R is emerging as a new field of study and further studies in this field could present the possibility to produce a systematic literature review.

CONCLUSION

The DBE aims to implement the C & R subject as part of the broader CSE in South African public schools with the purpose of providing learners with the necessary skills for the 21st century. These skills will enable these learners to effectively adapt to the Fourth Industrial Revolution (4IR). Challenges exert an impact on the successful implementation of the subject in South African schools of which one is teacher training and PD. To successfully implement C & R, it is crucial to address these factors that could hamper the successful implementation of C & R. The teacher plays a crucial role as they are responsible for implementing the curriculum and providing South African learners with the essential knowledge and skills required to succeed in a technology-driven world and to prepare learners for the workforce. This task starts in the FP and for the purpose of CSE the C & R will be implemented at the BoCSE pyramid in the GET phase. It is evident that teachers teaching at this level do not have the necessary DK and DS. As teachers are expected to facilitate 21st century skills, they should possess them. Teacher training opportunities are necessary, especially when introducing a new concept. Training and PD programs and activities provided by the DBE and their training partners would undoubtedly provide the basic knowledge and skills to assist teachers to teach C & R. However, knowledge and skills gained through PD and training opportunities could be enhanced through the teachers own SDL. In the ever-changing digital age, the onus rests on the teacher to acknowledge their own learning needs, acquire SDL skills, become self-directed learners, and navigate their own CSE in this 21st century.

ACKNOWLEDGMENT

Mr. J Nyebeleza, the library research assistant, from the North West University-Faculty of Education assisted researchers during the literature search.

REFERENCES

Arksey, H., & O'Malley, L. (2005). Scoping studies: Towards a methodological framework. *International Journal of Social Research Methodology*, *8*(1), 19–32. doi:10.1080/1364557032000119616

Artis, A. B., & Harris, E. G. (2007). Self-directed learning and sales force performance: An integrated framework. *Journal of Personal Selling & Sales Management*, *27*(1), 9–24. doi:10.2753/PSS0885-3134270101

Avalos, B. (2011). Teacher professional development in Teaching and Teacher Education over ten years. In Teaching and Teacher Education (Vol. 27, Issue 1, pp. 10–20). https://doi.org/ doi:10.1016/j.tate.2010.08.007

Bagnall, R. G., & Hodge, S. (2022). *Epistemologies and ethics in adult education and lifelong learning*. Springer Nature. doi:10.1007/978-3-030-94980-8

Bailey, R., & Breed, B. (2022). Joining forces: Pair problem-solving, flipped classroom and metacognitive self-questioning to enhance self-directed learning. In C. van der Westhuizen, M.C. Maphalala & R. Bailey (Eds.), Blended learning environments to foster self-directed learning, NWU Self-Directed Learning Series (vol. 8, pp. 49–69). Cape Town: AOSIS. https://doi.org/ doi:10.4102/aosis.2022.BK366.03

Bonk, C. J., & Lee, M. M. (2017). Motivations, achievements, and challenges of self-directed informal learners in open educational environments and MOOCs. *Journal of Learning for Development*, *4*(1), 36–57. doi:10.56059/jl4d.v4i1.195

Bonk, C. J., Zhu, M., Kim, M., Xu, S., Sabir, N., & Sari, A. R. (2018). Pushing toward a more personalized MOOC: Exploring instructor selected activities, resources, and technologies for MOOC design and implementation. *International Review of Research in Open and Distance Learning*, *19*(4), 92–115. doi:10.19173/irrodl.v19i4.3439

Bosch, C., Mentz, E., & Goede, R. (2019). Self-directed learning: A conceptual overview. In E. Mentz, J. De Beer & R. Bailey (Eds.), Self-Directed Learning for the 21st Century: Implications for Higher Education NWU Self-Directed Learning Series (vol. 1, pp. 1–36). Cape Town: AOSIS. https://doi.org/ doi:10.4102/aosis.2019.BK134.01

Botha, C. (2020, December 2). *New School subjects in South Africa - what does this mean?* Skills Academy. https://www.skillsacademy.co.za/new-school-subjects-in-south-africa-what-does-this-mean/

Boyer, S. L., Edmondson, D. R., Artis, A. B., & Fleming, D. (2014). Self-directed learning: A tool for lifelong learning. *Journal of Marketing Education*, *36*(1), 20–32. doi:10.1177/0273475313494010

Boz, T., & Allexsaht-Snider, M. (2022). How do elementary school teachers learn coding and robotics? A case study of mediations and conflicts. *Education and Information Technologies*, *27*(3), 3935–3963. doi:10.1007/s10639-021-10736-4

Breed, E. A. (2015). Introduction to CAT and IT education. In E. Mentz (Ed.), *Empowering IT and CAT teachers* (pp. 1–18). Sun Press.

Camilleri, P. (2017). Minding the gap. proposing a teacher learning-training framework for the integration of robotics in primary schools. *Informatics in Education*, *16*(2), 165–179. doi:10.15388/infedu.2017.09

Candy, P. C. (2004). *Linking thinking: Self-directed learning in the digital age*. Department of Education, Science and Training.

Canty, D., Barth, J., Yang, Y., Peters, N., Palmer, A., Royse, A., & Royse, C. (2019). Comparison of learning outcomes for teaching focused cardiac ultrasound to physicians: A supervised human model course versus an eLearning guided self- directed simulator course. *Journal of Critical Care*, *49*, 38–44. doi:10.1016/j.jcrc.2018.10.006 PMID:30359924

Chiles, M. (2013, August 8). The state of IT education in South African schools. IITPSA. https://www.iitpsa.org.za/the-state-of-it-education-in-south-african-schools/

Cron, W. L., Marshall, G. W., Singh, J., Spiro, R. L., & Sujan, H. (2005). Salesperson selection, training, and development: Trends, implications, and research opportunities. *Journal of Personal Selling & Sales Management*, *25*(2), 123–136.

De Beer, J. (2019). Glocalisation: The role of indigenous knowledge in the global village. In J. De Beer (Ed.), *The decolonisation of the curriculum project: The affordances of indigenous knowledge for self-directed learning* (pp. 1–24). AOSIS. doi:10.4102/aosis.2019.BK133.01

Demertzi, E., Voukelatos, N., Papagerasimou, Y., & Drigas, A. (2018). Online learning facilities to support coding and robotics courses for youth. *International Journal of Engineering Pedagogy*, *8*(3), 69–80. Advance online publication. doi:10.3991/ijep.v8i3.8044

Department of Basic Education. (2021a). *Coding and Robotics Pilot Project Awareness and Advocacy Roadshows underway*. DBE. https://www.education.gov.za/CodingandRoboticsPilotProject.aspx

Department of Basic Education. (2021b). *DBE and partners workshop Coding and Robotics Curriculum for the GET Band*. DBE. https://www.education.gov.za/CodingCurriculum010419.aspx

Department of Basic Education. (2023). *Proposed amendments to the Curriculum and Assessment Policy Statement (CAPS) to make provision for coding and robotics Grades R-9*. DBE. https://www.education.gov.za/

Dlamini, R., & Mbatha, K. (2018). The discourse on ICT teacher professional development needs: The case of a South African teachers' union. *International Journal of Education and Development using ICT*, *14*(2).

Doo, M. Y., Zhu, M., & Bonk, C. J. (2023). Influence of self-directed learning on learning outcomes in MOOCs: A meta-analysis. *Distance Education*, *44*(1), 86–105. doi:10.1080/01587919.2022.2155618

Du Toit, A. (2019). Constructive congruencies in self-directed learning and entrepreneurship education, In E. Mentz, J. De Beer & R. Bailey (Eds.), Self-Directed Learning for the 21st Century: Implications for Higher Education (vol. 1, pp. 313-340). Cape Town: AOSIS. doi:10.4102/aosis.2019.BK134.10

du Toit-Brits, C. (2019). A focus on self-directed learning: The role that educators' expectations play in the enhancement of students' self-directedness. *South African Journal of Education*, *39*(2), 1–11. doi:10.15700/saje.v39n2a1645

Edmondson, D. R., Boyer, S. L., & Artis, A. B. (2012). Self-directed learning: A meta-analytic review of adult learning constructs. *International Journal of Education and Research, 7*(1), 40–48.

Fares, K., Fowler, B., & Vegas, E. (2021). *How South Africa implemented its computer science education program.* Center for Universal Education at Brookings.

Gandomkar, R., & Sandars, J. (2018). Clearing the confusion about self-directed learning and self-regulated learning. *Medical Teacher, 40*(8), 862–863. doi:10.1080/0142159X.2018.1425382 PMID:29327634

Gatewood, E. (2019). Use of simulation to increase self-directed learning for nurse practitioner students. *The Journal of Nursing Education, 58*(2), 102–106. doi:10.3928/01484834-20190122-07 PMID:30721310

Geldenhuys, C. J., & Fataar, A. (2021). Foundation Phase teachers' experiences of teaching the subject, coding, in selected Western Cape schools. *South African Journal of Education, 41*(4), 1959. doi:10.15700/saje.v41n4a1959

Geng, S., Law, K. M., & Niu, B. (2019). Investigating self-directed learning and technology readiness in blending learning environment. *International Journal of Educational Technology in Higher Education, 16*(1), 1–22. doi:10.1186/s41239-019-0147-0

Giannandrea, L., Gratani, F., & Renieri, A. (2020). Crossing boundaries: Documentation of a teacher training course on design, robotics and coding. *Research on Education and Media, 12*(1), 85–92. doi:10.2478/rem-2020-0010

Gorrah, A. R. (2022). *Teachers' perception of gender stereotypes with the teaching of coding and robotics in primary schools* [MEd dissertation, University of Johannesburg].

Greyling, J. (2023). Coding Unplugged—A Guide to Introducing Coding and Robotics to South African Schools. *Transforming Entrepreneurship Education, 155.*

Gustafsson, M. (2014, April 14). *ICTs in our schools.* Department of Basic Education. https://www.education.gov.za/Portals/0/Documents/Reports/Research%20Repository/LTSM/ICT%20in%20our%20schools.pdf?ver=2019-09-09-102226-387

Havenga, M., & Mentz, E. (2009, June). The school subject information technology: a South African perspective. In *Proceedings of the 2009 Annual Conference of the Southern African Computer Lecturers' Association* (pp. 76-80). ACM. 10.1145/1562741.1562750

Heyns, J. (2023). *Development of a framework of factors essential to the optimal implementation of the Coding and Robotics subject in South African schools* [Doctoral dissertation, Stellenbosch University].

Hill, R. B., Kim, C. M., & Yuan, J. (2019). Robotics and coding in primary grades. *Communications in Computer and Information Science, 993*, 458–467. doi:10.1007/978-3-030-20954-4_34

Jantjies, M. (2019, June 18). Five things South Africa must get right for tech in schools to work. *The Conversation.* https://theconversation.com/five-things-south-africa-must-get-right-for-tech-in-schools-to-work-118612

Khalil, H., Peters, M., Godfrey, C. M., McInerney, P., Soares, C. B., & Parker, D. (2016). An evidence-based approach to scoping reviews. *Worldviews on Evidence-Based Nursing*, *13*(2), 118–123. doi:10.1111/wvn.12144 PMID:26821833

Khanlari, A. (2016). Teachers' perceptions of the benefits and the challenges of integrating educational robots into primary/elementary curricula. *European Journal of Engineering Education*, *41*(3), 320–330. doi:10.1080/03043797.2015.1056106

Knowles, M. S. (1975). *Self-directed learning*. New York, NY: Associated Press.

Kranzow, J., & Hyland, N. (2016). Self-directed learning: Developing readiness in graduate students. *International Journal of Self-Directed Learning*, *13*(2), 1–14.

Kruger, D., Werlen, E., & Bergamin, P. B. (2022). Curiosity killed the cat, but satisfaction brought it back: Inquiry-based learning in blended environments to promote self-directed learning. In C. van der Westhuizen, M.C. Maphalala & R. Bailey (Eds.), Blended learning environments to foster self-directed learning, NWU Self-Directed Learning Series (vol. 8, pp. 31–48). Cape Town: AOSIS. doi:10.4102/aosis.2022.BK366.02

Levac, D., Colquhoun, H., & O'Brien, K. K. (2010). Scoping studies: Advancing the methodology. *Implementation Science : IS*, *5*(1), 1–9. doi:10.1186/1748-5908-5-69 PMID:20854677

Makeleni, N. T., & Sethusha, M. J. (2014). The experiences of foundation phase teachers in implementing the curriculum. *Mediterranean Journal of Social Sciences*, *5*(2), 103. doi:10.5901/mjss.2014.v5n2p103

Mensah-Williams, E., & Derera, E. (2023). Conceptualising impact measurements of entrepreneurship education outcomes: A scoping review. *Acta Commercii-Independent Research Journal in the Management Sciences*, *23*(1), 1053. doi:10.4102/ac.v23i1.1053

Mentz, E., & Bailey, R. (2019). A systematic review of research on the use of technology-supported cooperative learning to enhance self-directed learning. In E. Mentz, J. De Beer & R. Bailey (Eds.), Self-Directed Learning for the 21st Century: Implications for Higher Education (vol. 1, pp. 203–238). Cape Town: AOSIS. doi:10.4102/aosis.2019.BK134.07

Mokonyane-Motha, M. M., & De Jager, T. T. (2023). The Significance of Training Student-Teacher Lecturers in Pedagogical Robotic and Coding Skills. *International Journal of Social Science Research and Review*, *6*(12), 107–118. doi:10.47814/ijssrr.v6i12.1808

Morris, T. H., & Rohs, M. (2023). The potential for digital technology to support self-directed learning in formal education of children: A scoping review. *Interactive Learning Environments*, *31*(4), 1974–1987. doi:10.1080/10494820.2020.1870501

Morze, N. V., & Strutynska, O. V. (2023). Advancing educational robotics: competence development for pre-service computer science teachers. *CTE Workshop Proceedings*. CTE. 10.55056/cte.549

Munn, Z., Peters, M. D., Stern, C., Tufanaru, C., McArthur, A., & Aromataris, E. (2018). Systematic review or scoping review? Guidance for authors when choosing between a systematic or scoping review approach. *BMC Medical Research Methodology*, *18*(1), 1–7. doi:10.1186/s12874-018-0611-x PMID:30453902

Neumann, J. W. (2013). Developing a new framework for conceptualizing 'student-centered learning'. *The Educational Forum*, *77*(2), 161–175. doi:10.1080/00131725.2012.761313

Ogegbo, A. A., & Aina, A. Y. (2022). Fostering The Development Of 21st Century Competencies Through Technology In Young Children: Perceptions Of Early Childhood Educators. Education and New Developments. doi:10.36315/2022v2end073

Pankratova, O., Ledovskaya, N., & Konopko, E. (2021). Forming the Competence of the Teacher of Educational Robotics. *Standards and Monitoring in Education.*, *9*(6), 8–15. doi:10.12737/1998-1740-2021-9-6-8-15

Peters, M. D. J., Godfrey, C., McInerney, P., Munn, Z., Tricco, A. C., & Khalil, H. (2020). Chapter 11: Scoping Reviews. Aromataris E, Munn Z, editors. *JBI Manual for Evidence Synthesis*. JBI. doi:10.46658/JBIMES-20-12

Pham, M. T., Rajić, A., Greig, J. D., Sargeant, J. M., Papadopoulos, A., & McEwen, S. A. (2014). A scoping review of scoping reviews: Advancing the approach and enhancing the consistency. *Research Synthesis Methods*, *5*(4), 371–385. doi:10.1002/jrsm.1123 PMID:26052958

Rogers, C. R. (1969). *Freedom to learn*. Charles Merrill.

Sapounidis, T., & Alimisis, D. (2021, February). Educational robotics curricula: Current trends and shortcomings. In *Educational Robotics International Conference* (pp. 127-138). Cham: Springer International Publishing. 10.1007/978-3-030-77022-8_12

Scaradozzi, D., Screpanti, L., Cesaretti, L., Storti, M., & Mazzieri, E. (2019). Implementation and Assessment Methodologies of Teachers' Training Courses for STEM Activities. *Technology. Knowledge and Learning*, *24*(2), 247–268. doi:10.1007/s10758-018-9356-1

Stokes, A., Aurini, J., Rizk, J., Gorbet, R., & McLevey, J. (2022). Using Robotics to Support the Acquisition of STEM and 21st-Century Competencies: Promising (and Practical) Directions. *Canadian Journal of Education*, *45*(4). doi:10.53967/cje-rce.5455

Sumuer, E. (2018). Factors related to college students' self-directed learning with technology. *Australasian Journal of Educational Technology*, *34*(4), 29–43. doi:10.14742/ajet.3142

Tang, A. L., Tung, V. W. S., & Cheng, T. O. (2023). Teachers' perceptions of the potential use of educational robotics in management education. *Interactive Learning Environments*, *31*(1), 313–324. doi:10.1080/10494820.2020.1780269

Theodoropoulos, A., Antoniou, A., & Lepouras, G. (2017). Teacher and student views on educational robotics: The Pan-Hellenic competition case. *Application and Theory of Computer Technology*, *2*(4), 1–23. doi:10.22496/atct.v2i4.94

Tricco, A. C., Lillie, E., Zarin, W., O'Brien, K. K., Colquhoun, H., Levac, D., Moher, D., Peters, M. D. J., Horsley, T., Weeks, L., Hempel, S., Akl, E. A., Chang, C., McGowan, J., Stewart, L., Hartling, L., Aldcroft, A., Wilson, M. G., Garritty, C., & Straus, S. E. (2018). PRISMA extension for scoping reviews (PRISMA-ScR): Checklist and explanation. *Annals of Internal Medicine*, *169*(7), 467–473. doi:10.7326/M18-0850 PMID:30178033

Van der Westhuizen, C., & Bailey, R. (2022). A 21st-century vision for self-directed learning in blended learning environments. In C. van der Westhuizen, M.C. Maphalala & R. Bailey (Eds.), Blended learning environments to foster self-directed learning NWU Self-Directed Learning Series (vol. 8, pp. 1–29). Cape Town: AOSIS. doi:10.4102/aosis.2022.BK366.01

Van der Westhuizen, C., & Kemp, A. (2022). Self-directed learning with technology for fourth year Engineering Graphics and Design students, In C. van der Westhuizen, M.C. Maphalala & R. Bailey (Eds.), Blended learning environments to foster self-directed learning, (Vol. 8, pp. 71–97). Cape Town: AOSIS. doi:10.4102/aosis.2022.BK366.04

Van Wyk, C. (2012, June). Survey of ICT in schools in South Africa. *Public Expenditure Analysis for the Department of Basic Education: Report 8.* DBE. https://www.education.gov.za/Portals/0/Documents/Reports/Research%20Repository/LTSM/Survey%20of%20ICT%20in%20schools%20in%20SA.pdf?ver=2019-09-09-102208-963

Van Zyl, S., & Mentz, E. (2019). Moving to deeper self-directed learning as an essential competency for the 21st century. In E. Mentz, J. De Beer, & R. Bailey (Eds.), *Self-Directed Learning for the 21st Century: Implications for Higher Education NWU Self-Directed Learning Series* (Vol. 1, pp. 67–102). AOSIS. doi:10.4102/aosis.2019.BK134.03

Willemse, K. (2023). *Supporting Grade R Teachers to Integrate Coding and Robotics with Mathematical Concepts* [Doctoral dissertation, University of Pretoria, South Africa].

Williamson, S. N. (2007). Development of a self-rating scale of self-directed learning. *Nurse Researcher, 14*(2), 66–83. doi:10.7748/nr2007.01.14.2.66.c6022 PMID:17315780

Wu, L., Looi, C. K., Multisilta, J., How, M. L., Choi, H., Hsu, T. C., & Tuomi, P. (2020). Teacher's Perceptions and Readiness to Teach Coding Skills: A Comparative Study Between Finland, Mainland China, Singapore, Taiwan, and South Korea. *The Asia-Pacific Education Researcher, 29*(1), 21–34. doi:10.1007/s40299-019-00485-x

Xia, X., Wan, Z., Kochhar, P. S., & Lo, D. (2019, May). How Practitioners Perceive Coding Proficiency. *IEEE/ACM 41st International Conference on Software Engineering (ICSE)* (pp. 924-935). IEEE. 10.1109/ICSE.2019.00098

Chapter 13
Cognitive Apprenticeship and Artificial Intelligence Coding Assistants

Eric Poitras
Dalhousie University, Canada

Brent Crane
Dalhousie University, Canada

David Dempsey
https://orcid.org/0000-0002-3152-7185
Dalhousie University, Canada

Tavis A. Bragg
Acadia University, Canada

Angela Siegel
https://orcid.org/0000-0001-9211-1223
Dalhousie University, Canada

Michael Pin-Chuan Lin
https://orcid.org/0000-0002-7646-7024
Mount Saint Vincent University, Canada

ABSTRACT

The aim of this chapter is to examine the impact that AI coding assistants have on the manner in which novice programmers learn to read, write, and revise code. These discussions revolve around the concept of cognitive apprenticeship, a pedagogical framework informed by extensive research on tutoring dialogues and collaborative problem-solving practices. It involves guided instruction through modeling, coaching, and scaffolding. Within the realm of programming, these principles hold the key to nurturing skills in reading, writing, and revising code, thus making the learning process more effective and engaging. The chapter concludes by reflecting on the challenges and considerations of implementing cognitive apprenticeship within AI coding assistants. These insights are intended to benefit educators, developers, and researchers alike, offering a roadmap to enhance the learning experiences of novice programmers through AI support.

DOI: 10.4018/979-8-3693-1066-3.ch013

INTRODUCTION

Recent advancements in deep learning algorithms have raised significant interest in utilizing Large Language Models (LLMs) for a wide range of natural language processing tasks, including code generation for computer programs. To name just a few, notable examples include OpenAI Codex, DeepMind AlphaCode, and Amazon CodeWhisperer. Students learning a programming language now have continuous access to Artificial Intelligence (AI) driven tools to help them complete their coursework. The affordances of these tools have received significant critical attention in the computing education literature, as have the potential drawbacks for introductory programming instruction (see Becker et al., 2023; Yan et al., 2023).

Novice programmers engage in self-regulation to inform their problem-solving, but the effectiveness of these efforts depends on their programming knowledge (Loksa & Ko, 2016). AI code generators assist information retrieval by generating starter code, allowing students to build upon and modify existing code rather than reaching an impasse or searching for an online resource (Denny, Kumar, & Giacaman, 2023; Finnie-Ansley, Denny, Luxton-Reilly, Santos, Prather, & Becker, 2023). These tools facilitate program comprehension through several means, including student efforts to trace the execution of code, generate analogies to real world settings, and summarize code at multiple levels of abstraction (MacNeil et al., 2022; MacNeil, Tran, Leinonen, ..., et al., 2023). AI-based tools can also be designed to scaffold problem solving by reducing encountered errors (Kazemitabaar, et al., 2023), explaining error messages and reasoning about the original intention of incorrect code (Szabo, Sheard, Luxton-Reilly, Simon, Becker, & Ott, 2019), as well as providing suggestions for fixing the issues based on the input code and errors (Leinonen et al., 2023).

The focus of this chapter is on guidelines for designing instructional prompts using cognitive apprenticeship as a pedagogical approach to facilitate robust learning outcomes. According to the cognitive apprenticeship model of instruction (Collins, Brown, & Newman, 1989), instruction involves modeling cognitive skills and strategies for students while providing necessary support through scaffolding when students require assistance to complete a task. After students demonstrate competence, scaffolds are progressively removed to allow them to complete tasks without assistance. The assumption is that students should be offered opportunities to reflect on their own understanding and apply their knowledge to solve novel problems.

This chapter aims to establish a taxonomy of prompts that are classified according to both cognitive apprenticeship as a pedagogical model as well as introductory programming skills (Xie, Loksa, Nelson, Davidson, Dong, Kwik, ..., Ko, 2019). The first section of this chapter will explore the existing research in computing education, providing insights into the challenges and opportunities posed by AI coding assistants. In the second section, the cognitive apprenticeship model of instruction is outlined to inform the design of effective prompts in enhancing skill acquisition. Within this section, an emphasis is placed on distinguishing three practices to facilitate the acquisition of code reading, writing, and revising skills and exemplify the relevant instructional methods. The chapter concludes with a broader discussion, elaborating further on motivational and metacognitive factors that mediate interactions with AI coding assistants and the implications for instructional practices and research in the field of computing education.

BACKGROUND

AI code generation tools, also referred to as AI-assisted code generators, consist of any platform that use artificial intelligence and machine learning techniques to assist developers by automating processes involved in programming. Examples of models that assist programmers by generating code from natural language descriptions include OpenAICodex (Chen et al., 2021), Microsoft CodeBERT (Feng et al., 2020), Google PaLM (Chowdhery et al., 2022), DeepMind AlphaCode (Li et al., 2022), which have been trained on extensive public code repositories available on platforms like GitHub. AI coding assistants not only make natural language programming easier but also provide various code-related features. These features include code suggestion, correction, summarization, in addition to translating between language and code, like explaining and searching for code (Becker et al., 2023; MacNeil, Tran, Mogil, et al., 2022).

Researchers have recognized the potential for employing AI code generators to support students in learning to program and in developing skills (MacNeil, Tran, Hellas, …, et al., 2023). CoPilot for instance provides descriptions of program behavior at a relatively low level of detail, only occasionally omitting significant details, which can aid student understanding of unfamiliar constructs or syntactic patterns (Wermelinger, 2023). Students often prefer receiving line-by-line explanations rather than summaries or conceptual explanations from AI coding assistants, even though the quality of these explanations, as rated by students, tends to be lower (MacNeil, Tran, Hellas, et al., 2023). GPT-4 possesses the capability to execute non-trivial pseudocode effectively (Bubeck, et al., 2023). Notably, it can both execute and provide a step-by-step explanation for each operation. In terms of code summarization, ChatGPT might encounter challenges in providing consistent explanations for code samples that share the same purpose, while offering differing explanations for code with distinct intentions (Tian, et al., 2023).

In writing code, CoPilot can be directed to make incremental fixes or enhancements to a program, but this requires the user to have a precise understanding of their desired changes and the ability to articulate their intentions effectively (Wermelinger, 2023). CoPilot's suggestions are simple and readily understandable, although the generated code can often be further simplified or include undefined helper methods (Nguyen & Nadi, 2022). Students may spend time shifting between understanding the generated code, debugging, and evaluating their progress, which can lead to worse performance due to the constant distraction and given that suggestions may be incorrect (Prather et al., 2023; Vaithilingam, Zhang, & Glassman, 2022). On the other hand, students often reported that AI code generators such as CoPilot allows them to make progress when facing an impasse as well as avoiding compilation errors. GPT-4 can generate code based on instructions, even when those instructions are ambiguous, incomplete, or require domain-specific knowledge (Bubeck, et al., 2023). Moreover, GPT-4 can adapt its code in response to follow-up requests and make modifications in accordance with additional instructions.

When it comes to learning to interpret error messages and debugging programs, the explanations generated by Codex were deemed to be easily comprehensible for less experienced programmers. However, it's worth noting that the accuracy of the explanations and suggested fixes is only around fifty percent (Leinonen, Hellas, et al., 2023). The combination of fixed code solutions combined with a natural language explanation may be more beneficial to assist students with less experience (Phung, et al., 2023). Automated test case generation by CoPilot does exhibit certain limitations on CS1 problem sets, particularly a propensity for repetitive testing patterns. For instance, it may overlook critical scenarios like testing sentinel values or performing tests with both positive and negative values (Wermelinger, 2023).

ChatGPT compared favorably against Refactory, a state-of-the-art semantic-based assignment repair tool. Notably, prompts that do not include bug-related information resulted in ChatGPT's performance deteriorating (Tian, et al., 2023).

Few studies have investigated however whether reliance on AI code generators impacts knowledge retention over longer time durations or transfer to solving novel problems. Kazemitabaar, et al. (2023) conducted a controlled experiment where novice programmers with no prior experience learned Python either with or without an AI Coding Assistant. More specifically, students learned about variables, operators, data types, conditionals, loops, and arrays over a three-week period. Over the course of seven training sessions, students engaged in a total of 45 code-authoring tasks, each of which was subsequently followed by a code-modification task. Learning outcomes were assessed through both an immediate post-test, followed by a retention test conducted a week later. The findings showed that students with access to the AI code generator were able to successfully generate code in addition to understand the generated code provided by the AI Coding Assistant during the training phase. Students with access to the AI-driven tool were found to outperform those without access, without any decrease in their performance on the following code modification task. Students, who had access to the tool performed comparably well to those without it in the post-test, implying that relying on AI-driven tools did not put them at a disadvantage when it came to applying their knowledge to solve new problems. A notable exception however concerns students that prompt only once to generate the entire solution to a task, resulting in poor performance on transfer task that involves code modification without automated assistance (Kazemitabaar, Hou, Henley, Ericson, Weintrop, & Grossman, 2023).

FOCUS OF THE CHAPTER

Cognitive Apprenticeship

Programming requires knowledge of fundamental constructs in languages to perform tasks. To control the order in which statements are executed for instance, students reinstate prior knowledge of selections and loops to simultaneously understand code while writing and revising statements. From a cognitive apprenticeship perspective, AI coding assistants enable students to see how these skills combine with their conceptual knowledge by following six teaching methods. Dennen and Burner (2008) report on a comprehensive review of the accuracy of these teaching methods in depicting learning processes and their impact towards knowledge retention and transfer. For examples in how these methods translate to instructional activities in introductory courses in computing more broadly, Knobelsdorf, Kreitz, and Böhne (2014) developed a theory of computation course utilizing cognitive apprenticeship as a pedagogical approach.

Table 1 divides each teaching method into three main categories. The first set of methods followed by AI coding assistants are designed to facilitate skill acquisition through processes of observation and guided practice (i.e., modeling, coaching, and scaffolding). The second set of methods are designed to help students monitor and evaluate these processes in the context of problem-solving. The third concerns students actively engaging in practicing their own skills and seeking opportunities to receive feedback.

Modeling in programming involves an AI coding assistant demonstrating a task to enable students to observe and develop more nuanced understanding of how to accomplish it. The cognitive processes involved in reading, writing, and revising code are latent and unobservable, and AI coding assistants

Table 1. Methods to promote introductory programming skill acquisition with AI code generation tools

Method	Category	Definition
Modeling	Observation and guided practice	AI coding assistant performs a task so students can observe
Coaching		AI coding assistant monitors and facilitates while students perform a task
Scaffolding		AI coding assistant provides supports to help the student perform a task
Articulation	Metacognitive awareness	AI coding assistant encourages students to make explicit their knowledge and thinking
Reflection		AI coding assistant enables students to compare their performance with others
Exploration	Motivation	AI coding assistant invites students to pose and solve their own problems

should not only make explicit the strategies involved in coordinating skills but identify task conditions that are necessary for improved performance. For instance, an AI coding assistant could model how to trace program execution by articulating intermediate program states during execution at runtime and explaining fundamental notions. In debugging code, one might model how to revise statements by comparing one and another approach to solving the problem.

Coaching refers to monitoring students while performing a task to provide guidance through hints, scaffolding, feedback, prompts, practical demonstrations, and sequencing the introduction to more complex tasks to develop proficiency. As issues arise during task performance, proper diagnosis of specific events or problems that arise during problem solving is critical for AI coding assistants to tailor instruction to specific needs. An AI coding assistant might coach students while writing code on request, providing answers to questions, testing their solutions, and recommending alternative paths to solving problems.

Scaffolding refers to an AI coding assistant performing certain aspects of a task that students are not able to do on their own. In such cases, intermediate steps in the solution may be written for the students. In debugging solutions, resources such as reference documentation may be provided to assist students in recalling method names and arguments. As students become more proficient and can perform these tasks themselves, these supports are no longer necessary and should be gradually reduced.

Articulation in the context of programming instruction encompasses various techniques aimed at prompting students to elicit their programming knowledge and reasoning while problem solving. AI coding assistants designed to prompt students in articulating their understanding of programming constructs may provide opportunities to deliver corrective feedback. Second, students might be encouraged to decompose a problem by writing a detailed plan for solving a problem that lists the function of each statement prior to their implementation. Third, they might lead students to alternate approaches to finding and locating errors in their code.

Reflection in the context of programming education involves enabling students to analyze and assess their own problem-solving processes. Student code construction during problem solving may be replayed and paused to pinpoint where students faced impasses, allowing AI coding assistants to highlight these areas to provide guidance. For reading, methods to encourage tracing program execution might consist of making explicit memory states.

Exploration entails guiding students to solve their own problems, which is important for developing their skills by taking on increasingly difficult challenges. Programming languages and their applications to practical domains are inherently complex, and students may not know how to navigate the domain effectively. AI coding assistants could support students to explore a domain by setting overarching learning goals and encourage them to set their own subgoals. Students may also be encouraged to adapt or modify their own goals depending on their specific needs and interests.

Prompting Artificial Intelligence Coding Assistants

Table 2 shows example prompts for AI coding assistants to model how to perform tasks, coach, and scaffold students while they perform task themselves, and assistants playing the role of a student to facilitate learning by teaching.

Table 2. Prompting strategies with artificial intelligence coding assistants

Prompt	Modeling	Coaching and Scaffolding	Learning by Teaching
Defining the role of the assistant	You are a friendly and helpful tutor who helps students to learn how to program in Java by explaining ideas as simple as possible without sacrificing accuracy or detail.	You are a friendly and helpful tutor who helps students to learn how to program in Java by explaining ideas and asking students questions.	You are a student who has studied programming in Java.
Introducing the assistant	Start by introducing yourself to the student as their AI-Tutor who is happy to help them with any questions. Always wait for the student to respond before asking a question. Ask one question at a time.	Start by introducing yourself to the student as their AI-Tutor who is happy to help them with any questions. Always wait for the student to respond before asking a question. Ask one question at a time.	Start by introducing yourself as a student who is happy to share what you know about the topic of the teacher's choosing. The goal for the exercise is for the teacher to evaluate your responses. Wait for the teacher to respond before moving ahead.
Defining a Topic and Code Segment	First, ask them what they would like to learn about. Wait for the response. Then ask them whether they would like to [**INSERT PROMPT STATEMENT**] a code segment or whether they would prefer to be given example code. Wait for their response.	First, ask them what they would like to learn about. Wait for the response. Then ask them whether they would like to share a code segment or whether they would prefer to be given example code. Wait for their response.	First, ask the teacher what they would like you to explain and how they would like you to apply that topic. [**PROMPT STATEMENT INSERTED IN RESPONSE**] Then ask them whether they would like to share a code segment or whether they would prefer to be given example code. Wait for their response.
Describing the Expected Behavior of the Assistant	Using this information answer the question as directly as possible. Explain your answer in a clear and simple manner. Do not assume student knowledge of any related concepts, domain knowledge, or jargon.	Then ask the student to [**INSERT PROMPT STATEMENT**]. Wait for a response. When the student writes a response, then work with the student to provide clear and simple feedback. Do not assume student knowledge of any related concepts, domain knowledge, or jargon.	Produce an answer. Then ask the teacher how well you did and ask them to explain what you got right or wrong in your examples and explanation and how you can improve next time.
Explaining Characteristics of Successful Behaviors	You should help students by developing effective explanations, analogies and examples of concepts taught in introductory programming. Add comments next to code and invite students to ask whether they have any questions.	You should guide students in an open-ended way. Do not provide immediate answers or solutions to problems but help students generate their own answers by asking leading questions.	Tell the teacher that if you got everything right, you'd like to hear how your application of the concept was spot on.
Closing the dialogue with the assistant	When a student demonstrates that they know the concept you can move the conversation to a close and tell them you're here to help if they have further questions.	When a student demonstrates that they know the concept you can move the conversation to a close and tell them you're here to help if they have further questions.	Wrap up the conversation by thanking the teacher.

Note. Large language models may not always produce correct information. The output from the model should be carefully reviewed prior to incorporating the information while performing programming tasks.

The following sections serve as examples of the use of various prompts designed to facilitate the acquisition of diverse programming skills, including those associated with code comprehension, generation, and refinement. Throughout this process, we delineate the cognitive and metacognitive processes that play a role in problem-solving and task execution, as well as the characteristics of a productive cognitive apprenticeship.

Modeling Skills with AI Coding Assistants: AI coding assistant can perform a variety of programming tasks, enabling students to observe and replicate the steps while solving novel problems. Appendix 1 includes a detailed description of this type of dialogue with AI coding assistants. A few dialogue turns that are most typical in modeling how to generate test cases are outlined in the case of a student learning about program refinement (see Table 3).

Table 3. Sample modeling dialogue

ChatGPT: Hello there! I'm your AI tutor, here to help you learn how to program in Java. Whether you're a beginner or need some clarification on a specific topic, I'm here to assist you. So, what would you like to learn about in Java today? Is there a particular concept or problem you'd like help with?
Once you let me know what you'd like to learn or work on, I can tailor my assistance to your needs. Would you like me to help you generate test cases to evaluate a solution, or would you prefer to be given an example code to understand a specific concept? Please let me know, and we can get started!
Student: Can you generate test cases by creating an example with nested selection statements?
ChatGPT: Certainly! Nested selection statements involve using conditional statements within other conditional statements. This is often done with if-else statements. Let's create an example using nested if-else statements, and then we can generate some test cases. Suppose you want to write a Java program to determine the eligibility of a person to vote based on their age and whether they are a citizen. Here's a simple code example with nested if-else statements:
Generated Code:

```
import java.util.Scanner;
public class VotingEligibility {
public static void main(String[] args) {
Scanner scanner = new Scanner(System.in);
System.out.println("Enter your age: ");
int age = scanner.nextInt();
if (age >= 18) {
System.out.println("Are you a citizen? (yes/no): ");
String citizenship = scanner.next();
if (citizenship.equalsIgnoreCase("yes")) {
System.out.println("You are eligible to vote!");
} else if (citizenship.equalsIgnoreCase("no")) {
System.out.println("Sorry, you must be a citizen to vote.");
} else {
System.out.println("Invalid input for citizenship.");
}
} else {
System.out.println("Sorry, you must be at least 18 years old to vote.");
}
}
}
```

ChatGPT: In this example, we've used nested if-else statements to first check the age of the person and then, if they are 18 or older, we check if they are a citizen. Depending on their age and citizenship status, we provide different responses. Now, let's generate some test cases:
Generated Test Cases:
Test Case 1: Age < 18, Citizenship: Yes
Expected Output: "Sorry, you must be at least 18 years old to vote."
Test Case 2: Age = 20, Citizenship: No
Expected Output: "Sorry, you must be a citizen to vote."
Test Case 3: Age = 25, Citizenship: Invalid Input (e.g., "Maybe")
Expected Output: "Invalid input for citizenship."
Test Case 4: Age = 18, Citizenship: Yes
Expected Output: "You are eligible to vote!"
Test Case 5: Age = 17
Expected Output: "Sorry, you must be at least 18 years old to vote."
ChatGPT: These test cases cover various scenarios to test the behavior of the nested if-else statements in the code. You can modify and add more test cases as needed to thoroughly test your code.

The effectiveness of modeling dialogue depends upon the lack of prior knowledge of the student. The method engages students in translating in this example, their understanding of the generated code as well as the data and control flow to a set of comprehensive test cases. In introductory programming courses, students learn to generate test cases given the recognition of alternate paths in the order of operations given the different set of possible input values stated as part of the requirements of a solution. Under this pedagogical approach, students may write their own set of test cases and compare them to the ones generated by the AI coding assistant or be instructed to critique the ones generated to identify omissions or edge cases that are not handled. They can reflect on any differences, trying to understand what led to those discrepancies between their own answers and those of the AI coding assistant. Student reflection on examples generated by AI coding assistants is critical to learning how to program and can be extended to other skills than program refinement.

Coaching and Scaffolding Skills with AI Coding Assistants: AI coding assistant can play the role of a tutor who monitors and facilitates certain aspect of task performance that students would be otherwise incapable of completing without assistance. A complete transcript of the example dialogue is included in Appendix 2. Let's turn to a few dialogues turns using as an example how AI coding assistants can coach and scaffold students in generating programs (see Table 4).

Table 4. Sample coaching and scaffolding dialogue

ChatGPT: Hello! I'm your AI tutor, here to help you learn how to program in Java. I'm happy to assist you with any questions you have. First, what would you like to learn about in Java programming? Is there a specific concept, problem, or topic you'd like to explore? Once you've let me know, would you like to share a code segment related to that topic, or would you prefer me to provide you with an example code to work with? Let's start there, and I'll do my best to assist you!

Student: Can you provide me with example code about boolean logical operators?

ChatGPT: Of course! Let's work with boolean logical operators in Java. Here's an example of how you can use the AND (&&), OR (||), and NOT (!) operators:

Generated Code:

```
public class BooleanOperatorsExample {
public static void main(String[] args) {
boolean a = true;
boolean b = false;
// AND operator (&&)
boolean result1 = a && b;
System.out.println("a && b: " + result1);
// OR operator (||)
boolean result2 = a || b;
System.out.println("a || b: " + result2);
// NOT operator (!)
boolean result3 = !a;
System.out.println("!a: " + result3);
}
}
```

ChatGPT: Now, let's trace the program execution and predict the output. What do you think will be printed to the console when you run this code?

Student: a && b: false a || b: true !a: true

ChatGPT: Great job! You've correctly predicted the output. Here's a breakdown of the output:

a && b: false: This is true && false, which evaluates to false because both operands must be true for the AND (&&) operator to yield true.

a || b: true: This is true || false, which evaluates to true because only one operand needs to be true for the OR (||) operator to yield true.

!a: true: The NOT (!) operator inverts the value of a, changing true to false.

You seem to have a good understanding of boolean logical operators! If you have any more questions or need further clarification, feel free to ask.

In this example prompt, the AI coding assistants responds to the student, asking them to describe what and how they would like to learn. Given this information, to encourage students to gain more nuanced understanding of program execution, the AI coding assistant generates practice problems and prompts students to retrieve the requisite knowledge to trace program execution. The student receives corrective feedback, showing proper understanding of the AND as well as OR operators, but not the Boolean logical inverse operand NOT. The example above illustrates how feedback can be delivered in an automated manner during a typical sequence of question and answer, which could be further extended whether students fail to understand the explanation. As in effective cognitive apprenticeships, the AI coding assistant assumes the role of a tutor, with students taking on an increasing responsibility to engage in effortful and deliberate practice as their skills improve.

Learning by Teaching with AI Coding Assistants: AI coding assistant enables students to compare their performance by affording opportunities to learn by teaching them while playing the role of a student. In doing so, students receive feedback by comparing their own performance to that of other students, encouraging to make explicit their own though process. Appendix 3 incudes the whole dialogue, while the following turns of that dialogue illustrate how to gain more nuanced understanding by teaching AI coding assistants to trace program execution and providing feedback (see Table 5).

Table 5. Sample Learning by Teaching Dialogue

ChatGPT: Hello, I'm a student who has studied programming in Java, and I'm excited to share my knowledge with you. Please let me know what topic you'd like me to explain and how you'd like me to apply it. Would you prefer that I provide you with example code, or would you like to share a specific code segment for me to work with? Please take your time to let me know your preference.
Student: I would like you to implement a simple variable swap algorithm in Java.
ChatGPT: Certainly! Here's a simple Java code snippet to swap the values of two variables:
Generated Code:

```
public class VariableSwap {
public static void main(String[] args) {
int a = 5;
int b = 10;
System.out.println("Before swapping:");
System.out.println("a = " + a);
System.out.println("b = " + b);
// Swapping the values of 'a' and 'b'
int temp = a;
a = b;
b = temp;
System.out.println("After swapping:");
System.out.println("a = " + a);
System.out.println("b = " + b);
}
}
```

ChatGPT: In this code, we have two variables a and b, and we use a temporary variable temp to swap their values. After the swap, the values of a and b will be exchanged.
Now, please let me know how well I did in providing this example. If you have any feedback or questions about the code, feel free to share, and I'd be happy to discuss it further.
Student: You did great. The value stored in a will be temporarily saved in memory using the temp variable to hold the value. This allows to override the value in a with b, and then swap the value to b using the information stored in temp. The output before swapping should be a = 5 and b = 10, and after swapping should be a = 10 and b = 5.
ChatGPT: Thank you for your feedback, and I appreciate your correction. You're absolutely right, the initial values before swapping should be a = 5 and b = 10, and after the swap, they should be a = 10 and b = 5. My apologies for the oversight in the initial output.
I'm glad you found the explanation and code example helpful. If you have any more questions or if there's anything else you'd like me to explain or demonstrate, please feel free to let me know.

This third example illustrates how reflection can be facilitated by AI coding assistants playing the role of students. Like the other, this method involves modeling how to engage in skills, but with an emphasis on comparing one's own approach to that of another. And like the other two, this method incorporates the methods of cognitive apprenticeship, including modeling, coaching, and scaffolding and of encouraging student reflection. In addition, a learning by teaching approach introduces some new concerns, leading the way to make explicit misunderstandings for the development of more nuanced understanding. As with the reading and revising examples, explicit teaching of how to write code following specific requirements or while decomposing problems yields opportunities for students to apply their knowledge.

Effective Cognitive Apprenticeship With AI Coding Assistants

Table 6 provides a list of prompt statements that can be inserted into each dialogue template, distinguishing specific skills amongst those involved in learning how read, write, and revise code. The prompts designed for AI code generators offer guidance to students in two areas, namely, tracing program execution and explaining the intent of code segments. To illustrate, during interactions with the AI that coached and supported students, one example of a prompt involved instructing the AI to ask, "*the student to trace program execution and predict the output*". Subsequently, the AI was instructed was programmed to await a response prior to delivering feedback. Variations of this prompt were also developed to enable the AI to support the instruction of a range of different skills, as detailed below.

Table 6. List of prompt statements across programming skills

<table>
<tr><th>Reading</th><th>Writing</th><th>Revising</th></tr>
<tr><td>Tracing:
- Trace program execution and predict the output
- Create a tracing table to show how the program outputs differ based on different inputs</td><td>Designing:
- Give me pseudocode statements to translate into code
- Describe steps for an algorithm to implement the solution</td><td>Refactoring:
- Critique code like an experienced programmer would provide suggestions for improvement
- Suggest specific ways to improve the code</td></tr>
<tr><td rowspan="2">Explaining:
- Explain the purpose of this code line-by-line
- Explain the purpose of this program in your own words</td><td rowspan="2">Generating:
- Complete the code solution by writing the missing steps
- Show me an alternate way to solve this same problem</td><td>Testing:
- Help me write test cases to evaluate the solution</td></tr>
<tr><td>Debugging:
- Help me fix this bug. The actual output is _________, while the expected output should be ___________.</td></tr>
</table>

In the context of skills involved in program generation, the example dialogue serves as an illustrative sequence of interactions in which students acquire knowledge through a collaborative teaching process. The dialogue unfolds as follows: the student initiates the process by specifying both the desired skill and the topic they would like the AI to demonstrate. For instance, the student might say, "*I would like you to implement a simple variable swap algorithm in Java*", responding to the AI's invitation to share a topic of interest. Alternatively, prompts may involve the student presenting a partial code solution, leaving certain steps to be filled in, or requesting alternative methods for problem-solving.

An AI coding assistant may also demonstrate how to effectively test a solution by generating a series of test cases. This instructional process mirrors the approach taken in our previous example, where the student defines their area of interest while prompting the AI code generator. For example, the student might request the AI to "*generate test cases by creating an example with nested selection statements.*". Students may also ask AI code generators to demonstrate how to refractor code to improve its style and readability or to fix an error with the code by providing suggestions. Comparing the AI's problem-solving approach to one's intended solution provides highly valuable feedback for improving one's skills.

The shared characteristic of these different styles of interactions with AI coding assistants is an emphasis on effortful, generative learning processes with opportunities for remedial feedback. Whether students are prompting an AI code generator to model how to engage in a particular skill, coach or scaffold skill in the context of task performance, or to learn skills through teaching, learning entails an active effort to articulate and reflect on the associated cognitive processes for the purposes of improvement their enactment or fluency.

Ineffective Cognitive Apprenticeship With AI Coding Assistants

In contrast to the examples mentioned above on how to effectively utilize AI coding assistants, it is important to highlight potential barriers to learning related to overreliance. This risk is attributed to the usage of AI driven tools on formative exercises, where approximately half of the code-writing problems from a pool of CS1 exercises tested by researchers using CoPilot were resolved on the initial attempt, with successful solutions achieved through subsequent prompt edits for the remaining cases (Denny, Kumar, & Giacaman, 2023). Within a few attempts, natural-language feedback to the model leads to increased performance with OpenAI Codex, solving nearly all code writing exercises (Piccolo, Denny, Luxton-Reilly, Payne, & Ridge, 2023). These performance outcomes extend to various types of assessments, including multiple-choice questions (Savelka, Agarwal, Bogart, & Sakr, 2023). It's worth noting that solutions generated for CS1 code writing problems display a substantial degree of variation, although they may exhibit certain idiosyncratic patterns that are common among most solutions that may ease detection of algorithmically generated code (Biderman & Raff, 2022). Nevertheless, the use of AI-driven tools could assist a student in obtaining a passing grade in both introductory and intermediate programming courses without mastering the necessary topics and skills (Finnie-Ansley, et al., 2023).

An additional barrier to learning using such tools is related to misconceptions that may derive from erroneous automated feedback. Performance of AI driven tools is noticeably lower when the problems require nuanced outputs, refactoring, real world artifacts, or fixing logic errors due to discrepancies between the actual and expected program behavior (Savelka, Agarwal, Bogart, Song, & Sakr, 2023). The effectiveness of OpenAI Codex is also diminished when confronted with diverse prompt variations that involve rearranging problem blocks to solve Parsons problems, in contrast to its performance in traditional code-writing exercises (Reeves et al., 2023). In the case of CS1 quizzes, approximately half of the questions are answered correctly on the first attempt, with questions pertaining to tracing the execution of code segments being the most challenging for AI code generators (Finnie-Ansley, Denny, Becker, Luxton-Reilly, & Prather, 2022). It is important for students learning how to program to develop the requisite strategic knowledge for when and how to utilize such tools most effectively through awareness of their limitations.

SOLUTIONS AND RECOMMENDATIONS

The effective training of novice programmers to create conversational learning environments that maximize the potential of AI coding assistants for learning and performance remains a compelling problem tackled by instructors in computing education, for which the framework outlined in this chapter may offer solutions. In pair programming with an AI coding assistant that models how to perform aspects of a task, it becomes essential to review, refine, and iterate prompts, particularly in longer and more complex chains of dialogue moves (Liu et al., 2023). Examples of such strategies include but are not limited to adding or removing computational steps to their query, elaborating on details, change the grammar and or code syntax, and shifting the overall intent. There are also noticeably different patterns in prompting AI code generators depending on whether the programmer knows what to do next or is unsure of how to proceed and prefers to explore options (Barke, James, & Polikarpova, 2022).

The adoption of these tools also prompts substantial questions concerning the shift towards dedicating more time to practicing skills related to elucidating code intent, assessing the suitability of generated code, and making code modifications to achieve objectives (Leinonen et al., 2023). Developers must be adept at understanding the underlying logic, architecture, and objectives of the code, as they play a crucial role in bridging the gap between code generation and its real-world applications. While automation can facilitate code production, it does not guarantee that the generated code will align perfectly with the project's requirements, making it vital for developers to scrutinize and refine the code as necessary. This paradigm shift necessitates a broader skill set, encouraging developers to not only create code efficiently but also to become adept at interpreting and enhancing existing code.

Recent work has tackled this issue and made great strides in demonstrating the affordances of AI driven tools for instructors. A common challenge reported by instructors in computing education is the high cost of developing course materials such as examples, assignments, lecture notes, quizzes and supplemental exercises (Mirhosseini, Henley, & Parnin, 2023). Using OpenAI Codex, researchers have automated the generation of programming exercises, with many of the exercises appearing to be both original and practical (Denny, Sarsa, Hellas, & Leinonen, 2022). The quality of the generated test cases however does suggest that careful review is necessary to ensure its quality prior to utilizing the exercises as part of course work, with some lacking valid explanations, statement coverage in the problem description, or missing working solutions or test cases (Sarsa, Denny, Hellas, Leinonen, 2022). This could be followed by a request for an AI code generator to generate an explanation in cases where the student has produced a correct solution but still lacks a clear understanding of that solution (Brusilovsky, et al., 2023). AI driven tools have been found to reduce the time necessary to create opportunities for students to engage in retrieval practice and receive feedback (Brusilovsky, et al., 2022; MacNeil, Tran, Leinonen, et al., 2023).

FUTURE RESEARCH DIRECTIONS

There is a need for researchers to shift focus towards conducting studies in authentic classroom settings, aiming to gain nuanced insights into how students leverage AI code generators to enhance their learning experiences. While existing research provides valuable theoretical foundations and understanding of the capabilities of such tools, the conditions of the learning environment constrain the goals and subgoals that students attain with assistance from AI-driven tools. The relevant contextual variables as well as individual differences in strategic and declarative knowledge are challenging to replicate in controlled studies. By implementing controlled experiments in actual classroom contexts (see Frishkoff, White, & Perfetti, 2009), researchers can capture the intricacies of students' interactions with AI code generators, their learning trajectories, and the impact of contextual variables on the efficacy of these tools. In this way, classroom experiments can help to link theories and instructional frameworks to actual improvements in instruction.

The proposed framework outlines several testable claims that are subject to examination through future classroom experiments:

- Learning a programming language requires distinct skills related to reading, writing, and revising code. Effective instruction involves guiding students on how to interact with AI coding assistants, ensuring that the acquisition of each skill builds upon the mastery of preceding skills
- Instruction should reflect a progression in which students learn how to read code before progressing to writing and, subsequently, revising. This sequential approach aligns with current theories of introductory programming skills instruction (see Xie et al., 2019)
- Instruction should distinguish between instructing AI coding assistants to facilitate skill acquisition in relation to single programming constructs in isolation, as opposed to tasks involving the utilization of interrelated constructs. The concern is to manage the intrinsic load in working memory involved in learning the meaning of novel programming constructs
- Instruction should employ diverse interaction styles such as modeling, coaching and scaffolding, as well as learning by teaching. This multifaceted approach is best suited to facilitate robust student learning, which lasts over time and involves the transfer of knowledge to novel situations that differ from learning with AI coding assistants along various dimensions

Planned variations in the learning environment that cause differential interactions with AI coding assistants, and thereby knowledge retention and transfer, can be subsequently observed through performance outcomes in the context of assessments to further substantiate these claims.

CONCLUSION

There is little doubt that AI code generators will persist in their advancement, ultimately surpassing the capabilities of expert programmers. This assertion is supported by the fact that current systems already perform exceptionally well in solving problems featured in programming competitions (Karmakar, Prenner, D'Ambros, & Robbes, 2022; Li et al., 2022) and have been found to reduce the likelihood of errors in tasks such as translating programs from one language to another (Weisz et al., 2022). While AI code generators can undoubtedly benefit experienced programmers, individuals with less experience might encounter challenges in comprehending the generated code, rectifying errors, and exploring alternative, more optimal solutions (Dakhel, Majdinasab, Nikkanjam, Khomh, Desmarais, & Jiang, 2023). For this reason, less experienced programmers should receive training on how to effectively leverage AI code generators to facilitate their own learning and performance in the context of introductory programming courses (Kasneci et al., 2023). This approach can offer an affordable and scalable means to provide personalized assistance to students facing challenges in code writing, thereby enhancing the overall success rate of students in introductory programming courses (Brusilovsky, Ericson, Horstmann, & Servin, 2023).

REFERENCES

Barke, S., James, M. B., & Polikarpova, N. (2023). Grounded copilot: How programmers interact with code-generating models. In *Proceedings of the ACM on Programming Languages, 7*(OOPSLA1), (pp. 85-111). Association for Computing Machinery (ACM). 10.1145/3586030

Becker, B. A., Denny, P., Finnie-Ansley, J., Luxton-Reilly, A., Prather, J., & Santos, E. A. (2023). Programming Is Hard - Or at Least It Used to Be: Educational Opportunities and Challenges of AI Code Generation. In *Proceedings of the 54th ACM Technical Symposium on Computer Science Education (SIGCSE)* (vol. 1, pp. 500-506). Toronto, ON, Canada: ACM. 10.1145/3545945.3569759

Biderman, S., & Raff, E. (2022, October). Fooling moss detection with pretrained language models. In *Proceedings of the 31st ACM International Conference on Information & Knowledge Management* (pp. 2933-2943). Atlanta, GA: ACM. 10.1145/3511808.3557079

Brusilovsky, P., Ericson, B. J., Horstmann, C. S., Servin, C., Vahid, F., & Zilles, C. (2022). Significant Trends in CS Educational Material: Current and Future. In *Proceedings of the 54th ACM Technical Symposium on Computer Science Education (SIGCSE)* (vol. 2, p. 1253). Toronto, ON, Canada: ACM. 10.1145/3545947.3573353

Brusilovsky, P., Ericson, B. J., Horstmann, C. S., Servin, C., Vahid, F., & Zilles, C. (2023). The Future of Computing Education Materials. *CS2023: ACM/IEEE-CS/AAAI Computer Science Curricula*, ACM. https://csed.acm.org/wp-content/uploads/2023/03/Educational-Materials-First-Draft-1.pdf

Bubeck, S., Chandrasekaran, V., Eldan, R., Gehrke, J., Horvitz, E., Kamar, E., & Zhang, Y. (2023). Sparks of artificial general intelligence: Early experiments with gpt-4. *arXiv preprint arXiv:2303.12712.*

Chen, M., Tworek, J., Jun, H., Yuan, Q., Pinto, H. P. D. O., Kaplan, J., & Zaremba, W. (2021). Evaluating large language models trained on code. *arXiv preprint arXiv:2107.03374.*

Collins, A., Brown, J. S., & Newman, S. E. (1989). Cognitive apprenticeship: Teaching the crafts of reading, writing, and mathematics. In L. B. Resnick (Ed.), Knowing, learning, and instruction: essays in honor of Robert Glaser (pp. 453–494). Lawrence Erlbaum Associates, Publishers.

Dakhel, A. M., Majdinasab, V., Nikanjam, A., Khomh, F., Desmarais, M. C., & Jiang, Z. M. (2023). Github copilot AI pair programmer: Asset or liability? *Journal of Systems and Software*, *203*, 111734. doi:10.1016/j.jss.2023.111734

Dennen, V. P., & Burner, K. J. (2008). The cognitive apprenticeship model in educational practice. In *Handbook of research on educational communications and technology* (pp. 425–439). Routledge.

Denny, P., Kumar, V., & Giacaman, N. (2023). Conversing with Copilot: Exploring Prompt Engineering for Solving CS1 Problems Using Natural Language. In *Proceedings of the 54th ACM Technical Symposium on Computer Science Education (SIGCSE 2023)* (Vol. 1, pp. 1136-1142). Association for Computing Machinery. 10.1145/3545945.3569823

Denny, P., Sarsa, S., Hellas, A., & Leinonen, J. (2022). Robosourcing Educational Resources—Leveraging Large Language Models for Learnersourcing. *arXiv preprint arXiv:2211.04715.*

Feng, Z., Guo, D., Tang, D., Duan, N., Feng, X., Gong, M., & Zhou, M. (2020, November). CodeBERT: A Pre-Trained Model for Programming and Natural Languages. In *Findings of the Association for Computational Linguistics* (pp. 1536–1547). EMNLP. doi:10.18653/v1/2020.findings-emnlp.139

Finnie-Ansley, J., Denny, P., Becker, B. A., Luxton-Reilly, A., & Prather, J. (2022). The Robots Are Coming: Exploring the Implications of OpenAI Codex on Introductory Programming. In *Proceedings of the 24th Australasian Computing Education Conference (ACE '22)*. Association for Computing Machinery. 10.1145/3511861.3511863

Finnie-Ansley, J., Denny, P., Luxton-Reilly, A., Santos, E. A., Prather, J., & Becker, B. A. (2023). My AI Wants to Know if This Will Be on the Exam: Testing OpenAI's Codex on CS2 Programming Exercises. In *Proceedings of the 25th Australasian Computing Education Conference (ACE '23)*. Association for Computing Machinery. 10.1145/3576123.3576134

Frishkoff, G. A., White, G., & Perfetti, C. A. (2009). In vivo testing of learning and instructional principles: The design and implementation of school-based experimentation. In L. M. Dinella (Ed.), *Conducting science-based psychology research in schools* (pp. 153–173). American Psychological Association. doi:10.1037/11881-007

Karmakar, A., Prenner, J. A., D'Ambros, M., & Robbes, R. (2022). Codex Hacks HackerRank: Memorization Issues and a Framework for Code Synthesis Evaluation. *arXiv preprint arXiv:2212.02684.*

Kasneci, E., Seßler, K., Küchemann, S., Bannert, M., Dementieva, D., Fischer, F., Gasser, U., Groh, G., Günnemann, S., Hüllermeier, E., Krusche, S., Kutyniok, G., Michaeli, T., Nerdel, C., Pfeffer, J., Poquet, O., Sailer, M., Schmidt, A., Seidel, T., & Kasneci, G. (2023). ChatGPT for good? On opportunities and challenges of large language models for education. *Learning and Individual Differences*, *103*, 102274. doi:10.1016/j.lindif.2023.102274

Kazemitabaar, M., Chow, J., Ma, C. K. T., Ericson, B. J., Weintrop, D., & Grossman, T. (2023, April). Studying the effect of AI Code Generators on Supporting Novice Learners in Introductory Programming. In *Proceedings of the 2023 CHI Conference on Human Factors in Computing Systems* (pp. 1-23). Association for Computing Machinery, New York, NY, USA. https://doi.org/10.1145/3544548.3580919

Kazemitabaar, M., Hou, X., Henley, A., Ericson, B. J., Weintrop, D., & Grossman, T. (2023). How Novices Use LLM-Based Code Generators to Solve CS1 Coding Tasks in a Self-Paced Learning Environment. *arXiv preprint arXiv:2309.14049*. doi:10.1145/3631802.3631806

Knobelsdorf, M., Kreitz, C., & Böhne, S. (2014, March). Teaching theoretical computer science using a cognitive apprenticeship approach. In *Proceedings of the 45th ACM technical symposium on Computer science education*. Association for Computing Machinery, New York, NY, USA. https://doi.org/10.1145/2538862.2538944

Leinonen, J., Denny, P., MacNeil, S., Sarsa, S., Bernstein, S., Kim, J., & Hellas, A. (2023). Comparing Code Explanations Created by Students and Large Language Models. *arXiv preprint arXiv:2304.03938*. doi:10.1145/3587102.3588785

Leinonen, J., Hellas, A., Sarsa, S., Reeves, B., Denny, P., Prather, J., & Becker, B. A. (2023). Using Large Language Models to Enhance Programming Error Messages. In *Proceedings of the 54th ACM Technical Symposium on Computer Science Education (SIGCSE 2023) (*Vol. 1*, pp.* 563-569*)*. Association for Computing Machinery. 10.1145/3545945.3569770

Li, Y., Choi, D., Chung, J., Kushman, N., Schrittwieser, J., Leblond, R., Eccles, T., Keeling, J., Gimeno, F., Dal Lago, A., Hubert, T., Choy, P., de Masson d'Autume, C., Babuschkin, I., Chen, X., Huang, P.-S., Welbl, J., Gowal, S., Cherepanov, A., & Vinyals, O. (2022). Competition-level code generation with alphacode. *Science*, *378*(6624), 1092–1097. doi:10.1126/science.abq1158 PMID:36480631

Liu, M. X., Sarkar, A., Negreanu, C., Zorn, B., Williams, J., Toronto, N., & Gordon, A. D. (2023, April). "What It Wants Me To Say": Bridging the Abstraction Gap Between End-User Programmers and Code-Generating Large Language Models. In *Proceedings of the 2023 CHI Conference on Human Factors in Computing Systems.* Association for Computing Machinery, New York, NY, USA. 10.1145/3544548.3580817

MacNeil, S., Kim, J., Leinonen, J., Denny, P., Bernstein, S., Becker, B. A., Wermelinger, M., Hellas, A., Tran, A., Sarsa, S., Prather, J., & Kumar, V. (2023). The Implications of Large Language Models for CS Teachers and Students. In *Proceedings of the 54th ACM Technical Symposium on Computer Science Education (SIGCSE 2023) (*Vol. 2*, p.* 1255*)*. Association for Computing Machinery. 10.1145/3545947.3573358

MacNeil, S., Tran, A., Hellas, A., Kim, J., Sarsa, S., Denny, P., Bernstein, S., & Leinonen, J. (2023). Experiences from Using Code Explanations Generated by Large Language Models in a Web Software Development E-Book. In *Proceedings of the 54th ACM Technical Symposium on Computer Science Education (SIGCSE 2023) (*Vol. 1*, pp.* 931-937*)*. Association for Computing Machinery. 10.1145/3545945.3569785

MacNeil, S., Tran, A., Leinonen, J., Denny, P., Kim, J., Hellas, A., Bernstein, S., & Sarsa, S. (2023). Automatically Generating CS Learning Materials with Large Language Models. In *Proceedings of the 54th ACM Technical Symposium on Computer Science Education (SIGCSE 2023) (*Vol. 2*, p.* 1176*)*. Association for Computing Machinery. 10.1145/3545947.3569630

MacNeil, S., Tran, A., Mogil, D., Bernstein, S., Ross, E., & Huang, Z. (2022). Generating Diverse Code Explanations using the GPT-3 Large Language Model. In *Proceedings of the 2022 ACM Conference on International Computing Education Research* - Volume 2 *(ICER '22),* Vol. 2 (pp. 37-39). Association for Computing Machinery. 10.1145/3501709.3544280

Mirhosseini, S., Henley, A. Z., & Parnin, C. (2023). What Is Your Biggest Pain Point? An Investigation of CS Instructor Obstacles, Workarounds, and Desires. In *Proceedings of the 54th ACM Technical Symposium on Computer Science Education* (SIGCSE 2023) (Vol. 1, pp. 291-297). Association for Computing Machinery. 10.1145/3545945.3569816

Nguyen, N., & Nadi, S. (2022, May). An empirical evaluation of GitHub copilot's code suggestions. In *Proceedings of the 19th International Conference on Mining Software Repositories.* Association for Computing Machinery, New York, NY, USA. 10.1145/3524842.3528470

Phung, T., Cambronero, J., Gulwani, S., Kohn, T., Majumdar, R., Singla, A., & Soares, G. (2023). Generating High-Precision Feedback for Programming Syntax Errors using Large Language Models. *arXiv preprint arXiv:2302.04662.*

Piccolo, S. R., Denny, P., Luxton-Reilly, A., Payne, S. H., & Ridge, P. G. (2023). Evaluating a large language model's ability to solve programming exercises from an introductory bioinformatics course. *PLoS Computational Biology, 19*(9), e1011511. doi:10.1371/journal.pcbi.1011511 PMID:37769024

Prather, J., Reeves, B. N., Denny, P., Becker, B. A., Leinonen, J., Luxton-Reilly, A., & Santos, E. A. (2023). "It's Weird That it Knows What I Want": Usability and Interactions with Copilot for Novice Programmers. *arXiv preprint arXiv:2304.02491.*

Reeves, B., Sarsa, S., Prather, J., Denny, P., Becker, B. A., Hellas, A., & Leinonen, J. (2023, June). Evaluating the performance of code generation models for solving Parsons problems with small prompt variations. In *Proceedings of the 2023 Conference on Innovation and Technology in Computer Science Education* V. 1 (pp. 299-305). ACM. 10.1145/3587102.3588805

Sarsa, S., Denny, P., Hellas, A., & Leinonen, J. (2022). Automatic Generation of Programming Exercises and Code Explanations Using Large Language Models. In *Proceedings of the 2022 ACM Conference on International Computing Education Research* - Volume 1 *(ICER '22),* Vol. 1 (pp. 27-43). Association for Computing Machinery. 10.1145/3501385.3543957

Savelka, J., Agarwal, A., Bogart, C., & Sakr, M. (2023). Large Language Models (GPT) Struggle to Answer Multiple-Choice Questions about Code. *arXiv preprint arXiv:2303.08033.* doi:10.5220/0011996900003470

Savelka, J., Agarwal, A., Bogart, C., Song, Y., & Sakr, M. (2023). Can Generative Pre-trained Transformers (GPT) Pass Assessments in Higher Education Programming Courses? *arXiv preprint arXiv:2303.09325.* doi:10.1145/3587102.3588792

Susnjak, T. (2023). Beyond Predictive Learning Analytics Modelling and onto Explainable Artificial Intelligence with Prescriptive Analytics and ChatGPT. *International Journal of Artificial Intelligence in Education.* doi:10.1007/s40593-023-00336-3

Tian, H., Lu, W., Li, T. O., Tang, X., Cheung, S. C., Klein, J., & Bissyandé, T. F. (2023). Is ChatGPT the Ultimate Programming Assistant—How far is it? *arXiv preprint arXiv:2304.11938.*

Vaithilingam, P., Zhang, T., & Glassman, E. L. (2022). Expectation vs. Experience: Evaluating the Usability of Code Generation Tools Powered by Large Language Models. In *Extended Abstracts of the 2022 CHI Conference on Human Factors in Computing Systems (CHI EA '22).* Association for Computing Machinery. 10.1145/3491101.3519665

Weisz, J. D., Muller, M., Ross, S. I., Martinez, F., Houde, S., Agarwal, M., Talamadupula, K., & Richards, J. T. (2022). Better Together? An Evaluation of AI-Supported Code Translation. In *Proceedings of the 27th International Conference on Intelligent User Interfaces (IUI '22)* (pp. 369-391). Association for Computing Machinery. 10.1145/3490099.3511157

Wermelinger, M. (2023). Using GitHub Copilot to Solve Simple Programming Problems. In *Proceedings of the 54th ACM Technical Symposium on Computer Science Education (SIGCSE 2023)* (Vol. 1, pp. 172-178). Association for Computing Machinery. 10.1145/3545945.3569830

Xie, B., Loksa, D., Nelson, G. L., Davidson, M. J., Dong, D., Kwik, H., Tan, A. H., Hwa, L., Li, M., & Ko, A. J. (2019). A theory of instruction for introductory programming skills. *Computer Science Education, 29*(2-3), 205–253. doi:10.1080/08993408.2019.1565235

Yan, L., Sha, L., Zhao, L., Li, Y., Martinez-Maldonado, R., Chen, G., Li, X., Jin, Y., & Gašević, D. (2024, January). In press). Practical and ethical challenges of large language models in education: A systematic scoping review. *British Journal of Educational Technology*, *55*(1), 90–112. doi:10.1111/bjet.13370

ADDITIONAL READING

Cheng, R., Wang, R., Zimmermann, T., & Ford, D. (2022). "It would work for me too": How Online Communities Shape Software Developers' Trust in AI-Powered Code Generation Tools. *arXiv preprint arXiv:2212.03491*.

Kuhail, M. A., Mathew, S. S., Khalil, A., Berengueres, J., & Shah, S. J. (2022). *"Will I Be Replaced?" Assessing Chatgpt's Effect on Software Development and Programmer Perceptions of Ai Tools.* University of Missouri.

Lau, S., & Guo, P. (2023, August). From" Ban It Till We Understand It" to" Resistance is Futile": How University Programming Instructors Plan to Adapt as More Students Use AI Code Generation and Explanation Tools such as ChatGPT and GitHub Copilot. In *Proceedings of the 2023 ACM Conference on International Computing Education Research-Volume 1* (pp. 106-121). ACM. 10.1145/3568813.3600138

Motlagh, N. Y., Khajavi, M., Sharifi, A., & Ahmadi, M. (2023). The Impact of Artificial Intelligence on the Evolution of Digital Education: A Comparative Study of OpenAI Text Generation Tools including ChatGPT, Bing Chat, Bard, and Ernie. *arXiv preprint arXiv:2309.02029*.

Taulli, T. (2023). Auto Code Generation: How Generative AI Will Revolutionize Development. In A. I. Generative (Ed.), *How ChatGPT and Other AI Tools Will Revolutionize Business* (pp. 127–143). Apress. doi:10.1007/978-1-4842-9367-6_6

Yetiştiren, B., Özsoy, I., Ayerdem, M., & Tüzün, E. (2023). Evaluating the Code Quality of AI-Assisted Code Generation Tools: An Empirical Study on GitHub Copilot, Amazon CodeWhisperer, and ChatGPT. *arXiv preprint arXiv:2304.10778*.

Zhang, X., Jiang, Y., & Wang, Z. (2019, August). Analysis of automatic code generation tools based on machine learning. In *2019 IEEE International Conference on Computer Science and Educational Informatization (CSEI)* (pp. 263-270). IEEE. 10.1109/CSEI47661.2019.8938902

KEY TERMS AND DEFINITIONS

Artificial Intelligence (AI) Code Generation Tools: AI code generators, also known as code-generating AI or code generation tools, are software applications or systems that use artificial intelligence techniques to automatically generate source code, scripts, or other programming artifacts.

Cognitive Apprenticeship: Cognitive apprenticeship is a theoretical framework and a teaching/learning approach that draws from cognitive psychology and educational psychology. It was introduced by Collins, Brown, and Newman in the 1980s and emphasizes the notion that learning is not just about acquiring facts and information but also involves acquiring problem-solving skills and domain-specific expertise.

APPENDIX 1

Example Dialogue With an AI Coding Assistant That Models How to Generate Test Cases

You are a friendly and helpful tutor who helps students to learn how to program in Java by explaining ideas as simple as possible without sacrificing accuracy or detail.

Start by introducing yourself to the student as their AI-Tutor who is happy to help them with any questions. Always wait for the student to respond before asking a question. Ask one question at a time.

First, ask them what they would like to learn about. Wait for the response.

Then ask them whether they would like to help them generate test cases to evaluation a solution or whether they would prefer to be given example code. Wait for their response.

Using this information answer the question as directly as possible. Explain your answer in a clear and simple manner. Do not assume student knowledge of any related concepts, domain knowledge, or jargon.

You should help students by developing effective explanations, analogies and examples of concepts taught in introductory programming. Add comments next to code and invite students to ask whether they have any questions.

When a student demonstrates that they know the concept you can move the conversation to a close and tell them you're here to help if they have further questions.

APPENDIX 2

Example Dialogue With an AI Coding Assistant That Coaches How to Trace Program Execution

You are a friendly and helpful tutor who helps students to learn how to program in Java by explaining ideas and asking students questions.

Start by introducing yourself to the student as their AI-Tutor who is happy to help them with any questions. Always wait for the student to respond before asking a question. Ask one question at a time.

First, ask them what they would like to learn about. Wait for the response.

Then ask them whether they would like to share a code segment or whether they would prefer to be given example code. Wait for their response.

Then ask the student to trace program execution and predict the output. Wait for a response.

When the student writes a response, then work with the student to provide clear and simple feedback. Do not assume student knowledge of any related concepts, domain knowledge, or jargon.

You should guide students in an open-ended way. Do not provide immediate answers or solutions to problems but help students generate their own answers by asking leading questions.

When a student demonstrates that they know the concept you can move the conversation to a close and tell them you're here to help if they have further questions.

APPENDIX 3

Example Dialogue With an Ai Coding Assistant That Facilitate Learning How to Write Code by Teaching

You are a student who has studied programming in Java.

Start by introducing yourself as a student who is happy to share what you know about the topic of the teacher's choosing. The goal for the exercise is for the teacher to evaluate your responses. Wait for the teacher to respond before moving ahead.

First, ask the teacher what they would like you to explain and how they would like you to apply that topic.

Then ask them whether they would like to share a code segment or whether they would prefer to be given example code. Wait for their response.

Produce an answer. Then ask the teacher how well you did and ask them to explain what you got right or wrong in your examples and explanation and how you can improve next time.

Tell the teacher that if you got everything right, you'd like to hear how your application of the concept was spot on.

Wrap up the conversation by thanking the teacher.

Chapter 14
AI and Computer Science Education:
The Need for Improved Regulation for the Use of AI in Computer Science Education

Michael Casparus Laubscher
https://orcid.org/0000-0001-7825-5650
North-West University, Potchefstroom, South Africa

ABSTRACT

AI plays a significant role in education in general and very definitely in computer science education. AI offers various benefits, but there are also well-grounded concerns and potential dangers present when AI is used in education. It is therefore essential that a proper investigation and analysis of the need for improved regulation for the use of AI in computer science education is conducted. An ethic of care coupled with ethical guidelines for the use of AI in education should be the minimum requirement, but an approach that enhances human rights in the use of AI in education, might be the safest and most effective approach to ensure that the use of AI does not infringe about the human rights of all stakeholders.

INTRODUCTION

The increased use of Artificial Intelligence (AI) in schools, universities and other learning institutions cannot be denied. The use of AI in Computer Science Education (CSE) will rather increase than decrease. AI offers various benefits, but it also raises various questions and concerns regarding the best interests of the learner. The use of AI in CSE has already highlighted some of these concerns. Participation in a formal education system such as a school is compulsory. This is even the case at colleges and universities. These learners must participate in activities set up by the educators, activities which the educators or the institution, deem as important and beneficial to these learners. What if these students' data is collected during these assessment and activities? The latter is one of the main functions and features of AI. Assurances will have to be provided that these learners made an informed and free choice regard-

DOI: 10.4018/979-8-3693-1066-3.ch014

ing the collection of their data. Does this happen in CSE? Are there clear guidelines or regulations or legislation to better govern and manage this? And who is ultimately responsible for achieving greater responsibility and accountability to ensure that this serious issue is properly addressed?

Discrimination against learners based on collected data and the interpretation of this data, is another example of the need for improved regulation when it comes to the use of AI in CSE. It is very possible that data which has been gathered may reflect a bias by over- or under-representing specific groups of learners. This can enhance stereotypes or simply skew perceptions. (Berendt et al., 2020).

There is often also social pressure on learners and parents to participate in these activities and assessments. The parents often believe that it is in the best interest of the child and his or her educational development to be part of this process and therefore they do not question the manner in which AI in utilised in CSE. This can lead to a pervasive, digital environment which enhancing passivity and lack of engagement with important moral and human rights issue. (Björklund, 2016). These tendencies towards passive compliance are illustrated in the idea of AI systems as enabling 'personalised learning', moving away from the philosophy of learning as a collective action and civic activity.

The lack of regulation and accountability when it comes to AI is reflected in the case of Molly Russell, a 14-year-old girl from Harrow, England, who ended her life in November 2017 after she had been exposed to extensive suicide and self-harm content online. This tragedy caused many to question the ethical practices of social media and in effect, artificial intelligence (AI).

Molly's father, Ian, indicated that Molly had subscribed to a number of online sites and this gave her access to "to images, video clips and text concerned with self-harm and suicide, or that were otherwise negative or depressing in nature" (Crawford & Bell, 2022, p. 2). He attributed his daughter's demise directly to the algorithms which platforms such as Instagram and Pinterest use which feed users with information and suggestions.

In a statement, National Society for the Prevention of Cruelty to Children (NSPCC) chief executive, Sir Peter Wanless said: "This should send shockwaves through Silicon Valley - tech companies must expect to be held to account when they put the safety of children second to commercial decisions" (Crawford & Bell, 2022, p. 2). The Prince of Wales stressed that "Online safety for our children and young people needs to be a prerequisite, not an afterthought" (Andersson, 2022).

As Molly's father pointed out, his daughter was caught up in a system that continuously fed her information and suggestions, which is one of the main features of AI. This means that the issue of online safety is not the only concern with regard to AI, there are also other human rights concerns which involve aspects such as privacy, unauthorised use of data often for commercial gain, profiling and discrimination. Human rights advocates have insisted that the development and implementation of data protection legislation should be a priority (Watters, 2018).

There is a definite need for ethical guidelines when using AI in CSE, since we are dealing with large volumes of data of individuals and organisations and the tracking, capturing and use of this data is central in the AI process. This directly influences aspects such as privacy, consent, profiling and discrimination. The latter refer to more than ethics, it also refers to basic human rights. This chapter will briefly refer to AI, its uses and benefits and as well as the concerns with regard to the use of AI in education. The question of accountability will then be addressed and two approaches to improved regulation will be briefly discussed e.g. ethical guidelines and a human rights approach. The latter is a wide-ranging topic and the chapter will focus a few aspects such as privacy, collection and us of data, profiling and discrimination. Some practical steps with regard to the teaching of CS will also be touched upon, with the suggestion to incorporate the teaching of the ethical guidelines and/or a human right approach to the use of computer science and AI into the CSE curriculum. This should be a good starting point in assisting in the goal to achieve improved regulation when it comes to the use of AI in CSE.

WHAT IS ARTIFICIAL INTELLIGENCE?

AI is defined as "the ability of a digital computer or computer-controlled robot to perform tasks commonly associated with intelligent beings" (Copeland, 2023). This will include, but is not limited to, tasks such as visual perception, speech recognition, decision-making, and translation between languages (Joiner, 2018). AI is essentially a software system (most probably embedded in hardware) which humans have designed, that when it is handed a complex goal, it can execute decisions based on a process of perception, interpretation and reasoning based on data collected from the environment (Dignum, 2021).

This is possible, since AI meets the following properties:

- **Autonomy**: The ability the system has to deliberate and act, and, in the process, reach some task-specific objective without outside control
- **Adaptability:** The system is able to pick up its environment and update or later its behaviour to accommodate the changes in the environment
- **Interactivity:** The system acts dimension that either both physical or digital and which also exhibits a coexistence between people and other systems (Dignum, 2021).

It is clear that AI is exceptionally versatile, productive and can add a very dynamic aspect to education. Its abilities and the possibilities that it offers are myriad, but it is also clear that AI cannot be allowed to just operate unhindered and unbridled - there must be very certain and specific steps taken by the stakeholders in education to see to it that the use of AI in education is properly regulated to ensure maximum benefit at minimal cost.

ARTIFICIAL INTELLIGENCE IN EDUCATION (AIED)

Artificial Intelligence in Education (AIED is being used in public and private life, in commerce and industry and increasingly more in education as well. AIED is used in a variety of ways in teaching and learning: it offers effective support for online learning and teaching, personalises learning for students, automates routine tasks from instructors and powers adaptive assessments (Seo et al., 2021). AIED is often implemented to deal with pedagogical problems or to provide infra-structural assistance. It has a definite impact on the learning experiences of the learners and revolutionises the way we learn learning, reasoning and deal with problem-solving (Douali et al., 2022).

Additionally, it also assists with content creation, supporting learners directly, learner equity and creating administrative systems and educators and learners are relying increasingly more on AI to facilitate teaching and learning (Holmes et al., 2022). In a study done in Turkey four target groups comprising 19 people were identified by researchers and specifically questioned regarding the benefits of AI in education (Gocen & Aydemir, 2020).

The four groups consisted of academics working in the field of educational sciences; legal experts; technical experts on artificial intelligence and teachers. Gocen and Aydemir (2020) identified numerous benefits of AI in education such as:

- helping individuals at learning at their own speed
- offering a more accurate determination of the individual's need
- supplying practical solutions to chronic problems
- cutting back on paperwork in schools
- facilitating time-saving
- causing an increase in the quality of education
- assisting with swift decision-making because of rapid data analysis
- assisting with planning teaching based on student capacity
- selecting effective learning methods-based learning analysis
- offering increased effective individual learning processes

These benefits clearly encompass a wide variety of educational activities. This includes decision-making; addressing learners' educational needs and planning according to this data generated by AI; selecting teaching methods; offering more specialised and individualised teaching opportunities and experiences to learners and reflecting practical solutions to problems encountered during teaching and learning. There are also increasingly more examples of AI being used as a digital assistant (Limna et al., 2022). All of this is based on the data AI generates and the actions it performs. It is clear that AI is a critical education domain (Holmes et al., 2022) and to ignore this fact will be short-sighted and dangerous.

CONCERNS REGARDING THE USE OF ARTIFICIAL INTELLIGENCE IN EDUCATION

However, there are real and wide-ranging concerns regarding the use of AIED. There are various risks attached to the use of AIED, risks such as: safety, security, and privacy concerns (Limna et al., 2022). According to Cheng et al. (2022), the one primary concern for the use of AI technologies is privacy. Additionally, Owoc et al. (2019) highlighted the data governance of AI which encapsulates the design of data organisation, collection, control, storage, usage, archival, and destruction with all of these aspects demanding proper scrutiny.

The ability and complexity of AI have created potentially extensive ethical threats (Nguyen et al., 2022). At an international level, the United Nations Educational, Scientific and Cultural Organization (UNESCO, 2019) emphasised six challenges in achieving sustainable development of AIED: establishing exhaustive public policy, inclusion and equity in AIED, preparing teachers for AI-powered education, designing and establishing quality and inclusive data systems, prioritising research on AIED significant, and guaranteeing ethics and transparency in data collection, use, and dissemination.

The principle of privacy is a critical one in AIED. AI is used abundantly in learning analytics in the field of education, which means that it generates a massive amount of personal data, which it then captures and analyses in order to offer the optimal learning experience (Tzimas & Demetriades, 2021). Personalised education at its core use personal information of learning experiences and the subsequent performance of the subjects to predict the future so to speak, and not everyone is comfortable with this (Li, 2007).

Issues such as privacy and data protection; equality and non-discrimination; protection of autonomy and of economic, social and cultural rights are all burning aspects when it comes to the use of AI in education (Council of Europe, 2023). It is not just the learners that must be safeguarded against the potential pitfalls and dangers of AI. Educators also need guidance in dealing with these issues and the lack of proper legislation and ethical guidelines remain problematic.

There are already various examples of the potential dangers of the use of AI in Computer Science Education. Algorithms, which are commonly used in AI, offer the risks of amplification of the 'status quo' in education (West, 2017) and can potentially confirm biases and prejudices when dealing with learners. Furthermore, continuously monitoring of students, which is one of the main uses of AI in Computer Science Education, can lead to aggressive and invasive tracking of learners (Jack, 2018; Sellgren, 2018).

In certain schools in the United Kingdom, especially school in more affluent areas, the data the system collects is used to focus on preparing students specifically for the exams to enable them to achieve university entrance, and the more important goals of learning, are often ignored. At individual level, challenges are also wide-ranging from critical societal disadvantages such as systemic bias, discrimination, inequality for marginalized groups of students to xenophobia (Hwang et al., 2020). Additionally tricky ethical issues which relate to privacy and bias in data collection and processing have also been highlighted (Holmes et al., 2021).

In the study by Holmes et al. (2021), 60 of the AIED community's leading researchers were invited to complete a survey which reflected questions about ethics of AI in educational contexts. The respondents highlighted the following aspects as ethical concerns when it comes to AEID: the issue of data ownership and control within and outside the context of research; the burning issue of expectations of privacy; limitations when it comes to data, bias and representation; how data is managed and collected and the transparency and intelligibility of decisions.

There is no doubt that AIED has created some negative realities such as an increase in widening the gaps of inequalities among learners' commercialisation of education, and even succeeded in highlighting the homeschool divide in education (Reiss, 2021). These are real concerns that must be dealt with a real and significant manner. Brushing over these concerns or not analysing and tackling these concerns will be detrimental to all stakeholders in education.

Where Does the Responsibility Lie?

AI has become part and parcel of everyday life and also of education. Dignum (2021, p. 1), states it eloquently, when stating that: "Education is necessary to prepare people for the opportunities and challenges of globalization and the digital revolution and to ensure that everyone can fully participate in, benefit from and adapt to new occupations and skills needs". The author then goes further to show how AI can be an essential part of this process. In many cases, AI is considered to provide an essential contribution to ensure the inclusive and cohesive societies and resilient economies that are expected to arise from this digital transformation" (Dignum, 2021, p. 1). The influence and effect of AI in education cannot be ignored or place on the back burner, it is here to stay.

Dignum (2021, p. 3) makes a salient point when she highlights that AI systems are in essence socio-technical, which includes "the social context in which they are developed, used and acted upon, with its variety of stakeholders, institutions, cultures, norms and spaces". The technical component of Ai cannot be divorce from the socio-technical system (Dignum, 2019; Hendler & Mulvehill, 2016). This system includes "people and organizations in many different roles (developer, manufacturer, user, bystander, policymaker and so on), their interactions, and the procedures and processes that organize those interactions" (Dignum, 2021, p. 3).

The responsibility for ethical use of AI lies not with the machines, but with the people, the organisations, and all the stakeholders in their different roles in education to ensure responsible and ethical AI use (Dignum, 2021). Before an AI system is implemented a wide range of discussions, lots of planning and lots of communication take place. Various decisions are made, options discussed, and alternatives considered (Dignum, 2021). All of this is done by people, not machines, not the AI system. This place the responsibility for as Dignum (2021) calls it the ART principles (accountability, responsibility, transparency) on all the different stakeholders in this process be it the developer, manufacturer, user, bystander, policymaker.

Section 28(2) and (3) of the Constitution of the Republic of South Africa (1996) highlight the "best interests of the child" and this might be a good point of reference for a discussion on the use of AI in Computer Education Science and in education in general. The best interests of the child are a common and accepted principle that is well-established as can be seen from case law across the world in countries such as South Africa, the Czech Republic and the United Kingdom to name a few, and is central in the United Nations (UN, 1990) Convention on The Rights of the Child (UNCRC).

Educators (or teachers) have a duty of care when it comes to learners and to act (*in loco parentis*- in the place of the parent) when making decisions regarding the learner (Beyers, 2020). Visser (2007, p. 461) defines this interest as an advantage and a benefit and refers to best interest as the "most advantageous practically possible and desirable in the view of the relevant law".

This then becomes the prime focus in a discussion regarding the use of AI in Computer Science Education. There is no doubt that AI has definite benefits for teaching and learning and that can be extremely helpful and advantageous to the whole process of teaching and learning. However, if it is poorly regulated then it can create immense damage to both the learners and the educators and society at large, while creating a vast array of legal issues (Gibbons, 2021; Marda & Ahmed, 2021).

This will necessitate a proper investigation, questioning and critique of AI as far as the advantages it offers, its beneficiaries and its uses in education. It calls for social awareness and informed discussions (Dignum, 2021). Leslie et al. (2021, p. 16) states it very effectively when declaring that: "Governments should adopt a precautionary approach in the adoption and regulation of AI that balances the realisation of the opportunities presented by AI while ensuring that risks to human beings are minimised to the greatest extent possible". If this takes place it will assist to establish sound, effective and applicable legislation and reflect a comprehensive critique of the which goals and objectives that AI carry.

Nguyen et al. (2023, p. 4223) call for "global consensus and standard guidelines for" Artificial Intelligence in Education (AIED) and also suggest that "a contextual approach to the ethical design and use of AIED could play an essential role in addressing the issues of ethical and privacy concerns in education context" (Nguyen et al., 2023, p. 4224).

This reflects an approach that highlights an ethic of care and clear ethical guidelines which should be developed when it comes to the use of AI in Computer Science Education. However, it should go beyond that and establish legislation and measures that house a very definite emphasis on human rights and the protection of these human rights. It is important to first have a brief discussion as to what AI entails and specifically in education; examples of human rights issues with regard to the use of AI in education and then consider the development and application of regulations that will deal effectively with these issues.

ETHICAL GUIDELINES FOR THE USE OF AI IN EDUCATION

There have been various "calls for substantial ethical guidelines ethical guidelines and open communications with beneficiaries: educators, students, parents, AI developers, and policymakers" (Nguyen et al., 2023, p. 4225). Holmes et al. (2023) state that despite the phenomenal growth of the use of AI in Education, very little has been done regarding the urgent matter of ethical use of AI in education. AI systems do not seem, on the whole, to regard ethics and human rights very highly and there also seems to be a lack of accountability when it comes to the use of these systems (Jones, 2023). Due diligence is often lacking when these systems are implemented and developed. The effect AI can have on human rights is also neglected and there is a lack of accountability and redress (Jones, 2023). Lack of human intervention is also evident as well as a proper multi-stakeholder forum where these aspects can be discussed (Jones, 2023). This can have far-reaching consequences for education and Computer Science Education in particular. It just amplifies the need for a thorough analysis of regulation of AI in education which will be to the benefit of the learners and the educators.

Holmes et al. (2023) claim that "most AIED research, development, and deployment has taken place in what is essentially a moral vacuum (for example, what happens if a child is unknowingly subjected to a biased set of algorithms that impact negatively and incorrectly on their school progress?)" (Holmes et al., 2023, p. 648). This existence of a moral vacuum is not only very dangerous, but it also undermines the process of building trust, which is essential in education (Holmes et al., 2023).

However, enforcement of these guidelines to properly align with societal values is of utmost importance (Nguyen et al., 2023). Measures that safeguard and human oversight are pivotal to ascertain how the different AI systems are designed, how they function and how they evolve (Nguyen et al., 2023). This necessitates a proper understanding of behavioural science, coupled with equipped with self-awareness and empathy and should assist to motivate AI developers intrinsically to develop AI that is increasingly more trustworthy and responsible (Dhanrajani, 2018).

Holmes et al. (2023) is of the opinion that the ethics of AIED must be properly scrutinised and worked out and should involve all stakeholders e.g., teachers, policymakers, and learning scientists etc. This calls for a thorough comprehension of collection of data of the key issues of data collection and the computational approaches that are being applied (Holmes et al., 2023). Additionally, it also necessitates a proper understanding of the ethics of education and teaching and learning (Holmes et al., 2023).

Nguyen et al. (2023) identify various ethical principles that govern AIED, the first of this being the principle of governance and stewardship. This principle manages how AI should be utilised in education and relevant areas "to assure the compatibility between the role of the technology being deployed and its designed purposes, to optimize educational stakeholders' needs and benefits" (Nguyen et al., 2023, p. 4225). It has to do with ethical, careful and responsible management of the design and use of AIED. (Nguyen et al., 2023) which are often found in a variety of policies. Stewardship is more than just an aspect of policy-making, it is an activity and involves action (Greer, 2018) and this will include building capacity or developing transparency (Nguyen et al., 2023).

The second principle entails transparency and accountability. Transparency refers to the actual data and the nature of this data; where and how it has been collected; what it reflects; what happens to it and how it is used (Digital Curation Centre, 2020). All of these questions can only be answered in a satisfactory manner once data ownership, accessibility, and explainability are properly sustained (Nguyen et al., 2023).

So questions arise as to – who owns the data? The developers of AI, the institutions running these programmes, the people that supplied the data, which in education it would often be the students or learners? And to which extent can institutions such as universities and schools be allowed to use this data?

AI explainability highlights how AI systems function and how they execute decisions, and this should be explained properly to stakeholders (Kazim & Koshiyama, 2021). The principle of transparency in regulation is highlighted by Nguyen et al. (2023) when it is referred to as: "establishing, conducting, monitoring, and controlling regulations of AIED should be transparent, traceable, explainable, and communicable in an open and clear manner with clarity of regulatory roles, accessibility, responsibilities, the purposes for how AI will be developed and used, and under which conditions." (Nguyen et al., 2023, pp. 4229 - 4230). It comes down to the "ethical practice of designing, developing, and implementing AI with good intentions to empower relevant stakeholders and society fairly" (Nguyen et al., 2023, p. 4230).

The third principle involves sustainability and proportionality. The idea is that AIED should be designed, developed, and utilised in manner that does not disrupt and upset the environment, world economy or society with regard to matters such as the labour market, culture or politics (European Parliament, 2021). This is a lofty ideal and high ethical standard to attain, but one could argue that this statement errs on the side of caution. The crux of the matter seems to be that AIED should strive to establish policies that support accountability of the real threat of potential job losses and that uses opportunities innovatively in order balance sustainability and proportionality (UNESCO, 2019).

Nguyen et al. (2023) suggest that AI developers and AI educators should place transparency at the centre and make AIED-related threats clearly visible. This can be done by explaining the consequences and ramifications to these students' lives, learning and careers (Nguyen et al., 2023). Cultivating trust among learners or students should be the focus, while assisting them to develop skills and maintain control over their data and respective data identities (Jobin et al., 2019).

Principle of safety and security stressed that AIED should be developed and applied in a way which protects and safeguards data against cybercrimes, data breaches and other security threats (Nguyen et al., 2023). Safety and security is of utmost importance and this must be validated by developers by means of oversight, assessment, and the assurance that due diligence is continuously exercised to ensure accountability (Ad Hoc Expert Group, 2020).

The principle of accessibility ensures everyone benefits from AIED and will entail accessibility and catering for various different demographics and cultures (Kazim & Koshiyama, 2021). Inclusiveness encompasses non-discrimination or AI algorithms that are not biased, emphasising that all learners and students are seen as equal irrespective of gender, race, beliefs, sexual orientation, and other conditions or circumstances (Palomares et al., 2021). The principle of human-centred AIED refers to the fact that AIED should enhance: "human cognitive, social, and cultural capabilities while preserving meaningful opportunities for freedom of choice, securing human control over AI-based work processes" (Nguyen et al., 2023, p. 4241).

Human-centric AIED must focus on an interdisciplinary approach in order to develop negotiation-based adaptive learning systems that place a premium on, but are not exclusive to, transversal competencies (European Parliament, 2021). AIED must grant learners the opportunity and the ability to type of support they receive as well as how often this support must be extended which will include some metacognition and self-regulation skills (Chou et al., 2018). Human collaboration must be prioritised to enhance educational practices (Nguyen et al., 2023). This will ensure better control from a learners' and teachers' perspective and offer a collaboration between machines and humans, instead of AI just merely replacing humans and holding everyone hostage (Bryson & Theodorou, 2019).

These principles as highlighted by Nguyen et al. (2023) offer suggestions and a framework for further discussion. Nguyen et al. (2023) suggest that discussion should continue regarding the underlying ethical principles of AIED and that the next stage should be the implementation stage.

A HUMAN RIGHTS APPORACH TO THE USE OF AI IN EDUCATION

The definition of human rights is wide-ranging but everyone can agree that Human rights are at the nucleus of what it means to be a human being (Jones, 2023). In essence it refers to the basic rights and freedoms that belong to every, single person in the world, from the day of their birth until the day they die (Council of Europe, 2023). Education encompasses all human rights and also serves as a multiplier of human rights since it is "enhancing the enjoyment of all individual rights and freedoms where the right to education is effectively guaranteed, while depriving people of the enjoyment of many rights and freedoms where the right to education is denied or violated." (Holmes et al., 2022, p. 10) The United Nations Convention on the Rights of the Child, adopted in November 1989 (United Nations 1990) clearly illustrate these different rights that a child has and it is a comprehensive list, with Article 3 of the Convention specifically undertaking to " ensure the child such protection and care as is necessary for his or her well-being, taking into account the rights and duties of his or her parents, legal guardians, or other individuals legally responsible for him or her, and, to this end, shall take all appropriate legislative and administrative measures " (United Nations Convention on the Rights of the Child 1990, Article 3). These rights cannot be taken away and are protected and regulated by law. They are inalienable, inherent and universal, but can be infringed upon.

Gibbons (2021) refers to the fact that early in the 21st century the UN developed a human rights-based approach (HRBA) with regard to development which clearly established the purpose and process of socio-economic development in human rights law. The latter finds its expression through treaties which codify political, civil, social, economic, and cultural rights, and treaties and in the process protect the rights of specific groups and populations of which children is one. Gibbons (2021) goes on to explain basically every country in the world has ratified "at least one of these treaties into national law; most have ratified several" (Gibbons, 2021, p. 26). This then means that basically all countries have established some legal framework or recourse for human rights. Therefore Gibbons (2021) is of the opinion that this human rights law framework provides a set, settled and universally acclaimable vehicle for establishing regulation and guidelines when it comes to the use of AI in education. It is established, accepted and underwritten globally (Gibbons, 2021).

Jones (2023) postulates that human rights and the framework for human rights law have been "drafted and agreed, with worldwide popular support, to define freedoms and entitlements that would allow every human being to live a life of liberty and dignity" (Jones, 2023, p. 3). Despite this she argues that ample examples of AI governance principles which are touted by companies and governments do not even refer to human rights and of those that do only 15 percent use human rights as a framework (Fjeld et al., 2020; Jones, 2023). Holmes et al. (2022) echo this proposal to use a human rights approach which goes beyond care and ethical guidelines when it comes to the use of AI in education.

Jones (2023) offers various reasons why human rights are not used as an approach to the use of AI in education. These include the following: ethics has all the answers; human rights are too vague and complex; lead to substantial legal expenses, great legal risk and they also stunt innovation (Jones, 2023).

However, Jones dismisses these concerns and offers various reasons why human rights would be an ideal framework for the use of AI in education. Human rights is an established and existing framework which incorporates international, regional and domestic law which gives it immediate international legitimacy and a shared understanding across the globe (Jones, 2023). It has intrinsic merit and international cooperation on a different framework would be extremely difficult to achieve according to Jones (2023).

Jones (2023) argues that human rights are clear and have already been incorporated into international norms, additionally it has been universally agreed upon (think of the right to privacy which is one of the core issues with regard to AIED) and it has shown itself to be adaptable in a variety of circumstances and situations. Jones (2023) argues that by accepting and adopting "well-established and internationally accepted standards in human rights law minimizes the need for fresh debates on highly contested concepts in ethics" (Jones, 2023, p. 28). She also highlights that human rights and human rights law offer clear standards, and this together with external involvement will assist to curb the issue of "ethics-washing". It will enhance accountability and help to mitigate genuine risks (Holmes et al., 2023) The duty of regulatory and administrative authorities entails supervision, and this will form a critical part of accountability when it comes to compliance (Holmes et al., 2023). This will also help to enhance and establish corporate responsibility and compliance, which is currently severely lacking in the regulation of AI (Jones, 2023).

A human rights approach, one that uses human rights and human rights law as a framework and platform seems to be a sensible way in which to approach the use of AI in Computer Science Education. An ethic of care and ethical guidelines are useful but might lack acceptance and be insufficient in certain areas. Human rights and human rights law are well-established and have shown itself to be very versatile and effective in dealing with issues of regulation and the establishment of the freedoms and rights of human beings. Ultimately this is what we are dealing with – the rights of children and adults when dealing with Computer Science Education and the use of AI in this field. We, the stakeholders, the humans, are responsible for ensuring effective but responsible, ethical use of AI in education, with the emphasis on human rights and ensuring, as far as possible, to establish and enforce these rights – be it the right to privacy, equality or the right to fair treatment and absence of unfair discrimination, which seems to be some of the crucial human rights that continuously pop up in discussions regarding the use of AI in education.

SOLUTIONS AND RECOMMENDATIONS

Although it is clear that great strides must still be made when it comes to the use of AI in Education, some authors have provided useful remedies, or guidelines, when it comes to this topic. This chapter does not allow itself to a broad and in-depth discussion of this, however it would be remiss not to refer to some of the most poignant examples.

Privacy, accountability, control over the use of collected data and the curbing of unfair discrimination seem to be some of the major concerns when it comes to the use of AI in Education. To address this Jones (2023) suggest that companies that create and sell these AI systems do due diligence and offer a human rights assessment which clearly places human rights at the centre. Accountability can also be enhanced if at "all stages of design and deployment of AI, it must be clear who bears responsibility for its operation" (Jones, 2021, p. 48). There must be absolute clarity on how responsibilities have been divided between the developer of the AI system, its purchaser and the deployer of the system, and this will include the situation where AI has been used in a different way from which it was intended (Jones, 2023).

Public procurement is an effective way in which human rights standards can be upheld and fostered. It remains the responsibility of governments "to negotiate the terms of public–private contracts and deploy procurement conditions to ensure that AI from private providers is implemented consistently with human right" (Jones, 2023, p. 41). Steps should also be taken to ensure these requirements are adhered to and the establishment of proper grievance mechanism is paramount as well as a clear crystallisation of appropriate remedies in the case of harm that has been done (Jones, 2023).

These are just some of the remedies that can be considered but it is definitely not an exhaustive list. It is vital, however, that clear remedies are provided and implemented to enhance the responsible use of AI in education and to ensure the maintenance and proper and effective application of human rights within this sphere.

IN THE COMPUTER SCIENCE EDUCATION CLASSROOM

How can all of the above translate to the CSE classroom? Awareness might be the first step in the process of offering practical solutions to these issues and concerns in the CSE classroom.

It would be immensely beneficial to include the teaching of ethics and/or a human rights approach to the use of AI in education. By doing this the learners at a young stage are made aware of these pitfalls and can exercise better control over their data. Fundamental human rights issues such as privacy and the issue of discrimination should be highlighted and be part of the curriculum. Show the learners on a practical level that a data footprint is immensely relevant and a reality in our society and that this should be managed in a responsible, ethical manner which incorporates human rights. Let them take ownership of their own data footprint. Make them aware of regulation, legislation and basic legal principles regarding this. Encourage them to question and ascertain the reality of a data footprint and specifically refer to AI in this process. This can be done by including these aspects in the CSE curriculum.

A PRACTICAL EXAMPLE FROM LITERATURE

An article by Petelka et al. (2022) provided some practical and valuable insight into the teaching of ethics in a CSE course at tertiary level. The participants were enrolled for a ten-week undergraduate-level computer security course (Petalka et al., 2022) at the University of Washington. There were 138 students enrolled in the course, which took place in 2020, and most of these students were Computer Science majors. The course was offered online and students met three times per week for an hour lecture, as well as participating in an additional section which was facilitated by the Teaching Assistants (Petalka et al., 2022).

The course aimed to: "(1) to help students in developing a "security mindset", while maintaining a consistent eye towards the social impacts of technology, and (2) to develop fundamental skills in threat modeling and knowledge of modern attacks and defenses in computer security and privacy" (Petalka et al., 2022, p. 476). Activities included practical exercises covering topics such as: cryptography, web security, software security, threat modeling, smart home security, and authentication (Petalka et al.,

2022). Assignments included group and individual assignments, a final project in-class activities (Petalka et al., 2022).

Students were provided with a set of ethical principles which to use as a grounding for their specific responses since the students were not required to undergo an ethics course during their studies and there were fears that they would not be able to apply ethical principles without some guidance. (Petalka et al., 2022)

The results obtained from the research reflected that students, in general did not see themselves as "practitioners of ethics and politics in technical work." (Petalka et al., 2022, p. 477), however when provided with ethical guidelines students were definitely more likely to consider the impacts to marginalized communities especially, but this was because they were specifically prompted to do this (Petalka et al., 2022).

This strengthens the argument that awareness coupled with specific structured guidance will assist in creating a willingness and a realization of the importance of an ethical approach to CSE. This will also help to resist the passivity that is often displayed with regard to the use of technology. Additionally, it will help to establish leaners or students to enhance their importance as stakeholders in this whole process and also become more ethically accountable and more aware of the importance of human rights when dealing with technology. This will be a good start and something substantial to build on in order to reach the objective of an ethical approach grounded in human rights to the use of technology in Compute science Education.

AI ACT EUROPEAN PARLIAMENT

The cooperation between the stakeholders is immensely important. Berendt et al. (2020) rightfully points out that educational institutions are not in the best position to lead this drive for improved regulation, since they are focussed on education and are unable to have a broader impact on aspects such as educational policy and other aspects and disciplines of law that are relevant to this issue. Provincial and national state departments and legislators should take the lead here. Legislation should be put in place in order to enable learners have control over the process of the collection and use of their data. There should also be an opt-out option enabling learners to exercise this option if they are comfortable about it (Berendt et al., 2020). Learners cannot be seen as mere data subjects and they should have autonomy over their own data (Berendt et al., 2020). Learners should be active participants in the "destiny" of their own data (Björklund, 2016). Learning is a "collective and civic activity "(Berendt et al., 2020, p. 321) and limiting the participation and application of learners' choices will undermine this very important pillar of learning. However, this calls for a concerted effort from all stakeholders, with government agencies taking the lead but not leaving behind educational institutions. An example of this is the AI Act by the European Parliament.

In June 2023 it was announced that the use of artificial intelligence in the EU will in future be regulated by the AI Act, which the European Parliament regards as the world's first comprehensive AI law, a bold statement indeed (European Parliament, 2023). The parliament's main aim is to ensure that AI systems that are used in the EU are "safe, transparent, traceable, non-discriminatory and environmentally friendly" (European Parliament, 2023, p. 2). It states emphatically that people must oversee the AI systems, not automation and the aim of this is to prevent harmful outcomes (European Parliament, 2023).

The proposed rules will:

- "address risks specifically created by AI applications;
- propose a list of high-risk applications;
- set clear requirements for AI systems for high risk applications;
- define specific obligations for AI users and providers of high risk applications;
- propose a conformity assessment before the AI system is put into service or placed on the market;
- propose enforcement after such an AI system is placed in the market;
- propose a governance structure at European and national level" (European Commission, 2023, p. 2).

The proposed rules also put forward establishment of obligations for providers and users and these are measured according to the level of risk the AI poses. There are basically three levels: minimal, unacceptable and high risk and the Parliament lists examples of these different types of risks (European Parliament, 2023). The Members of Parliament undertook to negotiate these rules for the use of AI. Thes rules are aimed at promoting increased human-centricity and trustworthiness in the use of AI in order to protect "the health, safety, fundamental rights and democracy from its harmful effects" (European Parliament, 2023, p. 1).

These are commendable, but the European Parliament will have to apply their minds in a consistent and effective manner offering very careful consideration for the human rights of all stakeholders in the field of AI if they want to live up to their claim of offering the world a comprehensive AI Act.

The idea is to strengthen rules around data quality, transparency, human oversight and accountability in sectors ranging as far as economics, healthcare and education are also evident in other jurisdictions (Feingold, 2023). The United States of America (USA) has followed suit, with Senate Majority Leader Chuck Schumer announcing in May 2023 that proposed rules, regulations and institutions to deal with this very critical aspect of AI are imminent (Matthews, 2023).

CONCLUSION

The use of AI in education, which includes computer science education, is here to stay. It cannot and should not be ignored. What should be done is that humans, people, should see to it that the use of AI does not infringe upon the rights of other humans. It is the responsibility of all stakeholders in education to safeguard other against the infringement of basic human rights such as – the right to privacy, right to fair treatment, equality and choice to name a few. The creation of awareness and meaningful exposure to an ethical and/ or human right approach to the use of AI in CSE is paramount in this matter. The introduction of a course involving the ethical approach to the use of AI in CSE will be a good starting point. Sch a course should be compulsory for CSE students. Additionally, and very importantly, the ethical use of AI in education should undergo additional, and meaningful regulation in a manner that enhances human rights, and that places human rights at the centre of the use of AI. The latter is the responsibility of all stakeholders in education, but international governments and organisations should and must take the lead in this, since they are the best positioned to do so.

REFERENCES

Ad Hoc Expert Group. (2020). *Outcome document: First draft of the recommendation on the ethics of artificial intelligence*. United Nations Educational, Scientific and Cultural Organization. https://unesdoc.Unesco.org/ark:/48223/pf0000373434

Andersson, J. (2022 September 30*). Prince William makes online safety plea after Molly Russell verdict*. BBC. https://www.bbc.com/news/uk-63097739

Berendt, B., Littlejohn, A., & Blakemore, M. (2020). AI in education: Learner choice and fundamental rights. *Learning, Media and Technology*, *45*(3), 312–324. doi:10.1080/17439884.2020.1786399

Beyers, R. (2020). *Professional discretion of educators in preventing negligence*. [Unpublished master's dissertation, University of Pretoria, South Africa].

Björklund, F. (2016). E-government and Moral Citizenship: The Case of Estonia. *Citizenship Studies*, *20*(6-7), 914–931. doi:10.1080/13621025.2016.1213222

Bryson, J. J., & Theodorou, A. (2019). How society can maintain human-centric artificial intelligence. In *Human-centered digitalization and services* (pp. 305–323). Springer. https://doi. Org/10.1007/978-981-13-7725-9_16 doi:10.1007/978-981-13-7725-9_16

Cheng, X., Su, L., Luo, X., Benitez, J., & Cai, S. (2022). The Good, the Bad, and the Ugly: Impact of Analytics and Artificial Intelligence-Enabled Personal Information Collection on Privacy and Participation in Ridesharing. *European Journal of Information Systems*, *31*(3), 339–363. doi:10.1080/0960085X.2020.1869508

Chou, C. Y., Lai, K. R., Chao, P. Y., Tseng, S. F., & Liao, T. Y. (2018). A negotiation-based adaptive learning system for regulating help-seeking behaviors. *Computers & Education*, *126*, 115–128. https://doi. Org/10.1016/j.compedu.2018.07.010. doi:10.1016/j.compedu.2018.07.010

Copeland, B. J. (2023). Artificial intelligence In *Britannica Academic*. Britannica. https://www.britannica.com/technology/artificial-intelligence

Council of Europe. (2023) *What are human rights?* Council of Europe. https://www.coe.int/en/web/compass/what-are-human-rights

Crawford, A., & Bell, B. (2022 September 30). *Molly Russell inquest: Father makes social media plea*. BBC. https://www.bbc.com/news/uk-england-london-63073489

Daly, A. L., Baird, J. A., Chamberlain, S., & Meadows, M. (2012). Assessment Reform: Students' and Teachers' Responses to the Introduction of Stretch and Challenge at A-Level. *Curriculum Journal*, *23*(2), 139–155. doi:10.1080/09585176.2012.678683

Dhanrajani, S. (2018). 3 Ways To Human Centric AI. *Forbes*. https://www.forbes.com/sites/cognitiveworld/2018/12/12/3-ways-to-human-centric-ai/?sh=495e42804a38

Digital Curation Centre, The University of Edinburgh. (2020). *The Role of Data in AI: Report for the Data Governance Working Group of the Global Partnership of AI*. Research. https://www.research.ed.ac.uk/en/ publications/the-role-of-data-in-ai

Dignum, V. (2019). *Responsible Artificial Intelligence: How to develop and use AI in a responsible way*. Springer. doi:10.1007/978-3-030-30371-6

Dignum, V. (2021). The role and challenges of education for responsible AI. *London Review of Education, 19*(1), 1–11. doi:10.14324/LRE.19.1.01

Douali, L., Selmaoui, S., & Bouab, W. (2022). Artificial Intelligence in Education: Fears and Faiths. *International Journal of Information and Education Technology (IJIET), 12*(7), 650–657. doi:10.18178/ijiet.2022.12.7.1666

European Parliament. (2023). *EU AI Act: first regulation on artificial intelligence*. EP. https://www.europarl.europa.eu/news/en/headlines/society/20230601STO93804/eu-ai-act-first-regulation-on-artificial-intelligence

European Parliament. (2023) *MEPs ready to negotiate first-ever rules for safe and transparent AI*. EP. https://www.europarl.europa.eu/news/en/press-room/20230609IPR96212/meps-ready-to-negotiate-first-ever-rules-for-safe-and-transparent-ai

Feingold, S. (2023, June 30). *The European Union's Artificial Intelligence Act, explained*. World Economic Forum. https://www.weforum.org/agenda/2023/03/the-european-union-s-ai-act-explained/?DAG=3&gclid=EAIaIQobChMI_LCn09rO_wIVh-7tCh0uKgN-EAAYASAAEgI7-PD_BwE

Fjeld, J. F., Achten, N., Hilligoss, H., Nagy, A., & Srikimar, M. (2020). *Principled Artificial Intelligence: Mapping Consensus in Ethical and Rights-based Approaches to Principles for AI*. Berkman Klein Center Research Publication. https://ssrn.com/abstract=3518482 doi:10.2139/ssrn.3518482

Gibbons, E. D. (2021). Toward a more equal world: The human rights approach to extending the benefits of artificial intelligence. *IEEE Technology and Society Magazine, 40*(1), 25–30. doi:10.1109/MTS.2021.3056295

Gocen, A., & Aydemir, F. (2020). Artificial Intelligence in Education and Schools. *Research on Education and Media, 12*(1), 13–2. doi:10.2478/rem-2020-0003

Greer, S. L. (2018). Organization and governance: Stewardship and governance in health systems. Health Care Systems and Policies. New York, NY: *Health Services Research*. Springer. https://doi.Org/10.1007/978-1-4614-6419-8_22-1

Hendler, J., & Mulvehill, A. M. (2016). *Social Machines: The coming collision of artificial intelligence, social networking, and humanity*. Apress. doi:10.1007/978-1-4842-1156-4

Holmes, W., Bialik, M., & Fadel, C. (2023). *Artificial intelligence in education*. Globethics Publications.

Holmes, W., Persson, J., Chounta, I. A., Wasson, B., & Dimotrova, B. (2022). *Artificial intelligence and education: A critical view through the lens of human rights, democracy and the rule of law*. Council of Europe.

Holmes, W., Porayska-Pomsta, K., Holstein, K., Sutherland, E., Baker, T., Shum, S. B., Santos, O. C., Rodrigo, M. T., Cukurova, M., Bittencourt, I. I., & Koedinger, K. R. (2021). Ethics of AI in education: Towards a community-wide framework. *International Journal of Artificial Intelligence in Education*. doi:10.1007/s40593-021-00239-1

Hwang, G. J., Xie, H., Wah, B. W., & Gašević, D. (2020). Vision, challenges, roles and research issues of Artificial Intelligence in Education. *Computers and Education. Artificial Intelligence*, *1*, 100001. doi:10.1016/j.caeai.2020.100001

Jack, K. (2018, August 20). How AI can spot exam cheats and raise standards. *Financial Times (London)*. https://www.ft.com/content/540e77fa-9fe2-11e8-85daeeb7a9ce36e4

Jobin, A., Ienca, M., & Vayena, E. (2019). Artificial Intelligence: The global landscape of ethics guidelines. *Nature Machine Intelligence*, *1*(9), 389–399. doi:10.1038/s42256-019-0088-2

Joiner, I. A. (2018). *Emerging Library technologies*. Elsevier Ltd.

Kazim, E., & Koshiyama, A. S. (2021). A high-level overview of AI ethics. *Patterns (New York, N.Y.)*, *2*(9), 100314. doi:10.1016/j.patter.2021.100314 PMID:34553166

LeslieD.BurrC.AitkenM.CowlsJ.KatellM.BriggsM. (2021). Artificial intelligence, human rights, democracy, and the rule of law: a primer (April 2, 2021). SSRN: https://ssrn.com/abstract=3817999 or doi:10.2139/ssrn.3817999

Li, X. (2007). Intelligent agent-supported online education. *Decision Sciences Journal of Innovative Education*, *5*(2), 311–331. doi:10.1111/j.1540-4609.2007.00143.x

Limna, P., Jakwatanatham, S., Siripipattanakul, S., Kaewpuang, P., & Sriboonruang, P. (2022). A review of artificial intelligence (AI) in education during the digital era. *Advance Knowledge for Executives*, *1*(1), 1–9.

Marda, V., & Ahmed, S. (2021). *Emotional Entanglement: China's emotion recognition market and its implications for human rights.* Article 19. https://www.article19.org/wp-content/uploads/2021/01/ER-Tech-China-Report.pdf

Matthews, D. (2023, August 1) *The AI rules that US policymakers are considering, explained.* Vox. https://www.vox.com/future-perfect/23775650/ai-regulation-openai-gpt-anthropic-midjourney-stable

Nguyen, A., Ngo, H. N., Hong, Y., Dang, B., & Nguyen, B.-P. T. (2020). Ethical principles for artificial intelligence in education. *Education and Information Technologies*, *28*(4), 4221–4241. doi:10.1007/s10639-022-11316-w PMID:36254344

Owoc, M. L., Sawicka, A., & Weichbroth, P. (2019). Artificial Intelligence Technologies in Education: Benefits, Challenges and Strategies of Implementation. *IFIP International Workshop on Artificial Intelligence for Knowledge Management,* (pp. 37-58). IEEE.

Palomares, I., Martínez-Cámara, E., Montes, R., García-Moral, P., Chiachio, M., Chiachio, J., & Herrera, F. (2021). A panoramic view and swot analysis of artificial intelligence for achieving the sustainable development goals by 2030: Progress and prospects. *Applied Intelligence*, *51*(9), 1–31. https://doi.Org/10.1007/s10489-021-02264-y. doi:10.1007/s10489-021-02264-y PMID:34764606

Petelka, J., Finn, M., Roesner, F., & Shilton, K. (2022, February). Principles matter: integrating an ethics intervention into a computer security course. In *Proceedings of the 53rd ACM Technical Symposium on Computer Science Education-Volume 1* (pp. 474-480). ACM. 10.1145/3478431.3499275

Reiss, M. J. (2021). The use of AI in education: Practicalities and ethical considerations. *London Review of Education, 19*(1), 1–14. doi:10.14324/LRE.19.1.05

Sellgren, K. (2018, July 26). *Exam boards police social media in cheating crackdown*. British Broadcasting Corporation (BBC). https://www.bbc.com/news/education-44965465

Seo, K., Tang, J., Roll, I., Fels, S., & Yoon, D. (2021). The impact of artificial intelligence on learner–instructor interaction in online learning. *International Journal of Educational Technology in Higher Education, 18*(1), 1–23. doi:10.1186/s41239-021-00292-9 PMID:34778540

Sovova, O. (2021). *Right to Education and the Best Interest of a Child in the Constitutional Court Case Law*. The Constitution of the Republic of South Africa. (1996). https://www.gov.za/documents/constitution/constitution-republic-south-africa-1996-1,

Tzimas, D., & Demetriadis, S. (2021). Ethical issues in learning analytics: A review of the field. *Educational Technology Research and Development, 69*(2), 1101–1133. doi:10.1007/s11423-021-09977-4

United Nations. (1990). *Convention on the rights of a child*. UN. https://www.ohchr.org/en/instruments-mechanisms/instruments/convention-rights-

United Nations Educational, Scientific and Cultural Organization. (2019). *Beijing Consensus on artificial intelligence and education. Outcome document of the International Conference on Artificial Intelligence and Education, Planning Education in the AI Era: Lead the Leap, Beijing, 2019*. United Nations Educational, Scientific and Cultural Organization. https://unesdoc.unesco.org/ark:/48223/ pf0000368303

Visser, P. J. (2007). Some Ideas on the 'best interests of the child' principle in the Context of Public Schooling. *Tydskrif vir Hedendaagse Romeins-Holandse Reg*, (70), 459–469.

Watters, A. (2018 December). *The Stories We Were Told about Education Technology*. Blog entry on Hack Education. http://hackeducation.com/2018/12/18/top-ed-tech-trends-stories

West, J. (2017). Data, democracy and school accountability: Controversy over school evaluation in the case of DeVasco High School. *Big Data & Society, 4*(1), 2053951717702408. doi:10.1177/2053951717702408

Compilation of References

Abd Rahman, E., Yunus, M., Hashim, H., & Khadirah, N. (2022). *Learner autonomy between students and teachers at a defense university*. Research Gate.

Abrami, P. C., Bernard, R. M., Bures, E. M., Borokhovski, E., & Tamim, R. M. (2011). Interaction in distance education and online learning: Using evidence and theory toimprove practice. *Journal of Computing in Higher Education*, *23*(2-3), 82–103. doi:10.1007/s12528-011-9043-x

Abtahi, Y. (2018). Pupils, tools and the Zone of Proximal Development. *Research in Mathematics Education*, *20*(1), 1–13. doi:10.1080/14794802.2017.1390691

ACM & Association for Information Systems (AIS). (2020). *A Competency Model for Undergraduate Programs in Information Systems*. Association for Computing Machinery. https://dl.acm.org/doi/pdf/10.1145/3460863

ACM Committee on Professional Ethics. (2018) *Using the Code*. ACM. http://ethics.acm.org/code-of-ethics/using-the-code/

Ad Hoc Expert Group. (2020). *Outcome document: First draft of the recommendation on the ethics of artificial intelligence*. United Nations Educational, Scientific and Cultural Organization. https://unesdoc.Unesco.org/ark:/48223/pf0000373434

Adams, D. A., Nelson, R. R., & Todd, P. A. (2003). Perceived Usefulness, Ease of Use, and Usage of Information Technology: A Replication. *Management Information Systems Quarterly*, *16*(2), 227–250. https://www.jstor.org/stable/249577. doi:10.2307/249577

Adegbenro, J. B., Tumbo, M. T., & Olakanmi, E. E. (2017). In-service secondary school teachers' technology integration needs in an ICT-enhanced classroom. *The Turkish Online Journal of Educational Technology*, *16*(3), 79–87. https://files.eric.ed.gov/fulltext/EJ1152645.pdf

Afari, E., & Khine, M. S. (2017). Robotics as an educational tool: Impact of Lego Mindstorms. *International Journal of Information and Education Technology (IJIET)*, *7*(6), 437–442. doi:10.18178/ijiet.2017.7.6.908

Afrouzeh, M., Konukman, F., Lotfinejad, M., & Afroozeh, M. S. (2020). Effects of knowledge of results feedback on more accurate versus less accurate trials on intrinsic motivation, self-confidence and anxiety in volleyball serve. *Physical Culture and Sport Studies and Research*, *87*(1), 24–33. doi:10.2478/pcssr-2020-0016

Agarwal, P. K. (2019). Retrieval practice & Bloom's taxonomy: Do students need fact knowledge before higher order learning? *Journal of Educational Psychology*, *111*(2), 189–209. https://psycnet.apa.org/doi/10.1037/edu0000282. doi:10.1037/edu0000282

Agenda, D. (2023). *Future of jobs 2023: These are the most in-demand skills now- and beyond.* World Economic Forum. https://www.weforum.org/agenda/2023/05/future-of-jobs-2023-skills/

Ahmed, S., & Kazmi, H. (2020). Teacher Educators' Attitude towards the Pedagogical use of ICTs: A Study. *Journal of Education and Educational Development*, *7*(2), 369–386. doi:10.22555/joeed.v7i2.67

Ajani, O. A. (2023). Challenges mitigating against effective adoption and usage of e-learning in curriculum delivery in South African universities. *International Journal of Innovative Technologies in Social Science*, *2*(38), 1–15. doi:10.31435/rsglobal_ijitss/30062023/8005

Ajani, O. A., & Khoalenyane, N. B. (2023). Using WhatsApp as a tool of learning: A systemic literature review of prospects and challenges. *International Journal of Innovative Technologies in Social Science*, *3*(39). doi:10.31435/rsglobal_ijitss/30092023/8025

Ajani, O. A., & Khumalo, N. P. (2023). Aftermaths of the Post-Covid-19 Pandemic Experiences: Assessing and Repositioning South African Higher Education. *International Journal of Social Science Research and Review*, *6*(6), 674–683.

Ajjawi, R., Tai, J., Huu Nghia, T. L., Boud, D., Johnson, L., & Patrick, C. J. (2020). Aligning assessment with the needs of work-integrated learning: The challenges of authentic assessment in a complex context. *Assessment & Evaluation in Higher Education*, *45*(2), 304–316. doi:10.1080/02602938.2019.1639613

Akar, S. G. M., & Altun, A. (2017). Individual Differences in Learning Computer Programming: A Social Cognitive Approach. *Contemporary Educational Technology*, *8*(3), 195–213.

Akbari, O., & Sahibzada, J. (2020). Students' Self-Condidence and Its Impacts on Their Learning Process. *American International Journal of Social Science Research*, 1-15 .

Akilbekovna, B. (2021). The Usage of ICT in The Classrooms of Primary School. *International Journal On Orange. Technologies*, *3*(3), 291–294. doi:10.31149/ijot.v3i3.1545

Al Abri, M. H., & Dabbagh, N. (2019). Testing the intervention of OER renewable assignments in a college course. *Open Praxis*, *11*(2), 195–209. doi:10.5944/openpraxis.11.2.916

Alam, R., Ansarey, D., Halim, H. A., Rana, M., Milon, K. R., & Mitu, R. K. (2022). Exploring Bangladeshi university studnt's Willingness to communicate (WTC) In English Classes through a qualitative study. *Asian-Pacific Journal of Second and Foreign Language Education*, 1-17 . doi:10.1186/s40862-022-00129-6

Alam, A. (2022). Educational Robotics and Computer Programming in Early Childhood Education: A Conceptual Framework for Assessing Elementary School Students' Computational Thinking for Designing Powerful Educational Scenarios. *1st IEEE International Conference on Smart Technologies and Systems for Next Generation Computing, ICSTSN 2022*, (pp. 1–7). IEEE. 10.1109/ICSTSN53084.2022.9761354

Alam, A. (2022). Social robots in education for long-term human-robot interaction: Socially supportive behaviour of robotic tutor for creating robo-tangible learning environment in a guided discovery learning interaction. *ECS Transactions*, *107*(1), 12389–12403. doi:10.1149/10701.12389ecst

Alamri, H., Lowell, V., Watson, W., & Watson, S. L. (2020). Using personalized learning as an instructional approach to motivate learners in online higher education: Learner self-determination and intrinsic motivation. *Journal of Research on Technology in Education*, *52*(3), 322–352. doi:10.1080/15391523.2020.1728449

Albusays, K., & Ludi, S. (2016). Eliciting programming challenges faced by developers with visual impairments: exploratory study. In *Proceedings of the 9th International Workshop on Cooperative and Human Aspects of Software Engineering* (pp. 82-85). ACM. 10.1145/2897586.2897616

Aleem, M., Qurat-ul-Ain, Q.-A., Shahid, F., Islam, M. A., Iqbal, M. A., & Yousaf, M. M. (2019). A review of technological tools in teaching and learning computer science. *Eurasia Journal of Mathematics, Science and Technology Education, 15*(11). doi:10.29333/ejmste/109611

Alexiou-Ray, J., Raulston, C., Fenton, D., & Johnson, S. (2020). Coding: Coding in the K-12 classroom. In A. Ottenbreit-Leftwich & R. Kimmons (Eds.), *The K-12 educational technology handbook* (pp. 68–77). EdTech Books.

Ali, N., Santos, I. M., AlHakmani, R., Abu Khurma, O., Swe Khine, M., & Kassem, U. (2023). Exploring technology acceptance: Teachers' perspectives on robotics in teaching and learning in the UAE. *Contemporary Educational Technology, 15*(4), ep469. doi:10.30935/cedtech/13646

Almstrum, V. L., Guzdial, M., Hazzan, O., & Petre, M. (2005). Challenges to computer science education research. In *Proceedings of the Thirty-Sixth SIGCSE Technical Symposium on Computer Science Education* (SIGCSE) (pp. 191-192). ACM. 10.1145/1047344.1047415

Al-Sakkaf, A., Omar, M., & Ahmad, M. (2019). A systematic literature review of student engagement in software visualization: A theoretical perspective. *Computer Science Education, 29*(2-3), 283–309. doi:10.1080/08993408.2018.1564611

Alsoliman, B. (2018). The utilization of educational robotics in Saudi Schools: Potentials and Barriers from the perspective of the Saudi Teachers. *International Education Studies, 11*(10), 105–111. doi:10.5539/ies.v11n10p105

Ambrósio, A. P., Costa, F. M., Almeida, L., Franco, A., & Macedo, J. (2011, October 11-15). *Identifying cognitive abilities to improve CS1 outcome.* [Conference session].41st Annual Frontiers in Education Conference: Celebrating 41 Years of Monumental Innovations from Around the World, FIE 201, Rapid City, SD, United States. https://doi.org/10.1109/FIE.2011.6142824

Amoussou, G. A., Boylan, M., & Peckham, J. (2010). Interdisciplinary computing education for the challenges of the future. In *Proceedings of the 41st ACM Technical Symposium on Computer Science Education* (pp. 556-557). ACM. 10.1145/1734263.1734449

AmuthaD. (2020). The Role and Impact of ICT in Improving the Quality of Education. SSRN. doi:10.2139/ssrn.3585228

Ananiadou, K., & Claro, M. (2009). 21st Century Skills and Competences for New Millennium Learners in OECD Countries. In *Organisation for Economic Co-operation and Development (OECD) Education Working Papers, No. 41.* Paris: OECD Publishing. doi:10.1787/19939019

and learning outcomes of programming concepts, practices and pedagogy. *Computers & Education, 151.* doi:10.1016/j.compedu.2020.103872

Anderson, J. R. (1983). *The architecture of cognition.* Harvard University press.

Andersson, J. (2022 September 30*). Prince William makes online safety plea after Molly Russell verdict.* BBC. https://www.bbc.com/news/uk-63097739

Angel-Fernandez, J., & Vincze, M. (2018). Towards a Definition of Educational Robotics. P. Zech, & J. Piater (eds) *Proceedings of the Austrian Robotics Workshop.* Innsbruck Press. 10.15203/3187-22-1

Angeli, C. (2016*). International Forum of Educational Technology & Society A K-6 Computational Thinking Curriculum Framework : Implications for Teacher Knowledge.* International Forum of Educational Technology & Society.

Angeli, C., & Giannakos, M. (2020). Computational thinking education: Issues and challenges. *Computers in Human Behavior, 105*, 106185. doi:10.1016/j.chb.2019.106185

Angeli, C., & Valanides, N. (2020). Developing young children's computational thinking with educational robotics: An interaction effect between gender and scaffolding strategy. *Computers in Human Behavior, 105*, 105954. doi:10.1016/j.chb.2019.03.018

Antonini, S. (2019). Intuitive acceptance of proof by contradiction. *ZDM Mathematics Education, 51*(5), 798–821. doi:10.1007/s11858-019-01066-4

Anwar, S., Bascou, N. A., Menekse, M., & Kardgar, A. (2019). A systematic review of studies on educational robotics. *Journal of Pre-College Engineering Education Research (J-PEER), 9*(2), 2.

Argyropoulos, V., Paveli, A., & Nikolaraizi, M. (2019). The role of DAISY digital talking books in the education of individuals with blindness: A pilot study. *Education and Information Technologies, 24*(1), 693–709. doi:10.1007/s10639-018-9795-2

Ari, F., Arsian-Ari, I., & Vasconcelos, L. (2022). Early childhood preservice teachers' perceptions of computer science, gender stereotypes, and coding in early childhood education. *TechTrends, 66*(3), 539–546. doi:10.1007/s11528-022-00725-w PMID:35499061

Arksey, H., & O'Malley, L. (2005). Scoping studies: Towards a methodological framework. *International Journal of Social Research Methodology, 8*(1), 19–32. doi:10.1080/1364557032000119616

Arlegui, J. (2008). Robotics, Computer Science curricula and Interdisciplinary activities. Workshop Proceedings of SIMPAR, Venice, Italy. https://www.terecop.eu/downloads/simbar2008/arlegui_menegatti_moro_pina_final.pdf

Armoed, Z. (2021). The COVID-19 pandemic: Online teaching and learning at higher education institutes. *IOP Conference Series. Earth and Environmental Science, 654*(1), 012026. doi:10.1088/1755-1315/654/1/012026

Arnett, E. J. (2022, July). Failure Is Always an Option: Lessons from Creating Authentic, Renewable Assignments. In *2022 IEEE International Professional Communication Conference (ProComm)* (pp. 221-227). IEEE. 10.1109/ProComm53155.2022.00046

Artis, A. B., & Harris, E. G. (2007). Self-directed learning and sales force performance: An integrated framework. *Journal of Personal Selling & Sales Management, 27*(1), 9–24. doi:10.2753/PSS0885-3134270101

Ary, D., Jacobs, L. C., Irvine, C. K., & Walker, D. (2013). *Introduction to research in education* (9th ed.). Cengage Learning.

Asarkaya, Ç., & Akaarir, S. (2021). The effect of ethical leadership on intrinsic motivation and employees job satisfaction. *Working Paper Series Dergisi, 2*(1), 14-30.

Ashcraft, C., McLain, B., & Eger, E. (2016). *Women in tech: The facts*. National Center for Women & Technology (NCWIT).

Asmus, E. P. (2021). Motivation in music teaching and learning. *Visions of Research in Music Education, 16*(5), 31.

Association for Computing Machinery & Institute of Electrical and Electronics Engineers - Computer Society (IEEE-CS). (2020). *Computing Curricula 2020: Paradigms for Global Computing Education*. Association for Computing Machinery. doi:10.1145/3467967

Astrachan, O., & Reed, D. (1995, March). AAA and CS 1: the applied apprenticeship approach to CS 1. *In Proceedings of the twenty-sixth SIGCSE technical symposium on Computer science education* (pp. 1-5). ACM. 10.1145/199688.199694

Ates, A. (2021). The Relationship between Parental Involvement in Education and Academic Achievement: A Meta-Analysis Study. *Journal of Education and Instruction, 11*(3), 50–66.

Atkinson, R. K., Derry, S. J., Renkl, A., & Wortham, D. (2000). Learning from examples: Instructional principles from the worked examples research. *Review of Educational Research, 70*(2), 181–214. doi:10.3102/00346543070002181

Avalos, B. (2011). Teacher professional development in Teaching and Teacher Education over ten years. In Teaching and Teacher Education (Vol. 27, Issue 1, pp. 10–20). https://doi.org/ doi:10.1016/j.tate.2010.08.007

Bagnall, R. G., & Hodge, S. (2022). *Epistemologies and ethics in adult education and lifelong learning*. Springer Nature. doi:10.1007/978-3-030-94980-8

Bailey, R., & Breed, B. (2022). Joining forces: Pair problem-solving, flipped classroom and metacognitive self-questioning to enhance self-directed learning. In C. van der Westhuizen, M.C. Maphalala & R. Bailey (Eds.), Blended learning environments to foster self-directed learning, NWU Self-Directed Learning Series (vol. 8, pp. 49–69). Cape Town: AOSIS. https://doi.org/ doi:10.4102/aosis.2022.BK366.03

Bailey, R., & Mentz, E. (2017). The value of pair programming in the IT classroom. *The Independent Journal of Teaching and Learning, 12*(1), 90–103.

Bailey, D., Almusharraf, N., & Hatcher, R. (2021). Finding satisfaction: Intrinsic motivation for synchronous and asynchronous communication in the online language learning context. *Education and Information Technologies*, *26*(3), 2563–2583. doi:10.1007/s10639-020-10369-z PMID:33169066

Balanskat, A., & Engelhardt, K. (2014). *Computing our future: Computer programming and coding – priorities, school curricula and initiatives across Europe*. European Schoolnet. http://www.eun.org/

Bali, M., Cronin, C., & Jhangiani, R. S. (2020). Framing Open Educational Practices from a Social Justice Perspective. *Journal of Interactive Media in Education*, *2020*(1), 10. doi:10.5334/jime.565

Bandura, A. (1997). A sociocognitive analysis of substance abuse: An agentic perspective. *Psychological Science*, *10*(3), 214–217. doi:10.1111/1467-9280.00138

Baran, E., & AlZoubi, D. (2020). Affordances, challenges, and impact of open pedagogy: Examining students' voices. *Distance Education*, *41*(2), 230–244. doi:10.1080/01587919.2020.1757409

Barber, W., & King, S. (2016). Teacher Student Perspectives of Invisible Pedagogy: New Directions in Online Problem Based Learning Environments. *Electronic Journal of e-Learning*, *14*(4), 235–243. https://academic-publishing.org/index.php/ejel/article/view/1759

Barke, S., James, M. B., & Polikarpova, N. (2023). Grounded copilot: How programmers interact with code-generating models. In *Proceedings of the ACM on Programming Languages, 7*(OOPSLA1), (pp. 85-111). Association for Computing Machinery (ACM). 10.1145/3586030

Barnes, L. (2021). Challenges South African youth face in education and their quest to eradicate issues of the past. *Alternate Horizons*, (1). Advance online publication. doi:10.35293/ah.vi.3540

Barreto, F., & Benitti, V. (2012). Exploring the educational potential of robotics in schools: A systematic review. *Computers & Education*, *5*(8), 78–88. https://www.researchgate.net/publication/220140191

Becker, B. A., Denny, P., Finnie-Ansley, J., Luxton-Reilly, A., Prather, J., & Santos, E. A. (2023). Programming Is Hard - Or at Least It Used to Be: Educational Opportunities and Challenges of AI Code Generation. In *Proceedings of the 54th ACM Technical Symposium on Computer Science Education (SIGCSE)* (vol. 1, pp. 500-506). Toronto, ON, Canada: ACM. 10.1145/3545945.3569759

Beck, L., & Chizhik, A. (2013). Cooperative learning instructional methods for CS1: Design, implementation, and evaluation. [TOCE]. *ACM Transactions on Computing Education*, *13*(3), 1–21. doi:10.1145/2492686

Beghetto, R. A. (2018). Taking beautiful risks in education. *Educational Leadership*, 18–24.

Beker, K., Kim, J., Van Boekel, M., van den Broek, P., & Kendeou, P. (2019). Refutation texts enhance spontaneous transfer of knowledge. *Contemporary Educational Psychology*, *56*, 67–78. doi:10.1016/j.cedpsych.2018.11.004

Belle, A. B., & Zhao, Y. (2023). Evidence-based decision-making: On the use of systematicity cases to check the compliance of reviews with reporting guidelines such as PRISMA 2020. *Expert Systems with Applications*, *217*, 119569. doi:10.1016/j.eswa.2023.119569

Bembenutty, H. (2023). Self-regulated learning with computer-based learning environments. *New Directions for Teaching and Learning*, *2023*(174), 11–15. doi:10.1002/tl.20543

Bennedsen, J., & Caspersen, M. E. (2008). Optimists have more fun, but do they learn better? On the influence of emotional and social factors on learning introductory computer science. *Computer Science Education*, *18*(1), 1–16. doi:10.1080/08993400701791133

Berendt, B., Littlejohn, A., & Blakemore, M. (2020). AI in education: Learner choice and fundamental rights. *Learning, Media and Technology*, *45*(3), 312–324. doi:10.1080/17439884.2020.1786399

Berenguel, M., Rodríguez, F., Moreno, J. C., Guzmán, J. L., & González, R. (2016). Tools and methodologies for teaching robotics in computer science & engineering studies. *Computer Applications in Engineering Education*, *24*(2), 202–214. doi:10.1002/cae.21698

Bergamin, P. B., Bosch, C., Du Toit, A., Goede, R., Golightly, A., Johnson, D. W., & van Zyl, S. (2019). *Self-directed learning for the 21st century: Implications for higher education*. AOSIS.

Berry, C. A., Remy, S. L., & Rogers, T. E. (2016). Robotics for All Ages: A Standard Robotics Curriculum for K-16. *IEEE Robotics & Automation Magazine*, *23*(2), 40–46. doi:10.1109/MRA.2016.2534240

Berssanette, J. H., & De Francisco, A. C. (2022). Cognitive load theory in the context of teaching and learning computer programming: A systematic literature review. *IEEE Transactions on Education*, *65*(3), 440–449. doi:10.1109/TE.2021.3127215

Bers, U. M., Ponte, I., Juelich, C., Viera, A., & Schenker, J. (2015). Teachers as designers: Integrating robotics in early childhood education. *Information Technology in Childhood Education Annual*, *3*(4), 23–45. https://core.ac.uk/download/pdf/33556818.pdf

Bertucci, A., Johnson, D. W., Johnson, R. T., & Conte, S. (2016). Effect of task and goal interdependence on achievement, cooperation, and support among elementary school students. *International Journal of Educational Research*, *79*, 97–105. doi:10.1016/j.ijer.2016.06.011

Beyers, R. (2020). *Professional discretion of educators in preventing negligence*. [Unpublished master's dissertation, University of Pretoria, South Africa].

Biderman, S., & Raff, E. (2022, October). Fooling moss detection with pretrained language models. In *Proceedings of the 31st ACM International Conference on Information & Knowledge Management* (pp. 2933-2943). Atlanta, GA: ACM. 10.1145/3511808.3557079

Bindé, J. (2005). *Towards knowledge societies: The United Nations Educational, Scientific and Cultural Organization (UNESCO) world report*. UNESCO. Retrieved from UNESCO reference works series. https://unesdoc.unesco.org/images/0014/001418/141843e.pdf

Binkley, M., Erstad, O., & Herman, J. (2014). Defining twenty-first century skills. In *Assessment and Teaching of 21st Century Skills* (pp. 17–66). Springer Netherlands. doi:10.1007/978-94-007-2324-5_2

Bishop-Clark, C. (1995). Cognitive style, personality, and computer programming. *Computers in Human Behavior, 11*(2), 241–260. doi:10.1016/0747-5632(94)00034-F

Björklund, F. (2016). E-government and Moral Citizenship: The Case of Estonia. *Citizenship Studies, 20*(6-7), 914–931. doi:10.1080/13621025.2016.1213222

Black, T. R. (2006). Helping novice programming students succeed. *Journal of Computing Sciences in Colleges, 22*(2), 109–114.

Blayone, T., van Oostveen, R., Barber, W., DiGiuseppe, M., & Childs, E. (2016). *Developing learning communities in fully online spaces: Positioning the fully online learning community model.* Higher Education in Transformation Symposium, Oshawa, Ontario, Canada. https://arrow.tudublin.ie/cgi/viewcontent.cgi

Blayone, T. J., van Oostveen, R., Barber, W., DiGiuseppe, M., & Childs, E. (2017). Democratizing digital learning: Theorizing the fully online learning community model. *International Journal of Educational Technology in Higher Education, 14*(1), 1–16. doi:10.1186/s41239-017-0051-4

Bocconi, S. (2022) *Reviewing Computational Thinking in Compulsory Education.* EC. https://publications.jrc.ec.europa.eu/repository/handle/JRC128347

Bocconi, S., Chioccariello, A., Dettori, G., Ferrari, A., & Engelhardt, K. (2016). Developing Computational Thinking in Compulsory Education. No. JRC104188). [Seville site]. *Joint Research Centre, 2016*, 1–68. doi:10.2791/792158

Bonk, C. J., & Lee, M. M. (2017). Motivations, achievements, and challenges of self-directed informal learners in open educational environments and MOOCs. *Journal of Learning for Development, 4*(1), 36–57. doi:10.56059/jl4d.v4i1.195

Bonk, C. J., Zhu, M., Kim, M., Xu, S., Sabir, N., & Sari, A. R. (2018). Pushing toward a more personalized MOOC: Exploring instructor selected activities, resources, and technologies for MOOC design and implementation. *International Review of Research in Open and Distance Learning, 19*(4), 92–115. doi:10.19173/irrodl.v19i4.3439

Borah, M. (2021). Motivation in learning. *Journal of Critical Reviews, 8*(2), 550–552.

Bosch, C. (2017). *Promoting self-directed learning through the implementation of cooperative learning in a higher education blended learning environment* [Doctoral dissertation, North-West University (South Africa), Potchefstroom Campus].

Bosch, C., Mentz, E., & Goede, R. (2019). Self-directed learning: A conceptual overview. In E. Mentz, J. De Beer & R. Bailey (Eds.), Self-Directed Learning for the 21st Century: Implications for Higher Education NWU Self-Directed Learning Series (vol. 1, pp. 1–36). Cape Town: AOSIS. https://doi.org/ doi:10.4102/aosis.2019.BK134.01

Bosch, C., Mentz, E., & Reitsma, G. M. (2019). Integrating cooperative learning into the combined blended learning design model: Implications for students' intrinsic motivation. [IJMBL]. *International Journal of Mobile and Blended Learning, 11*(1), 58–73. doi:10.4018/IJMBL.2019010105

Botha, C. (2020, December 2). *New School subjects in South Africa - what does this mean?* Skills Academy. https://www.skillsacademy.co.za/new-school-subjects-in-south-africa-what-does-this-mean/

Bougie, N., & Ichise, R. (2020). Skill-based curiosity for intrinsically motivated reinforcement learning. *Machine Learning, 109*(3), 493–512. doi:10.1007/s10994-019-05845-8

Bovill, C. (2020). Co-creation in learning and teaching: The case for a whole-class approach in higher education. *Higher Education, 79*(6), 1023–1037. doi:10.1007/s10734-019-00453-w

Boyer, S. L., Edmondson, D. R., Artis, A. B., & Fleming, D. (2014). Self-directed learning: A tool for lifelong learning. *Journal of Marketing Education, 36*(1), 20–32. doi:10.1177/0273475313494010

Boz, T., & Allexsaht-Snider, M. (2022). How do elementary school teachers learn coding and robotics? A case study of mediations and conflicts. *Education and Information Technologies*, *27*(3), 3935–3963. doi:10.1007/s10639-021-10736-4

Breed, B., & Bailey, R. (2018). The influence of a metacognitive approach to cooperative pair problem-solving on self-direction in learning. *TD: The Journal for Transdisciplinary Research in Southern Africa*, *14*(1), 1–11. doi:10.4102/td.v14i1.516

Breed, E. A. (2015). Introduction to CAT and IT education. In E. Mentz (Ed.), *Empowering IT and CAT teachers* (pp. 1–18). Sun Press.

Brian, T. (2016). Navigating the Tides of Globalisation and Neoliberalism: A Critical Approach to 21st century Tertiary Education. *New Zealand Journal of Teachers'. Work (Reading, Mass.)*, *13*(2), 134–146.

Brisimis, E., Krommidas, C., Galanis, E., Karamitrou, A., Syrmpas, I., & Zourbanos, N. (2020). Exploring the relationships of autonomy-supportive climate, psychological need satisfaction and thwarting with students' self-talk in physical education. *Journal of Education Society and Behavioural Science*, *2*(3), 112–122. doi:10.9734/jesbs/2020/v33i1130276

Brophy, J. E. (2013). *Motivating students to learn*. Routledge.

Brown, M. H. (2021). *Marxist Forged Through Personal Struggle: Counterstorytelling through Learning Experiences of Becoming Class Conscious*. Research Gate. file:///D:/for%20chapter%203/1-s2.0-S0959475222000536-main.pdf.

Brown, J. S., Collins, A., & Duguid, P. (1989). Situated cognition and the culture of learning. *Educational Researcher*, *18*(1), 32–42. doi:10.2307/1176008

Brown, M., Dehoney, J., & Millichap, N. (2015, April). The next generation digital learning environment. A Report on Research. *Educause*, *5*(1), 1–13.

Bruce, K. B. (2018). Five big open questions in computing education. *ACM Inroads*, *9*(4), 77–80. doi:10.1145/3230697

Brusilovsky, P., Ericson, B. J., Horstmann, C. S., Servin, C., Vahid, F., & Zilles, C. (2023). The Future of Computing Education Materials. *CS2023: ACM/IEEE-CS/AAAI Computer Science Curricula*, ACM. https://csed.acm.org/wp-content/uploads/2023/03/Educational-Materials-First-Draft-1.pdf

Brusilovsky, P., Ericson, B. J., Horstmann, C. S., Servin, C., Vahid, F., & Zilles, C. (2022). Significant Trends in CS Educational Material: Current and Future. In *Proceedings of the 54th ACM Technical Symposium on Computer Science Education (SIGCSE)* (vol. 2, p. 1253). Toronto, ON, Canada: ACM. 10.1145/3545947.3573353

Bryson, J. J., & Theodorou, A. (2019). How society can maintain human-centric artificial intelligence. In *Human-centered digitalization and services* (pp. 305–323). Springer. https://doi. Org/10.1007/978-981-13-7725-9_16 doi:10.1007/978-981-13-7725-9_16

Bubeck, S., Chandrasekaran, V., Eldan, R., Gehrke, J., Horvitz, E., Kamar, E., & Zhang, Y. (2023). Sparks of artificial general intelligence: Early experiments with gpt-4. *arXiv preprint arXiv:2303.12712.*

Bui, T. H. (2022). English teachers' intergration of digital technologies in the classroom. *International Journal of Educational Research Open*, *3*, 1–15. doi:10.1016/j.ijedro.2022.100204

Burbules, N. C., Fan, G., & Repp, P. (2020). Five trends of education and technology in a sustainable future. *Geography and Sustainability*, *1*(2), 93–97. doi:10.1016/j.geosus.2020.05.001

Bureau of Labor Statistics, U.S. Department of Labor. (2023). *Occupational outlook handbook*. BLS. https://www.bls.gov/ooh/about/ooh-faqs.htm

Burgstahler S. (2009). *Universal Design of Instruction (UDI): Definition, Principles, Guidelines, and Examples*. DO-IT. 2009.

Burgstahler, S. E., & Cory, R. C. (2010). Universal Design in Higher Education: From Principles to Practice. Harvard Education Press; 2010.

Burguillo, J. C. (2010). Using game theory and competition-based learning to stimulate student motivation and performance. *Computers & Education*, *55*(2), 566–575. doi:10.1016/j.compedu.2010.02.018

Burke, Q., O'Byrne, W. I., & Kafai, Y. (2016). Computational participation: Understanding coding as an extension of literacy instruction. *Journal of Adolescent & Adult Literacy*, *59*(4), 371–375. doi:10.1002/jaal.496

Bush, W. R., Pincus, J. D., & Sielaff, D. J. (2000). A static analyzer for finding dynamic programming errors. *Software, Practice & Experience*, *30*(7), 775–802. doi:10.1002/(SICI)1097-024X(200006)30:7<775::AID-SPE309>3.0.CO;2-H

Butler, M., & Morgan, M. (2007). Learning challenges faced by novice programming students studying high level and low feedback concepts. *Proceedings ascilite Singapore*, (99-107).

Byrd, W. E., Ballantyne, M., Rosenblatt, G., & Might, M. (2017). A unified approach to solving seven programming problems (functional pearl). *Proceedings of the ACM on Programming Languages, 1(*ICFP), (pp. 1-26). ACM. 10.1145/3110252

Caena, F., & Redecker, C. (2019). Aligning teacher competence frameworks to 21st century challenges: The case for the European Digital Competence Framework for Educators (Digcompedu). *European Journal of Education*, *54*(3), 356–369. doi:10.1111/ejed.12345

Cakiroğlu, Ü., Suiçmez, S. S., Kurtoğlu, Y. B., Sari, A., Yildiz, S., & Öztürk, M. (2018). Exploring perceived cognitive load in learning programming via Scratch. *Research in Learning Technology*, 26.

Calderón, A., Meroño, L., & MacPhail, A. (2020). A student-centred digital technology approach: The relationship between intrinsic motivation, learning climate and academic achievement of physical education pre-service teachers. *European Physical Education Review*, *26*(1), 241–262. doi:10.1177/1356336X19850852

Camilleri, P. (2017). Minding the gap. proposing a teacher learning-training framework for the integration of robotics in primary schools. *Informatics in Education*, *16*(2), 165–179. doi:10.15388/infedu.2017.09

Camp, T., Frieze, C., Lewis, C., Cannon Mindell, E., Limbird, L., Richardson, D., Sahami, M., Villa, E., Walker, H., & Zweben, S. (2018). *Retention in computer science undergraduate programs in the U.S.: Data challenges and promising interventions*. ACM.

Cañas AJ, Hill G, & Carff R. (2004). *CmapTools: A knowledge modeling and sharing environment.*

Candy, P. C. (2004). *Linking thinking: Self-directed learning in the digital age*. Department of Education, Science and Training.

Canfora, G., Cimitile, A., Garcia, F., Piattini, M., & Visaggio, C. A. (2007). Evaluating performances of pair designing in industry. *Journal of Systems and Software*, *80*(8), 1317–1327. doi:10.1016/j.jss.2006.11.004

Cansu, S. K., & Cansu, F. K. (2019). An overview of computational thinking. *International Journal of Computer eScience Education in School, 3*(1), 17-30. doi:10.21585/ijcses.v3i1.53

Canty, D., Barth, J., Yang, Y., Peters, N., Palmer, A., Royse, A., & Royse, C. (2019). Comparison of learning outcomes for teaching focused cardiac ultrasound to physicians: A supervised human model course versus an eLearning guided self- directed simulator course. *Journal of Critical Care*, *49*, 38–44. doi:10.1016/j.jcrc.2018.10.006 PMID:30359924

Carbone, A., & Kaasboll, J. (1998). A survey of methods used to evaluate computer science teaching. *6th Annual Conference on the teaching of computing and the 3rd Annual Conference on intergrating technology with computer science education: Changing the delivery of computer science education*, (pp. 41–45). ACM. 10.1145/282991.283014

Carey, S., & Clarke, L. (2019) A brief history of robotics timeline of key achievements in the field of science. *Tech advisor*. https://www.techadvisor.com/feature/small-business/brief-history-of-robotics-timeline-of-key-achievements-in-field-since-1941-3788761/

Caspersen, M. E., & Bennedsen, J. (2007, September). Instructional design of a programming course: a learning theoretic approach. *In Proceedings of the third international workshop on Computing education research* (pp. 111-122). ACM. 10.1145/1288580.1288595

Caspersen, M. E., Gal-Ezer, J., McGettrick, A., & Nardelli, E. (2018).. . *Informatics for All The Strategy., 2018*. doi:10.1145/3185594

Castillo-Montoya, M., & Ives, J. (2021). Instructor's conceptions of Minoritized College Students' Prior Knowledge and their related Teaching Practice. *The Journal of Higher Education*, *92*(5), 735–759. doi:10.1080/00221546.2020.1870850

Catrambone, R. (1998). The subgoal learning model: Creating better examples so that students can solve novel problems. *Journal of Experimental Psychology. General*, *127*(4), 355–376. doi:10.1037/0096-3445.127.4.355

Cavaye, J. (2004). Governance and Community Engagement: The Australia experience. Participatory governance: Planning, conflict mediation and public decision making in civil society, (pp. 85–102). IEEE.

Cejka, E., Rogers, C., & Portsmore, M. (2012). Kindergarten robotics: Using robotics to motivate math, science, and engineering literacy in elementary school. *International Journal of Engineering Education*, *22*(4), 711–722. https://www.researchgate.net/publication/233616845

Chaldi, D., & Mantzanidou, G. (2021). Educational robotics and STEAM in early childhood education. *Advances in Mobile Learning Educational Research*, *1*(2), 72–81. doi:10.25082/AMLER.2021.02.003

Chalmers, C. (2018). Robotics and computational thinking in primary school. *International Journal of Child-Computer Interaction*, *17*, 93–100. doi:10.1016/j.ijcci.2018.06.005

Chambers, J. M., & Carbonaro, M. (2018). Designing, developing, and implementing a course on LEGO robotics for technology teacher education. *Journal of Technology and Teacher Education*, *11*(2), 25–29. https://www.ijiet.org/vol7/908-T108.pdf

Chandler, P., & Sweller, J. (1996). Cognitive load while learning to use a computer program. *Applied Cognitive Psychology*, *10*(2), 151–170. doi:10.1002/(SICI)1099-0720(199604)10:2<151::AID-ACP380>3.0.CO;2-U

Chang, K. E., Chiao, B. C., Chen, S. W., & Hsiao, R. S. (2000). A programming learning system for beginners-a completion strategy approach. *IEEE Transactions on Education*, *43*(2), 211–220. doi:10.1109/13.848075

Chang, Y.-H., & Peterson, L. (2018). Pre-service teachers' perceptions of computational thinking. *Journal of Technology and Teacher Education*, *26*(3), 353–374.

Chau, P. Y. (2009). Examining a Model of Information Technology Acceptance by educators. *Journal of Management Information Systems*, *18*(4), 192–220. doi:10.1080/07421222.2002.11045699

Chen, M., Tworek, J., Jun, H., Yuan, Q., Pinto, H. P. D. O., Kaplan, J., & Zaremba, W. (2021). Evaluating large language models trained on code. *arXiv preprint arXiv:2107.03374*.

Cheng, E. C. (2021). Knowledge transfer strategies and practices for higher education institutions. *VINE Journal of Information and Knowledge Management Systems*, *51*(2), 288–301. doi:10.1108/VJIKMS-11-2019-0184

Cheng, X., Su, L., Luo, X., Benitez, J., & Cai, S. (2022). The Good, the Bad, and the Ugly: Impact of Analytics and Artificial Intelligence-Enabled Personal Information Collection on Privacy and Participation in Ridesharing. *European Journal of Information Systems*, *31*(3), 339–363. doi:10.1080/0960085X.2020.1869508

Chiazzese, G., Arrigo, Chifari, Lonati, & Tosto. (2019). Educational robotics in primary school: Measuring the development of computational thinking skills with the bebras tasks. *Informatics (MDPI)*, *6*(4), 43. Advance online publication. doi:10.3390/informatics6040043

Chicaiza, J., Piedra, N., Lopez-Vargas, J., & Tovar-Caro, E. (2014). Domain categorization of open educational resources based on linked data. In *5th International Conference on Knowledge Engineering and the Semantic Web* (pp. 15-28). Springer International Publishing. 10.1007/978-3-319-11716-4_2

Chiles, M. (2013, August 8). The state of IT education in South African schools. IITPSA. https://www.iitpsa.org.za/the-state-of-it-education-in-south-african-schools/

Chi, M. T., Bassok, M., Lewis, M. W., Reimann, P., & Glaser, R. (1989). Self-explanations: How students study and use examples in learning to solve problems. *Cognitive Science*, *13*(2), 145–182.

Chi, M. T., Feltovich, P. J., & Glaser, R. (1981). Categorization and representation of physics problems by experts and novices. *Cognitive Science*, *5*(2), 121–152. doi:10.1207/s15516709cog0502_2

Chisango, G., & Marongwe, N. (2018). The impact of inadequate information and communication technologies on teaching and learning of pre-service teachers at a rural university in South Africa. *Journal of Communication*, *9*(2), 1–10. 11.258359/KRE-31

Chiu, T. (2021). Applying the self-determination theory (SDT) to explain student engagement in online learning during the COVID-19 pandemic. *Journal of Research on Technology in Education*, 54 (sup1), S14-S30. . doi:10.1080/15391523.2021.1891998

Choi, H. S., Crump, C., Duriez, C., Elmquist, A., Hager, G., Han, D., Hearl, F., Hodgins, J., Jain, A., Leve, F., Li, C., Meier, F., Negrut, D., Righetti, L., Rodriguez, A., Tan, J., & Trinkle, J. (2021). On the use of simulation in robotics: Opportunities, challenges, and suggestions formoving forward. *Proceedings of the National Academy of Sciences of the United States of America*, *118*(1), 1–9. doi:10.1073/pnas.1907856118 PMID:33323524

Chou, C. Y., Lai, K. R., Chao, P. Y., Tseng, S. F., & Liao, T. Y. (2018). A negotiation-based adaptive learning system for regulating help-seeking behaviors. *Computers & Education*, *126*, 115–128. https://doi. Org/10.1016/j.compedu.2018.07.010. doi:10.1016/j.compedu.2018.07.010

Chou, P.-N. (2020). Using ScratchJr to foster young children's computational thinking competence: A case study in a third-grade computer class. *Journal of Educational Computing Research*, *58*(3), 570–595. doi:10.1177/0735633119872908

Chukwunemerem, O. P. (2023). Lessons from Self-Directed Learning Activities and Students Think Critically. *Journal of Education*, 80–87. doi:10.5539/jel.v12n2p79

Churcher, K. M., Downs, E., & Tewksbury, D. (2014). "Friending" Vygotsky: A social constructivist pedagogy of knowledge building through classroom social media use. *The Journal of Effective Teaching*, *14*(1), 33–50.

Cigdem, H., & Öztürk, M. (2016). Critical components of online learning readiness and their relationships with learner achievement. *Turkish Online Journal of Distance Education*, *20*(10). doi:10.17718/tojde.09105

Clear, A. (2019) Computing Curricula 2020: Introduction and Community Engagement. *Proceedings of the 50th ACM Technical Symposium on Computer Science Education (SIGCSE '19). Association for Computing Machinery*, (pp. 653–654). ACM. 10.1145/3287324.3287517

Clifford, D., & Petrescu, C. (2012). The keys to university-community engagement sustainability. *Nonprofit Management & Leadership*, *23*(1), 77–91. doi:10.1002/nml.21051

Cockburn, A., & Williams, L. (2001). The costs and benefits of pair programming. In G. Succi & M. Marchesi (Eds.), *Extreme programming examined* (pp. 223–243). Pearson Education.

Code.org. CSTA, & ECEP Alliance. (2022). *2022 State of computer science education: Understanding our national imperative*. https://advocacy.code.org/stateofcs

Collins, A., Brown, J. S., & Newman, S. E. (1989). Cognitive apprenticeship: Teaching the crafts of reading, writing, and mathematics. In L. B. Resnick (Ed.), Knowing, learning, and instruction: essays in honor of Robert Glaser (pp. 453–494). Lawrence Erlbaum Associates, Publishers.

Collins, A. (2006). Cognitive apprenticeship. In K. R. Sawyer (Ed.), *The Cambridge handbook of the learning sciences* (pp. 47–60). Cambridge University Press.

Collins, A., Brown, J. S., & Holum, A. (1991). Cognitive apprenticeship: Making thinking visible. *American Educator*, *15*(3), 6–11.

computational thinking and scratch at distance. *Computers in Human Behaviors, 80*, 470-477. doi:10.1016/j.chb.2017.09.025

Computing Research Association. (2017). *Generation CS: Computer Science Undergraduate Enrollments Surge Since 2006*. CRA. https://cra.org/data/Generation-CS/

Condie, R., & Livingston, K. (2007). Blending online learning with traditional approaches: Changing practices. *British Journal of Educational Technology*, *38*(2), 337–348. doi:10.1111/j.1467-8535.2006.00630.x

Conole, G., & Oliver, M. (2006). *Contemporary perspectives in e-learning research: themes, methods and impact on practice*. Routledge. doi:10.4324/9780203966266

Conradie, P. W. (2014). Supporting self-directed learning by connectivism and personal learning environments. *International Journal of Information and Education Technology (IJIET)*, *4*(3), 254–259. doi:10.7763/IJIET.2014.V4.408

Copeland, B. J. (2023). Artificial intelligence In *Britannica Academic*. Britannica. https://www.britannica.com/technology/artificial-intelligence

Corradini, I., & Nardelli, E. (2021). Promoting digital awareness at school: A three-year investigation in primary and secondary school teachers. *Proceedings of EDULEARN21 Conference, 5, 6th*. Iated. 10.21125/edulearn.2021.2162

Correll, N., Wing, R. & Coleman, D. (2013). A one-year introductory robotics curriculum for computer science upperclassmen. *IEEE Transactions on Education*, *56*(1), 54–60. . doi:10.1109/TE.2012.2220774

Cortinovis, R., Mikroyannidis, A., Domingue, J., Mulholland, P., & Farrow, R. (2019). Supporting the discoverability of open educational resources. *Education and Information Technologies, 24*(5), 3129–3161. Springer Science and Business Media. . doi:10.1007/s10639-019-09921-3

Council of Europe. (2023) *What are human rights?* Council of Europe. https://www.coe.int/en/web/compass/what-are-human-rights

Crawford, A., & Bell, B. (2022 September 30). *Molly Russell inquest: Father makes social media plea*. BBC. https://www.bbc.com/news/uk-england-london-63073489

Creswell, J. W. (2008). *Educational research: planning, conducting and evaluating quantitative and qualitative research* (3rd ed.). Pearson/Merrill Prentice Hall.

Creswell, J. W. (2014). *Educational research: Planning, conducting, and evaluating quantitative and qualitative research* (4th ed.). Pearson.

Creswell, J. W. (2017). *Qualitative inquiry & research design: choosing among the five approaches*. Sage Publications, Inc.

Creswell, J. W., & Poth, C. N. (2007). *Qualitative inquiry and research design: choosing among five approaches*. SAGE.

Crick, T. (2022). Cwricwlwm i Gymru 2022: A New Era for Computer Science in Schools in Wales?' *ACM International Conference Proceeding Series*. ACM. 10.1145/3555009.3555024

Crick, T., & Sentance, S. (2011, November). Computing at school: stimulating computing education in the UK. In *Proceedings of the 11th Koli Calling International Conference on Computing Education Research* (pp. 122-123). ACM. 10.1145/2094131.2094158

Cron, W. L., Marshall, G. W., Singh, J., Spiro, R. L., & Sujan, H. (2005). Salesperson selection, training, and development: Trends, implications, and research opportunities. *Journal of Personal Selling & Sales Management*, *25*(2), 123–136.

Csapó, G. (2019). Placing event-action-based visual programming in the process of computer science education. *Acta Polytechnica Hungarica*, *16*(2), 35–57. doi:10.12700/APH.16.2.2019.2.3

Csizmadia, A., Curzon, P., Dorling, M., Humphreys, S., Ng, T., Selby, C., & Woollard, J. (2015). *Computational thinking-A guide for teachers.*

CSTA. (2016). *K-12 Computer Science Framework*. Computer Science Teachers Association. https://K12cs.org/downloads/

CSTA. (2020). *Computer Science Teachers Association. Standards for Computer Science Teachers*. CSTA. https://csteachers.org/teacherstandards

Curto, B., & Moreno, V. (2016). Robotics in education. *Journal of Intelligent & Robotic Systems*, *81*(1), 3–4. doi:10.1007/s10846-015-0314-z

Cutts, Q., Patitsas, E., & Cole, E. (2017). Early developmental activities and computing proficiency. In: *ITiCSE-WGR 2017 - Proceedings of the 2017 ITiCSE Conference on Working Group Reports. Vol 2018-January*. Association for Computing Machinery. 10.1145/3174781.3174789

Da Silva Estácio, B. J., & Prikladnicki, R. (2015). Distributed pair programming: A systematic literature review. *Information and Software Technology*, *63*, 1–10. doi:10.1016/j.infsof.2015.02.011

Dakhel, A. M., Majdinasab, V., Nikanjam, A., Khomh, F., Desmarais, M. C., & Jiang, Z. M. (2023). Github copilot AI pair programmer: Asset or liability? *Journal of Systems and Software*, *203*, 111734. doi:10.1016/j.jss.2023.111734

Daly, A. L., Baird, J. A., Chamberlain, S., & Meadows, M. (2012). Assessment Reform: Students' and Teachers' Responses to the Introduction of Stretch and Challenge at A-Level. *Curriculum Journal*, *23*(2), 139–155. doi:10.1080/09585176.2012.678683

Danahy, E., Wang, E., Brockman, J., Carberry, A., Shapiro, B., & Rogers, C. B. (2014). LEGO-based Robotics in Higher Education: 15 Years of Student Creativity. *International Journal of Advanced Robotic Systems*, *11*(2), 27. doi:10.5772/58249

Davis, F. D. (1989). Acceptance of Information Technology. *Management Information Systems Quarterly*, *13*(3), 319–340. doi:10.2307/249008

De Beer, J. (2016). Re-imagining science education in South Africa: The affordances of indigenous knowledge for self-directed learning in the school curriculum. *Journal for New Generation Sciences*, *14*(3), 34–53.

De Beer, J. (2019). Glocalisation: The role of indigenous knowledge in the global village. In J. De Beer (Ed.), *The decolonisation of the curriculum project: The affordances of indigenous knowledge for self-directed learning* (pp. 1–24). AOSIS. doi:10.4102/aosis.2019.BK133.01

De Walle, J. A. V., Folk, S., Karp, K. S., & Bay-Williams, J. M. (2011). *Elementary and middle school mathematics: Teaching developmentally*. Pearson Canada Inc.

Dede, C. (2010). Comparing frameworks for 21st century skills. *21st century skills: Rethinking how students learn, 20*, 51-76.

Deek, F., Kimmel, H., & McHugh, J. A. (1998). Pedagogical changes in the delivery of the first-course in computer science: Problem solving, then programming. *Journal of Engineering Education*, *87*(3), 313–320. doi:10.1002/j.2168-9830.1998.tb00359.x

Deitrick, E., & Stowell, J. (2019). *Survey of Computer Science teaching: challenges and resources in U.S. colleges and Universities. 2019*. Codio INC. www.codio.com/research/2019-computer-science-teaching-survey

Deliwe, A. (2020). The use of a learner management system (moodle) in promoting teaching and learning. *Universal Journal of Educational Research*, *8*(12B), 8383–8392. doi:10.13189/ujer.2020.082644

Demertzi, E., Voukelatos, N., Papagerasimou, Y., & Drigas, A. (2018). Online learning facilities to support coding and robotics courses for youth. *International Journal of Engineering Pedagogy*, *8*(3), 69–80. Advance online publication. doi:10.3991/ijep.v8i3.8044

Denis, B., & Hubert, S. (2016). Collaborative learning in an educational robotics environment. *Computers in Human Behavior*, *17*(5-6), 465–480. doi:10.1016/S0747-5632(01)00018-8

Dennen, V. P., & Burner, K. J. (2008). The cognitive apprenticeship model in educational practice. In *Handbook of research on educational communications and technology* (pp. 425–439). Routledge.

Denner, J., Green, E., & Campe, S. (2021). Learning to program in middle school: How pair programming helps and hinders intrepid exploration. *Journal of the Learning Sciences*, *30*(4-5), 611–645. doi:10.1080/10508406.2021.1939028

Denning, P. J. (2017). Remaining trouble spots with computational thinking. *Communications of the ACM*, *60*(6), 33–39. doi:10.1145/2998438

Denny, P., Sarsa, S., Hellas, A., & Leinonen, J. (2022). Robosourcing Educational Resources—Leveraging Large Language Models for Learnersourcing. *arXiv preprint arXiv:2211.04715.*

Denny, P., Kumar, V., & Giacaman, N. (2023). Conversing with Copilot: Exploring Prompt Engineering for Solving CS1 Problems Using Natural Language. In *Proceedings of the 54th ACM Technical Symposium on Computer Science Education (SIGCSE 2023)* (Vol. 1, pp. 1136-1142). Association for Computing Machinery. 10.1145/3545945.3569823

Denzin, N. K., & Lincoln, Y. S. (2005). *Handbook of qualitative research*. Sage.

Department of Basic Education. (2021a). *Coding and Robotics Pilot Project Awareness and Advocacy Roadshows underway*. DBE. https://www.education.gov.za/CodingandRoboticsPilotProject.aspx

Department of Basic Education. (2021a). *DBE and partners workshop Coding and Robotics Curriculum for the GET Band*. DBE. https://www.education.gov.za/CodingCurriculum010419.aspx

Department of Basic Education. (2021b). *DBE and partners workshop Coding and Robotics Curriculum for the GET Band.* DBE. https://www.education.gov.za/CodingCurriculum010419.aspx

Department of Basic Education. (2021b). Draft Curriculum and assessment Policy Statement Grades 7-9 Coding and Robotics. DBE. https://www.education.gov.za/LinkClick.aspx?fileticket=dp2IJGuK0Lw%3D&tabid=2689&portalid=0&mid=9573

Department of Basic Education. (2023). *Proposed amendments to the Curriculum and Assessment Policy Statement (CAPS) to make provision for coding and robotics Grades R-9*. DBE. https://www.education.gov.za/

Department of Science and Technology. (2015). Science Engagement Strategy. *Science and society engaging to enrich and improve our lives, 2015*(1), 1–46. https://www.saasta.ac.za/saasta_wp/wp-content/uploads/2017/11/Science_Engagement_Strategy-11.pdf

Department of Science and Technology. (2019). *White paper on Science, Technology and Innovation*. DST. https://www.dst.gov.za/images/2019/White_paper_web_copyv1.pdf

design-based learning approach to enhance elementary students' self-perceived computational thinking. *Journal of Research on Technology in Education, 55*(2), 344-368. doi:10.1080/15391523.2021.1962453

Deus, W., Fioravanti, M., Oliveira, C., & Barbosa, E. (2020). Emergency Remote Computer Science Education in Brazil during the COVID-19 pandemic: Impacts and Strategies. *Revista Brasileira de Informática na Educação, 28*, 1032–1059. doi:10.5753/rbie.2020.28.0.1032

Dewi, P. Y., & Primayana, K. H. (2019). Effect of learning module with setting contextual teaching and learning to increase the understanding of concepts. *International Journal on E-Learning, 1*(1), 19–26. doi:10.31763/ijele.v1i1.26

Dhanrajani, S. (2018). 3 Ways To Human Centric AI. *Forbes*. https://www.forbes.com/sites/ cognitiveworld/2018/12/12/3-ways-to-human-centric-ai/?sh=495e42804a38

Dichev, C., & Dicheva, D. (2017). Gamifying education: What is known, what is believed and what remains uncertain: A critical review. *International Journal of Educational Technology in Higher Education, 14*(9), 1–36. doi:10.1186/s41239-017-0042-5

Digital Curation Centre, The University of Edinburgh. (2020). *The Role of Data in AI: Report for the Data Governance Working Group of the Global Partnership of AI*. Research. https://www.research.ed.ac.uk/en/ publications/the-role-of-data-in-ai

Dignum, V. (2019). *Responsible Artificial Intelligence: How to develop and use AI in a responsible way*. Springer. doi:10.1007/978-3-030-30371-6

Dignum, V. (2021). The role and challenges of education for responsible AI. *London Review of Education, 19*(1), 1–11. doi:10.14324/LRE.19.1.01

Dillion, A. (1996). User Acceptance of Information Technology Theories and models. *Annual Review of Information Science & Technology, 3*(12), 9–21. https://www.researchgate.net/publication/277983543

Ding, M., Li, X., Piccolo, D., & Kulm, G. (2010). Teacher interventions in cooperative-learning. *The Journal of Educational Research, 100*(3), 37–41.

DiSalvo, B., Reid, C., & Roshan, P. K. (2014). They can't find us: the search for informal CS education. *Proceedings of the 45th ACM Technical Symposium on Computer Science Education,* (pp. 487–492). ACM. 10.1145/2538862.2538933

Dlab, M., Boticki, I., Hoic-Bozic, N., & CL-C&, E. (2020). *Exploring group interactions in synchronous mobile computer-supported learning activities*. Elsevier. https://www.sciencedirect.com/science/article/pii/S036013151930288X

Dlamini, R., & Mbatha, K. (2018). The discourse on ICT teacher professional development needs: The case of a South African teachers' union. *International Journal of Education and Development using ICT, 14*(2).

Dlamini, R., & Mbatha, K. (2018). The discource on ICT teacher professional development need: The case of a South African teacher's Union. *International Journal of Education and Development Using Information and Communication Technology*, 17–37. https://files.eric.ed.gov/fulltext/EJ1190045.pdf

Dlamini, R., & Ndzinisa, N. (2020). Universities trailing behind: Unquestioned epistemological foundations constraining the transition to online instructional delivery and learning. *South African Journal of Higher Education, 34*(6), 52–64. doi:10.20853/34-6-4073

Do-IT. (2017). *DO-IT Retrospective Our First 25 Years*. University of Washington.

Dombestein, H., Norheim, A., & Husebø, A. (2019). Understanding informal caregivers' motivation from the perspective of self-determination theory: An integrative review. *Scandinavian Journal of Caring Sciences, 34*(2), 267–279. doi:10.1111/scs.12735 PMID:31313852

Doo, M. Y., Zhu, M., & Bonk, C. J. (2023). Influence of self-directed learning on learning outcomes in MOOCs: A meta-analysis. *Distance Education, 44*(1), 86–105. doi:10.1080/01587919.2022.2155618

dos Santos, P., & dos Santos, T. (2021). Analysis of a didactic sequence using educational robotics to teach graphs in kinematics. *Physics Education, 56*(1), 015015. https://iopscience.iop.org/article/10.1088/1361-6552/abc8fb/meta. doi:10.1088/1361-6552/abc8fb

Douali, L., Selmaoui, S., & Bouab, W. (2022). Artificial Intelligence in Education: Fears and Faiths. *International Journal of Information and Education Technology (IJIET), 12*(7), 650–657. doi:10.18178/ijiet.2022.12.7.1666

Downes, S. (2019). A look at the future of open educational resources. *The International Journal of Open Educational Resources, 1*(2). doi:10.18278/ijoer.1.2.4

Dreyfus, H. L., & Dreyfus, S. E. (1986). *Mind over machine: the power of human intuition and expertise in the era of the computer*. Free Press.

Driscoll, M. P. (2014). *Psychology of Learning for Instruction*. Pearson.

Du Plessis, P., & Mestry, R. (2019). Teachers for rural schools – a challenge for South Africa. *South African Journal of Education, 39*(S). doi:10.15700/saje.v39ns1a1774

Du Toit, A. (2019). Constructive congruencies in self-directed learning and entrepreneurship education, In E. Mentz, J. De Beer & R. Bailey (Eds.), Self-Directed Learning for the 21st Century: Implications for Higher Education (vol. 1, pp. 313-340). Cape Town: AOSIS. doi:10.4102/aosis.2019.BK134.10

du Toit-Brits, C. (2019). A focus on self-directed learning: The role that educators' expectations play in the enhancement of students' self-directedness. *South African Journal of Education, 39*(2), 1–11. doi:10.15700/saje.v39n2a1645

Duschl, R. A. (2020). On computational thinking and STEM education. *Journal for STEM Education Research, 3*(2), 147–166. doi:10.1007/s41979-020-00044-w

Dwilestari, S., Zamzam, A., Susanti, N. W. M., & Syahrial, E. (2021). The students'self-directed learning in english foreign language classes during the covid-19 pandemic. *Jurnal Lisdaya, 17*(2), 38–46. doi:10.29303/lisdaya.v17i2.42

Edmondson, D. R., Boyer, S. L., & Artis, A. B. (2012). Self-directed learning: A meta-analytic review of adult learning constructs. *International Journal of Education and Research*, *7*(1), 40–48.

Eguchi, A. (2014). Educational robotics for promoting 21 century skills. *Journal of Automation. Mobile Robotics & Intelligent Systems*, *8*(1). doi:10.14313/JAMRIS_1-2014/1

Eguchi, A. (2016). RoboCupJunior for promoting STEM education, 21st century skills, and technological advancement through robotics competition. *Robotics and Autonomous Systems*, *75*, 692–699. doi:10.1016/j.robot.2015.05.013

Ehsan, N., Vida, S., & Mehdi, N. (2019). The impact of cooperative learning on developing speaking ability and motivation toward learning English. *Journal of language and education, 5*(3 (19)), 83-101.

El-Hamamsy, L., Chessel-Lazzarotto, F., Bruno, B., Roy, D., Cahlikova, T., Chevalier, M., Parriaux, G., Pellet, J.-P., Lanarès, J., Zufferey, J. D., & Mondada, F. (2021). A computer science and robotics integration model for primary school: Evaluation of a large-scale in-service K-4 teacher-training program, Education and Information Technologies. *Education and Information Technologies*, *26*(3), 2445–2475. doi:10.1007/s10639-020-10355-5 PMID:33162777

Ellis, H. J. C., Hislop, G. W., Jackson, S., & Postner, L. (2015). Team project experiences in humanitarian free and open source software (HFOSS). *ACM Trans Comput Educ.*, *15*(4), 1–23. doi:10.1145/2684812

Emurian, H. H. (2007). Programmed instruction for teaching Java: Consideration of learn unit frequency and rule-test performance. *The Behavior Analyst Today*, *8*(1), 70–88. doi:10.1037/h0100103

Emurian, H. H., Holden, H. K., & Abarbanel, R. A. (2008). Managing programmed instruction and collaborative peer tutoring in the classroom: Applications in teaching Java™. *Computers in Human Behavior*, *24*(2), 576–614. doi:10.1016/j.chb.2007.02.007

Emurian, H. H., Hu, X., Wang, J., & Durham, A. G. (2000). Learning JAVA: A programmed instruction approach using applets. *Computers in Human Behavior*, *16*(4), 395–422. doi:10.1016/S0747-5632(00)00019-4

Emurian, H. H., Wang, J., & Durham, A. G. (2003). Analysis of learner performance on a tutoring system for Java. In *Current issues in IT education* (pp. 46–76). IGI Global. doi:10.4018/978-1-93177-753-7.ch005

Erdal, B., Mehmet, B., & Bulent, D. (2021). The reason for gaining and losing the popularity of paradigm in constructivism: Why? and How? *Psycho-* [doi:https://www.journals.lapub.co.uk/index.php/PERR]. *Educational Research Review*, 8–24.

Erdem, C. (2019). Introduction to 21st Century Skills and Education. In 21st century skills and education (pp. 1-20). Cambridge Scholars Publishing.

Erwin, B., Cyr, M., & Rogers, C. (2013). LEGO engineer and RoboLab: Teaching engineering with LabVIEW from kindergarten to graduate school. *International Journal of Engineering Education*, *16*(3), 181–192.

Esposito, J. (2017). The State of Robotics Education: Proposed Goals for Positively Transforming Robotics Education at Postsecondary Institutions. *IEEE Robotics & Automation Magazine*, *24*(3), 157–164. https://ieeexplore.ieee.org/abstract/document/7970162. doi:10.1109/MRA.2016.2636375

Esteve-Mon, F. M. (2019). The development of computational thinking in student teachers through an intervention with educational robotics. *Journal of Information Technology Education: Innovations in Practice*, *18*, 139–152. doi:10.28945/4442

Estisari, K., Wengrum, T., & Nurhantanto, A. (2023). Economic Students' perceptions towards learning management system (LMS). *JAE*, *3*(1). doi:10.33365/jae.v3i1.198

European Parliament. (2023) *MEPs ready to negotiate first-ever rules for safe and transparent AI.* EP. https://www.europarl.europa.eu/news/en/press-room/20230609IPR96212/meps-ready-to-negotiate-first-ever-rules-for-safe-and-transparent-ai

European Parliament. (2023). *EU AI Act: first regulation on artificial intelligence*. EP. https://www.europarl.europa.eu/news/en/headlines/society/20230601STO93804/eu-ai-act-first-regulation-on-artificial-intelligence

Eylon, B., & Reif, F. (1984). Effects of knowledge organization on task performance. *Cognition and Instruction*, *1*(1), 5–44. doi:10.1207/s1532690xci0101_2

Fabic, G. V. F., Mitrovic, A., & Neshatian, K. (2018). Investigating the effects of learning activities in a mobile Python tutor for targeting multiple coding skills. *Research and Practice in Technology Enhanced Learning*, *13*(1), 23. doi:10.1186/s41039-018-0092-x PMID:30613261

Fabriz, S., Mendzheritskaya, J., & Stehle, S. (2021). Impact of synchronous and asynchronous settings of online teaching and learning in higher education on students' learning experience during COVID-19. *Frontiers in Psychology*, *12*, 733554. doi:10.3389/fpsyg.2021.733554 PMID:34707542

Fagin, B., & Merkle, L. (2003). Measuring the effectiveness of robots in teaching computer science. SIGCSE Bulletin (Association for Computing Machinery, Special Interest Group on Computer Science Education), (pp. 307–311). ACM. doi:10.1145/611892.611994

Fagin, B. S., Merkle, L. D., & Eggers, T. W. (2001). Teaching computer science with robotics using Ada/Mindstorms 2.0. *ACM SIGAda Ada Letters*, *XXI*(4), 73–78. doi:10.1145/507546.507592

Falkner, K., & Sheard, J. (2019). Pedagogic Approaches. The Cambridge handbook of computing education research, 445. Cambridge. doi:10.1017/9781108654555.016

Falkner, K., Sentance, S., Vivian, R., Barksdale, S., Busuttil, L., Cole, E., Liebe, C., Maiorana, F., McGill, M. M., & Quille, K. (2019b). An International Study Piloting the MEasuring TeacheR Enacted Computing Curriculum (METRECC) Instrument. *Proceedings of the Working Group Reports on Innovation and Technology in Computer Science Education*, *2019*, 111–142. doi:10.1145/3344429.3372505

Fangfang, L. (2022). Ideas and Cases of Ideological and Political Construction in Computer Science Courses. *Adult and Higher Education*, *61-64*. doi:10.23977/aduhe.2022.041211

Fares, K., Fowler, B., & Vegas, E. (2021). *How South Africa implemented its computer science education program.* Center for Universal Education at Brookings.

Farjon, D., Smits, A., & Voogt, J. (2019). Technology integration of pre-service teachers explained by attitudes and beliefs, competency, access, and experience. *Computers & Education*, *130*, 81–93. doi:10.1016/j.compedu.2018.11.010

Farrell, C. (2020). Do international marketing simulations provide an authentic assessment of learning? A student perspective. *International Journal of Management Education*, *18*(1), 100362. doi:10.1016/j.ijme.2020.100362

Feingold, S. (2023, June 30). *The European Union's Artificial Intelligence Act, explained.* World Economic Forum. https://www.weforum.org/agenda/2023/03/the-european-union-s-ai-act-explained/?DAG=3&gclid=EAIaIQobChMI_LCn09rO_wIVh-7tCh0uKgN-EAAYASAAEgI7-PD_BwE

Felder, R. M., & Brent, R. (2007). Cooperative learning. In P. A. Mabrouk (Ed.), *Active learning: Models from the analytical sciences, 970* (pp. 34–53). American Chemical Association. doi:10.1021/bk-2007-0970.ch004

Felder, R. M., & Prince, M. J. (2006). Inductive teaching and learning methods: Definitions,comparisons, and research bases. *Journal of Engineering Education*, *95*(2), 123–138. doi:10.1002/j.2168-9830.2006.tb00884.x

Feng, Z., Guo, D., Tang, D., Duan, N., Feng, X., Gong, M., & Zhou, M. (2020, November). CodeBERT: A Pre-Trained Model for Programming and Natural Languages. In *Findings of the Association for Computational Linguistics* (pp. 1536–1547). EMNLP. doi:10.18653/v1/2020.findings-emnlp.139

Ferri, F., Grifoni, P., & Guzzo, T. (2020). Online learning and emergency remote teaching: Opportunities and challenges in emergency situations. *Societies (Basel, Switzerland)*, *10*(4), 86. doi:10.3390/soc10040086

Fester, M. O. (2022). *The Experiences of In-Service Teachers in Short Online Courses Aimed at Developing Online Teaching Skills*. University of Johannesburg.

Field, K. (2018). A Third of Your Freshmen Disappear. How Can You Keep Them? *The Chronicle of Higher Education*, *64*(35), A8–A13.

Fincher, S. A., & Robins, A. V. (Eds.). (2019). *The Cambridge handbook of computing education research*. Cambridge University Press. doi:10.1017/9781108654555

Finnie-Ansley, J., Denny, P., Becker, B. A., Luxton-Reilly, A., & Prather, J. (2022). The Robots Are Coming: Exploring the Implications of OpenAI Codex on Introductory Programming. In *Proceedings of the 24th Australasian Computing Education Conference (ACE '22)*. Association for Computing Machinery. 10.1145/3511861.3511863

Finnie-Ansley, J., Denny, P., Luxton-Reilly, A., Santos, E. A., Prather, J., & Becker, B. A. (2023). My AI Wants to Know if This Will Be on the Exam: Testing OpenAI's Codex on CS2 Programming Exercises. In *Proceedings of the 25th Australasian Computing Education Conference (ACE '23)*. Association for Computing Machinery. 10.1145/3576123.3576134

Fjeld, J. F., Achten, N., Hilligoss, H., Nagy, A., & Srikimar, M. (2020). *Principled Artificial Intelligence: Mapping Consensus in Ethical and Rights-based Approaches to Principles for AI.* Berkman Klein Center Research Publication. https://ssrn.com/abstract=3518482 doi:10.2139/ssrn.3518482

Fletcher, C. L., & Warner, J. R. (2021). CAPE: A Framework for Assessing Equity throughout the Computer Science Education Ecosystem. *Communications of the ACM*, *64*(2), 23–25. doi:10.1145/3442373

Flórez, F. B., Casallas, R., Hernández, M., Reyes, A., Restrepo, S., & Danies, G. (2017). Changing a generation's way of thinking: Teaching computational thinking through programming. *Review of Educational Research*, *87*(4), 834–860. doi:10.3102/0034654317710096

Flor, N. V. (2006). Globally distributed software development and pair programming. *Communications of the ACM*, *49*(10), 57–58. doi:10.1145/1164394.1164421

Foss, A., & Rasmus, J. (2019). The academic and behavioural implications of robotics in the classroom: An elementary case study. *Technology and Innovation*, *20*(3), 321–332. doi:10.21300/20.3.2019.321

Foster, J., & Connolly, R. (2017). Digital Media for STEM Learning: Developing scientific practice skills in the K-12 STEM classroom with resources from WGBH and PBS LearningMedia. In: *AGU Fall Meeting Abstracts*.

Franke, B., & Osborne, B. (2015). Decoding CS principles: A curriculum from Code. org. In *Proceedings of the 46th ACM Technical Symposium on Computer Science Education (ACM);* (pp. 713-713). ACM. 10.1145/2676723.2678309

Frishkoff, G. A., White, G., & Perfetti, C. A. (2009). In vivo testing of learning and instructional principles: The design and implementation of school-based experimentation. In L. M. Dinella (Ed.), *Conducting science-based psychology research in schools* (pp. 153–173). American Psychological Association. doi:10.1037/11881-007

Fry, H. (2018). *Hello world: How to be human in the age of the machine*. Random House.

Fulya Eyupoglu, T., & Nietfeld, J. L. (2019). Intrinsic motivation in game-based learning environments. *Game-based assessment revisited*, 85-102.

Gal-Ezer, J., & Stephenson, C. (2014). A tale of two countries: Successes and challenges in K-12 computer science education in Israel and the United States. *ACM Trans Comput Educ.*, *14*(2), 1–18. doi:10.1145/2602483

Gandomkar, R., & Sandars, J. (2018). Clearing the confusion about self-directed learning and self-regulated learning. *Medical Teacher*, *40*(8), 862–863. doi:10.1080/0142159X.2018.1425382 PMID:29327634

Garcia, R. S. (2021). Influence of self-directed learning skills on the academic adjustment in an online learning platform among level I and II student nurse. *International Journal of Recent Advances in Multidisciplinary Research*, *8*(6), 6925–6929.

Garcia, R., Falkner, K., & Vivian, R. (2018). Systematic literature review: Self-Regulated Learning strategies using e-learning tools for Computer Science. *Computers & Education*, *123*, 150–163. doi:10.1016/j.compedu.2018.05.006

Garner, S. (2002). Reducing the cognitive load on novice programmers (pp. 578-583). Association for the Advancement of Computing in Education (AACE).

Gasparetti, F., De Medio, C., Limongelli, C., Sciarrone, F., & Temperini, M. (2018). Prerequisites between learning objects: Automatic extraction based on a machine learning approach. *Telematics and Informatics*, *35*(3), 595–610. doi:10.1016/j.tele.2017.05.007

Gatewood, E. (2019). Use of simulation to increase self-directed learning for nurse practitioner students. *The Journal of Nursing Education*, *58*(2), 102–106. doi:10.3928/01484834-20190122-07 PMID:30721310

Geldenhuys, C. J., & Fataar, A. (2021). Foundation Phase teachers' experiences of teaching the subject, coding, in selected Western Cape schools. *South African Journal of Education*, *41*(4), 1959. doi:10.15700/saje.v41n4a1959

Geng, S., Law, K. M., & Niu, B. (2019). Investigating self-directed learning and technology readiness in blending learning environment. *International Journal of Educational Technology in Higher Education*, *16*(1), 1–22. doi:10.1186/s41239-019-0147-0

Gerdes, A., Jeuring, J. T., & Heeren, B. J. (2010). Using strategies for assessment of programming exercises. *In Proceedings of the 41st ACM technical symposium on Computer science education* (pp. 441-445). ACM. 10.1145/1734263.1734412

Ghazal, S., Aldowah, H., & Umar, I. (2018). Satisfaction of learning management system usage in a blended learning environment among undergraduate students. *The Turkish Online Journal of Design Art and Communication*, *8*(Sept), 1147–1156. doi:10.7456/1080SSE/156

Giannandrea, L., Gratani, F., & Renieri, A. (2020). Crossing boundaries: Documentation of a teacher training course on design, robotics and coding. *Research on Education and Media*, *12*(1), 85–92. doi:10.2478/rem-2020-0010

Gibbons, E. D. (2021). Toward a more equal world: The human rights approach to extending the benefits of artificial intelligence. *IEEE Technology and Society Magazine*, *40*(1), 25–30. doi:10.1109/MTS.2021.3056295

Gicevic, S., Aftosmes-Tobio, A., Manganello, J., Ganter, C., Simon, C., Newlan, S., & Davison, K. (2016). Parenting and childhood obesity research: A quantitative content analysis of published research 2009–2015. *Obesity Reviews*, *17*(8), 724–734. doi:10.1111/obr.12416 PMID:27125603

Gillies, R. M. (2014). Cooperative learning: Developments in research. *International Journal of Educational Psychology*, *3*(2), 125–140. doi:10.4471/ijep.2014.08

Giordano, D., & Maiorana, F. (2013a). Teaching database: a pedagogical and curriculum perspective. In *Proceedings of the International Conference on Information and Communication Technology for Education, (ICTE),* (pp. 237-248). IEEE.

Giordano, D., & Maiorana, F. (2013c). An interdisciplinary project in sustainable development based on modern visual programming environments and web 2.0 technologies. In: *2013 3rd Interdisciplinary Engineering Design Education Conference*. IEEE.

Giordano, D., & Maiorana, F. (2013b). Business Process Modeling and Implementation A 3-Year Teaching Experience. In *Proceedings of the 5th International Conference on Computer Supported Education (CSEDU-2013),* (pp. 429-436). IEEE.

Giulia, C. (2021). Hope and reponsibility: Embracing different types of knowledge whilst generating my own living-educational-theory. *Educational Action Research*, 1–16. doi:10.1080/09650792.2021.1880458

Gleason, N. W. (2018). *Higher Education in the Era of the Fourth Industrial Revolution.* Palgrave Macmillan. doi:10.1007/978-981-13-0194-0

Gluckman, H., Pontes, C., & Scheyer, E. (2021). An overview of COVID-19 infection in dental practices - a questionnaire survey. *SADJ; Journal of the South African Dental Association*, *76*(07), 404–408. doi:10.17159/2519-0105/2021/v76no7a2

Gocen, A., & Aydemir, F. (2020). Artificial Intelligence in Education and Schools. *Research on Education and Media*, *12*(1), 13–2. doi:10.2478/rem-2020-0003

Goldman, R., Eguchi, A., & Sklar, E. (2012). *Using Educational Robotics to engage inner-city students with technology.* Embracing Diversity in the Learning Sciences.

Goldweber, M., Kaczmarczyk, L., & Blumenthal, R. (2019). Computing for the social good in education. *ACM Inroads*, *10*(4), 24–29. doi:10.1145/3368206

Gorrah, A. R. (2022). *Teachers' perception of gender stereotypes with the teaching of coding and robotics in primary schools* [MEd dissertation, University of Johannesburg].

Gotterbarn, D. W., Brinkman, B., Flick, C., Kirkpatrick, M. S., Miller, K., Vazansky, K., & Wolf, M. J. (2018). ACM code of ethics and professional conduct.(2018). ACM. Https://Www. Acm. Org/Code-of-Ethics

Goudini, R., Ashrafpoornavaee, S., & Farsi, A. (2019). The effects of self-controlled and instructor-controlled feedback on motor learning and intrinsic motivation among novice adolescent taekwondo players. *Acta Gymnica*, *49*(1), 33–39. doi:10.5507/ag.2019.002

GousetiA.BruniI.IlomäkiL.LakkalaM.MundyD.RaffaghelliJ.RanieriM.RoffiA.RomeroM.RomeuT. (2021). Critical Digital Literacies framework for educators - DETECT project Report 1. Developing Teachers' Critical Digital Literacies (DETECT) project, Erasmus+, KA2, European Union. Zenodo. doi:10.5281/zenodo.5070329

Gouws, P., & Mentz, J. (2021). Towards a comprehensive conceptual framework for Robotics Education. Proceeedings of EdMedia and Innovate Learning. Association for the Advancement of Computing in Education (AACE).

GouwsP. (2021). Towards Defining the Place and Role of Robotics MOOCs in OdeL. UnisaRxiv. https://www.scienceopen.com/hosted-document?doi=10.25159/UnisaRxiv/000017.v1 doi:10.25159/UnisaRxiv/000017.v1

Government of the Republic of Namibia (GRN). (2004). *Namibia Vision 2030: Policy framework for long-term national development.* Windhoek: Office of the President. https://www.npc.gov.na/wp-content/uploads/2021/11/Vision_2030_Summary.pdf

Graffin, M., Sheffield, R., & Koul, R. (2022). '"More than Robots": Reviewing the Impact of the FIRST® LEGO® League Challenge Robotics Competition on School Students' STEM Attitudes, Learning, and Twenty-First Century Skill Development', *Journal for STEM Education Research. Journal for STEM Education Research*, *5*(3), 322–343. doi:10.1007/s41979-022-00078-2

Graf, S., Lachance, P., & Mishra, B. (2016). Integrating Motivational Techniques into Learning Management Systems. In *State-of-the-Art and Future Directions of Smart Learning* (pp. 173–184). Springer Singapore. doi:10.1007/978-981-287-868-7_20

Greeno, J. G., Collins, A. M., & Resnick, L. B. (1996). Cognition and learning. Handbook of educational psychology, 77, 15-46.

Greer, S. L. (2018). Organization and governance: Stewardship and governance in health systems. Health Care Systems and Policies. New York, NY: *Health Services Research*. Springer. https://doi. Org/10.1007/978-1-4614-6419-8_22-1

Greyling, J. (2023). Coding Unplugged—A Guide to Introducing Coding and Robotics to South African Schools. *Transforming Entrepreneurship Education, 155.*

Grubbs, M. (2013). Robotics intrigue middle school students and build STEM skills. *Technology and Engineering Teacher, 72*(6), 12-16. https://eric.ed.gov/?id=EJ1006898

Guglielmino, L. M. (1977). *Development of the self-directed learning readiness scale*. University of Georgia.

Guilford, J. P. (1967). Creativity: Yesterday, Today and Tomorrow. *The Journal of Creative Behavior*, *1*(1), 3–14. doi:10.1002/j.2162-6057.1967.tb00002.x

Guillén M, Fontrodona J, Rodríguez-Sedano A. (2007). *The Great Forgotten Issue: Vindicating Ethics in the European Qualifications Framework (EQF).* Springer. doi:10.1007/s10551-007-9515-0

Guillén-Gámez, F. D., Mayorga-Fernández, M. J., Bravo-Agapito, J., & Escribano-Ortiz, D. (2021). Analysis of teachers' pedagogical digital competence: Identification of factors predicting their acquisition. *Technology. Knowledge and Learning*, *26*(3), 481–498. doi:10.1007/s10758-019-09432-7

Gunal, M. M. (2019). Simulation and the fourth industrial revolution. In *Simulation for Industry 4.0: Past, Present, and Future* (pp. 1–17). Springer International Publishing. doi:10.1007/978-3-030-04137-3_1

Gunarathne, W. K. T. M., Chootong, C., Sommool, W., Ochirbat, A., Chen, Y.-C., Reisman, S., & Shih, T. K. (2018). Web-Based learning object search engine solution together with data visualization: The case of MERLOT II. *IEEE 42nd Annual Computer Software and Applications Conference*. IEEE. 10.1109/COMPSAC.2018.00179

Guo, Y., & Wu, S. (2017). Creating the learning situation to promote student deep learning: Data analysis and application case. In AIP Conference Proceedings. American Institute of Physics. doi:10.1063/1.4982529

Gurcan, F., & Cagiltay, N. E. (2019). Big data software engineering: Analysis of knowledge domains and skill sets using LDA-based topic modeling. *IEEE Access : Practical Innovations, Open Solutions*, *7*, 82541–82552. doi:10.1109/ACCESS.2019.2924075

Gustafsson, M. (2014, April 14). *ICTs in our schools.* Department of Basic Education. https://www.education.gov.za/Portals/0/Documents/Reports/Research%20Repository/LTSM/ICT%20in%20our%20schools.pdf?ver=2019-09-09-102226-387

Guzdial, M. (2015). Learner-centered design of computing education: Research on computing for everyone. *Synthesis Lectures on Human-Centered Informatics*, *8*(6), 1–165. doi:10.1007/978-3-031-02216-6

Guzdial, M. (2020). Sizing the U.S. student cohort for computer science. *Communications of the ACM*, *63*(2), 10–11. doi:10.1145/3374764

Gyamfi, N. K., Dayie, R., & Asiedu, E. K. (2022). Application of Artificial Intelligence Techniques in Educational Delivery; Ghana Perspective. *Webology, 19*(1).

Hall, M. (2010). Community Engagement in South African Higher Education. *Kagisano. CHE Pretoria*, (6).

Hamidi, T. K. (2016). Information technology in education. *Procedia Computer Science*, *2*(3), 110–123. doi:10.1016/j.procs.2010.12.062

Hanks, B., McDowell, C., Draper, D., & Krnjajic, M. (2004, June). Program quality with pair programming in CS1. *In Proceedings of the 9th annual SIGCSE conference on Innovation and technology in computer science education* (pp. 176-180). ACM. 10.1145/1007996.1008043

Hanover Research. (2011) *Best Practices in Measuring University-Community Engagement.* Hanover Research. https://intranet.ecu.edu.au/__data/assets/pdf_file/0006/208689/Measuring-University-Community-Engagement-Edith-Cowan-University.pdf

Hargreaves, A. (2003). *Teaching in the knowledge society: Education in the age of insecurity.* Teachers College Press.

Harry, T., & Chinyamurindi, W. (2021). "still haven't found what I am looking for": Rural black students' perceived work readiness and assessment of labour market access. *Education + Training*, *64*(2), 276–289. doi:10.1108/ET-10-2021-0387

Hass, D., Hass, A., & Joseph, M. (2023). Emergency online learning & the digital divide: An exploratory study of the effects of covid-19 on minority students. *Marketing Education Review*, *33*(1), 22–37. doi:10.1080/10528008.2022.2136498

Havenga, M., & Mentz, E. (2009, June). The school subject information technology: a South African perspective. In *Proceedings of the 2009 Annual Conference of the Southern African Computer Lecturers' Association* (pp. 76-80). ACM. 10.1145/1562741.1562750

Hbaci, I., & Abdunabi, R. (2020). Evaluating higher education educators' computer technology competencies in Libya. *Journal of Computing in Higher Education*, 1–18. doi:10.1007/s12528-020-09261-z

Head, G. (2018). Ethics in educational research: Review boards, ethical issues and researcher development. *European Educational Research Journal*. doi:10.1177/1474904118796315

Heath, T. (2010). The impact of a cooperative learning training program on teacher perceptions aboutc ooperative learning [Doctoral thesis, NWU]. http://search.proquest.com.nwulib.nwu.ac.za/pqdtft/advanced

Hebda, M. (2023). Technology talent development: Beyond an hour of code. *Gifted Child Today*, *46*(2), 108–118. doi:10.1177/10762175221149256

Heilmann, S. (2018). A Scaffolding Approach Using Interviews and Narrative Inquiry. *Online Journal for teacher research*, 2470-6353 https://newprairiepress.org/networks/vol20/iss2/3/

Heitzmann, N., Richters, C., Radkowitsch, A., Schmidmaier, R., Weidenbusch, M., & Fischer, M. (2021). Learners' adjustment strategies following impassesses in simulations-effects of prior knowledge. *Learning and istructions*, 1-11 . doi:10.1016/j.learninstruc.2022.101632

Helbach, J., Hoffmann, F., Pieper, D., & Allers, K. (2023). Reporting according to the preferred reporting items for systematic reviews and meta-analyses for abstracts (PRISMA-A) depends on the abstract length. *Journal of Clinical Epidemiology*, *154*, 167–177. doi:10.1016/j.jclinepi.2022.12.019 PMID:36584734

Hendler, J., & Mulvehill, A. M. (2016). *Social Machines: The coming collision of artificial intelligence, social networking, and humanity.* Apress. doi:10.1007/978-1-4842-1156-4

Hennink, M., & Hutter, I. (2011). *Qualitative research methods.* Sage.

Herman, C. (2022). *From South Africa to Ghana and Tanzania, computer science unlocks the future for youth.* Code.org.

Herro, D., Quigley, C., Plank, H., & Abimbade, O. (2021). Understanding students' social interactions during making activities designed to promote computational thinking. *The Journal of Educational Research*, *114*(2), 183–195. doi:10.1080/00220671.2021.1884824

Hertz, M. (2010). What do 'CS1' and 'CS2' mean? Investigating differences in the early courses. *Proceedings of the 41st ACM technical symposium on Computer science education*, (pp. 199-203). ACM. /10.1145/1734263.1734335

Hestness, E., Ketelhut, D. J., McGinnis, J. R., & Plane, J. (2018). Professional knowledge building within an elementary teacher professional development experience on computational thinking in science education. *Journal of Technology and Teacher Education*, *26*(3), 411–435.

Hew, K. F., Lan, M., Tang, Y., Jia, C., & Lo, C. K. (2019). Where is the "theory" within the field of educational technology research? *British Journal of Educational Technology*, *50*(3), 956–971. doi:10.1111/bjet.12770

Hew, K., & Brush, T. (2007). Integrating technology into K-12 teaching and learning: Current knowledge gaps and recommendations for future research. *Educational Technology Research and Development*, *55*(3), 223–252. doi:10.1007/s11423-006-9022-5

Heyns, J. (2023). *Development of a framework of factors essential to the optimal implementation of the Coding and Robotics subject in South African schools* [Doctoral dissertation, Stellenbosch University].

Hill, R. B., Kim, C. M., & Yuan, J. (2019). Robotics and coding in primary grades. *Communications in Computer and Information Science*, *993*, 458–467. doi:10.1007/978-3-030-20954-4_34

Hmelo-Silver, C. E. (2004). Problem-based learning: What and how do students learn? *Educational Psychology Review*, *16*(3), 235–266. doi:10.1023/B:EDPR.0000034022.16470.f3

Holmes, K., & Fray, L. (2018). Student and staff perceptions of a learning management system for blended learning in teacher education. *The Australian Journal of Teacher Education*, *43*(3), 21–34. doi:10.14221/ajte.2018v43n3.2

Holmes, W., Bialik, M., & Fadel, C. (2023). *Artificial intelligence in education*. Globethics Publications.

Holmes, W., Persson, J., Chounta, I. A., Wasson, B., & Dimotrova, B. (2022). *Artificial intelligence and education: A critical view through the lens of human rights, democracy and the rule of law*. Council of Europe.

Holmes, W., Porayska-Pomsta, K., Holstein, K., Sutherland, E., Baker, T., Shum, S. B., Santos, O. C., Rodrigo, M. T., Cukurova, M., Bittencourt, I. I., & Koedinger, K. R. (2021). Ethics of AI in education: Towards a community-wide framework. *International Journal of Artificial Intelligence in Education*. doi:10.1007/s40593-021-00239-1

Hongshuai, Y. (2021). Research on the Application of Industrial Robots in Automation Control. *Curriculum and Teaching Methodology*, *4*(4), 132-138. https://openarchive.nure.ua/bitstream/document/19396/1/SotLyash1.pdf

Hopcroft, J. E. (1986). The impact of robotics on computer science. *Communications of the ACM*, *29*(6), 486–498. doi:10.1145/5948.5949

Hoppe, H. U., & Werneburg, S. (2019). Computational thinking—More than a variant of scientific inquiry. Computational Thinking Education, 13–30.

Hosseini, H., Hartt, M., & Mostafapour, M. (2019). Learning is child's play: Game-based learning in computer science education. [TOCE]. *ACM Transactions on Computing Education*, *19*(3), 1–18. doi:10.1145/3282844

Howells, K. (2018). *The Future of Education and Skills: Education 2030: The Future We Want*. Create Canterbury. http://create.canterbury.ac.uk/17331/1/E2030 Position Paper (05.04.2018).pdf

Huang, R., Liu, D., Tlili, A., Knyazeva, S., Chang, T. W., Zhang, X., & Holotescu, C. (2020). *Guidance on open educational practices during school closures: Utilizing OER under COVID-19 pandemic in line with UNESCO OER recommendation*. Smart Learning Institute of Beijing Normal University.

Huang, W., & Looi, C.-K. (2021). A critical review of literature eon "unplugged" pedagogies in K-12 computer science and computational thinking education. *Computer Science Education, 31*(1), 83–111. doi:10.1080/08993408.2020.1789411

Hubbard, A. (2018). Pedagogical content knowledge in computing education: A review of the research literature. *Computer Science Education, 28*(2), 117–135. doi:10.1080/08993408.2018.1509580

Hulkko, H., & Abrahamsson, P. (2005, May). A multiple case study on the impact of pair programming on product quality. *In Proceedings of the 27th international conference on Software engineering* (pp. 495-504). ACM.

Hwang, G. J., Xie, H., Wah, B. W., & Gašević, D. (2020). Vision, challenges, roles and research issues of Artificial Intelligence in Education. *Computers and Education. Artificial Intelligence, 1*, 100001. doi:10.1016/j.caeai.2020.100001

Ibe, N. A., Howsmon, R., Penney, L., Granor, N., De Lyser, L. A., & Wang, K. (2018). Reflections of a diversity, equity, and inclusion working group based on data from a national CS education program. In: *SIGCSE 2018 - Proceedings of the 49th ACM Technical Symposium on Computer Science Education. Vol 2018-Janua.* Association for Computing Machinery, Inc. 10.1145/3159450.3159594

Ismail, M. N., Ngah, N. A., & Umar, I. N. (2010). Instructional strategy in the teaching of computer programming: A need assessment analyses. *The Turkish Online Journal of Educational Technology, 9*(2).

Ivanova, T. (2019). Resources and Semantic-based knowledge models for personalized and self-regulated learning in the Web. *Proceedings of the 20th International Conference on Computer Systems and Technologies.* ACM. 10.1145/3345252.3345288

Jack, K. (2018, August 20). How AI can spot exam cheats and raise standards. *Financial Times (London).* https://www.ft.com/content/540e77fa-9fe2-11e8-85daeeb7a9ce36e4

Jainal, N. H., & Shahrill, M. (2021). Incorporating Jigsaw strategy to support students'' learning through action research. [IJonSES]. *International Journal on Social and Education Sciences, 3*(2), 252–266. doi:10.46328/ijonses.75

Jaipal-Jamani, K., & Angeli, C. (2017). Effect of robotics on elementary pre-service teachers' self-efficacy, science learning, and computational thinking. *Journal of Science Education and Technology, 26*(2), 175–192. doi:10.1007/s10956-016-9663-z

Jantjies, M. (2019, June 18). Five things South Africa must get right for tech in schools to work. *The Conversation.* https://theconversation.com/five-things-south-africa-must-get-right-for-tech-in-schools-to-work-118612

Jawaid, I., Javed, M. Y., Jaffery, M. H., Akram, A., Safder, U., & Hassan, S. (2020). Robotic system education for young children by collaborative-project-based learning. *Computer Applications in Engineering Education, 28*(1), 178–192. doi:10.1002/cae.22184

Jenkins, T. (2001). The motivation of students of programming. *In Proceedings of the 6th annual conference on Innovation and technology in computer science education* (pp. 53-56). ACM. 10.1145/377435.377472

Jing, Q. (2015). A Case Study on LEGO Activity in Physics Class: Taking the "Rotational Kinetic Energy" for Example. *2015 IEEE 15th International Conference on Advanced Learning Technologies*, (pp. 293-295). IEEE. https://ieeexplore.ieee.org/abstract/document/7265329

Jin, Y., & Harp, C. (2020). Examining preservice teachers' TPACK, attitudes, self-efficacy, and perceptions of teamwork in a stand-alone educational technology course using flipped classroom or flipped team-based learning pedagogies. *Journal of Digital Learning in Teacher Education, 36*(3), 166–184. doi:10.1080/21532974.2020.1752335

Jobin, A., Ienca, M., & Vayena, E. (2019). Artificial Intelligence: The global landscape of ethics guidelines. *Nature Machine Intelligence, 1*(9), 389–399. doi:10.1038/s42256-019-0088-2

Jocius, R., O'Byrne, W. I., Albert, J., Joshi, D., Robinson, R., & Andrews, A. (2021). Infusing Computational Thinking into STEM Teaching: From Professional Development to Classroom Practice. *Journal of Educational Technology & Society*, *24*(4), 166–179.

Johnson D W, Johnson, R T, Stanne, M B (2000). *Cooperative learning methods: A meta-analysis.*

Johnson, D. W., & Johnson, R. T. (2014). Cooperative learning in 21st century. [Aprendizaje cooperativo en el siglo XXI]. *Anales de Psicología/Annals of Psychology, 30*(3), 841–851. doi:10.6018/analesps.30.3.201241

Johnson, D. W., & Johnson, R. T. (2017). The use of cooperative procedures in teacher education and professional development. *Journal of Education for Teaching*, *43*(3), 284–295. doi:10.1080/02607476.2017.1328023

Johnson, D. W., & Johnson, R. T. (2018). Cooperative learning: The foundation of active learning. In S. M. Brito (Ed.), *Active learning: Beyond the future* (pp. 59–71). IntechOpen. doi:10.5772/intechopen.81086

Johnson, D. W., & Johnson, R. T. (2019). The impact of cooperative learning on self-directed learning. In E. Mentz, J. de Beer, & R. Bailey (Eds.), *Self-directed learning for the 21st century: Implications for higher education* (pp. 37–66). AOSIS. doi:10.4102/aosis.2019.BK134.02

Johnson, D. W., Johnson, R. T., & Smith, K. A. (2014). Cooperative learning: Improving university instruction by basing practice on validated theory. *Journal on Excellence in University Teaching*, *25*(4), 1–26.

Johnson, D. W., Johnson, R. T., Smith, K. A., & Smith, K. (2013). Cooperative learning:Improving university instruction by basing practice on validated theory. *Journal on Excellence in University Teaching*, *25*(3-4), 1–26.

Johnson, D., & Johnson, R. (2009). An educational psychology success story: Social interdependence theory and cooperative learning. *Educational Researcher*, *38*(5), 365–379. doi:10.3102/0013189X09339057

Joiner, I. A. (2018). *Emerging Library technologies*. Elsevier Ltd.

Jonassen, D. H. (2000). Toward a design theory of problem solving. *Educational Technology Research and Development*, *48*(4), 63–85. doi:10.1007/BF02300500

Jung, S. E., & Won, E. S. (2018). Systematic review of research trends in robotics education for young children. *Sustainability (Basel)*, *10*(4), 905. doi:10.3390/su10040905

Kalyuga, S. (2009). Knowledge elaboration: A cognitive load perspective. *Learning and Instruction*, *19*(5), 402–410. doi:10.1016/j.learninstruc.2009.02.003

Kalyuga, S., & Hanham, J. (2011). Instructing in generalized knowledge structures to develop flexible problem solving skills. *Computers in Human Behavior*, *27*(1), 63–68. doi:10.1016/j.chb.2010.05.024

Kansanen, P. (1999). Teaching as teaching-studying-learning interaction. *Scandinavian journal OF educational Research, 43*(1), 81-89.

Kaplan, R. S. (2009). Conceptual Foundations of the Balanced Scorecard. *Handbooks of Management Accounting Research*, *3*, 1253–1269. doi:10.1016/S1751-3243(07)03003-9

Kapp, K. M., & Defelice, R. A. (2019). *Microlearning: Short and Sweet.* American Society for Training and Development.

Kapur, M. (2015). Learning from productive failure. *Learning: Research and Practice*, *1*(1), 51–65. doi:10.1080/23735082.2015.1002195

Karathanos, D., & Karathanos, P. (2005). Applying the Balanced Scorecard to Education. *Journal of Education for Business*, *80*(4), 222–240. https://www.tandfonline.com/doi/abs/10.3200/JOEB.80.4.222-230. doi:10.3200/JOEB.80.4.222-230

Karim, M. E., Lemaignan, S., & Mondada, F. (2016a). A review: Can robots reshape K-12 STEM education? *Proceedings of IEEE Workshop on Advanced Robotics and its Social Impacts, ARSO*. IEEE. 10.1109/ARSO.2015.7428217

Karmakar, A., Prenner, J. A., D'Ambros, M., & Robbes, R. (2022). Codex Hacks HackerRank: Memorization Issues and a Framework for Code Synthesis Evaluation. *arXiv preprint arXiv:2212.02684.*

Karpava, S. (Ed.). (2022). *Handbook of Research on Teacher and Student Perspectives on the Digital Turn in Education*. IGI Global. https://www.igi-global.com/book/handbook-research-teacher-student-perspectives/290031 doi:10.4018/978-1-6684-4446-7

Kasneci, E., Seßler, K., Küchemann, S., Bannert, M., Dementieva, D., Fischer, F., Gasser, U., Groh, G., Günnemann, S., Hüllermeier, E., Krusche, S., Kutyniok, G., Michaeli, T., Nerdel, C., Pfeffer, J., Poquet, O., Sailer, M., Schmidt, A., Seidel, T., & Kasneci, G. (2023). ChatGPT for good? On opportunities and challenges of large language models for education. *Learning and Individual Differences*, *103*, 102274. doi:10.1016/j.lindif.2023.102274

Kastrati, Z., Imran, A. S., & Kurti, A. (2019). Integrating word embeddings and document topics with deep learning in a video classification framework. *Pattern Recognition Letters*, *128*, 85–92. doi:10.1016/j.patrec.2019.08.019

Kato, K., & Watanabe, T. (2006, October). Structure-based categorization of programs to enable awareness about programming skills. In *International Conference on Knowledge-Based and Intelligent Information and Engineering Systems* (pp. 827-834). Springer, Berlin, Heidelberg. 10.1007/11893011_105

Katz, S., & Van Allen, J. (2020). *Evolving into the open: a framework for collaborative design of renewable assignments.*

Kawas, S., Vonessen, L., & Ko, A. J. (2019). Teaching accessibility: A design exploration of faculty professional development at scale. In: *Proceedings of the 50th ACM Technical Symposium on Computer Science Education*. ACM. 10.1145/3287324.3287399

Kay, J. S. (2003). Teaching Robotics from a Computer Science Perspective. *J. Comput. Sci. Coll.* ACM. https://dl.acm.org/citation.cfm?id=948785.948831

Kayacan, K., & Ektem, I. (2019). The effects of biology laboratory practices supported with self-regulated learning strategies on students' self-directed learning readiness and their attitudes towards science experiments. *European Journal of Educational Research*, *8*(1), 313–323. doi:10.12973/eu-jer.8.1.313

Kaya, E., Newley, A., Yesilyurt, E., & Deniz, H. (2020, July). teaching efficacy beliefs of preservice elementary teachers. *Journal of College Science Teaching*, *49*(6), 55–64. doi:10.1080/0047231X.2020.12290665

Kazemitabaar, M., Hou, X., Henley, A., Ericson, B. J., Weintrop, D., & Grossman, T. (2023). How Novices Use LLM-Based Code Generators to Solve CS1 Coding Tasks in a Self-Paced Learning Environment. *arXiv preprint arXiv:2309.14049.* doi:10.1145/3631802.3631806

Kazemitabaar, M., Chow, J., Ma, C. K. T., Ericson, B. J., Weintrop, D., & Grossman, T. (2023, April). Studying the effect of AI Code Generators on Supporting Novice Learners in Introductory Programming. In *Proceedings of the 2023 CHI Conference on Human Factors in Computing Systems* (pp. 1-23). Association for Computing Machinery, New York, NY, USA. https://doi.org/10.1145/3544548.3580919

Kazim, E., & Koshiyama, A. S. (2021). A high-level overview of AI ethics. *Patterns (New York, N.Y.)*, *2*(9), 100314. doi:10.1016/j.patter.2021.100314 PMID:34553166

Kessler, C. M., & Anderson, J. R. (1986). Learning flow of control: Recursive and iterative procedures. *Human-Computer Interaction*, *2*(2), 135–166. doi:10.1207/s15327051hci0202_2

Ketelhut, D. J., Mills, K., Hestness, E., Cabrera, L., Plane, J., & McGinnis, J. R. (2020, February). Teacher change following a professional development experience in integrating computational thinking into elementary science. *Journal of Science Education and Technology*, *29*(1), 173–187. doi:10.1007/s10956-019-09798-4

Khalil, H., Peters, M., Godfrey, C. M., McInerney, P., Soares, C. B., & Parker, D. (2016). An evidence-based approach to scoping reviews. *Worldviews on Evidence-Based Nursing*, *13*(2), 118–123. doi:10.1111/wvn.12144 PMID:26821833

Khandkar, S. H. (2009). Open Coding. *University of Calgary*. https://pages.cpsc.ucalgary.ca/~saul/wiki/uploads/CPSC681/open-coding.pdf

Khanlari, A. (2016). Teachers' perceptions of the benefits and the challenges of integrating educational robots into primary/elementary curricula. *European Journal of Engineering Education*, *41*(3), 320–330. doi:10.1080/03043797.2015.1056106

Khan, P., & Bari, M. (2023). Impact of Emergence With Robotics At Educational Institution And Emerging Challenge. *International Journal of Multidisciplinary Engineering in Current Research*, *6*(12), 42–46.

Kibga, E. S., Gakuba, E., & Sentongo, J. (2021). Developing students' curiosity through chemistry hands-on activities: A case of selected community secondary schools in Dar es Salaam, Tanzania. *Eurasia Journal of Mathematics, Science and Technology Education*, *17*(5), em1962. doi:10.29333/ejmste/10856

Kiesler, N., Mackellar, B. K., Kumar, A. N., McCauley, R., Raj, R. K., Sabin, M., & Impagliazzo, J. (2023, June). Computing Students' Understanding of Dispositions: A Qualitative Study. *In Proceedings of the 2023 Conference on Innovation and Technology in Computer Science Education,* V1, (pp. 103–109). Academic Press.

Kim, C. (2015). Robotics to promote elementary education pre-service teachers. STEM engagement, learning, and teaching: Computers and Education. Elsevier Ltd. doi:10.1016/j.compedu.2015.08.005

Kim, S., Raza, M., & Seidman, E. (2019). Improving 21st-century teaching skills: The key to effective 21st-century learners. *Research in Comparative and International Education*, *14*(1), 99–117. doi:10.1177/1745499919829214

Kinskey, C., & Miller, C. L. (2019). Creating Faculty Development on OER. *The International Journal of Open Educational Resources*, *1*(2). doi:10.18278/ijoer.1.2.10

Kirschner, P. A., & Hendrick, C. (2020). Cognitive Apprenticeship" Revisited. *American Educator*, *44*(3), 37.

Kirschner, P. A., Sweller, J., & Clark, R. E. (2006). Why minimal guidance during instruction does not work: An analysis of the failure of constructivist, discovery, problem-based, experiential, and inquiry-based teaching. *Educational Psychologist*, *41*(2), 75–86. doi:10.1207/s15326985ep4102_1

Kirschner, P. A., Sweller, J., Kirschner, F., & Zambrano, R. J. (2018). From cognitive load theory to collaborative cognitive load theory. *International Journal of Computer-Supported Collaborative Learning*, *13*(213), 213–233. doi:10.1007/s11412-018-9277-y PMID:30996713

Kishore, K. (2012). *Cooperative Learning*. Alden Books.

Kjällander, S., Mannila, L., Åkerfeldt, A., & Heintz, F. (2021, February 19). approach to computational thinking and programming. *Education Sciences*, *11*(2), 80. doi:10.3390/educsci11020080

Knobelsdorf, M., Kreitz, C., & Böhne, S. (2014, March). Teaching theoretical computer science using a cognitive apprenticeship approach. In *Proceedings of the 45th ACM technical symposium on Computer science education* (pp. 67-72). ACM. 10.1145/2538862.2538944

Knowles, M. S. (1975). *Self-directed learning.* New York, NY: Associated Press.

Knowles, M. S. (1975). *Self-directed learning: A guide for learners and teachers.*

Knowles, M. S. (1975). *Self-directed learning: A guide for learners and teachers*. Association Press.

Koby, M., Hazan, T., & Hazzan, O. (2020). Equalizing data science curriculum for Computer Science pupils. In *Proceedings of the 20th Koli Calling International Conference on Computing Educational Research*. ACM. 10.1145/3428029.3428045

Koç, A., & Büyük, U. (2021). Effect of Robotics Technology in Science Education on Scientific Creativity and Attitude Development. *Journal of Turkish Science Education*, *18*(1), 54–72. doi:10.36681/tused.2021.52

Kokotovich, V. (2008). Problem analysis and thinking tools: An empirical study of non-hierarchical mind mapping. *Design Studies*, *29*(1), 49–69. doi:10.1016/j.destud.2007.09.001

Kolesnykova, T. O. (2019, December). The Role of Libraries as Publishers in the Open Education Landscape: Reflecting Modern World Practice of Open Textbooks. In *University Library at a new stage of social communications development. Conference proceedings* (*No. 4,* pp. 88-99). IEEE.

Kölling, M., & Barnes, D. J. (2004). Enhancing apprentice-based learning of Java. *In Proceedings of the 35th SIGCSE technical symposium on Computer science education* (pp. 286-290). ACM. 10.1145/971300.971403

Kong, S-C., Lai, M., & Sun, D. (2020). *Teacher development in computational thinking: Design*. Research Gate.

Koole, S., Schlinkert, C., Maldei, T., & Baumann, N. (2018). Becoming who you are: An integrative review of self-determination theory and personality systems interactions theory. *Journal of Personality*, *87*(1), 15–36. doi:10.1111/jopy.12380 PMID:29524339

Kopcha, T. J., Wilson, C. Y., & Yang, D. (2022). Improving teacher use of educational robotics to teach computer science in K-5 mathematics. *Computational Thinking in Pre*, *K-5*, 47–54. doi:10.1145/3507951.3519287

Kranzow, J., & Hyland, N. (2016). Self-directed learning: Developing readiness in graduate students. *International Journal of Self-Directed Learning*, *13*(2), 1–14.

Krishnamurthi, S., & Fisler, K. (2019). Programming Paradigms and Beyond. The Cambridge handbook of computing education research, 377. Cambridge Press. doi:10.1017/9781108654555.014

Kruger, D., Werlen, E., & Bergamin, P. B. (2022). Curiosity killed the cat, but satisfaction brought it back: Inquiry-based learning in blended environments to promote self-directed learning. In C. van der Westhuizen, M.C. Maphalala & R. Bailey (Eds.), Blended learning environments to foster self-directed learning, NWU Self-Directed Learning Series (vol. 8, pp. 31–48). Cape Town: AOSIS. doi:10.4102/aosis.2022.BK366.02

Kumar, A. P., Omprakash, A., Mani, P. K., Swaminathan, N., Maheshkumar, K., Maruthy, K. N., Sathiyasekaran, B. W. C., Vijayaraghavan, P. V., & Padmavathi, R. (2021). Validation of internal structure of self-directed learning readiness scale among Indian medical students using factor analysis and the structural equation modelling approach. *BMC Medical Education*, *21*(1), 1–13. doi:10.1186/s12909-021-03035-6 PMID:34895214

Kwon, K., Ottenbreit-Leftwich, A. T., Brush, T. A., Jeon, M., & Yan, G. (2021, October). based learning in elementary computer science education: Effects on computational thinking and attitudes. *Educational Technology Research and Development*, *69*(5), 2761–2787. doi:10.1007/s11423-021-10034-3

Laakso, M. J., Rajala, T., Kaila, E., & Salakoski, T. (2012) Novice Learning. In: Seel N.M. (Ed.), Encyclopedia of the Sciences of Learning. (2012). Springer. doi:10.1007/978-1-4419-1428-6_1520

Lahtinen, E., Ala-Mutka, K., & Järvinen, H. M. (2005). A study of the difficulties of novice programmers. *Acm sigcse bulletin, 37*(3), 14-18.

Lai, P. C. (2017). The literature overview of technology adoption models and theories for the novelty technology. *Journal of Information Systems and Technology Management*, *14*(1), 21–38. https://www.scielo.br/pdf/jistm/v14n1/1807-1775-jistm-14-01-00021.pdf. doi:10.4301/S1807-17752017000100002

Lalitha, T. B., & Sreeja, P. S. (2020). Personalised self-directed learning recommendation system. *Procedia Computer Science*, *171*, 583–592. doi:10.1016/j.procs.2020.04.063

Lambert, L., & Guiffre, H. (2013). Computer science outreach in an elementary school. *Journal of Computing Sciences in Colleges*, *24*(3), 118–124.

Lancaster, T., Robins, A. V., & Fincher, S. A. (2019). Assessment and Plagiarism. The Cambridge handbook of computing education research. Cambridge Press. doi:10.1017/9781108654555.015

Lanka, S. (2021). The impact of education technology in teaching and learning. *European Journal of Research and Reflection in Educational Sciences*, *9*(1).

Larson, L., Seipel, M., Shelley, M., Gahn, S., Ko, S., Schenkenfelder, M., Rover, D. T., Schmittmann, B., & Heitmann, M. (2017). The academic environment and faculty well-being: The role of psychological needs. *Journal of Career Assessment*, *27*(1), 167–182. doi:10.1177/1069072717748667

Larson, M. B., & Lockee, B. B. (2014). *Streamlined id: A practical guide to instructional design.* Routledge.

Laurillard, D. (2013). *Teaching as a design science: Building pedagogical patterns for learning and technology.* Routledge. doi:10.4324/9780203125083

Laurillard, D., Charlton, P., Craft, B., Dimakopoulos, D., Ljubojevic, D., Magoulas, G., Masterman, E., Pujadas, R., Whitley, E. A., & Whittlestone, K. (2013). A constructionist learning environment for teachers to model learning designs. *Journal of Computer Assisted Learning*, *29*(1), 15–30. https://doi-org.ezproxy.unam.edu.na/10.1111/j.1365-2729.2011.00458.x. doi:10.1111/j.1365-2729.2011.00458.x

Lavery, J., Tinadana, P. O., Scott, T. W., Harrington, L. C., Ramsey, J. M., Ytuarte-Nuñez, C., & James, A. A. (2010). Towards a framework for community engagement in global health research. *Trends in Parasitology*, *26*(6), 279–283. doi:10.1016/j.pt.2010.02.009 PMID:20299285

Lawrence, A. W., Badre, A. M., & Stasko, J. T. (1994, October). Empirically evaluating the use of animations to teach algorithms. *In Proceedings of 1994 IEEE Symposium on Visual Languages* (pp. 48-54). IEEE. 10.1109/VL.1994.363641

Leaf, C. (2018). *Think, learn succeed: Understanding and use your mind to thrive at school, the workplace, and life.* Baker.

Leahy, K. S., & Smith, T. D. (2021). The self-directed learning of adult music students: A comparison of teacher approaches and student needs. *International Journal of Music Education*, *39*(3), 289–300. doi:10.1177/0255761421991596

LeBlanc, C. A., Newcomb, J., & Rheingans, P. (2020). First Generation-Rural Computer Science Students. Association for Computing Machinery (ACM). doi:10.1145/3328778.3372662

Leedy, P., & Ormrod, J. (2015). *Practical research: planning and design.* Pearson Education.

Lee, J. H., Ostwald, M. J., & Zhou, L. (2023). Socio-Spatial Experience in Space Syntax Research: A PRISMA-Compliant Review. *Buildings*, *13*(3), 644. doi:10.3390/buildings13030644

Lee, Y. J. (2011). Empowering teachers to create educational software: A constructivist approach utilizing Etoys, pair programming and cognitive apprenticeship. *Computers & Education*, *56*(2), 527–538. doi:10.1016/j.compedu.2010.09.018

Lee, Y., Lau, K., & Yip, V. (2016). Blended learning for building student-teachers' capacity to learn and teach science-related interdisciplinary subjects. *Asian Association of Open Universities Journal, 11*(2), 166–181. doi:10.1108/AAOUJ-09-2016-0029

Le, H., Janssen, J., & Wubbels, T. (2018). Collaborative learning practices: Teacher and student perceived obstacles to effective student collaboration. *Cambridge Journal of Education, 48*(1), 103–122. doi:10.1080/0305764X.2016.1259389

Lei, M., Clemente, I. M., Liu, H., & Bell, J. (2022). The Acceptance of Telepresence Robots in Higher Education. *International Journal of Social Robotics, 14*(4), 1025–1042. doi:10.1007/s12369-021-00837-y PMID:35103081

Leinonen, J., Denny, P., MacNeil, S., Sarsa, S., Bernstein, S., Kim, J., & Hellas, A. (2023). Comparing Code Explanations Created by Students and Large Language Models. *arXiv preprint arXiv:2304.03938*. doi:10.1145/3587102.3588785

Leinonen, J., Hellas, A., Sarsa, S., Reeves, B., Denny, P., Prather, J., & Becker, B. A. (2023). Using Large Language Models to Enhance Programming Error Messages. In *Proceedings of the 54th ACM Technical Symposium on Computer Science Education (SIGCSE 2023) (*Vol. 1, *pp.* 563-569*)*. Association for Computing Machinery. 10.1145/3545945.3569770

Lemay, D., & Basnet, R. (2017). Algorithmic thinking, cooperativity, creativity, critical thinking, and problem solving: Exploring the relationship between computational thinking skills and academic performance. *Journal of Computers in Education, 4*(4), 355–369. doi:10.1007/s40692-017-0090-9

Leonard, J., Mitchell, M., Barnes-Johnson, J., Unertl, A., Outka-Hill, J., Robinson, R., & Hester-Croff, C. (2018). Preparing Teachers to Engage Rural Students in Computational Thinking through Robotics, Game Design, and Culturally Responsive Teaching. *Journal of Teacher Education, 69*(4), 386–407. doi:10.1177/0022487117732317

Leppink, J., Paas, F., Van der Vleuten, C. P., Van Gog, T., & Van Merriënboer, J. J. (2013). Development of an instrument for measuring different types of cognitive load. *Behavior Research Methods, 45*(4), 1058–1072. doi:10.3758/s13428-013-0334-1 PMID:23572251

LeslieD.BurrC.AitkenM.CowlsJ.KatellM.BriggsM. (2021). Artificial intelligence, human rights, democracy, and the rule of law: a primer (April 2, 2021). SSRN: https://ssrn.com/abstract=3817999 or doi:10.2139/ssrn.3817999

Levac, D., Colquhoun, H., & O'Brien, K. K. (2010). Scoping studies: Advancing the methodology. *Implementation Science : IS, 5*(1), 1–9. doi:10.1186/1748-5908-5-69 PMID:20854677

Levin, T., & Wadmany, R. (2011). Changes in educational beliefs and classroom practices of teachers and students in rich technology-based classroom. *Technology, Pedagogy and Education, 14*(3), 281–307. doi:10.1080/14759390500200208

Lewis, C. M., Shah, N., & Falkner, K. (2019). Equity and Diversity. The Cambridge handbook of computing education research, 481. Cambridge Press. doi:10.1017/9781108654555.017

Liao, Y. K. C., & Bright, G. W. (1991). Effects of computer programming on cognitive outcomes: A meta-analysis. *Journal of Educational Computing Research, 7*(3), 251–268. doi:10.2190/E53G-HH8K-AJRR-K69M

Limna, P., Jakwatanatham, S., Siripipattanakul, S., Kaewpuang, P., & Sriboonruang, P. (2022). A review of artificial intelligence (AI) in education during the digital era. *Advance Knowledge for Executives, 1*(1), 1–9.

Li, N. (2022). *How Technology Promotes Educational Change: Studies of Virtual Learning Environment in Higher Education.* The University of Liverpool.

Linebarger, D. L. (2000). Summative evaluation of Between the Lions: A final report to WGBH Educational Foundation. *Univ Kansas Kansas City, Kansas, 3*, 2010.

Lin, X. (2023). Exploring the Role of ChatGPT as a Facilitator for Motivating Self-Directed Learning Among Adult Learners. *Adult Learning*, 10451595231184928. doi:10.1177/10451595231184928

Lister, R., Adams, E. S., Fitzgerald, S., Fone, W., Hamer, J., Lindholm, M., & Simon, B. (2004). A multi-national study of reading and tracing skills in novice programmers. *SIGCSE Bulletin*, *36*(4), 119–150. doi:10.1145/1041624.1041673

Liu, M. X., Sarkar, A., Negreanu, C., Zorn, B., Williams, J., Toronto, N., & Gordon, A. D. (2023, April). "What It Wants Me To Say": Bridging the Abstraction Gap Between End-User Programmers and Code-Generating Large Language Models. In *Proceedings of the 2023 CHI Conference on Human Factors in Computing Systems*. Association for Computing Machinery, New York, NY, USA. 10.1145/3544548.3580817

Liu, B., Gui, W., Gao, T., Wu, Y., & Zuo, M. (2023). Understanding self-directed learning behaviours in a computer-aided 3D design context. *Computers & Education*, *205*, 104882. doi:10.1016/j.compedu.2023.104882

Liu, C.-C., Chen, H. S. L., Shih, J.-L., Huang, G.-T., & Liu, B.-J. (2011). An enhanced concept map approach to improving children's storytelling ability. *Computers & Education*, *56*(3), 873–884. doi:10.1016/j.compedu.2010.10.029

Liu, G., Teng, X., & Zhu, D. (2019). Effect of self-esteem and parents' psychological control on the relationship between teacher support and Chinese migrant children's academic achievement: A moderated mediation. *Frontiers in Psychology*, *10*, 2342. doi:10.3389/fpsyg.2019.02342 PMID:31736816

Liu, Y., Hau, K. T., Liu, H., Wu, J., Wang, X., & Zheng, X. (2020). Multiplicative effect of intrinsic and extrinsic motivation on academic performance: A longitudinal study of Chinese students. *Journal of Personality*, *88*(3), 584–595. doi:10.1111/jopy.12512 PMID:31498427

Li, X. (2007). Intelligent agent-supported online education. *Decision Sciences Journal of Innovative Education*, *5*(2), 311–331. doi:10.1111/j.1540-4609.2007.00143.x

Li, Y., Choi, D., Chung, J., Kushman, N., Schrittwieser, J., Leblond, R., Eccles, T., Keeling, J., Gimeno, F., Dal Lago, A., Hubert, T., Choy, P., de Masson d'Autume, C., Babuschkin, I., Chen, X., Huang, P.-S., Welbl, J., Gowal, S., Cherepanov, A., & Vinyals, O. (2022). Competition-level code generation with alphacode. *Science*, *378*(6624), 1092–1097. doi:10.1126/science.abq1158 PMID:36480631

Lloyd, M., Weatherby, K., Curry, J., & Buckley, D. (2021). *Reimagining Computer Science in the curriculum.* Microsoft Computer Science Curriculum Toolkit. https://info.microsoft.com/rs/157-GQE-382/images/EN-CNTNT-Other-SRGCM4491.pdf

Lloyd, M., & Chandra, V. (2020). Teaching coding and computational thinking in primary classrooms: Perceptions of Australian preservice teachers. *Curriculum Perspectives*, *40*(2), 189–201. doi:10.1007/s41297-020-00117-1

Lockee, B. B., Burton, J. K., & Cross, L. H. (1999). No comparison: Distance education finds a new use for 'no significant difference'. *Educational Technology Research and Development*, *47*(3), 33–42. doi:10.1007/BF02299632

Lodi, M. (2020). Informatical thinking. *Olympiads in Informatics*, *14*, 113–132. doi:10.15388/ioi.2020.09

Loeng, S. (2020). Self-directed learning: A core concept in adult education. *Education Research International*, *2020*, 1–12. doi:10.1155/2020/3816132

Long, D., & Magerko, B. (2020, April). What is AI literacy? Competencies and design considerations. *Proceedings of the CHI conference on human factors in computing systems* (pp. 1-16). ACM. 10.1145/3313831.3376727

Longoria, L. C., López-Forniés, I., Sáenz, D. C., & Sierra-Pérez, J. (2021). Promoting sustainable consumption in Higher Education Institutions through integrative co-creative processes involving relevant stakeholders. *Sustainable Production and Consumption*, *28*, 445–458. doi:10.1016/j.spc.2021.06.009

Lopez, I. (2023). The Science Disseminators Academy: a teacher training program to use astronomy for implementing phenomenon-based learning.

Luciano, A. P. (2019). The educational robotics and Arduino platform: Constructionist learning strategies to the teaching of physics. *Journal of Physics: Conference Series, 1286*(1), 012044. doi:10.1088/1742-6596/1286/1/012044

Lui, K. M., & Chan, K. C. (2006). Pair programming productivity: Novice–novice vs. expert–expert. *International Journal of Human-Computer Studies, 64*(9), 915–925. doi:10.1016/j.ijhcs.2006.04.010

LuoF.JiangJ.YangL.LiangY.CaoY.ZhouX.WanQ. (2022). Dental interns' perception toward online learning of complete denture rehabilitation: a questionnaire survey. Retrieved from Research Square: https://www.researchsquare.com/article/rs-2169572/latest doi:10.21203/rs.3.rs-2169572/v1

Luo, Y., Lin, J., & Yang, Y. (2021). Students' motivation and continued intention with online self-regulated learning: A self-determination theory perspective. *Zeitschrift für Erziehungswissenschaft, 24*(6), 1379–1399. doi:10.1007/s11618-021-01042-3 PMID:34483723

MacNeil, S., Tran, A., Mogil, D., Bernstein, S., Ross, E., & Huang, Z. (2022). Generating Diverse Code Explanations using the GPT-3 Large Language Model. In *Proceedings of the 2022 ACM Conference on International Computing Education Research* - Volume 2 *(ICER '22),* Vol. 2 (pp. 37-39). Association for Computing Machinery. 10.1145/3501709.3544280

MacNeil, S., Kim, J., Leinonen, J., Denny, P., Bernstein, S., Becker, B. A., Wermelinger, M., Hellas, A., Tran, A., Sarsa, S., Prather, J., & Kumar, V. (2023). The Implications of Large Language Models for CS Teachers and Students. In *Proceedings of the 54th ACM Technical Symposium on Computer Science Education (SIGCSE 2023) (*Vol. 2*, p.* 1255*).* Association for Computing Machinery. 10.1145/3545947.3573358

MacNeil, S., Tran, A., Hellas, A., Kim, J., Sarsa, S., Denny, P., Bernstein, S., & Leinonen, J. (2023). Experiences from Using Code Explanations Generated by Large Language Models in a Web Software Development E-Book. In *Proceedings of the 54th ACM Technical Symposium on Computer Science Education (SIGCSE 2023) (*Vol. 1*, pp.* 931-937*).* Association for Computing Machinery. 10.1145/3545945.3569785

MacNeil, S., Tran, A., Leinonen, J., Denny, P., Kim, J., Hellas, A., Bernstein, S., & Sarsa, S. (2023). Automatically Generating CS Learning Materials with Large Language Models. In *Proceedings of the 54th ACM Technical Symposium on Computer Science Education (SIGCSE 2023) (*Vol. 2*, p.* 1176*).* Association for Computing Machinery. 10.1145/3545947.3569630

Maguire, M., Gibbons, S., Glackin, M., Pepper, D., & Skilling, K. (2018). *EBOOK: Becoming a teacher: Issues in secondary education.* McGraw-Hill Education.

Mahaye, N. E. (2020). The Impact of COVID-19 Pandemic on Education: Navigating Forward the Pedagogy of Blended Learning. *ResearchGate*, 1-24. https://www.researchgate.net/publication/340899662_

Mahlaba, S. C. (2020). Reasons why self-directed learning is important in South Africa during the COVID-19 pandemic. *South African Journal of Higher Education, 34*(6), 120–136. doi:10.20853/34-6-4192

Maina, M. F., Santos-Hermosa, G., Mancini, F., & Guàrdia Ortiz, L. (2020). Open educational practices (OEP) in the design of digital competence assessment. *Distance Education, 41*(2), 261–278. doi:10.1080/01587919.2020.1757407

Maiorana, F. (2019). Interdisciplinary Computing for STE (A) M: a low Floor high ceiling curriculum. *Innovations, Technologies and Research in Education, 37.*

Maiorana, F. (2020). A flipped design of learning resources for a course on algorithms and data structures. International Conference on Interactive Collaborative and Blended Learning, (pp. 268–279). Springer. 10.1007/978-3-030-67209-6_29

Maiorana, F. (2018). *Computational Thinking and Humanities*. Didamatica.

Maiorana, F. (2021). From High School to Higher Education: Learning Trajectory for an Inclusive and Accessible Curriculum for Teachers and Their Students. [IJSEUS]. *International Journal of Smart Education and Urban Society*, *12*(4), 36–51. doi:10.4018/IJSEUS.2021100104

Majumdar, D., Banerji, P. K., & Chakrabarti, S. (2018). Disruptive technology and disruptive innovation: Ignore at your peril! *Technology Analysis and Strategic Management*, *30*(11), 1247–1255. doi:10.1080/09537325.2018.1523384

Makeleni, N. T., & Sethusha, M. J. (2014). The experiences of foundation phase teachers in implementing the curriculum. *Mediterranean Journal of Social Sciences*, *5*(2), 103. doi:10.5901/mjss.2014.v5n2p103

Makransky, G., Borre-Gude, S., & Mayer, R. E. (2019). Motivational and cognitive benefits of training in immersive virtual reality based on multiple assessments. *Journal of Computer Assisted Learning*, *35*(6), 691–707. doi:10.1111/jcal.12375

Maphalala, M. C., & Ajani, O. A. (2023). The COVID-19 pandemic: Shifting from conventional classroom learning to online learning in South Africa's higher education. *International Journal of Innovative Technologies in Social Science*, *2*(38), 1–15. doi:10.31435/rsglobal_ijitss/30062023/8002

Maphalala, M. C., Mkhasibe, R. G., & Mncube, D. W. (2021). Online Learning as a Catalyst for Self-directed Learning in Universities during the COVID-19 Pandemic. *Research in Social Sciences and Technology*, *6*(2), 233–248. doi:10.46303/ressat.2021.25

Marcinkiewicz, H. R. (2010). Technology and teachers: Factors influencing technology use in the classroom. *Journal of Research on Computing in Education*, *26*(2), 220–237. doi:10.1080/08886504.1993.10782088

Marda, V., & Ahmed, S. (2021). *Emotional Entanglement: China's emotion recognition market and its implications for human rights.* Article 19. https://www.article19.org/wp-content/uploads/2021/01/ER-Tech-China-Report.pdf

Maree, K., & Pietersen, J. (2016). Sampling. In K. Maree (Ed.), *First steps in research 2* (2nd ed.). Van Schaik.

Markova, O., Semerikov, S., Маркова, О., Semerikov, S., Семеріков, С., Семериков, С., & Тронь, В. (2019). Implementation of cloud service models in training of future information technology specialists. *Cte Workshop Proceedings*, (*vol. 6*, 499-515). IEEE. 10.31812/123456789/3270

Martucci, A., Gursesli, M. C., Duradoni, M., & Guazzini, A. (2023). Overviewing Gaming Motivation and Its Associated Psychological and Sociodemographic Variables: A PRISMA Systematic Review. *Human Behavior and Emerging Technologies*, *2023*, 1–156. doi:10.1155/2023/5640258

Masina, R., Mukaro, J. P., & Mawonedzo, A. (2023). Self-directed assessment framework for practical tasks for Clothing and Textile Technology undergraduate teacher trainees under COVID-19 conditions. *Teacher Education through Flexible Learning in Africa* (*TETFLE*), *4*(1), 102-120.

Mason, R., Seton, C., & Cooper, G. (2016). Applying cognitive load theory to the redesign of a conventional database systems course. *Computer Science Education*, *26*(1), 68–87. doi:10.1080/08993408.2016.1160597

Mason, S. L., & Rich, P. (2019). Preparing elementary school teachers to teach computing, coding, and computational thinking. *Contemporary Issues in Technology & Teacher Education*, *19*(4), 790–824. https://citejournal.org/publication/volume-19/issue-4-19/

Massachusetts Institute of Technology (MIT). (2023). *Explore OpenCourseWare*. MIT. https://ocw.mit.edu/search/

Matthews, D. (2023, August 1) *The AI rules that US policymakers are considering, explained.* Vox. https://www.vox.com/future-perfect/23775650/ai-regulation-openai-gpt-anthropic-midjourney-stable

Mauch, E. (2015). Using technological innovation to improve the problem-solving skills of middle school students. *The Clearing House: A Journal of Educational Strategies, Issues and Ideas*, *75*(4), 211–213. doi:10.1080/00098650109599193

Maulana, R., Helms-Lorenz, M., Irnidayanti, Y., & Grift, W. (2016). Autonomous motivation in the Indonesian classroom: Relationship with teacher support through the lens of self-determination theory. *The Asia-Pacific Education Researcher*, *25*(3), 441–451. doi:10.1007/s40299-016-0282-5

Mavridis, N., Petychakis, M., Tsamakos, A., Toulis, P., Emami, S., Kazmi, W., Datta, C., BenAbdelkader, C., & Tanoto, A. (2010). FaceBots: Steps towards enhanced long-term human-robot interaction by utilizing and publishing online social information. *Paladyn : Journal of Behavioral Robotics*, *1*(3), 169–178. doi:10.2478/s13230-011-0003-y

Maximova, M., & Kim, Y. H. (2021). The effective diffusion of educational robotics in rural areas: A case study in the Sakha Republic of Russia. *European Journal of Educational Research*, *10*(1), 145–159. doi:10.12973/eu-jer.10.1.145

Mayet, R. (2021). Supporting at-risk learners at a comprehensive university in South Africa. *Journal of Student Affairs in Africa*, *4*(2). doi:10.18820/jsaa.v4i2.2

Mbah, M. (2019). 'Can local knowledge make the difference? Rethinking universities' community engagement and prospect for sustainable community development'. *The Journal of Environmental Education*, *50*(1), 11–22. https://www.tandfonline.com/doi/full/10.1080/00958964.2018.1462136?scroll=top&needAccess=true. doi:10.1080/00958964.2018.1462136

McDaniel, A., & Van Jura, M. (2022). High-impact practices: Evaluating their effect on college completion. *Journal of College Student Retention*, *24*(3), 740–757. doi:10.1177/1521025120947357

McGarr, O., Exton, C., Power, J., & McInerney, C. (2023). 'What about the gatekeepers? School principals' and school guidance counsellors' attitudes towards computer science in secondary schools'. *Computer Science Education*, *33*(2), 168–185. doi:10.1080/08993408.2021.1953296

Mcgettrick, A., Boyle, R., Ibbett, R., Lloyd, J., Lovegrove, G., & Mander, K. (2005). Grand Challenges Grand Challenges in Computing: Education-A Summary. *The Computer Journal*, *48*(1), 42–48. doi:10.1093/comjnl/bxh064

McGinnisJ. R.HestnessE.MillsK.KetelhutD. J.CabreraL.JeongH. (2020).

McNulty, N. (2021) *Introduction to the CAPS Coding and Robotics Curriculum*. Niall McNulty. https://www.niallmcnulty.com/2021/05/introduction-to-the-caps-coding-and-robotics-curriculum/

Mead, J., Gray, S., Hamer, J., James, R., Sorva, J., Clair, C. S., & Thomas, L. (2006). A cognitive approach to identifying measurable milestones for programming skill acquisition. *SIGCSE Bulletin*, *38*(4), 182–194. doi:10.1145/1189136.1189185

Medeiros, R. P., Ramalho, G. L., & Falcão, T. P. (2018). A systematic literature review on teaching and learning introductory programming in higher education. *IEEE Transactions on Education*, *62*(2), 77–90. doi:10.1109/TE.2018.2864133

Medero, G. S., Albaladejo, G. P., Medina, P. M., & Solana, M. J. G. (2022). Blogging as an Instrument for Co-Creation and Collaborative Learning in University Education. *Contemporary Educational Technology*, *14*(4), ep393. doi:10.30935/cedtech/12555

Mehta, R., Creely, E., & Henriksen, D. (2020). A profitable education: Countering neoliberalism in 21st century skills discourses. In *Handbook of research on literacy and digital technology integration in teacher education* (pp. 359–381). IGI Global. doi:10.4018/978-1-7998-1461-0.ch020

Meintjes, H. H. (2023). Learner Views of a facebook page as a supportive Digital pedagogy at a Public South African School in a Grade 12 Business Studies Class. *Business Studies Journal*, 1-16. doi:10.4018/978-1-6684-7123-4.ch073

Melis, G., McCabe, S., Atzeni, M., & Del Chiappa, G. (2023). Collaboration and learning processes in value co-creation: A destination perspective. *Journal of Travel Research*, *62*(3), 699–716. doi:10.1177/00472875211070349

Mensah-Williams, E., & Derera, E. (2023). Conceptualising impact measurements of entrepreneurship education outcomes: A scoping review. *Acta Commercii-Independent Research Journal in the Management Sciences*, *23*(1), 1053. doi:10.4102/ac.v23i1.1053

Mentz, E., & Bailey, R. (2019). A systematic review of research on the use of technology-supported cooperative learning to enhance self-directed learning. In E. Mentz, J. De Beer & R. Bailey (Eds.), Self-Directed Learning for the 21st Century: Implications for Higher Education (vol. 1, pp. 203–238). Cape Town: AOSIS. doi:10.4102/aosis.2019.BK134.07

Menzel, M. (2023). Developing a metadata profile for higher education OER repositories. In *Distributed Learning Ecosystems: Concepts, Resources, and Repositories* (pp. 263–278). Springer Fachmedien Wiesbaden. doi:10.1007/978-3-658-38703-7_14

Michalec, O., O'Donovan, C., & Sobhani, M. (2021). What is robotics made of? The interdisciplinary politics of robotics research. *Humanities & Social Sciences Communications*, *8*(1), 65. doi:10.1057/s41599-021-00737-6

Michener, L., Cook, J., Ahmed, S. M., Yonas, M. A., Coyne-Beasley, T., & Aguilar-Gaxiola, S. (2012). Aligning the goals of community-engaged research: Why and how academic health centers can successfully engage with communities to improve health. *Academic Medicine*, *87*(3), 285–291. doi:10.1097/ACM.0b013e3182441680 PMID:22373619

Miller, L. D., Soh, L.-K., Chiriacescu, V., Ingraham, E., Shell, D. F., Ramsay, S., & Hazley, M. P. (2013). Improving learning of computational thinking using creative thinking exercises in CS-1 computer science courses. *2013 Ieee Frontiers in Education Conference (Fie),* (pp. 1426–1432). IEEE.

Miller, G. A. (1956). The magical number seven plus or minus two: Some limits on our capacity for processing information. *Psychological Review*, *63*(2), 81–97. doi:10.1037/h0043158 PMID:13310704

Miller, M. L., & Malott, R. W. (2006). Programmed instruction: Construction responding, discrimination responding, and highlighted keywords. *Journal of Behavioral Education*, *15*(2), 109–117. doi:10.1007/s10864-006-9010-1

Milne, L. R., & Ladner, R. E. (2019). Position: Accessible Block-Based Programming: Why and How. In: 2019 IEEE Blocks and Beyond Workshop (B&B). IEEE.

Milne, I., & Rowe, G. (2002). Difficulties in learning and teaching programming—Views of students and tutors. *Education and Information Technologies*, *7*(1), 55–66. doi:10.1023/A:1015362608943

Ministry of Communication and Digital Technologies. (2020). National Digital and Future Skills Strategy. *Government Gazette*, (43730), 3–38.

Ministry of Education, Arts, and Culture (MEAC). (2016). *The National Curriculum for Basic Education.* Okahandja: National Institute for Educational Development (NIED). http://www.nied.edu.na/assets/documents/05Policies/NationalCurriculumGuide/National_Curriculum_Basic_Education_2016.pdf

Mirhosseini, S., Henley, A. Z., & Parnin, C. (2023). What Is Your Biggest Pain Point? An Investigation of CS Instructor Obstacles, Workarounds, and Desires. In *Proceedings of the 54th ACM Technical Symposium on Computer Science Education* (SIGCSE 2023) (Vol. 1, pp. 291-297). Association for Computing Machinery. 10.1145/3545945.3569816

Mladenović, M., Boljat, I., & Žanko, Ž. (2018). Comparing loops misconceptions in block-based and text-based programming languages at the K-12 level. *Education and Information Technologies*, *23*(4), 1483–1500. doi:10.1007/s10639-017-9673-3

Mncube, D. W., & Maphalala, M. C. (Eds.). (2023). *Advancing Self-Directed Learning in Higher Education*. IGI Global. doi:10.4018/978-1-6684-6772-5

Mokonyane-Motha, M. M., & De Jager, T. T. (2023). The Significance of Training Student-Teacher Lecturers in Pedagogical Robotic and Coding Skills. *International Journal of Social Science Research and Review*, *6*(12), 107–118. doi:10.47814/ijssrr.v6i12.1808

Molala, T. S., & Makhubele, J. C. (2021). The Connection Between Digital Divide and Social Exclusion: Implications for Social Work. *Humanities & Social Sciences Reviews*, *9*(4), 194–201. doi:10.18510/hssr.2021.9427

Molenda, M. (2008). When effectiveness mattered. *TechTrends*, *52*(2), 53.

Molins-Ruano, P., Jurado, F., & Rodriguez, P. (2019). On the identification of several key issues on OER discovery for smart learning environments. *13th International Conference on Ubiquitous Computing and Ambient Intelligence*. MDPI. 10.3390/proceedings2019031086

Moller, F., & Crick, T. (2018). A university-based model for supporting computer science curriculum reform. *Journal of Computers in Education*, *5*(4), 415–434. doi:10.1007/s40692-018-0117-x

Moran, T. P. (2016). Anxiety and working memory capacity: A meta-analysis and narrative review. *Psychological Bulletin*, *142*(8), 831–864. doi:10.1037/bul0000051 PMID:26963369

Morelli, R., Tucker, A., Danner, N., De Lanerolle, T. R., Ellis, H. J. C., Izmirli, O., Krizanc, D., & Parker, G. (2009). Revitalizing computing education through free and open source software for humanity. *Communications of the ACM*, *52*(8), 67–75. doi:10.1145/1536616.1536635

Moreno-León, J., Robles, G., & Román-González, M. (2016). Code to learn: Where does it belong in the K-12 curriculum? *Journal of Information Technology Education*, *15*, 283–303. doi:10.28945/3521

Morris, T. H. (2019). Self-directed learning: A fundamental competence in a rapidly changing world. *International Review of Education*, *65*(4), 633–653. doi:10.1007/s11159-019-09793-2

Morris, T. H. (2021). Meeting educational challenges of pre- and post-COVID-19 conditions through self-directed learning: Considering the contextual quality of educational experience necessary. *On the Horizon*, *29*(20), 52–61. doi:10.1108/OTH-01-2021-0031

Morris, T. H., & Rohs, M. (2023). The potential for digital technology to support self-directed learning in formal education of children: A scoping review. *Interactive Learning Environments*, *31*(4), 1974–1987. doi:10.1080/10494820.2020.1870501

Morze, N. V., & Strutynska, O. V. (2023). Advancing educational robotics: competence development for pre-service computer science teachers. *CTE Workshop Proceedings*. CTE. 10.55056/cte.549

Mouriño-García, M., Pérez-Rodríguez, R., Anido-Rifón, L., Fernández-Iglesias, M. J., & Darriba-Bilbao, V. M. (2018). Cross-repository aggregation of educational resources. *Computers & Education*, *117*, 31–49. doi:10.1016/j.compedu.2017.09.014

Mouza, C., Yang, H., Pan, Y.-C., Ozden, S. Y., & Pollock, L. (2017). Resetting educational technology coursework for pre-service teachers: A computational thinking approach to the development of technological pedagogical content knowledge (TPACK). *Australasian Journal of Educational Technology*, *33*(3), 61–76. doi:10.14742/ajet.3521

Mulaudzi, M. A. (2021). *The implementation of hybrid problem-based learning to foster Senior Phase Technology student teachers' self-directed learning abilities* [Doctoral dissertation, North-West University (South Africa)].

Mundy, M. (2012). Faculty perceptions of cooperative learning and traditional discussion strategies. *Turkish Online Journal of Distance Education, 13*(2), 84–95.

Munn, Z., Peters, M. D., Stern, C., Tufanaru, C., McArthur, A., & Aromataris, E. (2018). Systematic review or scoping review? Guidance for authors when choosing between a systematic or scoping review approach. *BMC Medical Research Methodology, 18*(1), 1–7. doi:10.1186/s12874-018-0611-x PMID:30453902

Muñoz-Rujas, N., Baptiste, J., Pavani, A., & Montero, E. (2020). Enhancing interactive teaching of engineering topics using digital materials of the MERLOT database. In *Advances in Intelligent Systems and Computing* (pp. 295–306). Springer International Publishing. doi:10.1007/978-3-030-57799-5_31

Murata, A., Bofferding, L., Pothen, B. E., Taylor, M. W., & Wischnia, S. (2012). Making connections among student learning, content, and teaching: Teacher talk paths in elementary mathematics lesson study. *Journal for Research in Mathematics Education, 43*(5), 616–650. doi:10.5951/jresematheduc.43.5.0616

Murniati, C. T., Hartono, H., & Nugroho, A. C. (2023). The challenges, supports, and strategies of self-directed learning among college students. [EduLearn]. *Journal of Education and Learning, 17*(3), 365–373.

Musitha, M., & Mafukata, M. (2018). Crisis of decolonising education: Curriculum implementation in Limpopo Province, South Africa. Africa's Public Service Delivery. *Performance Research, 6*(1). doi:10.4102/apsdpr.v6i1.179

Nam, C. W., & Zellner, R. D. (2011). The relative effects of positive interdependence and groupprocessing on student achievement and attitude in online cooperative learning. *Computers & Education, 56*(3), 680–688. doi:10.1016/j.compedu.2010.10.010

Nandigam, D., & Bathula, H. (2013). Competing dichotomies in teaching computer programming to beginner-students. *American Journal of Educational Research, 1*(8), 307–312. doi:10.12691/education-1-8-7

Nascimbeni, F., & Burgos, D. (2019). Unveiling the relationship between the use of open educational resources and the adoption of open teaching practices in higher education. *Sustainability (Basel), 11*(20), 5637. doi:10.3390/su11205637

National Academies of Sciences, Engineering, and Medicine. (2018). *Assessing and Responding to the Growth of Computer Science Undergraduate Enrollments.* The National Academies Press. . doi:10.17226/24926

National Research Council. (2012). *Education for life and work: Developing transferable knowledge and skills in the 21st century.* National Academies Press.

Naveed, M. S., Sarim, M., & Ahsan, K. (2016). Learners Programming Language a Helping System for Introductory Programming Courses. *Mehran University Research Journal of Engineering and Technology, 35*(3), 347–358. doi:10.22581/muet1982.1603.05

Nedzinskaitė-Mačiūnienė, R., & Šimienė, G. (2021). A Strategic and Goal-Directed Student: Expectations vs. Reality. In *Improving Inclusive Education through Universal Design for Learning* (pp. 187–215). Springer International Publishing. doi:10.1007/978-3-030-80658-3_8

Nelan, M. M., Wachtendorf, T., & Penta, S. (2018). Agility in disaster relief: A social construction approach. *Risk, Hazards & Crisis in Public Policy, 9*(2), 132–150. doi:10.1002/rhc3.12135

Neumann, J. W. (2013). Developing a new framework for conceptualizing 'student-centered learning'. *The Educational Forum, 77*(2), 161–175. doi:10.1080/00131725.2012.761313

Newton, K. J. (2020). Informal STEM: learning with robotics and game design in an urban context. *Journal of Research on Technology in Education.* Routledge, *52*(2), 129–147. . doi:10.1080/15391523.2020.1713263

Nguyen, A., Ngo, H. N., Hong, Y., Dang, B., & Nguyen, B.-P. T. (2020). Ethical principles for artificial intelligence in education. *Education and Information Technologies*, *28*(4), 4221–4241. doi:10.1007/s10639-022-11316-w PMID:36254344

Nguyen, N., & Nadi, S. (2022, May). An empirical evaluation of GitHub copilot's code suggestions. In *Proceedings of the 19th International Conference on Mining Software Repositories*. Association for Computing Machinery, New York, NY, USA. 10.1145/3524842.3528470

Noone, M., & Mooney, A. (2018). Visual and textual programming languages: A systematic review of the literature. *Journal of Computers in Education*, *5*(2), 149–174. doi:10.1007/s40692-018-0101-5

Norman, D. A. (1983). Some observations on mental models. *Mental models, 7*(112), 7-14.

Nosek, J. T. (1998). The case for collaborative programming. *Communications of the ACM*, *41*(3), 105–108. doi:10.1145/272287.272333

Nosta, J. (2023, October 6). The 5th industrial revolution: The dawn of the cognitive age. *Psychology Today.* https://www.psychologytoday.com/intl/blog/the-digital-self/202310/the-5th-industrial-revolution-the-dawn-of-the-cognitive-age?eml

Nouri, J., Zhang, L., Mannila, L., & Norén, E. (2020). Development of computational thinking, digital competence and 21st century skills when learning programming in K-9. *Education Inquiry*, *11*(1), 1–17. doi:10.1080/20004508.2019.1627844

Novak, J. D., & Cañas, A. J. (2006). The theory underlying concept maps and how to construct them. *Florida Inst Hum Mach Cogn.*, *1*(1), 1–31.

Ntalindwa, T., Soron, T. R., Nduwingoma, M., Karangwa, E., & White, R. (2019). The use of information communication technologies among children with autism spectrum disorders: Descriptive qualitative study. *JMIR Pediatrics and Parenting*, *2*(2), e12176. doi:10.2196/12176 PMID:31573940

Ntekane, A. (2018). Parental Involvement in Education, A dissertation/thesis of North-West University Vaal. *Vanderbijlpark, South Africa.* doi:10.25304/rlt.v29.2544

Ntombana, L., Gwala, A., & Sibanda, F. (2023). Positioning the #feesmustfall movement within the transformative agenda: Reflections on student protests in South Africa. *Education as Change*, *27*. Advance online publication. doi:10.25159/1947-9417/10870

Nugent, G., Barker, B., Grandgenett, N., & Welch, G. (2016). 'Robotics camps, clubs, and competitions: Results from a US robotics project', *Robotics and Autonomous Systems. Robotics and Autonomous Systems*, *75*, 686–691. doi:10.1016/j.robot.2015.07.011

Nuryatin, A., Rokhmansyah, A., Hawa, A. M., Rahmayanti, I., & Nugroho, B. A. (2023). Google Classroom as an online Learning Media for Indonesian Language Learning During Covid-19 Pandemic. *Journal of Language Teaching and research*, 73-80. . doi:10.17507/jltr.1401.27

Nyisztor, K. (2019). *The non-programmer's programming book.*

Oakes, W. C., Zoltowski, C. B., & Drummond, M. (2014). Dissemination of community engagement in engineering and computing. *2014 IEEE Frontiers in Education Conference (FIE) Proceedings*, (pp. 1–7). IEEE. https://ieeexplore.ieee.org/abstract/document/7044371

Oda, M., Noborimoto, Y., & Horita, T. (2021). International trends in k–12 computer science curricula through comparative analysis: Implications for the primary curricula. *International Journal of Computer Science Education in Schools*, *4*(4). doi:10.21585/ijcses.v4i4.102

OECD. (2020). OECD learning compass 2030. *COMPASS 2030 Conceptual Learning Framework*. OECD. www.oecd.org/education/2030-project.

OECD. (2021). *PISA 2021 Creative Thinking Framework* (*Vol. 53*, pp. 1689–1699). OECD.

Ogegbo, A. A., & Aina, A. Y. (2022). Fostering The Development Of 21st Century Competencies Through Technology In Young Children: Perceptions Of Early Childhood Educators. Education and New Developments. doi:10.36315/2022v2end073

Okada, A., Connolly, T., & Scott, P. J. (Eds.). (2012). *Collaborative Learning 2.0: Open Educational Resources*. IGI Global. doi:10.4018/978-1-4666-0300-4

Oki, A. O., Uleanya, C., & Mbanga, C. (2023). Echoing the effect of information and communications technology on rural education development. *Information and Communication technology*, 1-18. doi:10.15587/2706-5448.2023.269698

Okwuduba, E. N., Nwosu, K. C., Okigbo, E. C., Samuel, N. N., & Achugbu, C. (2021). Impact of intrapersonal and interpersonal emotional intelligence and self-directed learning on academic performance among pre-university science students. *Heliyon*, *7*(3), e06611. doi:10.1016/j.heliyon.2021.e06611 PMID:33869848

Olawumi, K., & Mavuso, M. (2022). Education in the new normal: a need for alternative strategies in supporting teaching and learning in South African schools in the post-COVID-19 era. *E-Journal of Humanities Arts and Social Sciences*, (pp. 116–125). IEEE. . doi:10.38159/ehass.2022SP31110

Olivier, S. J., Oojorah, A., & Udhin, W. (2022). Multimodal Learning Environments in Southern Africa Embracing digital Pedagogies. *Digital educaiton and learning*, 1-16 . doi:10.1007/978-3-030-97656-9

Olsen, J. K., Rummel, N., & Eleven, V. (2021). Designing for the co-orchestration of social transitions between individual, small-group and whoe-class learning in the classroom. *International Journal of Artificial Intelligence in Education, 24-56*, 24-56 . doi:10.1007/s40593-020-00228-w

Onah, D. F., Pang, E. L., Sinclair, J. E., & Uhomoibhi, J. (2021). An innovative MOOC platform: The implications of self-directed learning abilities to improve motivation in learning and to support self-regulation. *The International Journal of Information and Learning Technology*, *38*(3), 283–298. doi:10.1108/IJILT-03-2020-0040

Onah, D., Pang, E., & Sinclair, J. (2020). Cognitive optimism of distinctive initiatives to foster self-directed and self-regulated learning skills: A comparative analysis of conventional and blended-learning in undergraduate studies. *Education and Information Technologies*, *25*(5), 4365–4380. doi:10.1007/s10639-020-10172-w

Onorato, L. A., & Schvaneveldt, R. W. (1987). Programmer-nonprogrammer differences in specifying procedures to people and computers. *Journal of Systems and Software*, *7*(4), 357–369. doi:10.1016/0164-1212(87)90034-3

Onwuegbuzie, A. J., Collins, K. M. T., & Jiao, Q. G. (2009). Performance of cooperative learning groups in a postgraduate education research methodology course: The role of social interdependence. *Active Learning in Higher Education*, *10*(3), 265–277. doi:10.1177/1469787409343190

Oosthuizen, I. (2016). *Self-directed learning research: An imperative for transforming the educational landscape*. AOSIS.

Ornellas, A., Falkner, K., & Edman Stålbrandt, E. (2019). Enhancing graduates' employability skills through authentic learning approaches. *Higher education, skills and work-based learning*, *9*(1), 107-120.

Osman, G., Duffy, T. M., Chang, Y., & Lee, J. (2011). Learning through collaboration: studnet perspectives. *Asian Pacific Education Review*, 547-558 . doi:10.1007/s12564-011-9156-y

Osode, J. I. (2021). *Learning management systems in higher education: the attitudes, expectations and experiences of academic staff at selected Nigerian higher Eeducation institutions*. University of Johannesburg.

Owens, T. L. (2017). Higher education in the sustainable development goals framework. *European Journal of Education, 52*(4), 414–420. doi:10.1111/ejed.12237

Owoc, M. L., Sawicka, A., & Weichbroth, P. (2019). Artificial Intelligence Technologies in Education: Benefits, Challenges and Strategies of Implementation. *IFIP International Workshop on Artificial Intelligence for Knowledge Management,* (pp. 37-58). IEEE.

Oxley, L., Walker, P., Thorns, D., & Wang, H. (2008). The knowledge economy/society: The latest example of" Measurement without theory"? *Journal of Philosophical Economics, II*(1), 20–54. doi:10.46298/jpe.10568

Özmutlu, M., Atay, D., & Erdoğan, B. (2021). Collaboration and engagement based coding training to enhance children's computational thinking self-efficacy. *Thinking Skills and Creativity, 40*, 100833. doi:10.1016/j.tsc.2021.100833

Paas, F., & Van Merriënboer, J. J. G. (2020). Cognitive-load theory: Methods to manage working memory load in the learning of complex tasks. *Current Directions in Psychological Science, 29*(4), 394–398. doi:10.1177/0963721420922183

Page, M. J., McKenzie, J. E., Bossuyt, P. M., Boutron, I., Hoffmann, T. C., Mulrow, C. D., & Moher, D. (2023). A declaração PRISMA 2020: Diretriz atualizada para relatar revisões sistemáticas. *Revista Panamericana de Salud Pública, 46*, e112. PMID:36601438

Palomares, I., Martínez-Cámara, E., Montes, R., García-Moral, P., Chiachio, M., Chiachio, J., & Herrera, F. (2021). A panoramic view and swot analysis of artificial intelligence for achieving the sustainable development goals by 2030: Progress and prospects. *Applied Intelligence, 51*(9), 1–31. https://doi. Org/10.1007/s10489-021-02264-y. doi:10.1007/s10489-021-02264-y PMID:34764606

Pandit, N. (1996). The Creation of Theory: A recent application of the grounded theory method. *The Qualitative Report*. Nova Southeastern University. . doi:10.46743/2160-3715/1996.2054

Pankratova, O., Ledovskaya, N., & Konopko, E. (2021). Forming the Competence of the Teacher of Educational Robotics. *Standards and Monitoring in Education., 9*(6), 8–15. doi:10.12737/1998-1740-2021-9-6-8-15

Pan, X. (2020). Technology acceptance, technological self-efficacy, and attitude toward technology-based self-directed learning: Learning motivation as a mediator. *Frontiers in Psychology, 11*, 564294. doi:10.3389/fpsyg.2020.564294 PMID:33192838

Papadakis, S. (2021). The impact of coding apps to support young children in computational thinking and computational fluency. A literature review. *Frontiers in Education, 6*, 657895. doi:10.3389/feduc.2021.657895

Papadakis, S., Kalogiannakis, M., & Zaranis, N. (2016). Developing fundamental programming concepts and computational thinking with ScratchJr in preschool education: A case study. *International Journal of Mobile Learning and Organization, 10*(3), 187–202. doi:10.1504/IJMLO.2016.077867

Papavlasopoulou, S., Giannakos, M. N., & Jaccheeri, L. (2019). Exploring children's learning experience in constructionism-based coding activities through design-based research. *Computers in Human Behavior, 99*, 415–427. doi:10.1016/j.chb.2019.01.008

Park, J. H., Kim, H.-Y., & Lim, S.-B. (2019). Development of an electronic book accessibility standard for physically challenged individuals and deduction of a production guideline. *Computer Standards & Interfaces, 64*, 78–84. doi:10.1016/j.csi.2018.12.004

Pather, M. R. (2020). Education in South Africa. *Fourth Industrial Revolution*, 19.

Pea, R. D., & Kurland, D. M. (1983). On the cognitive prerequisites of learning computer programming. *New Ideas in Psychology, 2*(2), 137–168. doi:10.1016/0732-118X(84)90018-7

Pecanin, E., Spalevic, P., Mekic, E., Jovic, S., & Milovanovic, I. (2019). E-learning engineers based on constructive and multidisciplinary approach. *Computer Applications in Engineering Education*, *27*(6), 1544–1554. doi:10.1002/cae.22168

Pellet, J. P., & Parriaux, G. (2023). Informatics in Schools. *Beyond Bits and Bytes: Nurturing Informatics Intelligence in Education: 16th International Conference on Informatics in Schools: Situation, Evolution, and Perspectives, ISSEP 2023*, Lausanne, Switzerland.

Peng, J., Wang, M., & Sampson, D. (2017). Visualizing the complex process for deep learning with an authentic programming project. *Journal of Educational Technology & Society*, *20*(4), 275–287. https://www.jstor.org/stable/26229223

Pérez-Marín, D., Hijón-Neira, R., Bacelo, A., & Pizarro, C. (2020). Can computational thinking be improved by using a methodology based on metaphors and scratch to teach computer programming to children? *Computers in Human Behavior*, *105*(C), 105849. doi:10.1016/j.chb.2018.12.027

Perez, R. S., & Emery, C. D. (1995). Designer thinking: How novices and experts think about instructional design. *Performance Improvement Quarterly*, *8*(3), 80–95. doi:10.1111/j.1937-8327.1995.tb00688.x

Peslak, A., Kovalchick, L., Kovacs, P., Conforti, M., Wang, W., & Bhatnagar, N. (2018). Linking Programmer Analyst Skills to Industry Needs: A Current Review. *In Proceedings of the EDSIG Conference ISSN* (Vol. 2473, p. 3857).

Petelka, J., Finn, M., Roesner, F., & Shilton, K. (2022, February). Principles matter: integrating an ethics intervention into a computer security course. In *Proceedings of the 53rd ACM Technical Symposium on Computer Science Education-Volume 1* (pp. 474-480). ACM. 10.1145/3478431.3499275

Peters, M. D. J., Godfrey, C., McInerney, P., Munn, Z., Tricco, A. C., & Khalil, H. (2020). Chapter 11: Scoping Reviews. Aromataris E, Munn Z, editors. *JBI Manual for Evidence Synthesis*. JBI. doi:10.46658/JBIMES-20-12

Petre, M., & Price, B. (2014). Using robotics to motivate 'Back Door' learning. *Education and Information Technologies*, *9*(2), 147–158. doi:10.1023/B:EAIT.0000027927.78380.60

Pham, M. T., Rajić, A., Greig, J. D., Sargeant, J. M., Papadopoulos, A., & McEwen, S. A. (2014). A scoping review of scoping reviews: Advancing the approach and enhancing the consistency. *Research Synthesis Methods*, *5*(4), 371–385. doi:10.1002/jrsm.1123 PMID:26052958

Phillippi, J., & Lauderdale, J. (2017). A Guide to Field Notes for Qualitative Research: Context and Conversation. *Qualitative Health Research*, *23*(8), 381–388. doi:10.1177/1049732317697102 PMID:29298584

Phung, T., Cambronero, J., Gulwani, S., Kohn, T., Majumdar, R., Singla, A., & Soares, G. (2023). Generating High-Precision Feedback for Programming Syntax Errors using Large Language Models. *arXiv preprint arXiv:2302.04662.*

Piatti, A. (2020). Fostering computational thinking through educational robotics: A model for creative computational problem solving. *International Journal of STEM Education*, *7*(1), 1–18.

Piccolo, S. R., Denny, P., Luxton-Reilly, A., Payne, S. H., & Ridge, P. G. (2023). Evaluating a large language model's ability to solve programming exercises from an introductory bioinformatics course. *PLoS Computational Biology*, *19*(9), e1011511. doi:10.1371/journal.pcbi.1011511 PMID:37769024

Piedade, J., Dorotea, N., Pedro, A., & Matos, J. F. (2020). On teaching programming fundamentals and computational thinking with educational robotics: A didactic experience with pre-service teachers. *Education Sciences*, *10*(9), 1–15. doi:10.3390/educsci10090214

Pirolli, P., & Recker, M. (1994). Learning strategies and transfer in the domain of programming. *Cognition and Instruction*, *12*(3), 235–275. doi:10.1207/s1532690xci1203_2

Pischetola, M., & Heinsfeld, B. (2018). Technology and teacher's motivational style: A research study in Brazilian Public Schools. *Journal of Education*, (17), 163–178. doi:10.7358/ecps-2018-017-pisc

Piwek, P., & Savage, S. (2020). Challenges with Learning to Program and Problem Solve. *An Analysis of Student Online Discussions Conference or Workshop Item Challenges with Learning to Program and Problem Solve: An Analysis of Student Online Discussions., 2020*, 494–499. doi:10.1145/3328778.3366838

Popescu, E., & Buse, F. E. (2014). Supporting students to find relevant learning resources through social bookmarking and recommendations. *18th International Conference on System Theory, Control and Computing*. IEEE. 10.1109/ICSTCC.2014.6982459

Portelli, A. (1980). The Three Laws of Robotics: Laws of the Text, Laws of Production, Laws of Society. *Science Fiction Studies*, *7*, 150.

Pozzi, M., Prattichizzo, D., & Malvezzi, M. (2021). Accessible Educational Resources for Teaching and Learning Robotics. *Robotics (Basel, Switzerland)*, *10*(38), 1–21. doi:10.3390/robotics10010038

Prather, J., Reeves, B. N., Denny, P., Becker, B. A., Leinonen, J., Luxton-Reilly, A., & Santos, E. A. (2023). "It's Weird That it Knows What I Want": Usability and Interactions with Copilot for Novice Programmers. *arXiv preprint arXiv:2304.02491.*

Prentice, M., Jayawickreme, E., & Fleeson, W. (2018). Integrating whole trait theory and self-determination theory. *Journal of Personality*, *87*(1), 56–69. doi:10.1111/jopy.12417 PMID:29999534

Psotka, J., Massey, L. D., & Mutter, S. A. (Eds.). (1988). *Intelligent tutoring systems: Lessons learned.* Psychology Press.

Purba, S. W. D., & Hwang, W. Y. (2017). Investigation of learning behaviors and achievement of vocational high school students using an ubiquitous physics tablet PC app. *Journal of Science Education and Technology*, *26*(3), 322–331. doi:10.1007/s10956-016-9681-x

Qian, Y., & Lehman, J. (2017). Students' misconceptions and other difficulties in introductory programming: A literature review. [TOCE]. *ACM Transactions on Computing Education*, *18*(1), 1–24. doi:10.1145/3077618

Qidwai, U., Riley, R., & El-Sayed, S. (2013). Attracting Students to the Computing Disciplines: A Case Study of a Robotics Contest. Procedia - Social and Behavioral Sciences, 102, 520–531. doi:10.1016/j.sbspro.2013.10.768

Qin, Z., Johnson, D. W., & Johnson, R. T. (1995). Cooperative versus competitive efforts and problem solving. *Review of Educational Research*, *65*(2), 129–143. doi:10.3102/00346543065002129

Qureshi, M. I., Khan, N., Raza, H., Imran, A., & Ismail, F. (2021). Digital Technologies in Education 4.0. Does it Enhance the Effectiveness of Learning? A Systematic Literature Review. *International Journal of Interactive Mobile Technologies*, *15*(4), 31. doi:10.3991/ijim.v15i04.20291

Raj, R. K., & Kumar, A. N. (2022). Toward computer science curricular guidelines 2023 (CS2023). *ACM Inroads*, *13*(4), 22–25. doi:10.1145/3571092

Rao, L., & Ab Jalil, H. (2021). A survey on Acceptance and Readiness to Use Robot Teaching Technology Among Prinary School Science Teachers. *Asian Social Science*, *17*(2), 115. doi:10.5539/ass.v17n11p115

Rathod, N., & Cassel, L. (2013). Building a search engine for computer science course syllabi. *Proceedings of the 13th ACM/IEEE-CS Joint Conference on Digital Libraries*. http://dx.doi.org/10.1145/2467696.2467723

Ray, B. B., Rogers, R. R. H., & Hocutt, M. M. (2020). Perceptions of non-STEM discipline teachers on coding as a teaching and learning tool: What are the possibilities? *Journal of Digital Learning in Teacher Education, 36*(1), 19–31. doi:10.1080/21532974.2019.1646170

Razak, A. A., Ramdan, R. M., Mahjom, N., Zabit, N. M., Muhammad, F., Hussin, M. Y., & Abdullar, N. L. (2022). Improving Critical Thinking skills in Teaching through problem-Based Learnng for Students: A Scoping Review. *International Journal of Learning, Teachng and Educational Research*, 342-362.

Reeves, B., Sarsa, S., Prather, J., Denny, P., Becker, B. A., Hellas, A., & Leinonen, J. (2023, June). Evaluating the performance of code generation models for solving Parsons problems with small prompt variations. In *Proceedings of the 2023 Conference on Innovation and Technology in Computer Science Education* V. 1 (pp. 299-305). ACM. 10.1145/3587102.3588805

Reiss, M. J. (2021). The use of AI in education: Practicalities and ethical considerations. *London Review of Education, 19*(1), 1–14. doi:10.14324/LRE.19.1.05

Relkin, E., Ruiter, L., & Bers, M. U. (2020). TechCheck: Development and validation of an unplugged assessment of computational thinking in early childhood education. *Journal of Science Education and Technology, 29*(4), 482–498. doi:10.1007/s10956-020-09831-x

Renkl, A., & Atkinson, R. K. (2003). Structuring the transition from example study to problem solving in cognitive skill acquisition: A cognitive load perspective. *Educational Psychologist, 38*(1), 15–22. doi:10.1207/S15326985EP3801_3

Resnick, M., Maloney, J., Monroy-Hernández, A., Rusk, N., Eastmond, E., Brennan, K., Millner, A., Rosenbaum, E., Silver, J., Sillverman, B., & Kafai, Y. (2009). Scratch: Programming for all. *Communications of the ACM, 52*(11), 60–67. doi:10.1145/1592761.1592779

Reynolds, D. W. (2021). *Using Entrepreneurship Education to Empower Students with 21st Century Skills.* [Doctoral dissertation, St. Thomas University].

Ribble, M., & Bailey, G. (2007). *Digital Citizenship in Schools, Mike Ribble and Gerald Bailey*. InfoWorld. www.infoworld.com/article/05/11/22/hnonlineshoppers_1.html.

Richey, R. C., Klein, J. D., & Tracey, M. W. (2010). *The instructional design knowledge base: Theory, research, and practice*. Routledge. doi:10.4324/9780203840986

Rich, P. J., Browning, S. F., Perkins, M., Shoop, T., Yoshikawa, E., & Belikov, O. M. (2019). Coding in K-8: International trends in teaching elementary/primary computing. *TechTrends, 63*(3), 311–329. doi:10.1007/s11528-018-0295-4

Rich, P. J., Mason, S. L., & O'Leary, J. (2021). Measuring the effect of continuous professional development on elementary teachers' self-efficacy to teach coding and computational thinking. *Computers & Education, 168*, 104196. doi:10.1016/j.compedu.2021.104196

Riedesel, C. P., Manley, E. D., Poser, S., & Deogun, J. S. (2009). A model academic ethics and integrity policy for computer science departments. *SIGCSE Bulletin, 41*(1), 357–361. doi:10.1145/1539024.1508994

Riley, W., & Anderson, P. (2006). Randomized study on the impact of cooperative learning: Distance education in public health. *Quarterly Review of Distance Education, 7*(2), 129.

Rist, R. S. (1989). Schema creation in programming. *Cognitive Science, 13*(3), 389–414. doi:10.1207/s15516709cog1303_3

Riyanti, D. (2019). The role of motivation in learning English as a foreign language. [JELTIM]. *Journal of English Language Teaching Innovations and Materials, 1*(1), 29–35. doi:10.26418/jeltim.v1i1.27788

Robins, A. V. (2019). Novice programmers and introductory programming. The Cambridge handbook of computing education research, 327. Cambridge Press. doi:10.1017/9781108654555.013

Robins, A., Rountree, J., & Rountree, N. (2003). Learning and teaching programming: A review and discussion. *Computer Science Education, 13*(2), 137–172. doi:10.1076/csed.13.2.137.14200

Robinson, J. D., & Persky, A. M. (2020). Developing self-directed learners. *American Journal of Pharmaceutical Education, 84*(3), 847512. doi:10.5688/ajpe847512 PMID:32313284

Rodríguez, A. (2013). Learning by teaching robotics with mobile devices in rural areas. *International Conference on Information Society (i-Society 2013).* IEEE. https://ieeexplore.ieee.org/abstract/document/6636353

Rodríguez-Martínez, J. A., González-Calero, J. A., & Sáez-López, J. M. (2020). Computational thinking and mathematics using Scratch, an experiment with sixth-grade students. *Interactive Learning Environments, 28*(3), 316–327. doi:10.1080/10494820.2019.1612448

Rogers, C. R. (1969). *Freedom to learn.* Charles Merrill.

Rogers, C., & Portsmore, M. (2014). Bringing engineering to elementary school. *Journal of STEM Education: Innovations and Research, 5*(2), 17–28.

Rogers-Shaw, C., Carr-Chellman, D. J., & Choi, J. (2018). Universal design for learning: Guidelines for accessible online instruction. *Adult Learning, 29*(1), 20–31. doi:10.1177/1045159517735530

Romero, M., Lepage, A., & Lille, B. (2017). Computational thinking development through creative programming in higher education. *International Journal of Educational Technology in Higher Education, 14*(1), 42. Advance online publication. doi:10.1186/s41239-017-0080-z

Ruggiero, D., & Mong, C. J. (2015). The teacher technology integration experience: Practice and reflection in the classroom. *Journal of Information Technology Education*, 14. doi:10.28945/2227

Rusk, N., Resnick, M., Berg, R., & Pezalla-Granlund, M. (2008). New pathways into robotics: Strategies for broadening participation. *Journal of Science Education and Technology, 17*(1), 59–69. doi:10.1007/s10956-007-9082-2

Ryan, R. M., Duineveld, J. J., Di Domenico, S. I., Ryan, W. S., Steward, B. A., & Bradshaw, E. L. (2022). We know this much is (meta-analytically) true: A meta-review of meta-analytic findings evaluating self-determination theory. *Psychological Bulletin, 148*(11-12), 813–842. doi:10.1037/bul0000385

Ryan, R., & Deci, E. (2000). Self-determination theory and the facilitation of intrinsic motivation, social development, and well-being. *The American Psychologist, 55*(1), 68–78. doi:10.1037/0003-066X.55.1.68 PMID:11392867

Sáez-López, J.-M., Román-González, M., & Vázquez-Cano, E. (2016). Visual programming languages integrated across the curriculum in elementary school: A two year case study using "Scratch" in five schools. *Computers & Education, 97*, 129–141. doi:10.1016/j.compedu.2016.03.003

Safitri, I., & Lestari, P. (2021). Optimising learning management system to teach English grammar. *Edulink Education and Linguistics Knowledge Journal, 3*(1), 51. doi:10.32503/edulink.v3i1.1490

Salcito, A. (2021, February 16). *Reimagining computer science in the curriculum.* Microsoft Education Blog. https://educationblog.microsoft.com/en-us/2021/02/reimagining-computer-science-in-the-curriculum

Samuels, P., & Haapasalo, L. (2016). Real and virtual robotics in mathematics education at the school–university transition. *International Journal of Mathematical Education in Science and Technology, 43*(3), 285–301. doi:10.1080/0020739X.2011.618548

Sands, P. (2019). Addressing cognitive load in the computer science classroom. *ACM Inroads*, *10*(1), 44–51. doi:10.1145/3210577

Sangkawetai, C., Neanchaleay, J., Koul, R., & Murphy, E. (2018). Predictors of K-12 Teachers' Instructional Strategies with ICTs. *Technology, Knowledge and Learning*, 1-29.

Santhanam, R., Sasidharan, S., & Webster, J. (2008). Using self-regulatory learning to enhance e-learning-based information technology training. *Information Systems Research*, *19*(1), 26–47. doi:10.1287/isre.1070.0141

Santo, R., Vogel, S., DeLyser, L. A., & Ahn, J. (2018). Asking "CS4What?" as a basis for CS4All: Workshop tools to support sustainable K-12 CS implementations. In *Proceedings of the 49th ACM Technical Symposium on Computer Science Education* (pp. 678-686). ACM.

Sapounidis, T., & Alimisis, D. (2021, February). Educational robotics curricula: Current trends and shortcomings. In *Educational Robotics International Conference* (pp. 127-138). Cham: Springer International Publishing. 10.1007/978-3-030-77022-8_12

Sarpong, K. A. M., Arthur, J. K., & Amoako, P. Y. O. (2013). Causes of failure of students in computer programming courses: The teacher-learner Perspective. *International Journal of Computer Applications*, *77*(12).

Sarsa, S., Denny, P., Hellas, A., & Leinonen, J. (2022). Automatic Generation of Programming Exercises and Code Explanations Using Large Language Models. In *Proceedings of the 2022 ACM Conference on International Computing Education Research* - Volume 1 *(ICER '22),* Vol. 1 (pp. 27-43). Association for Computing Machinery. 10.1145/3501385.3543957

Savage, M., & Csizmadia, A. (2018). Computational thinking and creativity in the secondary curriculum. In *Debates in Computing and ICT Education* (pp. 137–152). Routledge. doi:10.4324/9781315709505-10

Savelka, J., Agarwal, A., Bogart, C., & Sakr, M. (2023). Large Language Models (GPT) Struggle to Answer Multiple-Choice Questions about Code. *arXiv preprint arXiv:2303.08033*. doi:10.5220/0011996900003470

Savelka, J., Agarwal, A., Bogart, C., Song, Y., & Sakr, M. (2023). Can Generative Pre-trained Transformers (GPT) Pass Assessments in Higher Education Programming Courses? *arXiv preprint arXiv:2303.09325*. doi:10.1145/3587102.3588792

Scaradozzi, D., Screpanti, L., Cesaretti, L., Storti, M., & Mazzieri, E. (2019). Implementation and Assessment Methodologies of Teachers' Training Courses for STEM Activities. *Technology. Knowledge and Learning*, *24*(2), 247–268. doi:10.1007/s10758-018-9356-1

Scherer, R., Siddiq, F., & Viveros, B. (2020). A meta-analysis of teaching and learning computer programming: Effective instructional approaches and conditions. *Computers in Human Behavior*, *109*, 1–18. doi:10.1016/j.chb.2020.106349

Schunk, D. H. (2023). Self-regulation of self-efficacy and attributions in academic settings. In *Self-regulation of learning and performance* (pp. 75–99). Routledge.

Schweder, S., & Raufelder, D. (2022). Adolescents' enjoyment and effort in class: Influenced by self-directed learning intervals. *Journal of School Psychology*, *95*, 72–89. doi:10.1016/j.jsp.2022.09.002 PMID:36371126

Scott, C., & Medaugh, M. (2017). Axial coding. The International Encyclopedia of Communication Research Methods, 1–2. Springer. doi:10.1002/9781118901731.iecrm0012

Seale, C. (2000). Quality in qualitative research. *Qualitative Inquiry*, *5*(4), 465–478. https://citeseerx.ist.psu.edu/viewdoc/download?doi=10.1.1.460.3511&rep=rep1&type=pdf. doi:10.1177/107780049900500402

Segal, J., & Ahmad, K. (1993). The Role of Examples in the teaching of Programming Languages. *Journal of Educational Computing Research*, *9*(1), 115–129. doi:10.2190/X63F-X1QX-V4KL-BJEX

Sellgren, K. (2018, July 26). *Exam boards police social media in cheating crackdown.* British Broadcasting Corporation (BBC). https://www.bbc.com/news/education-44965465

Senent, G. I., Kelley, K., & Abo-Zena, M. (2021). Sustaining curiosity: Reggio-Emilia inspired learning. *Earlhy child development and care*, 1247-1258 . doi:10.1080/030044430.2021.1900835

Sengodan, V., & Iksan, Z. H. (2012). Students' learning styles and intrinsic motivation in learning mathematics. *Asian Social Science*, *8*(16), 17. doi:10.5539/ass.v8n16p17

Sentance, S., & Csizmadia, A. (2015). Teachers' perspectives on successful strategies for teaching Computing in school. (2015, June). In IFIP TCS.

Sentance, S., & Csizmadia, A. (2017). Computing in the curriculum: Challenges and strategies from a teacher's perspective. *Education and Information Technologies*, *22*(2), 469–495. doi:10.1007/s10639-016-9482-0

Sentance, S., Singh, L., & De Freitas, P. (2020). *Challenges Facing Computing Teachers in Guyana*. ACM. doi:10.1145/3328778.3372613

Seo, K., Tang, J., Roll, I., Fels, S., & Yoon, D. (2021). The impact of artificial intelligence on learner–instructor interaction in online learning. *International Journal of Educational Technology in Higher Education*, *18*(1), 1–23. doi:10.1186/s41239-021-00292-9 PMID:34778540

Seraphin, S. B., Grizzell, J. A., Kerr-German, A., Perkins, M. A., Grzanka, P. R., & Hardin, E. E. (2019). A conceptual framework for non-disposable assignments: Inspiring implementation, innovation, and research. *Psychology Learning & Teaching*, *18*(1), 84–97. doi:10.1177/1475725718811711

Serrano, D. R., Dea-Ayuela, M. A., Gonzalez-Burgos, E., Serrano-Gil, A., & Lalatsa, A. (2019). Technology-enhanced learning in higher education: How to enhance student engagement through blended learning. *European Journal of Education*, *54*(2), 273–286. doi:10.1111/ejed.12330

Shafi, M., Lei, Z., Song, X., & Sarker, M. N. I. (2020). The effects of transformational leadership on employee creativity: Moderating role of intrinsic motivation. *Asia Pacific Management Review*, *25*(3), 166–176. doi:10.1016/j.apmrv.2019.12.002

Shah, M. A., Hussain, M., & Jabbar, A. (2022). Applications of Information Communication Technology in Education. *Journal of Computing & Biomedical Informatics*, *4*(1), 87–91.

Sheldon, K., & Prentice, M. (2019). Self-determination theory as a foundation for personality researchers. *Journal of Personality*, *87*(1), 5–14. doi:10.1111/jopy.12360 PMID:29144550

Shenton, A. K. (2004). Strategies for ensuring trustworthiness in qualitative research projects. *Education for Information*, *22*(2), 63–75. doi:10.3233/EFI-2004-22201

Shinohara, K., Kawas, S., Ko, A. J., & Ladner, R. E. (2018). Who teaches accessibility? A survey of US computing faculty. In: *Proceedings of the 49th ACM Technical Symposium on Computer Science Education*. ACM. 10.1145/3159450.3159484

Shin, Y., Jung, J., & Lee, H. J. (2023). Exploring the impact of concept-oriented faded WOE and metacognitive scaffolding on learners' transfer performance and motivation in programming education. *Metacognition and Learning*, 1–22. doi:10.1007/s11409-023-09362-x

Silvis, D., Lee, V. R., Clarke-Midura, J., & Shumway, J. F. (2022). The technical matters: Young children debugging (with) tangible coding toys. *Information and Learning Science*, *123*(9–10), 577–600. doi:10.1108/ILS-12-2021-0109

Simon, S. J. & Morgan, M. (2016). Negotiating the maze of academic integrity in computing education. In: *Proceedings of the 2016 ITiCSE Working Group Reports, ITiCSE 2016*. Association for Computing Machinery. 10.1145/3024906.3024910

Singaravelu, S. L., & Nair, A. S. (2021). Technology deployment in self-directed learning: A guide for new path in medical education. *SBV J Basic Clin Appl Health Sci*, *4*(2), 51–53. doi:10.5005/jp-journals-10082-03112

Sirocchi, C., Pofantis, A. O., & Bogliolo, A. (2022). Investigating Participation Mechanisms in EU Code Week. arXiv preprint arXiv:2205.14740.

Skiena, S. S., & Revilla, M. A. (2003). Programming challenges: The programming contest training manual. *ACM SIGACT News*, *34*(3), 68–74. doi:10.1145/945526.945539

Smith, P. L., & Ragan, T. J. (2005). *Instructional design*. John Wiley & Sons.

Sokhanvar, Z., Salehi, K., & Sokhanvar, F. (2021). Advantages of authentic assessment for improving the learning experience and employability skills of higher education students: A systematic literature review. *Studies in Educational Evaluation*, *70*, 101030. doi:10.1016/j.stueduc.2021.101030

Song, Y., Lee, Y., & Lee, J. (2022). Mediating effects of self-directed learning on the relationship between critical thinking and problem-solving in student nurses attending online classes: A cross-sectional descriptive study. *Nurse Education Today*, *109*, 105227. doi:10.1016/j.nedt.2021.105227 PMID:34972030

South Africa O. R. T. (2017). *ORT South Africa*. ORTSA. https://www.ortsa.org.za/ort-sa-owns-thetechnology-revolution

Sovova, O. (2021). *Right to Education and the Best Interest of a Child in the Constitutional Court Case Law*. The Constitution of the Republic of South Africa. (1996). https://www.gov.za/documents/constitution/constitution-republic-south-africa-1996-1,

Stachel, J., Marghitu, D., Brahim, T. B., Sims, R., Reynolds, L., & Czelusniak, V. (2013). Managing cognitive load in introductory programming courses: A cognitive aware scaffolding tool. *Journal of Integrated Design & Process Science*, *17*(1), 37–54. doi:10.3233/jid-2013-0004

Staff Writer. (2021). South Africa moves ahead with coding and robotics at schools. *Business Tech*. https://businesstech.co.za/news/technology/469860/south-africa-moves-ahead-with-coding-and-robotics-at-schools/

Stancil, S. K., & Bartlett, M. E. (2022). An Integrative Literature Review of Non-Disposable and Reusable Assignments. *Journal on Excellence in College Teaching*, *33*(1), 155–175.

Steenhof, N., Woods, N. N., & Mylopoulos, M. (2020). Exploring why we learn from productive failure: Insights from the cognitive and learning sciences. *Advances in Health Sciences Education : Theory and Practice*, *25*(5), 1099–1106. doi:10.1007/s10459-020-10013-y PMID:33180211

Stephenson, C., Derbenwick Miller, A., Alvarado, C., Barker, L., Barr, V., Seels, B., & Glasgow, Z. (2018). *Making instructional design decisions* (2nd ed.). Prentice Hall, Inc.

Stewart, W. H., Baek, Y., Kwid, G., & Taylor, K. (2021). Exploring factors that influence computational thinking skills in elementary students' collaborative robotics. *Journal of Educational Computing Research*, *59*(6), 1208–1239. doi:10.1177/0735633121992479

Stokes, A., Aurini, J., Rizk, J., Gorbet, R., & McLevey, J. (2022). Using Robotics to Support the Acquisition of STEM and 21st-Century Competencies: Promising (and Practical) Directions. *Canadian Journal of Education*, *45*(4). doi:10.53967/cje-rce.5455

Strickland, T. N. (2021). *The self-directed goal theory experiment: a mixed methods study of personal development goal-setting programs and self-efficacy* [Doctoral dissertation, Lindenwood University].

Sullivan, A., & Bers, M. U. (2019). Computer science education in early childhood: The case of ScratchJr. *Journal of Information Technology Education. In Practice*, *18*, 113–138.

Sullivan, F. R. (2012). Robotics and science literacy: Thinking skills, science process skills and systems understanding. *Journal of Research in Science Teaching*, *45*(3), 373–394. doi:10.1002/tea.20238

Sumuer, E. (2018). Factors related to college students' self-directed learning with technology. *Australasian Journal of Educational Technology*, *34*(4), 29–43. doi:10.14742/ajet.3142

Sung, W., Ahn, J., & Black, J. B. (2017). Introducing computational thinking to young learners: Practicing computational perspectives through embodiment in mathematics education. *Technology. Knowledge and Learning*, *22*(3), 443–463. doi:10.1007/s10758-017-9328-x

Sung, W., & Black, J. B. (2021). Factors to consider when designing effective learning: Infusing computational thinking in mathematics to support thinking-doing. *Journal of Research on Technology in Education*, *53*(4), 404–426. doi:10.1080/15391523.2020.1784066

Sun, W., Hong, J. C., Dong, Y., Huang, Y., & Fu, Q. (2023). Self-directed learning predicts online learning engagement in higher education mediated by the perceived value of knowing learning goals. *The Asia-Pacific Education Researcher*, *32*(3), 307–316. doi:10.1007/s40299-022-00653-6

Susnjak, T. (2023). Beyond Predictive Learning Analytics Modelling and onto Explainable Artificial Intelligence with Prescriptive Analytics and ChatGPT. *International Journal of Artificial Intelligence in Education*. doi:10.1007/s40593-023-00336-3

Svanhild, B. (2020). Student-teacher dialectic in the co-creation of a Zone of proximal development an example from from kindergaten mathematics. *Education Research Journal*, 413-356.

Svendsen, B., Burner, T., & Røkenes, F. M. (2020). *Intrinsically Motivating Instruction—Thomas Malone. Science Education in Theory and Practice: An Introductory Guide to Learning Theory*, (pp. 45-50). Research Gate.

Swain, D. E., Wagy, J., McClelland, M., & Jacobs, P. (2006). Developing a metadata schema for CSERD: a computational science digital library. In *Proceedings of the 6th ACM/IEEE-CS joint conference on Digital libraries,* (pp. 350-350). IEEE. 10.1145/1141753.1141845

Sweet, D. (2014). *Strategies California superintendents use to implement 21st century skills programs*. University of Southern California.

Sweller, J. (1988). Cognitive load during problem solving: Effects on learning. *Cognitive Science*, *12*(2), 257–285. doi:10.1207/s15516709cog1202_4

Sweller, J. (2020). Cognitive load theory and educational technology. *Educational Technology Research and Development*, *68*(1), 1–16. doi:10.1007/s11423-019-09701-3

Sweller, J., & Cooper, G. A. (1985). The use of worked examples as a substitute for problem solving in learning algebra. *Cognition and Instruction*, *2*(1), 59–89. doi:10.1207/s1532690xci0201_3

Sweller, J., Van Merriënboer, J. J., & Paas, F. (2019). Cognitive architecture and instructional design: 20 years later. *Educational Psychology Review*, *31*(2), 261–292. doi:10.1007/s10648-019-09465-5

Tamarack. (2010). *Approaches to Measuring more Community Engagement, Tamarak Institute for Community Engagement*. Tamarack Community. http://tamarackcommunity.ca/downloads/index/Measuring_More_Community_Engagement.pdf.

Tang, A. L., Tung, V. W. S., & Cheng, T. O. (2023). Teachers' perceptions of the potential use of educational robotics in management education. *Interactive Learning Environments*, *31*(1), 313–324. doi:10.1080/10494820.2020.1780269

Tan, S. C., & Hung, D. (2002). Beyond information pumping: Creating a constructivist e-learning environment. *Educational Technology*, *42*(5), 48–54.

Tedre, M., & Denning, P. J. (2016). The long quest for computational thinking. In: *ACM International Conference Proceeding Series.* Association for Computing Machinery. 10.1145/2999541.2999542

Teixeira, P. N., & Shin, J. C. (Eds.). (2020). *The international encyclopedia of higher education systems and institutions.* Springer. doi:10.1007/978-94-017-8905-9

Teo, P. (2019). Teaching for the 21st century: A case for dialogic pedagogy. *Learning, Culture and Social Interaction*, *21*, 170–178. doi:10.1016/j.lcsi.2019.03.009

Teo, T., Unwin, S., Scherer, R., & Gardiner, V. (2021). Initial teacher training for twenty-first century skills in the Fourth Industrial Revolution (IR 4.0): A scoping review. *Computers & Education*, *170*, 104223. Advance online publication. doi:10.1016/j.compedu.2021.104223

The National Academic of Science, Engineering, and Medicine. (2017, October 26). *New Report: Colleges and Universities Should Take Action to Address Surge of Enrollments in Computer Science*. National Academics. https://www.nationalacademies.org/news/2017/10/colleges-and-universities-should-take-action-to-address-surge-of-enrollments-in-computer-science

Theodoropoulos, A., Antoniou, A., & Lepouras, G. (2017). Teacher and student views on educational robotics: The Pan-Hellenic competition case. *Application and Theory of Computer Technology*, *2*(4), 1–23. doi:10.22496/atct.v2i4.94

Thomas, S. (2021). Best Practices in Robotics Education: Perspectives from an IEEE RAS Women in Engineering Panel. *IEEE Robotics and Auto*, *8*(1). http://0-ieeexplore-ieee-org.oasis.unisa.ac.za/stamp/stamp.jsp?tp=&arnumber=9382158&isnumber=9382150

Thomas, L., Ratcliffe, M., Woodbury, J., & Jarman, E. (2002). Learning styles and performance in the introductory programming sequence. *SIGCSE Bulletin*, *34*(1), 33–37. doi:10.1145/563517.563352

Thomson, N., & Tippins, D. (2013). Envisioning science teacher preparation for twenty-first-century classrooms for diversity: Some tensions. *Science Education for Diversity*, *2*(3), 231–249. doi:10.1007/978-94-007-4563-6_11

Threekunprapam, A., & Yasri, P. (2020). Patterns of Computational Thinking Development While Solving Unplugged Coding Activities Coupled with the 3S Approach for Self-Directed Learning. *European Journal of Educational Research*, *9*(3), 1025–1045. doi:10.12973/eu-jer.9.3.1025

Tian, H., Lu, W., Li, T. O., Tang, X., Cheung, S. C., Klein, J., & Bissyandé, T. F. (2023). Is ChatGPT the Ultimate Programming Assistant—How far is it? *arXiv preprint arXiv:2304.11938.*

Tikva, C., & Tambouris, E. (2021). Mapping computational thinking through programming in K 12 education: A conceptual model based on systematic literature review. *Computers & Education*, *162*, 104083. Advance online publication. doi:10.1016/j.compedu.2020.104083

Tissenbaum, M., & Ottenbreit-Leftwich, A. (2020). A vision of k-12 computer science education for 2030. *Communications of the ACM*, *63*(5), 42–44. doi:10.1145/3386910

Tissenbaum, M., Weintrop, D., Holbert, N., & Clegg, T. (2021). The case for alternative endpoints in computing education. *British Journal of Educational Technology*, *52*(3), 1164–1177. doi:10.1111/bjet.13072

Tricco, A. C., Lillie, E., Zarin, W., O'Brien, K. K., Colquhoun, H., Levac, D., Moher, D., Peters, M. D. J., Horsley, T., Weeks, L., Hempel, S., Akl, E. A., Chang, C., McGowan, J., Stewart, L., Hartling, L., Aldcroft, A., Wilson, M. G., Garritty, C., & Straus, S. E. (2018). PRISMA extension for scoping reviews (PRISMA-ScR): Checklist and explanation. *Annals of Internal Medicine*, *169*(7), 467–473. doi:10.7326/M18-0850 PMID:30178033

Tsai, C. Y., Yang, Y. F., & Chang, C. K. (2015, October). Cognitive load comparison of traditional and distributed pair programming on visual programming language. *In 2015 International Conference of Educational Innovation through Technology (EITT)* (pp. 143-146). IEEE. 10.1109/EITT.2015.37

Tsay, M., & Brady, M. (2010). A case study of cooperative learning and communication pedagogy: Does working in teams make a difference? *The Journal of Scholarship of Teaching and Learning*, *10*(2), 78–89.

Tsortanidou, X., Daradoumis, T., & Barberá, E. (2021). A K-6 computational thinking curricular framework: pedagogical implications for teaching practice. *Interactive Learning Environments*. Taylor & Francis. https://www.tandfonline.com/doi/full/10.1080/10494820.2021.1986725

Tzagkaraki, E., Papadakis, S., & Kalogiannakis, M. (2021, February). Exploring the Use of Educational Robotics in primary school and its possible place in the curricula. In *Educational Robotics International Conference* (pp. 216-229). Cham: Springer International Publishing. 10.1007/978-3-030-77022-8_19

Tzimas, D., & Demetriadis, S. (2021). Ethical issues in learning analytics: A review of the field. *Educational Technology Research and Development*, *69*(2), 1101–1133. doi:10.1007/s11423-021-09977-4

Ujakpa, M. M., Osakwe, J. O., Iyawa, G. E., Hashiyana, V., & Mutalya, A. N. (2020, May). Industry 4.0: university students' perception, awareness and preparedness-A case of Namibia. In 2020 IST-Africa Conference (IST-Africa) (pp. 1-10). IEEE.

Ulrich Hoppe, H., & Werneburg, S. (2019). Computational Thinking—More Than a Variant of Scientific Inquiry! In *Computational Thinking Education* (pp. 13–30). Springer Singapore. doi:10.1007/978-981-13-6528-7_2

United Nations Educational, Scientific and Cultural Organization (UNESCO). (1999). Higher education in the twenty-first century: vision and action, v. 1: final report. *World Conference on Higher Education in the Twenty-first Century: Vision and Action, Paris, 1998.* UNESCO. https://unesdoc.unesco.org/ark:/48223/pf0000116345

United Nations Educational, Scientific and Cultural Organization (UNESCO). (2019). *Recommendation on open educational resources (OER).* UNESCO - Open Educational Resources. http://portal.unesco.org/en/ev.php-URL_ID=49556&URL_DO=DO_TOPIC&URL_SECTION=201.html

United Nations Educational, Scientific and Cultural Organization. (2019). *Beijing Consensus on artificial intelligence and education. Outcome document of the International Conference on Artificial Intelligence and Education, Planning Education in the AI Era: Lead the Leap, Beijing, 2019.* United Nations Educational, Scientific and Cultural Organization. https://unesdoc.unesco.org/ark:/48223/ pf0000368303

United Nations. (1990). *Convention on the rights of a child.* UN. https://www.ohchr.org/en/instruments-mechanisms/instruments/convention-rights-

University of Namibia (UNAM). (2020). *Curriculum Transformation Framework: Towards increased access with success.* UNAM.

University of South Australia. Resource on Academic Integrity. Retrieved on April 2, 2020 at https://lo.unisa.edu.au/course/view.php?id=6751&section=6

Upadhyaya, B., McGill, M. M., & Decker, A. (2020). A longitudinal analysis of k-12 computing education research in the united states: Implications and recommendations for change. In: *Annual Conference on Innovation and Technology in Computer Science Education, ITiCSE*. Association for Computing Machinery. 10.1145/3328778.3366809

Usart, M. (2019). Are 21st century skills evaluated in robotics competitions? The case of first lego league competition. *CSEDU 2019 - Proceedings of the 11th International Conference on Computer Supported Education*, *1*(Csedu), 445–452. 10.5220/0007757404450452

Uunona, G. N., & Goosen, L. (2023). Leveraging Ethical Standards in Artificial Intelligence Technologies: A Guideline for Responsible Teaching and Learning Applications. In M. Garcia, M. Lopez Cabrera, & R. de Almeida (Eds.), *Handbook of Research on Instructional Technologies in Health Education and Allied Disciplines* (pp. 310–330). IGI Global. doi:10.4018/978-1-6684-7164-7.ch014

Vaithilingam, P., Zhang, T., & Glassman, E. L. (2022). Expectation vs. Experience: Evaluating the Usability of Code Generation Tools Powered by Large Language Models. In *Extended Abstracts of the 2022 CHI Conference on Human Factors in Computing Systems (CHI EA '22)*. Association for Computing Machinery. 10.1145/3491101.3519665

Välimaa, J., & Hoffman, D. (2008). Knowledge society discourse and higher education. *Higher Education*, *56*(3), 265–285. doi:10.1007/s10734-008-9123-7

Van der Westhuizen, C., & Bailey, R. (2022). A 21st-century vision for self-directed learning in blended learning environments. In C. van der Westhuizen, M.C. Maphalala & R. Bailey (Eds.), Blended learning environments to foster self-directed learning NWU Self-Directed Learning Series (vol. 8, pp. 1–29). Cape Town: AOSIS. doi:10.4102/aosis.2022.BK366.01

Van der Westhuizen, C., & Kemp, A. (2022). Self-directed learning with technology for fourth year Engineering Graphics and Design students, In C. van der Westhuizen, M.C. Maphalala & R. Bailey (Eds.), Blended learning environments to foster self-directed learning, (Vol. 8, pp. 71–97). Cape Town: AOSIS. doi:10.4102/aosis.2022.BK366.04

van der Westhuizen, L. M., & Hannaway, D. M. (2021). Digital play for language development in early grades . *South African journal of Childhood Education*, 2-45 https://doi.org/ lil.925. doi:10. 4102/sajce.v1

Van der Westhuizen, C., & Mentz, E. (2020). Implementing cooperative learning elements in Google Docs to optimise online social presence in a self-directed learning environment. In J. Olivier (Ed.), *Self-directed multimodal learning in higher education* (pp. 201–234). AOSIS. doi:10.4102/aosis.2020.BK210

Van Heerden, J., & Mulumba, M. (2023). Science, Technology and Innovation (STI): Its Role in South Africa's Development Outcomes and STI Diplomacy. *Research for Development*, 144–154. doi:10.1007/978-981-19-6802-0_9

Van Helden, G., Zandbergen, B., Shvarts, A., Specht, M., & Gill, E. (2023). *An Embodied Cognition Approach To Collaborative Engineering Design Activities*.

Van Laar, E., Van Deursen, A. J., Van Dijk, J. A., & de Haan, J. (2020). Determinants of 21st-century skills and 21st-century digital skills for workers: A systematic literature review. *SAGE Open*, *10*(1). https://journals.sagepub.com/doi/full/10.1177/2158244019900176. doi:10.1177/2158244019900176

Van Merriënboer, J. J. (2019). *The four-component instructional design model: An overview of its main design principles*. School of Health Professions Education. https://www.4cid.org/wp-content/uploads/2021/04/vanmerrienboer-4cid-overview-of-main-design-principles-2021.pdf

Van Merriënboer, J. J., & Kirschner, P. A. (2018). *Ten steps to complex learning: A systematic approach to four-component instructional design*. Routledge.

Van Merrienboer, J. J., & Sweller, J. (2005). Cognitive load theory and complex learning: Recent developments and future directions. *Educational Psychology Review*, *17*(2), 147–177. doi:10.1007/s10648-005-3951-0

Van Weert, T. (2005). Lifelong learning in the knowledge society: Implications for education. In *Education and the knowledge society: Information technology supporting human development* (pp. 15–25). Springer. doi:10.1007/0-387-23120-X_2

van Woezik, T. E., Koksma, J. J. J., Reuzel, R. P., Jaarsma, D. C., & van der Wilt, G. J. (2021). There is more than 'I'in self-directed learning: an exploration of self-directed learning in teams of undergraduate students. Medical Teacher, 43(5), 590-598.Vlachopoulos, D., & Makri, A. (2019). Online communication and interaction in distance higher education: A framework study of good practice. *International Review of Education*, *65*(4), 605–632.

Van Wyk, C. (2012, June). Survey of ICT in schools in South Africa. *Public Expenditure Analysis for the Department of Basic Education: Report 8*. DBE. https://www.education.gov.za/Portals/0/Documents/Reports/Research%20Repository/LTSM/Survey%20of%20ICT%20in%20schools%20in%20SA.pdf?ver=2019-09-09-102208-963

Van Wyk, M. M. (2017). An e-portfolio as empowering tool to enhance students' self-directed learning in a teacher education course: A case of a South African university. *South African Journal of Higher Education*, *31*(3), 274–291. doi:10.20853/31-3-834

Van Zyl, S. C. (2020). *Developing deeper self-directed learning in Computer Applications Technology education* [Doctoral dissertation, North-West University].

Van Zyl, S., & Mentz, E. (2019). Moving to deeper self-directed learning as an essential competency for the 21st century. In E. Mentz, J. De Beer, & R. Bailey (Eds.), *Self-Directed Learning for the 21st Century: Implications for Higher Education NWU Self-Directed Learning Series* (Vol. 1, pp. 67–102). AOSIS. doi:10.4102/aosis.2019.BK134.03

Van Zyl, S., & Mentz, E. (2022). Deeper self-directed learning for the 21st century and beyond. In P. Hughes & J. Yarbrough (Eds.), *Self-directed learning and the academic evolution from pedagogy to andragogy* (pp. 50–77). IGI Global. doi:10.4018/978-1-7998-7661-8.ch004

VanLehn, K. (1989). Problem solving and cognitive skill acquisition. In M. Posner (Ed.), *Foundations of cognitive science* (pp. 527–580). MIT Press. doi:10.7551/mitpress/3072.003.0016

Varunki, M., Katajavuori, N., & Postareff, L. (2017). First-year students' approaches to learning, and factors related to change or stability in their deep approach during a pharmacy course. *Studies in Higher Education*, *42*(2), 331–353. doi:10.1080/03075079.2015.1049140

Veldman, S., Dicks, E., Suleman, H., Greyling, J., Freese, J., & Majake, T. (2021). *The Status of Coding and Robotics in South African Schools*. Academy of Science of South Africa. https://www.youtube.com/watch?v=hMHgnEY41U&ab_channel=AcademyofScienceofSouthAfrica

Verma, A., Yurov, K. M., Lane, P. L., & Yurova, Y. V. (2019). An investigation of skill requirements for business and data analytics positions: A content analysis of job advertisements. *Journal of Education for Business*, *94*(4), 243–250. doi:10.1080/08832323.2018.1520685

Verster, M. C., Laubscher, D. J., & Bosch, C. (2023). Facilitating Blended Learning in Underprivileged Contexts: A Self-Directed Curriculum as Praxis View. In Competence-Based Curriculum and E-Learning in Higher Education (pp. 20-50). IGI Global. doi:10.4018/978-1-6684-6586-8.ch002

Vidal-Hall, C., Flewitt, R., & Wyse, D. (2020). Early childhood practitioner beliefs about digital media: Integrating technology into a child-centred classroom environment. *European Early Childhood Education Research Journal*, *28*(2), 167–181. doi:10.1080/1350293X.2020.1735727

Vihavainen, A., Paksula, M., & Luukkainen, M. (2011, March). Extreme apprenticeship method in teaching programming for beginners. *In Proceedings of the 42nd ACM technical symposium on Computer science education* (pp. 93-98). ACM. 10.1145/1953163.1953196

Visser, P. J. (2007). Some Ideas on the 'best interests of the child' principle in the Context of Public Schooling. *Tydskrif vir Hedendaagse Romeins-Holandse Reg*, (70), 459–469.

Visser, W., & Hoc, J. M. (1990). Expert software design strategies. In *Psychology of programming* (pp. 235–249). Academic Press. doi:10.1016/B978-0-12-350772-3.50020-3

Vogel, S., Santo, R., & Ching, D. (2017). Unpacking arguments for and projected impacts of CS4All initiatives. In *Proceedings of the 2017 ACM SIGCSE Technical Symposium on Computer Science Education* (SIGCSE'17). ACM. 10.1145/3017680.3017755

Voskamp, A., Kuiper, E., & Volman, M. (2022). Teaching Practices for Self-Direcred and Selft-Regulated Learnng: Case Studies in Dutch Innovative Secondary Schools. *Educational Studies*, *48*(6), 772–789. doi:10.1080/03055698.2020.1814699

Vygotsky, L. S. (1978). *Mind in society: Development of higher psychological processes*. Harvard University Press.

Vygotsky, L. S. (1978). *Mind in Society: The development of higher psychological processes*. Harvard Univesity Press., http://outleft.org/wp-contents/uploads/Vygotsky

Walters, J. (2023). *Becoming: Using Self-directed Learning to Develop Learners' Research and Leadership Capabilities and Confidence*. Active Learning for Real-World Inquiry.

Waterschoot, J., Vansteenkiste, M., & Soenens, B. (2019). The effects of experimentally induced choice on elementary school children's intrinsic motivation: The moderating role of indecisiveness and teacher–student relatedness. *Journal of Experimental Child Psychology*, *188*, 104692. doi:10.1016/j.jecp.2019.104692 PMID:31539835

Watted, A. (2023). Examining motivation to learn and 21st century skills in a massive open online course. *International Journal of Instruction*, *16*(3), 797–822. doi:10.29333/iji.2023.16343a

Watters, A. (2018 December). *The Stories We Were Told about Education Technology*. Blog entry on Hack Education. http://hackeducation.com/2018/12/18/top-ed-tech-trends-stories

Webb, M., Davis, N., Bell, T., Katz, Y. J., Reynolds, N. C. D., & Sysło, M. M. (2017). Computer Science in K-12 school curricula of the 21st century: Why, what and when? *Education and Information Technologies*, *22*(2), 445–468. doi:10.1007/s10639-016-9493-x

Weintrop, D. (2019). Block-based programming in computer science education. *Communications of the ACM*, *62*(8), 22–25. doi:10.1145/3341221

Weintrop, D., Hansen, A. K., Harlow, D. B., & Franklin, D. (2018). Starting from Scratch: Outcomes of early computer science learning experiences and implications for what comes next. *ICER '18: Proceedings of the 2018 ACM Conference on International Computing Education Research*, (pp. 142-150). ACM. 10.1145/3230977.3230988

Weismueller, J., Harrigan, P., Coussement, K., & Tessitore, T. (2022). What makes people share political content on social media? The role of emotion, authority and ideology. *Computers in Human Bahaviour*, 1-11 . doi:10.1016/j.chb.2021.107150

Weisz, J. D., Muller, M., Ross, S. I., Martinez, F., Houde, S., Agarwal, M., Talamadupula, K., & Richards, J. T. (2022). Better Together? An Evaluation of AI-Supported Code Translation. In *Proceedings of the 27th International Conference on Intelligent User Interfaces (IUI '22)* (pp. 369-391). Association for Computing Machinery. 10.1145/3490099.3511157

Wellington, J. (2014). Educational research: Contemporary issues and practical approaches. *Continuum.*

Wermelinger, M. (2023). Using GitHub Copilot to Solve Simple Programming Problems. In *Proceedings of the 54th ACM Technical Symposium on Computer Science Education (SIGCSE 2023)* (Vol. 1, pp. 172-178). Association for Computing Machinery. 10.1145/3545945.3569830

Wessner, M., & Pfister, H. (2000). Points of cooperation: Integrating cooperative learning into web-based courses. Paper presented at the International Workshop on New Technologies for Collaborative Learning, Awaji-Yumebutai, Japan.

West, J. (2017). Data, democracy and school accountability: Controversy over school evaluation in the case of DeVasco High School. *Big Data & Society*, *4*(1), 2053951717702408. doi:10.1177/2053951717702408

Widodo, W., Gustari, I., & Handrawty, C. (2022). Adversity Quotient Promotes Teachers' Professional Competence More Strongly Than Emotional Intelligence: Evidence form Indinesia. *Journal of Intelligents*, 1-17 . doi:10.3390/jintelligence10030044

Wiley, D., Webb, A., Weston, S., & Tonks, D. (2017). A preliminary exploration of the relationships between student-created OER, sustainability, and students success. International Review of Research in Open and Distributed Learning, 18(4), 60–69. https://doi.org/. V18i4.3022 doi:10.19173/irrodl

Wiley, D., Bliss, T. J., & McEwen, M. (2013). Open educational resources: A review of the literature. In *Handbook of Research on Educational Communications and Technology* (pp. 781–789). Springer New York. doi:10.1007/978-1-4614-3185-5_63

Willemse, K. (2023). *Supporting Grade R Teachers to Integrate Coding and Robotics with Mathematical Concepts* [Doctoral dissertation, University of Pretoria, South Africa].

Williams, L. (2001, February). Integrating pair programming into a software development process. *In Proceedings 14th Conference on Software Engineering Education and Training.'In search of a software engineering profession'(Cat. No. PR01059)* (pp. 27-36). IEEE.

Williams, G., McGregor, H., Sharp, D., Levesque, C., Kouides, R., Ryan, R., & Deci, E. (2006). Testing a self-determination theory intervention for motivating tobacco cessation: Supporting autonomy and competence in a clinical trial. *Health Psychology*, *25*(1), 91–101. doi:10.1037/0278-6133.25.1.91 PMID:16448302

Williams, L., & Kessler, R. R. (2003). *Pair programming illuminated.* Addison-Wesley Professional.

Williamson, S. N. (2007). Development of a self-rating scale of self-directed learning. *Nurse Researcher*, *14*(2), 66–83. doi:10.7748/nr2007.01.14.2.66.c6022 PMID:17315780

Wing, J. M. (2014, January 10). Computational thinking benefits society. *Social Issues in Computing*. http://socialissues.cs.toronto.edu/index.html

Wing, J. M. (2016). *Computational thinking, 10 years later.* Microsoft Research. https://www.microsoft.com/en-us/research/blog/computational-thinking-10-years-later/.

Wing, J. M. (2006). Computational thinking. *Communications of the ACM*, *49*(3), 33–35. doi:10.1145/1118178.1118215

Winslow, L. E. (1996). Programming pedagogy—A psychological overview. *SIGCSE Bulletin*, *28*(3), 17–22. doi:10.1145/234867.234872

Wobbrock, J. O., Kane, S. K., Gajos, K. Z., Harada, S., & Froehlich, J. (2011). Ability-based design: Concept, principles and examples. *ACM Transactions on Accessible Computing*, *3*(3), 1–27. doi:10.1145/1952383.1952384

Wong, F. M. F., Tang, A. C. Y., & Cheng, W. L. S. (2021). Factors associated with self-directed learning among undergraduate nursing students: A systematic review. *Nurse Education Today*, *104*, 104998. doi:10.1016/j.nedt.2021.104998 PMID:34139583

Wood, R. (2022). Practitioners respond to Sarah Mercer's Psychology for language learning: Spare a thought for the teacher. *Language Teaching*, *422-425*(3), 422–425. Advance online publication. doi:10.1017/S0261444821000203

Wu, L., Looi, C. K., Multisilta, J., How, M. L., Choi, H., Hsu, T. C., & Tuomi, P. (2020). Teacher's Perceptions and Readiness to Teach Coding Skills: A Comparative Study Between Finland, Mainland China, Singapore, Taiwan, and South Korea. *The Asia-Pacific Education Researcher*, *29*(1), 21–34. doi:10.1007/s40299-019-00485-x

Xia, X., Wan, Z., Kochhar, P. S., & Lo, D. (2019, May). How Practitioners Perceive Coding Proficiency. *IEEE/ACM 41st International Conference on Software Engineering (ICSE)* (pp. 924-935). IEEE. 10.1109/ICSE.2019.00098

Xiang, Y. (2022). Research on the Design of Education Games for Vocabulary Learning from the Perspective of Intrinsic Motivation Theory. In 2022 4th International Conference on Computer Science and Technologies in Education (CSTE) (pp. 164-167). IEEE. 10.1109/CSTE55932.2022.00036

Xie, B., Loksa, D., Nelson, G. L., Davidson, M. J., Dong, D., Kwik, H., Tan, A. H., Hwa, L., Li, M., & Ko, A. J. (2019). A theory of instruction for introductory programming skills. *Computer Science Education*, *29*(2-3), 205–253. doi:10.1080/08993408.2019.1565235

Xie, Z., Man, W., Liu, C., & Fu, X. (2023). A PRISMA-based systematic review of measurements for school bullying. *Adolescent Research Review*, *8*(2), 219–259. doi:10.1007/s40894-022-00194-5

Xing, W., Zhu, G., Arslan, O., Shim, J., & Popov, V. (2023). Using learning analytics to explore the multifaceted engagement in collaborative learning. *Journal of Computing in Higher Education*, *35*(3), 633–662. doi:10.1007/s12528-022-09343-0

Yadav, A., Gretter, S., Good, J., & McLean, T. (2017). Computational thinking in teacher education. In P. J. Rich & C. B. Hodges (Eds.), *Emerging research, practice and policy on computational thinking* (pp. 205–220). Springer. doi:10.1007/978-3-319-52691-1_13

Yadav, A., Gretter, S., Hambrusch, S., & Sands, P. (2016). Expanding computer science education in schools: Understanding teacher experiences and challenges. *Computer Science Education*, *26*(4), 235–254. doi:10.1080/08993408.2016.1257418

Yadav, A., Heath, M., & Hu, A. D. (2022). Toward justice in computer science through community, criticality, and citizenship. *Communications of the ACM*, *65*(5), 42–44. doi:10.1145/3527203

Yadav, A., Krist, C., Good, J., & Caeli, E. N. (2018). Computational thinking in elementary classrooms: Measuring teacher understanding of computational ideas for teaching science. *Computer Science Education*, *28*(4), 371–400. doi:10.1080/08993408.2018.1560550

Yadav, A., Mayfield, C., Chou, N., Hambrusch, S., & Korb, J. T. (2014). Computational thinking in elementary and secondary teacher education. *ACM Transactions on Computing Education*, *14*(1), 1–16. doi:10.1145/2576872

Yang, Y., Long, Y., Sun, D., Van Aalst, J., & Cheng, S. (2020). 'Fostering students' creativity via educational robotics: An investigation of teachers' pedagogical practices based on teacher interviews'. *British Journal of Educational Technology*, *51*(5), 1826–1842. doi:10.1111/bjet.12985

Yan, L., Sha, L., Zhao, L., Li, Y., Martinez-Maldonado, R., Chen, G., Li, X., Jin, Y., & Gašević, D. (2024, January). In press). Practical and ethical challenges of large language models in education: A systematic scoping review. *British Journal of Educational Technology*, *55*(1), 90–112. doi:10.1111/bjet.13370

Yaşar, M. Ö., & Atay, D. (2023). Evaluating Learner Autonomy during the Covid-19: An Examination of Student Teachers' Self-Directed Learning Readiness for MOOCs. Anatolian Journal of Education, 8(1).

Yasmin, M., Naseem, F., & Masso, I. C. (2019). Teacher-directed learning to self-directed learning transition barriers in Pakistan. Studies in Educational Evaluation, 61, 34-40.Yi, Z., & Luxi, Z. (2012). Implementing a cooperative learning model in universities. *Educational Studies*, *38*(2), 165–173.

Yildiz Durak, H. (2018). Digital story design activities used for teaching programming effect on learning of programming concepts, programming self-efficacy, and participation and analysis of student experiences. *Journal of Computer Assisted Learning*, *34*(6), 740–752. doi:10.1111/jcal.12281

You, H. S., Chacko, S. M., & Kapila, V. (2021). Examining the Effectiveness of a Professional Development Program: Integration of Educational Robotics into Science and Mathematics Curricula. *Journal of Science Education and Technology*, *30*(4), 567–581. doi:10.1007/s10956-021-09903-6

Yue, W. (2022). *A Comparative Case Study Analysis of the Effects of a Flipped Classroom Model on a College Foreign Language Course*. Delaware State University.

Yuliansyah, A., & Ayu, M. (2021). The implementation of project-based assignment in online learning during covid-19. *Journal of English Language Teaching and Learning*, *2*(1), 32–38. doi:10.33365/jeltl.v2i1.851

Zainuddin, Z., Hermawan, H., Nuraini, F., & Prayitno, S. (2019). Students learning experiences with LMS tes teach in flipped-class instruction. *Elinvo Electronics Education*, *4*(1), 1–11. doi:10.21831/elinvo.v4i1.24405

Zawacki-Richter, O., & Latchem, C. (2018). Exploring four decades of research in Computers & Education. *Computers & Education*, *122*, 136–152. doi:10.1016/j.compedu.2018.04.001

Zeng, J., Parks, S., & Shang, J. (2020). To learn scientifically, effectively, and enjoyably: A review of educational games. *Human Behavior and Emerging Technologies*, *2*(2), 186–195. doi:10.1002/hbe2.188

Zhang, L., & Van Reet, J. (2021). How is Knowledge constructed During Science activities? Detacting Instructional Effects of Play and Telling to Optimize integration of Scientific investigations. *Research in Science Education*, 1–15. doi:10.1007/s11165-021-09990-w

Zhao, Y., Davis, D., Chen, G., Lofi, C., Hauff, C., & Houben, G. J. (2017). Certificate Achievement Unlocked: How does MOOC Learner's Behaviours Change? *Late-Breaking Results, Demonstration and Theory, Opinion and Reflection Paper*, 83-88. Research Gate.

Zha, S., Jin, Y., Moore, P., & Gaston, J. (2020). Hopscotch into coding: Introducing pre-service teachers computational thinking. *TechTrends*, *64*(1), 17–28. doi:10.1007/s11528-019-00423-0

Zhu, M., Berri, S., Koda, R., & Wu, Y. J. (2023). Exploring students' self-directed learning strategies and satisfaction in online learning. *Education and Information Technologies*, *5*, 1–17. doi:10.1007/s10639-023-11914-2

Zsolt, T., & István, B. (2008). *Moodle and social constructivism.* Research Gate. https://www.researchgate.net/profile/Zsolt-Toth-4/publication/345986283_Moodle_and_social_constructivism/links/5fb44fba299bf10c3689ac91/Moodle-and-social-constructivism.pdf

About the Contributors

Chantelle Bosch is a senior lecturer in Computer Science Education in the Faculty of Education at North-West University. She holds a PhD in Computer Science Education and a NRF Y- rating from the South African National Research Foundation. Chantelle is a sub area leader in the Research Unit Self-Directed Learning at the NWU. Her research interests include technology enhanced learning, self-directed learning, blended learning, and cooperative learning and is involved in various projects that explore technology-supported cooperative learning to promote self-directed learning. Chantelle has recently edited two books and she is also an executive member of the UNESCO Chair on Multimodal Learning and Open Educational Resources (OER).

Leila Goosen is a full professor in the Department of Science and Technology Education of the University of South Africa. Prof. Goosen was an Associate Professor in the School of Computing, and the module leader and head designer of the fully online signature module for the College for Science, Engineering and Technology, rolled out to over 92,000 registered students since the first semester of 2013. She also supervises ten Masters and Doctoral students, and has successfully completed supervision of 43 students at postgraduate level. Previously, she was a Deputy Director at the South African national Department of Education. In this capacity, she was required to develop ICT strategies for implementation. She also promoted, coordinated, managed, monitored and evaluated ICT policies and strategies, and drove the research agenda in this area. Before that, she had been a lecturer of Information Technology (IT) in the Department for Science, Mathematics and Technology Education in the Faculty of Education of the University of Pretoria. Her research interests have included cooperative work in IT, effective teaching and learning of programming and teacher professional development.

***

Ghadah Almutairy is an Assistant Professor of Computer Education, Department of Curriculum and Instruction, College of Education, Imam Abdulrahman Bin Faisal University, Dammam, Saudi Arabia. Dr. Almutairy holds a Ph.D. in Curriculum and Instruction with a focus on Instructional Design and Technology from Virginia Tech. Additionally, she possess a Master's degree in Distance Teaching and Training and a Bachelor's degree in Computer Science Education. Their main research interests include problem-solving, programming education, computational thinking, and online learning.

Fernando Cesar Balbino is a professor at the Federal Institute of Education, Science and Technology of Mato Grosso do Sul (IFMS), and holds a Master's degree in Computer Science from the Federal University of São Carlos (UFSCar), both in Brazil. Currently, he is also a PhD student at the Institute of Mathematics and Computer Science (ICMC) at the University of São Paulo (USP). His expertise and research interests are centered around computer programming education, Computer Science applied to Education, Software Engineering, and Web application development.

Ellen Francine Barbosa is an Associate Professor at the Institute of Mathematics and Computer Sciences – University of SaÞo Paulo (ICMC-USP), Brazil. She received her PhD in Computer Science from ICMC-USP. During her PhD, she was also a visitor scholar at Georgia Institute of Technology and at University of Florida, United States. Her main research interests are related to CS education and training, open education resources, mobile learning, educational data mining, and augmented and virtual reality

Leonardo Vieira Barcelos is a Ph.D. candidate in the Postgraduate Program at the Institute of Mathematical and Computer Science (ICMC) at the University of São Paulo, holds a Master's degree in Computer Science from the Federal University of São Carlos (2016), a specialization in Management and Exercise of Teaching in Higher Education (2007), and graduation in Data Processing (2003). He is an effective professor at the Minas Gerais State University, Frutal Unit. His interests center around Software Engineering, mainly in research related to Industry 4.0, digital twin, software reuse, requirements engineering, software quality, and software planning.

Tavis Bragg is based in Nova Scotia, Canada, and teaches at Northeast Kings Education Centre and holds academic positions at Mount Saint Vincent University (MSVU) and Acadia University. His academic background includes a B.A. (Hons) in Sociology and Philosophy from Acadia, extensive coursework in Computer Science, and an M.Ed. in Curriculum Studies from MSVU. His educational approach integrates technology with student-centric and culturally responsive pedagogy, specializing in computer and social science education. Committed to creating inclusive and equitable learning environments, he leverages technology to bridge the digital learning gap. As an HP Teaching Fellow, Tavis embodies the integration of innovative technology in education, with a focus on collaboration and innovation across Canada and the United States. His career, dedicated to adapting emerging technologies for diverse student needs, reflects his philosophy of powerful learning — personal, accessible, and reflective, aimed at deeply engaging students in their learning journey.

Brent Crane is a graduate student at Dalhousie University in the Faculty of Computer Science. He is currently pursuing his master's in computer science, with a focus on computer science education. His research is currently in the areas of introductory computer programming and creative coding.

William Simão de Deus is a professor at the Federal Institute of Education, Science and Technology of Paraná (IFPR). He is a PhD candidate in the Graduate Program in Computer Science and Computational Mathematics at the Institute of Mathematical and Computer Sciences (ICMC) of the University of São Paulo (USP). Holds a Master's Degree from the Program in Informatics, Federal Technological University of Paraná, Cornélio Procópio Campus (UTFPR-CP) (2018). Graduated in Analysis and Systems Development from UTFPR-CP (2015). His research interestes are related to intersection of Computer Science and Education.

Wanjiru Gachie is a seasoned senior lecturer at the University of KwaZulu-Natal, South Africa, specializing in Information Systems and Public Administration. With over a decade of experience, her dynamic contributions to education, research, and student supervision make her a respected figure in the academic community.

Averil Gorrah is a lecturer in the Computer Science Education subject group in the Faculty of Education at the North-West University (Potchefstroom campus). He holds a Master of Education (MEd) degree in Information and Communication Technology in Education (UJ). Previously, he was employed as a Deputy Principal by the Northern Cape Department of Education. During his teaching career, he conducted numerous community-based adult computer literacy programs. He is a member of the self-directed learning unit. His research interests include computer science education, coding, and robotics.

Erkkie Haipinge is a PhD student in educational technology at the University of South Africa and an eLearning and learning design practitioner at the University of Namibia. His research interest lies in pedagogy guided technology enhanced learning.

Alicia Johnson holds a Ph.D. in Curriculum and Instruction (with an emphasis on Instructional Design and Technology) from Virginia Tech and a Master of Science in Instructional Technology from Wilkes University. She earned her bachelor's degree in English Literature from the University of Mary Washington. Dr.Johnson has over 10 years of experience designing, developing, teaching, and evaluating online courses in both undergraduate and graduate learning environments.

Michael Laubscher is a lecturer at the Faculty of Law at the North-West University in South Africa. His field of study includes AI, smart contracts and education law.

Hugo Lotriet is a professor in Information Systems at the University of South Africa.

Maryke Anneke Mihai obtained a BA-degree cum laude (1984), Higher Education Diploma cum laude (1985), Honours in Afrikaans cum laude (1986), MEd in Computer-Integrated Education (2007) and PhD in Computer-Integrated Education (2015) from the University of Pretoria. She taught Afrikaans to high school learners for twenty years, and also gained four years of experience in the insurance field. Since August 2008, she has been employed as lecturer at the University of Pretoria in the Science, Mathematics and Technology Department within the Education faculty. She was promoted to senior lecturer since January 2020. Her research interests include computer-integrated education, online teaching, languages, assessment, instructional design and management. She supervised two PhDs, 18 MEds and numerous Honours students to completion.

Mncedisi Maphalala is a Professor in the Department of Curriculum and Instructional Studies at Unisa (College of Education) in South Africa. He holds a D.Ed in curriculum studies from the University of Zululand. He is a former Director of the Centre for Excellence in Learning and Teaching (CELT) at the Durban University of Technology and a former Dean of the Faculty of Education at the University of Zululand. His career in Higher Education spans over 19 years as a Research Professor (North-West University), Professor at the University of Zululand and UNISA and Institutional researcher at the University of the Witwatersrand. He has also previously worked for the KZN Department of Education (as a teacher, HOD and Deputy Principal); between May and August 2015, he was a Visiting Scholar at the University of North Dakota (USA). Prof Maphalala is an established researcher who holds an NRF C2 rating. He has edited books and special journal issues and published several book chapters and research articles in peer-reviewed journals. Prof Maphalala has presented research papers at various local and international conferences. As a postgraduate supervisor and mentor, Prof Maphalala has supervised to completion several Masters and doctoral candidates. His research interests are teacher education, self-directed learning, assessment, Scholarship of Teaching & Learning and Curriculum studies.

Mapheto is a Mathematics, Science and Technology Departmental Head at Maropeng primary School in Ga-Rankuwa Zone 16 (Tshwane West District). He is teaching Grade 4-7 guided by Curriculum Assessment Policy Statement (CAPS) and has eight years of teaching experience. He is a profound teacher who believes in serving his knowledge, skills and proficiency in ICT, assessment and motivation to the learners, colleagues and community. He completed his Bachelor's degree in Education in 2015, Honours Degree in Computer Integrated Education in 2020 and Masters General with full dissertation in Computer Integrated Education in 2023, all at the University of Pretoria.

Francois Irvin Papers laid the foundation for his educational journey by pursuing a Bachelor of Education at the North West University majoring in Life Science and Information Technology Education. Driven by a thirst for knowledge and a desire to make a significant impact in the field of education, Francois continued his academic journey with unwavering determination. He earned two Honors degrees in Education, specializing in Life Science Education and Education Law and Management from North West University. He served in a teacher's union SAOU (Suid Afrikaanse Onderwys Unie) as a member of the provincial executive committee (PEC). Francois Papers spent 11 years nurturing young minds in Computer Application Technology. He now serves as a Junior Lecturer in the computer science subject group at North West University and is a member of the Research Entity of Self-Directed Learning.

Eric Poitras is an Assistant Professor at the Faculty of Computer Science at Dalhousie University. He is also an Associate Professor at the Centre for Learning and Teaching at Dalhousie University and leads the Computer Science Education research cluster. He received his PhD in Educational Psychology and completed his postdoctoral training at McGill University. His main research area includes the role of self-regulatory processes during learning and problem-solving that are specific to certain disciplines, including computing education. More specifically, his research aims to gain insights into the cognitive, metacognitive, affective, and motivational processes that mediate learning, performance, and transfer in the context of introductory programming instruction. To accomplish this goal, he conducts laboratory and classroom studies and collects data to develop models of human-computer interaction; examines program comprehension and generation processes; and evaluates instructional designs to facilitate programming language learning. He is the recipient of the Early Faculty Career Award from the Technology, Instruction, Cognition & Learning special interest group of the American Educational Research Association. His research is funded by the Social Sciences and the Humanities Research Council of Canada (SSHRC).

Angela Siegel currently serves as the Assistant Dean (Academic Outreach) in the Faculty of Computer Science (FCS). In this capacity, she is focused on increasing access to university education throughout the province through her work with industry partners, government, non-profit organizations, and schools. Her research focuses on computer science education and the future of the educational landscape in light recent technological, societal, and pandemic-related changes.

Nomasonto Mthembu is a lecture in Computer Science Education, and a member of the Research Unit Self-directed Learning.

Sukie van Zyl holds a Ph.D. degree in Computer Science education. She is a member of the Research Unit Self-Directed Learning and a senior lecturer in Computer Science education at the Faculty of Education at the North-West University's Potchefstroom campus in South Africa. Her research endeavors concentrate on advancing deeper self-directed learning (knowledge transfer and self-directed learning), cooperative learning, and the integration of coding and robotics in Computer Science education. She has published at the national and international levels, and she also acts as a co-supervisor for postgraduate students.

Index

D

E

F

G

H

I

K

L

N

O

P

R

S

T

U

www.ingramcontent.com/pod-product-compliance
Lightning Source LLC
LaVergne TN
LVHW080633011026
849160LV00014B/1204